J. Michael Morgan
Western Kentucky University

McGRAW-HILL BOOK COMPANY

New York   St. Louis   San Francisco   Auckland   Bogotá
Hamburg   Johannesburg   London   Madrid   Mexico
Montreal   New Delhi   Panama   Paris   São Paulo
Singapore   Sydney   Tokyo   Toronto

Study Guide to Accompany FISCHER/DORNBUSCH
Economics

To

JAN, MATT, AND JESSIE

Study Guide
to Accompany
FISCHER/DORNBUSCH
ECONOMICS

Copyright © 1983 by McGraw-Hill, Inc.
All rights reserved.
Printed in the United States of America.
Except as permitted under the United States Copyright Act of 1976,
no part of this publication may be reproduced or distributed
in any form or by any means, or stored in a data base or retrieval system,
without the prior written permission of the publisher.

1 2 3 4 5 6 7 8 9 0   SEMSEM   8 9 8 7 6 5 4 3

ISBN 0-07-017759-7

This book was set in Highland by Automated Composition Service, Inc.
The editors were Peter J. Dougherty, Marjorie Singer, and James B. Armstrong;
the designer was Nicholas Krenitsky;
the production supervisor was Dominick Petrellese.
The drawings were done by Fine Line Illustrations, Inc.
Semline, Inc., was printer and binder.

Contents

	To the Student	v
1	An Introduction to Economics and the Economy	1
2	The Tools Economists Use	8
3	Demand, Supply, and the Market	17
4	The Demand Curve: Adjustments to Price and Income Changes	26
5	Special Topics in Demand	34
6	The Firm: Costs and Output	46
7	Production, Costs, and the Firm's Output Decisions	55
8	Market Structure and Competitive Markets	65
9	Monopoly and Imperfect Competition	77
10	Oligopoly and Monopolistic Competition	90
11	Antitrust and Regulation of Natural Monopolies	101
12	The Public Interest, Externalities, and Regulation	111
13	Factor Markets and Derived Demand: Labor	119
14	Human Capital, Discrimination, and Trade Unions	130
15	Capital and Land	138
16	Applied Economics in Action	150
17	The Government and Resource Allocation	154
18	City Economics and the Problems of the Cities	164
19	Uncertainty in Economic Life	173
20	General Equilibrium and Welfare Economics	181
21	An Introduction to Macroeconomics	189
22	National Income Accounting	195
23	The Business Cycle, Output, and Aggregate Demand	203
24	The Budget, Fiscal Policy, and Aggregate Demand	211
25	Money and Banking	223
26	Central Banking and the Monetary System	232
27	Money, Investment, and the Economy	243
28	Full-Employment Output and the Price Level	253
29	Aggregate Supply, the Price Level, and Unemployment	262
30	Unemployment	269

31	The Inflation Problem	276	
32	Money, Deficits, and Inflation	285	
33	Growth and Investment	292	
34	International Trade and the Balance of Payments	299	
35	The Gains from Trade and Problems of Trade	306	
36	The Economics of Exchange Rates and International Finance	314	
37	Problems of Developing Countries in the World Economy	320	
38	Income Distribution and Poverty in the United States	328	
39	Alternative Economic Approaches and Systems	335	
	Answers	343	

To the Student

This study guide has one purpose: to help you understand and apply the economic principles developed in the textbook *Economics* by Stanley Fischer and Rudiger Dornbusch. It is a supplement to, not a substitute for, the textbook. In writing it, my main objective has been to develop a learning tool which would assist you in a self-paced study of introductory economics. Economics is a fascinating subject. Once you have an understanding of the principles involved, you will have learned a new way of thinking about social relationships.

Each chapter of the study guide corresponds to a chapter in the textbook and contains nine separate components.

1. An *overview* at the beginning of each chapter sets the stage for what you are about to study in the textbook chapter. Each overview offers a brief summary of the text chapter, and some also offer suggestions about what you should look for in that chapter.

2. A *chapter outline* organizes the chapter in two or three pages. Most of the outlines are rather detailed and present a summary of the important points in each section and subsection of the text chapter.

3. *Important terms and their meaning* lists the new vocabulary developed in the chapter. This section of the study guide is more than a simple list of terms. I have used a matching format for the vocabulary drill because you must know how economic terminology is used if you are to understand the principles. A word of caution, though: Don't simply memorize the definitions; understand the meanings.

4. The *exercises* contained in each chapter allow you to apply some of the newly developed principles. This is one of the more rigorous sections; it is also a very important one. Don't be discouraged by the amount of graphical (and in some chapters numerical) analysis required, because it is here that you see the interrelationships of economic principles.

5. The *fill-in questions* are your initial check of the facts and general concepts presented in the text chapter. In many of the questions, you have a selection from which to choose the correct answer; in others, you must supply the answer.

6. The *true-false*, and *multiple choice questions* are the sixth and seventh components of each study guide chapter. These questions serve as a test, a quick indicator of how well you understand the material presented in the textbook.

7. *At this point, you should be able to . . .* is a list of learning objectives. After completing the text chapter and the study guide chapter, you should be able to meet these specified objectives.

8. The *questions for thought* are designed to stimulate class discussion and to identify important concepts in the chapter. Some questions require you to use your imagination, while others are rather straightforward. All answers, except those for *questions for thought*, are presented in the back of the study guide.

As I stated earlier, this study guide is designed to help you learn introductory economics. How should it be used? You should first read the chapter overview, the important terms, and the learning objectives. These components provide a brief idea of what is covered in the chapter and what you are expected to know. Next, carefully read the text, but keep the study guide close by. After reading a major section in the text, write one or two sentences which give the key points, and list any new terms. Then read that section in the chapter outline of the study guide, because it provides a review and summary of what you have just read. When you have completed the chapter, work on your vocabulary. Try to match as many of the terms with their meaning without looking back at the text. After you have completed the terms, refer to the text for the meaning of any new vocabulary you were initially unable to identify. Be sure that you understand all terms.

Next, work the exercises. In many chapters there are several exercises which progress in degree of difficulty. When you begin an exercise, reread the relevant sections of your textbook. Each of the exercises is designed to reveal principles presented in the text. Complete the exercises before checking the answers.

At this point, you should again read the chapter overview and outline, because you are now ready to test yourself on both general and specific points in the text. Answer as many of the fill-in, true-false, and multiple choice questions as you can without looking at the text.

If you cannot complete all of them, go back to the textbook and find the answers. When you have completed these three components of the study guide, check the answers provided. For any questions missed, you should reread the sections of the text covering the particular question. Don't leave these questions before you have mastered them. Read again the learning objectives and ask yourself whether you can do each of the things listed. Be honest. If you have trouble with some, go back to the text. Finally, study the questions for thought. You don't need to write down the answers, but you do need to think about general answers.

There is at least one question (fill-in, true-false, or multiple choice) for each section of the text. Ideally, you should answer all the questions and work all the exercises. Realistically, though, you will often be tempted to answer some questions and omit others. My only advice is to be careful in your selection.

ACKNOWLEDGMENTS

A number of people have helped me develop this study guide by reading chapters, working problems, suggesting questions, and pointing out errors. Special thanks go to Professors Marvin Snowbarger (San Jose State University), Timothy Keely (Tacoma Community College), John Wassom (Western Kentucky University), and Karen Russell (Western Kentucky University). Each of these individuals read most of the manuscript, worked the exercises and questions, and offered valuable suggestions. Professors Richard Cantrell, Carolyn Fost, William Davis, and Roy Howsen, all colleagues at Western Kentucky, and Stanley Fischer and Rudiger Dornbusch of M.I.T reviewed various chapters of the manuscript. Marjorie Singer of McGraw-Hill offered direction and encouragement. Freda Powell did a professional job of typing the manuscript under what were at times very trying conditions.

J. Michael Morgan

1 An Introduction to Economics and the Economy

In Chapter 1 you begin your study of economics. Human needs are practically unlimited, while the resources available to produce goods which satisfy those needs are limited. The central problem in economics is allocating resources in a manner which satisfies as many of these needs as possible. Every society faces this central economic problem and must answer the following questions: "What is to be produced?" "How is production to take place?" and "For whom are the goods and services produced?" Economics is the study of how society decides these "what," "how," and "for whom" questions.

Chapter 1 begins by discussing three economic issues which show how society deals with the problem of scarce resources and unlimited needs. The issues presented are the impact of the oil price increases of the 1970s, the distribution of income, and the role of government in a market economy. Each of these issues causes a response by society as it changes the allocation of its scarce resources, and so the answers to the basic questions change.

An important concept in economics is the production possibilities frontier. This frontier shows that society has a limit to what can be produced with its given resources and that more of one good can be produced only at the expense of other goods. The trade-off illustrated by the production possibilities frontier shows that using resources to produce one type of good costs society other goods. Society must choose where to be on the frontier. When this choice is made, the "what" and "how" questions are answered.

Society can answer the basic questions in different ways. One way is through markets. In a free market, government does not intervene. Buyers and sellers of goods come together for the purpose of trade. Each buyer and seller tries to maximize his self-interest, and this leads to the best interest of society as well. A command economy is another way in which society can try to promote its best interest, but in this system government decides the "what," "how," and "for whom" questions. Most countries have a mixed economy in which both government and markets interact in solving the basic questions.

Economists not only explain how society makes choices about consumption, production, and exchange, they also offer suggestions for improving the economy's performance. Positive economics deals with objective explanations of how the economy works. Normative economics offers prescriptions for the economy and is based on the economists' values.

All specialized areas in economics are based on microeconomic and macroeconomic principles. Microeconomic analysis studies the operation and behavior of individual economic units, while macroeconomics examines the operation of the entire economy.

CHAPTER OUTLINE

1. Economics is the study of how society makes choices about what, how, and for whom output is to be produced and thus decides how its scarce resources are to be allocated among competing alternatives. Three specific issues illustrate how society answers these three economic questions.
    a. The first issue is the impact of OPEC's oil price increase on both the domestic and the world economy. When the oil price shocks occurred during the middle and late 1970s, the price of petroleum products increased relative to the prices of other goods. Producers of goods using petroleum began to reduce their consumption of oil products as firms tried to find more fuel-efficient ways of producing output. The "how" question is answered in this case by having the firms produce in a more petroleum-efficient manner. The "what" question is answered as higher oil prices induce both households and firms to conserve on the use of petroleum so that goods that use less (or no) oil products are produced and consumed. The answer to the "for whom" question stems from OPEC's vastly increased wealth after the oil price increases. As this increased wealth flowed into the OPEC countries, they demanded more

goods and services. OPEC's share of world output increased, and less was left for everyone else.
  b. The second issue is the way income is divided among different groups both within the United States and among nations. More than half the world's population lives in low-income countries, and so we find low standards of living in much of the world. The industrialized countries have less than one-fifth of the world's population but receive 60 percent of the world's income. The "for whom" question is answered simply. The world economy produces primarily for people in the upper-income countries because they can afford to buy the output. The "what" question is also answered simply because output is produced primarily to satisfy the wants of people in the rich countries. The answer to the "how" question helps explain the differences in the distribution of output and income. In the rich countries, production takes place using a larger amount of machines and skilled labor, while in the poor countries, the production process involves a larger quantity of unskilled labor and fewer machines. The number of goods produced per worker per hour is higher in the industrialized countries than in the low-income countries, and so labor in the industrialized nations receives a much higher income. Within a particular country, the distribution of income is determined by the type of work performed by labor and the ownership of wealth. The distribution of income within a country influences the type of goods produced, who receives the goods, and how production takes place.
  c. The third issue is the way in which governments affect the allocation of resources and influence society's decisions on the "what," "how," and "for whom" questions. Governments provide services to society and make transfer payments (no services are provided by the recipient) to some citizens. In order to pay for these services and transfer payments, governments levy taxes. Governments affect the "what" question when they purchase particular goods and services; the "for whom" question is affected by taxing some citizens while making transfer payments to others; and the "how" question is affected when governments impose regulations on production. The role of government in economic activity is controversial. Some economists argue that government intervention into the economy causes disincentives to work and lowers overall production efficiency, while others argue that government participation improves society's overall well-being.
2. The production possibilities frontier illustrates both the concept of scarcity in an economic system and the problem of making choices about what is to be produced and how production is to take place. Given society's limited resources and a definite number of goods which can be produced, more of one good is produced only at the expense of other goods. This happens because of the law of diminishing returns. As resources are transferred from the production of all other goods into the production of only one good, the additional output of these extra resources falls. If society wants more of one good, it must transfer more and more resources out of the production of all other goods. If an economy produces only two goods, the production possibilities frontier shows for each level of the output of one good the maximum amount of the other good which can be produced. Each point on the curve is efficient because it's the best society can do. Points below the frontier are attainable but inefficient, while points outside the curve are not attainable. Where society chooses to be on its production possibilities frontier determines the types of goods produced and how (in terms of resource use) production takes place. In many economies, market activities primarily determine where society is on its frontier and answer the "what," "how," and "for whom" questions.
3. Buyers and sellers of goods and services come together in the market. The market is where households express decisions about their consumption of goods, firms decide what and how to produce, and workers decide how much and for whom to work. Because markets respond to the prices of both goods and resources, they allocate resources into the production of goods which society wants. Some economic systems, however, do not use markets to answer the three fundamental questions.
  a. In a command economy, the government makes the decisions about what will be produced, how, and for whom and then instructs firms and workers about its decisions. Even in a command economy, though, some markets exist to a small degree.
  b. When the government does not intervene in market activities, free markets exist. The invisible hand concept argues that as individuals in free markets pursue their own self-interest, the interests of others and of society as a whole are promoted. There is no need for any central direction by government, since the free market answers the basic economic questions.
  c. Completely free markets with individuals and

AN INTRODUCTION TO ECONOMICS AND THE ECONOMY

firms free to pursue their own self-interest and absolute command economies with their suppression of personal and economic freedoms are two opposite approaches society can take in answering the basic economic questions. These extremes, however, do not exist. Most countries have, to varying degrees, a mixed economic system. In a mixed economy, both the government and the private sector interact in solving the "what," "how," and "for whom" questions. The degree of government intervention in the economies of the industrialized countries differs. In the United States, most economists favor a free market, yet many still see areas in which government intervention might benefit society.

4. Economists are called upon to explain how the economy works and to make recommendations about how economic performance can be improved. When an economist objectively states a fact about the operation of the economy, positive economics is being practiced; the economist serves as a detached scientist. When statements are made about or prescriptions are made for an economic system on the basis of personal value judgments, normative economics is being practiced. Although positive and normative economics ideally should be kept separate, most economists find this difficult to do.

5. The fundamental principles on which all of economic analysis is based are classified as either microeconomics or macroeconomics. Microeconomics studies the behavior of individual economic agents and of particular markets or industries. In microeconomic analysis, emphasis is placed on the relative prices of goods, not the overall level of prices in the economy. Macroeconomics examines the activities and behavior of the economy as a whole. Three of the more frequently used macroeconomic concepts are gross national product, the aggregate price level, and the unemployment rate.

IMPORTANT TERMS AND THEIR MEANING

Match the following terms with the correct definition or phrase.

1. __i__ A society in which government makes all of the decisions about production and consumption

2. __q__ The value of all goods and services produced in the economy in a given time period

3. __e__ Offers prescriptions for an economy on the basis of personal value judgments

4. __o__ Term used to describe a falling aggregate price level

5. __a__ Examines the activities and behavior of the economy as a whole

6. __s__ Shows for each level of output of one good the maximum amount of the other good that can be produced

7. __l__ Shows how income is divided among different groups

8. __r__ Describes a market in which there is no government intervention and individuals are not restricted in the pursuit of their own self-interest

9. __f__ There is only a limited amount of land, labor, and machines which can be used to satisfy society's virtually unlimited needs

10. __n__ Examines the activities and behavior of individual economic agents

11. __g__ The most output possible is being produced with the resources available to society; any point on the production possibilities frontier

12. __c__ Term used to describe an increasing aggregate price level

13. __k__ Adding more and more workers to a given industry causes the number of goods produced by the extra workers to fall because each has less of the other resources with which to work

14. __p__ Deals with objective or scientific explanations of the working of an economy

15. __t__ Payments made to individuals without their providing a service in return

a. Macroeconomics
b. Trade-off
c. Inflation
d. Invisible hand
e. Normative economics
f. Scarcity
g. Efficiency
h. Adam Smith
i. Command economy
j. Unemployment
k. Diminishing returns
l. Income distribution
m. Mixed economy
n. Microeconomics
o. Deflation

16. _h_ Author of the *Wealth of Nations* (1776), who argued that society would benefit if individuals pursued their own self-interest

17. _m_ The government and private sector interact in solving the basic economic questions

18. _j_ The situation in which individuals are in the labor force, want to work, but cannot find a job

19. _d_ Argues that individuals pursuing their own self-interest are led to do things that are in the interest of others and of society as a whole

20. _b_ Because all resources have alternative uses, in order to get one good, another good which could have been produced has to be given up

p. Positive economics

q. Gross national product

r. The free market

s. Production possibilities frontier

t. Transfers

EXERCISES

1. Presented in the table below is the production possibilities schedule for a hypothetical economy. It is assumed that the economy produces only two goods: movies and steaks. It is also assumed that all resources are employed in the production of either movies or steaks. The table shows six alternative output possibilities.

			POSSIBILITY			
GOOD	A	B	C	D	E	F
Steaks	15	14	12	9	5	0
Movies	0	1	2	3	4	5

a. This table shows what the economy (can/should) __CAN__ produce and would be described as (positive/normative) __POSITIVE__ economics.

b. In order to produce the first movie, society must give up __ONE__ unit(s) of steak.

c. As society chooses to produce more movies, people must give up (more/fewer) __MORE__ steaks for each extra movie produced. This happens because as resources continue to transfer out of the production of __STEAKS__ into the production of __MOVIES__, the law of __Diminishing Returns__ applies.

d. It (is/is not) __IS NOT__ possible for society to produce 14 steaks and 3 movies.

e. Every time an additional movie is produced, it costs society something in terms of steaks. In the table below, complete the column labeled "cost of movies in terms of steaks" by entering the number of steaks which must be given up in order to produce one more movie.

MOVIES	COST OF MOVIES IN TERMS OF STEAKS
First movie	1
Second movie	2
Third movie	3
Fourth movie	4
Fifth movie	5

f. This table shows that as society produces more of one good, its costs (increase/decrease) __INCREASE__ in terms of the other good so that the trade-off (is/is not) __IS NOT__ constant.

2. Figure 1-1 shows the six production possibilities for movies and steaks presented in Exercise 1.

a. Connect the six possibilities and label your curve PPF.

b. If society is (on/below/beyond) __ON__ the PPF, the economy is producing efficiently, but any point (on/below/beyond) __BELOW__ the PPF shows that resources are being wasted.

c. Suppose that the economy was producing 3 movies but only 5 steaks. Find the point which represents this combination of goods and label it point G. At point G, society is producing (efficiently/inefficiently) __INEFF.__ because it could produce __9 STEAKS__ units

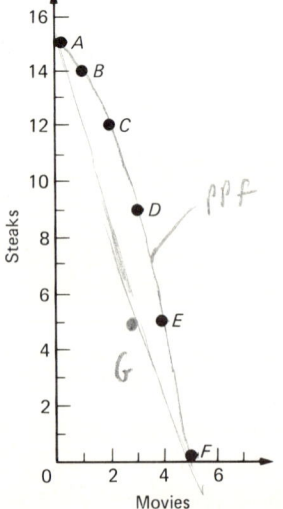

FIGURE 1-1

AN INTRODUCTION TO ECONOMICS AND THE ECONOMY

of steaks and 3 movies or 5 units of steak and __4__ movies.

d. Suppose now that the law of diminishing returns does not hold and that steaks can be traded for movies at the rate of 3 steaks for each movie. The maximum number of steaks which can be produced (assuming no movies) is 15. The maximum number of movies which can be produced (assuming no steaks) is 5. Draw a new PPF to reflect this constant trade-off and label if PPF'.

The PPF' is now a __STRAIGHT__ line because the cost of movies in terms of steak (does/does not) __DOES NOT__ increase as more movies and fewer steaks are produced.

3. Below are six statements which the economist might find interesting. In the blank beside each statement, indicate whether it is a positive (P) or normative (N) statement.

   a. __P__ Sanitation workers in San Francisco have an average salary of $20,000 per year.

   b. __N__ Craftsmen from the Appalachian region of the United States are the best in the country.

   c. __N__ The average salary of sanitation workers in San Francisco is too high.

   d. __P__ In August 1982, the price of gold again topped the $400 per ounce mark.

   e. __P__ In 1924, the value of GNP in the United States was $85 billion.

   f. __N__ Because the market system promotes an unfair distribution of income, it should be done away with, and economic planning should take its place.

4. In the spaces below, list and give one-sentence definitions of three frequently used macroeconomic concepts.

   a. __GNP Value of wealth produced via goods and services in a given time__

   b. __Average prices, calculate on no. & value of goods__

   c. __Unemployment rate % working population out of work__

FILL-IN QUESTIONS

1. The __unemployment rate__ is the percentage of individuals in the labor force who would like to find work but cannot.

2. The price of a gallon of gasoline, the number of workers hired by a firm, and the satisfaction received by a consumer from eating a hamburger are examples of topics studied in (micro/macro) __micro__ economics.

3. Economics is the study of how society decides __what__ is to be produced, __how__ it is to be produced, and __for whom__.

4. The dramatic price increases of petroleum products during the 1970s were called __oil price__ shocks, and as a result the OPEC countries had (more/less) __more__ money to spend.

5. In a command economy, the __government__ plans the production and distribution activities of the entire economy, but in a market economy, these decisions are made by __individuals__ as they each pursue their own __end__.

6. By levying taxes and making transfer payments, governments directly influence how society answers the (how/for whom) __for whom__ question.

7. With its given level of resources, there (is/is not) __is__ a definite amount of goods and services a society can produce during a certain period of time; if society wants more of one good, it must give up increasingly (more/less) __more__ of other goods.

8. The __law of D. Ret__ states that as we add additional workers to an industry, the amount each extra worker adds to output declines.

9. Adam Smith argued that it (was/was not) __was__ possible for society's well-being to be promoted when each individual pursued his own __ends__.

10. In a __mixed__ economy, both the government and the private sector interact in solving the fundamental economic questions. This (is/is not) __is__ the most frequently encountered type of economic system.

11. Normative economics reflects __economic__ judgments which are based on an individual's feelings about an issue.

TRUE-FALSE QUESTIONS

1. __T__ To say that the rate of inflation is 6.2 percent per year is a positive statement about a macroeconomic concept.

2. __F__ The distribution of income tells how much a country produced during a particular period of time and serves as an indicator of the citizens' standard of living.

3. _T_ A frequently heard argument against government transfer payments and income taxes is that they create disincentives to work and affect the way society allocates its scarce resources.

4. _T_ Any point along a production possibilities frontier is efficient because it shows the most that society can produce with its given resources.

5. _F_ Once society determines its production possibilities in a market system, it is up to economists to decide where production should take place and what goods should be produced.

6. _F_ In an absolute command economy, the government determines what is to be produced and who receives the output, but it leaves the decisions about how to produce up to private citizens.

7. _T_ The United States, the Soviet Union, and Hong Kong all have mixed economies, but they all have different degrees of market orientation.

8. _F_ When economists make normative statements about market performance, they are simply stating facts about prices, output, income, and employment.

9. _T_ All of the specialized areas of economics have as their basis either microeconomics or macroeconomics.

10. _F_ The OPEC price increases during the 1970s had little or no effect on either how or what the U.S. economy produced.

MULTIPLE CHOICE QUESTIONS

Circle the correct answer.

1. The production possibilities frontier is concave to the origin because
   a. if society wants an extra unit of one good, it has to give up increasing amounts of the other good
   b. the extra output produced by resources declines as more and more are added to a given industry
   c. the law of diminishing returns applies
   d. it shows that as more of one good is produced, its cost in terms of other goods increases
   e. all of the above

2. Economics can be defined as
   a. the study of the stock market
   b. the study of how society answers the "what," "how," and "for whom" questions
   c. the study of how government influences market behavior
   d. the study of how to increase personal financial well-being

3. All of the following are classified as low-income countries except
   a. Brazil   c. China
   b. India   d. Uganda

4. In a country where assets are privately owned and highly concentrated in the hands of a few, we would expect
   a. income to be equally distributed across the population
   b. a larger percentage of the population living in poverty and a small percentage being very wealthy
   c. a large percentage of the population being very wealthy and a small percentage living in poverty
   d. none of the above

5. When governments tax and make transfer payments to households, they are most directly affecting
   a. what is to be produced
   b. how production is to take place
   c. the location of the production possibilities frontier
   d. for whom output is produced

6. When society chooses a point on its production possibilities frontier, it answers all of the following except
   a. how to produce
   b. what to produce
   c. for whom to produce
   d. where production takes place efficiently

7. The term "free markets" describes
   a. markets in which there is an absence of government intervention and the invisible hand is operating
   b. markets in which the government establishes the prices producers must charge for their output
   c. markets in which employers must pay labor a minimum wage and produce according to government regulations
   d. markets in which government prohibits the price of certain goods from rising above a certain level

8. The United States, Canada, and Great Britain are said to have mixed economies because
   a. firms produce only with the approval of the government
   b. government exercises no influence over the market
   c. both government and the private sector interact to solve the basic economic questions
   d. there are no trade barriers between the three nations

9. All of the following are positive economic statements except
  a. in August 1982, the Fed lowered its discount rate to 10 percent
  b. the unemployment rate during 1981 exceeded 9 percent
  c. the Federal income tax is unfair to middle-income households
  d. the Social Security tax base is now greater than $30,000

10. Microeconomics examines all of the following except
  a. the level of output produced by a firm
  b. increases or decreases in the level of unemployment
  c. the impact on sales of a higher federal excise tax on a bottle of whiskey
  d. the number of workers hired in a particular industry

11. Which of the following statements is incorrect?
  a. in a mixed economy, the organization of all markets is the same  *as well*
  b. markets can answer the basic economic questions
  c. a market can exist only if there are buyers and sellers
  d. markets are one way society can determine the allocation of its scarce resources

12. All of the following are characteristics of an absolute command economy except
  a. government decides what, how, and for whom to produce
  b. there is a strong central government
  c. there is an absence of markets
  d. there is private ownership and allocation of resources

AT THIS POINT YOU SHOULD BE ABLE TO . . .

1. Write a definition of economics and explain the problem of scarcity.
2. Using one of the issues presented in this chapter, explain how society deals with the allocation of scarce resources among competing demands.
3. Construct a production possibilities frontier and explain the principles behind the curve.
4. State the effect of the law of diminishing returns on the shape of the production possibilities frontier.
5. Explain the concept of a free market and a command economy and state how each answers the basic economic questions.
6. Describe how the invisible hand can produce a coherent society.
7. Explain why most countries have a mixed economy rather than either of the two absolute extremes.
8. Give an example of positive and normative economic statements.
9. State the difference between microeconomics and macroeconomics and list two topics covered in each.

QUESTIONS FOR THOUGHT

1. What are some of the arguments both for and against active government participation in market activities? In your opinion, is the role of government in our economy good or bad? Explain.
2. The production possibilities frontier emphasizes the notion of scarcity and the problem of choosing what is to be produced. Why is the term "frontier" used? Under what conditions would the frontier shift outward? Explain.
3. If you had to define economics to a friend, what would you say? Why do you think people study economics?
4. Explain the difference between microeconomics and macroeconomics. Professors Fischer and Dornbusch state that nearly all economic issues fall into either microeconomics or macroeconomics. Explain what they mean by this statement.
5. Explain the difference between a free market and a command economy. How does each answer the basic economic questions?

2

The Tools Economists Use

Chapter 2 introduces some basic concepts and techniques employed by economists in their attempt to understand economic events. Economists, like physicists or chemists, use a scientific approach to problem solving but, unlike pure scientists, do not have the luxury of a controlled laboratory environment. Using the scientific method, economists formulate theories, specify models, collect data, advance hypotheses, and then test the hypotheses to either substantiate or refute the theory.

Chapter 2 is organized into nine main parts, and the emphasis is on correctly formulating, building, and testing economic models. When you have mastered Chapter 2, you will have learned the basic foundation for a new way of thinking.

Chapter 2 begins by locating some of the more frequently used data sources and emphasizes the importance of using tables and charts in economic analysis. The main discussion of economic data centers on the meanings and descriptions of time series and cross section data. Time series data are measurements of economic variables over a period of time (weeks, months, or years). Cross section data, on the other hand, are measurements of a given variable taken at a particular time for different economic units. All data used in your textbook belong to one of these two types and are frequently presented in tabular or graphic form. Weighted averages are commonly used in the analysis of time series data.

Index numbers, which are numbers expressing time series data in terms of a common base value, permit economists to compare different economic data over time. The best known index number is the consumer price index (CPI).

Economic data can be either real or nominal. A variable's nominal value is expressed in current dollars; it is the variable's money value. The real value of a variable equals its purchasing power. An index of prices allows an economist to convert nominal values into real values. Economists are interested in how variables change. When analyzing time series data, they want to know how much a variable changes over time. When studying cross section data, they want to know how much a variable changes among different groups. Two ratios commonly used to measure changes in variables are the percentage change and the growth rate.

Economists build models to help organize their thinking processes and to express relationships among economic variables. Models may be very formal mathematical expressions or very informal arguments about the perceived relationships among variables. Diagrams are used in model building to help us visualize how variables interact with one another. By plotting data in a scatter diagram and then fitting a line to the data, it is possible to determine quickly whether variables are related. Economic theory alone may not tell this.

Economic models often incorporate simplifying assumptions in order to reach a conclusion. One simplifying assumption is "other things equal." This assumption is needed because there are many economic factors in an actual situation, and this makes analysis difficult. The economist attempts to make the situation less complex by eliminating some factors. The economist must be aware that although other things may be assumed equal, they often are not.

Although economists follow the scientific method when observing economic phenomena by advancing a theory to explain the phenomena and then testing hypotheses with data in an attempt to accept or refute the theory, the absence of a controlled experimental environment makes economics an inexact science.

CHAPTER OUTLINE

1. Economists use data to describe economic events which occur in society. Data also serve as inputs into theoretical and descriptive models. A first step to any serious study of economics is the development of an understanding of data collection, organization, and tabulation techniques.
    a. Some common sources of economic data are government and trade publications as well as private data banks. Among the most frequently

used government publications are the *Statistical Abstract of the U.S.* and *The Economic Report of the President.*
- b. Once data are collected, they can be presented in the form of tables and charts. A table has a title, specifics of data measurement, a legend, and any other description specific to the data being presented.
- c. Data collected at different points in time (weeks, months, or years) are called time series data and show how variables change over time. Time series data are often presented diagrammatically in charts. In a chart, both the vertical and horizontal axes are labeled in the appropriate units (the horizontal axis may measure time), and the data points are plotted in the space between the axes. Although charts are a convenient way of presenting data, caution must be taken not to mislead or be misled by the graphical presentations. In both charts and tables, time series data are often presented as averages.
- d. In contrast to time series data, cross section data measure a given variable for different economic units at the same moment of time. Cross section data can also be presented in tables or charts.
  - (1) The median of any set of data is the middle point when the data are arranged by size. The mean is the average of the data. The mean may be influenced or distorted by extreme values in the data, but the median is not affected by such values.
2. When economic data are measured in different units, an index number allows the comparison of the different data sets. An index number expresses data relative to a given base value and is calculated by the formula

$$\text{Index number} = \frac{\text{value of observed data}}{\text{value of base}} \times 100$$

Index numbers provide a quick and convenient method of comparing data over different time periods or different data series.
- a. An important use of index numbers is to describe the behavior of several different economic variables and express this behavior in a single number. To develop a single index number for a group of variables, an index for each variable to be included is first calculated and then weighted. The weighted average of the index for the group of variables (the single index number) is calculated by adding all of the individually weighted indices. The weighted average provides an index number which allows an analysis of the overall behavior of the group of variables.
- b. One of the most frequently cited indices is the consumer price index (CPI). The CPI measures the price behavior of a broad group of commodities often consumed by households, and so it is a weighted average. The index is a measure of inflation and tells how prices, on average, change.
- c. Indices can be developed to measure such diverse data as wages, production, manufacturing, and stock prices. To create an index for a set of time series data, a base year must be established and assigned a value of 100. All other data are then expressed in relation to the base year.
3. Economic data are at times measured in real terms and at other times measured in nominal terms. Real data are adjusted for changes in the price level. Nominal data are expressed in terms of current prices. The nominal value of economic data is simply its money value, but the data's real value shows what the data will buy. Economists are often interested in how real values change over time or within a specific time period because such information is important in understanding the effects of inflation on the economy.
- a. The real (relative) price of a good is its price measured relative to the prices of other goods. The real price of a good is adjusted for changes in the general level of prices. The nominal price of a good is simply the price measured in dollars. Consumers are often more concerned with the relative prices of goods than with nominal prices.
- b. The purchasing power of money is an index of the amount of goods that can be bought with a dollar. Real income is a measure of the purchasing power of income because prices are held constant. All real variables are measured in constant dollars because the effect of changes in the price level is removed so that the purchasing power of money remains the same. Nominal variables are measured in current dollars because no adjustment is made for changes in the purchasing power of these dollars.
4. Economists usually want to know how much a variable changes, and so two widely used measures are the percentage change and the growth rate.
- a. The percentage change in either time series or cross section data provides a unit-free statistic. A percentage change in an index number (or other economic data such as price, quantity,

or income) from one period to the next is calculated by the formula

Percentage change
$$= \frac{\begin{pmatrix} \text{ending} & \text{beginning} \\ \text{observation} - \text{observation} \end{pmatrix}}{\text{beginning observation}} \times 100$$

The percentage change can be either positive or negative, depending on the direction of the change.

b. When time series data are being examined, it is useful to measure the growth rate of the variable over time. The growth rate is the percentage rate per period by which a variable is changing. For any two time periods, the growth rate can be calculated as a percentage change, using the formula in 4a.

5. As economists establish relationships between variables and use these relationships to make predictions, building an economic model helps organize the thinking and reasoning process. An economic model is a simplified picture of reality and provides a logical framework for examining an issue. The construction of an economic model begins with the observation of economic events in the real world. Although some elements of the model may be given, others, through a process of theoretical abstraction, may be assumed constant (other things equal). Through either statistics or logical means, the model is specified.

   a. The main purpose of model building is to provide a systematic way of thinking about a problem. Models may be very simple or very elaborate, but they should all simplify reality. There is no easy answer to the question of how far models should go in simplifying the real world.

6. During the specification and definition of the basic framework of a model, the actual relationship between variables is unknown. The model tells what the relevant facts (data) are.

   a. Examining historical or cross sectional data on the variables in either tabular or graphic form may help establish their relationship.
   b. The scatter diagram is a quick and convenient method of determining how two variables are related. If a relationship exists between two variables, the scatter diagram also provides a general idea about its strength.

7. Besides showing the combined observations on two variables, the scatter diagram shows that if a relationship exists, it may be either positive or negative.

   a. When a scatter diagram contains many observations, we can fit a line through the points on the diagram. Fitting a line through the data is a statistical technique usually performed by an econometrician. The significance of the fitted line is that it establishes an approximate quantitative relationship between the two variables.

   b. The quantitative relationship established by the econometrician between two variables takes the form of an equation, or an algebraic statement of the fitted line. The equation shows the exact relationship between two variables.

   c. Economic relationships are often presented in diagrams. An equation showing the relationship between two variables is easily plotted and states the slope and intercept of the line. The slope of a line indicates its steepness, while the intercept is the point at which the line crosses the vertical axis. The slope of a line may be positive or negative. When the slope is negative, the relationship between the variables is negative. A negative relationship between two variables means that higher values of one imply lower values of the other; the variables move in opposite directions. A positive relationship means that higher values of one imply higher values of the other; the variables move in the same direction. Not all economic relationships plot as straight lines.

8. Economists often make the simplifying assumption of "all other things equal" as they build models. This assumption is made in order to remove all the market interactions which might affect the variables under analysis. When a model specifies a relationship between two variables and all other things are assumed equal, you must be aware that some of the things that are assumed away may affect the model's results. It is not uncommon for variables to be omitted from a model when they should have been included.

9. Economists do not have the luxury of controlled laboratory experiments. However, by observing economic phenomena, presenting a theory or model to explain the phenomena, and then testing the theory, economists are learning how a complex economic system works. As theories are tested, retested, and substantiated, they are accepted as facts.

IMPORTANT TERMS AND THEIR MEANING

Match the following terms with the correct definition or phrase.

1. __ℓ__ In a graphic presentation of an equation, this number tells how much Y changes when X changes

   a. Consumer price index

2. __k__ Dollars which have not been adjusted for the price level; a nominal measure

3. __l__ The arithmetic average of a group of data

4. __p__ A direct relationship between two variables; when one variable increases, the other variable increases

5. __x__ An index of the amount of goods that can be bought with a dollar

6. __a__ An index number of the prices of goods that households consume

7. __d__ Calculated by using the formula

$$\left(\frac{\text{ending observation} - \text{beginning observation}}{\text{beginning observation}}\right) \times 100$$

8. __u__ In an equation, the value of Y when X is zero; the point where a line cuts the vertical axis

9. __q__ Graphic presentation showing the combined observations on two variables and indicating whether an obvious relationship exists between the two variables

10. __b__ A commodity's price measured relative to the price of other goods; the real price of a commodity

11. __g__ A logical, organized framework for examining an issue which may take the form of verbal arguments, equations, or diagrams; a simplified picture of reality

12. __i__ Shorthand for "depends on" and written as $f(\ )$

13. __w__ A collection of measurements of a variable at different points or intervals of time

14. __f__ Expresses data relative to a given base value

15. __r__ The growth rate of prices

16. __h__ The measurement of economic variables after the effects of price changes have been removed

17. __c__ The middle number in a group of data when the data are organized by size

18. __v__ A simplifying assumption often made by economists in order to remove the problem of the interaction of many economic forces

19. __o__ The percentage rate per period by which a variable is increasing

20. __n__ Variables expressed in money (dollar) terms

21. __m__ Information organized for analysis; facts

22. __s__ Data measurement of a given variable for different economic units

23. __j__ A relationship between two variables in which they move in opposite directions; when one increases, the other decreases

24. __t__ Using a particular year for comparison, dollars are expressed in terms of their real purchasing power

b. Relative price
c. Median
d. Percentage change
e. Slope of a line
f. Index numbers
g. Model
h. Real variables
i. Function
j. Negative relationship
k. Current dollars
l. Mean
m. Data
n. Nominal variables
o. Growth rate
p. Positive relationship
q. Scatter diagram
r. Inflation rate
s. Cross section data
t. Constant dollars
u. Intercept of a line
v. Other things equal
w. Time series data
x. Purchasing power of money

EXERCISES

1. Listed in Table 2-1 are seven different data sets. In the blanks beside each set, identify the data as being cross section or time series. Place a check (√) in the appropriate column.

2. a. Suppose you are given the following data from the U.S. Bureau of Labor Statistics *News*, May 7, 1982, about unemployment rates for February, March, and April 1982. The unemployment rates are expressed as a percentage of the labor force. All workers: Feb. = 8.8, Mar. = 9.0, April = 9.4. Adult men: Feb. = 7.6, Mar. = 7.9, April = 8.2. Adult women: Feb. = 7.6, Mar. = 7.9, April = 8.3. Teenagers: Feb. = 22.3, Mar. = 21.9, April = 23.0. Construct a table presenting these data. Be sure to give your table a title.

CHAPTER 2

TABLE 2-1

DATA SET	TIME SERIES	CROSS SECTION
a. The number of eggs supplied by farmers at different prices		✓
b. Yearly change in the average output per worker in manufacturing between 1950 and 1980	✓	
c. The amount people are willing to save at different income levels		✓
d. The average earnings per worker for different levels of education		✓
e. The monthly unemployment rate for 1982	✓	
f. The amount of revenue acquired by a firm in an industry as a result of selling different levels of output		✓
g. The hourly earnings index for production workers, by industry, during quarters 1, 2, 3, and 4 of 1981	✓	

b. Plot the four sets of time series data on graph paper. Label the vertical axis "percentage unemployment" and the horizontal axis "time." On the horizontal axis, every 8 spaces should indicate one of the months. Do you need a break (squiggly line) on the axis? Identify each curve by its worker classification. You will have to approximate some of the percentages.

3. Table 2-2 presents the weights for the consumer price index (CPI) as shown in Table 2-7 of your text. Also in the table are hypothetical price indices for each component in the CPI for 2 years.

a. In Table 2-2, the sum of the weights is __1__. Complete the table by calculating the weighted price index for each component listed.

b. In order to calculate the weighted component index, it is necessary to multiply the component price index by its respective __weight %__.

c. From your calculations, the weighted CPI for 1980 is __238.8__, and for 1981 it is __251.1__.

d. From 1980 to 1981, the CPI (increased/decreased) __increased__ by __12.3__, while prices grew at a rate of __5.15__ percent.

4. In Table 2-3, annual sales and promotional expenditures are presented for invisible goldfish for the years 1970 through 1980.

a. Plot a scatter diagram of the observations on graph paper. It is reasonable to assume that the number of fish sold is a function of the amount of money spent on promotion of the product, or

Fish sold = f(promotion expenditures)

The vertical axis should be labeled "number of fish sold," and the horizontal axis should be labeled "promotion expenditure." On your grid, let two squares represent 1 unit of promotion expenditure and 1 unit of fish sold.

b. Your scatter diagram plots (times series/cross section) __cross section__ data and suggests that a (positive/negative) __positive__ relationship exists between promotion expenditures and sales since as expenditures increase, sales (increase/decrease) __increase__.

c. If you made a general statement about the relationship between the number of fish sold and promotional expenditures, you would be stating a (hypothesis/prediction) __prediction × Hypothesis__

d. In the scatter diagram, draw a line which you think best fits the data. The line will be an approximation, and there may be one or two observations in the data which lie some distance from the line.

e. The intercept of the line drawn in the scatter diagram (is/is not) __is not__ zero, and its slope is (positive/negative) __positive__. From the line, it appears that each 1-unit increase in promotion expenditures results in an increase of approximately __0.65__ fish sold, and this approximates the (intercept/slope) __slope__ of the line.

5. Graph each of the following equations by assigning X the values of 0, 1, 2, 3, 4, and 5.

TABLE 2-2
HYPOTHETICAL CONSUMER PRICE INDEX DATA (1972 = 100)

COMPONENT	WEIGHT, %	COMPONENT PRICE INDEX, 1980	WEIGHTED COMPONENT INDEX, 1980	COMPONENT PRICE INDEX, 1981	WEIGHTED COMPONENT INDEX, 1981
Food	.192	214.7	41.2	224.7	43.1
Housing	.443	291.6	129.2	306.4	135.7
Apparel and upkeep	.055	183.4	10.1	197.2	10.8
Transportation	.177	205.9	36.4	211.5	37.4
Medical care	.050	176.3	8.8	187.8	9.4
Entertainment	.040	165.5	6.6	179.4	7.2
Other goods and services	.043	150.0	6.5	170.9	7.3

238.8   251.1

THE TOOLS ECONOMISTS USE

TABLE 2-3
INVISIBLE GOLDFISH: NUMBER OF FISH SOLD AND PROMOTIONAL EXPENDITURES FOR YEARS 1970–1980

	1970	1971	1972	1973	1974	1975	1976	1977	1978	1979	1980
Promotional expenditures, $	1.5	2.5	3.0	2.0	3.5	6.5	4.5	5.5	6.0	4.0	5.0
Number of fish sold	2	5	4	3	9	10	6	7	11	8	12

a. $Y = 5 + 2X$ b. $Y = 5 - 2X$

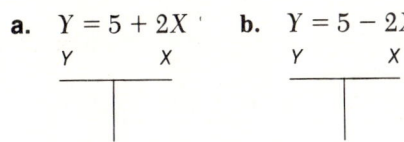

c. Equation (a) represents a __positive__ relationship between Y and X with an intercept of __five__ and a slope of __2__, while equation (b) is a __negative__ relationship between Y and X with an intercept of __5__ and a slope of __-2__.

6. On graph paper, plot the following schedules. Smooth the curves as best as possible.

a. Y	X	b. Y	X
−1½	1	7½	1
0	2	4	2
2	3	2½	3
3½	4	2	4
4	5	1½	5
3½	6	2	6
2	7	2½	7
0	8	4	8
−1½	9	7½	9

7. In the spaces below, list the three steps generally followed by economists in their approach to problem solving.

a. __spot a relation__

b. __build model__

c. __test model__

FILL-IN QUESTIONS

1. The major reason for indexing various data sets is to improve the (calculation/comparison) __comparison__ of the data over time.

2. The problem of interdependence among economic forces is often overcome by invoking the __other things =__ assumption.

3. Economists often develop a __model__ which permits an organized way of looking at various phenomena and often (is/is not) __is__ a simplified picture of the real world.

4. In order for typical students of economics to be successful, it is necessary that they possess the ability to organize data in __tables__ and __charts__, since these are the two main methods for data presentation.

5. The __[Economist] GOD KNOWS__ is one of the best general sources of many types of data.

6. If an analyst uses average data over a long period of time, short-term fluctuations become (more/less) __less__ important in influencing the data set.

7. The relationship between income levels and consumption expenditures in the United States is an example of (cross section/time series) __cross section__ data, while change in consumption and income patterns since World War II is an example of (cross section/time series) __time series__ data.

8. In a set of data, the middle number in the set is the (median/mean) __median__, while the average of the data is the (median/mean) __mean__.

9. The Dow Jones average is a __weighted__ average of the price of different stocks.

10. Economists often use the (absolute/percentage) __%__ change in a variable because it is more easily compared to changes in other data series since it (is/is not) __is not__ expressed in units.

11. If we wanted to examine a (theoretical/statistical) __statistical__ relationship, we could plot the data in a __scatter__ diagram.

12. __econometrics__ is the branch of economics concerned primarily with measuring and quantifying the relationship among economic variables.

13. Any graphed relationship, either linear or non-linear, can be described by the characteristics of its ___slope___ and ___intercept___.

14. If an economic model is explicitly stated but misspecified, we have (included/excluded) ___excluded___ important factors from the model, and it (will/will not) ___will not___ perform satisfactorily in explaining the relationships among the data.

15. An economic theory that has been tested and accepted over a long period of time becomes accepted as a ___theory___ (law).

TRUE-FALSE QUESTIONS

1. __F__ To state that $Y = f(x)$ is to state a specific relationship, in equation form, between variables X and Y.

2. __T__ In contrast to cross section data, time series data measure the changes over time of a particular variable or a set of different variables.

3. __T__ Data presented in graphic form can be misleading and can suggest results not substantiated by the facts.

4. __T__ Given any data set, the observation having the greatest distance from the mean can significantly influence the mean of the data.

5. __F__ The first step in solving any economic problem is to advance a hypothesis in order to predict how the problem might be solved.

6. __F__ In order to construct a CPI, all prices must be added, divided by the price level in a given base year, and multiplied by 100.

7. __F__ The only areas in which indices can be used effectively are those involving wage or price data.

8. __T__ A measure of the purchasing power of a good in terms of a general basket of goods is a measure of its real value.

9. __F__ For a table with the title "Annual Index of Beef Prices, 1965–1982 (1972 = 100)," the base year is 1965.

10. __X__ When the term "economic growth" is used in casual conversation, it usually refers to the average standard of living.

11. __T__ For any economic theory, its ultimate (and only) test is how well it predicts economic events.

12. __T__ There are some variables within an economic system over which analysts and model builders have no control.

13. __T__ If X and Y exhibit a positive relationship, as one increases, so will the other.

14. __T__ The equation $Y = 10 - 5X$ shows a negative relationship between X and Y; it has an intercept of 10 and a slope of -5.

15. __F__ A major disadvantage faced by economists which biologists do not have is that economists cannot conduct controlled experiments in a "laboratory" setting.

MULTIPLE CHOICE QUESTIONS

Circle the correct answer.

1. The major reason why economists develop models is that
 a. a model is necessary to test a hypothesis
 b. a model helps clarify and organize the thinking process about an issue
 c. a model is required in order to determine an index number
 d. only real variables are used in a model

2. In April 1981 the index of industrial production was 151.9 (1967 = 100), and in April 1982 the index was 140.7. It can be concluded that the percentage change in the index over the year's period is approximately
 a. 7.4 percent   c. −7.9 percent
 b. 7.9 percent   **d.** −7.4 percent

3. All of the following are steps in the economist's approach to problem solving except
 a. disregarding previous theories
 b. collection and organization of available data
 c. observation and model building
 d. testing of hypotheses

4. Which of the following statements is correct?
 a. if X and Y are positively related, an increase in the value of X results in a decrease in the value of Y
 b. if X and Y are negatively related, a negative change in X results in a negative change in Y
 c. if X and Y are positively related, a graph of the values of X and Y will slope upward and to the right
 d. if X and Y are unrelated, a graph of the values of X and Y will slope downward

5. The presence of market interaction
 a. is unimportant in the economist's model building
 b. exerts little or no influence on the behavior of price and quantity in markets
 c. often is simply assumed away by economists
 d. suggests that markets are completely independent of each other

6. As prices change over time, the indices of the real value of a good

a. experience no change in their numerical value
   b. hold nominal changes constant
   c. change less frequently than prices
   d. present a more accurate picture of time series data than do indices of nominal values

7. Economic theories
   a. serve no relevant purpose in the study of economics
   b. can be tested by the application of data to a model
   c. are indisputable most of the time
   d. cannot be tested because they are based primarily on abstract ideas

8. The dollar value of the wage rate in the textile manufacturing industry between 1950 and 1980 is an example of
   a. time series data
   b. cross section data
   c. real data values
   d. economic predictions

9. If the consumer price index in March 1981 was 261.5 and in March 1982 was 283.4, prices have grown at a rate of
   a. 10.37 percent   c. 8.37 percent
   b. −7.73 percent   d. 9.42 percent

10. To say that an index is a weighted average means that
    a. it is the sum of the indices of the weighted components
    b. it will range between the upper and lower index values of its components
    c. it incorporates some predetermined weighting scheme for its components
    d. it more nearly reflects the index value of the component with the largest weight
    e. all of the above

11. The likelihood of finding the average wage paid vineyard workers in France would be greatest if you consulted
    a. *Economic Report of the President*
    b. *Handbook of Labor Statistics*
    c. *International Financial Statistics*
    d. *Statistical Abstract of the U.S.*

12. The average household income in New York by age and ethnic origin is an example of
    a. cross section data   c. real value data
    b. time series data   d. none of the above

13. If the index of poultry prices in 1982 was 217.3 and the GNP deflator was 287.4, the index of the real price of poultry in 1982 was
    a. 124.2   c. 261.9
    b. 88.7   d. 75.6

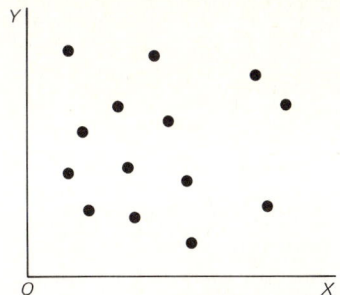

FIGURE 2-1

14. Figure 2-1 suggests
    a. a linear relationship between X and Y
    b. no relationship between X and Y
    c. a positive relationship between X and Y
    d. a negative relationship between X and Y

15. Suppose the prices of widgets in five different cities are $2, $5, $9, $21, and $23. The median price and the mean price are
    a. median $12, mean $9
    b. median $2, mean $21
    c. median $9, mean $12
    d. median $12, mean $12
    e. cannot be determined

AT THIS POINT YOU SHOULD BE ABLE TO . . .

1. State two ways in which data interact with models, prepare a set of data for presentation using both tables and charts, and explain the differences between time series and cross section data.
2. State an example of how the graphic presentation of data can be misleading.
3. Calculate an index number from raw data, explain why indices are used in data presentation, and state why the base value is important to any index.
4. Explain how the consumer price index is a weighted average of component prices and state the procedure for weighting a group of data.
5. Distinguish between nominal and real variables.
6. Calculate both the percentage change and the growth rate between two numbers.
7. Write one or two sentences stating the purpose of an economic model and explain the importance of the "other things equal" assumption in economic model building.
8. Distinguish between functional notation $f(\ )$ and an equation.
9. Plot a scatter diagram from a given set of data and state the observed relationship between the variables.
10. Define a positive and negative relationship between variables and draw a graph of each type.
11. State how an equation shows a positive or negative relationship between variables, define a curve's

intercept and slope, and identify the intercept and slope components in an equation.

12. List three generally accepted steps followed in solving economic problems.

QUESTIONS FOR THOUGHT

1. The use of charts to present data is commonplace in economics and business since they are a convenient and easily understood tool. Charts, however, can be misleading. Explain how.

2. Explain this statement from your text: "Index numbers are used to describe the behavior over time of a group's 'basket' of economic data series." Why is such a description desirable?

3. At several places in your text, you saw the terms "relative," "relative to," and "relatively." What is meant exactly when economists use these terms? Why do you think they are important?

4. In the presentation of scatter diagrams, line fitting, and equations, only two variables were used to describe the graphs. Certainly an equation can have more than two variables. Why is it that only two variables were used in the graphs and equations in your text?

5. The "other things equal" assumption is used frequently in economic analysis; however, it can be a dangerous assumption. Explain why this is so.

6. Do you think that the absence of controlled experiments in economics weakens the discipline? Explain why or why not.

7. In a few sentences, briefly construct what you think might be the basic framework of a model for beef in the United States.

8. Explain how an economic model might be used to justify a university charging students less than nonstudents to attend football games.

Demand, Supply, and the Market

The basic framework of a market economy is presented in Chapter 3. A market brings buyers and sellers of a good together for the purpose of trade. The basic questions of "what," "how," and "for whom" and hence the problem of allocating society's scarce resources can be answered through the market system.

Every market consists of two basic forces: supply and demand. These forces result from the behavior of independent buyers and sellers. The interaction of supply and demand determines the types, prices, and quantities of goods produced.

Demand reflects the behavior of consumers and is represented by a demand schedule. The demand schedule shows the amounts of a good consumers want to buy at different prices. The demand schedule is depicted graphically by a demand curve which slopes downward. At any point on a demand curve, one price is associated with only one quantity. The downward slope shows that more of a good will be purchased at lower prices and less at higher prices. Any movement along the demand curve shows that quantity demanded changes because price changes. The demand curve itself will shift when consumers' incomes or tastes or the prices of related goods change. Such a shift in the demand curve is a change in demand.

Supply, the other basic force at work in a market, reflects the behavior of sellers and is represented by a supply schedule. The supply schedule shows the amount of a good sellers are willing to sell at different prices. The supply schedule can be presented graphically as a supply curve which slopes upward. As with the demand curve, any point on the supply curve shows one price associated with only one quantity. Unlike the demand curve, however, the supply curve shows that sellers are willing to offer more of a good on the market only at higher prices and less only at lower prices. A movement along the supply curve occurs only because price has changed and reflects a change in quantity supplied. A movement of the supply curve itself is called a change in supply and is caused by a change in the technology of production, resource prices, or government policies toward business.

A market's equilibrium price is established at the price level where quantity demanded and quantity supplied are equal. A market clears itself when it is at the point of equilibrium and there is no tendency to move from the equilibrium price. A change in either supply or demand results in a new equilibrium price and quantity.

If a market's price is either above or below the equilibrium price, an excess supply or excess demand is present. As buyers and sellers engage in trading, price moves toward equilibrium, and the excesses are removed. In the case of government price controls, however, the market cannot clear itself by price changes, and the excesses remain unless eliminated by changes in demand or supply.

Chapter 3 discusses the nature of the demand and supply schedules and provides you with the necessary background and tools to determine equilibrium price and quantity.

CHAPTER OUTLINE

1. One approach to answering the "what," "how," and "for whom" questions faced by economies (and hence determine the allocation of resources) is through the market. A market is a set of arrangements by which buyers and sellers of a good are in contact to trade that good. The market may be structured (such as the New York Stock Exchange or the Chicago Board of Trade) or unstructured (such as the classified section of a newspaper). In the market, prices and quantities of goods bought and sold are determined. The forces which determine prices and quantities are demand and supply.
2. Demand describes consumer behavior and shows the quantities of a good buyers want to purchase at different prices; supply, which describes seller behavior, shows the quantities sellers want to sell at different prices. The terms "supply" and "demand" indicate the quantities of a good bought and sold at different prices rather than just one particular quantity at one particular price.
   a. At each different price, a specific quantity

will be demanded. Quantity demanded varies negatively with the price of the good: At lower prices, quantity demanded will increase, while higher prices cause quantity demanded to fall. Quantity demanded will be greater than or equal to zero.

    b. At each different price, a specific quantity will be supplied. Quantity supplied will vary positively with the price of good: At lower prices, quantity supplied will fall, while higher prices cause quantity supplied to increase. Quantity supplied will always be greater than or equal to zero.

    c. For a specific geographic area and time period, there exists in the market for a particular good an equilibrium price and a corresponding equilibrium quantity at which quantity demanded and quantity supplied are equal. At the equilibrium price, the market clears. For any price above the equilibrium price, quantity supplied exceeds quantity demanded, and there are surplus goods on the market. When a surplus is present, suppliers reduce their asking price, quantity demanded increases, and quantity supplied decreases until the surplus is removed. For any price below the equilibrium price, quantity demanded exceeds quantity supplied, and there is excess demand (a shortage) of goods on the market. When a shortage is present, sellers raise the price and try to increase the quantity supplied; quantity demanded decreases until the shortage is removed.

3. The price and quantity relationships for demand and supply can be presented graphically by the demand curve and the supply curve. The demand curve shows the quantity demanded at each price. The demand curve slopes downward because of the negative relationship between price and quantity demanded. Any movement along the demand curve reflects a change in price and a change in quantity demanded. The supply curve shows the quantity supplied at each price. The supply curve slopes upward because of the positive relationship between price and quantity supplied.

    a. The intersection of the demand and supply curves establishes the market equilibrium price and quantity. For prices above the equilibrium price, the horizontal distance between the supply curve and the demand curve is excess supply. For prices below the equilibrium price, excess demand is determined by the horizontal distance between the demand curve and the supply curve.

4. The relationship between price and quantity demanded assumes that buyer tastes and incomes, as well as the prices of related goods, remain constant. These are the determinants of demand.

    a. Since a good may be either a substitute or a complement for other goods, a change in the price of related goods can affect demand for the first good.

    b. A change in buyers' income will influence the demand for a good. The manner in which demand is affected will depend on whether the good is normal or inferior. When a good is normal, changes in demand and changes in income are in the same direction. When a good is inferior, changes in income and changes in demand are in opposite directions.

    c. Buyer tastes are considered to be stable and are determined in part by habits and institutions; however, any change in tastes can influence the demand for a good.

5. Changes in any one of the determinants of demand will result in either an increase or a decrease in demand. If there is an increase in demand, the demand curve shifts upward. This indicates that at each price a greater quantity will be demanded. Equilibrium price will rise (assuming supply doesn't change). If there is a decrease in demand, the demand curve shifts downward so that at each price less quantity is demanded. Equilibrium price falls (again assuming supply doesn't change). A change in the demand for a good can also cause the prices of other goods to change.

6. The supply curve slopes upward because for more resources to be forthcoming to produce additional quantities of a good, the rewards to producers (price of the good) must be higher. The upward-sloping supply curve is based on the assumption that the technology of the firm, the cost of using the factors of production, and government regulation and taxation are constant. These are the three determinants of supply.

    a. A change in any one of the determinants of supply can either increase or decrease the cost of producing a good at every level of output. If the cost of producing a good changes for every level of output, supply changes and the supply curve shifts.

    b. When the statement "other things being equal" is made, the main determinants of demand (tastes, income, and prices of other goods) and supply (input prices, technology, and regulation) are assumed constant even though these factors may influence demand and supply.

    c. Assuming a constant demand, an increase in supply shifts the supply curve downward and to the right, causing the equilibrium price to

DEMAND, SUPPLY, AND THE MARKET

fall and quantity to rise; a greater quantity is supplied at every price. A decrease in supply shifts the supply curve upward and to the left, causing the equilibrium price to rise and quantity to fall; a smaller quantity is supplied at every price.

7. When the Pope in 1966 allowed Catholics to eat meat on Friday, the demand for fish fell, and a new equilibrium in the fish market was established at a lower price and quantity.

8. The presence of price controls in a market will prohibit the adjustment of quantity demanded and quantity supplied. An equilibrium price cannot be reached because buyers and sellers are prevented from behaving in a normal manner. Prices are said to be in disequilibrium. Two types of price controls which have been used by the government are the price ceiling and the price floor. The imposition of a price ceiling on the market for a good prohibits the market price from rising above the established ceiling. The market cannot reach an equilibrium, and as a result, disequilibrium prices and quantities prevail in the form of excess demand. Rent controls provide an example. A price floor prohibits the market price from falling below the established price. Again, equilibrium cannot be reached, and disequilibrium prices and quantities prevail in the form of excess supply. Milk prices supports provide an example.

9. The facts strongly suggest that buyers are responsive to changes in the prices charged for goods.
   a. When the world price of sugar doubled in the early 1970s, the quantity of sugar demanded per person fell. During the latter part of the decade, prices fell substantially, but quantity demanded increased only slightly because substitutes for sugar were found.
   b. In 1977, the world supply of coffee fell and its price rose because of a severe frost in Brazil. Quantity demanded per person fell, and the demand for tea (a substitute) increased. When coffee prices declined, the quantity demanded increased.
   c. Improvements in technology lowered the cost of producing digital watches, so the supply of watches increased. This increase caused the market price to fall. When the price fell, quantity demanded increased.

10. In a free market, society can answer the "what," "how," and "for whom" questions. The market decides how much of a particular good ("what") to produce by finding the price which makes quantity demanded and quantity supplied equal. The "for whom" question is answered by consumers who are willing and able to pay at least the equilibrium price of the good in order to have it. The "how" question is answered once information about the production side of the economy is known. The way society wants its resources allocated and the way they are allocated in a free market may not be the same.

IMPORTANT TERMS AND THEIR MEANING

Match the following terms with the correct definition or phrase.

1. ____ Demand for the good increases when income rises
2. ____ A price control below which market price cannot fall; results in a surplus of the good on the market
3. ____ A set of arrangements by which buyers and sellers of a good are in contact to trade that good
4. ____ Factors such as technology and resource costs which influence the amount of a good a producer will supply at different prices
5. ____ The amount of a good actually purchased at a particular price
6. ____ The amount of a good buyers want to purchase at different prices
7. ____ The price of one good rises, and the demand for another good falls
8. ____ Demand for the good falls when income rises
9. ____ The amount of a good actually offered for sale at a particular price
10. ____ The price at which quantity demanded equals quantity supplied
11. ____ The price-determined movement along a demand curve as opposed to the non-price-determined movement of the demand curve

a. Market
b. Demand
c. Supply
d. Quantity demanded
e. Quantity supplied
f. Equilibrium price
g. Excess demand
h. Excess supply
i. Demand curve
j. Supply curve
k. Determinants of demand

12. _____ A graphical representation of the quantity demanded at each price

13. _____ A price control above which market price cannot rise; results in a shortage of the good on the market

14. _____ Factors such as incomes, prices of related goods, and tastes which influence the amount of a good buyers will purchase at each price

15. _____ The price of one good falls, and the demand for another good falls

16. _____ The horizontal distance between the demand and supply curves when quantity demanded exceeds quantity supplied at a given price

17. _____ The amount of a good sellers want to sell at different prices

18. _____ A graphical presentation of the quantity supplied at each price

19. _____ The horizontal distance between the demand and supply curves when quantity supplied exceeds quantity demanded at a given price

l. Normal good

m. Inferior good

n. Determinants of supply

o. Price ceiling

p. Price floor

q. Change in quantity demanded versus change in demand

r. Substitutes

s. Complements

EXERCISES

1. Table 3-1 is a set of data showing the market for whatnots.

   a. On your graph paper, carefully plot and label both the demand curve and the supply curve for whatnots. Be sure to label the axes clearly.

   b. From your graph, when price goes up, quantity demanded _____, and quantity supplied _____.

   c. Has an equilibrium price been determined? _____ If so, the equilibrium price is $_____ and the equilibrium quantity is _____ units.

   d. If the price for whatnots increases to $4, quantity demanded is now _____ units and quantity supplied is _____ units. As a result, a (surplus/shortage) _____ of _____ units is present on the market.

   e. Before a shortage would appear on the market, price would have to be below $_____ per unit.

2. Presented in Table 3-2 are the market data for long-playing phonograph albums. The second column shows demand (all things equal), and the third column shows the new demand relationship after the price of stereos falls. Supply is given in the fourth column.

TABLE 3-1

PRICE, $	DEMAND, thousands of units	SUPPLY, thousands of units
6	0	12
5	2	10
4	4	8
3	6	6
2	8	4
1	10	2
0	12	0

TABLE 3-2

(1) PRICE, $	(2) DEMAND D_1, tens of thousands of units	(3) DEMAND D_2, tens of thousands of units	(4) SUPPLY S, tens of thousands of units
7.50	0	0	50
7.00	0	5	45
6.50	0	10	40
6.00	5	15	35
5.50	10	20	30
5.00	15	25	25
4.50	20	30	20
4.00	25	35	15
3.50	30	40	10
3.00	35	45	5

   a. Carefully plot the supply schedule and the demand schedule in the second column. Label the demand curve D_1 and the supply curve S. Label the axes properly.

   b. The initial equilibrium price and quantity are $_____ and _____ albums.

   c. Now assume that the price of stereos falls. The new demand schedule is shown in the third column. Plot this new demand schedule and label your curve D_2.

   d. After the reduction in the price of stereo components, the new equilibrium price is $_____,

DEMAND, SUPPLY, AND THE MARKET

and the new quantity is _____ albums. There has been a change in (demand/quantity demanded) _____ for albums.

e. The above analysis suggests that the stereo components and long-playing albums are (substitutes/complements) _____ since when the price of one falls, the demand for the other increases. The increase in demand for albums is indicated by a (shift to the right/shift to the left) _____ of the demand curve.

3. Suppose that Table 3-3 represents the market for studio apartments in New York City.

TABLE 3-3

RENT/APARTMENTS, $	DEMAND FOR APARTMENTS, hundreds	SUPPLY OF APARTMENTS, hundreds
700	30	180
600	50	150
500	70	120
400	90	90
300	110	60
200	130	30
100	150	0

a. Plot the demand and supply curves on graph paper. Be sure to label the curves and axes.

b. The equilibrium price is $_____, and equilibrium quantity is _____ units.

c. If the New York City government placed price controls on the rents that could be charged so that the maximum rental fee was $300, these controls (would/would not) _____ force the market from equilibrium.

d. As a result of the price controls in c, the quantity demanded of apartments would now be _____ units and the quantity supplied would fall to _____ units. Draw a line from the new price to the demand curve.

e. The apartment rental market after price controls has an (excess demand/excess supply) _____ of _____ rental units.

f. The type of price control placed on the apartment rental market is a (price ceiling/price floor) _____, and there (would/would not) _____ be a tendency for the market to return to equilibrium.

4. Listed in Table 3-4 are several factors which could have an impact on the market for sailboats. Indicate the effect each of the factors might have on the market, using a (√) to represent a increase, an (X) to represent a decrease, and a (0) to represent no change.

5. Consider the market model presented in Figure 3-1.

a. The initial equilibrium price for curves DD and SS is $_____, with the associated quantity of _____ units.

b. The distance AB represents an _____ of _____ units, while the distance CD is an _____ of _____ units.

c. A price ceiling would be effective at any price

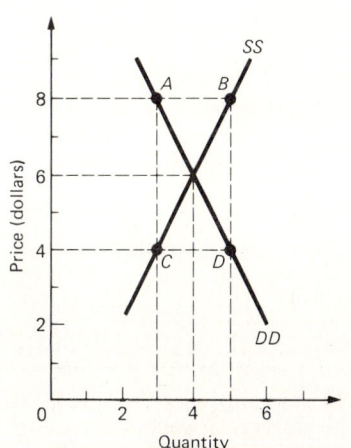

FIGURE 3-1

TABLE 3-4

	DEMAND	SUPPLY	PRICE	QUANTITY
a. The prices of powerboats increase	____	____	____	____
b. Consumers decide to spend more of their leisure time at nearby lakes and beaches	____	____	____	____
c. Fiberglass, a basic component in hull construction, falls in price	____	____	____	____
d. The average household income increases significantly	____	____	____	____
e. The government prohibits powerboats from all public water recreation areas because of pollution problems	____	____	____	____
f. The wages of sail makers and the price of masts increase	____	____	____	____
g. The average sailor gets seasick on a sailboat	____	____	____	____

below $_____, while for a price floor to be effective, it must be above $_____.

FILL-IN QUESTIONS

1. The (positive/negative) _____ slope of a demand curve is due to the (positive/negative) _____ relationship between the price and the quantity demanded of a good.

2. If buyers' income went up, they could be expected to buy more of a good if it was (normal/inferior) _____.

3. The U.S. government supporting the price of tobacco is an example of a (price ceiling/price floor) _____.

4. A shortage of a good on the market at a particular price results when (quantity demanded/quantity supplied) _____ exceeds (quantity demanded/quantity supplied) _____.

5. We expect price to (rise/fall) _____ if suppliers try to sell more than buyers want because the sellers' asking price is (above/below) _____ the market equilibrium price.

6. With a given demand, an improvement in technology will result in (an increase/a decrease) _____ in supply, causing equilibrium price to (rise/fall) _____ and equilibrium quantity to (increase/decrease) _____.

7. If there is a decrease in demand, the demand curve shifts to the (right/left) _____ and buyers demand (more/less) _____ at every price.

8. The presence of either buyers or sellers of a good (is/is not) _____ sufficient for a market to exist.

9. If the price of a good goes up, we expect the supply schedule to (increase/remain the same/decrease) _____.

10. In the market for good A, if the price is $10 and quantity demanded is 50 units, quantity supplied must be _____ units and price $_____ to be in equilibrium.

11. If a price ceiling was imposed at a level above the price which cleared the market, a market disequilibrium (would/would not) _____ occur.

12. When there is no tendency for price and quantity demanded and supplied to change, the market is said to be in _____.

13. In plotting both the demand and supply curves, we label the vertical axis as (price/quantity) _____ and the horizontal axis as (price/quantity) _____. Equilibrium is shown by the _____ of the two curves.

14. Gasoline and automobiles are (substitute/complementary) _____ goods, while coffee and tea are (substitutes/complements) _____.

TRUE-FALSE QUESTIONS

1. _____ Rent controls are an example of a price floor.

2. _____ The basis for the allocation of resources in a market economy is the interaction of buyers and sellers.

3. _____ In most markets, the general tendency is for the price to be at a disequilibrium level.

4. _____ Based on statistical data, price controls have provided an excellent method of efficient resource allocation.

5. _____ A market will clear only at the price at which quantity demanded equals quantity supplied.

6. _____ The supply curve illustrates a positive relationship between price and quantity supplied.

7. _____ When there is excess demand on the market, the natural tendency is for price to rise.

8. _____ For any two related goods A and B, if the price of A goes down and the demand for B decreases, the goods are substitutes.

9. _____ Changes in the price of a particular good will not have any influence on the prices of other goods.

10. _____ All other things equal, the effect of the government imposing antipollution standards on the steel industry would be to shift the supply curve of steel downward and to the right.

11. _____ If there is a decrease in demand for a good, the new equilibrium price will always rise, other things equal.

12. _____ In 1977, the price of coffee increased sharply and caused the quantity demanded of the complement tea to increase.

13. _____ A change in the price of a good causes both a movement along and a shift of the supply curve.

14. _____ Soybean filler, often used to extend hamburger, is an example of an inferior good.

15. _____ In 1979, the demand curve for pet rocks shifted to the left because buyers' tastes changed and pet rocks were no longer a fad.

16. _____ When the Pope relaxed the requirement that Catholics could eat only fish on Fridays, the price of fish increased.

17. _____ Statistical evidence suggests that buyers are indeed responsive to the price of goods and that the forces of supply and demand do work in the marketplace.

MULTIPLE CHOICE QUESTIONS

Circle the correct answer.

1. All of the following will cause a shift of the demand curve for a good except
  a. buyers' incomes change
  b. the price of the good falls
  c. the price of a closely related good falls
  d. buyers' tastes change

2. A decrease in the price of a gallon of gasoline would probably
  a. increase the demand for gasoline
  b. increase the demand for public transportation
  c. increase the demand for motor oil
  d. decrease the demand for motel rooms

3. An increase in the wages paid to construction workers would
  a. shift the supply curve of new houses to the left and raise the equilibrium price
  b. shift the supply curve to the right and lower the price of new houses
  c. shift the demand curve for new houses to the left and lower their price
  d. shift the demand curve for new houses to the right and raise their price
  e. none of the above

4. If excess demand is present in the market for a good, it must be the case that
  a. the good's price is above the equilibrium price
  b. the good is inferior
  c. quantity supplied exceeds quantity demanded
  d. the good's price is below the equilibrium price

5. To say that a market has established its equilibrium price suggests that
  a. there is pressure on the price to rise
  b. there is pressure on the price to fall
  c. there is no pressure on the price to either rise or fall
  d. there is pressure on the demand to increase
  e. none of the above

6. The government's sale of butter to New Zealand in late 1981 at a price below that currently established by the market was a result of
  a. a price ceiling for dairy products which resulted in a surplus of butter
  b. a price floor for dairy products which resulted in a shortage of butter
  c. a price floor for dairy products which resulted in a surplus of butter
  d. a price ceiling for dairy products which resulted in a shortage of butter

7. If buyers' tastes suddenly changed in favor of fish, and simultaneously there was an improvement in commercial fishing technology, we would expect
  a. a shift to the right of both the demand and supply curves and an increase in both equilibrium price and quantity
  b. a shift to the right of both the demand and supply curves and a decrease in both equilibrium price and quantity
  c. a shift to the left of both the demand and supply curves with an increase in equilibrium price and a decrease in equilibrium quantity
  d. a shift to the right of both the demand and supply curves with an increase in equilibrium quantity and either a rise or a fall in equilibrium price
  e. none of the above

8. In the fall of 1981, WKU students for the first time had to pay to attend university football games; as a result, every game had many empty seats. This decline in attendance suggests that
  a. attending a football game is an inferior good
  b. the quantity demanded of football games declined
  c. the demand for football games declined
  d. attending a football game is a normal good

9. Which of the following statements is not correct?
  a. the initial impact of a reduction in supply is to increase price
  b. when the price of a good increases, consumers will seek lower-priced substitutes in other markets
  c. the overall effect of a reduction in the supply of a good will be confined to that good's market
  d. when the price of a good increases, the equilibrium price in other markets can be influenced

10. The demand curve slopes downward and to the right because
   a. consumers will consume a greater quantity of a good only at lower prices, other things equal
   b. consumers' incomes are neither equal nor constant
   c. the higher the price, the greater the quantity demanded
   d. tastes are never constant

11. The supply curve slopes upward and to the right because
   a. the costs of production are relatively constant in the short term
   b. technology is not fixed in the short term
   c. government policies and regulation of businesses change very slowly
   d. suppliers will place more goods on the market, other things equal, only at higher prices
   e. all of the above

12. If goods A and B are substitutes, a decrease in the price of good A would cause
   a. the demand curve for good A to shift to the right
   b. the demand curve for good A to shift to the left
   c. the demand curve for good B to shift to the right
   d. the quantity demanded of good B to increase
   e. none of the above

13. Two goods which are considered to be rather close substitutes are
   a. coffee and tea
   b. bread and butter
   c. scotch and soda
   d. gasoline and toothpaste

14. Which of the following statements is not correct?
   a. demand and supply are the two primary components of a market system
   b. for a market system to operate efficiently, government must take an active role
   c. an antique auction is an example of a market
   d. a market system can determine how society's scarce resources are allocated

15. Consider Figure 3-2 for good Z.

All of the following could cause the movement from A to B except
   a. the government reduced income taxes by 50 percent
   b. the price of good Z changed
   c. consumers suddenly preferred more of good Z
   d. the price of good Y, a substitute, increased.

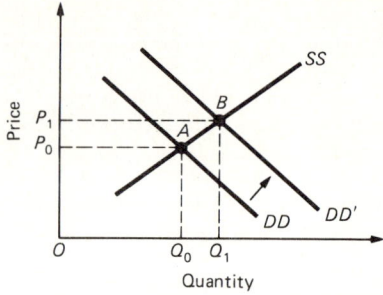

FIGURE 3-2

AT THIS POINT YOU SHOULD BE ABLE TO . . .

1. Define the concept of a market.
2. Define demand, supply, and market equilibrium.
3. Distinguish between changes in demand, quantity demanded, supply, and quantity supplied.
4. Graphically present and explain the demand and supply curves and determine the equilibrium price and quantity.
5. List the determinants of demand and explain how changes in these determinants affect demand.
6. List the determinants of supply and explain how changes in these determinants affect supply.
7. Explain the effect on a good's equilibrium price and quantity when there is a change in demand or a change in supply.
8. Define substitute, complementary, normal, and inferior goods.
9. Explain both verbally and graphically the impact of price ceilings and price floors on market quantity and market price.
10. Explain how price increases in one market can influence the behavior of prices in other markets.

QUESTIONS FOR THOUGHT

1. Early in this chapter, Professors Fischer and Dornbusch made the statement that a market system was one method of answering the "what," "how," and "for whom" questions faced by every society. Briefly explain.

2. During the late 1970s, a price ceiling existed on gasoline. President Carter presented to Congress a standby rationing plan for gasoline to be activated should the need arise. Each motorist could only buy a certain number of gallons each week. What would such a plan have done to the operation of the gasoline market? In terms of supply and demand, why do you think President Carter wanted the plan?

3. If you were asked to explain how a change in supply or demand in one market might influence the activity of other markets, what would you say?

4. When beef prices rise, more pork, poultry, and fish are sold. After a time, beef prices fall and the prices of pork, poultry, and fish rise. Explain how this can happen.

5. Early in 1982, a glut appeared on the diamond market. The DeBeers Organization, the world's leading producer and marketer of diamonds, began to buy large amounts of crude stones. Why do you think they engaged in such purchases? Did they act rationally? What effect do you think their actions had on the price of diamonds?

6. Define normal, inferior, substitute, and complementary goods. List three goods of each type (substitutes and complements must be listed in pairs). Explain the influence each type of good can have on the demand curve.

7. Suppose you were asked to speak to your alma mater's junior achievement club. The topic of your speech has been designated as the difference between quantity demanded as opposed to demand and quantity supplied as opposed to supply. Briefly list the main points of your speech.

4

The Demand Curve: Adjustments to Price and Income Changes

Chapter 4 is a continuation of your study of demand. Previously you learned how demand and supply together determine the market price and quantity of a good. You saw how the demand curve illustrates the negative relationship between price and quantity demanded. Chapter 4 examines the sensitivity of quantity demanded to price changes and develops the tools necessary to measure the effect of price changes on quantity. Chapter 4 also develops tools which are used to show the responsiveness of demand to changes in consumer income and changes in the price of related goods.

The sensitivity, or responsiveness, of quantity demanded to a change in price is measured by the price elasticity of demand. The price elasticity of demand is calculated by using the formula

$$\text{Price elasticity} = \frac{\text{percentage change in quantity demanded}}{\text{percentage change in price}}$$

The resulting quotient is always a negative number because price and quantity demanded move in opposite directions; that is, as price goes up, quantity demanded goes down. Even though elasticity is negative, it is the size of the number and not the sign that is important. Economists usually evaluate elasticity by its absolute value, and this removes the negative sign.

When elasticity is less than 1, demand is inelastic and quantity demanded is not very responsive to a price change. If the elasticity of demand equals 1, demand is unitary-elastic. When elasticity is greater than 1, demand is elastic, and the percentage change in quantity demanded is greater than the percentage change in price.

The total spending on a good by consumers is the product of the good's price and the number of units bought. This total spending by consumers is equal to the total revenue received by the suppliers of the good. The elasticity of demand tells us how total spending changes when a good's price changes. If demand is elastic and the price of a good falls, the percentage increase in quantity demanded exceeds the percentage decrease in price, and so total spending rises. When demand is unitary-elastic, the percentage fall in price equals the percentage increase in quantity demanded, and so total spending doesn't change. If demand is inelastic, the percentage fall in price is greater than the percentage increase in quantity demanded, and total spending falls.

Not only does a change in a good's own price affect the amount purchased, so do the income of consumers and the prices of related goods. When consumers' income or the prices of related goods change, the demand curve shifts. The cross-elasticity of demand shows the effect of a change in the price of one good on the demand for another. The cross-elasticity may be either positive or negative and shows whether goods are substitutes or complements. When income changes, the income elasticity of demand may be either positive or negative. The income elasticity of demand shows whether goods are normal or inferior. When the income elasticity for a good is greater than 1, the good is a luxury, because for any percentage increase in income, a larger percentage is spent on the good.

As you study Chapter 4, pay particular attention to the formulas used to compute the price and the cross-elasticity and income elasticity of demand. Also, be sure that you know when demand is elastic, unitary-elastic, and inelastic and what happens to total revenue when price changes under each of these demand conditions.

CHAPTER OUTLINE

1. The demand curve with its downward slope shows that as price falls, quantity demanded increases, and as price rises, quantity demanded decreases. The demand curve does not show the responsiveness of quantity demanded to price changes. Economists use the price elasticity of demand to get a measure of how sensitive quantity demanded is to price changes of a good.
   a. The price elasticity of demand is the ratio of the percentage change in quantity demanded to the percentage change in price. The elasticity formula is

THE DEMAND CURVE

$$\text{Price elasticity of demand} = \frac{\text{percentage change in quantity demanded}}{\text{percentage change in price}}$$

The price elasticity is always a negative number because of the negative relationship between price and quantity demanded. Economists use the absolute value of price elasticity and treat the number as positive.

b. Two special points which should be noted about the elasticity of demand are the use of arc elasticities and the use of the elasticity formula for both straight-line and curved demand curves.

(1) The arc elasticity of demand avoids the confusion often encountered when selecting the reference price and quantity used in the elasticity formula. The arc elasticity uses the average of the two prices and quantities as the reference point, and so it is a measure of the elasticity between two prices on the demand curve. The formula for arc elasticity is

$$\text{Arc elasticity of demand} = \frac{\text{change in quantity}}{\text{average quantity}} \div \frac{\text{change in price}}{\text{average price}}$$

(2) The elasticity of demand formula (including arc elasticity) can always be applied to a demand curve. It makes no difference whether the demand curve is linear or nonlinear.

c. Demand is elastic if the absolute value of the price elasticity is more than 1. When demand is elastic, quantity demanded is sensitive to price and changes by a larger percentage than price. Demand is inelastic if the absolute value of the price elasticity is less than 1. When demand is inelastic, quantity demanded is less sensitive to price and changes by a smaller percentage than price. Demand is unitary-elastic if the absolute value of the price elasticity equals 1. When demand is unitary-elastic, quantity demanded changes by the same percentage as price. On the demand curve, unitary elasticity occurs at the curve's midpoint. For prices above the midpoint on the demand curve, demand is elastic; for prices below the midpoint, demand is inelastic.

(1) The primary determinants of the price elasticity of demand for a good are consumer tastes and the ease of substitution between goods. The elasticity of demand increases as the number of substitutes for a good increases.

(2) Statistics show that basic goods such as food and shelter are price-inelastic, while some goods which are not considered necessities are very price-elastic.

d. The price elasticity of demand is useful when determining the pricing policy for goods produced in the marketplace and provided by government.

2. The total spending on a commodity by consumers is equal to the total revenue received by producers, because the amount spent in the market for a good must be the same amount received by the suppliers of the good. The total spending on a good is the good's price times the quantity demanded. When demand is elastic, total spending on a good changes in the opposite direction from a price change. For a price increase, total spending falls; for a price decrease, total spending rises. When demand is inelastic, total spending changes in the same direction as a price change. For a price increase, total spending rises; for a price decrease, total spending falls. When demand is unitary-elastic, total spending does not change as price changes.

a. When demand for a good is elastic and its price is reduced, total revenue rises; but when its price increases, total revenue falls. If demand is inelastic, total revenue falls when price is reduced and rises when price increases. Total revenue is maximized at the midpoint of the demand curve, where demand is unitary-elastic.

3. The relationship between price elasticities and spending is useful in studying the pricing decisions of firms.

a. Once the price elasticity of demand is known, the producer knows in which direction to move prices.

b. The demand for oil is inelastic, and so during the 1970s, oil producers restricted their supply, increased market prices, and increased their revenue.

c. The frost in Brazil in 1977 destroyed much of the coffee crop; world supply fell, and market prices increased. Producers' revenue increased since the demand for coffee is price-inelastic. Even with the substitutes available, consumer tastes influence how much buyers are willing to substitute one good for another.

d. During bad harvest years, farmers as a group may be better off since the demand for food is inelastic. Poor harvests reduce supply, increase prices, and increase the farmers' revenue because consumer spending on food increases.

4. The time period in which consumers adjust their quantity demanded in response to a change in price affects the price elasticity of demand for a good. Demand is less elastic in the short run, when adjustments to price are incomplete, than it is in the long run, when the adjustment process is complete.
   a. The long run is not a set number of years. It is the period of time in which all adjustments to price can be made, and it depends on the types of adjustments required.
5. The cross-elasticity of demand is a measure of the responsiveness in the quantity demanded of one good to a price change in a related good. The cross-elasticity of demand may be either positive or negative and is calculated by the formula

$$\text{Cross-elasticity of demand} = \frac{\text{percentage change in quantity demanded of one good}}{\text{percentage change in price of related good}}$$

When the cross-elasticity of demand is positive, the two goods are substitutes. When cross-elasticity is negative, the goods are complements. A good's own price elasticity of demand is usually larger than its cross-elasticities with other goods.

6. As consumers' income changes, the demand for goods changes; however, the proportion of the consumers' income spent on a good may not change by the same amount as income. The proportion of income spent on a particular commodity is the expenditure (budget) share and is calculated by the formula

$$\text{Budget share of good} = \frac{\text{price} \times \text{quantity demanded}}{\text{total consumer spending}}$$

A measure of the consumer responsiveness to changes in income on demand (the shift of the demand curve) when price is held constant is the income elasticity of demand. The income elasticity of demand is defined as

$$\text{Income elasticity of demand} = \frac{\text{percentage change in quantity demanded}}{\text{percentage change in income}}$$

The income elasticity may be either positive or negative. A positive elasticity may be less than 1.
   a. The income elasticity of demand is used to define normal and inferior goods. A normal good has a positive income elasticity of demand. When a good is inferior, the income elasticity of demand is negative. When a good is a necessity, its income elasticity of demand is between zero and 1. The share of income spent on necessities falls as income rises. The income elasticity of demand is greater than 1 if the good is a luxury. The share of income spent on luxuries increases as income increases.
   b. One reason why demand responds to changes in income is that consumers spend more on higher-quality and higher-priced items as income rises.
   c. Income elasticities of demand are used to forecast consumer behavior and growth in different sectors of the economy. Government uses income elasticities when it makes decisions about the allocation of resources for public investment.
7. The elasticity of supply measures the responsiveness of changes in quantity supplied to changes in price. The formula for the elasticity of supply is as follows:

$$\text{Elasticity of supply} = \frac{\text{percentage change in quantity supplied}}{\text{percentage change in price}}$$

The elasticity of supply is a positive number and indicates how much price and quantity change when there is a shift in demand.

IMPORTANT TERMS AND THEIR MEANING

Match the following terms with the correct definition or phrase.

1. _____ The period of time in which all consumer adjustments to a price change have been made

2. _____ Has an income elasticity of demand greater than 1

3. _____ Total expenditures made by the consumer but received by the seller

4. _____ Measures the elasticity of demand between two points on the basis of average prices and average quantities

5. _____ Measures the responsiveness of quantity supplied to a change in price

6. _____ $\dfrac{\text{Percentage change in quantity demanded}}{\text{Percentage change in income}}$

a. Price elasticity of demand
b. Elastic
c. Inelastic
d. Unitary-elastic
e. Price elasticity of demand formula
f. Cross price elasticity of demand

THE DEMAND CURVE

7. _____ Quantity demanded is highly responsive to price changes; the absolute value of the elasticity measure is greater than 1

8. _____ The income elasticity of demand is greater than zero but less than 1

9. _____ Consumption increases as income increases; has a positive income elasticity

10. _____ Fraction of income or household spending used for a commodity

11. _____ The period of time in which all consumer adjustments to a price change have not been made

12. _____ Measures the responsiveness of demand to changes in income

13. _____ $\dfrac{\text{Percentage change in quantity supplied}}{\text{Percentage change in price}}$

14. _____ Quantity demanded is not very responsive to changes in price; the absolute value of the elasticity measure is less than 1

15. _____ Measures the responsiveness of the quantity of a good demanded to changes in the prices of related goods

16. _____ $\dfrac{\text{Percentage change in quantity demanded}}{\text{Percentage change in price}}$

17. _____ From the consumers' standpoint: price × quantity demanded

18. _____ A measure of the responsiveness of quantity demanded of a good to changes in the good's price

19. _____ $\dfrac{\text{Percentage change in quantity of good } i \text{ demanded}}{\text{Percentage change in price of good } j}$

g. Normal goods

h. Total spending on a good

i. Arc elasticity

j. Elasticity of supply

k. Cross price elasticity formula

l. Substitutes

m. Luxury good

n. Expenditure share

o. Short run

p. Income elasticity of demand

q. Necessity

r. Inferior good

s. Complements

20. _____ When the price of a good changes, the percentage change in quantity demanded equals the percentage change in price

21. _____ Goods with a positive cross-elasticity of demand

22. _____ Consumption of the good decreases as income increases; the good has a negative income elasticity of demand

23. _____ Goods with a negative cross-elasticity of demand

t. Long run

u. Total revenue

v. Income elasticity formula

w. Elasticity of supply formula

EXERCISES

1. Suppose that the demand schedule for good X is as shown in Table 4-1.

TABLE 4-1

PRICE, $	QUANTITY DEMANDED	TOTAL REVENUE (TR), $	PRICE ELASTICITY (Ed)
6.00	10	_____	_____
5.00	20	_____	_____
4.00	30	_____	_____
3.50	35	_____	_____
3.00	40	_____	_____
2.00	50	_____	_____
1.00	60	_____	_____

   a. Plot the demand curve on graph paper. Be sure to label the axes.
   b. Compute the total revenue (expenditures) at each price and fill in the third column.
   c. Compute the price elasticity of demand for each change in price (beginning with $6.00) and fill in the fourth column.
   d. On the graph, indicate the range of elastic demand and inelastic demand.
   e. A unitary-elastic demand will occur at the price of $_____.

2. Using the demand data from Exercise 1, plot the total revenue curve. Label the vertical axis "revenue" and the horizontal axis "price."
   a. Total revenue is maximum at a price of $_____, and the price elasticity of demand is _____.
   b. For prices below $3, total revenue (decreases/increases) _____ as price rises and demand is

(price-elastic/price-inelastic/unitary-elastic) _____;
while for prices above $4, total expenditures (decrease/
increase) _____ as price rises and demand is
(price-elastic/price-inelastic/unitary-elastic) _____.

3. Suppose the demand schedule in Table 4-2 shows the consumption of coffee per month. Use the arc elasticity formula to compute any elasticities required.

TABLE 4-2

(1) PRICE PER POUND, $	(2) QUANTITY DEMANDED, pounds	(3) QUANTITY DEMANDED, pounds
3.00	1	_____
2.50	2	_____
2.00	3	_____
1.50	4	_____
1.00	5	_____
.50	6	_____

a. Over the price range $1.50 to $1.00 per pound, demand (is/is not) _____ price-elastic since the elasticity coefficient is _____, while over the range $3.00 to $2.50, demand (is/is not) _____ price-elastic with an elasticity coefficient of _____.

b. Assume now that consumer incomes go up and that they now purchase 1 pound more of coffee at every price. Enter the new quantity demanded data in the third column.

c. Over the price range $1.50 to $1.00, the price elasticity of demand is _____, while over the price range $3.00 to $2.50, the price elasticity of demand is _____.

d. Plot the two demand curves. Label the initial demand curve DD_1 and the second demand curve DD_2.

4. In Figure 4-1 two demand curves for a particular good are presented, each representing a different length of time in which the consumer can adapt to

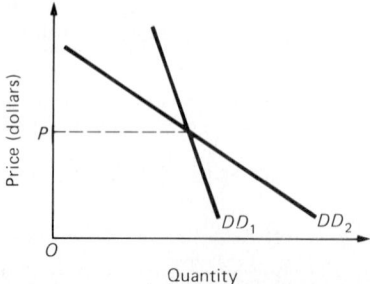

FIGURE 4-1

changes in price. Each curve reflects different elasticities.

a. The curve representing the shortest period of time for adjustment is _____, while the longer period is represented by curve _____.

b. Curve _____ is not as steep as curve _____ and will show a greater responsiveness to changes in price.

c. If curve DD_2 became almost horizontal, the elasticity of demand would be _____.

5. If the income elasticity of demand for cigarettes is 0.75, an increase in income of _____ percent would be necessary to increase the consumption by 2 percent.

FILL-IN QUESTIONS

1. If the price elasticity of demand is equal to 1, demand is said to be (elastic/inelastic/unitary-elastic) _____, and a change in price will cause total revenue to (rise/fall/remain the same) _____.

2. In the (long run/short run) _____, consumers can make some, but not complete, adjustments in their spending patterns as a result of a price change.

3. For any straight-line (linear) demand curve, as the price falls, the price elasticity of demand (increases/decreases/remains the same) _____.

4. A measure of the responsiveness of changes in quantity demanded to changes in income is the _____ elasticity of demand.

5. The _____ is defined as the product of price and quantity demanded divided by total consumer spending.

6. The percentage change in quantity demanded resulting from a 1 percent change in price provides a measure of the sensitivity of quantity demanded to price changes and is known as the _____ elasticity of demand.

7. If a particular good has an income elasticity of demand of −1.03, we say that it is a (normal/inferior/necessity/luxury) _____ good.

8. The number of available _____ and the ease with which changes of goods can be made is the primary determinant of the price elasticity of demand.

9. When the price elasticity of demand exceeds 1, demand is said to be (elastic/inelastic/unitary-elastic) _____, and an increase in price will cause total revenues to (rise/fall/remain the same) _____.

10. A luxury good has an income elasticity of demand which is (negative/positive but less than 1/positive and greater than 1) _____, and this indicates that for a percentage increase in income, demand for the good will (increase/decrease) _____ by a (greater/lesser) _____ percentage.

11. When price falls and as a result total revenue falls, the price elasticity of demand is (greater than/less than/equal to) _____ 1, and demand is said to be (elastic/inelastic/unitary-elastic) _____.

12. If demand is elastic, the (gain/loss) _____ in total revenue resulting from a price decrease is (greater than/less than) _____ the (gain/loss) _____ in total revenue resulting from the increase in quantity demanded at the lower price.

13. Above the midpoint on a linear (straight-line) demand curve, demand is (elastic/inelastic/unitary-elastic) _____, while below the midpoint, demand is (elastic/inelastic/unitary-elastic) _____.

14. If demand is inelastic, the (gain/loss) _____ in total revenue resulting from a price decrease is (greater than/less than/equal to) _____ the (gain/loss) _____ in total revenue resulting from the increase in quantity demanded at the lower price.

15. If the cross-elasticity of demand between goods A and B is −0.73, the goods are (complements/inferior/substitutes) _____.

TRUE-FALSE QUESTIONS

1. ____ It is reasonable to expect the income elasticity of demand for bread and potatoes to be greater than 1.

2. ____ If a particular commodity has no substitutes, its demand is highly elastic.

3. ____ Total revenue for sellers is generated by total expenditures of consumers.

4. ____ The relationship between price and quantity demanded shown by the demand curve does not tell us directly how responsive quantity demanded will be to price changes.

5. ____ If coffee prices increase, we would expect total expenditures on coffee to increase because the demand for coffee is inelastic.

6. ____ Demand for most commodities will be less elastic in the short run than in the long run.

7. ____ When we compute the income elasticity of demand, we allow price as well as income to change.

8. ____ A luxury good such as a mink coat has an income elasticity coefficient greater than 1.

9. ____ An industry producing a good with a low income elasticity of demand will experience a larger growth rate than an industry producing a good with a high income elasticity of demand.

10. ____ In order to raise revenue in a market with a very low price elasticity of demand, the proper strategy would be to increase price sharply.

11. ____ When the arc elasticity formula is used to compute the elasticity of demand, the problem of which price and quantity to use as reference points is removed.

12. ____ If a demand curve is not a straight line, the arc elasticity formula cannot be applied.

13. ____ When there is a shortage in a market, the price elasticity of demand can indicate the price change required to remove the shortage.

14. ____ If the elasticity of demand for public transportation in Atlanta equals 1, revenue can be raised if the transit fares are lowered.

15. ____ Because the demand for oil products is inelastic, in the 1970s OPEC was able to restrict the supply of petroleum, raise prices, and increase revenue for the oil-producing countries.

16. ____ The price elasticity of demand for a product is greater in the short run than in the long run because consumers have time to adjust to a price change in the good.

17. ____ Even though farmers may have a poor harvest, it is still possible for their overall revenue to increase.

18. ____ When the price of coffee increased in 1976 as a result of a frost in Brazil, the amount of money consumers spent on coffee increased. This shows that at higher prices, consumers may buy more of a good.

MULTIPLE CHOICE QUESTIONS

Circle the correct answer.

1. Suppose that the price elasticity of demand for a particular good is −2.0 when there is a 25 percent increase in quantity demanded. The percentage decrease in price necessary to result in an elasticity of −2.0 is
   a. 20 percent
   b. 12.5 percent
   c. 10.5 percent
   d. 50 percent
   e. impossible to determine from the information given

2. If there are many firms in an industry producing a standardized product, we would expect the demand for any one firm's product to be
   a. highly elastic
   b. highly inelastic
   c. unitary-elastic
   d. slightly elastic

3. If a 1 percent increase in income results in a decrease in the consumption of a good by 3 percent, the good is
   a. normal
   b. a necessity
   c. a luxury
   d. inferior

4. If demand is price-elastic for a particular commodity, an increase in price will
   a. lower total expenditures
   b. leave total expenditures unchanged
   c. increase total expenditures
   d. slightly increase total expenditures

5. Of the following goods, which would not be considered a luxury according to the income elasticities presented in your text?
   a. sports goods
   b. shelter
   c. taxicab transportation
   d. medical care

6. As income levels increased, we would expect the percentage of income spent on food to
   a. increase greatly
   b. increase slightly
   c. decline
   d. remain the same

7. If both a long-run and a short-run demand curve for a particular product were given, we would expect
   a. the long-run demand curve to be less elastic and hence flatter than the short-run curve
   b. the long-run demand curve to be less elastic and hence steeper than the short-run curve
   c. both demand curves to have the same elasticity and hence be equally steep
   d. the long-run demand curve to be more elastic and hence flatter than the short-run curve
   e. that the slope of the demand curve would have nothing to do with the price elasticity of demand for a good

8. For a particular good X, when price falls from $50 to $40, quantity demanded increases from 75 to 100 units. The price elasticity of demand is
   a. −1.0
   b. −1.67
   c. 2.45
   d. 1.89

9. The price elasticity of demand is calculated by using the formula
   a. percentage change in price divided by percentage change in quantity demanded
   b. absolute change in price divided by absolute change in quantity demanded
   c. percentage change in quantity demanded divided by percentage change in price
   d. absolute change in quantity demanded divided by absolute change in price

10. If total revenue declines as price declines, demand is
    a. elastic
    b. inelastic
    c. unitary-elastic
    d. inferior

11. One major determinant of the price elasticity of demand is
    a. consumer income
    b. whether or not a good is normal
    c. whether or not a good is a necessity or a luxury
    d. the ease and availability of substitutes

12. For a given demand curve
    a. demand is elastic at the lower price ranges
    b. demand is inelastic at the higher price ranges
    c. demand is inelastic at the midpoint
    d. demand is unitary-elastic at the midpoint

13. The income elasticity of demand is calculated by using the formula
    a. percentage change in quantity demanded divided by percentage change in income
    b. percentage change in income divided by change in quantity demanded
    c. absolute change in quantity demanded divided by absolute change in income
    d. absolute change in income divided by absolute change in quantity demanded

14. If the supply curve is infinitely elastic, an increase in demand causes
    a. the quantity supplied to increase and market price to decrease
    b. no change in price but an increase in the quantity supplied
    c. no change in price but a decrease in the quantity supplied
    d. no change in quantity supplied but an increase in price

15. If the number of zaflings sold falls from 500 to 425

when the price of skylids falls from $3.00 to $2.90 per unit, the cross-elasticity of demand between the two goods is

    a. −8.7   **c.** 0.87
    b. 4.5   **d.** −3.3

16. When the price of widgets increases from $10 to $12 each, the quantity supplied by producers increases from 1000 to 1500. Using the arc elasticity formula, the elasticity of supply is

    a. 2.2   **c.** 3.0
    b. 2.5   **d.** 1.5

17. If the cross-elasticity of demand between goods X and Y is −2.3, it can be concluded that

    a. X and Y are substitutes
    b. X and Y are normal goods
    c. X and Y are inferior goods
    d. X and Y are complements

AT THIS POINT YOU SHOULD BE ABLE TO . . .

1. Define the concept of the price elasticity and cross price elasticity of demand and tell why they are useful in the study of markets.

2. Calculate the price elasticity of demand; state when demand is elastic, inelastic, and unitary-elastic; and explain the meaning of each term.

3. State and explain the major determinants of the price elasticity of demand.

4. Explain the relationship between the price elasticity of demand and total expenditures and total revenue.

5. Graphically show how the price elasticity of demand changes over the range of the demand curve.

6. Explain the importance of the time period for adjustment of consumer expenditures on the price elasticity of demand for a good.

7. State some examples and uses of the price elasticity of demand and the cross-price elasticity of demand.

8. Define the concept of income elasticity of demand.

9. Calculate the budget share and the income elasticity of demand.

10. Define the meaning of and income elasticity value for normal goods, inferior goods, luxury goods, and necessities.

11. State some examples and uses of the income elasticity of demand.

QUESTIONS FOR THOUGHT

1. From time to time, Brazil has actually destroyed coffee beans rather than put them on the market for sale. Is this rational behavior for a major producer of coffee? Why? Explain your answer in terms of the price elasticity of demand.

2. **a.** Your text gives the income elasticity of demand for the following goods: clothing = 0.77, shelter = 0.89, medical care = 1.9, and toilet articles = 3.6. What would happen to the demand for each of these goods if income increased 1 percent? Are the goods normal, inferior, luxuries, or necessities?

    b. Suppose the income elasticity of flour is −0.26. What effect will a 1 percent increase in income have on the demand for flour? What type of good is flour?

3. Suppose you are president of a firm which produces and sells four products. Each product has the following price elasticity of demand.

PRODUCTS	ELASTICITY
Zaflings	−2.34
Widgets	−1.0
Skylids	− .71
Bluars	− .36

You are concerned with your firm's profit structure and want to increase revenue if possible. What would your pricing strategy be on each of the products (assume costs are constant)? Explain your decisions.

4. Explain why a short-run price elasticity of demand should not be considered the appropriate elasticity for the long run.

5. If the price elasticity of demand for theater tickets in New York City is −0.71, would it seem a reasonable policy to increase the municipal tax on the tickets as a source of additional revenue for the city even though this would cause the price of tickets to go up? Explain.

6. Are the income elasticity of demand and the price elasticity of demand useful concepts in practical situations? Explain why or why not.

7. When the income elasticity of demand is calculated, prices are assumed constant. Why is this assumption necessary? What would be the impact on our calculations if prices varied?

5

Special Topics in Demand

The central theme of Chapter 5 is that markets are seldom completely independent. A price or income change in one market spills over into secondary markets, and as a result, prices and quantities in these secondary markets change.

Chapter 5 begins by developing a simple model of consumer choice as a first step toward understanding how a change in price and quantity in one market is transmitted to other markets. The model assumes that the consumer can rank his preferences for combinations of goods and, with income and prices constant, select the combination which maximizes his utility or satisfaction.

Using the model of consumer choice, you can determine what happens when either the consumer's income or the market price of a good changes. An increase in income permits the consumer to buy more of both goods. A decrease means that the consumer can afford less of both goods. Whether a good is normal or inferior depends on consumer response to changes in income. A change in the price of a good with other prices remaining constant includes both an income effect (purchasing power has changed) and a substitution effect (the relative price ratio has changed). This means that both the rate at which one good can be traded for another and the amount of all goods a consumer can purchase change.

The income and substitution effects are used to examine a good's own price elasticity of demand and the cross price elasticity of demand. The cross price elasticity of demand measures the responsiveness of changes in quantity demanded of one good to changes in the price of another good. The cross price elasticity determines whether goods are substitutes, complements, or neutral.

The downward slope of the individual consumer's demand curve and hence the negative relationship between price and quantity is also explained by the income and substitution effects. The market demand curve for a good with its downward slope is the horizontal summation of all individual curves.

The effect of a price change in one particular market as it spills over into other markets may also be explained by using the income and substitution effects.

Using a model of consumer choice, we can examine changes in overall consumer welfare and predict the preferences of consumers toward in-kind versus direct cash transfers.

Chapter 5 describes tools designed to help explain observed consumer behavior in the marketplace.

CHAPTER OUTLINE

1. Consumer choice theory analyzes the effects of changing market conditions on the consumer's behavior. The theory also provides a basis for predictions about consumer responsiveness to changes in income and prices. There are four elements required for a model of consumer choice.
    a. The first two elements are that the consumer has a given income and that the prices of all goods are given. These two elements determine the consumer's budget constraint and restrict the possible combinations of goods the consumer can purchase. For a given budget constraint, a consumer can purchase more of one good only if less of others is purchased, and so a trade-off exists between goods.
        (1) When there are only two goods, the budget constraint can be graphed and forms the consumer's budget line. The budget line shows the maximum amounts of both goods a consumer can buy with a given income and prices. The line is constructed by plotting alternative consumption baskets. The intercepts of the budget line are determined by dividing the consumer's money income by the price of each respective good. The negative slope of the budget line is constant and is determined by the ratio of the prices of the two goods. The slope shows how many units of one good must be given up in order to get 1 more unit of the other, and so any movement along the budget line shows the trade-offs the con-

sumer can make. Any point beyond the budget line is not possible for the consumer because his income is too small to reach that combination of goods. Any point below the line is attainable, but all of the consumer's income would not be spent. In the model, we assume that the consumer spends all of his income. Thus, only the points along the line are relevant for the model of consumer choice.
- **b.** The consumer ranks each bundle of goods by the utility or satisfaction received from each. Although we assume that the consumer prefers more goods to less, consumer tastes are an important factor in the ranking process. For any two bundles of goods A and B, one of the following conditions must hold: (1) Bundle A is liked better than bundle B, and so A is preferred to B, (2) bundle B is liked better than bundle A, and so B is preferred to A, or (3) bundle A and bundle B are liked equally well, and so the consumer is indifferent between A and B.
- **c.** The consumer's goal in the market is to maximize utility, and so he behaves in such a manner that the bundle of goods chosen yields the highest level of satisfaction possible, given the budget constraint. The optimal combination of goods lies on the budget line and is determined by both the principle of diminishing marginal utility and the consumer's ability to substitute one good for another.
  - **(1)** The marginal utility of a good is the increase in the consumer's total utility that results from consuming 1 more unit of a good. As more and more of a good is consumed, each additional unit adds less and less to total utility so that marginal utility diminishes. As less and less of a good is consumed, the marginal utility of the good rises.
  - **(2)** The consumer substitutes one good for the other by changing his spending up to the point where the marginal utility of an extra dollar spent on one good exactly equals the marginal utility from an extra dollar spent on the other. This is the consumer's optimum position (given the budget constraint) because he cannot be made any better off by changing the combination of goods consumed.
2. An increase in the consumer's income causes the budget line to shift outward. The new budget line is parallel to the old one as long as the price ratio remains the same. If there are only two goods and both are normal, an increase in income causes more of both goods to be consumed. If one of the two goods is inferior, an increase in income causes less of the inferior good and proportionately more of the normal good to be consumed. A fall in income causes the budget line to shift inward toward the origin.
3. A change in the price of a good causes a change in quantity demanded. The responsiveness of changes in quantity to changes in price is given by the good's own price elasticity of demand. But the demand for goods in other markets can be affected, too. The cross price elasticity of demand illustrates the responsiveness of quantity demanded of one good when the price of another good changes. These cross price elasticities are usually smaller than the good's own price elasticity, and they may be either positive or negative.
   - **a.** For the two-good case, a change in the price of one good causes the budget line to rotate about the intercept on the axis for the good whose price does not change. The budget line rotates either clockwise or counterclockwise, depending on whether price increases or decreases. A price change causes the household's purchasing power and consumption opportunities to change, and so its standard of living changes.
   - **b.** A change in the price of a good involves both an income effect and a substitution effect on consumer demand. The income effect of a price change is the adjustment in the consumption of all goods as a result of the change in the purchasing power of a buyer's income. The substitution effect of a price change is the adjustment in the composition of the goods purchased because of the change in relative prices. The substitution effect assumes that the consumer's purchasing power does not change when the price of one good changes, and it examines the influence on consumer choice of the new relative price ratio.
     - **(1)** When only the income effect is considered and both goods are normal, a change in price changes the demand for both goods in the same direction as the change in the purchasing power of income.
     - **(2)** When the price of one good changes and there is no change in the purchasing power of income, that good's cost in terms of other goods changes. The consumer buys more of the relatively less expensive good and less of the relatively more expensive good by substituting one good for the other. The substitution effect of a good's own price change on the

quantity demanded is always negative, but the effect on other goods may be positive or negative.

(3) The net effect on quantity demanded of a good's own price change is negative since price and quantity demanded change in opposite directions. The net effect of a good's own price change on other goods is less well defined and depends on whether the income or the substitution effect dominates.

4. The income and substitution effects taken together determine the downward slope of the demand curve and the negative relationship between price and quantity demanded.

   a. The market demand curve for a particular good is the sum of all individual consumers' demand curves; the individual demand curves are summed horizontally. The negative relationship between price and quantity demanded exists in the market, just as it does for individual consumers.

   b. For some goods, the substitution effect is negligible. If the item commands a relatively large part of the consumer's budget, the income effect is predominant for a price change in the particular good. For goods which command a relatively small part of the consumer's budget and which have substitutes, the substitution effect dominates a price change of a particular good. When goods are substitutes, the cross price elasticities are positive.

   c. When there are many goods on the market, some may be consumed jointly. Goods used jointly are called complementary goods and have a negative cross price elasticity of demand. An increase in the price and a decrease in the quantity of a good cause the amount consumed of its complement to decrease also.

   d. If two goods are close substitutes and the price of each good changes in the same direction, the substitution effect is dampened and the net effect on each good's own price elasticity of demand is lower. Often the prices of goods which are close substitutes rise together.

5. A price change in one market is not confined only to that market; through the income and substitution effects, other markets are influenced. A price increase in one market causes an increase in demand for the good's substitute and shifts its demand curve so that the price of the substitute also increases. The prices in substitute markets can increase or decrease together as demand rises or falls.

6. The consumer behavior model suggests that some households receive less utility from in-kind assistance programs than they would receive from a direct cash grant equivalent to the in-kind transfers. Cash transfers in place of in-kind transfers are politically unpopular.

7. The model of consumer behavior and observations on income, prices, and consumption may allow us to evaluate consumer well-being over time. Given a consumer's income and the price level in the current year, if last year's goods could be purchased but were not, the consumer must be at a higher level of utility. Consumer welfare has improved. Observations on prices, incomes, and consumption from one time period to the next are the basis for the construction of cost-of-living index numbers.

IMPORTANT TERMS AND THEIR MEANING

Match the following terms with the correct definition or phrase.

1. _____ The horizontal sum of all individual demand curves in a market

2. _____ A particular good's price elasticity of demand

3. _____ The satisfaction received from the consumption of a good

4. _____ The theory describing how the consumer responds to changes in market conditions

5. _____ Observations of income and prices over time which are used to measure changes in real income and changes in consumers' standard of living

6. _____ The consumer chooses the bundle of goods which yields the greatest level of satisfaction, given the budget constraint

7. _____ States that the additional satisfaction received by the consumption of an extra unit of a good adds less to total utility the more of that good the individual is already consuming

8. _____ The price of one good in terms of the price of another good

9. _____ Assistance in some form other than cash

a. Budget constraint
b. Budget line
c. Relative price
d. Utility maximization
e. Utility
f. Tastes
g. Cost-of-living comparison
h. Marginal utility
i. Consumption basket

SPECIAL TOPICS IN DEMAND

10. _____ The set of combinations of goods the consumer can purchase, given income and prices

11. _____ The effect of a disturbance in one market on the behavior of other markets

12. _____ The extra satisfaction gained by consuming 1 more unit of a good

13. _____ Measures the effect a price change in one good has on the quantity demanded of another

14. _____ Any particular combination of goods purchased or considered for purchase by the consumer

15. _____ Assuming purchasing power constant, a price change of a good causes more of the less expensive good and less of the more expensive good to be consumed

16. _____ Describes goods which are consumed jointly

17. _____ The change in the demand for goods caused by a change in the consumer's purchasing power

18. _____ Graphical presentation of the budget constraint, showing the maximum combination of goods that the consumer can buy, given income and prices

19. _____ Income effect plus substitution effect

20. _____ Determines the consumer's ranking of alternative bundles of goods

j. Cross price elasticity

k. Own price elasticity

l. Consumer choice

m. Diminishing marginal utility

n. Income effect

o. Substitution effect

p. Net effect of a price change

q. Market demand curve

r. Spillover effect

s. Complementarity

t. In-kind transfers

EXERCISES

1. Suppose that freshman Sam has a weekly budget of $40 and must decide what his consumption possibilities are. Since Mom and Dad pay for room and board, Sam buys only two goods with his budget: beer and record albums. If beer is priced at $8 per case and albums are $5 each, plot Sam's budget line on graph paper. Label the vertical axis "cases of beer" and the horizontal axis "albums." The vertical intercept should be labeled A and the horizontal intercept B.

   a. The feasible budget region for Sam's consumption choice is triangle _____.

   b. The trade-off between beer and record albums faced by Sam is _____ cases of beer for every record album. The rate at which beer can be traded off for albums is the (intercept/slope/range) _____ of the budget line.

   c. If the price of record albums increased from $5 to $8 each, the budget line would (shift/rotate) _____ (outward/inward) _____, indicating that Sam could buy (more/fewer) _____ albums.

   d. On your graph, draw a new budget line for Sam if the price of albums is $8. The new trade-off between cases of beer and albums is _____ case(s) of beer given up for every additional album. The slope of the new budget line is _____.

   e. Let the price of beer decrease to $5 per case while albums remain at $8 each. Draw the new budget line.

2. Suppose that your income is $100 and that you purchase only the two goods X and Y. The price of X is $10 per unit, and the price of Y is $20 per unit.

   a. On graph paper plot your budget line. Label the vertical axis Y, the horizontal axis X, the vertical intercept K, and the horizontal intercept M.

   b. The feasible region for consumer choice and the region within which you must determine your optimal budget allocation is given by _____. The trade-off of Y for X is _____ units of Y for every unit of X.

   c. Assume that you have the following baskets from which to make your choice:

BASKET	UNITS OF Y	UNITS OF X
A	2	2
B	1	7
C	2	6
D	3	8
K	5	0
M	0	10

On your graph, plot each of the commodity baskets.

   d. Based on your graph, any point below line KM is (less preferred than/preferred to) _____ any point on or above the line. Baskets _____ will be preferred less than baskets _____.

Basket _____ contains only good Y and no X, while basket _____ contains no Y and all X. It (is/is not) _____ reasonable to assume that you prefer some of both goods as opposed to all of only one good. As a result, you (are/are not) _____ indifferent to bundles K, C, and M. Your optimal basket, given the budget constraint, is thus _____, where you consume _____ units of X and _____ units of Y and have $_____ remaining. Being a rational consumer, you prefer basket _____ to basket C; however, your income (is/is not) _____ sufficient to purchase the basket.

e. If your income increased by $40, the budget line would (shift/rotate) _____ outward. With the higher budget of $140, you could buy _____ units of Y, or _____ units of X, or some other combination outside the initial constraint.

f. Draw your new budget line. Point D (is/is not) _____ now attainable. The trade-off of Y for X is _____ units of Y for every unit of X.

3. Table 5-1 presents the individual demand data for three consumers of widgets. Determine the quantity demanded of widgets in the market at each price. Graph each individual demand curve and the market demand schedule on paper. Be sure to label the curves.

4. Table 5-2 presents the satisfaction gained by Joan as she consumes lobster dainties. The table shows how total utility behaves as total consumption goes up. You are to first compute the marginal utility of each additional lobster dainty consumed. Next, plot the total utility curve. Label the vertical axis "utility" and the horizontal axis "quantity." On a separate graph, plot the marginal utility curve. Plot the marginal values at the midpoints on the quantity axis.

TABLE 5-1

PRICE PER UNIT, $	ROBERT, quantity	EDWARD, quantity	ALICE, quantity	MARKET DEMAND
7	0	0	3	____
6	1	0	4	____
5	2	1	5	____
4	3	2	6	____
3	4	3	7	____
2	5	4	8	____
1	6	5	9	____

TABLE 5-2

QUANTITY	TOTAL UTILITY	MARGINAL UTILITY
0	0	
1	7	____
2	13	____
3	18	____
4	22	____
5	25	____
6	27	____
7	28	____
8	28	____
9	27	____

a. Marginal utility (does/does not) _____ fall as more dainties are consumed.

b. When total utility is (maximized/minimized) _____, marginal utility is (greater than/equal to/less than) _____ zero.

5. Presented below is a table containing hypothetical own and cross price elasticities of demand for three goods A, B, and C. Your task is to determine whether the goods are substitutes or complements.

ELASTICITY OF DEMAND FOR	WITH RESPECT TO THE PRICE OF		
	A	B	C
A	−1.71	−1.05	.76
B	−.76	−0.43	1.24
C	.55	.91	−1.0

a. If the goods are substitutes, circle the appropriate elasticity.

b. If the goods are complements, put a square around the elasticity.

c. Indicate the own elasticity by underlining it.

FILL-IN QUESTIONS

1. For a decrease in income and with prices remaining constant, the budget line will shift (upward and to the right/downward and to the left) _____, and the ratio of relative prices will (increase/decrease/remain constant) _____.

2. For a particular good, if the price increases and both the income and substitution effects are negative, the total effect of the price change on quantity demanded will be (positive/negative/uncertain) _____.

3. The term (substitutability/complementarity) _____ designates goods which are consumed together.

SPECIAL TOPICS IN DEMAND

4. Food stamps and low-income housing are examples of (cash transfers/in-kind transfers) _____ which the theory of consumer choice suggests yield (more/less) _____ consumer welfare than a _____.

5. When the price of a commodity with close substitutes available increases, we expect _____ effects in the substitute goods markets to (increase/decrease/not influence) _____ prices as the demand curve for the substitute (shifts upward and to the right/shifts downward and to the left/remains constant) _____.

6. If food is plotted on the horizontal axis and entertainment is plotted on the vertical axis, a price increase for food causes the budget line to rotate and become (less steep/steeper) _____, while a price decrease for food causes the budget line to rotate and become (flatter/steeper) _____.

7. The (utility/relative price ratio/income constraint) _____ measures the price of one good in terms of another good.

8. The rational consumer will prefer (more/less) _____ of a good to (more/less) _____ of it as he attempts to maximize (utility/income/price) _____ in consumption.

9. To be in equilibrium, a consumer with a given income and facing constant market prices should consume goods until the _____ of an extra dollar spent on all goods is equal.

10. For the two-good case, a change in the price of one good will cause the _____ ratio to change as one good becomes more expensive in terms of the other good. The consumer's purchasing power will (increase/decrease/remain constant) _____ if the price falls and (increase/decrease/remain constant) _____ if the price rises.

11. (Utility/Marginal utility/Income) _____ is a measure of the total satisfaction received by consuming a good.

12. The _____ curve for a good is determined by adding individual demand curves.

13. The cross price elasticity of demand for substitutes is (positive/negative/zero) _____, while for complementary goods, the cross price elasticity is (positive/negative/zero) _____.

14. Any point on the budget line is (attainable/unattainable) _____, while any point above the budget line is (attainable/unattainable) _____.

15. Assuming all goods are normal, a fall in the price of Scotch whiskey will cause (more/less/no change in) _____ consumption of Scotch, (more/less/no change in) _____ consumption of other goods because of the substitution effect, and (more/less/no change in) _____ consumption of all other goods because of the income effect.

TRUE-FALSE QUESTIONS

1. _____ Complementary goods will have a positive cross price elasticity of demand.

2. _____ Given consumer preferences and income, no consumption bundle with more goods will ever be less preferred to a consumption bundle with fewer of the same goods.

3. _____ The income and substitution effects explain why the individual's demand curve slopes downward and to the right.

4. _____ The substitution effect for price changes of a good will always be negative.

5. _____ One important element in the model of consumer choice is that the consumers' tastes are meaningless.

6. _____ The budget constraint defines the feasible area within which consumer choices are made.

7. _____ If there is a price increase in the market for a particular good, we would expect a price decrease in the markets for substitute goods since their demand curves will shift to the left.

8. _____ When economists speak of trade-offs, they are describing the presence of spillover effects in related markets.

9. _____ For a price change of a particular good, the income effect may be either positive or negative.

10. _____ The consumer is in equilibrium when the marginal utility of an extra dollar spent on a particular good equals the marginal utility of an extra dollar spent on other goods.

11. _____ For an inferior good, the relationship between a price change and the income effect is negative.

12. _____ Given income and prices, a consumer will be in equilibrium either on or above the budget line.

13. _____ The model of consumer behavior developed in this chapter indicates that a consumer's well-being will be greater from an in-kind transfer than from a cash transfer.

14. _____ Information on prices, incomes, and consumption baskets can be used to examine consumer welfare from one time period to the next.

15. _____ The rational consumer tries to maximize total utility in consumption subject to a set of given constraints.

16. _____ A change in consumer income rotates the budget line around one of the intercepts.

17. _____ The cross price elasticities for goods which are close substitutes are both large and positive.

MULTIPLE CHOICE QUESTIONS

Circle the correct answer.

1. If a person consumes 9 units of good X for a total utility in consumption of 38 utils and then consumes a tenth unit of the good for a total utility of 45 utils, you can conclude that the marginal utility of the last-unit consumed is
    a. 45 utils
    b. 10 utils
    c. 7 utils
    d. 5 utils
    e. none of the above

2. Suppose that the quantity demanded of good X goes up by 10 percent when the price of good Y goes up by 4 percent. You can conclude that
    a. X and Y are substitutes with a cross price elasticity demand of +2.5
    b. X and Y are substitutes with a cross price elasticity of demand of −2.5
    c. X and Y are complements with a cross price elasticity of demand of +2.5
    d. X and Y are complements with a cross price elasticity of demand of −2.5

3. Which of the following statements concerning the model of consumer choice is incorrect?
    a. the consumer has to make choices subject to a given income constraint
    b. the prices of goods in the consumption basket are assumed to be given
    c. the consumer seeks to arrange goods in his consumption basket so that utility is maximized
    d. tastes allow the consumer to rank alternative bundles of goods
    e. none of the above statements is correct

4. The substitution effect for the two-good case is always negative because
    a. when a price changes, the consumer's purchasing power will change
    b. when the price of one good changes relative to another, more of the less expensive good will be consumed at the expense of the other good
    c. of the concept of complementarity
    d. of the spillover effects in other markets

5. A market demand curve for a good
    a. slopes downward and to the right
    b. is to the right of an individual's demand curve
    c. shows that at higher prices, consumers buy less of a good
    d. is determined by adding all individual demand curves
    e. all of the above

6. The initial impact of a price decrease of one good on the markets for substitute goods is that
    a. the demand curves in the substitute markets shift to the right
    b. the supply curves of the substitutes shift to the right
    c. the price of the substitutes increases
    d. the demand curves for the substitutes shift to the left

7. An in-kind transfer may cause some consumers to
    a. attain a higher level of utility than would be the case with a cash transfer
    b. attain a lower level of utility than would be the case with a cash transfer
    c. not change their consumption baskets
    d. move to a lower budget constraint

8. A price change for one good will cause the budget line to
    a. shift upward and to the right
    b. shift downward and to the left
    c. rotate about the intercept for the good whose price remains constant
    d. rotate about the intercept for the good whose price changes

9. Consumer choice models require that the consumer
    a. be able to explicitly determine the amount of utility received from all consumption baskets
    b. be able to rank, in order of preference, consumption baskets
    c. spend some but not all of his income
    d. none of the above

10. Which of the following goods would have a negative cross price elasticity of demand?
    a. gasoline and automobile tires
    b. natural gas and electricity
    c. coffee and tea
    d. meat and fish

AT THIS POINT YOU SHOULD BE ABLE TO . . .

1. State the four elements of a consumer choice model.
2. Explain the meaning of a budget constraint and draw a budget line from a given set of income and price data.
3. Explain why a consumer will never be above or below his budget line if he tries to maximize utility.
4. State the condition for the optimal consumption point in terms of marginal utility.
5. Define and explain the income, substitution, and net effects on the consumption of a good when the good's price changes.
6. Use the income and substitution effects to explain why the consumer's demand curve slopes downward and to the right.
7. Define cross price elasticity of demand and explain how the elasticity is influenced by the income and substitution effects.
8. Define the market demand curve for a good in terms of individual demand curves.
9. Explain and show how price and income changes affect a consumer's budget line.
10. Show how a price change in one market can spill over into and influence the markets for substitutes and complements.
11. Present the argument that transfers in cash are preferred to transfers in kind by the recipients.
12. Explain how information on changes in prices and incomes can be used to make general statements about consumer welfare.

QUESTIONS FOR THOUGHT

1. Even though total utility and marginal utility cannot be measured, explain how and why the concepts are so useful in consumer theory.
2. Suppose that a consumer is purchasing two goods X and Y and that the marginal utility of the extra dollar spent on good X is greater than the marginal utility of the extra dollar spent on good Y. Is the consumer in equilibrium? Why? If not, explain what actions the consumer should take to achieve his optimal consumption basket.
3. The income and substitution effects show how a consumer behaves when the price of a good changes. Assuming the two-good case, what do you think would happen if both prices increased by 10 percent and income increased by 10 percent? Explain.
4. Cross price elasticities of demand tell us how one good responds to price changes in other goods. Why do you think such elasticities are important? List two or three cases in which cross price elasticities can be used.
5. Marginal utility is defined as the change in total utility as a result of consuming 1 more unit of a good. Suppose you had 10 apples to eat and could indicate whether each apple gave you more or less satisfaction than the previous one. Do you think that the marginal utility from each apple would be the same (constant)? Why or why not? What do you think would happen to the marginal utility generated by each additional apple consumed? Explain.
6. Explain how the application of the theory of consumer choice to government assistance programs can provide information about whether individuals are better off with in-kind assistance or direct cash transfers. What are the political arguments against paying individuals a direct cash subsidy?

APPENDIX: INDIFFERENCE CURVE ANALYSIS

The appendix to Chapter 5 presents an extension and a different way of viewing the concept of consumer equilibrium. The extension consists of the introduction of a consumer's indifference curve. The indifference curve approach shows that consumers can rank a market basket of goods in order of preference and can substitute baskets so that a constant overall level of satisfaction (utility) is maintained. The indifference curve shows all combinations of goods that yield a constant level of utility. As the consumer gets more of both goods, we know that utility will increase, and the consumer moves to a higher indifference curve. Every possible basket of goods is a point on some indifference curve.

For the two-good case, the consumer, knowing prices and given an income, will rearrange his consumption baskets until he reaches the point where the budget line is just tangent to an indifference curve. This point represents the utility-maximizing level for the consumer, given the income and price constraints. Any change in the price of a good will rotate the budget line, and any change in income (prices held constant) will cause a parallel shift of the budget line. After either price or income changes, the consumer will reach a new equilibrium on another indifference curve. The consumer is in an equilibrium position when the ratio of the marginal utilities of goods consumed equals the relative price ratio.

CHAPTER OUTLINE

1. An indifference curve shows all possible combinations of consumption baskets which generate the same level of utility.
   a. Since more goods are preferred to less, baskets containing more of both goods yield higher levels of utility, and their indifference curves lie above and to the right of the curves for baskets with fewer goods. A basket of goods may lie on only one indifference curve.
   b. Consumer choice theory requires that indifference curves adhere to four fundamental rules:
      (1) Indifference curves cannot cross.
      (2) Higher indifference curves correspond to higher levels of utility.
      (3) Indifference curves are negatively sloped, indicating consumer willingness to substitute goods.
      (4) As the consumer moves down and along his indifference curve, the slope of the curve becomes flatter.
   c. The marginal rate of substitution is the slope of an indifference curve and shows the rate at which the consumer is willing to trade off one good for another. As one good is substituted for another, the willingness of the consumer to continue substitution diminishes.
2. With a given income and price, the consumer reaches an equilibrium when the budget line is just tangent to an indifference curve. This indifference curve reflects the highest attainable level of utility, given the income constraint. At any point other than the tangency point, the consumer can attain a higher level of satisfaction by rearranging the consumption baskets and moving to a higher indifference curve.
3. The equilibrium point for the consumer requires the slope of the budget line and the slope of the indifference curve to be equal since they must be tangent. Another way of writing the condition is that the ratio of the marginal utilities of the goods consumed (slope of the indifference curve) equals the ratio of the goods' prices (slope of the budget line).
4. A change in the price of one good causes the budget line to rotate and thus changes its slope. A new equilibrium point is established on either a higher or a lower indifference curve, and its slope equals the new price ratio. By observing how a consumer rearranges his consumption basket after a change in the price of one good, it is possible to determine whether other goods are substitutes or complements.
5. Assuming no changes in price, a change in income causes a parallel shift in the budget line. The new equilibrium point is established at the point of tangency between the new budget line and a new indifference curve.

IMPORTANT TERMS AND THEIR MEANING

Match the following terms with the correct definition or phrase.

1. _____ The rate at which the consumer is willing to trade one good for another
   a. Equilibrium condition

2. _____ The locus of consumption baskets yielding the consumer a constant level of satisfaction
   b. Marginal rate of substitution

3. _____ The ratio of the marginal utilities of goods consumed must equal the ratio of relative prices
   c. Indifference curve

EXERCISES

1. Table 5-3 presents the indifference schedules for three levels of utility. Two goods, food (F) and entertainment (E), are being consumed.

TABLE 5-3

SCHEDULE UU_1		SCHEDULE UU_2		SCHEDULE UU_3	
F	E	F	E	F	E
8	25	1	29	1	23
9	21	2	23	2	19
10	17	3	20	3	17
11	14	4	18	4	15
12	12	6	15	6	12
14	10	8	12	6	10
15	9	10	10	10	8
18	7	12	8	12	6
20	6	15	6	14	5
		17	5	16	4
		19	4	19	3

a. Draw the three indifference curves on your graph paper by plotting each basket of goods and connecting each point. Number both the horizontal and vertical axes from 1 to 30. Label the vertical axis "entertainment" and the horizontal axis "food."

b. Indifference curve UU_1 represents a (higher/lower) _____ level of satisfaction than indifference curve UU_2.

c. The consumer (is/is not) _____ indifferent between the basket containing 12 units of food and 12 units of entertainment and the basket containing 9 units of food and 21 units of entertainment.

SPECIAL TOPICS IN DEMAND

He (is/is not) _____ indifferent between the basket containing 12 units of food and 12 units of entertainment and the basket containing 4 units of food and 18 units of entertainment.

d. All of the indifference curves have a (positive/negative) _____ slope, and as one moves farther downward and to the right on every curve, the slope (increases/diminishes) _____ as the consumer becomes (more/less) _____ willing to give up entertainment for more food.

e. It (is/is not) _____ now possible to determine the consumer's optimal consumption basket.

2. Using the indifference curves from Exercise 1, assume that the consumer has a budget of $300. Let the price of entertainment be $10 and the price of food be $15. Draw the consumer's budget line.

a. The maximum amount of entertainment that can be purchased if no food is purchased is _____ units, while the maximum amount of food that can be purchased if no entertainment is consumed is _____ units.

b. The slope of the budget line is _____.

c. The consumer attains an equilibrium by consuming _____ units of entertainment and _____ units of food. At equilibrium, the slopes of the indifference curve and budget line (are/are not) _____ equal.

d. In equilibrium, the consumer spends $_____ for the purchase of entertainment and $_____ for the purchase of food.

e. The highest level of utility that can be reached is shown by indifference curve _____.

f. The consumer (would/would not) _____ consume any basket shown on curves UU_2 and UU_3 because he (would/would not) _____ be maximizing utility.

3. Now let the price of entertainment increase from $10 to $20 per unit. The price increase will (shift/rotate) _____ the budget line. Draw the new budget line, leaving the price of food at $15 per unit.

a. The maximum amount of entertainment that can be purchased if no food is bought is _____ units. The new budget line is (steeper/flatter) _____ than the original, and its slope is _____.

b. The consumer is forced to a new equilibrium point on indifference curve _____ and consumes _____ units of entertainment and _____ units of food. The overall level of satisfaction has (increased/decreased) _____ for the consumer.

4. The table below presents an indifference curve for goods A and B. Draw the curve and show good A on the vertical axis and good B on the horizontal. Label the indifference curve U_0.

A	B
1	5
2	4
3	3
4	2
5	1

a. Indifference curve U_0 is (linear/nonlinear) _____, and the marginal rate of substitution (does/does not) _____ diminish as B is substituted for A.

b. An indifference curve such as U_0 reflects goods which are (perfect/imperfect) _____ substitutes.

FILL-IN QUESTIONS

1. When a consumer is in equilibrium, his budget has been allocated among goods so that the ratio of the _____ utilities equals the _____ ratio.

2. If there is an increase in the price of one good, other things equal, the budget line (shifts/rotates) _____ and the consumer is forced to a (higher/lower) _____ indifference curve.

3. An indifference curve shows all combinations of goods which yield a constant level of _____, is (concave/convex) _____ to the origin, and has a slope which (increases/decreases/remains constant) _____ as one moves from left to right along the curve.

4. In order to determine a consumer's equilibrium, we must know not only the consumer's preferences rankings but also his _____ and the _____ of goods.

5. When a consumer is in equilibrium and the price of

one good changes, the _____ effect and _____ effect will move the consumer to a different level of utility.

6. (Higher/lower) _____ indifference curves reflect greater levels of satisfaction since they represent (more/less) _____ of both goods.

7. A utility-maximizing consumer will always consume goods up to the point where an indifference curve and the budget line are _____ since any other combination is either (attainable/unattainable) _____ or yields a lower level of _____.

8. The willingness of a consumer to give up one good in exchange for another good as more of the other good is consumed (increases/decreases) _____, and this is known as the _____.

TRUE-FALSE QUESTIONS

1. ____ If income increases, all other things constant, the consumer will move to a higher indifference curve.

2. ____ Even though two indifference curves intersect, it is still possible to attain a consumer equilibrium.

3. ____ Any movement along an indifference curve involves more of both goods being consumed.

4. ____ As indifference curves approach the origin, the level of utility increases.

5. ____ Every possible combination of goods lies on some indifference curve.

6. ____ In the two-good case, if the ratio of the goods' marginal utilities exceeds the ratio of the goods' prices, the consumer is not in a position of equilibrium.

MULTIPLE CHOICE QUESTIONS

Circle the correct answer.

1. One of the basic assumptions of indifference curve theory is that
   a. the consumer's income is neither known nor fixed
   b. indifference curves slope upward and to the right
   c. indifference curves cannot intersect
   d. the rate at which one good can be substituted for another is constant

2. The indifference curve approach to consumer choice requires that the consumer must be able to
   a. rank commodity bundles in order of preference
   b. numerically quantify the level of utility associated with each basket of goods consumed
   c. have linear preferences
   d. none of the above

3. If all prices were reduced by one-half, the consumer would
   a. remain on the same indifference curve
   b. move to a higher indifference curve
   c. move to a lower indifference curve
   d. move along the original indifference curves

4. The indifference curve shows
   a. that as more of one good is consumed, more and more of another good has to be given up
   b. that utility changes as we substitute one good for another
   c. that the marginal utilities of the two goods remain constant for movements along the curve
   d. the quantities of two goods that can be purchased, given prices

Answer Questions 5 and 6 on the basis of Figure 5-1. The initial budget line is KR, and the initial basket of goods is Y_1X_1.

5. In Figure A5-1
   a. the income of the consumer increased
   b. the income of the consumer decreased
   c. the price of Y increased
   d. the price of X decreased

6. Figure A5-1 shows goods which
   a. are substitutes
   b. are complements
   c. are independent
   d. cannot be determined

AT THIS POINT YOU SHOULD BE ABLE TO . . .

1. Define the concept of an indifference curve.
2. State the four rules which apply to indifference curve analysis.
3. Explain why indifference curves are convex in

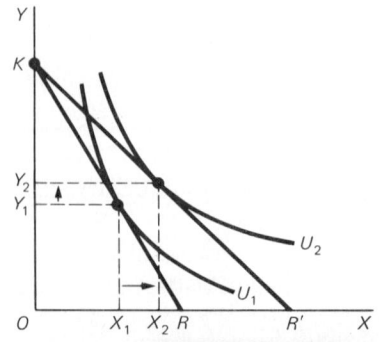

FIGURE 5-1

terms of the diminishing marginal rate of substitution.

4. Explain and draw the consumer's equilibrium position for a given income level, prices, and preferences.

5. Show the effect of a change in the price of one good on the consumer's equilibrium position using indifference curves.

6. Identify substitute and complementary goods using indifference curves.

7. Explain why in equilibrium the consumer's optimal consumption basket will be the combination of goods at which the ratio of their marginal utilities equals the ratio of their prices.

QUESTIONS FOR THOUGHT

1. If one good has a marginal utility of 4 with a price of $2 while another good has a marginal utility of 9 with a price of $3, is the consumer in equilibrium? Why or why not? What should the consumer do?

2. When a consumer purchases goods so that all of his income is spent but MU_x/MU_y is not equal to P_x/P_y, how would the indifference curve and budget line appear graphically? Should the consumer change his consumption basket? Why or why not?

3. Explain and show graphically the concepts of substitute goods and complementary goods. How do the income effect and the substitution effect enter into your analysis?

4. What would be the effect of two indifference curves intersecting? Draw a set of intersecting indifference curves and explain why such an occurrence is logically impossible.

6

The Firm: Costs and Output

Chapter 6 presents an introduction to the demand and cost conditions faced by the firm. More specifically, the chapter introduces a decision faced by the profit-maximizing firm, namely, what level of output to produce.

The first part of Chapter 6 describes the three primary forms of business organization. The proprietorship is a business firm owned by an individual. It is the most common form of business in the United States. The partnership is a business owned by two or more people and is the least common type of business organization. The corporation is the dominant type of organization measured by the value of output produced. The corporation is a legal entity and is owned by the stockholders. The owners usually have limited influence over the management of the firm.

Chapter 6 introduces the basic accounting concepts and practices found in most firms. The balance sheet shows the firm's financial condition at a given time by listing its assets, liabilities, and net worth. The income statement records the firm's performance during a given time period and shows revenue, expenses, and profits. The income statement includes a firm's accounting costs and accounting profits but not the opportunity costs incurred as a result of failing to value resources in their best alternative use. The calculation of economic profit incorporates the concept of both opportunity costs and accounting costs. Economic profit is always less than the accounting profit.

The major emphasis of Chapter 6 is the firm's production decision as it tries to maximize profits by choosing the optimal level of output to produce. The output decision in turn depends on the costs of production and the demand for the firm's product.

The total cost of production is the sum of the costs which do not change as the level of output changes and the costs which do change with output. Total costs rise as the level of output increases; however, costs and output do not increase at the same rate.

A firm's total revenue is the dollar amount of consumer expenditures for the firm's product and is calculated simply as price times quantity. The revenue of a firm increases as the level of output increases, but since more can be sold only at lower and lower prices, total revenue will reach a maximum and eventually fall.

The difference between a firm's total revenue and total costs is its profit. Profits can be either positive or negative (a loss). The profit-maximizing firm must decide what level of output generates the greatest positive difference between total revenue and total costs.

An alternative approach presented in the latter sections of Chapter 6 is based on marginal revenue and marginal cost. A firm's marginal revenue is the contribution made to total revenue when 1 additional unit of output is sold. Marginal revenue declines over all ranges of output, is zero when total revenue is maximum, and becomes negative when total revenue falls. Marginal cost is the addition to total costs when output increases by 1 unit. Marginal cost initially falls, reaches a minimum, and then rises primarily as a result of the available production techniques. As long as profits are positive, the firm maximizes these profits by selecting the output level which equates marginal cost and marginal revenue.

The material presented in Chapter 6 is your introduction to the factors which determine a firm's supply schedule. Chapters 7 and 8 further refine and expand the concept. The use of marginal analysis, especially the marginal cost-marginal revenue approach, is a tool used in many of the following chapters.

CHAPTER OUTLINE

1. In the U.S. economy, there are three main types of business organizations: individual proprietorships, partnerships, and corporations. The individual proprietorship is the most common type of business organization and is owned by an individual who is responsible for any profits or losses made by the business. The individual proprietorship has unlimited liability since the debts of the business are not limited to its assets but extend to the owner's personal wealth. A partnership is a very specific form of business which is owned by two or more individuals and which, like the proprietorship, has unlimited liability. The partnership is the least

common form of business. The corporation is a legal entity separate from the owners, and it is permitted to carry on certain business activities. Individuals who hold shares of stock in the corporation own it. The corporation sells shares of ownership (stock) in order to obtain financing to run the business. The corporation has limited liability. If it goes bankrupt, none of the owners' personal wealth is jeopardized; the assets of the corporation serve as security for its debts. In terms of economic importance, the corporation is the main type of business organization. Some of the profits are paid to the owners (shareholders) in the form of dividends, and some profits are held by the firm in the form of retained earnings for use in replacing capital and expanding capacity.

2. The revenue a firm receives from selling its goods minus the cost of producing those goods yields the profit received by the firm. Profits can be negative (loss), zero, or positive. An income statement shows the firm's revenue, expenses, and profit or loss. There are four complications which affect the calculation of a firm's profits. First, there may be outstanding bills owed by the firm, and there may be money owed to the firm at the end of an accounting period. Outstanding bills either owed by or due to the firm affect its cash flow. The economist's concern is with the revenues and costs associated with the firm during the accounting period, not with the timing of payments. The second complication is the firm's physical capital and depreciation. Physical capital has a useful life of several time periods. This year's purchases are therefore not counted entirely as expenses for this year. Rather, capital is depreciated over its useful life. Each year the value of capital used in production is added to the firm's cost. The third complication is inventories. Inventories are goods held in stock for future sales. Inventories are treated like capital. Only net inventories that are used up are included in current operating costs. The final complication affecting the calculation of a firm's profit or loss is borrowing. Any interest paid on borrowed money is included in current operating costs because it is a cost of doing business.

   a. The balance sheet shows a firm's assets (what it owns), its liabilities (what it owes), and its net worth (assets minus liabilities) at a given date. Besides its net worth, the value of a firm also includes its goodwill as a proven business.
   b. The balance sheet adjusts for some of the difficulties (especially the time differences between payments received and payments made) encountered when calculating profit and loss with an income statement.
   c. When a firm earns profits, it can pay all or some out to shareholders as dividends or it can keep some or all as retained earnings. If the firm keeps retained earnings, the balance sheet is influenced.
   d. The income statement and balance sheet of a firm record accounting costs, not economic costs. The economic costs of production include both accounting costs and opportunity costs. Opportunity costs are the amounts lost by not using scarce resources, including the owner's financial capital, in their best alternative use. Because the accounting costs and economic costs are different, accounting profits and economic profits are different.

3. Although economic analysis assumes that the motive of business is profit maximization, some economists and businessmen question this assumption because they believe that firms have other aims as well.
   a. Most large corporations are run by managers and not owners. Some managers may act to promote their own and not the stockholders' best interest. As a result, firms may actually have goals other than profit maximization.
   b. Whether firms have a social conscience is an unanswered question. Even if firms have multiple goals, profit maximization is assumed to be the primary objective.

4. In pursuing its profit-maximizing goal, a firm must decide the best level of output to produce, subject to the cost of production and the demand for its output.
   a. A profit-maximizing firm produces a given level of output at minimum costs; otherwise, profits are not maximized.
   b. A firm incurs some cost even when it produces no output. This is the cost of being in business. When a firm's output rises, its total cost of production rises; however, they may increase at different rates.
   c. The demand for a firm's output determines the total revenue it receives. Total revenue is the number of units sold times the market price at which the output is sold. The difference between total revenue and total cost is the firm's profit. There is a profit level (even though it may be negative) associated with each level of output. When the firm chooses the level of output which maximizes profits, the difference between total revenue and total cost is greatest. There is no reason to expect that total revenue will be maximized when profits are maximized. Maximum profits and maximum revenue are not the same thing.

5. Marginal cost is the increase in the firm's total cost when output is increased by 1 unit. Marginal

revenue is the change in the firm's total revenue when 1 more unit of output is sold. Marginal revenue and marginal costs can be used to show the producer the level of output the firm should produce and sell so that profits are maximized.
   a. Because of the production techniques employed by the firm, marginal costs are typically high for low levels of output, decrease as output increases, and then increase as output continues to expand. There is no law in economics which states that marginal cost changes in the same way for all firms.
   b. Marginal revenue falls throughout the range of output sold and becomes negative at low market prices. The reason for this decline is that any firm facing a downward-sloping demand curve for its product must lower the price in order to sell more units. When the firm lowers the price, it does so not only for the extra units sold but for all previous units that could be sold at higher prices as well. When the firm lowers prices and sells an extra unit, it gains revenue. It also loses revenue because it sells the existing level of output (which could have been sold at a higher price) at the new lower price. The increase in total revenue falls when 1 unit is sold.
      (1) The marginal revenue curve depends on the firm's demand curve for its output. When the firm faces a downward-sloping demand curve, the marginal revenue curve declines as output sold increases. The only exception to the downward-sloping marginal revenue curve is a firm controlling a very small part of a large market. This kind of firm sells all it wants at the going market price, and so its marginal revenue curve is horizontal.
   c. When marginal revenue exceeds marginal cost, output should be expanded since the contribution to total revenue of 1 more unit of output is greater than the contribution to total cost. When marginal cost exceeds marginal revenue, output should not be increased because total cost is increasing by more than total revenue.
   d. The marginal revenue-marginal cost approach yields the same output results as the total revenue-total cost approach. Marginal analysis is used more frequently because it permits an evaluation of the effect of small changes on the firm. When using marginal analysis, the firm should be sure that a profit and not a loss is being made.
   e. The firm maximizes profits at the level of output at which the marginal revenue and marginal cost curves cross.

6. Assuming that the firm is not confined to producing strictly integer levels of output (fractions of a unit can be produced), the marginal revenue MR curve declines continuously; it is not broken by steps. The marginal cost curve MC is smoothly falling at first, reaching a minimum and then rising. The intersection of the curves ($MC = MR$) establishes the optimal output level.
   a. A change in the firm's cost of production shifts the marginal cost curve and causes the profit-maximizing output to change.
   b. A change in demand for the firm's output shifts both the demand curve and the marginal revenue curve. A shift in the marginal revenue curve causes a change in the firm's level of output.

IMPORTANT TERMS AND THEIR MEANING

Match the following terms with the correct definition or phrase.

1. ____ A firm's profit and loss statement showing revenue received and expenses incurred over some time period
2. ____ The addition to total cost as a result of increasing output by 1 unit
3. ____ The net amount of money a firm receives in a given period
4. ____ The value of a firm as a going and proven business
5. ____ A legal business entity having an existence separate from the owners
6. ____ The owners of a firm are not liable for more money than they committed to the business
7. ____ The loss of a machine's value resulting from its use during a given time period
8. ____ The form of business organization with two or more owners each having unlimited liability
9. ____ The excess of a firm's assets over its liabilities
10. ____ The return paid to the owners of a corporation on their

a. Marginal cost
b. Profits
c. Net worth
d. Limited liability
e. Opportunity costs
f. Dividends
g. Economic costs
h. Shareholder
i. Capital gains
j. Cash flow

THE FIRM: COSTS AND OUTPUT

personal investment

11. _____ The excess of a firm's total revenue over its total costs

12. _____ Total business receipts of a firm; equal to the total expenditures by consumers for the firm's product

13. _____ The addition to total revenue as a result of a firm selling 1 more unit of its product

14. _____ The owners of stock and thus of a corporation

15. _____ A listing of a firm's assets and liabilities at a point in time

16. _____ A type of business organization owned by an individual

17. _____ Cost incurred by not using a resource in its best alternative use

18. _____ That part of corporate profits not disbursed as dividends

19. _____ Accounting cost plus opportunity costs

20. _____ The positive difference between what is paid for an asset and what is received from the asset when it is sold

21. _____ All costs of production including those which vary with the level of output and those which do not

k. Retained earnings
l. Proprietorship
m. Income statement
n. Total costs
o. Depreciation
p. Corporation
q. Total revenue
r. Balance sheet
s. Partnership
t. Marginal revenue
u. Goodwill

EXERCISES

1. Presented below are the year-end accounts for the Widget Company, a sole proprietorship:

a.	cash on hand	$ 60,000
b.	factory building owned (original value $85,000)	70,000
c.	wage expense (10,000 hours @ $8 per hour)	80,000
d.	loan from bank payable	240,000
e.	inventories	130,000
f.	office supplies expense	10,000
g.	cost (expense) of materials used in production	300,000
h.	real estate mortgage payable	50,000
i.	other current assets	10,000
j.	200,000 units of output sold @ $4 each	800,000
k.	office operating expense	20,000
l.	salaries payable	30,000
m.	capital equipment (original value $800,000)	600,000
n.	accounts receivable	50,000
o.	advertising and selling expense	60,000
p.	accounts payable	30,000
q.	rental expense on warehouse	100,000
r.	wages payable	20,000
s.	other current liabilities	80,000

The Widget Company has been in operation for only 1 year, and it is up to you to prepare the necessary statements for Mr. Smith, the proprietor.

a. Carefully identify the expenses (costs) and revenue for the first year of operation and prepare the company's income statement. (See Table 6-1.)

TABLE 6-1

WIDGET COMPANY
INCOME STATEMENT FOR THE YEAR
ENDING DECEMBER 31, 1983

Revenues:

Expenses:

Net income: $_____

b. Identify the assets and liabilities of the company and prepare a year-end balance sheet. Be sure to set up both statements as shown in your text. (See Table 6-2.)

TABLE 6-2

WIDGET COMPANY
BALANCE SHEET AS OF DECEMBER 31, 1983

Assets	Liabilities

Total assets: $_____   Total liabilities: $_____
Net worth: $_____

c. From your income statement, the expenses listed represent (accounting/economic) _____ costs, and Mr. Smith's company had a net (economic/accounting) _____ profit of $_____.

d. The balance sheet shows total assets of $_____, total liabilities of $_____, and a net worth of the company of $_____. The balance sheet (does/does not) _____ reflect any value of goodwill associated with the firm.

e. Mr. Smith is a highly qualified manager and could be earning a salary of $75,000 if he worked for one of several firms. Also, Mr. Smith invested $300,000 of his own money in order to start up the Widget Company. The $300,000 could currently be invested in commercial paper and earn 14.5 percent per year. Adjust your income statement (see Table 6-3) to reflect the opportunity costs incurred by Mr. Smith. The total value of the accounting costs plus opportunity cost is $_____, and as a result, Mr. Smith earns an economic profit of $_____ as opposed to an accounting profit of $_____.

TABLE 6-3

WIDGET COMPANY
ADJUSTED INCOME STATEMENT FOR THE YEAR
ENDING DECEMBER 31, 1983

Revenues:

Expenses:

$_____

2. Table 6-4 presents hypothetical price and quantity data for a firm.

a. Complete the table by completing the total and marginal revenue values.

b. The data in the table suggest that as long as total revenue continues to increase, marginal revenue is (positive/negative/zero) _____, and when total revenue is maximum (between the sixth and seventh units), marginal revenue is (positive/negative/zero) _____.

c. To say that marginal revenue is negative means that an additional price reduction and increase in quantity causes total revenue to _____.

d. Marginal revenue is negative after the _____ unit produced.

3. The cost of producing the output listed in Question 2 is presented in Table 6-5.

TABLE 6-5

QUANTITY PRODUCED, per week	TOTAL COST, $	MARGINAL COST (MC), $
0	22	
1	26	_____
2	29	_____
3	31	_____
4	36	_____
5	45	_____
6	59	_____
7	79	_____

a. Complete the cost schedule in Table 6-5 by computing the marginal cost for each additional unit of output produced.

b. Marginal cost first (decreases/increases) _____ as output expands and then (decreases/increases) _____ between the _____ and _____ units produced.

c. The total cost of production (increases/decreases) _____ slowly until the third unit is produced, but then it increases at a faster rate.

d. A cost of $_____ has to be paid by the firm even if it is producing zero output.

4. Plot the graphs of both the marginal cost and marginal revenue schedules from Exercises 2 and 3. Associate each marginal value at the midpoint of each quantity interval. Label the vertical axis "dollars" and the horizontal axis "quantity."

a. From the graph, $MR = MC$ at an output level between the _____ and _____ units, and the price associated with the level of output from Table 6-4 in Exercise 2 is between $_____ and $_____ per unit.

b. The graph of the MC curve shows marginal cost beginning to increase between the _____ and _____ units.

TABLE 6-4

QUANTITY PRODUCED, per week	PRICE RECEIVED, $	TOTAL REVENUE (TR), $	MARGINAL REVENUE (MR), $
0	12	_____	
1	11	_____	_____
2	10	_____	_____
3	9	_____	_____
4	8	_____	_____
5	7	_____	_____
6	6	_____	_____
7	5	_____	_____

THE FIRM: COSTS AND OUTPUT

TABLE 6-6

QUANTITY PRODUCED, per week	PRICE RECEIVED, per unit, $	TOTAL REVENUE (TR), $	TOTAL COSTS (TC), $	MARGINAL REVENUE (MR), $	MARGINAL COSTS (MC), $	PROFIT (Π), $
0	19	_____	20	_____	_____	_____
1	18	_____	30	_____	_____	_____
2	17	_____	38	_____	_____	_____
3	16	_____	44	_____	_____	_____
4	15	_____	48	_____	_____	_____
5	14	_____	54	_____	_____	_____
6	13	_____	62	_____	_____	_____
7	12	_____	72	_____	_____	_____
8	11	_____	84	_____	_____	_____

5. The price, output, and cost data for a firm are presented in Table 6-6.

  a. Complete Table 6-6 by computing total revenue, marginal revenue, marginal costs, and profits.

  b. From the table, profit is maximized between the _____ and _____ units with $MR =$ _____ and $MC =$ _____.

  c. Profit is negative when (total cost/total revenue) _____ is greater than (total cost/total revenue) _____, becomes positive, increases, and then begins to (increase/decrease) _____ as total cost increases (faster/slower) _____ than total revenue.

  d. The marginal cost of producing the fifth unit is $_____, and it contributes $_____ to total revenue. The marginal cost of producing the sixth unit is $_____, and it contributes $_____ to total revenue. As a result, the net change in profits is _____ when the sixth unit is produced.

FILL-IN QUESTION

1. One of the underlying assumptions when studying the behavior of the firm is that it tries to (maximize/minimize) _____ profits.

2. If more customers entered the market for a good, we would expect the (marginal cost/total cost/marginal revenue) _____ curve to (shift/rotate) _____ and the optimal level of output produced by the firm to (increase/decrease/remain constant) _____.

3. Profits are maximized when total revenue minus _____ is (greatest/least) _____.

4. Using capital equipment causes the machinery to (appreciate/depreciate) _____ over time.

5. If a firm pays out more money than it receives during a particular time period, its _____ flow will be (positive/negative/zero) _____.

6. A shareholder of a corporation is the firm's (owner/creditor/manager) _____ and expects to receive a return on his investment in the form of both (interest/dividends/salary) _____ and (rent/capital gains/capital depreciation) _____.

7. If marginal cost exceeds marginal revenue at a particular level of output, the firm should (increase/decrease) _____ output until the point at which (marginal revenue exceeds marginal cost/marginal revenue equals marginal cost) _____ in order to maximize (costs/revenue/profits) _____.

8. One advantage of the corporation over the proprietorship and partnership is (limited liability/unlimited liability/product quality) _____.

9. The (income statement/balance sheet/net cash flow) _____ shows the liabilities of a firm, while the (income statement/balance sheet/net cash flow) _____ shows the firm's operating expenses.

10. If a firm is small relative to the market and provides only a very small part of total market output, its marginal revenue curve will be (sloping downward and to the right/horizontal/sloping upward and to the right) _____.

11. The cost of using self-owned resources in a firm as opposed to their best alternative use is (accounting costs/opportunity costs/production costs) _____.

12. When all costs of production are considered, economic profits will be (greater than/less than/equal to) _____ accounting profits.

13. Given production techniques and costs, at low levels of output, a firm's marginal cost will be (high/low) _____; as output increases, marginal costs initially (fall/rise/remain constant) _____ and then (fall/rise/remain constant) as output continues to expand.

14. A firm attempts to maximize profits by adjusting the level of output produced, and this requires adjustment of the level of _____ used by the firm, which in turn affects the _____ of production.

15. Profit maximization implies the minimization of (costs/revenue) _____.

TRUE-FALSE QUESTIONS

1. _____ During any particular time period, the cost of manufacturing goods and the cost of manufacturing goods sold are identical.

2. _____ The typical corporation will always seek to maximize its profits.

3. _____ Even when profits are high, it is possible for a firm to have a low cash flow.

4. _____ The balance sheet of a firm will show its profits or losses for a particular time period.

5. _____ The opportunity costs of doing business are not reflected in a firm's income statement.

6. _____ A firm maximizes profits by producing the level of output at which $MC = MR$.

7. _____ Although the idea of a firm's revenues, profits, and costs is simple, actually calculating them can be very difficult.

8. _____ When a firm increases its output, total costs of production increase; however, output and cost do not increase at the same rate.

9. _____ When a firm increases output and sells an additional unit, the increase in revenue is called marginal costs.

10. _____ If a firm seeks to maximize profits, it must first maximize its revenue.

11. _____ An improvement in the techniques of production could be expected to lower marginal cost and lower the optimal level of output.

12. _____ When prices are very low, selling 1 more unit of output could cause marginal revenue to be negative and total revenue to fall.

13. _____ If marginal revenue is greater than marginal cost, the firm can increase its profits by selling an additional unit of the good.

14. _____ The dominant type of business organization in the United States in terms of average revenue is the corporation.

15. _____ The value of a company's goodwill is reflected in its net worth on the balance sheet.

16. _____ The firm's balance sheet shows all income and expenses listed on its income statement plus capital depreciation, liabilities, and net worth.

17. _____ Because the ownership and management of most corporations are separate, the goals of the managers may not be those of the owners.

18. _____ Everyone accepts the argument that corporations exist only to maximize profits.

19. _____ The approach most frequently used to establish the profit-maximizing level of output is marginal cost and marginal revenue.

20. _____ When the marginal cost curve crosses the marginal revenue curve, profits are maximized.

MULTIPLE CHOICE QUESTIONS

Circle the correct answer.

1. An advantage of the corporation which the partnership and proprietorship do not have is
   a. limited liability
   b. an easier access to capital markets
   c. unlimited liability
   d. *a* and *b* above
   e. none of the above

2. In terms of the value of output produced, the most important type of business firm is the
   a. partnership   c. proprietorship
   b. corporation   d. monopoly

3. The balance sheet of a firm will show all of the following except
   a. the firm's total assets
   b. any money the firm owes
   c. the operating expenses incurred by the firm
   d. the firm's net worth

4. The accounting statements of a firm usually do not reflect
   a. the depreciation of capital
   b. the value lost because a resource was not used in its best alternative use

THE FIRM: COSTS AND OUTPUT

   c. interest paid on debt owed by the firm
   d. the owner's equity in the firm

5. Which of the following statements is incorrect?
   a. economists assume that the goal of the firm is to maximize profits
   b. when the profits are maximized, total revenue exceeds total cost by the greatest amount
   c. profit maximization implies that total revenue is maximized
   d. when profits are at a maximum, the amount of revenue generated by selling 1 more unit of the good just equals the cost of producing the good

6. All of the following would cause a shift of the marginal cost curve except
   a. an increase in the firm's output
   b. production techniques changing substantially
   c. the minimum wage increasing to $4.50 per hour
   d. the price of a firm's raw material increasing

7. Marginal revenue declines because
   a. the demand curve faced by a typical firm declines
   b. in order to sell more of its product, the firm must reduce its product price, thereby both losing and gaining revenue
   c. when price is reduced in order to sell more, the price reduction applies to all quantities that could have been sold at higher prices
   d. all of the above

8. If a firm produces an output up to a point where $MC > MR$, it should
   a. do nothing since profits are being maximized
   b. reduce output since profits can be expanded
   c. increase output in order to cause marginal revenue to increase
   d. none of the above

9. All of the following would cause the marginal revenue curve to shift except
   a. a change in consumer tastes
   b. a change in consumer income
   c. a change in the number of consumers in the market
   d. a change in the price of the good

10. A profit-maximizing firm
    a. maximizes output
    b. minimizes marginal cost
    c. minimizes costs
    d. maximizes marginal revenue

11. In Figure 6-1, if MC_1 is the initial marginal cost curve and the firm is producing output level Q_3
    a. the firm should cut back production to Q_4 so that marginal costs will fall

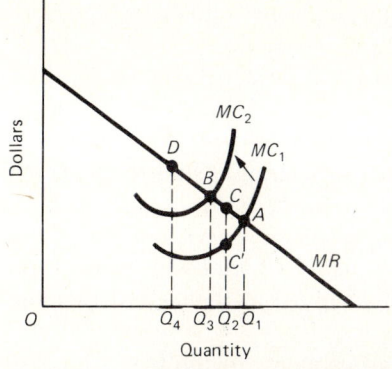

FIGURE 6-1

   b. the firm should increase production to output level Q_1
   c. the optimal output level is being produced at Q_3
   d. none of the above

12. In Figure 6-1, if the firm is producing at output Q_1 and the marginal cost curve shifts from MC_1 to MC_2,
    a. there has been an increase in the level of marginal cost, and the firm should reduce output to Q_3
    b. there has been a decrease in the level of marginal cost, and the firm should reduce output to Q_2
    c. there has been an increase in marginal costs, and the firm should cut output to Q_4 to produce at the new minimum marginal cost
    d. none of the above

13. Which of the following statements is not correct?
    a. retained earnings may be kept by the corporation to help finance future expansion of the firm
    b. retained earnings affect the firm's net worth
    c. that portion of after-tax profits not held by the firm as retained earnings is paid to stockholders as dividends
    d. retained earnings appear only on the firm's income statement because they are a part of after-tax profits

AT THIS POINT YOU SHOULD BE ABLE TO . . .

1. Explain (and distinguish between) the different types of business organizations.
2. Distinguish between the owners and the managers of a corporation and state why the goals of each may be different.
3. Explain what is both included and excluded in an income statement and a balance sheet.
4. Define the concepts of accounting costs, opportunity costs, economic costs, and profits.
5. Describe the concept of profit maximization using the total revenue-total cost approach.
6. State the meaning of marginal cost and marginal revenue.

7. Explain why marginal costs initially is high, then falls, then rises as output increases.

8. Explain how demand influences marginal revenue and state why marginal revenue falls as output increases.

9. List some factors which might shift the marginal revenue and marginal cost schedules.

10. Draw both a marginal cost curve and a marginal revenue curve and explain how and why the optimal level of output is determined at their point of intersection.

11. Explain what adjustments to the firm's level of output would be necessary if marginal cost were either greater than or less than marginal revenue.

QUESTIONS FOR THOUGHT

1. The question is still unanswered whether firms have a social conscience or simply try to maximize their level of profits by appearing to promote the social welfare. Briefly give your opinion on the issue.

2. In the modern corporation, the owners usually are separate from those who control it. Explain how this separation can occur. What are some of the implications of such a separation?

3. Explain how the income statement and balance sheet of a firm can provide an insight into its financial and economic well-being. What shortcomings might such statements have?

4. What are some of the advantages and disadvantages of each of the three types of business organizations?

5. Fischer and Dornbusch state that as the level of output produced by a firm increases, both total costs and total revenue increase, but they increase at different rates. Explain how this might happen and how it can influence the firm's attempts to maximize profits.

6. Suppose you had to explain the differences between accounting cost, accounting profit, economic costs, and economic profit to your roommate who is an accounting major. What would you say?

7. Are a corporate manager's motives necessarily in the best interest of the stockholders? Is the profit maximization assumption valid for the modern corporation? Explain.

8. Explain why a profit-maximizing firm may not necessarily try to maximize total revenue.

9. Describe how the manager of a firm maximizes profits by adjusting output, using both the total cost-total revenue approach and the marginal cost-marginal revenue approach.

10. Explain why the marginal cost curve has its particular shape.

11. Does it really make sense to say that marginal revenue could become negative? Under what condition could this happen? What effect would a negative marginal revenue have on total revenue and profits?

7

Production, Costs, and the Firm's Output Decisions

Chapter 7 further develops and extends the concepts of the firm's production, cost, and output initially presented in Chapter 6. The underlying theme of Chapter 7 is why the firm's costs change when the level of output produced is expanded or contracted. The text pays particular attention to the conditions under which a firm must choose between continuing production and closing down. Chapter 7 also addresses the problem of selecting the production technique which produces output in the most efficient (minimum cost) manner. Any change in input prices or production methods affects the firm's costs. These costs in turn influence the firm's output in both the short run and the long run as it attempts to maximize profits.

You are introduced to many new terms and concepts in Chapter 7. Don't simply memorize the definitions, because your success in later chapters depends on a thorough understanding of the costs of production. If you realize initially that total, marginal, and average costs are the three basic cost relationships for any firm in both the long run and the short run, it will be easier for you to learn the other cost concepts presented in this chapter. When you study the cost of production, you are studying the fundamentals of supply.

The first two sections of Chapter 7 are a foundation for your study of the firm's cost schedules. They examine the nature of the production function and the influence of the production function on the firm's choice of production technique. Any change in either the production function or input prices affects the choice of production methods.

Chapter 7 next introduces long-run costs. In the long run, the firm has time to make any adjustments it wishes in order to maximize profits. Long-run adjustments affect the scale of operation and plant size since all inputs are variable. The firm selects the scale of operation which minimizes long-run average cost for the output produced and results in maximum profit. The firm cannot continually increase its size of operation without encountering economies and diseconomies of scale. Economies and diseconomies of scale determine the shape of the firm's long-run average cost curve. The long-run output level is determined by producing the level of output at which long-run marginal cost and marginal revenue are equal. The price of the firm's output must not be less than the long-run average cost or the firm will go out of business.

Short-run costs are determined by input prices and the short-run production function. The law of diminishing returns is a short-run concept which states that as more units of a variable input are added to a given quantity of a fixed input, each additional unit of the variable factor will produce less and less output. The marginal product of a factor exhibiting diminishing returns is the basis for the firm's short-run marginal cost schedule. The short-run average cost schedule is simply total cost (total fixed plus total variable) divided by the level of output. The average cost schedule gives a per unit cost of output at various levels of production. In the short run, some inputs are fixed, and so there are some costs which are fixed. These fixed costs do not change with the level of output produced and must be paid even if the firm shuts down.

The firm in the short run determines the optimal output level by equating short-run marginal cost and marginal revenue. As long as output price equals or exceeds the average variable cost of production, the firm produces. Otherwise, it shuts down and loses an amount equal to its fixed cost.

In this chapter you should not only master the definitions of costs, cost schedules, and the cost calculations, you should understand why the costs of production change with changes in output. This understanding will require you to connect the production function to the cost schedules. In the long run, the cost schedules are affected by returns to scale.

CHAPTER OUTLINE

1. An input is any good or service used to produce an output. Inputs are also called the factors of production. Inputs can be combined in many different combinations to produce an output.

a. The production function shows the efficient methods of combining inputs to produce an output. Production is efficient in the sense that scarce resources are not wasted. Given any specific production function, it is possible to calculate the maximum output level which can be produced from any set of inputs.
   b. Although the production function describes a firm's production possibilities, the specific technology of production is not provided. The manager of a firm needs more information than just the production function if the business is to succeed.
2. The production function and given input prices permit the firm to minimize the cost of producing each output level and hence obtain the total cost curve.
   a. Given a production function and input prices, the firm calculates the minimum total cost of producing different levels of output using different input combinations. The marginal cost curve is derived from the total cost curve by calculating how much total cost changes when output changes by 1 unit.
      (1) The intensity of input use describes the production method in which one input is used more relative to other inputs.
   b. When the price of one input increases relative to others, the firm changes production techniques and substitutes the less expensive input for the more expensive factors as it attempts to maintain the level of output at the lowest possible cost. The firm's total cost increases for every level of output when the price of any input increases.
3. The firm's adjustment to changes in market conditions distinguishes the short run from the long run. The long run is some period of time in which the firm can adjust all of its inputs to changing market conditions. All inputs are variable and change with the level of output; none are fixed. In the short run, the firm cannot make a complete adjustment to changing market conditions; at least one input remains fixed and does not change with the level of output. The long-run total cost curve shows the lowest-cost way of producing each level of output when the firm can make any necessary adjustment to all of its inputs.
   a. In the long run, total cost is zero if the firm does not produce any output; the firm goes out of business. As long-run output increases, so does total cost. Long-run marginal cost *LMC* shows the increase in the total cost when output increases by 1 unit.
   b. The long-run average cost *LAC* of production is the total cost of production divided by the level of output. *LAC* provides a cost per unit of output produced. The *LAC* curve is U-shaped because it falls over the initial range of output, reaches a minimum, and then rises as output continues to expand. The reason for this behavior of the long-run average cost curve is returns to scale.
4. Economies of (increasing returns to) scale are present when *LAC* falls as output rises. Constant returns to scale means that *LAC* is constant at all levels of output. Diseconomies of (decreasing return to) scale are present when *LAC* rises as output increases.
   a. Economies of scale arise for three reasons. First, some inputs are required for the firm to be in business and do not change with the level of output. As output increases, the costs of these factors are spread over more output, and so long-run average cost falls. The second reason is specialization. As the firm gets larger and hires more specialized labor, the cost per unit of output produced falls. The third reason is that larger firms use better and more specialized machinery.
   b. Economies of scale apply primarily to manufacturing industries. Diseconomies of scale arise primarily because management becomes more and more complicated (managerial diseconomies). For any particular firm, the *LAC* curve may or may not be U-shaped.
   c. Evidence from some manufacturing firms suggests that diseconomies of scale are not present and that after a certain level of output is produced, economies of scale become unimportant.
5. Long-run average and long-run marginal costs both fall, reach a minimum, and then rise. The rates of change in these costs are different, but there is a close connection between the behavior of marginal and average costs. When *LMC* is below *LAC*, the average cost of production falls because the cost of producing 1 extra unit is lower than the average cost per unit. If marginal cost is greater than the average cost per unit, the cost of producing the extra unit pulls the overall average up. Average cost is at its minimum when average cost and marginal cost are equal.
6. To maximize profits in the long run, the firm produces that level of output at which marginal revenue equals long-run marginal cost ($MR = LMC$). Production takes place at this level as long as the product price is not less than the long-run average cost. Otherwise, the firm suffers a loss and should go out of business.
7. In the short run, the firm has at least one fixed factor of production and cannot fully adjust to changing

market conditions. When a factor of production is fixed, the amount used cannot be changed, and so the costs of these factors are fixed. Fixed costs do not vary with the level of output produced. The firm must pay its fixed costs even if it does not produce any output.

   a. The variable costs of production depend on the level of output produced by the firm, and so they change as output changes. Short-run fixed cost *SFC* plus short-run variable cost *SVC* yield short-run total cost *STC*. Marginal cost in the short run *SMC* is the increase in short-run total cost when output is increased by 1 unit.
   b. The marginal product of labor is the increase in output which results when an additional unit of labor is hired and all other inputs remain constant. As more and more units of any variable input are added to the fixed inputs, the law of diminishing returns states that the marginal product of the variable input declines or diminishes. This happens because an extra unit of the variable input has less and less of the fixed input with which to work. At very low levels of output, marginal product may actually increase as more of the variable input is used; however, beyond some input level, the law of diminishing returns takes effect.
   c. The shape of the marginal product curve implies the shape of the short-run marginal cost curve. When marginal product is rising, marginal costs are falling. When marginal product is falling, marginal costs are rising. Marginal cost begins to rise when diminishing returns set in. The marginal product curve is determined by the production function, and so the marginal cost and total cost curves are also influenced by the production function.
   d. Short-run fixed cost divided by the level of output yields short-run average fixed cost *SAFC*. Short-run variable cost divided by the level of output yields short-run average cost *SAVC*. Short-run average total cost *SATC* is calculated as the sum of *SAFC* plus *SVC* or determined by dividing short-run total cost by the level of output produced. The average cost measure shows the cost per unit of output produced. *SAFC* initially is high since total fixed costs have to be allocated over a low level of output. As output increases, *SAFC* declines throughout as the fixed costs are allocated over more and more units; *SAVC* initially is high but falls as output increases. Eventually, *SAVC* increases as output continues to expand. *SATC* is high at low levels of output, declines as output increases, and then increases as output continues to expand. The behavior of *SATC* is based upon the dominance of *SAFC* or *SAVC* for a particular level of output. The *SMC* curve intersects both the *SAVC* curve and the *SATC* curve at the minimum point of each. As long as *SMC* is less than *SAVC*, the *SAVC* curve falls. When *SMC* is greater than *SAVC*, the *SAVC* curve rises because the cost of producing an extra unit of output is greater than the average cost per unit, and so the average cost must go up.

8. The short-run decisions faced by a firm are whether to produce, and if production takes place, how much to produce. The decision criterion is *SMC* = *MR* at some particular level of output. When *SMC* = *MR* and the product price exceeds *SATC*, the firm should continue to produce because it makes a profit. If *SMC* = *MR* and product price is less than *SATC* but greater than *SAVC*, the firm should continue to produce even though a loss is incurred. Since price exceeds *SAVC*, some of the firm's revenue can be used to offset part of the fixed cost of production. When *SMC* = *MR* and the price does not equal or exceed *SAVC*, the firm should not produce any output because all of the fixed and some of the variable costs are not covered. The firm minimizes its losses by not producing and losing only fixed costs.

   a. Although a firm may operate with a loss in the short run when price is between *SAVC* and *SATC*, in the long run it will not. In the long run, if demand for the firm's products doesn't increase or if the firm can't reduce its operating costs, the firm should go out of business.

9. Over the long run, the firm can adjust plant size and production capacity in response to changing market conditions. Adjusting plant size and production capacity affects both short-run and long-run average costs.

   a. Every point on the *LAC* curve corresponds to a different size of plant and a different *SATC* curve. The point of tangency between an *SATC* curve and the *LAC* curve is the correct plant size for producing the given level of output at the lowest possible long-run cost. If a firm is producing with a plant size which is not optimal in the long run, it can increase profits by making the appropriate adjustments to plant size.

IMPORTANT TERMS AND THEIR MEANING

Match the following terms with the correct definition or phrase.

1. _____ The marginal product of a factor falls as the input of the factor rises
   a. U-shaped *LAC* curve

2. _____ When one method of production uses significantly more of one input relative to other inputs

3. _____ A short-run cost declining throughout every level of output

4. _____ Transformed in the production process into an output

5. _____ The sum of total fixed plus total variable costs

6. _____ That period of time in which all inputs are variable

7. _____ States that after some level of output is reached, the marginal product of the variable factor falls

8. _____ Takes its particular shape because of economies and diseconomies of scale

9. _____ Specifies the maximum output level that can be produced using some given amount of inputs

10. _____ Selection of the production method which produces the desired level of output at minimum cost

11. _____ The belief that sunk costs should be considered in a firm's operating decision

12. _____ In the short run, input usage is constant regardless of the level of output

13. _____ An equal increase in all inputs results in a greater increase in output, and so the long-run cost per unit of output falls

14. _____ Short-run variable costs divided by the level of output; provides variable cost per unit of output

15. _____ A curve showing how average cost changes with the level of output in the long run; assumed to be U-shaped

16. _____ Describes the lowest-cost way of producing each given level of output when the firm is able to adjust all its inputs optimally

17. _____ That period of time in which at least one input cannot be changed

18. _____ A proportionate change in all inputs results in a less than proportionate change in output, so the long-run average cost per unit of output increases.

19. _____ In the short run, those costs which change as the level of output changes

20. _____ The change in output resulting from a 1-unit change in the labor input, other inputs constant

21. _____ When at least one input is fixed, the change in total cost when an extra unit of output is produced

22. _____ Costs which remain constant for any level of output

23. _____ Created when inputs are combined in the production process

24. _____ Shows the change in total cost which results from the production of 1 more unit of output when all inputs are variable

25. _____ The change in output when all inputs are changed; the source of economies and diseconomies of scale

26. _____ The sum of $SAVC$ and $SAFC$; the short-run average total cost per unit of output produced

b. Short-run total cost (STC)
c. Sunk-cost fallacy
d. Short run
e. Choice of technique
f. Marginal product of labor
g. Short-run average variable cost ($SAVC$)
h. Inputs
i. Diminishing marginal returns
j. Decreasing returns to (diseconomies of) scale
k. Factor intensity
l. Outputs
m. Law of diminishing (marginal) returns
n. Short-run average fixed cost ($SAFC$)
o. Returns to scale
p. Production function
q. Short-run variable cost (SVC)
r. Long run
s. Short-run average total cost ($SATC$)
t. Long-run marginal cost curve
u. Short-run fixed factors
v. Short-run marginal cost
w. Long-run average cost curve
x. Increasing returns to (economies of) scale
y. Short-run fixed cost (SFC)
z. Long-run total cost curve

EXERCISES

1. Table 7-1 presents the output and labor input for a firm producing zaflings. There are only two inputs—capital and labor—and capital is fixed. Complete the table by computing the marginal product of labor.

   a. As more of the variable input is added to a

PRODUCTION, COSTS, AND THE FIRM'S OUTPUT DECISIONS

TABLE 7-1

LABOR INPUT	TOTAL OUTPUT	MARGINAL PRODUCT OF LABOR (MP_L)
0	0	
1	3	
2	9	
3	14	
4	18	
5	21	
6	23	
7	24	
8	24	
9	23	

fixed amount of capital, total output (increases/decreases) _____ until _____ units of labor are used.

 b. Diminishing returns to labor set in between the _____ and _____ units of labor, and as more labor is used, the marginal product of labor (increases/decreases) _____.

 c. When total output is at a maximum, marginal product has a value of _____. If more labor is added to capital, total output (increases/decreases) _____ as marginal product becomes _____.

 d. Over low levels of output, (labor/capital) _____ is the factor used intensively, while at high levels of output, (capital/labor) _____ is the intensive factor.

 e. Plot the total output and marginal product curves. Label the vertical axis "output" and the horizontal axis "labor input." Be sure to plot marginal product between the integers on the labor input axis. Assume continuous data. Try to draw the curves as smoothly as possible.

2. Table 7-2 presents production techniques for producing 1000 widgets per week. Each technique uses some combination of only two inputs: labor and capital. Complete the table.

 a. The firm should choose technique _____ since the 1000 widgets can be produced at a cost of $_____, which is the lowest cost of the four alternatives.

 b. If the price of capital falls from $400 to $230 per unit, the firm should substitute _____ for _____ and select technique _____, which produces the output for a total cost of $_____.

 c. If after the price of capital falls to $230 per unit, labor accepts a cut in pay from $250 to $240 per unit, the firm will use technique _____ since the price of labor (has/has not) _____ fallen enough relative to the price of capital.

3. Table 7-3 presents the output, fixed, and variable cost data for a firm using only labor (variable) and capital (fixed) inputs. The fixed cost of production is $10.

 a. Compute each entry in the table by calculating the appropriate cost.

 b. As output increases, the total cost of production (increases/decreases) _____, but at a (constant/nonconstant) _____ rate.

 c. Average fixed cost starts out high and (falls/increases) _____ throughout every level of output. Average variable and average total costs at first (increase/decrease) _____ as output increases, but both reach a (maximum/minimum) _____ and then begin to (increase/decrease) _____.

 d. The difference between average total and average variable cost is _____, and this difference (increases/diminishes) _____ as output expands.

 e. Marginal cost at first (rises/falls) _____ because of (increasing/decreasing) _____ returns to the labor factor, but between an output of 5 and 6 units, marginal cost begins to (rise/fall)

TABLE 7-2
ALTERNATIVE PRODUCTION TECHNIQUES FOR 1000 WIDGETS

TECHNIQUE	CAPITAL	LABOR	PRICE PER UNIT OF CAPITAL, $	PRICE PER UNIT OF LABOR, $	TOTAL CAPITAL COST (TCC), $	TOTAL LABOR COST (TLC), $	TOTAL COST (TC), $
1	2	7	400	250			
2	4	5	400	250			
3	6	3	400	250			
4	8	1	400	250			

TABLE 7-3

OUTPUT	FIXED COSTS, $	SHORT-RUN VARIABLE COST (SVC), $	SHORT-RUN TOTAL COST (STC), $	SHORT-RUN AVERAGE TOTAL COST (SATC), $	SHORT-RUN AVERAGE FIXED COST (SAFC), $	SHORT-RUN AVERAGE VARIABLE COST (SAVC), $	SHORT-RUN MARGINAL COST (SMC), $
0	10	—					
1	10	24					
2	10	39					
3	10	52					
4	10	63					
5	10	72					
6	10	82					
7	10	94					
8	10	108					
9	10	124					
10	10	142					
11	10	162					

_____ as (increasing/diminishing) _____ returns to labor begin. Between an output of 8 and 9 units, marginal cost will intersect and exceed (SATC/SAVC) _____.

4. The average and marginal cost data of a firm in production are as shown in Table 7-4. On your graph paper, plot the short-run average total, average variable, average fixed, and marginal cost curves. Assume continuous data and smooth your curves if possible. Be sure to plot marginal cost between the integers on the output axis. Label your cost curves.

5. Presented in Figure 7-1 are the cost curves and marginal revenue curves for a hypothetical firm operating in the short run. On the vertical axis, the measurement is in dollars. By measuring the vertical axis in dollars, you can read both revenue and cost.

a. By equating marginal revenue and marginal cost, the firm produces output level Q and incurs an average total cost of production of _____ dollars per unit. For the firm to break even, it must receive a price of _____ dollars for each unit of output sold.

b. If the firm received a price lower than OS_1 but greater than OS_2, it (would/would not) _____ continue to operate. For any price between OS_1 and OS_2, the firm makes a (profit/loss) _____ on each unit sold.

c. The distance AB shows the (average variable/

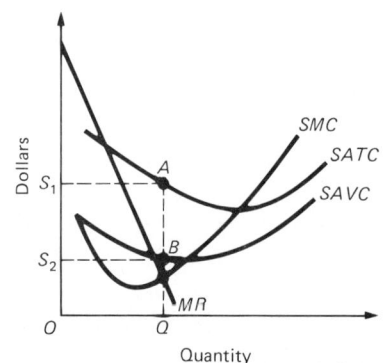

FIGURE 7-1

TABLE 7-4

OUTPUT	SHORT-RUN AVERAGE TOTAL COST	SHORT-RUN AVERAGE FIXED COST	SHORT-RUN AVERAGE VARIABLE COST	SHORT-RUN MARGINAL COST
0	—	—	—	
1	20	10	10	10
2	14	5	9	8
3	11.3	3.3	8	6
4	9.5	2.5	7	4
5	8.8	2	6.8	6
6	8.7	1.7	7	8
7	8.9	1.5	7.4	10
8	9.3	1.3	8	12
9	9.8	1.1	8.7	14

average fixed) _____ cost of producing OQ units of output.

   d. If the firm received a price below OS_2 dollars per unit, it (would/would not) _____ shut down. At a price below OS_2, none of the _____ costs and only some of the _____ costs are being covered.

   e. For any price above OS_1, the firm is making a (profit/loss) _____.

   f. The area of the rectangle OS_1AQ is nothing but _____.

6. Figure 7-2 shows four separate short-run average cost curves for a firm, with each curve representing a different scale of operation and plant size.

   a. Over the range of output OQ_3, if the firm expanded its plant size, it would experience (economies of/diseconomies of) _____ scale as the average cost of producing additional output (increased/decreased) _____.

   b. In the long run, the most efficient size of plant and output is shown by the curve _____ and _____ units of output.

   c. If the firm initially produced at output level OQ_1, the plant represented by _____ would be the most efficient; however, if the market demand for the firm's product increased to OQ_2, in the short run the firm would operate with the plant size _____ and incur a higher average cost of production. A long-run adjustment would be to expand to the plant, which is represented by _____.

   d. Beyond the scale of operation represented by $SATC_3$, any increase in the firm's scale results in _____.

   e. Draw the long-run average cost curve faced by this firm.

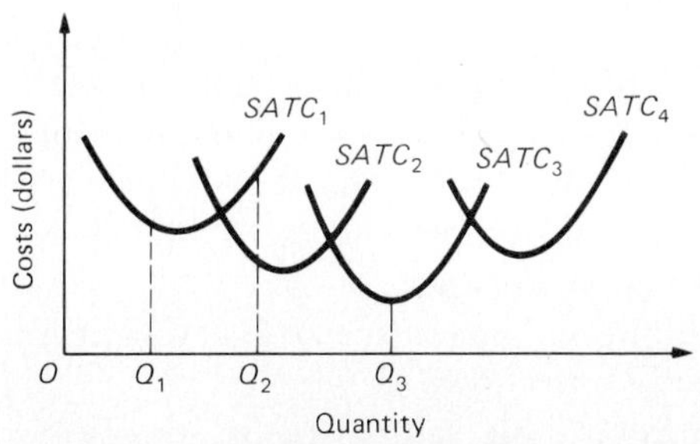

FIGURE 7-2

FILL-IN QUESTIONS

1. For any firm operating in the short run, its total cost of production will be made up of both _____ costs and _____ costs, while the same firm in the long run has only _____ costs.

2. An (input/output) _____ is anything that the firm uses to produce its product.

3. The law of _____ states that the marginal product of a factor will at some level of output begin to fall as more of the input is used.

4. The long-run average cost curve falls when there are (economies/diseconomies) _____ of scale and rises when there are (economies/diseconomies) _____ of scale.

5. Average variable cost can be calculated by dividing total variable cost by _____ or by subtracting _____ cost from _____ cost.

6. The (average total/average variable/marginal) _____ cost of production is the change in total variable cost which results from a 1-unit increase in output.

7. The total cost of production schedule can be calculated by determining the (maximum/minimum) _____ cost of producing various level of output.

8. The production function (does/does not) _____ provide directly the cost of producing various levels of output.

9. The choice of a production technique is determined by both the _____ function and the (input/output) _____ prices.

10. A firm will maximize its short-run profit or minimize losses by producing at the level of output where _____ equals _____ as long as the price of the product exceeds the _____ costs of producing the output. Otherwise, the firm (should/should not) _____ produce.

11. When average total cost is falling, marginal cost will be (above/below/equal to) _____ the average total cost curve; when average total cost is rising, marginal cost is (greater than/less than/equal to)

_____ average total cost; and when average total cost is at a minimum, marginal cost is (greater than/less than/equal to) _____ average total cost.

12. When the marginal cost curve is falling over some range of output, there are (increasing/diminishing) _____ returns to the variable factor, and when marginal cost rises, there are (increasing/diminishing) _____ returns to the variable input.

13. The (total/variable/fixed/sunk) _____ cost of a firm should not be considered a primary determinant in the firm's production decision.

14. The firm's adjustment in the long run involves primarily changing the _____ size.

15. In the long run, the firm produces the level of output where long-run _____ equals _____ as long as the product _____ exceeds _____ costs.

TRUE-FALSE QUESTIONS

1. _____ If the short-run marginal cost curve were horizontal throughout all levels of output, the firm would not experience diminishing returns to the variable factor.

2. _____ If a factor is used intensively, the firm uses substantially more of the factor relative to other inputs.

3. _____ A change in the price of one input relative to others will not generally affect the firm's technique of production.

4. _____ In the long run, the firm can adjust all of its inputs in response to changes in business conditions.

5. _____ Long-run fixed costs are present because some inputs are fixed even in the long run.

6. _____ The only essential information an individual needs to open and operate a business is the production function and the availability of inputs.

7. _____ The difference between marginal variable cost and marginal total cost is average variable cost.

8. _____ Studies have suggested that economies and diseconomies of scale are very prominent for firms in the manufacturing industry.

9. _____ If $MC = MR$ and $AVC < P < ATC$, the firm should continue producing even though it is incurring a loss.

10. _____ The long-run average cost curve is tangent to numerous short-run average cost curves at the minimum point of each.

11. _____ When a firm experiences diminishing returns to a factor, its total cost curve will at some point increase at an increasing rate.

12. _____ If the firm knows the prices of the inputs used in production, the production function can be used to calculate the total cost curve.

13. _____ Data indicate that in the service industries, economies of scale are not very important in reducing long-run costs.

14. _____ A primary explanation for the presence of diseconomies of scale is that as a firm continues to get bigger, management complexities reduce efficiency.

15. As a firm gets larger and experiences a falling average total cost of production, the total costs of production are also falling.

16. _____ The LAC curve faced by every firm has to be U-shaped because of the law of diminishing returns.

17. _____ In the long run, the firm produces the level of output where $LMC = MR$ as long as output price is not less than LAC.

18. _____ Fixed costs are applicable to either the long-run or short-run analysis of a firm's production behavior because some factors will always be fixed.

19. _____ If output price is less than $SATC$ but greater than $SAVC$, and the firm expects the demand for its product to increase in the future, it should stay in business.

MULTIPLE CHOICE QUESTIONS

Circle the correct answer.

1. If a firm increases its output from 90 to 91 units and its total costs increases from $362 to $381, the marginal cost of the extra output is
   a. $381   **d.** $15
   b. $19   **e.** cannot be determined
   c. $362

2. Which of the following statements is incorrect?
   a. diminishing returns occur when the firm's total output is increasing
   b. when diminishing returns occur, the firm's marginal product curve declines
   c. when diminishing returns begin, the firm's marginal cost curve turns upward
   d. when diminishing returns begin, the firm's marginal product is zero

3. All of the following can be used to explain the presence of economies of scale except
   a. specialization of labor
   b. an increasing managerial bureaucracy
   c. better use of capital equipment
   d. spreading out of the firm's costs over a greater amount of output

4. All of the following statements are correct except
   a. any point on the LAC curve is the minimum cost of producing that particular level of output
   b. the SATC curve associated with each plant size is below the LAC curve
   c. there is a plant size corresponding to every point on the LAC curve
   d. each SATC curve touches the LAC curve at some point

5. A typical production function will
   a. have all inputs fixed only in the short run
   b. have some fixed inputs only in the long run
   c. have at least one fixed input in the short run
   d. show only inefficient levels of output

6. Increasing marginal returns to a factor will cause
   a. marginal product to rise
   b. total product to increase at an increasing rate
   c. marginal cost to fall
   d. all of the above

7. When marginal cost is below average total cost
   a. average total cost will be rising
   b. average variable cost may be either rising or falling
   c. total cost will be falling
   d. average variable cost will be rising

8. Average fixed cost
   a. declines throughout all levels of output
   b. is total fixed cost divided by the level of output
   c. can approach but never equal zero
   d. is the difference between average total and average variable costs
   e. all of the above

9. The variable costs of production
   a. are a cost incurred simply because the firm is in business
   b. are not present in the long run
   c. change with the level of output produced
   d. are incurred even if the firm produces a zero level of output

10. Interest payments, property taxes, and depreciation are examples of
    a. variable costs
    b. fixed costs
    c. sunk costs
    d. all of the above
    e. none of the above

11. If the market price of a product exceeds the average total cost of production, the firm
    a. is making a profit on each unit of output sold
    b. is making a loss but should stay in business
    c. is breaking even
    d. is making a loss and should shut down

12. A firm should shut down in the short run if
    a. it cannot cover its variable costs
    b. it can cover its variable costs but not its total costs
    c. all of its variable and some of its fixed costs are being covered
    d. total costs are just covered

13. All of the following would be a long-run decision except
    a. building a new plant
    b. purchasing new capital equipment
    c. hiring 200 additional workers
    d. acquiring another company

14. The long-run marginal cost curve
    a. is unimportant when determining the firm's long-run pricing strategy
    b. equals long-run average cost when LAC is at a minimum
    c. is linear and slopes upward and to the right
    d. none of the above

15. Total cost of production equals
    a. TVC plus TFC
    b. TVC minus TFC
    c. AFC plus AVC
    d. AVC minus AFC

16. If a firm experiences constant returns to scale, the LAC curve is
    a. rising
    b. vertical
    c. falling
    d. horizontal

AT THIS POINT YOU SHOULD BE ABLE TO . . .

1. Define the concept of a production function and explain the meaning of efficient production.
2. Define factor intensity and explain how input prices influence the choice of a production technique.
3. Define the concept of the long run and explain long-run total costs in terms of the inputs of production.
4. Explain the relationship between long-run total costs, long-run average costs, and long-run marginal costs.
5. Explain how economies and diseconomies of scale affect the shape of the long-run average cost curve and list some sources of economies and diseconomies of scale.
6. Using graphs, show and explain the firm's long-run output decision.
7. Define the marginal product of a factor and explain the law of diminishing returns.

8. Define and give examples of total, variable, and fixed costs of production.

9. Define, compute, and graph short-run average total cost, short-run average fixed cost, short-run average variable costs, and short-run marginal costs.

10. Explain the relationship between returns to a factor of production and the firm's marginal cost curve.

11. State and explain the firm's short-run profit-maximizing (loss-minimizing) output decision.

12. Explain the difference between short-run and long-run costs of production and explain why every point on the long-run average cost curve corresponds to a particular size of plant.

QUESTIONS FOR THOUGHT

1. Business managers are always concerned about the short-run and long-run performance of their companies. Why do you think the distinction between the two time periods is so important for business?

2. Short-run total costs usually increase rather rapidly over low levels of output, increase more slowly as output continues to increase, and then increase rapidly again so that output gets larger and larger. Explain why this happens. Use the concept of the production function in your answer.

3. Suppose a firm's marginal cost curve is horizontal. What can be said about the firm's total cost curve? About its average total cost curve? Explain.

4. Suppose you had to explain the concept of long-run average cost and output to your friends. What would you say?

5. Explain how returns to scale influence the firm's long-run average cost curve.

6. There is a difference between returns to factors (a short-run concept) and returns to scale (a long-run concept). Can you explain the difference?

7. Why does marginal cost equal average variable cost and average total cost at their minimum points? Explain the curves for each cost.

8. Can you think of any economies and diseconomies of scale not presented in your text?

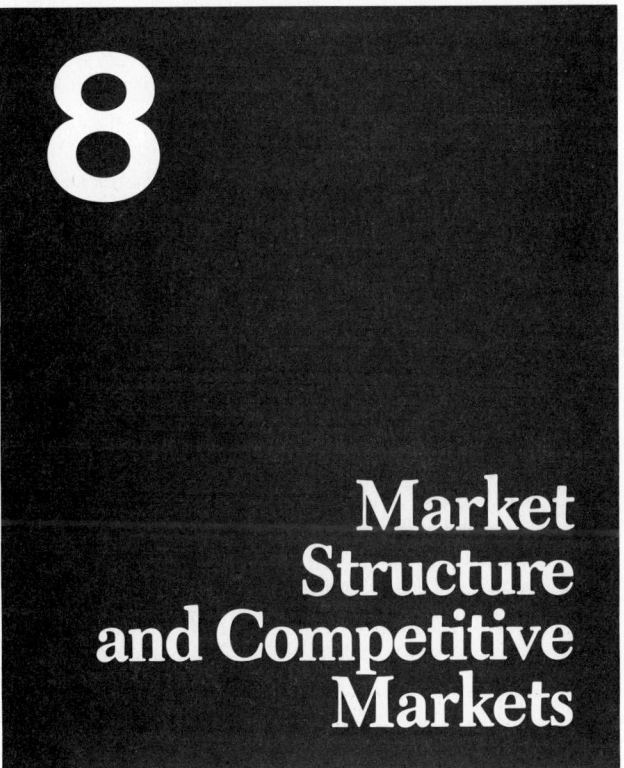

8

Market Structure and Competitive Markets

In Chapter 8 you begin the study of market structure. This is the first of three chapters which show the effects of different market structures on the price and output decision of both the firm and the industry. Each of the three chapters discusses different market structures from the standpoint of both short-run and long-run analysis. In the discussions, you will use the principles of demand and supply developed in earlier chapters. The analysis in Chapter 8 assumes that every firm is a profit maximizer and tries to establish the price and output level that generates the greatest amount of profit. The price charged for a product determines the firm's revenue and depends on the market demand faced by the firm. The level of output that can be produced is determined by the production function. The production function and input prices in turn determine the firm's costs. Different types of markets face different demand curves, and so different pricing, production, and profit possibilities exist. Chapter 8 presents a market structure in which the firm takes prices as given and can change its revenue only by changing output.

Chapter 8 begins with an introduction to the basic types of market studied by the economist. These are perfect competition, monopoly, monopolistic competition, and oligopoly. Monopoly, monopolistic competition, and oligopoly are imperfectly competitive since the market participants to some extent take into account the effect of their own actions on market price. Perfectly competitive firms, on the other hand, take the price determined by the interaction of all buyers and sellers in the marketplace as given and pay no attention to the behavior of individual economic units. Firms in a perfectly competitive environment must in the long run produce as efficiently as possible or they will not survive. In a competitive market, firms enter and leave the industry in response to long-run profit potential or loss minimization. This activity ensures that industry resources are allocated efficiently.

One of the distinguishing characteristics of the competitive firm is the equality of MC, MR, and P. The firm can sell any level of output it wishes at the going market price, and so its marginal revenue schedule is constant and equal to market price. The firm tries to equate the marginal cost at a particular level of output with the marginal revenue (price) gained from the sale of an additional unit in order to maximize profit. The competitive firm's short-run supply curve is that segment of the marginal cost curve that is above minimum average variable cost; as long as price exceeds minimum average variable cost, the firm will supply some quantity of output. If market price is below average variable cost, the firm will shut down. In the long run, the firm's supply curve is the segment of the long-run marginal cost curve above minimum long-run average costs. The supply curve thus shows the cost of producing 1 extra unit of output. Although a firm can make excess profits in the short run, in the long run it cannot.

The competitive industry's supply curve is the horizontal sum of each individual firm's supply curve. In the long run, the industry's supply curve is flatter (more elastic) than that for the short run primarily because of plant size adjustment and unrestricted entry of other firms into the industry.

A competitive industry adjusts itself in response to changing market conditions. As market supply or demand changes, it is possible that existing firms in the industry will overshoot the long-run equilibrium price in response to the change. Such an overshooting sends a signal, in the form of windfall profits, to potential competitors to enter the industry. As the industry expands, the market price approaches its long-run equilibrium price.

Applications of the adjustment process in and the operation of competitive markets are presented in the latter sections of Chapter 8. Competition in world markets and the effect of changes in either the domestic or the foreign market for goods are linked in a world economy. If free trade exists, the law of one price states that the price of a given good approaches a world price. If transportation costs are removed, a world price is attained.

The last section of Chapter 8 is an application of the competitive market structure to agriculture. Quite often, some agricultural commodities are not at their free-market equilibrium price; this is due in part to government price support programs. Although such programs increase farmers' income, they cause an inefficient allocation of resources.

CHAPTER OUTLINE

1. The term "market structure" describes the behavior of buyers and sellers in a market. There are four basic types of market structure: (1) perfect competition—buyers and sellers believe their own behavior has no effect on market price; (2) monopoly—there is only one firm in the industry, and so it determines industry price; (3) monopolistic competition—many sellers produce close substitutes and exert limited control over product price; and (4) oligopoly—a few sellers in the industry are able to influence product price. The last three types of markets are classified as imperfect competition since some control over product price is present in each. The classification and delineation of markets under imperfect competition is difficult. Three criteria used in the identification of market types are the number of firms in the industry, whether the typical firm in the industry can influence price, and the ease of entry and exit of new firms into and out of the industry.
    a. Although market structure is usually defined according to the behavior of sellers, it can also be defined in terms of the behavior of buyers. Oligopsony and monopsony are terms used to identify markets with a few buyers or a single buyer.
    b. Market structure differs across industries because of the ability of existing firms to prevent the entry of new firms into the industry. The two primary barriers to entry are economies of scale and the political power of the existing firms.
    c. A free market exists when a market is competitive and there is no government intervention into the market. Although markets may be competitive, they may not be free of government intervention.
2. A firm maximizes profit or minimizes losses by producing that output at which $SMC = MR$, assuming that it produces at all. Perfectly competitive firms follow the same profit-maximizing criterion.
    a. Perfectly competitive firms believe that they can sell all that they produce at the going market price, and so each firm faces a horizontal demand curve. Each additional unit of output changes total revenue by an amount equal to the product's price. Marginal revenue for the perfectly competitive firm is product price, while for a firm in imperfect competition, marginal revenue and price are not equal.
    b. The perfectly competitive firm produces that output level at which price equals marginal cost ($P = SMC$). In the short run, as long as MC is not less than $SAVC$, the firm produces and has a positively sloped supply curve. If $P = SMC$ is greater than $SAVC$ but less than $SATC$, the firm produces even though it suffers a loss, since all of the variable and only some of the fixed costs are covered. If SMC is greater than $SATC$, the firm produces where $P = SMC$ and therefore earns a greater than normal profit. The short-run supply curve for the competitive firm is that part of the SMC curve which is above the $SAVC$ curve. Any price below the minimum $SAVC$ is a shutdown price since the firm will not produce any output.
    c. In the long run, the competitive firm's supply curve is that portion of the LMC curve which is above LAC. Unless long-run average costs are paid, the firm's output is zero. The shutdown price in the long run is less than the minimum LAC of production. For any price above the minimum LAC, the firm earns above-normal profits. The firm's long-run supply curve is that part of the LMC curve which is above the minimum LAC.
        (1) In the long run, the price at which the competitive firm just earns a normal profit occurs at the minimum LAC. This price is called the entry or exit price because if market price falls below minimum LAC, the firm leaves the industry. Prices above minimum LAC cause firms to enter the industry because above-normal profits are made.
    d. The long-run supply curve for a perfectly competitive firm is flatter (more elastic) than the short-run supply curve since the firm has time to adjust all factors of production in response to price changes. However, the competitive firm has a lower shutdown price in the short run than in the long run since it is willing to absorb some short-run losses.
3. The short-run supply curve for an industry is derived for a constant number of firms, each with some fixed factors of production. The long-run supply curve is based on the number of firms in the industry changing.
    a. The short-run supply curve for the industry is the horizontal sum of each individual firm's supply curve. Each firm enters the industry and is included in the industry supply curve when market price equals or exceeds its minimum $SAVC$.

- **b.** The industry long-run supply curve is flatter (more elastic) than its short-run supply curve. The reasons for the different slopes of the long-run and short-run supply curves are that each firm in the industry has time to adjust all input factors and that there is time for firms to enter or leave the industry in response to price changes.
    - **(1)** In a competitive industry, there is at least one firm whose entry or exit price is very close to the current market price. This is the marginal firm, and it is this firm which enters or leaves the industry when market price changes.
    - **(2)** Since each firm's supply curve is its MC curve when price and MC are not less than $SAVC$, a competitive industry's supply curve is the industry's MC curve. On the industry supply curve, $P = MC$ for each firm that produces.
- **c.** If all firms in an industry have identical production technology and face the same average and marginal cost curves, the long-run industry supply curve may very well be horizontal. When the supply curve is horizontal, only normal profits are being made and there are no incentives for firms to enter or leave the industry. If firms don't face identical production techniques or if input prices rise, the long-run supply curve may slope upward.
- **d.** Firms may earn above-normal profits or suffer losses in the short run; however, because of entry and exit of firms into the industry, no firm earns an above-normal profit in the long run as long as the cost conditions faced by all firms are the same. If the cost conditions are not the same in the long run, only the marginal firm does not earn above-normal profits.

4. An example of the long-run adjustment process is the adjustment of the coal industry in response to increased petroleum prices during 1973–1974. The initial increase in oil prices prompted the substitution of coal for oil, and the demand curve for coal shifted outward. Given the short-run fixed capacity of existing mining operations, both coal prices and output increased. As new mining operations entered the industry and capacity expanded, coal prices fell as output increased. A long-run equilibrium was reached with a price higher than the initial price but lower than the short-run adjustment price as well as an expanded output.

5. If price and quantity are plotted over time, the response of price to increases in demand is usually to overshoot its long-run value as quantity expands. This initial overshooting of price is essential to the long-run adjustment process.
    - **a.** The short-run overshooting of price often leads to windfall profits for producers. These profits signal potential competitors that it is profitable to enter the industry. The windfall profits are an important signaling device for the long-run adjustment of the industry.

6. In the competitive wool market, the introduction of synthetic fibers caused a fall in the demand for wool. Some producers left the market, and production capacity declined. The long-run equilibrium real price and quantity of wool fell. Since the late 1970s, wool prices have increased because of increased petroleum prices (a major input in synthetic fiber production) and adverse weather conditions in Australia.

7. Linkages exist between international markets, and so changing market conditions in one country affect market activity in other countries. If markets are competitive and no obstacles to trade exist, prices of a particular good will be the same worldwide. However, obstacles such as tariffs, quotas, and transportation costs do exist.
    - **a.** When free trade is permitted and price differentials for a particular good exist in different countries, producers in the country with the lower price export their products to the country with higher prices. As a result, prices in the lower-priced country rise as quantity supplied falls, and prices in the higher-priced country fall as the market becomes flooded with the imports. An international equilibrium price is established when producers become indifferent as to whether they sell at home or abroad and no buyer can get the commodity at a lower price in one country than another. In equilibrium, world quantity demanded equals world quantity supplied. The world equilibrium price settles between the international high and low prices.
    - **b.** Changes in the world price of a commodity affect the national economy by changing the quantity demanded and supplied domestically and by changing the amount of imports into the nation.
    - **c.** As a result of foreign trade, domestic prices change less when there are changes in supply or demand than would be the case if the United States were a closed economy. Foreign producers and consumers absorb some of the shock from shifting demand or supply curves through the process of trading and the international flow of goods from lower- to higher-priced nations.

8. Although agriculture is highly competitive, there are government programs which influence the price of agricultural commodities.

a. The prices of agricultural products in free markets fluctuate widely because the demand for and supply of (after planting) these products is inelastic. Demand is price-inelastic because consumers do not alter their eating habits in the short run, and so a change in supply can significantly change prices. With an inelastic supply, prices fluctuate because of changes in demand. Government intervenes to stabilize prices.
b. Government stabilization programs are designed to reduce price fluctuations by having the government act as a buyer or seller. The government is willing to buy or sell a supported commodity at a fixed price. With government acting as both buyer and seller, prices are stabilized for both producers and consumers when there are changes in market conditions.
c. In an attempt to stabilize prices for suppliers only, government may buy products from producers at a fixed price and sell to consumers at another price. When there are changes in demand for or supply of the product, the supported supply price is stable for the farmer, but the price paid by consumers changes.
d. Two methods used by government to stabilize agricultural prices are the commodity loan program and the direct purchase of agricultural goods by government.
   (1) Under the loan program, the government sets a support price and lends farmers money (using their crops as collateral) if the market price falls below the support price. If the market price is above the support price, farmers sell their crops on the market, repay the loan, and keep the difference. If the market price remains below the supported price, the farmer defaults on the loan, and the government gets the crops.
   (2) The government buys some commodities directly from farmers to keep prices at or above the supported price. The price government pays for the commodities is determined by the parity ratio. The parity ratio is designed to help maintain the purchasing power of farmers.

IMPORTANT TERMS AND THEIR MEANING

Match the following terms with the correct definition or phrase.

1. ____ A description of the action of buyers and sellers in a particular market

2. ____ One of the mechanisms by which long-run industry supply changes; this occurs when market price is less than minimum LAC and losses are being made by some firms

3. ____ States that if free trade exists between countries, the price of a particular good will be the same worldwide

4. ____ A firm just covering the average costs of production and on the borderline between continuing production and shutting down

5. ____ Market structure in which there are many sellers of a good with close substitutes, and each seller has limited control over product price

6. ____ Describes the observation that price changes are dampened in a country when market conditions change as long as there is international trade

7. ____ Describes a market structure in which there is only one buyer of a product

8. ____ A market environment characterized by perfect competition and an absence of government

9. ____ An attempt by government to prevent wide fluctuations in the price of agricultural commodities

10. ____ A short-run adjustment of market price in response to changes in supply or demand which results in a price higher than that necessary for a long-run equilibrium

11. ____ One of the mechanisms by which industry supply changes; this occurs when market price is greater than minimum average total cost and above-normal profits are being made by some firms

12. ____ A market structure in

a. Marginal firm
b. Monopsony
c. Overshooting
d. Market structure
e. Free markets
f. Parity ratio
g. Windfall profits
h. Shutdown Price
i. Monopoly
j. Entry (of new firms into the industry)
k. Oligopsony
l. Perfect competition

MARKET STRUCTURE AND COMPETITIVE MARKETS

which there is only one seller of a product

13. _____ An element in the long-run adjustment process in any industry which is caused by producers overshooting the long-run equilibrium price; this serves to signal new firms to enter the market

14. _____ An industry in which a few firms are dominant and each takes into account the effects of its actions on industry output and price

15. _____ The market price is less than $SAVC$ in the short run or LAC in the long run

16. _____ A market having only a few buyers of a product

17. _____ Markets in which either buyers or sellers take into account the effects of their own actions on market price

18. _____ Expresses the purchasing power of agricultural products in terms of the prices farmers pay for goods and services

19. _____ A market in which buyers and sellers assume that their actions have no effects on market price

m. Law of one price

n. Imperfect competition

o. Exit (of existing firms from the industry)

p. Oligopoly

q. Shock absorbers

r. Monopolistic competition

s. Price stabilization

EXERCISES

1. Table 8-1 presents the cost data for a firm in a perfectly competitive industry. The average data have been rounded to the nearest unit.

Table 8-2 presents a separate demand, revenue, and profit schedule for each of three prices. Complete the table by computing total revenue and profits in each schedule. To answer the questions, you will need to refer back to Table 8-1.

a. When the market price is $50, the firm will minimize its losses if it (operates/shuts down) _____ and produces _____ units of output. At a market price of $50, the firm's marginal revenue is $_____. Although $SMC = MR$ between the _____ and _____ units of output, $SAVC$ is (greater than/less than) _____ SMC. For the firm to produce any amount of output, market price must be above $_____.

b. When the market price is $90, the firm will produce _____ units of output and make a profit of $_____. The $SMC = MR$ criterion holds between the _____ and _____ unit of output.

c. When market price is $240, the $SMC = MR$ criterion holds between the _____ and _____ units of output, and the producer offers _____ units for sale. The producer realizes a profit of $_____ and (would/

TABLE 8-1

OUTPUT	TOTAL FIXED COSTS, $	SHORT-RUN VARIABLE COSTS, $	SHORT-RUN TOTAL COSTS, $	SHORT-RUN AVERAGE TOTAL COST, $	SHORT-RUN AVERAGE FIXED COSTS, $	SHORT-RUN AVERAGE VARIABLE COSTS, $	SHORT-RUN MARGINAL COSTS, $
0	100	—	100	—	—	—	
1	100	120	220	220	100	120	120
2	100	195	295	148	50	98	76
3	100	260	360	120	33	87	64
4	100	315	415	104	25	79	56
5	100	360	460	92	20	72	44
6	100	410	510	85	17	68	50
7	100	470	570	81	14	67	60
8	100	540	640	80	13	68	70
9	100	620	720	80	11	69	80
10	100	710	810	81	10	71	90
11	100	810	910	83	9	74	100
12	100	980	1080	90	8	82	170
13	100	1220	1320	102	7	94	240

TABLE 8-2

OUTPUT	WHEN MARKET PRICE IS $50 PER UNIT			WHEN MARKET PRICE IS $90 PER UNIT			WHEN MARKET PRICE IS $240 PER UNIT		
	TOTAL REVENUE (TR_1), $	TOTAL COST, $	PROFIT (Π_1), $	TOTAL REVENUE (TR_2), $	TOTAL COST, $	PROFIT (Π_2), $	TOTAL REVENUE (TR_3), $	TOTAL COST, $	PROFIT (Π_3), $
0	0	100	____	0	100	0	0	100	0
1	____	220	____	____	220	____	____	220	____
2	____	295	____	____	295	____	____	295	____
3	____	360	____	____	360	____	____	360	____
4	____	415	____	____	415	____	____	415	____
5	____	460	____	____	460	____	____	460	____
6	____	510	____	____	510	____	____	510	____
7	____	570	____	____	570	____	____	570	____
8	____	640	____	____	640	____	____	640	____
9	____	720	____	____	720	____	____	720	____
10	____	810	____	____	810	____	____	810	____
11	____	910	____	____	910	____	____	910	____
12	____	1080	____	____	1080	____	____	1080	____
13	____	1320	____	____	1320	____	____	1320	____

would not) _____ produce an additional unit since _____ cost would exceed _____ revenue.

2. Figure 8-1 is for a perfectly competitive firm in the short run.

   a. The shutdown price faced by this firm is _____ since for any lower price, _____ cost exceeds _____ cost and the firm produces zero units of output.

   b. If the market price is OS_3, the firm has a total revenue shown by rectangle _____, a total cost shown by rectangle _____, and a total profit shown by rectangle _____.

   c. If market price is between OS_1 and OS_2, the firm (will/will not) _____ produce since (none/some/all) _____ of the variable costs and (none/some/all) _____ of the fixed costs are covered. If the firm operates in the price range OS_1, OS_2, it makes a (profit/loss) _____.

   d. The supply curve for this firm is given by the segment of the marginal cost curve above point _____.

3. In Table 8-3 you are presented with the cost data for a firm in perfect competition.

   a. Complete Table 8-4 for this schedule.

   b. Plot the firm's supply curve on your graph paper.

   c. For any price below $_____, the firm produces zero units of output, and this is the firm's shutdown price.

   d. The firm will not produce only quantities 1, 2,

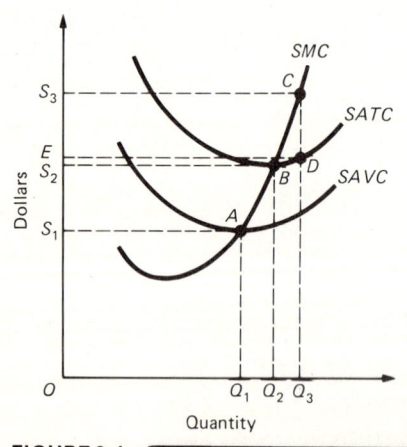

FIGURE 8-1

TABLE 8-3

QUANTITY	SATC	SAVC	MC
1	170	70	70
2	115	65	60
3	93	60	50
4	80	55	40
5	74	50	50
6	72	55	60
7	71.5	57	70
8	74	61	90
9	78	67	110
10	83	73	130
11	90	81	150

MARKET STRUCTURE AND COMPETITIVE MARKETS

TABLE 8-4

PRICE	QUANTITY SUPPLIED
$150	_____
130	_____
110	_____
90	_____
70	_____
60	_____
50	_____
40	_____

TABLE 8-6

PRICE PER BUSHEL	QUANTITY DEMANDED, bushels	QUANTITY SUPPLIED, bushels
$4.50	125	325
4.00	150	300
3.50	175	275
3.00	200	250
2.50	225	225
2.00	250	200
1.50	275	175
1.00	300	150
.50	325	125

3, or 4 because _____ cost is greater than _____ cost. If market price is $70, at outputs of both 1 and 7 units, the $MC = MR$ criterion holds; however, the firm will not produce an output of only 1 unit since MC is (rising/falling) _____ and the firm would incur a loss of $_____. If the firm produces 7 units where $MC = MR = \$70$, it incurs a loss of only $_____. The firm will have a positive profit when marginal revenue and marginal costs exceed _____ costs.

4. Table 8-1 of your text presents the general characteristics of each of the four types of market structure introduced in this chapter. Table 8-5 reproduces Table 8-1 except that some of the entries have been omitted. Your task is to complete the table without looking at the text.

5. Table 8-6 presents hypothetical demand and supply data for the soybean market.

   a. Plot the demand and supply curves. Identify the equilibrium price and quantity.

   b. The market equilibrium price for soybeans is $_____ per bushel. At this price, quantity demanded and quantity supplied equal _____ bushels.

   c. In equilibrium, farmers receive an income of $_____ from the production of soybeans.

   d. Suppose that a bumper crop of 300 bushels is harvested. Although farmers are willing to sell the 300 bushels at $_____ per bushel, consumers are willing to pay only $_____ per bushel. This means that farmers' incomes (rise/fall) _____ to $_____.

   e. On your graph, draw a line from the price which consumers are willing to pay for the 300 bushels to the demand curve.

   f. If a government price support program is in place which guarantees the farmers $4 per bushel for their beans, consumers will buy only _____ bushels at the supported price, and thus a surplus of _____ bushels remain. The government buys this surplus for a price of $_____ per bushel. Farmers receive an income of $_____, which represents an increase of $_____ over what they would have earned had they sold the soybeans on the free market.

   g. On your graph, identify the supported price and the market surplus by drawing a line from the price axis to the supply curve.

TABLE 8-5

| | MARKET STRUCTURE | | | |
| | | IMPERFECT COMPETITION | | |
CHARACTERISTIC	PERFECT COMPETITION	MONOPOLISTIC COMPETITION	OLIGOPOLY	MONOPOLY
Number of sellers	**a.** _____	Many	**e.** _____	One
Ability to affect price	None	**c.** _____	**f.** _____	**g.** _____
Limitations on entry	**b.** _____	**d.** _____	Some	**h.** _____
Example	Agriculture	Drugstores	automobiles, breakfast cereals	deBeers diamonds

TABLE 8-7

POUND PRICE, $	UNITED STATES QUANTITY DEMANDED, millions of pounds	QUANTITY SUPPLIED, millions of pounds
14	2	7
12	4	6
10	6	5
8	8	4
6	10	3
4	12	2
2	14	1

TABLE 8-8

POUND PRICE, U.S. dollars	AUSTRALIA QUANTITY DEMANDED, millions of pounds	QUANTITY SUPPLIED, millions of pounds
14	1	14
12	2	12
10	3	10
8	4	8
6	5	6
4	6	6
2	7	2

6. Tables 8-7 and 8-8 present the markets for raw wool in both the United States and Australia.

 a. Assuming that the United States and Australia are the world wool market and that no barriers to trade or transportation cost exist, an equilibrium will occur in the world wool market at a price of $_____ and a quantity of _____ million pounds of wool.

 b. In the world wool market (United States/Australia) _____ will export wool to the other country since at the world equilibrium price, it has a surplus of _____ million pounds while its trading partner has a shortage of _____ million pounds.

 c. If the United States levies a $4 import tariff per pound, exports will (increase/decrease) _____ and imports will (increase/decrease) _____ since the price of imported wool is relatively (more/less) _____ expensive than wool that is produced domestically.

 d. If U.S. producers, because of a remarkable improvement in production technology, suddenly are able to increase their output by 6 million pounds at each price (supply has shifted), the world market price for wool (increases/decreases) _____ to $_____ per pound and (imports into/exports from) _____ the country (increase/decrease) _____ to _____ million pounds.

FILL-IN QUESTIONS

1. For any firm in an industry which cannot affect the price of its product, the firm is said to be _____, and each firm has a (large/small) _____ part of the market.

2. In the long run, if there are no barriers to entry in an industry, above-normal profits will signal firms to (enter/leave) _____, and this (promotes/removes) _____ the excess profit so that long-run equilibrium price equals _____ at its minimum.

3. In the short run, a competitive firm produces that output at which _____ costs equals _____ which also equals market _____ as long as it exceeds _____.

4. The supply curve for a perfectly competitive industry is the horizontal _____ of each individual firm's _____ curve.

5. In the long run, an industry's supply curve (is/is not) _____ more elastic than its short-run supply curve since there (has/has not) _____ been time for market adjustments to be made.

6. As a result of changes in the price of petroleum in 1973, the supply of coal (increased/decreased) _____ as (more/fewer) _____ mining operations started up.

7. If identical firms in a competitive industry are equally efficient and face constant costs, the industry's long-run supply curve is (upward-sloping/horizontal) _____ and any change in demand results in a change in _____ but not market _____.

8. Windfall profits (do/do not) _____ serve a purpose in the long-run adjustment process of an industry.

9. _____, _____, and _____

are three obstacles to international trade and serve to promote price (equality/differentials) _____ for a particular good in the world market.

10. In the international economy, if no obstacles to trade are present, imports of a good flow into nations with a (high/low) _____ price, causing the price in some countries to (rise/fall) _____ and in others to (rise/fall) _____ until the international quantity _____ equals the quantity _____.

11. An objective of government agricultural programs is to (raise/stabilize/lower) _____ the prices of farm products, which can fluctuate widely as a result of the (elastic/inelastic) _____ nature of the demand for and supply of agricultural products.

12. In price support programs, government may serve as both a _____ and a _____ of agricultural products.

13. The _____ ratio attempts to maintain the _____ power of farm products and is used to determine the _____ paid by government for some commodities.

14. For a competitive firm in the short run, its supply curve is nothing but its _____ curve as long as prices are above the minimum _____.

15. It is unlikely that a competitive industry's long-run supply curve will be perfectly elastic (flat) because as more firms enter the industry, input prices may (increase/decrease) _____, which causes the cost of production to _____.

TRUE-FALSE QUESTIONS

1. _____ In the long run, a perfectly competitive firm will attain its equilibrium output level at the most efficient plant size.

2. _____ If the United States were a closed economy, any change in market conditions would result in lower price changes than would be the case if the nation actively engaged in foreign trade.

3. _____ The demand curve for agricultural products is inelastic because consumers readily and constantly change their eating habits in the short run.

4. _____ The government subsidy of milk production is an example of an agricultural loan program.

5. _____ If commodity A is produced in a country with a relatively low commodity price with respect to other countries, opening the countries to international trade will increase production at home and raise the domestic prices consumers pay for commodity A.

6. _____ Two major reasons why the law of one price is not working in international trade are import (export) restrictions and international transportation costs.

7. _____ The use of synthetic fibers, beginning in the early 1960s, resulted in an increase of 30 percent in U.S. production and consumption of wool products.

8. _____ For an industry in which all firms face identical costs, a reduction in market demand for the product will cause both long-run price and quantity to fall since some firms will leave the industry.

9. _____ If commodity A is produced in a competitive market and the price of B (a close substitute for A) increases, we would expect both the price and quantity produced of A to increase in the short run.

10. _____ The long-run supply curve for a competitive industry is obtained by adding vertically the supply curves of each firm in the industry.

11. _____ If the market price faced by a competitive firm is such that the firm can cover none of its fixed and only some of its variable costs, the firm should shut down and produce zero output.

12. _____ A competitive firm must determine both the quantity of output to be produced and the price at which to sell its output.

13. _____ The optimal level of output in a competitive firm is established at the point where $MC = MR < P$.

14. _____ A firm would never operate in the short run unless the price of its product was greater than short-run average total costs.

15. _____ The supply curve of a perfectly competitive firm is the section of the marginal cost curve lying above minimum average variable costs.

16. _____ The presence of competition does not ensure the existence of free markets.

MULTIPLE CHOICE QUESTIONS

Circle the correct answer.

1. Which of the following statements applies to an oligopolistic market?
   a. since there is only one seller in the market, the

firm does not need to be concerned about actions influencing the price charged by competitors

b. the presence of so many sellers and buyers in the market, with each selling and buying identical goods, prohibits sellers from influencing market price

c. the fact that only a few sellers are in the market suggests that each seller is aware of his rival's activities

d. the presence of many sellers of goods which are close substitutes permits only a limited control over market price

2. The typical firm in a perfectly competitive industry

a. regards the market price of its product as given

b. can exercise some, but not complete, control over the entry of new firms into the industry

c. can sell more of a product only if it lowers the product's price

d. sells a product which is unique compared with products sold by other firms in the industry

3. The equilibrium level of output of the competitive firm is established where
a. $MC = SAVC$ c. $MC = SATC$
b. $MC = P$ d. $MC = SAFC$

4. The long-run equilibrium for a perfectly competitive industry ensures that resources are most efficiently allocated, and this occurs when
a. $MR = LAC = MC$ c. $P = MR < MC$
b. $MR > LAC = MC$ d. $P > MC = LAC$

5. Suppose the widget industry consists of 3000 firms, each equally efficient and facing the same input prices, and that the industry's marginal cost of the tenth unit per month is $10, the marginal cost of the eleventh unit per month is $12, and the marginal cost of producing the twelfth unit per month is $16. If the short-run average variable costs for 10, 11, and 12 units are $15, $12, and $15, respectively, and the market price per unit is $9, the industry will supply
a. 30,000 units per month
b. 33,000 units per month
c. 36,000 units per month
d. zero units

6. In the international economy, if wine prices in the United States are very high relative to the rest of the world and there are no barriers to the international flow of goods, it is reasonable to expect

a. wine prices to continue to rise since domestic producers curtail production and foreign producers export more wine to the United States

b. wine prices to fall in the United States and rise in the rest of the world as more and more wine is imported into the United States at the expense of foreign consumption

c. wine prices to remain relatively stable because U.S. production will increase

d. wine prices to remain stable as U.S. producers try to export their surplus to foreign markets

7. All of the following agricultural commodities are eligible for federal loan programs except
a. cotton   c. cheese
b. sugar   d. tobacco

8. The long-run market supply curve for a perfectly competitive industry may be influenced by
a. the number of firms in the industry
b. the price of inputs
c. the state of the technological arts
d. the size of the plants of the firms in the industry
e. all of the above

9. In Figure 8-2, if the market price is P_1, this firm

a. produces output level Q_2 and experiences maximum profit shown by the rectangle $C_2 C_1 DE$

b. produces output level Q_1 and experiences maximum profit shown by the rectangle $C_1 P_1 GD$

c. produces output level Q_3 and makes a profit of $OP_3 AQ_3$

d. shuts down

10. The supply curve of this firm is shown by
a. that part of the marginal cost curve below point A
b. that part of the marginal cost curve above point A but below point B
c. that segment of the $SATC$ curve above (but not including) point D
d. that part of the MC curve above point A

11. The quantity supplied by the firm is zero below price
a. OP_2 c. OP_1
b. OP_3 d. cannot be determined

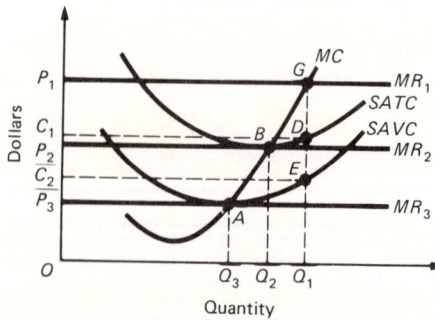

FIGURE 8-2

12. If the government taxes all of the short-run windfall profits in a competitive industry which result from an increase in market demand, it is reasonable to expect that

　a. new firms are reluctant to enter the market; hence, the long-run adjustment process is weakened

　b. after adjustment over the long run, equilibrium prices fall and quantity increases

　c. demand decreases because consumer disposable income is reduced by the tax

　d. new firms enter the industry and expand industry supply significantly

13. In practical terms, the law of one price suggests that

　a. the prices of a given good in different countries move in opposite directions

　b. the prices of different goods in different countries move in the same direction

　c. the prices of a given good in different countries move in the same direction

　d. the prices of different goods in the same country move in the same direction

14. All of the following are recognized as aims of agricultural price programs except

　a. dampening the fluctuations in agricultural commodity prices

　b. maintaining some purchasing power of agricultural households

　c. shifting the elastic demand curve for agricultural commodities

　d. appeasing some politically powerful special interest groups

15. Which of the following statements is incorrect?

　a. in the long run, a competitive firm will never produce if price is below minimum LAC

　b. in the short run, a competitive firm will never produce when price is between $SAVC$ and $SATC$ since it makes a loss

　c. in the short run, a competitive firm will never produce if price is below $SAVC$ since it incurs a loss

　d. in the short run, a competitive firm will produce if price is above $SATC$

AT THIS POINT YOU SHOULD BE ABLE TO . . .

1. State the characteristics of perfectly competitive, monopolistic, oligopolistic, and monopolistic competitive markets and give an example of each type of market.

2. Define the concept of a free market.

3. Explain why $P = MR = MC$ determines the competitive firm's profit-maximizing (loss-minimizing) level of output and state when the firm shuts down rather than produce.

4. Explain the derivation and construction of both the long-run supply curve and the short-run supply curve of the firm and state the role of average variable costs in determining supply.

5. State two input decisions of the competitive firm and state the basic condition of both short-run and long-run production.

6. Explain why the competitive firm adjusts quantity and not price.

7. Explain the derivation and construction of the competitive industry's short-run and long-run supply curves and explain why, in terms of market adjustment, the long-run supply curve for a competitive industry is flatter (more elastic) than its short-run supply curve.

8. Explain how price overshooting and windfall profits in the short run can be an important adjustment factor in the long run.

9. For an industry with a horizontal LAC curve, derive the long-run supply curve and state its meaning.

10. Explain the meaning of equilibrium and the adjustment process in international markets in terms of the law of one price and show, using diagrams, how a change in the foreign markets for a good can affect the domestic market for the good.

11. Using diagrams, explain how an agricultural price stabilization program works.

12. List and explain two agricultural price support programs undertaken by the U.S. government.

QUESTIONS FOR THOUGHT

1. The competitive firm reaches an optimal output level where $MC = MR = P$. Explain this "rule" in words and explain why the firm attains an optimal point when the rule holds.

2. Why will a competitive firm not incur a loss in the long run when it will in the short run? Is there any difference in the concept of shutting down in the short run as opposed to the long run?

3. Why is a competitive firm's short-run supply curve truncated at a lower price than its long-run supply curve? Does the same hold true for a competitive industry? Why or why not?

4. In a long-run competitive equilibrium, why are we assured that each firm operates with the most efficient size of plant? Can any conclusions be drawn about the efficient allocation of resources in the industry? Explain.

5. A competitive market facing a horizontal LAC curve faces constant long-run average costs of production. Does it seem reasonable that a market could face a downward-sloping *LAC* curve throughout the relevant range of production? Explain why or why not. What would such a curve mean?

6. Why should we not think of international trade as only a source of market disturbances in the United States?

7. Explain the reason for and approaches used in the government's agricultural price stabilization programs. What do you think would happen to the price of a gallon of milk and a pound of cheese if dairy price supports were removed? Explain.

9

Monopoly and Imperfect Competition

Chapter 9 is the second of three chapters in your study of market structure. It focuses on the purest form of imperfect competition—the monopoly. A monopoly exists when an industry consist of one firm; thus, the firm's demand curve is the industry's demand curve. To actually classify a firm as an absolute or pure monopoly is very difficult; however, in Chapter 9 you study how a market behaves when there is only one seller. There are some industries in the United States in which a few large firms essentially control the market, and so your understanding of monopolistic behavior is important when you begin to analyze the other types of market structures.

As you study Chapter 9, make sure that you can explain how the monopolist determines the level of output produced and the price charged for its product. Although the "decision rules" are the same for the monopolist and the perfect competitor, the outcomes are different. You also need to master the determination of the monopolist's profits, production efficiency, and costs. As you work through the material in Chapter 9, compare monopolistic behavior with that of the perfect competitor, because each represents an extreme type of market structure. You will also see that society's welfare is reduced when a competitive market is monopolized.

Chapter 9 begins with a review and expansion of the firm's demand curve, its total revenue, and its marginal revenue. Since the monopolist faces a downward-sloping demand curve, total revenue changes as price and quantity change. When total revenue changes, marginal revenue also changes. When the monopolist's demand curve is linear, marginal revenue decreases throughout the complete range of the demand curve and becomes negative when the absolute value of price elasticity of demand is less than 1.

A monopolist tries to minimize the costs of production and maximize profits. The profit-maximizing level of output is established at the point where $MR = MC$, as with the perfect competitor. Unlike the competitive industry, however, the monopolist may make monopoly or excess profits since $P > MC$. Because the monopolist faces no other firms in the industry, excess profits may be present in the long run. When the monopolist establishes the optimal level of output, the market demand curve sets the price at which this level of output can be sold. The degree of control which any firm exerts on the price of its product is one measure of the firm's monopoly power.

In equilibrium, a monopolist produces a lower output and charges a higher price for this output than does the competitive industry with similar cost curves. As a result, there exists a social cost of monopoly, since the lower output levels reduce society's overall welfare. As long as the market price of a commodity is greater than the marginal cost of producing an extra unit of that good, society can be made better off by producing more.

A monopolist discriminates if different groups are charged different prices for the same commodity. In order to practice price discrimination, the monopolist must be able to divide the total market into submarkets, with each submarket having a different price elasticity of demand. Even if the monopolist can effectively divide the market, the problem of resale of this good by those customers who initially paid a lower price than other customers must be solved.

The monopolist can exist only if other firms are kept out of the market. The presence of pronounced economies of scale and government permission to monopolize an industry are two reasons why there may be only one firm in an industry. If economies of scale are so pronounced, a natural monopoly exists, since the industry cannot survive with many firms. In such a circumstance, government regulates the monopoly and takes away some, if not all, of the excess profits. The goal of government regulation is a more socially optimal output level; however, problems arise when an agency attempts to establish market price or quantity.

CHAPTER OUTLINE

1. Although the monopolist is the only firm in an industry, its goal (like that of the perfect competitor) is profit maximization. The monopolist maximizes profit by choosing the level of output at which $MC = MR$; however, the firm must consider

the effect of its output level on market price. The monopolist is a price setter. Unlike a perfect competitor, the monopolist's marginal revenue is less than market price for every level of output.

  a. For a firm facing a downward-sloping linear demand curve, total revenue (price times quantity) changes along the curve. At high prices, total revenue initially increases. As prices are lowered, total revenue reaches a maximum (at the midpoint of the demand curve), but it decreases as prices are reduced further. Graphically, total revenue can be presented as a curve going up over some range of quantity, reaching a peak, and then descending as quantity continues to increase and price continues to decrease. Total revenue can also be shown as the area under a particular point on the demand curve. Marginal revenue MR is the change in total revenue generated by selling 1 more unit of a good. In imperfectly competitive markets, marginal revenue and price are not equal; marginal revenue is less than price for all levels of output. Marginal revenue is less than price because the firm must lower price in order to sell an additional unit of output. The price reduction applies not only to the additional unit sold but to all previous units sold at higher prices. Thus marginal revenue can be defined as the price at which the extra unit of output is sold minus the loss in revenues resulting from previous units now selling at a lower price. Graphically, the marginal revenue curve begins at the same point (on the vertical axis) as the demand curve and lies below the demand curve throughout. Marginal revenue equals zero and cuts the horizontal axis at the midpoint of the demand curve. This midpoint corresponds to the point of maximum total revenue. The marginal revenue curve falls twice as fast (is twice as steep) as the demand curve. As long as marginal revenue is positive (above the horizontal axis), total revenue is increasing. When marginal revenue is negative (below the horizontal axis), total revenue falls when an additional unit of output is sold.
  b. The monopolist (like the perfect competitor) tries to minimize the cost of producing at any level of output. As long as the monopolist and the competitive firm purchase resources in the same input market and face the same production technology, the marginal cost MC curve faced by the monopolist is the same as that faced by a firm in perfect competition.
  c. At the point where $MC = MR$, the monopolist must check to be sure that all costs are covered. The monopolist produces in the short run, where $SMC = MR$ as long as $P \geq SAVC$. In the long run, the monopolist produces where $LMC = MR$ as long as $P \geq LAC$. Otherwise, the monopolist shuts down. If $P > SATC$ or $P > LAC$, the firm makes monopoly profits above what is required to maintain resources in the industry. There is no way these profits can be lost through competition.
   (1) The monopolist is a price setter because once the optimal level of output is determined by equating MC and MR, there is only one price at which this output can be sold. The price is determined by finding the point on the firm's demand curve associated with the optimal output and charging the price at which the quantity can be sold.
   (2) One measure of the monopoly power (the degree of control over price) exercised by a firm is obtained from the difference between price and marginal cost. The greater the difference between price and marginal cost, the greater the degree of monopoly power.
   (3) When demand is price-elastic, marginal revenue is positive, and a reduction in price results in an increase in total revenue. When demand is unitary-elastic, marginal revenue is zero, and total revenue is at a maximum. When demand is price-inelastic, marginal revenue is negative, and a reduction in price causes total revenue to fall. The profit-maximizing monopolist always produces an output level at or above the midpoint on its demand curve.
   (4) In equilibrium, the monopolist's price is above its marginal costs since price is greater than marginal revenue.
2. Because the competitive firm believes that it can sell any amount of its product at the going market price, it is in equilibrium when $P = MC = MR$. The monopolist must lower price to sell additional units, and it reaches an equilibrium when $P > MC = MR$. The monopolist charges a higher price for its output and produces fewer units. Assuming that the demand and cost curves faced by both the perfectly competitive industry and the monopolist are equal, the competitive industry produces more output at a lower price than the monopolist. The monopolist is often charged with restricting output and charging higher prices than a competitive industry.
3. By using market price as a measure of the worth to consumers of an additional unit of a good (the

marginal social valuation of a commodity) and the marginal cost curves as a measure of the cost to society of producing 1 more unit of output (since resources must be taken from other industries to produce the extra output), it is possible to determine the cost to society of monopoly pricing as opposed to competitive pricing. In a competitive industry equilibrium, $P = MC$, and so the social worth (valuation) of the level of output equals the marginal cost to society of producing the output. The competitive industry equilibrium is socially optimal. Under monopoly, social well-being is increased when output is increased because society's valuation of an additional unit (P) exceeds the cost to society of producing an extra unit (MC). At the monopolist's equilibrium ($P > MC = MR$), the welfare cost of the monopoly is the cumulative excess of the marginal social valuation over the marginal cost to society from the monopolist's output to the competitive output. Even if the monopolist faced no production or operating costs, its output would still be restricted and its price would still be higher than that charged if consumers were allowed to consume up to the point at which they would be willing to pay nothing for an extra unit of the good.

4. The monopolist responds to an increase in demand by increasing both price and equilibrium output since marginal revenue is raised relative to marginal cost. In a competitive industry, an increase in demand results in both price and output increasing. In competition, if price changes, quantity supplied changes, while for the monopolist, changes in marginal revenue cause changes in the quantity supplied. If marginal costs increase, the monopolist increases price and decreases output.

5. If a monopolist can divide its market so that each submarket has a different price elasticity of demand (each faces a different demand curve), it can discriminate in the prices charged for the same commodity. Price discrimination is practiced in order to increase monopoly profits. Higher prices are charged in the submarket with the relatively inelastic demand, while the submarket with the relatively elastic demand is charged a lower price. The group with the lower elasticity of demand "subsidizes" the group with the more elastic demand by paying a higher price for the product. The price-discriminating monopolist must be able to keep the markets separate or the discriminatory practices will cease to be effective.

6. There are three major reasons which cause the existence of monopoly and explain its ability to keep potential competitors out of the industry. First, scale economies may be very pronounced so that one firm can produce the output more cheaply than many firms. If the average cost of production declines throughout (decreasing-cost industry), marginal cost is less than average cost. There can be no competitive equilibrium since one firm can produce more cheaply than many firms. Second, one firm may have control over some essential resource or technique needed in production. Patents provide a monopoly for a period of 17 years. A third reason for the existence of monopoly is that the firm is given or purchases the right to be a monopoly. In some states a liquor monopoly exists, while in most states utility companies function as monopolists.

7. A natural monopoly exists when economies of scale are so pronounced in an industry that it cannot sustain competitive firms. As long as $P > MC$, social welfare is increased by having the monopolist produce more and charge a lower price up to the point at which $P = MC$. The monopolist is unwilling to produce that output at which $P = MC$ since its profits are not maximized. Methods frequently employed to regulate the monopolist are providing subsidies (if the firm has increasing returns to scale), establishing price ceilings, and granting permission to just cover costs by setting price equal to average total cost. When $P = ATC$, the monopolist earns no excess profits. If regulators permit the monopolist to just cover the cost, the incentive for cost minimization disappears. A difficulty encountered when establishing a price ceiling is that regulators usually do not know the price at which the monopolist will not receive excess profits or incur a loss. An alternative to the monopoly problem is state-run monopolies.

8. Joseph Schumpeter argued that large firms are desirable since they are more innovative and adopt new production techniques more readily than competitive firms. Schumpeter argued that larger firms undertake more research and development, and evidence supports this up to a point. Firms that are monopolistic may not be very innovative if there is no threat of competition.

IMPORTANT TERMS AND THEIR MEANING

Match the following terms with the correct definition or phrase.

1. _____ The return earned by a firm above its average total costs of production and in excess of the return needed to keep resources in the industry

   a. Monopoly power

2. _____ Incurred by society as a result of the monopolist

   b. Joseph Schumpeter

producing a level of output at which $P > MC$; based on the observation that society values the consumption of an extra unit of the monopolist's output more than it costs to produce the extra unit

3. _____ The area under any point on a demand curve, calculated as price times quantity

4. _____ A measure of the extent to which a few firms dominate an industry

5. _____ An index of the degree of control exercised by a firm over its product price in the market

6. _____ An industry in which economies of scale are very pronounced and which cannot sustain competitive firms; public utilities are an example

7. _____ A firm which has the ability to separate its market into different submarkets, each with a different price elasticity of demand, and which charges each submarket a different price for the same commodity

8. _____ Argued that monopolies, or big firms, are desirable because they promote technological change

9. _____ Describes a market structure in which only a few firms dominate an industry

10. _____ Describes a firm having the ability to change its product price; the firm does not regard market price as fixed; the opposite of a price taker

11. _____ The change in total revenue resulting from a 1-unit change in sales

12. _____ The purest form of imperfect competition; an industry containing only one firm

13. _____ An industry with the AC curve falling throughout the relevant range of output and with MC below AC

14. _____ Firms having absolutely no control over the market price of their product

15. _____ A market structure in which many firms sell a slightly differentiated product with each having some limited control over market price

16. _____ An attempt to increase the output offered for sale and reduce the price charged by a monopolist through such policies as price ceilings, subsidies, and setting price equal to AC

17. _____ Describes market structures in which the firm's demand curve is downward-sloping so that it has some control over the market output and price

18. _____ The introduction of new techniques of production and the promotion of technological change

c. Decreasing-cost industry

d. Price setter

e. Imperfect competition

f. Social cost of monopoly

g. Marginal revenue

h. Natural monopoly

i. Monopoly profits

j. Oligopoly

k. Concentration ratios

l. Discriminating monopoly

m. Innovation

n. Price takers

o. Total revenue

p. Monopoly

q. Monopolistic competition

r. Regulation of monopoly

EXERCISES

1. Figure 9-1 shows the effects of the monopolization of a competitive industry. The competitive industry supply curve is the horizontal sum of each firm's marginal cost curve ($MC = S$), and the demand curve is D.

   a. From the diagram, the equilibrium price charged by the competitive firm is _____ and the equilibrium quantity is _____. At this

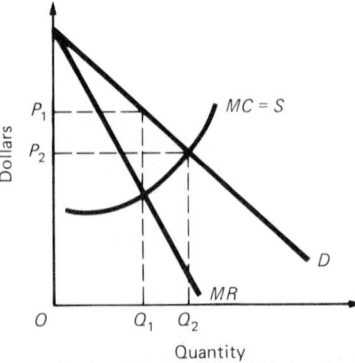

FIGURE 9-1

point, _____ demanded equals _____ supplied.

b. If the industry is monopolized and its costs do not change, there is now only _____ firm in the industry, and so the demand curve faced by the firm is (the same as/different from) _____ that faced by the industry.

c. The firm's marginal revenue is now (greater than/equal to/less than) _____ price at all levels of output since the demand curve is downward-sloping.

d. The monopolistic producer, like the competitor, equates _____ and _____ when establishing its equilibrium quantity.

e. The monopolist maximizes profits or minimizes losses by producing an output of _____ units and charging a price of _____.

f. The effect of the monopolization of this previously competitive industry is for output to (rise/fall) _____ and price to (increase/decrease) _____.

2. Figure 9-2 is for a monopoly producer.
a. Label the demand, marginal revenue, average total cost, and marginal cost curves.
b. Determine the price charged and quantity produced by the monopolist in order to maximize profits. Designate the equilibrium price as P_m and the equilibrium quantity as Q_m.
c. Determine the short-run average total cost of producing the equilibrium level of output and label this cost C.
d. Indicate on the graph the amount of monopoly profits made by the firm by shading the area representing the excess profits.

3. Table 9-1 presents the demand schedule for a monopolist.

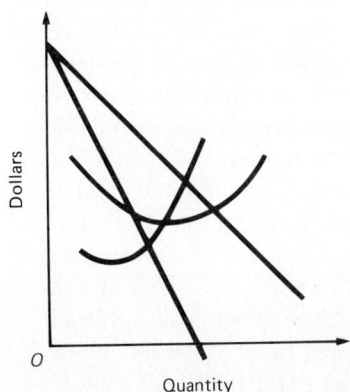

FIGURE 9-2

TABLE 9-1

PRICE, $	QUANTITY DEMANDED	TOTAL REVENUE (TR), $	MARGINAL REVENUE (MR), $
150	0	_____	_____
140	1	_____	_____
130	2	_____	_____
120	3	_____	_____
110	4	_____	_____
100	5	_____	_____
90	6	_____	_____
80	7	_____	_____
70	8	_____	_____
60	9	_____	_____
50	10	_____	_____
40	11	_____	_____
30	12	_____	_____
20	13	_____	_____
10	14	_____	_____

a. Complete Table 9-1 by calculating both total and marginal revenue for each price and quantity.

b. Plot the demand and marginal revenue curves on graph paper. Be sure to plot the marginal values at the midpoint between each quantity value. Label the vertical axis "$" and the horizontal axis "quantity."

c. For a price decrease from $120 to $110, the price elasticity of demand is _____, while for a price decrease from $30 to $20, the price elasticity of demand is _____.

d. Total revenue is maximized when price is between $_____ and $_____ and quantity demanded is between _____ and _____ units. When total revenue is at a maximum, marginal revenue is _____.

4. Table 9-2 presents revenue and cost data for a monopolist.
a. Complete Table 9-2 by calculating marginal revenue, short-run average total costs, marginal cost, and monopoly profits.
b. According to your calculations, the monopolist maximizes profits by selling _____ units of output and charging a price of $_____ per unit. Total profits are $_____.
c. $MC = MR$ between the _____ and _____ units of output when both have a value of $_____.
d. In order to verify your conclusions, plot the demand, marginal revenue, marginal cost, and average cost curves. Be sure to plot your marginal value at the midpoint on the quantity axis.

TABLE 9-2

PRICE, $	QUANTITY	TOTAL REVENUE, $	MARGINAL REVENUE (MR), $	TOTAL COST (TC), $	AVERAGE TOTAL COST (ATC), $	MARGINAL COST (MC), $	PROFIT (Π), $
150	0	—		50			
140	1	140		140			
130	2	260		200			
120	3	360		240			
110	4	440		270			
100	5	500		330			
90	6	540		420			
80	7	560		550			
70	8	560		720			
60	9	540		960			

e. If the quantities were infinitely divisible, the graph indicates that the monopolist would produce _____ units of output and charge a price of $_____ in order to maximize profits.

f. If consumers suddenly want to buy more of the monopolist's product at every price, the monopolist produces (more/less) _____ output and charges a (higher/lower) _____ price.

g. This producer is operating in the (elastic/inelastic) _____ range of the demand curve since MR is (greater than/less than) _____ zero.

5. Figure 9-3 shows a decreasing-cost monopoly.

a. The unregulated monopolist produces _____ units of output and charges a price of $_____ per unit. The monopolist generates a total revenue of $_____, incurs a total cost of $_____,

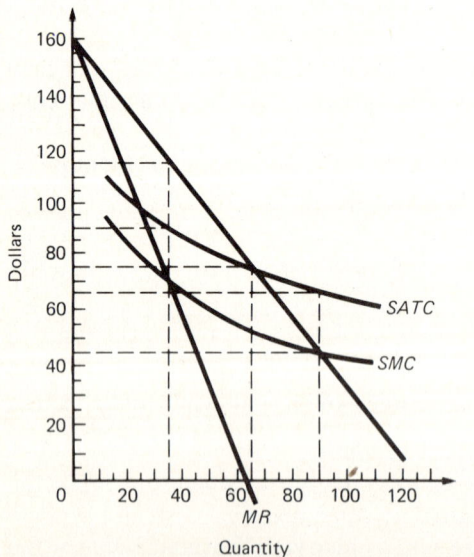

FIGURE 9-3

and thus makes a monopoly profit of $_____.

b. If a regulatory agency attempts to prohibit the monopolist from making excess profits and permits only a "fair" rate of return, the agency establishes a maximum price of $_____, and the monopolist produces _____ units of output. At this price and output, total revenue and total cost (are/are not) _____ equal and monopoly profits are $_____.

c. If the regulatory agency forces the monopolist to produce the socially optimum level of output, _____ units are produced and the regulated price is $_____. At this socially optimal level of output, however, total revenue is $_____ while total cost is $_____. The monopolist thus makes a (profit/loss) _____ of $_____. If the socially optimal output level is produced, government must pay a _____ of $_____ per unit to the monopolist.

6. Presented in Figure 9-4 is the model for a monopolist practicing price discrimination. The monopolist is able to segregate the market effectively, as shown by demand curves D_1 and D_2. Associated with each demand curve is a marginal revenue curve, MR_1 and MR_2. Each of the two demand curves reflects a different price elasticity of demand for the firm's product. The firm faces only one set of cost curves even though it sells in two separate markets. As a result, there is only one average total cost curve and marginal cost curve. The aggregate marginal revenue curve faced by the monopolist is simply the sum of the marginal revenue curves in each market ($MR_1 + MR_2$). The price-discriminating monopolist must allocate output in each submarket and establish the prices charged in each market so that it maximizes profits. The allocation of

MONOPOLY AND IMPERFECT COMPETITION

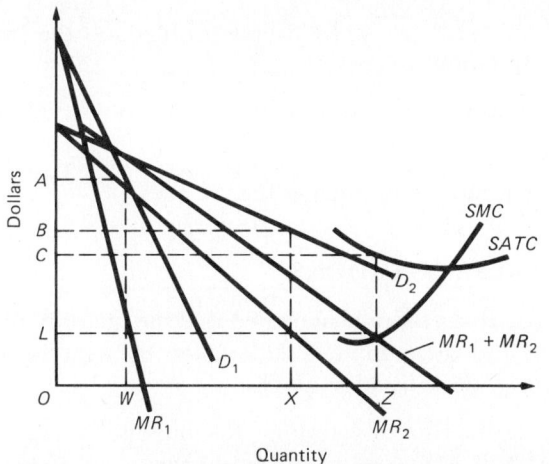

FIGURE 9-4

output in each market is determined by the rule $MC = MR_1 = MR_2 = MR$, or MC equals the MR in each market as well as aggregate MR. Once the quantities have been allocated, prices are read directly from each demand curve. On the basis of the above discussion and Figure 9-4, answer the following questions.

   a. The intersection of aggregate _____ revenue and _____ cost establishes a total output of _____ units produced by the monopolist.

   b. Total output is divided among the two markets, with the firm selling _____ units in market 1 and _____ units in market 2. The sum of the outputs sold in each market equals the distance _____ on the horizontal axis.

   c. Demand curve D_1 is (more/less) _____ elastic than demand curve D_2, and the firm should charge a (higher/lower) _____ price in market 1 than in market 2 since consumers are (more/less) _____ responsive to price in market 1.

   d. The price charged in market 1 when the firm allocates the optimal output for this market is $_____ per unit, while the price in market 2 is $_____. The price in market 2 (is/is not) _____ lower than that charged in market 1.

   e. The average total cost per unit of output is $_____.

7. List three reasons for the existence of monopolies.
   a. _____
   b. _____
   c. _____

FILL-IN QUESTIONS

1. In oligopolistic industries, there (is/is not) _____ control by individual firms over product price as well as (independence/interactions) _____ among the firms in regard to the pricing policies of other members in the industry.

2. According to 1977 data, the cigarette industry is (more/less) _____ concentrated than the petroleum-refining industry. The higher an industry's concentration ratio, the (more/fewer) _____ firms dominate the industry.

3. The industry structure in the United States (is/is not) _____ in general dominated by extreme concentration since sectors with a high degree of concentration (do/do not) _____ account for the majority of economic activity in the nation.

4. Because a monopolist must (raise/lower) _____ price in order to sell more output, price is (greater than/less than) _____ marginal revenue for all levels of output.

5. When total revenue is at a maximum, marginal revenue is (positive/zero/negative) _____, and this corresponds to a price elasticity of demand (greater than/equal to/less than) _____ 1. Such an elasticity corresponds to the _____ of the demand curve.

6. If the monopolist faces the same cost conditions as those faced by a competitive firm, the monopolist produces that level of output at which _____ equals _____. At this level of output, monopoly price is (greater than/equal to/less than) _____ marginal costs, and as long as price exceeds _____ costs, excess profits are made. The monopoly profits are excess profits since they (are/are not) _____ required by the industry in order to maintain the resources in the industry.

7. The monopolist can be described as a price (setter/taker) _____ since it (does/does not) _____ directly determine the price at which to sell its optimal output.

8. The _____ possessed by a firm is a measure or indication of the degree of control the firm exercises over its product price.

9. The monopolist's price is (greater than/equal to/less than) _____ the market price in a competitive industry, and the optimal output level is (greater/less) _____ than that produced in the competitive market.

10. Monopolies impose a social cost when the _____ of an extra unit by consumers, as indicated by product _____, exceeds the _____ cost of society of producing the extra unit. As long as _____ exceeds _____ cost, there is a loss of welfare to society. The socially optimal price and level of output is that attained by an industry in perfect _____.

11. Given demand, an increase in the costs faced by a monopolist causes prices to (increase/decrease) _____ and output to (increase/decrease) _____, while if costs are given, a decrease in demand causes price to (rise/fall) _____ and output to (rise/fall) _____.

12. In order for a monopolist to practice price discrimination effectively, it must be able to _____ its market into submarkets with each having a different _____ of demand. The submarket with the relatively more elastic demand is charged a (higher/lower) _____ price than the submarket with the relatively inelastic demand curve.

13. A(n) (decreasing/constant/increasing) _____-cost monopolist is characterized by a downward-sloping average total cost curve throughout the relevant range of output. As a result, the industry (can/cannot) _____ have a competitive equilibrium.

14. A _____ is issued by the government and permits the firm to have a monopoly over a specific product or technique of production for a given period of time.

15. When the economies of scale in an industry are pronounced, government may permit the industry to be a _____ monopoly.

16. If government regulates a monopoly by setting price equal to average cost, the firm (does/does not) _____ make excess profits, and the incentive to minimize cost _____.

17. According to Schumpeter, larger firms (do/do not) _____ engage in research and development more than smaller firms.

TRUE-FALSE QUESTIONS

1. _____ It is generally accepted that the majority of research and development undertaken by American industries is done by monopolies.

2. _____ In order to determine the monopolist's supply curve, it is necessary to obtain that part of the marginal cost curve above minimum average total costs.

3. _____ There is no reason to expect that a government agency responsible for regulating a monopoly will know the price which just permits the firm to cover its costs.

4. _____ One of the main reasons for the existence of monopolies is the presence of significant economies of scale so that output can be produced less expensively when there is only one firm in an industry.

5. _____ When a monopolist discriminates in price, a problem that must be solved is how to keep the markets separate.

6. _____ An example of price discrimination is charging senior citizens less for admission to a theater than is charged for individuals between 25 and 50 years old.

7. _____ Any time that marginal revenue increases while marginal costs do not change, the monopolist will decrease output.

8. _____ Monopoly generates a social cost because it costs society more to produce an extra unit of output than the value society places on the extra output.

9. _____ If a monopolist and a competitive industry faced identical demand and cost conditions, both would produce the same level of output and charge the same product price.

10. _____ A profit-maximizing monopolist establishes the optimal output level at which $MC = MR$, and this output is in the elastic range of the firm's demand curve.

11. _____ Although it is the usual case for monopoly that $P > MR$, under some circumstances, it is possible for $MR > P$.

12. _____ The profit-maximizing monopolist always attempts to maximize total revenue.

13. _____ Monopolists do not charge the highest prices that they could charge.

14. ____ For a monopolist facing a linear demand curve, total revenue can be increased by reducing price over every segment of the demand curve.

15. ____ If a monopolist purchases its inputs from a perfectly competitive input market, the appropriate market structure in which the producer operates is monopolistic competition.

16. ____ According to 1977 data, the industry with the highest four-firm concentration ratio is passenger cars.

MULTIPLE CHOICE

Circle the correct answer.

1. Which of the following could best be described as belonging to an oligopolistic industry?
   a. screw machine products
   b. telephone communications
   c. automobile production
   d. retail food outlets

2. If a monopolist faces a demand schedule given by the equation price = 30 − (2 × quantity), what is the firm's total revenue when quantity is 10 units?
   a. $100   c. $170
   b. $25   d. $200

3. For a monopolist with a linear demand curve, when total revenue is increasing,
   a. marginal revenue is positive and increasing
   b. marginal revenue is positive but decreasing
   c. marginal revenue equals zero
   d. marginal revenue is negative but approaching zero
   e. none of the above

4. The monopolistic firm maximizes profits when
   a. $P = MC = AC$ c. $P > MR = AC$
   b. $P > MR = MC$ d. $P > MC = AC$

5. If market price is above average total costs and marginal revenue is greater than marginal costs, an increase in sales of 1 unit by the monopolist
   a. has no effect on overall profits but narrows the difference between marginal revenue and marginal costs
   b. causes a reduction in profits by the amount it costs to produce the additional unit
   c. reduces total revenue received by the firm by the amount $P - AC$
   d. increases profits by the amount $MR - MC$ and narrows the difference between marginal revenue and marginal cost

6. If the monopolist's long-run average costs exceed market price, the firm should
   a. stay in business since it is making a normal return on its capital
   b. stay in business even though all of its fixed costs are not being covered
   c. go out of business and liquidate its assets
   d. shut down the business only temporarily

7. Monopoly or excess profits
   a. are not a cost since they do not represent an alternative cost for the resources used in production
   b. cannot be earned by a monopolist in the long run since price must equal LAC at the optimal output level
   c. are necessary to ensure that capital continues to be forthcoming into the industry
   d. can be earned by the competitive firm as well as the monopolistic firm in the long run

8. The unregulated, profit-maximizing monopolist
   a. will not produce an output beyond the midpoint of its demand curve
   b. will produce an output at which the price elasticity of demand is greater than 1 but diminishing
   c. will not produce when marginal revenue is negative
   d. produces at an output level at which $P > MC = MR$
   e. all of the above

9. Which of the following statements is correct?
   a. when compared with a competitive industry in long-run equilibrium, the monopolist produces output and uses resources more efficiently
   b. given identical demand and cost conditions, the monopolist's output and price are higher than those of a competitive industry in long-run equilibrium
   c. given identical demand and cost conditions, the competitive industry in long-run equilibrium produces a greater output at a lower price than the monopolist
   d. all of the above statements are incorrect

10. To say that a socially optimal price exists in a market means that
    a. individuals in society value the consumption of an additional unit of output more than it costs society to produce the extra unit
    b. there will be neither a surplus nor a shortage of a good on the market
    c. the value placed by society on the consumption of an extra unit of output equals the cost to society of producing the extra unit
    d. the market is functioning so that every consumer wanting an extra unit of the the commodity can obtain the marginal unit at the going market price

11. In equilibrium, the market structure assured of generating a social optimum is

a. monopoly
b. perfect competition
c. oligopoly
d. monopolistic competition

12. When there is an increase in market demand, the monopolist
    a. reacts to the increase in marginal revenue by increasing output
    b. reacts to the increase in price by increasing output
    c. reacts to the increase in marginal cost by decreasing output
    d. reacts to the decrease in price by decreasing output

13. All of the following are required for effective price discrimination except
    a. the ability to separate a market
    b. a large inelastic aggregate demand
    c. different price elasticities of demand for each submarket
    d. the ability to keep the markets separated and prevent the resale of the good by the customers facing the relatively elastic demand curve

14. For a monopolistic industry with increasing returns to scale
    a. firms will enter the industry in order to take advantage of the industry's monopoly profits
    b. the firm's marginal cost will be greater than average total costs
    c. the firm can approach a competitive equilibrium as more firms enter the industry
    d. there generally will not be more than one firm in the industry

15. If a regulatory agency placed a ceiling price on a monopolist so that only its costs of production could be covered and no economic profit could be made, price would be equal to
    a. marginal revenue
    b. marginal cost
    c. average total cost
    d. average variable costs

AT THIS POINT YOU SHOULD BE ABLE TO . . .

1. Define the term "concentration ratio" and state how the measure is used to indicate the presence of oligopolistic markets.
2. State the definition of "monopoly," give the characteristics of a monopolistic industry, give two examples of monopolistic industries, and state the monopolist's profit-maximizing rule.
3. Explain both verbally and graphically the relationship between the monopolist's demand, marginal, and total revenue curves, and the price elasticity of demand.
4. Explain why under conditions of imperfect competition, price and marginal revenue are not equal, and state three characteristics of the marginal revenue curve.
5. Define "monopoly power" and "monopoly profits," explain how firms possessing monopoly power in the market may earn monopoly profits, and distinguish between firms which are price setters and those which are price takers.
6. Explain and show graphically the difference between the equilibrium price and output of a monopolist and that of a perfectly competitive industry.
7. Explain both verbally and graphically the social costs of monopoly, state why a competitive equilibrium is socially optimal, and show the social cost of monopoly triangle.
8. Using diagrams, show the effects of a change in the costs of production or demand conditions on the monopolist's equilibrium price and output level.
9. Define price discrimination, describe the conditions which must be present for a monopolist to practice price discrimination, and state three examples of discriminatory practices.
10. List and explain three reasons for the existence of monopolies.
11. Define and state the major characteristics of a natural monopoly.
12. Explain the meaning of and justification for monopoly regulation, list two regulatory approaches which may be applied to monopolistic industries, and state a major difficulty encountered when monopoly regulation is undertaken.

QUESTIONS FOR THOUGHT

1. What does it mean when a firm is designated as a monopoly? Why should monopoly be thought of as only a matter of degree rather than an absolute? Explain.

2. When the monopolist equates marginal revenue and marginal cost, profits are maximized. This is the same criterion employed by the perfectly competitive firm, but clearly, output and prices differ between the two market structures. Explain why this difference occurs even if the marginal cost schedules are identical for both the monopolist and the competitive firm.

3. Explain why the terms "monopoly profits" and "excess profits" are used interchangeably. How can a firm have excess profits when it is assumed that a firm's goal is to maximize profit?

4. What does it mean to designate a firm as a price setter? Do you think that the firm really sets its market price? Explain.

MONOPOLY AND IMPERFECT COMPETITION

5. Why will the monopolist generally not operate in the inelastic range of its demand curve? Why should it not be a goal of the monopolist to produce that level of output associated at the precise midpoint of its demand curve even though at this point the firm's total revenue is at a maximum? Explain.

6. Explain the difference between the price and output level established by the competitive industry and that established by the monopolist. In your opinion, is the presence of monopoly in a market a bad thing? Explain your answer.

7. Suppose that an unregulated monopolist earns zero excess profits and receives only a normal return on its investment. Is such a situation socially optimal? Explain why or why not.

8. Suppose your employer (the president of a monopoly firm) assigns you the task of determining the profitability of beginning a policy of price discrimination in the firm's product market. What characteristics of the market must you look for? Explain.

9. Explain the objectives of monopoly regulation. Describe two approaches to regulating monopoly and give the shortcomings of each. Is it desirable to have government subsidize natural monopolies? Explain.

APPENDIX: CONSUMERS' SURPLUS AND PRODUCERS' SURPLUS

The appendix to Chapter 9 presents the concepts of consumers' and producers' surplus. These are important topics in welfare economics which economists examine in order to predict the effects of different market structures and pricing strategies on social welfare. Consumers' surplus arises because buyers are often willing to pay more for a product than they actually pay, and so a positive benefit accrues to society. Producers' surplus, on the other hand, is created when the producer is able to produce and sell a product at a market price above the marginal cost of production. It has already been established that a competitive equilibrium is socially optimal because (assuming that the good is not free and that the producer faces some positive costs of production) both consumers' and producers' surplus are maximized at this price and output level. A monopoly equilibrium is not optimal, and so there is a loss of both consumers' and producers' surplus. This appendix examines the competitive optimum and the monopoly equilibrium in terms of the surpluses.

CHAPTER OUTLINE

1. Consumers' surplus, a measure of the social costs of monopoly, is the difference between the price a consumer is willing to pay for a good and the price actually paid for the good.
   a. At each quantity of a commodity, the demand curve shows the price which consumers are willing to pay. It also shows what consumers are willing to pay for an additional unit of the good. If the market price paid for a particular quantity of a commodity is less than society is willing to pay, a surplus accrues to consumers. A measure of this surplus is the area under the demand curve above and up to the market price paid.
   b. A problem encountered when using consumers' surplus as a measure of a social cost is that everyone's valuation of a product is weighted equally when actually it may not be equal. At the individual level, a consumer's surplus poses no difficulty as a measure of individual gain.

2. A producer capable of producing and offering for sale an additional unit of a product at a market price above the marginal cost of production receives a producer's surplus. The producer's surplus is maximized at the point at which $P = MC$.

3. Because a competitive output is socially optimal, the monopolist's price and quantity reduce both the consumers' and producers' surplus, and so social welfare falls. Part of the consumers' surplus is transferred to the monopolist in the form of higher (excess) profits; however, part of both consumers' and producers' surplus is a deadweight loss—no one gets it. There is a misallocation of resources since society could be made better off by increasing production.

IMPORTANT TERMS AND THEIR MEANING

Match the following terms with the correct definition or phrase.

1. _____ That part of both consumers' and producers' surplus which is not transferred and does not accrue to society as a result of monopoly pricing and output.

a. Consumers' surplus

2. _____ A measure of a social cost of monopoly defined as the excess of the amount that individuals would be willing to pay for a good over the amount they actually pay

b. Producers' surplus

3. ____ That part of consumers' surplus received by the monopolist as a result of charging higher prices and producing a reduced output when compared with a competitive equilibrium

c. Deadweight loss

4. ____ The difference between the price received by a firm from selling an additional unit of output and the marginal cost of producing the extra output

d. Transfers

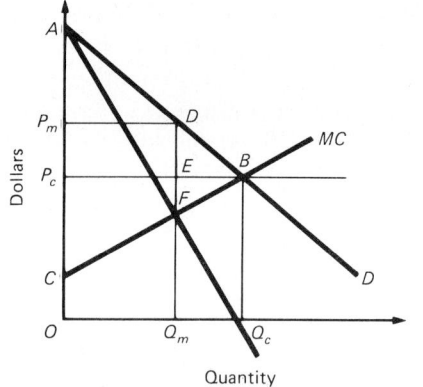

FIGURE 9-6

EXERCISES

1. Figure 9-5 presents both a "stepped" demand curve and a marginal cost curve with a market price of P.

a. Identify by labeling 1, 2, 3, etc., the consumer's surplus accruing to society for each unit above the market price P.

b. Identify by labeling a, b, c, etc., the producer's surplus accruing to the producer for each unit produced and offered for sale.

c. Calculate a numerical value for both consumers' and producers' surplus.

2. Figure 9-6 below illustrates the social costs of monopoly in terms of consumers' surplus and producers' surplus. The competitive price and quantity are P_c and Q_c, and the monopoly price and quantity are P_m and Q_m. Answer the questions based on Figure 9-6.

a. In a competitive equilibrium, the consumers' surplus is illustrated by triangle _____, and the producers' surplus is given by triangle ____. This output level (is/is not) _____ socially optimal.

b. At the monopoly price and quantity, triangle AP_mD measures the remaining _____, and this is (greater than/smaller than) _____ triangle AP_cB.

c. Triangle DEB is that part of _____ surplus lost to society, and triangle BEF is that part of _____ surplus lost. Triangle DBF thus represents the _____ loss.

d. Rectangle P_mP_cED is that part of the consumers' surplus/producers' surplus) _____ which is (lost/transferred) _____ to the firm in the form of _____ profits.

AT THIS POINT YOU SHOULD BE ABLE TO . . .

1. Define consumers' surplus, deadweight loss, producers' surplus, and transfer; state how consumers' surplus is a gain to society.
2. Show graphically that a competitive equilibrium yields a maximum consumers' and producers' surplus.
3. Explain how both consumers' surplus and producers' surplus can be shown graphically, and present a major difficulty with using consumers' surplus as a measure of social benefit.
4. State and explain the maximizing condition for producers' surplus.
5. Show graphically and explain the effect of monopoly pricing and output on society's well-being in terms of consumers' surplus and producers' surplus.
6. Explain how a deadweight loss is a net loss to society and how it reflects a misallocation of society's resources.

QUESTIONS FOR THOUGHT

1. Exactly what does it mean to say that monopoly behavior generates a deadweight loss to society? What would be the overall effect on society's welfare if the

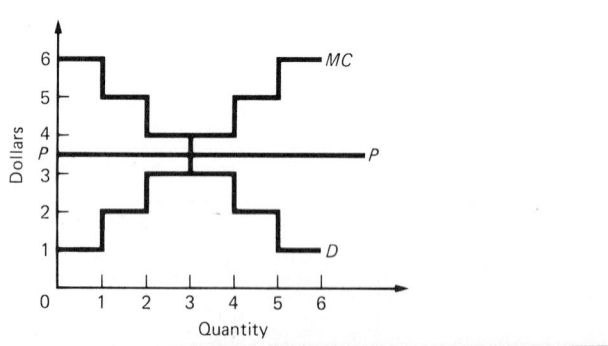

FIGURE 9-5

area of the deadweight loss was simply transferred to the monopolist? Explain.

2. What would be the effect on consumers' surplus if a price-discriminating monopolist was able to price each unit of its output separately at the price each individual consumer was willing to pay for the good? Explain. Can you show this graphically? Do the monopolist's demand and marginal revenue curves remain the same?

3. Explain any difficulty in comparing consumer's surplus with consumers' surplus.

10
Oligopoly and Monopolistic Competition

Chapter 10 examines oligopoly and monopolistic competition. These types of markets, which are common in our economy, fall between free, or competitive, markets and monopolies. If we view the market structures studied in Chapters 8 through 10 as a spectrum, the ends of the spectrum would be perfect competition and pure monopoly, with oligopoly and monopolistic competition inserted in between.

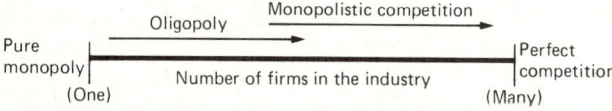

You should begin the study of oligopoly and monopolistic competition by mastering the definitions of each term. An industry is classified as oligopolistic when it consists of or is dominated by only a few sellers. The demand curve faced by an oligopolist is downward-sloping, and the oligopolist's pricing decision is influenced by the behavior of other firms in the industry. An industry is monopolistically competitive when it consists of many firms, each selling a differentiated product and having some control over product price. In monopolistic competition, new firms or products enter the market easily. The pricing and production decisions in both markets will generally lie between those of pure monopoly and perfect competition.

Oligopolies exist because there is an incentive for firms to collude, either explicitly or implicitly, in order to set prices above those which would be found in a perfectly competitive market. Often, the costs of technology and economies of scale favor large firms or an industry with a few large firms.

Most of Chapter 10 is devoted to coverage of oligopoly pricing behavior. The chapter begins with a discussion of the role of oligopoly profits and barriers to entry in creating this type of market structure. If oligopolists practice perfect collusion, they charge a monopoly price, produce the monopoly output, and divide the monopoly profits among all members in the industry. Such cooperation by the firms indicates that the industry is a cartel. Because there is no one model which fully describes oligopoly behavior, several models are presented. If the firms in the industry cooperate, the full collusion model and the price leadership model describe how industry price and quantity may be established. Each model has a different strategic assumption; however, the market price approximates that of the monopolist.

It is possible that some firms in the industry will fail to cooperate and instead cheat on the established price in order to raise individual profits. Such non-cooperative behavior is described by the Cournot, Bertrand, and kinked demand curve models. Each model involves different strategic assumptions about the industry participants, and so the price outcome of each is different. The final market price for non-cooperating firms may vary from the competitive price to nearly that of the monopolist, depending on the strategic assumptions of each model. The kinked demand curve model argues that prices are stable in oligopolies.

The seventh section of Chapter 10 introduces monopolistic competition. The monopolistically competitive industry is characterized by the presence of many firms, each with a downward-sloping demand curve. The market offers a large variety of goods, with each firm's product being similar to that of its competitors. Each firm tries to differentiate its product so that the demand curve faced by the firm can be regarded as its own. The individual firm tries to behave like a monopolist in its own market by attempting to maximize profits and producing that level of output at which $MC = MR$. The typical firm may earn short-run excess profits, but in the long run it only earns a normal return. This happens because the entry of new firms into the industry competes away the monopoly profits. In the long run, a tangency equilibrium exists for the monopolistically competitive firm at the point where $P = LAC$. The fact that the tangency equilibrium does not occur at the minimum LAC indicates that the monopolistically competitive firm is not producing as efficiently as possible.

The final two sections of Chapter 10 present the topics of product variety and advertising in monopolistically competitive markets. The question arises whether there are too many different products on the market.

The production of so many different goods involves the use of economic resources. Since the typical firm produces at a less than optimal scale, fewer products and fewer firms may improve the overall efficiency of the market. Advertising as a method of product differentiation and promotion raises questions about its social usefulness. Advertising may serve both to inform and to manipulate consumers.

CHAPTER OUTLINE

1. The presence of oligopolistic markets can be attributed to barriers to entry into the industry which keep out potential competitors and to the possibility of firms in the industry making oligopoly profits by selling a reduced output at increased prices. Excessive competition among the existing firms and the potential entry of new firms must be avoided if oligopoly profits are to be made.
   a. If the existing firms in an industry cooperate, they can behave like a monopolist. Together they make monopoly profits by equating industry MC and MR, producing a monopoly output level, and charging a monopoly price. The monopoly quantity the oligopolists produce is allocated among the different firms in the industry in such a manner that each firm has a share of the monopoly profits. A problem the oligopolist faces is the difficulty of getting all firms together so that price and quantity can be set without some member(s) cheating on the established price in an attempt to increase individual profits. Having fewer firms in an industry makes it easier to enforce price and output agreements among the individual firms.
   b. If new firms are attracted to the industry because of oligopoly profits, they can undercut the established price and damage the established market. This is why oligopolistic industries require effective barriers to the entry of new firms. Barriers to entry may be in the form of the ownership of essential resources, patents on products and techniques of production, economies of scale, or any combination of these. A potential entrant into an industry finds it very difficult to compete with the existing firms when these barriers are present.
      (1) The existence of economies of scale may create a situation in which the market can support only the very few firms which experience decreasing costs, and so large firms produce more efficiently than smaller ones which just start up. The most efficient scale of operation for a firm may represent a significant part of market output; thus the industry can support only a few firms. In such a situation, the industry is said to be a natural oligopoly. Natural oligopolies do exist in the United States.
2. Unlike perfect competition and monopoly, no single theory explains oligopoly pricing behavior because firms have both a common interest in setting prices so that monopoly profits are made and an individual interest in trying to get the maximum profit possible. These interests work in opposite directions, and so firms may collude by establishing a mutually agreed upon price and output. Collusion among firms pulls the market toward the monopolist's price and output; however, if firms cheat on the established agreements, a competitive solution is approached. Models of oligopoly pricing and output have been developed to reflect both the cooperative and noncooperative behavior of firms. Since explicit collusion is illegal in the United States, oligopolists rely primarily on implicit agreements to limit entry and maintain profits at an acceptable level.
   a. The collusive pricing model describes totally cooperating firms. Each firm knows that it is in its own best interest to establish and maintain a monopoly price and output level. Each firm recognizes that such a pricing strategy is also in the industry's best interest and is reluctant to cheat on the established price and quantity. The collusive pricing model may require no explicit agreement as firms cooperate to keep price at the monopoly level.
   b. The Bertrand model shows the industry outcome for noncooperating oligopolists. The model analyzes a duopoly and shows that if a firm believes its competitor will adhere to the established monopoly price, by reducing its price that firm can capture part of its competitor's market. The competitor (believing that the other firm will maintain its price) reacts by reducing its price below the initial price cut and increases its sales at the expense of the other firm. In the end, this price war terminates when a competitive price is reached. The Bertrand model does not provide a satisfactory explanation of long-run oligopoly pricing behavior.
3. Cooperative behavior among oligopolistic firms can be based on either implicit or explicit agreements. The goal of cooperative behavior is monopoly profits.
   a. A cartel exists (if legally permitted) when there is an explicit agreement on pricing and output policies among firms in an industry. OPEC is

the most famous cartel. If some firms begin to violate the established agreement by cutting prices, the cartel collapses.

    b. The dominant firm model describes a market consisting of one large firm providing a major fraction of total industry supply and a competitive fringe of smaller firms, each selling all it wants to at the going market price. The dominant firm establishes market price above the competitive level. Since the competitive fringe sells all it wants at the market price, the dominant firm regards the difference between market demand and the amount supplied by the competitive fringe (the excess demand in the market) as its demand curve. The dominant firm establishes price by equating the marginal revenue associated with its demand curve and its marginal cost. The competitive fringe regards this price as the market price. Saudi Arabia acts as the dominant firm in OPEC. Explicit cooperative behavior by firms to establish price and output was made illegal in the United States by the Sherman Act of 1890.

    c. It is possible for firms to bypass the legal barriers to explicit cooperation by entering into implicit agreements for pricing and output policies. The implicit agreement must be able to communicate the chosen price to members of the industry and provide a method for policing member firms to ensure that no individual firm cuts price below the established market price. Market price is usually determined by a price leader and then communicated to the other firms. If the other firms agree with the price, they follow the price leader; otherwise, the price leader rescinds the new price. The price leader may be the largest firm in the industry or just a barometric price leader.

    d. Cooperation among firms is easiest when it is legally permitted and when barriers to entry are strong. Licensing arrangements represent control over the entry of new firms into the industry. A small number of firms, stable cost and demand conditions, and product homogeneity promote cooperation among firms in an industry.

4. In the absence of cooperation, oligopolistic behavior becomes unpredictable because each firm tries to guess the actions of competing firms. If a challenging firm lowers prices and does not believe that other firms will react to its pricing policies (and they do react), the market price will be lower and the output higher than those of colluding oligopolists. Each firm must make certain assumptions about its demand curve and the reactions of its rivals to price changes.

    a. The Cournot model argues that the challenging firm believes its rivals will not change the quantity they sell and will continue to sell at the initially established market price. No firm considers the industry's common interest, and the outcome is a market price lower than, and an output level higher than, that established by a monopolist. In the Cournot model, each firm's optimal output level is determined at the point where its marginal revenue and marginal cost are equal. Given an initial price reduction by a challenging firm, the other firms in the industry react by reducing their output and raising price in an attempt to restore profits. In response, the challenging firm again reduces price, thus triggering another response by the established firms. Through a process of price and output adjustments, the challenging firm and the established firms charge the same price, and further price cutting does not occur.

    b. Noncooperating oligopolists need to know what assumptions and reaction strategies each firm makes about its rivals' pricing policies. The kinked oligopoly demand curve assumes that if one firm cuts its price, the other producers follow, and the firm's demand curve becomes inelastic. If the firm raises its price, the other producers do not follow the increase, and so the demand curve faced by the firm is highly elastic. The sharp difference in the elasticities of demand causes the firm's demand curve to be kinked at the prevailing market price. The kink causes the firm's marginal revenue curve to be discontinuous, and the marginal cost curve passes through the broken segment of this *MR* curve. The result of this model is that producers are reluctant to change price (prices are sticky) and the firm maximizes profit at the established price. Evidence supports the conclusion that oligopolists are reluctant to reduce prices but does not support the conclusion that oligopoly prices are more stable than those of the monopolist.

5. Oligopolists may practice limit pricing or predatory pricing in order to discourage potential entrants into the industry. Limit pricing occurs when the existing firms charge a price just low enough so that new firms do not find it profitable to enter the industry. The limit price is below the monopoly price. The goal of predatory pricing is to drive out new firms that enter the industry. When predatory pricing is practiced, the established firms may reduce their price to the point at which they incur losses in hopes of causing the new firm to fail. The success of predatory pricing practices depends on how long the established firms can withstand losses. The attempt to limit entry into the industry often serves to keep the oligopolists' price below the monopoly price.

6. Using the ratio of net profits to asset value as a measure of profits, evidence supports the theory that industries with high concentration ratios experience higher profits. Data also indicate that the presence of oligopolies in the retail grocery markets results in higher prices (for the same goods) than in more competitive markets.

7. Monopolistic competition describes a common type of market structure in which there are a variety of goods. The typical firm exhibits a few characteristics of monopoly and many of the characteristics of competition. The typical monopolistically competitive firm faces a downward-sloping though highly elastic demand curve, and so it has some control over its product price. Reductions in price increase quantity demanded primarily by capturing part of the competitor's market. Firms in the industry produce very similar products, with each good being a close substitute for the others. Because producers try to differentiate their products, each firm faces its own demand curve. In its own market, the monopolistically competitive firm determines price like a monopolist.

   a. In the short run, the monopolistically competitive firm sets price by equating marginal cost and marginal revenue. The firm may earn short-run excess profits.

   b. Although short-run excess profits may be earned, the entry of new firms, the introduction of new products, and changes in the price of substitute goods cause all firms to earn zero excess profits in the long run. In the long run, each firm's product price equals its average total costs, but it is greater than marginal costs. The long-run equilibrium for the monopolistically competitive firm is a tangency equilibrium since its demand curve is tangent to its average total cost curve. The monopolistically competitive firm does not produce at minimum average costs in either the long run or the short run. Since $P > MC$, each firm is willing to sell additional units of output, but it does not because MC would then exceed MR. It has been argued that the theory of monopolistic competition is unnecessary since it predicts the same outcomes as the competitive model.

8. As a compensation for underproduction and higher per unit costs, the monopolistically competitive industry offers substantial product variety. There are costs associated with product variety, and after a point, such variety may be wasteful. It is possible for the monopolistically competitive industry to produce a smaller variety of output and offer it for sale at a lower price.

9. Advertising is used to promote goods produced by oligopolies and monopolistic competitors. Expenditures on advertising are not costs of products in the same sense as payments for land, labor, and capital. Whether advertising is informative or manipulative is a judgment which results in unanswered questions about its social usefulness.

IMPORTANT TERMS AND THEIR MEANING

Match the following terms with the correct definition or phrase.

1. _____ A market structure containing many firms and a variety of goods, with each firm producing a product which is a close substitute of its competitors' products

2. _____ Firms which recognize the presence of a dominant producer in the industry and establish their price and output levels according to the price and output of this producer

3. _____ A model of noncooperative oligopoly behavior which has as the final outcome each firm producing at the competitive price

4. _____ A firm that can measure the pressure of demand in an industry, adjust price, and have other firms follow without explicit communication

5. _____ A demand curve which reflects a drastic change in the price elasticity and is used to support the argument of stable oligopoly prices

6. _____ Describes firms implicitly or explicitly agreeing on price and output in order to get maximum profits

7. _____ An industry with few sellers or dominated by a few sellers

8. _____ The production unit of a firm

9. _____ Market in which industry output is most

a. Oligopoly

b. Barriers to entry

c. Oligopoly profits

d. Natural oligopoly

e. Plant

f. Dominant firm

g. Competitive fringe

h. Firm

i. Bertrand model

efficiently and least expensively produced by only a few firms

10. ____ Differences in the products of various producers (either physical or perceived) designed to cause the buyer to prefer the output of one firm to that of another

j. Duopoly

11. ____ Describes the practice of existing firms in an industry establishing a price just low enough for it not to be profitable for new firms to enter the market

k. Price leader

12. ____ Designed to keep new firms out of an oligopolistic market; may take the form of ownership of resources, patents, and economies of scale

l. Sherman Act of 1980

13. ____ A firm which controls a significant percentage of an industry's supply and essentially determines the market price and output for its competitive fringe

m. Cartel

14. ____ Describes a monopolistically competitive firm's long-run equilibrium occurring where price equals average costs

n. Barometric price leader

15. ____ The practice of existing firms drastically cutting prices (and possibly suffering losses) in order to discourage or drive out new firms in an industry

o. Cournot model

16. ____ An industry consisting of only two firms

p. Limit pricing

17. ____ The excess of total revenue over total costs arising because a group of firms agree to behave as if they were a single monopolist

q. Monopolistic competition

18. ____ A model of noncooperative oligopoly behavior in which each firm in the industry assumes its competitors keep quantity unchanged, with the outcome being a market price and quantity between that of the monopoly and the perfectly competitive solution

r. Kinked oligopoly demand curve

19. ____ A business organization using resources and producing an output, which may consist of one or many plants

s. Product differentiation

20. ____ A law passed in the late nineteenth century which states that "every contract, combination . . . or conspiracy in restraint of trade or commerce . . . is hereby declared to be illegal."

t. Tangency equilibrium

21. ____ An explicit agreement among firms to establish prices and/or divide markets in order to make monopoly profits

u. Collude

22. ____ A firm which normally precedes all other firms in the industry in changing its price, with the remaining firms following

v. Predatory pricing

EXERCISES

1. For each of the producers listed below, indicate whether it can best be described as being competitive (C), monopolistic (M), monopolistically competitive (MC), or oligopolistic (O) by placing the appropriate letter in the space indicated.

    a. ____ wheat farmers

    b. ____ automobile manufacturers

    c. ____ retail food stores

    d. ____ the telephone system

    e. ____ drug stores

    f. ____ primary aluminum producers

    g. ____ tobacco growers

    h. ____ local utilities

    i. ____ ladies retail clothing stores

2. The data presented in Table 10-1 are price and quantity for an oligopolistic industry in which one large firm is dominant and several smaller firms make up a competitive fringe. Also presented are the marginal cost data for the dominant firm.

    a. Compute the dominant firm's demand, total, and marginal revenue schedules. Enter your computations in Table 10-1.

OLIGOPOLY AND MONOPOLISTIC COMPETITION

TABLE 10-1

PRICE, $	INDUSTRY DEMAND	COMPETITIVE FRINGE SUPPLY	DOMINANT FIRM DEMAND (DFD)	TOTAL REVENUE DOMINANT FIRM (TRDF)	MARGINAL REVENUE DOMINANT FIRM (MRDF)	MARGINAL COST (DOMINANT FIRM)
10	3	15	_____	_____		0
9	8	14	_____	_____	_____	0
8	13	13	_____	_____	_____	3
7	18	12	_____	_____	_____	5
6	23	11	_____	_____	_____	7
5	28	10	_____	_____	_____	10
4	33	9	_____	_____	_____	14
3	38	8	_____	_____	_____	20
2	43	7	_____	_____	_____	27
1	48	6	_____	_____	_____	

b. Based on your computations, the market price established in this industry is $_____ per unit, and the total market demand at this price is _____ units.

c. At the going market price, the amount supplied by the competitive fringe is _____ units and the quantity supplied by the dominant firm is _____. The total quantity supplied in the market is _____ units.

d. If the costs of production increase so that it now costs $4 more for each additional unit produced, the dominant firm (increases/decreases) _____ production to _____ units and the competitive fringe now produces _____ units in order to meet a total market demand of _____ units. The market price (increases/decreases) _____ to $_____ per unit.

3. Figure 10-1 presents the model for a typical firm in monopolistic competition.

a. Label the firm's demand, marginal revenue, average cost, and marginal cost curves.

b. In order to determine the price charged and quantities produced by this firm it is necessary to equate _____ and _____ cost.

c. Label the optimal quantity Q' and the market price P'.

d. This firm (does/does not) _____ produce at the most efficient level of output since the quantity produced (is/is not) _____ at the minimum _____ cost.

e. The firm (is/is not) _____ in a short-run equilibrium.

f. List two forces which will drive the firm toward its long-run equilibrium.

(1) _____

(2) _____

4. Figure 10-2 presents an oligopolist's demand, marginal revenue, average cost, and marginal cost curves. Use SMC_1 and $SATC_1$ as the initial cost curves. After studying Figure 10-2, answer the questions below.

a. This firm maximizes its initial profits by producing _____ units of output and charging $_____ per unit.

b. The producer earns a total revenue of $_____ and incurs a total cost of production of $_____. The profit earned is

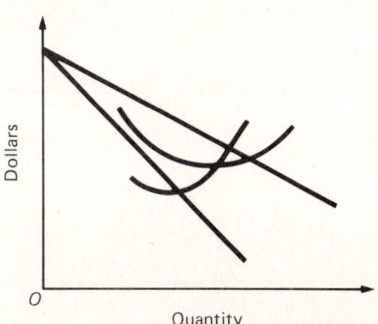

FIGURE 10-1

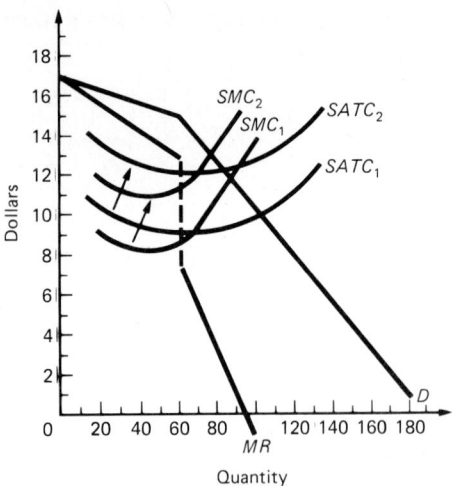

FIGURE 10-2

$_____.

   c. The marginal cost of producing the equilibrium level of output is approximately $_____.

   d. If there is an increase in the costs of production so that both the average and marginal cost curves shift upward as shown by $SATC_2$ and SMC_2, the output sold by the producer is _____ units and the price charged in the market is $_____.

   e. The fact that price (does/does not) _____ change after marginal cost increases from SMC_1 to SMC_2 illustrates the statement that oligopoly prices are (flexible/sticky) _____.

   f. After the increase in the cost of production, the firm's total profits are $_____.

   g. The oligopolist will continue to produce 60 units until SMC exceeds $_____ per unit. After that happens, the producer (increases/decreases) _____ output and (increases/decreases) _____ price.

5. In **a** through **c** below, list three conditions which promote collaboration among oligopolies. In **d** through **f**, list three conditions which promote the breakdown of cooperating oligopolies.

   a. _____
   b. _____
   c. _____
   d. _____
   e. _____
   f. _____

6. Figure 10-3 illustrates price leadership in an imperfectly competitive industry when the low-cost firm is the price leader. The diagram shows two firms (firm 1 and firm 2), with firm 2 being the lowest-cost producer. There is an overall market demand curve D, and it is assumed that each firm has exactly one-half of the market. With each firm having one-half of the market, each faces the demand curve D' and the marginal revenue curve MR' (the marginal revenue curve associated with D'). The fact that firm 2 is the low-cost producer is shown by $SATC_2$ and SMC_2 being below $SATC_1$ and SMC_1 for the same levels of output. Based on the above discussion and Figure 10-3, answer the following questions.

   a. Firm 2 will establish a price of _____ per unit and produce _____ units of output. Firm 2's equilibrium level of output is determined by the intersection of _____ cost 2 and _____ revenue. The total profit made by firm 2 is shown by the area of rectangle _____.

   b. Firm 1 would ideally like to charge a price of _____ and produce a quantity of _____ units in order to maximize its profits, as shown by rectangle _____. However, it must follow the price leader and charge a price of _____.

   c. At firm 2's established price, firm 1 would like to produce quantity Q_1; however, we assumed that the market was divided equally between the two producers. Thus, at the established market price, the output of firms 1 and 2 are (the same/different) _____. At the established market price, firm 1 produces _____ units of output and

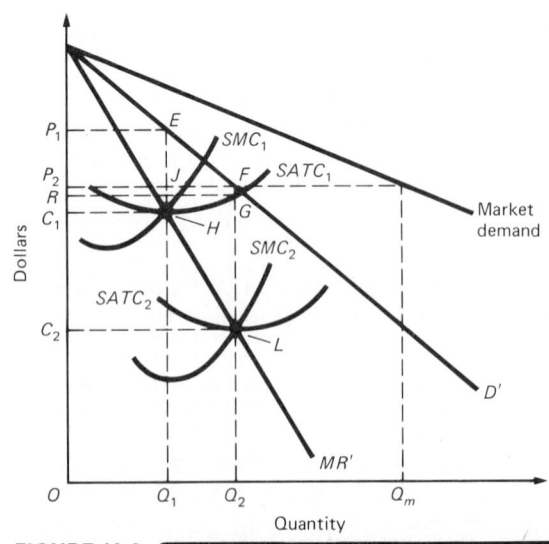

FIGURE 10-3

receives an excess profit shown by the area _____, which is (greater than/less than/equal to) _____ the profit earned by firm 2.

d. If firm 1 charged a price higher than that established by firm 2, it would (gain more/lose some or all) _____ of its share of the market.

e. At the established market price, the total quantity sold in the market is _____ units.

FILL-IN QUESTIONS

1. Two factors which tend to create and promote the existence of oligopolies are the presence of _____ into the industry and the possibility of making _____.

2. In a competitive industry, $MC = MR = P$; however, in monopolistically competitive or oligopolistic industries, $MC = MR$, and this is (greater than/equal to/less than) _____ the price established in the industry.

3. When cooperation among firms is legal, it is advantageous for the producers to establish a (cartel/plant) _____ in order to set prices, divide the market, and increase (the number of firms/costs/profits) _____.

4. In an oligopoly market, if all of the firms follow the pricing behavior of one of its members, the firm which sets the price is called the _____.

5. In a monopolistically competitive industry, entry is relatively (easy/difficult) _____, and there are a (large/small) _____ number of producers with each producing a (similar/unique) _____ product.

6. When an oligopolist practices limit pricing, the goal is to set prices (high/low) _____ enough so that other firms will be (encouraged to enter/discouraged from entering) _____ the market.

7. In the OPEC cartel, Saudia Arabia assumes the role of a _____ firm in the determination of market price and quantity.

8. The greater the number of firms in an oligopolistic industry, the (easier/more difficult) _____ it is to collude.

9. In a duopoly with each firm not cooperating with the other and assuming that the other keeps its price unchanged, the Bertrand model predicts that each firm produces the (monopoly/competitive) _____ level of output and charges the (competitive/monopoly) _____ price.

10. Stable (sticky) prices is the prediction of the (Cournot/kinked demand curve/dominant firm) _____ model of oligopoly behavior.

11. Under conditions of monopolistic competition, firms try to make their products (standardized/different/the same) _____, and this results in a large _____ of products on the market.

12. Although the relationship between industrial concentration and profits is not yet definitely established, recent evidence does indicate that oligopolies have (higher/about the same/lower) _____ profits than more competitive industries.

13. Firms which fully cooperate and practice collusive pricing will charge the same price as that established by the pure _____.

14. A tangency equilibrium for monopolistically competitive firms (does/does not) _____ yield the most efficient level of output.

15. When compared with a firm in perfect competition, a monopolistically competitive firm will have (greater/the same/less) _____ profits in the long run; it will produce (a greater/about the same/a lower) _____ level of output, and it will charge (a higher/about the same/a lower) _____ price.

TRUE-FALSE QUESTIONS

1. _____ Oligopolies always have higher profits than more competitive firms.

2. _____ In the kinked demand curve model of oligopoly behavior, for any increase in the cost of production, the model argues that after careful consideration, producers will more than likely raise their price.

3. _____ The avoidance of excessive competition among the existing firms is essential for the success of oligopolistic markets.

4. _____ At one time the Standard Oil Company, in an attempt to maintain its oligopoly profits, purchased many of its competitors.

5. ____ The Sherman Act permits firms to enter into explicit agreements with regard to price determination.

6. ____ A firm in monopolistic competition must always take into consideration the reaction of its competitors when setting its price.

7. ____ One of the most common forms of collusion among firms in the United States is to explicitly conspire to set prices.

8. ____ The Bertrand model predicts that each member of the industry will eventually produce at the competitive price level.

9. ____ The Cournot model, like the Bertrand model, is based on the assumption that each firm believes that all other firms will not change their price in response to an initial price reduction; however, unlike the Bertrand model, the Cournot solution has the final price between that of monopoly and that of competition.

10. ____ In the grocery market, data indicate that oligopolies do charge higher prices than competitive firms.

11. ____ In a monopolistically competitive industry, the cost of production could be reduced if the variety of goods on the market could be limited.

12. ____ The objective of predatory pricing is for the existing firms in an industry to cut their prices so severely that new firms will fail.

13. ____ If oligopolists produced a slightly differentiated product, they would never be in conflict over which price to charge and which quantity to produce.

14. ____ In a monopolistically competitive industry, the products of each firm are unique.

15. ____ A major reason explaining the failure of cartels is that some member firms begin to reduce their prices.

MULTIPLE CHOICE QUESTIONS

Circle the correct answer.

1. All of the following are characteristics of advertising expenditures except
 a. they serve to differentiate a product
 b. they account for 20 percent of GNP
 c. they can serve as a barrier to entry into an industry
 d. some are pure waste

2. Suppose a six-firm industry exists with a market price established at $P°$ ($P°$ is greater than the AC associated with production of the equilibrium level of output). A new firm enters the industry, and as a result, the original six producers cut their price to P' (P' is less than the AC of production.) This price-cutting behavior is an example of
 a. peak-load pricing
 b. limit pricing
 c. marginal cost pricing
 d. predatory pricing

3. In an attempt to attain joint profit maximization, firms may organize themselves into a
 a. monopolistically competitive market
 b. cartel
 c. homogeneous environment
 d. corporation

4. All of the following conditions are favorable to collusion among firms except
 a. only a few firms are in the market
 b. all firms produce a totally different product
 c. cost and demand conditions remain relatively stable
 d. entry into the industry is limited

5. The kinked demand curve shows that
 a. demand is elastic above and inelastic below the established price
 b. the market price is stable
 c. marginal revenue is discontinuous at the kink
 d. competitors do not respond to price increases but do respond to price decreases
 e. all of the above

6. The kinked demand curve, the Cournot model, and the Bertrand model are all examples of
 a. noncooperative oligopoly behavior
 b. collusive behavior
 c. a duopoly
 d. a cartel

7. The price leader in an oligopoly can be
 a. the dominant firm in the industry
 b. the firm recognized by competitors as the price leader
 c. the firm with the lowest cost of production
 d. a firm which can accurately predict the correct time and amount of a price change
 e. all of the above

8. If a cartel exercises complete control over price and quantity, it will behave like a(n)
 a. monopoly
 b. perfectly competitive firm
 c. industry
 d. price leader

9. A tangency equilibrium for a firm in monopolistic competition will ensure that
 a. MC equals minimum AC
 b. total cost exceeds total revenue
 c. P equals AC
 d. MC equals demand

10. It can be said that a natural oligopoly exists if
   a. the firms in the industry can be most cost-efficient when they produce a variety of products
   b. only a few firms in an industry can produce an output at the lowest cost
   c. industry output can be produced most cheaply by one firm
   d. there are not significant economies of scale present in the industry

11. The price established by an oligopolist which is just below that needed by a new firm potentially entering the market to recover its cost of production is known as the
   a. predatory price
   b. limit price
   c. monopoly price
   d. dominant firm price

12. The demand curve for a monopolistically competitive firm is
   a. perfectly elastic
   b. perfectly inelastic
   c. highly elastic
   d. highly inelastic
   e. kinked

13. OPEC is an example of a
   a. competitive firm
   b. monopolistically competitive firm
   c. noncooperating oligopoly
   d. cartel

14. For the kinked demand curve, if marginal cost increased significantly so that it no longer intersected MR in the discontinuous "gap," we would expect
   a. prices to be lowered and quantities increased
   b. marginal revenue to shift downward
   c. the demand curve to become less elastic
   d. prices to remain constant
   e. none of the above

AT THIS POINT YOU SHOULD BE ABLE TO . . .

1. Define oligopoly and monopolistic competition and state where each market structure stands with respect to pure monopoly and perfect competition.
2. List two factors which promote the creation and existence of oligopolies and explain the role of each.
3. Describe "cooperative" and "noncooperative" oligopoly behavior.
4. State the strategic assumptions and the resulting market price of the full collusive (cartel) and price leadership oligopoly pricing models.
5. State the strategic assumptions and price outcome of the dominant firm pricing model and show graphically how price is established in the dominant firm model.
6. List five conditions favorable to cooperative behavior among oligopolists, identify the major reason(s) why cooperation among firms may break down, and state the effect of such a breakdown on market price.
7. Show graphically the kinked demand curve model and use the model to explain oligopolists' reluctance to change prices.
8. Define limit pricing and predatory pricing in terms of a firm's entry into an industry.
9. Explain what the empirical data suggest about oligopolies and excess profits.
10. List four characteristics of monopolistic competition.
11. Explain the role of product differentiation in monopolistically competitive markets, show graphically how a firm in monopolistic competition determines its price and output, and show that it can make excess profits in the short run.
12. Explain the long-run adjustment process of monopolistic competition and show that although $P > MC$, the excess profits are zero.
13. Explain the meaning of a tangency equilibrium.
14. Describe the role of product variety and advertising in monopolistic competition and explain why some advertising is socially wasteful.

QUESTIONS FOR THOUGHT

1. "Oligopolies and big corporations gouge prices, rip off the public, and make tremendous profits." Do you agree with this statement? What does the empirical evidence suggest about oligopoly profits?

2. Occasionally, price wars break out in certain industries. The steel, aluminum, and gasoline distribution industries have all experienced periods of sharp price cuts. How can price wars be explained by the principles of oligopoly and monopolistic competition? Would you expect to see price wars in either a highly competitive industry or a monopoly? Explain.

3. In the long run, a monopolistically competitive firm produces a level of output at less than maximum efficiency and minimum cost per unit. How do you explain this equilibrium outcome? How does the long-run equilibrium of a monopolistically competitive firm compare with that of a perfect competitor? A pure monopolist?

4. The Bertrand model and the Cournot model describe noncooperative oligopoly behavior; however, each yields a different price outcome because of the assumptions made. Explain the assumptions for each model and explain how the established firms might react to a challenger.

5. What is the difference between limit pricing and predatory pricing practices? Are the objectives of both the same? Explain.

6. What are the characteristics of an oligopoly market? Is it possible for an oligopolist to behave like a pure monopolist? Explain.

7. Why can it be said that a monopolistically competitive firm sets price like a monopolist but earns only competitive profits in the long run?

8. The kinked demand curve model argues that oligopoly prices are stable and do not change very often. Do data support this argument? Why does the kink occur? Explain why the marginal revenue curve takes its particular shape.

9. Suppose that a monopolistically competitive industry suddenly organized itself into a cartel. What would be the effect on industry price, output, and profits? Since this cartel would consist of many firms, would you expect its life expectancy to be very long? Explain why or why not.

10. Why are product variety and product differentiation present in monopolistically competitive and oligopolistic industries? Explain why some economists argue that too much variety and advertising is socially wasteful.

11. Explain why it is in the firms' best interest to get together and fix prices.

Antitrust and Regulation of Natural Monopolies

Chapter 11 presents the problem of monopoly and monopoly power in our economic system. Monopoly imposes a cost on society. There is a loss of social welfare as price and output approach the level set by a monopolistic firm. This social welfare loss is attributed in part to a misallocation of resources by the monopolistic firm as it attempts to maximize excess profits. When any firm or industry exercises a significant degree of monopoly power, it has the ability to keep price above marginal costs and to widen the difference between them. As a firm exercises its monopoly power, economic inefficiency is promoted and competition is reduced. Certain industries, however, cannot sustain competing firms in the marketplace and still operate efficiently. Such firms experience decreasing costs of production throughout the relevant range of output and are called natural monopolies. If production efficiency is maximized by having only one firm in the industry, society benefits by having a natural monopoly. Public policies toward the monopoly problem take the form of antitrust legislation and the regulation of natural monopolies. Chapter 11 emphasizes these policies toward monopoly.

Chapter 11 begins with a review of the costs of monopolistic and oligopolistic market behavior presented in Chapters 9 and 10. The welfare cost triangle arises when part of consumers' surplus is lost because prices are above the competitive level. Part of the consumers' surplus is transferred to the monopolist in the form of excess profits. These excess profits represent a redistribution of income from consumers to the producer and are often called a privately collected tax. The welfare loss resulting from monopoly has not been estimated precisely.

The first serious attempts to control monopolies in the United States were the Sherman Act (1890) and the Clayton Act (1914). The Clayton Act was amended by the Robinson-Patman Act (1936) and the Celler-Kefauver Act (1954). These acts prohibit certain practices by firms and provide substantial penalties for violators. A firm can be charged with antitrust violations by either the government or the private sector. If found guilty of a violation, a firm may be assessed a fine, its officers may be imprisoned, and the firm may be forced to pay treble damages to any injured parties.

There is no definitive answer to the question of whether antitrust laws have worked; however, it is reasonable to conclude that the presence of the laws has reduced firms' attempts to monopolize.

If society's best interests are served with a single producer of a good or service, a method of regulating the natural monopoly is needed to ensure that the firm behaves properly. Public utilities are usually considered natural monopolies because of the significant production and transmission economies inherent in the industry. Regulatory commissions must consider the interests of both the firm and society. If the firm is allowed to charge a fair return price, the problem of underproduction is removed, and no monopoly profits are earned.

Chapter 11 concludes with an example of public utility rate determination and a discussion of problems encountered when attempts are made to regulate a natural monopoly. A major problem is the regulatory lag involved when setting prices during a period of rapid inflation.

As you read Chapter 11, don't confuse monopoly with bigness; they are not the same. Also, the term "monopoly" as used in this chapter does not mean pure monopoly; it means control of a significant portion of market supply by one or a few firms capable of influencing market price significantly.

CHAPTER OUTLINE

1. The most obvious cost of monopoly and oligopoly is a lower output and higher prices than for competitive industries. The social cost of monopoly (the deadweight loss presented in Chapter 9) created when $P > MC$ has been estimated as being between 1 and 7 percent of GNP. The traditional estimate is 1 percent of GNP. This low figure is caused by the observation that very few firms earn large profits over a period of time. One possible explanation for this is that the antitrust laws prevent

the use of monopoly power. Also, the usual estimate of social welfare costs ($P - MC$) may not include all of the costs associated with monopolies. These nonmeasured costs include the possible failure of monopolies to operate efficiently, the waste of resources as firms attempt to enhance their monopoly power, and the effect of monopoly power on the political process.

   a. Monopoly profits (the profits above a normal return to capital) are not a social cost of monopoly but represent a transfer of income from consumers to the producer. This redistribution of income is often called a privately collected tax. Whether monopoly profits are good or bad requires a value judgment.

2. As a result of the first major merger movement in the United States, many competitive industries were transformed into near-monopolies. The government responded by passing laws to restrict the monopolization of U.S. industry.

   a. The major antimonopoly and oligopoly laws in the United States are the Sherman Act of 1890, the Clayton Act of 1914, the Robinson-Patman Act of 1936, and the Celler-Kefauver Act of 1954. The FTC was formed in 1914.

      (1) Sections 1 and 2 of the Sherman Act prohibit monopolization and the restraint of trade. Under the act, monopoly itself is not illegal, but the establishment of new monopolies by using anticompetitive practices is a violation. Section 2 of the Clayton Act and its amendments in the Robinson-Patman Act prohibit price discrimination if its effect is to lessen competition or create a monopoly. If price discrimination arises from differences in the cost of production or distribution, consumers can be charged different prices. Section 7 of the Clayton Act and its amendments in the Celler-Kefauver Act prohibit the merger of firms if competition within an industry is lessened. Violators can be charged with criminal acts, fined, and imprisoned and can be forced to pay private claimants treble damages for any injuries suffered.

      (2) The Justice Department and the FTC have primary responsibility for the enforcement of the antitrust laws; however, private interests may also be represented by filing civil claims for damages resulting from a firm's monopolistic practices. Most antitrust actions are brought by the private sector. Violators of the Sherman Act can be fined and imprisoned.

      (3) In the 1960s, the Westinghouse Corporation and other electrical contractors were found guilty of price fixing. The firms paid large fines, and some executives received prison sentences. During the late 1970s, three grocery chains in Cleveland, Ohio, were found guilty of price fixing and other anticompetitive practices. The courts assessed fines and suspended prison sentences but required the violators to provide compensation in kind to 1 million customers over a 5-year period.

      (4) Anticompetitive practices and attempts to monopolize a market are difficult to establish under the Sherman Act because overt conspiracy is often absent. The definition of the firm's relevant market is difficult since many products can be substituted for each other, and this may involve a large number of firms.

      (5) When large firms want to merge, they are subject to review by the Justice Department. Government approval is needed before firms in highly concentrated industries are permitted to merge.

   b. In the absence of antitrust legislation, it is reasonable to expect that there would have been a reduction in the overall competitiveness of the U.S. economy and that firms would have more readily engaged in price fixing and collusive practices. The social cost of monopoly and monopolistic practices would probably be greater, and so the antitrust laws have in general benefited society. The governments of many countries, however, do not prohibit, and in fact promote, monopoly behavior. Although little was done initially to enforce the antitrust laws, both government and private interests have actively pursued antitrust litigation since World War II.

   c. Antitrust policies are not totally accepted by all groups in the United States. It is often argued that since merged firms usually are large, they produce more efficiently. Thus, if the cost saving which results from monopolization exceeds the social welfare loss incurred because an industry has fewer firms, antitrust laws work against the best interest of society. When domestic firms are highly concentrated in a particular market, the presence of foreign firms can make the market more competitive. Some also argue that vigorous competitive practices by big firms are not the same as monopolistic behavior and should not be subjected to antitrust litigation. The important

point is the effect on the consumer of firm size and concentration.
3. If an industry is a natural monopoly, the question arises whether the cost advantages resulting from the significant economies of scale experienced by the industry ultimately benefit the consumer.
   a. In a decreasing-cost natural monopoly, the competitive price and output level are not socially optimal because many firms cannot fully utilize the economies of scale. The objective of regulation in this case is twofold: permitting a natural monopoly to take advantage of the economies of scale and at the same time limiting the monopoly price and increasing output so that society's best interests are served. Public utilities are usually natural monopolies.
   b. If a regulatory commission promotes marginal cost pricing on the part of the natural monopolist so that a social optimum is approached, it must be prepared to allow the firm to undertake additional pricing methods to ensure efficient production and a normal rate of return. A two-part tariff (often used by public utilities) allows the firm to charge a fixed fee plus the marginal cost of units sold. Regulators may also simply fix a price close to the socially optimal price; however, underproduction may very well occur in this case. If a regulatory approach allows the firm to earn a long-run normal return, both excessive profits and excessive underproduction are avoided. Regulators must be aware that the firm may reduce efficiency and inflate its production costs since the incentive for cost minimization is removed.
   c. A fair rate of return is that price which just covers the firm's long-run average costs. One method of calculating the fair return is to use the ratio of total costs to output.
   d. If the return to capital in public utilities is permitted, through regulation, to fall below the opportunity cost of capital, the utility experiences a reduction in capacity and a decrease in service. If the return to capital exceeds the opportunity cost of capital, the utility's costs (and prices) are higher. Regulatory lag is a problem in public utility regulation. It can cause frequent adjustments in prices as well as reduce the profitability and level of investment in the utility.

IMPORTANT TERMS AND THEIR MEANING

Match the following terms with the correct definition or phrase.

1. ____ The absorption of one company by another; may also be in the form of a takeover or simply a combination of two companies

2. ____ The price charged by a firm which just equals the average cost of production and permits a normal return to capital

3. ____ Prohibited certain forms of price discrimination and restricted certain types of mergers

4. ____ The time period involved in setting new prices which can be charged by natural monopolies

5. ____ Charging different prices to different customers for commodities of the same grade and quality; may cause a reduction in market competitiveness

6. ____ Prohibits contracts, combinations, and conspiracies which lessen competition and prohibits the establishment of new monopolies

7. ____ A natural monopoly supplying an essential good or service, often encountering significant transmission economies, and subject to regulation by government

8. ____ The practice of existing firms dramatically cutting prices (and possibly suffering losses) in order to discourage or drive out new entrants into an industry

9. ____ The practice of setting market price at the point where the demand curve cuts the rising marginal cost curve; maximizes society's economic welfare

10. ____ An industry in which economies of scale are so pronounced that it cannot sustain competitive firms and still produce as efficiently

a. Sherman Act
b. Regulatory lag
c. Predatory pricing
d. Natural monopoly
e. Conscious parallelism
f. Merger
g. Two-part tariff
h. Clayton Act
i. Treble damages
j. Social costs of monopoly

11. ____ Compensation to an injured party in the amount of three times the damages actually suffered as a result of a firm's price fixing in the market

k. Fair return price

12. ____ Price leadership in an oligopolistic market even though there is no explicit conspiracy to reduce competition and increase profits

l. Price discrimination

13. ____ A pricing method often used by public utilities in which users pay a fixed sum for access to the service and then pay the marginal cost of production for the units of the service consumed

m. Marginal cost pricing

14. ____ Incurred by society as a result of the monopolist producing a level of output at which $P > MC$; based on the observation that society values the consumption of an extra unit of the monopolist's output more than it costs to produce this extra unit

n. Public utility

EXERCISES

1. The following is a brief summary of an antitrust case argued before the U.S. Supreme Court in 1967. As you read the next few paragraphs, think about the FTC's arguments and answer the questions that follow the brief.

United States Federal Trade Commission
v.
Proctor and Gamble Company

In 1957, the Procter and Gamble Company (P&G) acquired the assets of the Clorox Company. This acquisition marked P&G's first major entry into the liquid bleach market. Clorox at the time controlled approximately 48 percent of the national market for liquid bleach. Along with the three other leading bleach producers, the top four firms controlled nearly 80 percent of the national market. The liquid bleach industry is highly concentrated.

P&G is the major producer of soap and laundry detergents in the country. In 1957, the firm controlled approximately 55 percent of the packaged laundry detergent market. The three top producers of laundry detergents controlled over 80 percent of the market. P&G had one of the largest advertising budgets in the industry and received substantial discounts from all media services. In addition, the types of products (liquid bleach and laundry detergent) were so similar that cost savings could be obtained by P&G's production and distribution of Clorox.

The Federal Trade Commission (FTC) challenged the acquisition on the grounds that P&G had engaged in a product extension merger which would significantly lessen current and potential competition. The FTC argued that P&G was a potential entrant into the liquid bleach market, but with the acquisition of Clorox, P&G removed itself from the possibility of entry as a competitor in the market. Given P&G's size, production efficiencies, and marketing and advertising expenditures as well as the nature of the products, the FTC argued that potential entrants into the liquid bleach market would be discouraged from entering and that active competition would be lessened. It was possible that the two products could be integrated into a single marketing and distribution program, and so the remaining firms in the liquid bleach industry would be placed at a significant competitive disadvantage. The FTC also argued that P&G might possibly engage in predatory pricing and subsidize the loss from the sale of lower-priced Clorox with revenue from its other product lines.

The FTC ordered P&G to divest itself of the Clorox Company.

The Sixth United States Circuit Court of Appeals reversed the FTC's order and argued that no evidence had been presented which showed that the merger would lessen competition and result in a more monopolistic liquid bleach market.

The case was appealed to the U.S. Supreme Court, and in April 1967 the decision of the Court of Appeals was reversed. P&G was ordered to divest itself of Clorox, and the Supreme Court upheld the FTC's contentions that competition would indeed be lessened.

The Wall Street Journal for Thursday, June 24, 1982, had an article with the following headlines: "P&G Wants to Market Bleach; Clorox Prepares for Big Fight."

It has been more than 15 years since the courts ordered the divestiture of Clorox, and P&G is now entering the household bleach market with its own product. Clorox is preparing for the fight to defend its market share by introducing a new bleach product and increasing its marketing budget.

Based on the above case, answer the following questions in the spaces provided.

a. Under which of the antitrust acts studied in Chapter 11 of your text do you think the FTC charged P&G with violations? Explain why.

_____

_____

_____

_____

b. The acquisition of Clorox was called a product

ANTITRUST AND REGULATION OF NATURAL MONOPOLIES

extension merger by the FTC and the Supreme Court. What does the term "product extension merger" mean?

___

c. What type of products (substitutes or complements) were those of Clorox and P&G? How could this lessen competition in the liquid bleach market?

___

d. What role did potential or actual economies of scale play in the Supreme Court's decision? Where might some of the economies arise? How could the acquisition of Clorox by P&G raise the barriers to new entrants into the liquid bleach market?

___

e. The FTC argued that P&G could practice predatory pricing with its Clorox product. Why should the FTC and Supreme Court be worried about such pricing tactics? Explain.

___

f. Prior to the merger, could both industries (household bleach and soap and detergents) be classified as oligopolistic? Explain why.

___

2. Suppose that you are the chief economist for a state public utility regulatory commission and that it is time for the biennial review of the rates charged by the statewide electric company. Your job is to recommend a flat rate per kilowatt hour (KWH) to the commission. The recommended rate should permit the utility to earn only a normal profit (return) on its investment. Both your and the utility company's data indicate that within 9 months, the state's economy will be entering a period of high unemployment and reduced production. It is reasonable to expect that in the second year of the biennium, electricity demand will be falling while the prices of variable inputs and interest rates increase. The utility has overbuilt and currently is operating at less than full capacity. The estimated costs and output data for both years of the biennium are presented in Table 11-1.

a. In year 1, the utility will generate _____ billion KWH of electricity, and in year 2 it will generate _____ billion KWH.

b. Based on the above information data, what revenue must the utility receive in order to cover its costs? Year 1 $_____ billion; year 2 $_____ billion.

c. What rate per KWH will you recommend to the commission so that the utility can make a normal return? Year 1: _____ cents per KWH; year 2: _____ cents per KWH

FILL-IN QUESTIONS

1. To say that a monopolist opens up a difference between the marginal cost of output and the price of an additional unit of the good means that a social (loss/gain) _____ is created.

TABLE 11-1

COST AND OUTPUT DATA	YEAR 1	YEAR 2
1. Machinery and plant capacity	50 billion KWH	50 billion KWH
2. Current and projected utilization rate of plant and equipment	70%	63%
3. Variable costs of operation for 1 year	$1 billion	$1.2 billion
4. Value of asset base (capital and land)	$4 billion	$4.1 billion
5. Required rate of return to capital (opportunity costs of capital)	12.5%	14%

2. When monopoly profits are earned by a firm, the social costs of monopoly (are/are not) _____ removed since part of the consumers' surplus (is/is not) _____ captured by either consumers or producers.

3. The purpose of the antitrust laws is to regulate business activities which might reduce both _____ and social _____.

4. If a firm charges different prices to different purchasers of an identical commodity and as a result competition in the marketplace is reduced, the government may bring charges against the producer under section _____ of the _____ Act; however, if the firm can show that the different prices resulted from differences in the _____ of production and distribution and that competition was not reduced, the charges may be dropped.

5. Those who violate the antitrust laws may be charged with (criminal/civil/both civil and criminal) _____ violations, may have to pay _____ damages to parties injured by their actions, and (may/may not) _____ serve time in prison.

6. The government's charge in its suit against IBM was that the firm practiced (marginal cost/predatory/competitive) _____ pricing, while AT&T was charged with _____ access to an essential input to local telephone networks.

7. Antitrust actions can be initiated by the _____ Department of the federal government, by _____ who believe that they have been injured by a firm's anticompetitive practices, or by the FTC.

8. If the monopolization of an industry results in substantial _____ savings, the monopoly may be socially desirable.

9. Public utilities are usually natural _____ if they experience scale economies in the production and _____ of their service and if the market (can/cannot) _____ support competitors.

10. A _____ tariff permits a public utility to charge a flat fee for access to a service as well as the _____ cost for units consumed and is often used when the regulated price (does/does not) _____ generate enough revenue for the producer.

11. If a producer of electricity incurs an average cost of 9.5 cents (including a normal return) per unit in order to satisfy market demand, the regulated price would be set at _____ cents to ensure a fair return to the utility.

TRUE-FALSE QUESTIONS

1. _____ One reason why the estimates of the welfare costs of monopoly are low is that most firms do not earn huge rates of profits over a period of time.

2. _____ The industry exhibiting the highest welfare cost as a result of its monopoly power (based on 1963 data) was the auto industry.

3. _____ When a firm produces at the point at which $P = LAC$, monopoly profits are being made and are in excess of the normal return to capital.

4. _____ The Sherman Act of 1890 prohibits the existence of all monopolies.

5. _____ Monopoly power is present in a market if price exceeds the marginal cost of production over a period of time.

6. _____ With the passage of the Sherman Act of 1890, the government began a very intense attack on monopolies, and its antitrust activities are still present today.

7. _____ Westinghouse was charged under section 1 of the Sherman Act in the 1960s for practicing price discrimination.

8. _____ In order for the government to prosecute effectively under section 2 of the Sherman Act, it is necessary for the firm's market to be well defined.

9. _____ Government approval is needed if two firms in a highly concentrated industry begin merger proceedings.

10. _____ Following the role of the United States, practically all governments in the world have passed some type of antimonopoly laws.

11. _____ The Titanium Dioxide case established the precedent that the very fact that a company is big provides sufficient grounds for antitrust proceedings.

12. _____ Electric and gas companies are examples of natural monopolies.

13. _____ The purpose of marginal cost pricing is to

ensure a price and output level which is socially optimal.

14. ____ If a public utility company did not receive a rate of return on capital at least equal to its opportunity costs, we would expect the firm to expand capacity and increase efficiency in order to raise its profits.

15. ____ A vertical merger involves different firms at the same stage of production of the same good.

MULTIPLE CHOICE QUESTIONS

Circle the correct answer.

1. Regulatory lag
   a. can be a serious problem if the costs of operation and the rate of increase in prices require frequent changes in utility rates
   b. can be a serious problem because of the time difference between the time when antitrust violations are first observed and the time when the government first takes action against the firm
   c. can be a serious problem because of the difficulty in defining a firm's relevant market properly
   d. is not a serious problem because most regulatory commissions collect sufficient data on the utility subject to regulation

2. If a public utility creates and sells 10 billion units of output, has $4 billion in capital assets, and incurs $300 million in operating costs, and the opportunity cost of capital is 10 percent, the fair return price per unit of output is
   a. 5.5 cents per unit
   b. 8.5 cents per unit
   c. 7.0 cents per unit
   d. 6.0 cents per unit
   e. none of the above

3. All of the following are considerations which public utility regulators might use as guidelines in their regulatory function except
   a. establishing a range of acceptable excess profits
   b. encouraging the efficient production of output
   c. establishing prices so that the utility earns a normal return on its capital
   d. trying to adhere as closely as possible to the principle of marginal cost pricing

4. The Sherman Antitrust Act of 1890 prohibited
   a. mergers
   b. price discrimination
   c. all monopolies
   d. conspiracies to restrict trade

5. An agency which often pursues antitrust activity on behalf of the government is the
   a. Environmental Protection Agency (EPA)
   b. Interstate Commerce Commission (ICC)
   c. Federal Trade Commission (FTC)
   d. Food and Drug Administration (FDA)
   e. none of the above

6. If the courts declare that firm A has suffered damages in the amount of $5 million as a result of firm B's illegal price fixing, the maximum monetary award which firm A may receive from firm B is
   a. $5 million   c. $10 million
   b. $15 million   d. $25 million

7. Conscious parallelism among firms in an industry
   a. is ground for antitrust proceedings under the Clayton Act
   b. is an explicit attempt to fix prices
   c. can be easily established by government as a conspiracy to restrain trade
   d. describes price leadership in an oligopoly
   e. none of the above

Answer Question 8 on the basis of Figure 11-1, which describes an industry which is initially competitive but becomes monopolized with a reduction in costs from LMC_1 to LMC_2.

8. According to Figure 11-1
   a. society is worse off because the loss in social welfare is more than the gain from the reduction in costs
   b. society is better off because triangle A is greater than rectangle B
   c. society is better off because the cost savings exceed the loss in consumers' surplus
   d. society is worse off because the area of rectangle B exceeds that of triangle A
   e. society is neither better off nor worse off

9. All of the following characterize natural monopolies except that

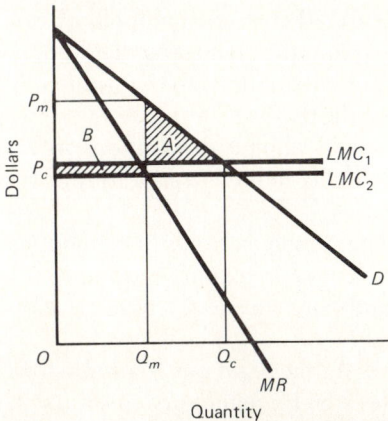

FIGURE 11-1

a. they are operated in the public's best interest
   b. they experience significant economies in the production and distribution of goods and services
   c. they submit to regulation only if assured of earning a monopoly profit
   d. they cannot produce a socially optimal level of output if competitors are in the industry

10. It can be said that antitrust laws
   a. are very infrequently applied to firms because of the potential power of the business community
   b. have had an overall positive effect by reducing the attempts by firms to monopolize
   c. were most frequently applied during the period 1890–1920
   d. provide civil but not criminal penalties for violators

AT THIS POINT YOU SHOULD BE ABLE TO . . .

1. Explain and show graphically the social costs incurred as a result of monopolistic and oligopolistic pricing.
2. Show graphically the transfer of consumers' surplus to the monopolist as a result of the monopolization of a competitive market and identify the welfare loss.
3. State the major provisions of the Sherman Act of 1890 (sections 1 and 2) and the Clayton Act of 1914 (sections 2 and 7).
4. List three remedies for monopolistic practices as set forth by the antitrust acts.
5. List two firms that have been subject to antitrust proceedings, state the offense of each, and state the resolution of these actions.
6. Define "relevant market" and state why this is an important and difficult concept in antitrust actions.
7. State and explain four issues which must be addressed in an evaluation of the effectiveness of U.S. antitrust laws.
8. Explain, in terms of its costs, how an industry which is highly concentrated or even monopolistic can benefit society, and explain the statement that "being big is not the issue but rather how the consumer is served or hurt by the industry."
9. Describe the general impact of vigorous international trade on a highly concentrated domestic industry.
10. Define a natural monopoly in terms of economies of production and transmission, list three examples of natural monopolies, and state why such a classification is appropriate.
11. Explain the role of public regulatory commissions and list three guidelines which a regulatory commission might follow.
12. Show graphically and mathematically how a fair rate of return might be established for a public utility and explain two major problems with the regulation of public utilities.

QUESTIONS FOR THOUGHT

1. Explain why monopoly profits are called by some economists a "privately collected tax."

2. What are the three remedies which society can impose on monopolistic behavior? Which sector of society (public or private) has been most active in initiating antitrust proceedings? Can you offer an explanation why?

3. The terms "monopoly," "monopolistic practices," and "monopolistic behavior" have been used throughout Chapter 11. Are the terms used in the same way that they were in Chapter 9 when the model for pure monopoly was presented? Explain.

4. Explain the difference between "conscious parallelism" and a conspiracy to fix prices. From the standpoint of economic analysis, which is the least harmful to society? Explain.

5. A firm must be able to define its market effectively in order to adopt and promote the appropriate marketing strategies. The identification of a firm's relevant market is of primary importance to the government in antitrust proceedings against a suspected violator. Why must the government be able to define the firm's relevant market effectively? What could be the results of an error in definition? What effect does product substitution have on market definition? Cite an example.

6. What is the rationale behind the antitrust laws? Who usually benefits from firms setting prices? Has the attitude toward antitrust enforcement changed over time? Explain.

7. It is generally accepted that the monopolization of a relatively competitive industry will reduce society's well-being; however, Professors Fischer and Dornbusch describe an exception. Explain how and under what conditions the monopolization of an industry can improve social welfare.

8. Define a "natural monopoly." Why are natural monopolies often found in public utilities? How does society try to assure itself that a natural monopoly operates in an acceptable manner?

9. A regulatory commission represents the public interest, yet it must be somewhat sensitive to the interests of the firm. What three guidelines might be helpful to the commission?

10. When might a two-part tariff be useful as a pricing policy for a natural monopoly? Explain how the tariff might work.

11. Why did the authors of your text state that a normal rate of return is a desirable criterion for the natural monopolist?

12. A politician once made the statement: "Big business is bad and benefits no one except the stockholders. The government should actively undertake a program to break up the monopolies and restore our competitive economy." Do you agree with this statement? Explain your reasons.

13. What are the most important provisions of the Sherman Act and the Clayton Act (as amended)?

12

The Public Interest, Externalities, and Regulation

Chapter 12 discusses government regulation in a market economy when there is market failure. Markets fail in their allocative functions when the marginal social costs of production are not equal to the marginal social benefits of the good consumed. Although a market equilibrium may be established, market failure prevents the attainment of a social optimum. The role of government becomes that of a regulator as it tries to determine an optimal price and output level. Whenever markets break down, someone is hurt because all costs of production are not internalized or because someone does not get the full benefits from consuming goods. The private and social costs of production and the private and social benefits are unequal, and so the government steps in.

Chapter 12 begins with explanations of the four sources of market distortion, each of which can lead to market failure. Three of the distortions—externalities, imperfect information, and social priorities—are the sources of market failure presented in Chapter 12.

An externality (which may be positive or negative) exists when spillover effects are not properly priced in the marketplace. In production, firms do not pay the full price of their activities; in consumption, consumers do not receive full benefit. In each case, spillover effects are not included in the market price of a good, and so resources are misallocated. The externality selected for analysis in Chapter 12 is pollution, which arises when firms discharge their wastes into a common area. Private property rights do not apply to public areas, resulting in part of the social cost of production being paid by individuals and other firms in the form of programs designed to clean up the environment. When an industry generates spillover costs, the market overproduces goods and establishes a price that is too low; resources are overallocated to the industry.

Pollution control measures currently exist in the form of pollution standards imposed by government through the EPA. The EPA is responsible for controlling air and water pollution as well as the use and disposal of hazardous materials. Firms violating EPA standards are punished with fines and denial of certification for installations and equipment. Through its regulations, the EPA tries to force the firm to internalize some of its external costs of production and thus approach a more socially desirable level of output. Pollution control and abatement does not mean zero pollution; this would require so many resources that it is not economically rational. The marginal costs of pollution control increase rapidly after a certain point, while the marginal benefits decrease. It has been argued that the best approach to pollution control is to have the EPA simply set a uniform price for pollution privileges. Such an approach would provide the least expensive way to attain a given reduction in the pollution level. Using prices, however, does present problems.

Another source of market failure discussed in Chapter 12 is the lack of complete information possessed by households and firms about goods and jobs in the marketplace. The government's regulatory agencies in the area of health, safety, and quality standards are the FDA, CPSC, NHTSA, and OSHA. By imposing standards which promote the safety of products and the workplace, the producer's marginal cost curve shifts upward, and market output is reduced. The demand curve for unsafe products falls when the consumer is given full information about goods which could be hazardous if consumed. Sometimes the agencies responsible for providing more complete information and standards abuse their regulatory power and establish rather absurd requirements which create problems by themselves.

The regulator's behavior is explained by both the capture hypothesis (which argues that they eventually promote the interest of the firms they are supposed to regulate) and the "share the gains, share the pains" hypothesis (which argues that since regulators are either elected or appointed, they try to please everybody by making all elements of their constituencies feel that their interests have been promoted at least somewhat).

The last section of Chapter 12 examines the current trend toward deregulation of some industries. As an example, deregulation in the airline industry is examined. Data indicate that the industry is becoming more competitive and efficient.

THE PUBLIC INTEREST, EXTERNALITIES, AND REGULATION

The role of regulation in American industry is very controversial, and many arguments have been made by proponents of both regulation and deregulation.

CHAPTER OUTLINE

1. Market failure occurs when resources are allocated in a nonoptimal manner. In a market system, price is the mechanism by which resources are allocated into the production and consumption of goods and services. A competitive market attains an optimal allocation of resources at the point at which quantity demanded equals quantity supplied. At this point, market price equals the marginal cost of producing 1 more unit, and so the value to consumers of 1 extra unit consumed equals the cost of producing it. Any deviation from this market clearing price can be undertaken only at someone's expense. In imperfectly competitive markets, a price may be established at the point where the market clears; however, price is greater than marginal cost, and so the allocation of resources is not optimal. When market price does not equal both the marginal social cost of producing a good and the marginal social valuation in consumption of a good, a market distortion exists. Distortions may arise from monopolies and oligopolies, externalities (spillover effects are improperly priced), imperfect information about goods or jobs, and social priorities other than production efficiency.

2. An externality exists when the production or consumption of a good involves spillover effects which are not included in its market price. Externalities may be positive (spillover benefit) or negative (spillover costs). Whenever there are spillover effects, a misallocation of resources occurs.
   a. When the production of a commodity reflects only the marginal private costs of production (the cost to the industry of producing 1 more unit) and none of the marginal social cost, externalities are present. If the market clearing price paid by consumers just equals the firm's marginal private costs (and none of the marginal social costs are considered), there is an overallocation of resources into the industry. The overallocation is shown by the fact that the sum of marginal private costs and marginal social costs exceeds the market price; the total marginal costs of producing an extra unit exceed society's marginal valuation of consuming an extra unit. The commodity is underpriced. By reducing output and increasing price (moving up on the market demand curve), a social optimum is attained in which price equals the sum of both marginal private costs and marginal social costs. When marginal social costs are not taken into consideration, the market equilibrium does not equate the social costs and social benefits of production and consumption, and this reflects market failure. The ability of some producers to pass the cost of pollution on to society is an example of a negative externality (spillover cost) and market failure.

3. In a free-market economy, the failure to price pollution externalities imposes a social cost which results in market failure. Since it is very difficult to charge producers for an amount equal to the marginal cost of their externalities (this would be ideal), society regulates the amount of pollution permitted by producers.
   a. It is the responsibility of the EPA (created in 1970) to administer various programs designed to reduce the social cost of pollution. Specifically, the EPA is responsible for controlling air pollution, water pollution, and hazardous materials. The EPA sets standards for achieving desired levels of environmental quality, informs producers about the technologies required to achieve these standards, monitors compliance with the standards, and prosecutes violators. The EPA's punitive actions against violators are fines and denial of installation certification.
   b. The optimal level of pollution occurs at the quantity at which the marginal benefit received by society from reducing the pollution level by an extra unit equals the marginal cost to society of reducing pollution by the extra unit. The marginal benefit of pollution abatement decreases as the environment is cleaned up, but the marginal costs rise. It does not make economic sense to attempt to reduce pollution beyond the point at which the marginal benefit equals the marginal cost to society because the cost incurred would be greater than the benefits received.
   c. Relative to total GNP, air pollution has decreased since 1970, but water pollution still remains a serious problem. Thus, the EPA has experienced mixed success in reducing pollution.
   d. The EPA could use a pricing mechanism to control or reduce pollution since producers would then generate the externality only to the point at which the price charged for an extra unit equals the marginal cost of reducing pollution by 1 more unit. At this point, the firm's pollution abatement costs are minimized. Pollution is efficiently allocated under

this method because all producers are charged the same price for polluting. Two reasons for using prices to reduce pollution are that the costs of pollution control are minimized and that the EPA does not have to set pollution standards and regulations for each individual firm. Arguments against using the price mechanism are that it is very difficult to measure the amount of pollution produced by each firm and that it is difficult to determine the appropriate price to charge the firm.

4. The presence of incomplete information about products or jobs is another source of market failure. This type of market failure occurs because the cost of information gathering can be very high. As a result, the costs of producing the good are less than the true social costs of the resources used. The federal government attempts to reduce the impact of this type of market failure through such regulatory agencies as the FDA, NHTSA, CPSC, and OSHA. Each agency's role is to provide information to the market so that resources are allocated more efficiently and to establish standards designed to reduce injury or death.

   a. A full information demand schedule provides the true marginal valuation by consumers of extra units of a good. Full information in the marketplace shifts the free-market demand curve, changes prices, and improves the efficiency of resource allocation.

   b. Regulatory agencies may not only supply information to the market but also impose operating and performance standards. Such standards increase the firm's costs of operation at every level of output, and so the supply curve shifts upward and to the left. The cost of imposing standards functions like a tax on the industry.

   c. The FDA sets standards for the food and drug industries. The FDA has been charged with following a very conservative approach in its approval and certification of new drugs. Critics argue that consumers must wait too long before getting a new drug. It has been argued that if the pharmaceutical industry operated in a free market, society would be assured of effective and safe drugs. The time and cost required for the industry to regulate itself, however, are too great, and so external regulation is socially desirable. Establishing objective governmental standards to ensure the quality and safety of unfamiliar drugs generates a saving to society since the cost of gathering information is reduced. The role of the government in monitoring adherence to these standards is not very clear since private certification of the safety and quantity of products (assuring compliance with the established standards) is often accepted in the marketplace. Another accepted role of government is that of information broker to consumers on the potential risks or unsafe nature of certain products on the market. This information transfer is left to government because of the scale economies required to patrol the marketplace routinely.

   d. Regulatory agencies have been criticized for their ineffective and inefficient enforcement of standards. OSHA provides an example of such regulatory ineffectiveness. Since its creation in 1970, the only sectors in which there have been significant reductions in job-related fatalities are agriculture and mining. How much of the reduction in deaths and injuries can be attributed to OSHA's regulation is uncertain; however, it is thought to be insignificant.

   e. Social priorities in the area of health and safety provide a basis for regulation. Although it is often politically popular to argue that the value of a human life cannot be calculated, the economic argument is that people knowingly risk their health and safety and that society cannot afford to implement across the board policies which guarantee everyone's health and safety. The costs of pursuing a zero-risk regulation would greatly outweigh the benefits, and so this is not economically rational.

5. Two major theories have been advanced to explain the behavior of regulatory agencies. These theories are the "capture" hypothesis and the "share the gains, share the pains" theory.

   a. The capture hypothesis argues that although regulatory agencies are initially established to protect consumers' (society's) best interests, they eventually shift to promoting the best interests of the firms they regulate. The reason for this shift is that the industry "captures" the regulators. The capture takes place because the regulators have usually been associated at one time or another with the industry which they regulate and because the firms are usually much better prepared (in terms of information and financial resources) for regulatory hearings than are consumers.

   b. The "share the gains, share the pains" theory argues that when regulators are selected or appointed, they try to win approval for their actions from their entire constituency. The regulators are reluctant to offend legislators, industry, or consumers; as a result, they pursue policies designed to split the difference. The agencies want each sector of their constituency to feel that its interest has been served to some degree.

6. It is possible that the decade of the 1980s will be a period of deregulation of American industry. Some social-interest groups and legislators as well as the regulators themselves still argue that more regulation is needed. Industry and many taxpayers argue that regulation reduces productivity and should be curtailed.

a. Until recently, the CAB regulated practically every aspect of the airline industry, thereby removing all price competition. Entry into the industry was almost nonexistent. In 1978, Congress enacted deregulatory measures which permitted the airline industry to become more competitive. New firms entered to compete with the established airlines, active competition in air fares on many routes burgeoned, and the number of passenger-miles traveled increased significantly. Although some airlines failed (Braniff and Laker), they failed because a less regulated, more competitive market system cannot sustain inefficiencies. Firms that use society's resources efficiently do well in a deregulated environment.

IMPORTANT TERMS AND THEIR MEANING

Match the following terms with the correct definition or phrase.

1. _____ The cost of additional resources used by an industry to produce an extra unit of output
2. _____ The regulatory agency responsible for setting the standards for labeling foods and for approving drugs for public use
3. _____ States that regulators eventually operate in the best interest of the firms they are suppose to regulate
4. _____ The price charged for the outflow of pollution into public areas
5. _____ Requires the FDA to ban all foods which cause cancer in humans or animals
6. _____ The removal of regulatory constraints from industry, permitting a more competitive market to operate
7. _____ The regulatory agency responsible for setting safety standards in the workplace
8. _____ Occurs when prices fail to bring about a proper allocation of resources and society's wants and best interest are not satisfied
9. _____ A method of analysis used to evaluate the allocation of resources in terms of a socially optimal level of utilization
10. _____ Argues that regulators try not to offend anyone and promote policies which allow all segments of their constituency to feel that their interests have been served to some degree
11. _____ Exist when market prices are not equal to both the marginal social valuation of a good and the marginal social costs of producing the good
12. _____ The right to own, maintain, enjoy, and dispose of land and other assets either as a private citizen or in common with other citizens
13. _____ Arise any time the production or consumption of a good has spillover effects beyond the consumers or producers involved in the market and these spillover effects are not fully reflected in the market price

a. Effluent charge
b. Deregulation
c. Market failure
d. Property rights
e. Marginal private costs
f. Distortions
g. FDA
h. Share the gains, share the pains hypothesis
i. Externalities
j. Cost-benefit analysis
k. Capture hypothesis
l. OSHA
m. Delaney amendment

EXERCISES

1. Listed below are several activities which various government regulatory agencies consider within their sphere of control. Some of the activities may seem humorous; however, official statements have been made by one agency or another about each one. In the blank beside each statement, indicate which agency you think is responsible for the activity. Use the abbreviations FDA, EPA, OSHA, NHTSA, CPSC, and CAB. Some may be used more than once.

a. Issued warnings that infant wear treated with the flame-retardant chemical TRIS could pose health hazards for young children. _____

b. In its publication *Safety with Beef Cattle* (1976), farmers were warned to be careful when working on floors which were "wet and slippery with manure"; also in the same publication, farmers were told to try to keep a fence between themselves and cattle and to be careful not to fall into manure pits. _____

c. Issued standards designed to reduce auto emissions into the atmosphere by the mid-1980s. _____

d. Issued standards requiring seat belts in passenger automobiles. _____

e. Ruled that Laetrile was of no value in the treatment of certain forms of cancer. _____

f. Issued standards prohibiting construction workers from using ladders with broken or missing rungs or with split side rails. _____

g. Established requirements for equipping ambulances which are used in highway rescue activities. _____

h. Prohibited commercial airline flights between certain cities by certain airlines. _____

i. Established the maximum level of impurities which can be contained in processed foods. _____

j. Warned that some missile-firing toy spaceships could potentially cause a choking hazard for small children. _____

2. Table 12-1 presents market demand, marginal private costs MPC, and marginal social cost MSC data for an industry producing a hypothetical commodity. The MPC is assumed to be constant.

a. Compute the total marginal cost to society (MC) for producing various quantities of this good. Enter your calculations in the column labeled "MC."

b. The competitive equilibrium is attained at a price of $_____ per unit and an output level of _____ units. At this point, market price and MPC equal $_____.

c. A (positive/negative) _____ externality exists since society's marginal valuation of the last unit produced and consumed is (greater than/less than) _____ the MC of the last unit. At the competitive equilibrium, resoures are (underallocated/over allocated) _____.

d. The value of the externality of the last unit consumed is $_____, and this occurs because producers (do/do not) _____ have to pay for the full costs of production.

e. The social optimum for the production and consumption of this good requires that output be (increased/reduced) _____ to a level of _____ units and that price (increase/decrease) _____ to $_____ per unit. At the social optimum, the total MC of production equals the good's _____.

3. Suppose the federal government has six alternatives for reducing water pollution. Each alternative can be undertaken only at increasingly greater costs, but each alternative yields a greater purity of water. Table 12-2 presents the alternatives.

a. Complete Table 12-3 by computing the marginal costs and marginal benefits for each alternative. Enter your computations in the appropriate columns.

b. In Table 12-4, compute the ratio of marginal benefits to marginal costs. Enter your computations in the last column.

c. According to the data, the government (should/should not) _____ undertake a program to reduce water pollution.

TABLE 12-1

PRICE, $	QUANTITY DEMANDED	MPC, $	MSC, $	MC, $
15.50	4	8.50	.50	_____
14.50	5	8.50	.60	_____
13.50	6	8.50	.80	_____
12.50	7	8.50	1.10	_____
11.50	8	8.50	1.50	_____
10.50	9	8.50	2.00	_____
9.50	10	8.50	2.60	_____
8.50	11	8.50	3.30	_____
7.50	12	8.50	4.10	_____

TABLE 12-2

ALTERNATIVE	TOTAL COSTS, $	TOTAL BENEFIT, $	CLEAN WATER, %
1. Do nothing	0	0	0
2. Sludge removal	1000	1300	39
3. Sludge removal and aeration	1500	2300	63
4. Sludge removal, aeration, and treatment plant	2200	3000	80
5. Sludge removal, aeration, treatment plant, and special filters	3100	3400	85
6. Sludge removal, aeration, treatment plant, special filters, and genetically altered enzymes	4200	3500	88

THE PUBLIC INTEREST, EXTERNALITIES, AND REGULATION

TABLE 12-3

ALTERNATIVE	MARGINAL COST (MC), $	MARGINAL BENEFIT (MB), $
1		
2		
3		
4		
5		
6		

TABLE 12-4

ALTERNATIVE	WATER PURITY, %	MARGINAL BENEFITS / MARGINAL COSTS
1	0	
2	39	
3	63	
4	80	
5	85	
6	88	

d. Given the choices, alternative _____ should be chosen, and water purity would be raised to _____ percent.

e. It (is/is not) _____ possible to improve water purity further; however, the _____ of increased purity are greater than the _____ attained.

f. At the optimal level of water purity, the ratio of marginal benefits to marginal costs is equal to _____. For some alternatives, the ratio is less than _____, and this indicates that the attempt to improve water quality further (is/is not) _____ an economically rational effort since marginal _____ are greater than marginal _____.

g. For alternatives with a ratio greater than 1, the government (should/should not) _____ continue to improve water purity since marginal benefits are (greater than/less than) _____ marginal social costs.

4. Figure 12-1 presents a market equilibrium in a competitive industry. The market supply curve (recall from Chapter 8) is the sum of the firms' marginal cost curves. The demand curve reflects the marginal valuation of consumers for 1 extra unit of the good. The competitive price is P_e, and quantity is Q_e. At this point, the marginal cost equals marginal *private* benefits. Assume now that the consumption of this good generates positive externalities so that society benefits. At point A, marginal social benefits equal the marginal cost of producing the good.

a. Draw a curve which reflects the marginal social benefits from the consumption of the good. The curve must go through point A. Label the curve "marginal social benefits."

b. Draw a line from point A to both the quantity axis and the price axis. Label the new quantity Q_o and the new price P_o. Also, where your line AQ_o crosses the demand curve, label the intersection point B.

c. The competitive equilibrium has (underallocated/overallocated) _____ resources to the production of this good since society _____ from its consumption.

d. In this example, a social optimum requires a (larger/smaller) _____ quantity of the good to be consumed than is the case for the competitive equilibrium.

e. The area of triangle _____ is a measure of the positive externality.

f. Which of the following goods might best be represented by the above model?
    (1) television sets   (3) college education
    (2) automobiles   (4) refrigerators

5. In spaces **a** and **b** below, list two advantages of using prices instead of government regulations to regulate pollution. In spaces **c** and **d**, list two disadvantages of using prices.

a. _____
b. _____
c. _____
d. _____

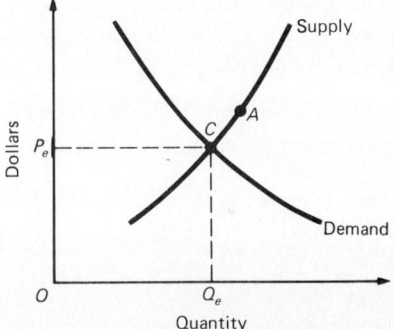

FIGURE 12-1

FILL-IN QUESTIONS

1. Market _____ is used as a major argument that regulations should be improved.

2. The central allocative mechanism is (price/quantity/government) _____ in a market; however, when the market clears, the equilibrium established may not be socially _____ in the sense that the consumers' marginal _____ equals the marginal _____ of producing an extra unit of output.

3. Externalities may be either _____ or _____ because some of the benefits or costs of consumption may spill over onto society.

4. If an externality exists, there is a _____ of resources in the market, and this (is/is not) _____ reflected in the market price of a good.

5. Pollution externalities arise primarily because (public/private) _____ property rights are not enforced.

6. The tasks of the EPA center on controlling _____, _____, and _____.

7. When the marginal _____ from cleaner air equals the marginal _____ of cleaning up the atmosphere, the _____ amount of pollution has been established since any attempt to reduce pollution below this amount (is/is not) _____ economically rational.

8. The role of the federal government has (expanded/contracted) _____ in the area of health and safety because of the difficulty of households and firms acquiring full _____ about products.

9. The (CPCS/FDA/EPA) _____ is the federal agency responsible for prohibiting impure or contaminated foods from being placed on the market.

10. If consumers had full information about a hazardous product, we would expect the socially optimal price to be (higher/lower) _____ and quantity to be (higher/lower) _____ because of a(n) (decrease/increase) _____ in market demand.

11. The _____ amendment prohibits any food which causes cancer in humans or animals from being sold.

12. It (would/would not) _____ be in society's best interest to promote standards designed to provide an absolutely hazard-free environment because the (benefits/costs/returns) _____ would be prohibitive.

13. The _____ hypothesis argues that regulators eventually promote the interests of the industries they are suppose to regulate.

14. A major attempt at deregulation has occurred in the _____ industry, and early results indicate that fares have (fallen/increased) _____ and that the level of competition has (decreased/increased) _____.

TRUE-FALSE QUESTIONS

1. _____ To say that a distortion exists in the marketplace means that both the marginal social valuation and the marginal cost of an extra unit of a good are equal.

2. _____ Imperfect competition and imperfect information can be sources of market distortions.

3. _____ If a spillover benefit is positive, society benefits from the private consumption of a good.

4. _____ Market failure can occur only when there is an equality of social costs and benefits.

5. _____ If $MSB > MSC$, society's resources have been overallocated in the production of the good, and output should be reduced.

6. _____ One of the best known efforts of the EPA is the reduction of automobile emissions.

7. _____ The socially optimal level of air pollution is that level at which the marginal value to society of an extra degree of cleanliness just equals the cost to society of producing the extra degree.

8. _____ If all spillover costs were included, the demand for a product would increase.

9. _____ All economists agree that the best method of reducing pollution is through a system of prices.

10. _____ The reason the FDA sets drug standards and requires certification of new drugs is that most consumers lack full information about pharmaceutical products.

11. _____ Since the formation of OSHA, death rates in U.S. manufacturing industries have fallen dramatically.

12. _____ An economist might respond to a government program to maintain a hazardfree environment with the statement that individuals in consumption, production, and recreation take risks and expose themselves to hazards.

13. _____ The source of "capture" in the capture hypothesis of the regulator is that the regulator tries to promote, at least to some degree, the interests of all parties.

14. _____ Most members of the business community are rather indifferent toward the current level of regulation in the U.S. economy.

15. _____ Part of the aim of airline deregulation is to permit efficient firms to have the opportunity to show how much better they can do than the less efficient firms.

MULTIPLE-CHOICE QUESTIONS

Circle the correct answer.

1. An externality can be defined as
   a. a cost of production arising from the use of land, capital, and labor
   b. a distortion which results from not pricing spillover effects properly
   c. an event which occurs because society prefers an outcome other than that of the free market
   d. a benefit which occurs because the market does not have complete information about a product

2. Which of the following statements is incorrect?
   a. if prices clear a free market, market failure cannot occur
   b. the primary allocative mechanism in a market economy is price
   c. imperfect competition results in market failure since output is underproduced
   d. when markets fail, some form of regulation is justified since someone can be made better off without making someone else worse off

3. In a free market, goods with positive externalities
   a. will be overproduced in the marketplace
   b. will have the marginal valuation of the externality reflected in their price
   c. will be produced to the point at which the marginal social benefit just equals the marginal social cost of the last unit produced
   d. will be underproduced at the market equilibrium

4. All of the following are responsibilities of the EPA except
   a. advising firms of the technologies available which comply with the agency's regulations
   b. establishing the standards for levels of water and air pollution
   c. issuing warnings of hazardous occupational practices
   d. monitoring compliance with established standards

5. In using cost-benefit analysis to evaluate regulatory programs, all of the following are true except
   a. at the social optimum, the ratio of marginal costs to marginal benefits equals 1
   b. all relevant costs and benefits are easily measured
   c. marginal social benefits decline throughout the relevant range of output
   d. a social optimum will be attained at some point where marginal costs are rising

6. The EPA has made progress in removing most air pollutants except
   a. nitrous oxides   c. hydrocarbons
   b. sulfur oxides   d. particulates

7. If prices were used to control pollution,
   a. a social optimum could not be attained because some firms are more efficient and would have lower marginal pollution costs
   b. it would not be necessary to have a measure of pollution generated by each individual firm
   c. all pollution could be controlled easily
   d. regulations would not have to be specified for each firm

8. All of the following are functions of the CPSC, OSHA, NHTSA, and FDA except
   a. imposing occupational and consumption taxes to promote an efficient allocation of resources
   b. providing both consumers and producers information in order to achieve a more efficient allocation of resources
   c. establishing standards designed to promote consumer and producer safety
   d. enforcing the established standards

9. When a regulatory agency imposes standards for safety
   a. the agency is providing more complete information for the consumer or producer
   b. some of the standards may have no relation to economic costs and benefits
   c. the market equilibrium price and output might change
   d. all of the above
   e. none of the above

10. The agency associated with the Delaney amendment is
    a. CPSC   c. EPA
    b. FDA   d. OSHA

11. The "share the gains, share the pains" hypothesis predicts that
   a. regulators will eventually serve the interests of the firms they should be regulating
   b. regulators almost always act prudently
   c. regulators are usually selected from the industry to be regulated
   d. regulators pay little or no attention to the interests of their constituencies

12. The industry regulated by the CAB is
   a. interstate trucking
   b. airlines
   c. drugs and pharmaceuticals
   d. steel

AT THIS POINT YOU SHOULD BE ABLE TO . . .

1. Define market failure and state why government regulation might be justified in such a situation.

2. Show the effect of market failure on price and output and explain why a social optimum cannot be reached.

3. Define the meaning of market distortion and list four sources of such distortions.

4. Explain the meaning of an externality and give an example of both a positive and a negative externality.

5. State the condition for a social optimum in terms of marginal social costs and marginal social benefits.

6. Explain and show graphically how a negative externality can prevent a market in equilibrium from attaining a social optimum and state how an optimum can be reached.

7. List three tasks for which the EPA is responsible and list four things the agency does in an attempt to fulfill these tasks.

8. Explain why it does not make economic sense to set as a goal the reduction of all water pollution to a zero level.

9. List two reasons for and two reasons against using the price mechanism as a method of reducing pollution, and describe how prices might be used to reduce the level of pollution.

10. Identify four federal agencies responsible for improving the transfer of information to producers and consumers, and state two major roles of each.

11. Discuss the reasons for having the FDA regulate drugs on the market and explain why some individuals argue that the FDA does a disservice by keeping good drugs off the market for a long period of time.

12. State both the capture hypothesis and the share the gains, share the pains hypothesis.

QUESTIONS FOR THOUGHT

1. When Alfred Kahn headed the CAB, he argued strongly in favor of airline deregulation in the belief that the airlines could become more competitive. Explain why Kahn supported the deregulation of the industry he was responsible for regulating.

2. What are four sources of distortion in a market economy? Explain the sources and also explain how each can lead to market failure.

3. Why does a market economy not place a price on pollution? What recourse do citizens injured by pollution have against firms? If all pollution occurred on private property, would it be easier to control? Explain.

4. Can there be too little pollution? Explain why or why not.

5. What is an alternative to using government regulations as a means to control pollution? Explain how this alternative might work and give both positive and negative arguments for using this pollution control measure.

6. What is the effect of the imposition of standards by a regulatory agency on industry price and output? Explain how this adjustment process occurs.

7. Distinguish between the "capture hypothesis" and the "share the gains, share the pains" hypothesis as an explanation of the behavior of regulators. Which approach do you think is more realistic? Why?

8. Suppose that as a member of a debating team at a national tournament you must present an argument against the government actively regulating firms in a market economy. Briefly sketch an outline of the major points that you would want to make. What arguments do you think you opponent might make? How would you counter these arguments?

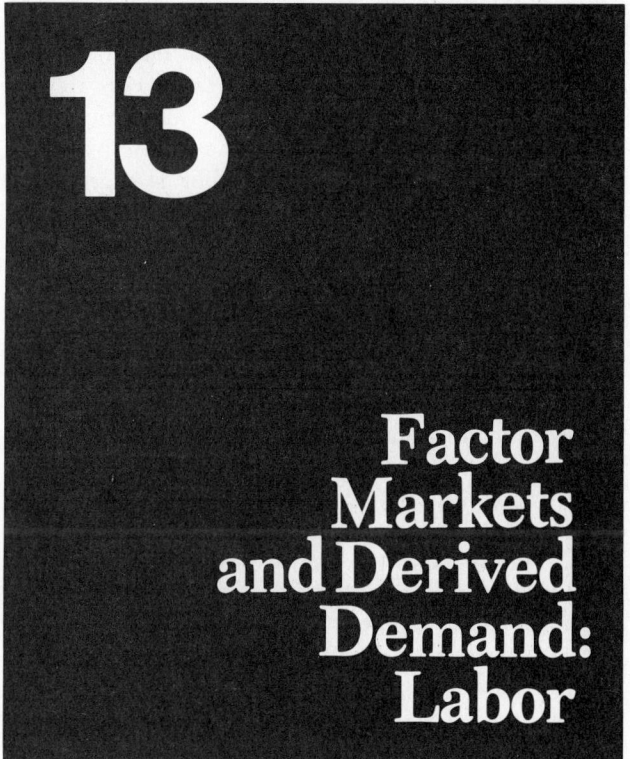

13

Factor Markets and Derived Demand: Labor

This is the first of three chapters which present the markets for the factors of production. In Chapter 13, you study how the principles of supply and demand are used to establish an equilibrium price and quantity for labor. Employers buy labor to produce their products. As the employer uses labor in production, his costs of production are influenced by both the quantity used and the price paid for the resource. You should understand as you begin reading Chapter 13 that the demand for labor as well as any other factor of production is a derived demand because firms hire resources only if their output can be sold on the product market. Thus, any change in product demand affects the demand for resources. Households supply labor. Payments made by producers are the major component of household income.

Chapter 13 begins with a review of the firm's choice of production technique, which initially was presented in Chapter 7. Two new concepts are introduced: the wage-rental ratio and capital-labor ratio. These show the relative cost of using inputs and the intensity of input use. The ratios indicate the type of production technique a firm will select, based on input prices and factor availability.

The firm's demand for labor depends on the marginal value product of labor $MVPL$. Although similar to the firm's marginal revenue schedule, which shows the change in revenue brought about by selling 1 more unit of output, the $MVPL$ shows the change in the value of a firm's output resulting from the employment of one additional worker. The $MVPL$ reflects the diminishing marginal product of labor. The firm hires labor until the $MVPL$ of the last worker employed just equals the cost of obtaining that worker. The cost of labor is the wage rate. Any change in the marginal product of labor or the market price of a firm's output causes the firm's $MPVL$ curve (its demand for labor curve) to shift.

The industry demand curve for labor is not simply the sum of each individual firm's demand curve but is obtained by taking into account the effect of changing wages, employment, and output prices on each firm's demand for labor. Unlike the firm, the industry demand for labor cannot take output price as given, since any change in employment affects output supply and price. Industry demand for labor is determined by the ease of input substitution and the output price elasticity of demand.

The other side of the labor market consists of labor supply. Whether an individual works more as wages increase depends on the dominance of the income effect or the substitution effect. It is possible that as wages increase beyond some level, the income effect dominates the worker's choice between income and leisure, and so fewer hours of labor are supplied. In such a situation, the worker's labor supply curve is backward-bending (negatively sloped). At both the industry and economy levels, as wages increase, more labor is supplied primarily because the rate of labor force participation increases. The supply curve for the industry and the economy are upward-sloping.

The industry equilibrium wage and quantity are determined by the intersection of labor demand and supply. Changes in productivity, wages, or product price influence wages and employment in other industries as labor moves from contracting to expanding industries. The mobility of labor is one important link in achieving a labor market equilibrium.

Chapter 13 concludes with a discussion of economic rents. An economic rent is the excess of a factor payment above the amount necessary to obtain that factor for a particular use. Rents occur when factor supply is either fixed or highly inelastic.

You will recognize many similarities between the output and input markets. In the output market, households are buyers, and firms are sellers. The roles are reversed in factor markets. Two of the more important concepts in Chapter 13 are the marginal value product of labor and the rule for expanding employment. These two concepts will be seen again in Chapter 14 as the topics of labor skills improvement and labor market imperfections are presented.

CHAPTER OUTLINE

1. A firm's demand for a factor of production is a derived demand since it is the demand for the

firm's output which determines the required factor level and factor type used. Factor intensity and production technique are determined by the cost and productivity of one factor relative to another. As the price of one factor changes while other factor prices do not, substitution occurs toward the relatively less expensive factor.

2. When the firm is operating in the short run with a fixed stock of capital, the primary input decision is the amount of labor to employ, and this determines the level of output produced. The firm's demand for labor is determined by the marginal value product of labor. The marginal value product of labor shows the increase in the value of the firm's output as a result of employing one additional worker. The marginal value product of labor is calculated by multiplying the marginal product of labor by the price of the firm's output. Because of diminishing marginal product, the marginal value product of labor declines. The firm is at its equilibrium level of employment when the wage paid for labor (the cost of the additional unit of labor) equals the marginal value product of labor (the value created by the additional unit).

3. Any change in the wage rate, labor productivity, or output price will change the firm's demand for labor. The firm's labor demand curve is the marginal value product of labor curve. With everything else constant, a negative relationship exists between the quantity of labor demanded and the wage rate. The slope of the marginal value product of labor curve depends on the degree of substitutability between capital and labor and relates changes in the amount of labor demanded to changes in the wage rate. A change in output price or labor productivity causes the marginal value product curve of labor to shift so that the firm's demand for labor curve shifts. Considering changes in wages and output prices simultaneously, the firm's demand for labor becomes a function of the real wage rate. The level of a firm's capital stock affects its employment decision because it influences the productivity of labor. A large capital stock increases the marginal product of labor so that the marginal value product of labor is higher, and the firm thus hires more workers. An increase in the capital stock shifts the firm's demand curve for labor.

4. The total demand for labor by all firms in an industry is determined by horizontally adding each firm's marginal value product of labor curve at a given output price; however, the industry demand curve for labor is not this aggregate sum. At the industry level, a change in wage rates changes the amount of labor employed, which changes industry supply. As supply changes, product price changes, causing a change in the relevant marginal value product of labor. The industry cannot consider the output price as constant when it responds to changes in the wage rate. The elasticity of the industry demand curve for labor is determined primarily by the substitutability between labor and capital for each firm and the price elasticity of demand for industry output.

5. An equilibrium wage and employment level is determined by combining both the industry's demand for and households' supply of labor. The individual worker's decision-making process determines how much labor is supplied, which in turn affects wages and employment in the industry and the economy.

   a. The number of hours worked by an individual depends on the real wage, because this measures how much can be purchased with the nominal wage. The income and substitution effects are present when real wages change. If real wages rise, workers want to work more since it now costs more not to work. The substitution effect causes the individual to substitute work for leisure. But the income effect of an increase in real wages causes the worker to consume more leisure (along with all other goods) and do less work. The relative strengths of the income and substitution effects determine whether the slope of the individual's labor supply curve will be upward-sloping or backward-bending. Data suggest that for men in their prime work years, the income and substitution effects cancel each other out so that the supply of labor curve is almost vertical.

      (1) An increase in wages may induce individuals to enter labor force because not working becomes more expensive, and this changes the labor force participation rate. It is unlikely that individuals drop out of the labor force when wages rise. Labor force participation has changed over the past 20 years as male participation rates dropped while those of females increased.

      (2) As long as it does not increase their costs, firms generally adjust their hours of work to satisfy the preferences of their workers.

   b. The labor supply curve for the economy is upward-sloping primarily because labor force participation increases as wages rise.

   c. In the short run, an industry's supply of labor depends on the wages paid by that industry relative to other industries. Small industries using unskilled labor face a flat labor supply curve, while large industries using skilled work-

FACTOR MARKETS AND DERIVED DEMAND: LABOR

ers face an upward-sloping labor supply curve. In the long run, the wage differences between industries narrow, and so the long-run supply curve faced by an industry is flatter than the short-run supply curve.

6. The industry labor market equilibrium is determined by the intersection of the upward-sloping labor supply curve and the downward-sloping demand for labor curve. At this intersection, an equilibrium wage and equilibrium employment are established. A change in labor productivity, output price, output demand, wages in other sectors of the economy, and the level of capital investment within the industry are some factors which cause industry demand for or supply of labor to change. When industry demand for or supply of labor changes, the equilibrium wage and equilibrium employment change. Worker mobility promotes a reallocation of labor from declining industries with lower wages to expanding industries with higher wages.

7. The average real wage in the economy is determined by the aggregate supply of and aggregate demand for labor. This wage depends on labor's attitudes toward work and its acquired human capital, the capital stock in the economy, and overall labor productivity. Any change in aggregate supply or aggregate labor demand will change the average real wages; however, the adjustment process to a new equilibrium wage occurs only over a period of time.

8. The imposition of a minimum wage increases the level of unemployment for those workers for whom the value of their marginal products is less than the established minimum wage. These workers are usually young and unskilled. In a competitive labor market, the competition of profit-maximizing firms for productive labor drives the wage paid up to the value of the worker's marginal product, and so the market wage is above the minimum wage.

9. The excess payment to a factor of production above the payment necessary to obtain the factor for a particular use is defined as an economic rent. Economic rents arise because the demand for factors of production is a derived demand and because factor supply is inelastic.

IMPORTANT TERMS AND THEIR MEANING

Match the following terms with the correct definition or phrase.

1. _____ The acquired skills of the labor force including education and on-the-job training

2. _____ The marginal product of labor times the price of a firm's output; measures the value generated for a firm by an additional worker

3. _____ The purchasing power of wages; nominal wages divided by an index of the price level

4. _____ The ratio of input use; declines as labor becomes relatively inexpensive

5. _____ The ability of workers to leave low-paying jobs and move to industries paying a higher wage

6. _____ At higher wage rates, the quantity of labor supplied falls; the income effect is dominant

7. _____ A measure of labor costs relative to capital costs; shows the relative cost of using labor

8. _____ The differences in the wages paid between industries

9. _____ The excess paid to a factor of production above the minimum amount that would have to be paid to get that quantity of the factor supplied for a particular use

10. _____ Continue to employ or terminate labor until the wage paid to the last worker just equals his marginal value product

11. _____ The lowest money wage, established by the federal government, which must be paid to workers

12. _____ The percentage of a given group who are in the labor force, either working or looking for work

13. _____ The demand for a factor of production; present because of the demand for a firm's output

a. Minimum wage
b. Labor force participation
c. Wage-rental ratio
d. Mobility of labor
e. Derived demand
f. Average real wage
g. Optimal employment rule
h. Human capital
i. Real wage
j. Capital-labor ratio
k. Economic rent
l. Interindustry wage differentials
m. Backward-bending labor supply curve

14. _____ The average price of labor in the economy; determined by the aggregate supply of and demand for labor

n. Equalizing differentials

15. _____ Differences in wages resulting from differences in job attractiveness

o. Marginal value product of labor

EXERCISES

1. Table 13-1 presents basic production function information for a firm as it employs variable amounts of labor and a fixed amount of capital.

a. Complete the third column of Table 13-1 by computing the marginal product of labor.

b. If the product can be sold on the market at a price of $5 for each unit, compute total revenue and enter each value in the table. Also, compute and enter the marginal value product of labor.

c. On your graph paper, plot the firm's marginal value product of labor curve. Label the vertical axis "dollars" and the horizontal axis "employment." Be sure to plot the marginal values at the midpoints on the horizontal axis.

d. Using the information just computed, determine the firm's demand schedule for labor in Table 13-2.

Other than the fact that we plotted out MVPL quantities in the middle of the employment interval, if the demand schedule was plotted, would there be any difference between the firm's *MVPL* curve and its demand for labor curve?

2. Suppose that the labor employed in Exercise 1 is unskilled and is paid a wage of $25 daily. Place your computations of *MVPL* in column 2 in Table 13-3. Given the $25 daily wage and the *MVPL* you calculated, compute the contribution to profits of each worker and place this computation in column 4.

a. Based on your calculations, all workers before

TABLE 13-2

WAGE RATE PER DAY, $	QUANTITY OF LABOR DEMANDED
95	0
85	_____
75	_____
65	_____
55	_____
45	_____
35	_____
25	_____
15	_____
5	_____

the _____ worker add a positive amount to profits, while workers _____ and _____ not only add nothing to profits but actually cause profits to fall. The firm should hire _____ workers if it is a profit maximizer.

b. Suppose the product's market price falls from $5 to $3. The new *MVPL* is now (greater than/less than) _____ the original *MVPL* for every quantity of labor, and the firm will hire (more/fewer) _____ workers. At a new price, the firm hires _____ units of labor in order to maximize profits.

c. Since the firm in Exercises 1 and 2 can sell any amount of output produced at a going market price of $5 ($3 after the fall) and can hire any amount of labor at a wage rate of $25 per day, it can be concluded that the firm is in a (competitive/imperfectly competitive) _____ market for both its outputs and inputs.

3. Figure 13-1 shows the market for labor. Initially assume that there are no constraints on the market and that it is competitive. The market demand for labor curve (*D*) incorporates each individual firm's *MVP* of

TABLE 13-1

QUANTITY OF LABOR	TOTAL OUTPUT	MARGINAL PRODUCT OF LABOR (MP_L)	TOTAL REVENUE (*TR*)	MARGINAL VALUE PRODUCT OF LABOR (*MVPL*)
0	0			
1	17	_____	_____	_____
2	32	_____	_____	_____
3	45	_____	_____	_____
4	56	_____	_____	_____
5	65	_____	_____	_____
6	72	_____	_____	_____
7	77	_____	_____	_____
8	80	_____	_____	_____
9	81	_____	_____	_____

FACTOR MARKETS AND DERIVED DEMAND: LABOR

TABLE 13-3

QUANTITY OF LABOR	MARGINAL VALUE PRODUCT OF LABOR ($MVPL$)	WAGE RATE PER DAY, $	CONTRIBUTION TO PROFITS PER DAY, $
0		25	
1	_____	25	_____
2	_____	25	_____
3	_____	25	_____
4	_____	25	_____
5	_____	25	_____
6	_____	25	_____
7	_____	25	_____
8	_____	25	_____
9	_____	25	_____

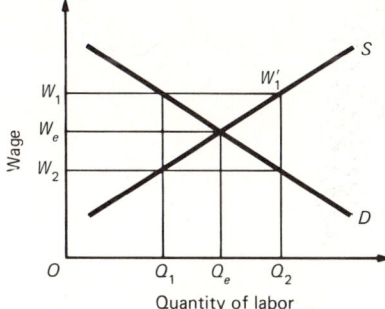

FIGURE 13-1

labor curve. The labor supply curve (S) incorporates all workers' preferences for work and leisure.

a. In the competitive market, the equilibrium wage is _____ and the equilibrium quantity of labor is _____. At this wage, the market (has a surplus/clears/has a shortage) _____. Any worker who wants a job (can/cannot) _____ find one at the equilibrium wage, and employers (can/cannot) _____ fill their job vacancies at this price for labor.

b. If the government makes it illegal for firms to pay labor any wage below W_1, it has established a _____ wage. At wage W_1, (more/fewer) _____ workers are willing to work than employers are willing to hire, and so there is (surplus/shortage) _____ of labor in the amount ($OQ_2 - OQ_1$ or $OQ_2 - OQ_e$ or $OQ_e - OQ_1$) _____.

c. The industry equates the marginal value product of labor and the _____ rate, and so with higher wages, less labor is demanded. The line $WW_1'S$, in effect, becomes the (demand for/supply of) _____ labor curve because no labor is offered or hired below wage W_1.

d. The wage established by the government serves as a price (ceiling/floor) _____.

e. If the government established the minimum wage at W_2, there (would/would not) _____ be a disequilibrium in the market because the competitive wage is (higher/lower) _____ than the government-established wage. Any minimum wage legislation below W_e (will/will not) _____ be effective.

4. Table 13-4 presents a supply schedule for an individual worker. Nominal wages (first column) and

TABLE 13-4

(1) NOMINAL WAGE PER HOUR, $	(2) REAL WAGE PER HOUR, $	(3) QUANTITY OF HOURS WORKED
17		8
15	_____	10
13	_____	12
11	_____	14
9	_____	12
7	_____	10
5	_____	8
3	_____	6
2	_____	4

TABLE 13-5

	CAPITAL	LABOR	RENTAL RATE, $ per week	WAGE RATE, $ per week	UNIT COST	WAGE-RENTAL RATIO	CAPITAL-LABOR RATIO
Technique 1	12	12	150	100	_____	_____	_____
Technique 2	6	18	150	100	_____	_____	_____
Technique 1	12	12	150	175	_____	_____	_____
Technique 2	6	18	150	175	_____	_____	_____

quantity of hours worked (third column) are provided. Assuming a price level index of 250 percent, calculate the real wage for each nominal wage.

   a. Graph the supply of labor curve for this worker. Label the vertical axis "real wage" and the horizontal axis "number of hours worked."

   b. For real wages between 0.80 and 4.40 per hour, the (income/substitution) _____ effect dominates, while at a real wage greater than 4.40, the (income/substitution) _____ effect is dominant.

   c. The supply curve you drew in **a** is called the _____ supply of labor curve.

5. Table 13-5 presents two alternative production techniques, each capable of producing 500 widgets per week.

   a. Compute the unit cost of producing the 500 widgets, the wage-rental ratio, and the capital-labor ratio. Complete the table.

   b. Technique 2 is (more/less) _____ labor-intensive than technique 1 as shown by the (wage-rental/capital-labor) _____ ratio.

   c. When labor costs $100 per unit and capital costs $150 per unit, the firm will select technique _____ to produce widgets since the unit costs are lowest.

   d. If labor costs increase to $175, the firm selects technique _____, and production becomes more _____-intensive as shown by the _____ ratio.

FILL-IN QUESTIONS

1. The firm's *MVPL* curve is its _____ curve for labor and is based upon the _____ of labor and the _____ of the firm's output.

2. If capital and labor are poor substitutes in production, the industry demand curve for labor is (more/less) _____ elastic and (steeper/flatter) _____ than the demand curve would be if capital and labor were close substitutes.

3. The demand for a factor of production is a _____ demand since it depends on the demand for the firm's output.

4. When the real wage goes up, the individual worker is expected to supply more labor if the (income/substitution) _____ effect dominates and less labor if the (income/substitution) _____ effect is dominant.

5. At the aggregate level, the labor supply curve for the economy is thought to be (upward-sloping/backward-bending) _____ since any change in wages affects the _____ participation rate as people either enter or leave the labor force.

6. In its attempt to maximize profits, a firm will hire additional units of a factor up to the point at which the _____ of the extra unit hired equals the extra _____ created by the factor for the firm.

7. The industry demand curve for labor (is/is not) _____ simply the sum of each individual firm's *MVPL* schedule.

8. As wages increase relative to the cost of capital, we would expect the wage-rental ratio to (increase/decrease) _____ and the capital-labor ratio to (increase/decrease) _____ as (more/less) _____ capital is substituted for labor.

9. A change in output price or a change in the productivity of labor causes the firm's demand curve for labor to _____, while a change in the wage rate causes a (shift in/movement along) _____ the *MVPL* curve.

10. The equilibrium wage and employment level in an industry are determined by the intersection of the industry _____ for and the market _____ of labor.

11. Better education, job training, and health can

FACTOR MARKETS AND DERIVED DEMAND: LABOR

improve the economy's stock of _____ capital.

12. If a factor of production has a completely inelastic supply, it is likely that an _____ will be paid to the factor.

TRUE-FALSE QUESTIONS

1. _____ If the wage-rental ratio changed from 13.4 to 0.872, we would expect more capital and less labor to be used in production.

2. _____ If the *MVPL* is less than the wage paid for labor, the firm can increase its profits by reducing the amount of labor hired.

3. _____ The backward-bending supply of labor curve suggests that at higher wages, workers supply more labor, and their income increases.

4. _____ The real wage reflects the purchasing power of the nominal wage.

5. _____ For a given product demand schedule, an increase in industry supply can drive the wages paid to labor downward.

6. _____ Relatively small industries employing unskilled labor face an upward-sloping supply of labor curve.

7. _____ For a given product price, the marginal value product of labor curve is downward-sloping because the marginal product of labor declines as more labor is used.

8. _____ The wages paid in one industry will never influence the wages paid in other industries.

9. _____ Increases in investment in either physical or human capital cause the quantity demanded for the labor input to increase at a given real wage and hence put pressure on the real wage to rise.

10. _____ For men of prime working age, evidence suggests that the income effect of a wage change dominates the substitution effect; hence, the supply of labor curve is backward-bending.

11. _____ An increase in the wage might cause more workers to enter the market and look for work, but since they are unemployed, the labor force participation rate falls.

12. _____ It is not uncommon for firms over the long run to adjust their work schedule to suit their employees, assuming any costs are minimal.

13. _____ There is no basis at all for the argument that the minimum wage increases the level of unemployment.

MULTIPLE CHOICE QUESTIONS

Circle the correct answer.

1. Which of the following statements is incorrect?
   a. economic rents initially were applied only to the money paid for the use of the land factor
   b. for an inelastic supply of a factor, rent is the difference between what is actually paid for the factor and the amount it would take to get the factor into its existing use
   c. rents are present because the demand for factors is a derived demand
   d. all of the above statements are incorrect

2. The equalizing differential in wages exists because
   a. all jobs require an equal productivity of labor
   b. there is a difference in the attractiveness of jobs
   c. different industries have different demands for labor
   d. there are large differences across countries in the capital-labor ratio used in the same industries

3. If there is an overall increase in the productivity of labor employed by a firm and the market wage doesn't change, the firm will
   a. hire more workers at the going wage rate
   b. hire fewer workers at the going wage rate
   c. hire more workers only if the wage falls
   d. cause the firm to substitute more capital for labor

4. The industry demand for labor curve is influenced by
   a. price changes in the industry's output
   b. the substitutability between capital and labor
   c. the elasticity of demand for the industry's product
   d. all of the above
   e. none of the above

5. The individual's backward-bending supply of labor curve might occur because
   a. the income effect is dominated by the substitution effect
   b. the supply of labor curve for the economy begins to bend backward at higher wages
   c. the income effect dominates the substitution effect
   d. individuals always want to work more at higher wages

6. A small, highly competitive, nonspecialized firm will face a supply of labor curve which is
   a. backward-bending   **c.** highly inelastic
   b. highly elastic   **d.** vertical

7. In an expanding industry, we would expect

a. wages to be higher than in nonexpanding industries
b. labor to move from declining industries to the expanding industry
c. a large quantity demanded of labor in the expanding industry
d. increasing wages in the industry relative to wages in some other sectors and a decreasing level of employment in contracting industries
e. all of the above

8. The average real wage in the economy is determined by
a. the capital stock
b. the stock of human capital
c. social customs
d. all of the above
e. none of the above

9. The marginal value product of labor
a. measures the cost of hiring one additional worker
b. measures the contribution to revenue of hiring one additional worker
c. measures the contribution to total revenue as a result of selling 1 more unit of output
d. reflects the cost of hiring labor

10. We would say that all of the following reflect the concept of derived demand except
a. the demand for automobiles increases, and as a result, the demand for auto workers increases
b. an increase in the demand for shoes causes the demand for shoe leather to increase
c. a decline in beef prices causes the demand for pork to fall
d. an increase in the demand for toothpicks causes the demand for lumber to increase

AT THIS POINT YOU SHOULD BE ABLE TO . . .

1. Define and give examples of the concept of derived demand for a factor of production.
2. Explain the meaning of and reasons for the existence of equalizing differentials in wages between jobs.
3. Explain the meaning of the wage-rental ratio and the capital-labor ratio, and explain the roles played by these ratios in determining a firm's optimal technique of production.
4. Define the marginal value product of labor and state the impact of a change in either labor productivity or output price on the firm's demand for labor.
5. Determine the marginal value product of labor curve from a given set of production, output, and price data; state the optimal employment rule; and explain how a firm determines its equilibrium level of employment.
6. List the determinants of labor demand and explain how the firm's demand schedule changes when the determinants change.
7. Explain the importance of input substitution in determining the firm's optimal production technique.
8. Define both nominal wages and real wages.
9. Show how the industry demand schedule for labor is determined and how it differs from that of a firm, and state the determinants of the elasticity of industry demand for labor.
10. Explain how the supply of labor curve differs for an individual, the industry, and the economy.
11. Show diagrammatically how an industry labor market equilibrium is established.
12. Define the concept of an economic rent.

QUESTIONS FOR THOUGHT

1. The optimal employment rule states that a firm will hire labor up to the point at which *MVPL* equals the wage paid for the last worker. Verbally and graphically explain the operation of the rule and explain why the firm stops hiring when *MVPL* equals wage.

2. Some businessmen and conservative politicians argue that the reason so many young people are unemployed is that the minimum wage is too high. In order to increase employment, they argue, the minimum wage should be lowered. Explain their reasoning in terms of a firm's and industry's demand for labor schedule. Do you think that employment assistance to firms in the form of either a direct cash subsidy or a tax credit will induce firms to hire workers when their *MVPL* is less than the minimum wage? Explain.

3. Why does the firm's demand curve for labor slope downward? How are the demand curve for labor and the consumer's demand curve for the firm's output similar? How are they different?

4. Suppose that an industry hired two types of labor: highly skilled and nonskilled. Which group would exhibit the more elastic demand? Explain.

5. One of your friends recently complained about certain NFL players receiving such ridiculously high salaries (when they are not on strike) relative to members of other professions. It is up to you to calm him down. How would you explain such salaries in terms of economic rents? Be specific.

6. Explain the backward-bending supply of labor curve for an individual and also explain how such a curve would be transformed into an upward-sloping supply of labor curve for the economy in general.

APPENDIX: ISOQUANTS AND THE CHOICE OF PRODUCTION TECHNIQUE

The appendix to Chapter 13 presents a different way of describing how the firm chooses the optimal technique of production and its input combination. In the appendix, you see how isoquants and the firm's operating budget are used to determine the input combination which minimizes the cost of producing a specific level of output. An isoquant shows the many combinations of inputs which can produce a given level of output. The producer has numerous possible combinations available, with each capable of generating the desired output level. Every possible combination of inputs will be on some isoquant contained in the firm's isoquant map.

The producer selects the input combination which generates a tangency between the firm's operating budget line and an isoquant. This input combination will be optimal in the sense that the highest output possible is being produced, given input prices and the operating budget. A change in input prices or in the operating budget causes the producer to search for a new optimal input combination, output level, and production technique.

CHAPTER OUTLINE

1. An isoquant shows the different input combinations capable of producing a given level of output. An isoquant map is a complete listing of all production techniques which can produce all possible output levels.
2. Any point on an isoquant corresponds to a particular production technique capable of producing a given level of output. On the isoquant map, production techniques requiring more of both inputs corresponds to higher output levels and are located on higher isoquants.
3. An isoquant map exhibits four important properties.
   a. Isoquants cannot intersect since each corresponds to a different level of output.
   b. The spacing of isoquants is caused by returns to scale.
   c. Isoquants are downward-sloping.
   d. The slope of an isoquant decreases, which causes the isoquant to curve inward. The decreasing slope is significant because it represents the increasing difficulties of input substitution as the producer moves toward either input extreme.
4. The firm's operating budget can be drawn in the space containing the isoquant map. The operating budget is graphed as a straight line with a slope equal to the ratio of input prices (wage-rental ratio). The slope shows the trade-off existing among the inputs. Any point on the operating budget line is an input combination which can be achieved and will exhaust the firm's operating budget. The firm chooses the optimal production technique and input combination by moving to the point of tangency between an isoquant and the operating budget line. The point of tangency shows the highest output level attainable given the operating budget and input prices.
5. Any change in the relative price of factors causes the operating budget line to rotate. The firm substitutes inputs and changes its production technique.

EXERCISES

1. Table 13-6 presents two production schedules for widgets. The schedule $Q_1 = f_1(K,L)$ and $Q_2 = f_2(K,L)$ use inputs of capital K and labor L. Schedule Q_1 shows the different combinations of capital and labor capable of producing 500 units of output per week, while schedule Q_2 shows the input combinations capable of producing 300 units per week. The firm has an operating budget of $1200. Capital costs $40 per unit, and the wage rate is $30 per unit of labor.

TABLE 13-6

$Q_1 = 500$		$Q_2 = 300$	
CAPITAL (K)	LABOR (L)	CAPITAL (K)	LABOR (L)
30	10	34	6
24	12	26	8
18	16	18	12
14	24	14	16
12	32	10	20
		8	26
		6	32

The firm's operating budget can be written as:

Total cost = (price of capital)(K) + (price of labor)(L)

$$TC = P_K K + P_L L$$

   a. Given your operating budget, on graph paper plot the operating budget constraint. Measure units of capital on the vertical axis in increments of 2 from zero to 40. On the horizontal axis, measure units of labor in increments of 2 from zero to 56. If the firm purchased no labor, the maximum amount of capital that could be purchased is _____ units. The slope of this operating budget constraint is the ratio of input prices, just as the slope of the consumer's budget line is the ratio of good prices.

   b. Plot the two production schedules Q_1 and Q_2 on

your graph. Smooth the curves as well as you can. You have drawn the production isoquants.

c. Label the isoquants $Q_1 = 500$; $Q_2 = 300$. Isoquant Q_1 lies (above/below) _____ isoquant Q_2 and reflects a greater output level. Any isoquant above and to the right of isoquant Q_1 would represent a (greater/lesser) _____ output.

d. Given the operating budget and the production schedules, the maximum amount of output the firm can produce is _____ widgets. In order to produce this level of output, the firm uses _____ units of capital and _____ units of labor and has $_____ of its operating budget remaining.

e. Label your equilibrium point A. At the equilibrium point, the capital-labor ratio is _____, and the wage-rental (price of labor to price of capital) ratio is _____.

f. Draw a line from the origin to the tangency point between the operating budget constraint and the isoquant. The slope of the line OA from the origin can be computed by selecting a vertical quantity on the line and dividing by the corresponding horizontal quantity. The measure of the vertical quantity is (capital/labor) _____, and the measure of the horizontal is (capital/labor) _____; hence, the slope of the line through the origin is the _____ ratio.

g. Now let the price of capital increase from $40 to $60. The operating budget constraint will (shift/rotate) _____ and intersect the vertical axis at _____ units of capital. The slope of the operating budget constraint has (increased/decreased) _____. Draw the new operating budget constraint. The increase in the price of capital relative to the price of labor forces the producer to attain a new equilibrium on isoquant _____; output has (increased/decreased) _____.

h. On isoquant Q_2, the producer uses _____ units of the more expensive capital and _____ units of the relatively less expensive labor; the producer has substituted _____ for _____.

The new capital-labor ratio is _____. Label the tangency point between Q_2 and the new operating budget constraint B. A line from the origin (line OB) is the capital-labor ratio and is (steeper/flatter) _____ than line OA, the initial capital-labor ratio. At point B, the wage-rental ratio is _____.

i. Suppose that the producer must produce 500 widgets per week, even if the price of capital has increased. The firm will need (more/less) _____ money for its operating budget. Draw a new operating budget line exactly parallel to the line tangent to isoquant Q_2 at point B. This new parallel line must be drawn so that it is tangent to some point on isoquant Q_1 since the producer has to produce 500 units of output. The new operating budget line reflects the price of capital as $60 and the price of labor as $30 since it has the same slope as the operating budget line after the price of capital increased.

j. Label the point of tangency between the new parallel operating budget constraint and the isoquant Q_1 as point C. At point C, the firm uses _____ units of capital and _____ units of labor. The capital-labor ratio is _____. Draw a line from the origin to C (line OC) to reflect the new capital-labor ratio. The line OC is (steeper/flatter) _____ than line OB.

k. In order for the firm to produce 500 widgets after the price of capital rises from $40 to $60 and the price of labor remains at $30, the original operating budget of $1200 must be increased by $_____ to $_____.

FILL-IN QUESTIONS

1. Each point on an isoquant corresponds to a particular production _____ which can be used to produce a given level of output.

2. The presence of numerous isoquants, each representing different output levels capable of being produced by different techniques, is called an _____.

3. As we move down an isoquant, the rate at which one input can be subsituted for another in production (increases/decreases) _____, and as a result, the slope of an isoquant (is/is not) _____ constant.

4. The producer can maximize output for a given level of costs by producing with the technique which provides a point of tangency between the _____ and the _____.

5. Any change in the price of one input will cause the

operating budget line to (shift/rotate) _____; the _____ ratio will change, the producer _____ the relatively less expensive input for the more expensive, and overall output (does/does not) _____ change.

TRUE-FALSE QUESTIONS

1. ____ For any isoquant map, as you move upward from the origin, the level of output decreases.

2. ____ The slope of the operating budget line is negative and is the ratio of the input prices.

3. ____ If the firm's operating budget increases, given input prices, the operating budget line makes a parallel shift away from the origin.

4. ____ For any two isoquants which intersect, the output level shown by the higher isoquant is greater than the output shown in the lower curve.

5. ____ If the ratio of relative factor prices changes, the firm will attain a new equilibrium on a different isoquant.

MULTIPLE-CHOICE QUESTIONS

Circle the correct answer.

1. The operating budget line is like the
   a. demand curve faced by the consumer
   b. consumer's budget line
   c. firm's total revenue curve
   d. long-run total cost curve

2. A profit-maximizing firm would not use an input combination to produce a given output other than that represented by the tangency point between an isoquant and the operating budget line because
   a. it would not be producing the desired level of output
   b. output can be increased while costs remain constant
   c. a different production technique will result in higher output
   d. it is not maximizing output for a given level of cost
   e. all of the above

3. Any point on an isoquant is
   a. a given input combination capable of producing various levels of output
   b. a particular combination of inputs capable of producing a given level of output
   c. a point of minimum production costs
   d. none of the above

4. For any set of isoquants, the distance between the curves reflects
   a. diminishing returns to factors
   b. the cost of production, given input costs and requirements
   c. returns to scale
   d. returns to factors
   e. none of the above

5. If all input prices increase by 20 percent
   a. the firm's operating budget line shifts to the left toward the origin
   b. the operating budget line shifts to the right away from the origin
   c. the operating budget line rotates about its vertical axis intercept
   d. the operating budget line rotates about the horizontal axis intercept

AT THIS POINT YOU SHOULD BE ABLE TO . . .

1. Define an isoquant and an isoquant map.
2. Show how different input combinations capable of producing a particular output level can be joined to form an isoquant.
3. Define the firm's operating budget and show how the operating budget line can be presented graphically for given input prices.
4. Use the isoquant and operating budget line to determine the firm's optimal input combination required for the production of a particular level of output.
5. Explain the effect of a change in factor prices on the firm's operating budget line, optimal input combination, and level of output.
6. Explain the process of input substitution using isoquants and the operating budget line.
7. State how returns to scale can be shown using isoquants.

QUESTIONS FOR THOUGHT

1. Suppose an isoquant is a straight line. What does such an isoquant suggest about the rate of substitution of the inputs? Can anything be said about the substitutability of the inputs?

14

Human Capital, Discrimination, and Trade Unions

The central theme of Chapter 14 is that different types and qualities of labor are present in the labor market, and so wage differentials exist. In Chapter 13, you learned that the wage rate was determined by the demand for and supply of labor. The demand for labor was determined by the marginal value product of labor, which assumes that within a particular occupation, all labor is equally productive. This means that the marginal productivity of labor is equal. In the real world, however, productivity and wages differ within the same occupation. Chapter 14 examines the reasons for such differences and argues that to some extent wage inequality may be explained by both qualitative and productivity differentials of labor. But in many cases, differences in wages are present for other reasons.

Chapter 14 begins with a discussion of human capital. Human capital is the income-earning potential embodied in individuals. People possess different quantities and types of human capital, and this explains some of the wage differences observed in the labor market. One of the basic investments in human capital is education. As an individual invests in education through formal schooling or on-the-job training, certain skills are developed. These skills improve the productivity of labor, and it is reasonable to expect the firm to distinguish between different productivities of labor by paying different wages.

Not all observed wage differences are explained by the human capital approach, however. Sex and race discrimination occur in the labor market. When some workers are discriminated against, it affects not only the wages they receive but also the types of jobs they secure. In the past, the jobs open to women and nonwhites paid relatively poorly and provided very little prestige. Even within the same occupation, women and nonwhites often are paid less than their white male counterparts. Discrimination occurs not only in job access but in the access to educational skills as well.

A third source of wage differences is organized labor. Unions seek to raise wages by controlling the supply of labor to industry, and so they assume the role of a monopolist. Because of a restricted labor supply, union wages are higher than those paid to nonunion workers. The working conditions for union workers are often less desirable than the conditions faced by nonunion workers, and some economists see the wage differentials as a compensation for the different working conditions and types of work performed by union labor.

CHAPTER OUTLINE

1. Human capital is the value of the income earnings potential embodied in individuals as a result of investments in the individual. Investment in human capital enhances the productivity and thus the income potential of the human factor of production. The payoff from investment in human capital is usually in the form of a higher earnings stream; however, it may also take nonmonetary forms. A major type of investment in human capital is investment in education.

   a. Age-earnings profiles of white male workers show that education increases earning ability. Two possible reasons for this increased earning capacity are that people who attain higher levels of education have greater natural ability than those with less education and that education gives the individual special skills and organizing abilities which are useful in production.

   b. In the market for educated workers, employers usually are willing to pay a premium for individuals who have completed a college degree as opposed to workers who have completed only high school. The underlying reason for such a wage premium is the belief that the college graduate is more productive. In the long run, the wage differential between college graduates and high school graduates narrows as the market forces of supply and demand operate to either increase or decrease the demand for and supply of college-trained workers. Higher wages paid to college graduates encourage more high school graduates to

attend college, and so the overall supply of college-educated workers increases in the long run.
- c. The high school graduate faces two major career choices: whether to enter college or enter the labor force. If the individual considers only the investment component of attaining a college degree, he must weigh both the costs and benefits of the additional years of education. The individual costs of education consist of the direct out-of-pocket costs for tuition, books, supplies, etc., and the opportunity cost of forgoing 4 years of income which is lost as a result of the individual not being in the labor market. The benefits are primarily in the form of higher earnings for the individual after completing a college education. When making the decision whether to attend college, the rational individual weighs both the costs and benefits.
    - (1) If the costs of an education are treated as an investment expenditure which pays a future return in the form of benefits, it is possible to determine the rate of interest which is required to generate this stream of future benefits, given the initial investment. This interest rate is called the rate of return to a college education.
    - (2) Studies show that the rate of return to college training in the United States is in excess of 10 percent. Any change in the cost of going to college or the benefits received from a college education changes the rate of return and the financial payoff.
    - (3) Because of the length of time involved in obtaining a college degree, market conditions can change as surpluses or shortages of college graduates appear on the job market. It is possible that quantity supplied and price fluctuate around, but do not attain, a market equilibrium.
- d. Like formal education, time spent on a job and on-the-job training can generate higher income levels, higher age-earnings profiles, and greater wage differentials. On-the-job training provides the worker with both firm-specific and general human capital. The longer the worker stays on the job and the more firm-specific on-the-job training is acquired, the more valuable he is to the firm. This leads to higher wages.
- e. Human capital and the market forces of demand and supply can be used to analyze the returns to professional athletes and artists. Such professions require extensive training, skill development, and talent.
- f. The return to human capital and higher education can be used to explain some pay differentials between college faculty members who teach different subjects.
- g. The signaling hypothesis argues that education itself does not necessarily enhance a worker's productivity. According to the hypothesis, education signals potential employers that the job applicant is proficient at performing certain tasks that might also be useful in the workplace. Evidence on the signaling hypothesis is limited, and so no conclusions can be drawn as to whether college training itself contributes anything to enhance worker productivity.

2. Income levels, access to jobs, and access to economic opportunities are not the same for members of different groups in the labor force. Such labor market inequalities are a result of discrimination.
    - a. Discrimination in access to good jobs, access to education, and higher wages accounts for the main difference in economic status between different groups in the labor force.
        - (1) Employment and income data show that in many occupations, women and nonwhite workers are more often in low-paying, less desirable jobs whereas white men dominate the higher-paying, more desirable jobs. The major reason for the dominance by white men in the better-paying jobs is sexual and racial discrimination. This lack of access to better jobs explains in part why blacks have a higher unemployment rate than whites. Statistical discrimination in access to jobs occurs when the employer judges an applicant not on the basis of individual qualifications but rather on the basis of the average qualifications of the applicant's peer group. Under such discriminatory conditions, the incentive to invest in education is reduced.
        - (2) If discrimination prevents members of different groups and those with different backgrounds from having access to quality education, members of these groups will be hindered in the choice of jobs and the ability to improve their economic well-being.
        - (3) Both sexual and racial discrimination frequently take the form of unequal pay for equal work.
    - b. Since the 1960s, the earnings differential between male and female, white and nonwhite

workers has narrowed significantly; however, the differential still exists. Also, there is easier access to better jobs and education for members of minority groups and women. The reasons for these improvements can be found in the general tendency not to discriminate. The Civil Rights Act of 1964 and other laws were designed to provide better economic opportunities for all groups and resulted in improved motivation by nonwhites for education. These reasons for improvement, however, are not accepted by everyone.
   c. Discrimination in any form is economically costly in terms of income and profits forgone as well as a general misallocation of labor and reduced aggregate output.
3. The role of unions in the labor market as they influence wages and working conditions is controversial. Unions are seen by some as being a balancing force whose purpose is to protect labor's interests against powerful industries.
   a. The percentage of the labor force belonging to unions has been declining since the early 1960s. The establishment of the American Federation of Labor (AFL) in 1886 by Samuel Gompers marked the beginning of the trade union movement in the United States. Under Gompers, labor unions worked within the capitalist system and were not aligned to any political party. Gompers's view of the role of unions differed from that of the more socialist European labor organization, which believed that unionism and politics were interwoven.
      (1) The creation of the Congress of Industrial Organization (CIO) in 1936 and the passage of the Wagner Act in 1935 are the two major reasons for union membership nearly doubling between 1936 and 1938. The CIO's main objective was to organize labor by industry. The Wagner Act made it easier for unions to organize in factories and permitted unions to take legal action against employers who opposed unionization of their work force.
      (2) The Taft-Hartley Act was passed in response to a general attitude that unions were too powerful, and it greatly weakened the unions. This act outlawed the closed shop but permitted the existence of the union shop. It also permitted states to pass right-to-work laws designed to outlaw the union shop. The act also permits the President to postpone strikes by unions for a period of 80 days.
      (3) In 1955, after a split of 19 years, the AFL-CIO reunited; it remains today the major U.S. labor organization.
      (4) Generally, union membership has been declining in recent years because the demand for goods has decreased, resulting in a decrease in the demand for blue-collar labor, and because formal opposition to organized labor has increased. The only area in which union membership has increased is among public employees.
   b. The traditional union function is to offset the firm's relative strength in controlling its employees. The union also tries to improve its members' economic well-being by controlling and restricting the supply of labor to the firm.
      (1) By controlling the supply of labor, the union acts as a monopoly seller to the firm and can increase the wages of its members. However, by establishing a wage higher than that which would be established in a competitive labor market, the union reduces the quantity of labor demanded by the firm, and so the union's membership potential falls. The elasticity of the firm's demand curve for labor determines the union's success in raising wages as it restricts the labor supply. As unions raise the relative wage of union labor, the relative costs and prices of goods produced by union labor increase.
      (2) The percentage of employees unionized within various occupations can produce substantial wage differentials between unionized and nonunion labor.
      (3) The union wage differential results from the union's monopoly power as it restricts the labor supply and from the compensating differential paid to labor for working in more structured settings. Unionized firms expect labor to be more productive, accept inflexible hours and overtime, and set a faster work pace. However, the unions' ability to restrict the labor supply is a major factor in explaining the wage differential.
   c. Strikes by unions against firms cause only a small loss in workdays per employee per year. The possibility of a strike is an element in the bargaining process between labor and management; however, strikes are not the usual method of reaching agreements between labor and management.

IMPORTANT TERMS AND THEIR MEANING

Match the following terms with the correct definition or phrase.

1. _____ Formed in 1886; represents the beginning of modern trade unionism in the United States

2. _____ The value of the income-earning potential embodied in individuals

3. _____ Describes the firm which is prohibited from hiring any workers unless they belong to the union

4. _____ Judging qualifications of members of a particular group on the characteristics of that group; two equally qualified individuals who are from different groups are judged differently

5. _____ The nonmonetary value of a college education

6. _____ Outlawed the closed shop and permitted the President to order an 80-day cooling-off period during labor disputes

7. _____ The relationship between income and age for a particular individual or group of individuals

8. _____ Attempts to organize labor by industries instead of crafts

9. _____ Special training for labor which is useful only in a particular firm

10. _____ Founder of the modern labor movement in the United States; headed the AFL

11. _____ The interest rate needed to produce the benefits of education, given the costs of gaining an education

12. _____ The hypothesis that college training does not increase the productivity of graduates but simply demonstrates to employers that graduates have certain desirable characteristics

13. _____ Adopted by some states; prohibits union membership from being a condition of employment

14. _____ Knowledge that can be used by the worker on any job

15. _____ Prohibited employers from engaging in unfair labor practices and made it easy for workers to organize into unions

16. _____ Requirement that anyone hired by a unionized firm must become a union member within 30 days.

a. Union shop
b. Consumption value of education
c. Right-to-work law
d. AFL
e. Signaling
f. General human capital
g. Samuel Gompers
h. Statistical discrimination
i. Human capital
j. CIO
k. Firm-specific capital
l. Wagner Act
m. Rate of return to education
n. Age-earnings profile
o. Closed shop
p. Taft-Hartley Act

EXERCISES

1. Presented in Table 14-1 are five possible college degree programs: A, B, C, D, and E. The expected annual income after 4 years of college is presented in the first column. The second column shows what could have been earned if employment had begun immediately after high school, assuming an hourly wage of $7.21. It costs $28,000 out of pocket and $2000 in interest (since some money is borrowed) to attend college. These cost data are presented in the fourth and fifth columns. While in school, you earn nothing. All data are hypothetical. An 18-year-old high school graduate may choose to work or go to college. Mandatory retirement age is 58 years. The earnings are assumed to be constant over the individual's working life.

   a. Based on the above data, complete Table 14-2.
   b. The major generating the highest net contribution to lifetime earnings is _____. The opportunity cost of the 4 years of college is $_____.
   c. If an individual selects major C, the net con-

TABLE 14-1

MAJOR	(1) ANNUAL INCOME AFTER COLLEGE DEGREE, $	(2) ANNUAL INCOME WITHOUT COLLEGE TRAINING, $	TOTAL OUT-OF-POCKET COSTS, $	INTEREST COSTS, $
A	20,000	15,000	28,000	2000
B	31,000	15,000	28,000	2000
C	16,000	15,000	28,000	2000
D	50,000	15,000	28,000	2000
E	18,500	15,000	28,000	2000

TABLE 14-2

MAJOR	PROJECTED LIFETIME INCOME WITH COLLEGE, $	PROJECTED LIFTEIME INCOME WITHOUT COLLEGE, $	TOTAL COST OF EDUCATION, $	NET CONTRIBUTION TO LIFETIME EARNINGS OF COLLEGE DEGREE, $
A				
B				
C				
D				
E				

tribution of going to college is (positive/negative) _____; selecting such a program of study probably indicates a very high (consumption/investment) _____ value placed on the course content of the major.

2. The demand for labor schedules for two firms (A and B) are presented in Table 14-3.

TABLE 14-3

WAGE, $	QUANTITY OF LABOR DEMANDED, FIRM A	QUANTITY OF LABOR DEMANDED, FIRM B
15	4	0
12	5	3
9	6	6
6	7	9
3	8	12

  a. Draw both demand for labor curves on graph paper. Lable firm A's demand curve $MVPL_A$ and firm B's curve $MVPL_B$.
  b. Firm A's demand for labor curve is (more/less) _____ elastic than firm B's, and so we would expect firm A to be (more/less) _____ responsive to a wage change.
  c. If the initial equilibrium wage rate is $9 per unit of labor, both firms hire _____ units. Draw a line from $9 to the MVPL curves.
  d. Suppose a union negotiates wages up to $12 per unit. Firm A hires _____ units, and firm B hires _____ units. If possible, the union would prefer that all demand for labor curves be like that of firm _____ since a large increase in wages results in a relatively small cutback in _____. Draw a line from $12 on the vertical axis to the MVPL curves.

FILL-IN QUESTIONS

1. The human capital theory argues that by investing in education, labor's _____ productivity increases, and as a result, higher wages are paid.

2. In the short run, the supply of college graduates is highly (elastic/inelastic) _____; however, in the long run, the supply curve becomes more (vertical/horizontal) _____.

3. Nonpecuniary returns on the (consumption/investment) _____ value of education often cause the rate of return to college education to be (understated/overstated) _____.

4. The (real/money) _____ rate of return to an investment in a college education adjust the interest rate for inflation.

5. (Firm-specific/General) _____ human capital can be moved easily with workers as they change jobs.

6. The signaling hypothesis argues that a college education (may/may not) _____ contribute to worker productivity.

7. The main sources of differences in economic status between groups in the labor force are the _____ held by each group and differences in _____ received for the same job.

8. Statistical discrimination occurs when an employer judges an individual on the basis of the characteristics exhibited by the (individual/group) _____ and can serve to (increase/reduce) _____ the investment in education for those who consider themselves discriminated against.

9. On-the-job discrimination often takes the form of paying workers (the same/differently) _____ for performing the same tasks.

10. The American Federation of Labor was organized primarily to include only (craft/industrial) _____ workers, while the CIO was organized to include (craft/industrial) _____ workers.

HUMAN CAPITAL, DISCRIMINATION, AND TRADE UNIONS

11. Requiring that firms bargain in good faith with unions was a provision of the (Taft-Hartley Act/Wagner Act/Right-to-work laws) _____.

12. A union acts as (a monopolist/an oligopolist/a competitor) _____ by restricting the supply of labor to the firm and as a result can gain a (higher/lower) _____ relative wage for its members.

13. The presence of _____ laws in some states makes it (easier/more difficult) _____ for unions to organize.

14. One view of union wages is that part of the wage differential (taxes/compensates) _____ labor for having to work in a more rigid environment.

15. Unions usually (do/do not) _____ resort to a strike against the firm in order to settle disputes.

TRUE-FALSE QUESTIONS

1. _____ The premium paid to college graduates is the difference between their wages and the wages paid to high school graduates.

2. _____ An example of personal investment in human capital is the auto mechanic buying a new set of metric wrenches.

3. _____ In 1979, 16 percent of the population over age 25 had a college degree.

4. _____ Generally speaking, the wage differentials between college graduates and high school graduates is not an important factor in deciding whether to attend college.

5. _____ Proponents of the signaling hypothesis believe that college signals potential employers that because individuals have attended college, they are more productive.

6. _____ The jobs least open to women and nonwhites are those requiring professional training.

7. _____ One way in which discrimination has been practiced is by denying minorities access to education.

8. _____ The majority of clerical jobs in the United States in 1980 were held by women, while men dominated the craft industries.

9. _____ The Civil Rights Act of 1964 permitted the federal government to use its powers to prohibit age, sexual, or racial discrimination.

10. _____ Most unions in the United States take an active political role in shaping national policy.

11. _____ Under the Wagner Act of 1935, firms could prohibit workers from organizing.

12. _____ In any state with a right-to-work law, the influence of unions is reduced.

13. _____ The percentage of the work force currently belonging to a union has declined during the past two decades.

14. _____ The union's only goal is to increase the income of its members.

15. _____ If new members are easily admitted to union membership, the union will not be as effective in raising relative wages.

16. _____ Much of union labor enjoys better working conditions and more break-time and has higher quit rates than nonunion labor.

17. _____ When labor and management have disagreements, the union probably will call for a strike.

MULTIPLE CHOICE QUESTIONS

1. One of the early leaders of the American labor movement was
    a. Samuel Gompers   **c.** Howard Taft
    b. James Hoffa   **d.** George Meany

2. Wage differentials in the United States can be attributed to
    a. different levels of human capital embodied in labor
    b. labor market discrimination
    c. the presence of unions in some industries
    d. all of the above
    e. none of the above

3. A labor union assumes the role of a(n)
    a. oligopolist   **d.** price leader
    b. cartel   **e.** none of the above
    c. monopolist

4. Which of the following describe age-earnings profiles?
    a. they tend to become flatter as workers enter middle age
    b. the more educated an individual, the higher the profile
    c. the more educated individual has a larger forgone income because of later entry into the labor force
    d. all of the above
    e. none of the above

5. If the demand curve for college graduates shifted to the left, we would expect
  a. the short-run equilibrium wage to rise
  b. the short-run equilibrium wage to fall
  c. the long-run equilibrium wage to rise
  d. the short-run equilibrium quantity to rise
  e. none of the above

6. When deciding whether to attend college, the rational individual must consider the
  a. direct out-of-pocket costs
  b. increased income stream after graduation
  c. consumption value of education
  d. forgone income as a result of not working
  e. all of the above

7. Training a worker to perform a task which is useful only on his current job is an example of
  a. statistical discrimination
  b. firm-specific human capital
  c. general human capital
  d. generalized on-the-job training

8. Under the signaling hypothesis, it is believed that
  a. a college degree doesn't add directly to a worker's marginal productivity
  b. pay differentials result from different productivities of labor
  c. a college degree informs potential employers about certain desirable attributes possessed by the graduate
  d. all of the above
  e. none of the above

9. The nonwhite to white male earnings ratio in 1978 was
  a. 0.60   **c.** 0.74
  b. 0.57   **d.** 0.93

10. According to Table 15-7 in your text, nonwhite women are most rarely found in which of the following occupations?
  a. service workers   **c.** nonfarm labor
  b. crafts   **d.** professionals

11. Which of the following statements best describes the general attitudes toward the government programs in the equal opportunity field in the 1960s and 1970s?
  a. the programs have had mixed results
  b. the programs have been highly successful
  c. the programs have been a dismal failure
  d. none of the above

12. Some economists believe that discrimination will disappear without government intervention because
  a. by not hiring a well-qualified applicant because of personal biases, the producer loses profits
  b. minority groups will become frustrated and leave the labor market
  c. social attitudes are changing toward the direction of complete assimilation of all groups into the mainstream of society
  d. those who are discriminated against often do not buy the output of the producer

AT THIS POINT YOU SHOULD BE ABLE TO . . .

1. Define human capital and state the general argument about the effect of an individual's stock of human capital on earnings.

2. Define and state the characteristics of the age-earnings profile, incorporating into your characteristics the effect of education on the profile.

3. Explain the long-run adjustment processes in the market for educated workers and its effect on the long-run wage differential.

4. Explain the investment component of a college education, define the rate of return to education, and state the principle involved in the use of cost-benefit analysis as applied to education.

5. Explain the relationship between on-the-job training and the age-earnings profile.

6. Describe the progress made in the past two decades in resolving discrimination and define the costs of discrimination.

7. Discuss the early union movement in the United States and state the significance of the Wagner Act, the Taft-Hartley Act, and the right-to-work laws.

8. Define AFL, CIO, union shop, and closed shop; state the reason(s) for the current decline in union membership.

9. Describe how unions attempt to raise members' wages.

10. Graphically present the model showing the union's effect on wages and employment and show how the elasticity of the firm's derived demand curve for labor determines employment levels as unions attempt to raise wages.

11. Explain how unionization influences relative wage levels and explain the role of a union strike in the bargaining process.

QUESTIONS FOR THOUGHT

1. One of the early studies on the rates of return to investment in education was conducted by Professor W. Lee Hansen. The marginal rates of return for different ages and educational levels are presented in Table 14-4.

Looking over Table 14-4, you probably notice that the highest marginal rate of return to investment in education is for an eighth grade education. Explain why the marginal rate of return is highest for the eighth grade.

2. Explain how an investment in human capital in-

TABLE 14-4

U.S. MALES, 1949: MARGINAL RATES OF RETURN TO TOTAL RESOURCE INVESTMENT IN SCHOOLING

AGE	GRADE	MARGINAL RATE OF RETURN, %
7	1–2	8.9
11	3–6	14.5
13	7–8	29.2
15	9–10	9.5
17	11–12	13.7
19	13–14	5.4
21	15–16	15.6

Source: W. Lee Hansen, "Total and Private Rates of Return to Investment in Schooling," *Journal of Political Economy*, LXXXI (April 1963), pp. 128–140.

creases the productivity of labor, raises wages, and increases worker income. Do you agree with this theory? Explain why or why not. Can you identify any weaknesses with the human capital approach to increasing worker income?

3. In a general sense, what are the goals of the equal opportunity programs that began in the 1960s and 1970s? Have these programs been successful? Explain. What is meant by the "statistical illusion" argument that the equal opportunity programs have not been successful?

4. Professors Dornbusch and Fischer state that discrimination imposes costs on the entire economy. What do you think some of these social costs are? Explain.

5. Union membership in the United States as a percentage of the labor force has been declining over the past two decades. What are some of the major reasons for this decline in membership?

6. If you were an owner of a business about to be organized by a union, would you prefer a closed shop or a union shop? Would you support efforts in your state to pass right-to-work laws? Explain your reasons.

7. How do unions attempt to raise wages for their members? What effect do union wages have on the relative wage differential in an area? Can the relative wage differential between union and nonunion labor be explained entirely in terms of productivity differences? Explain.

15 Capital and Land

Chapter 15 is the last of three chapters in which you study factor markets. Chapter 15 focuses on the derived demand for capital and land resources and examines interest and rents as the return to owners of these resources. Interest is earned by the owners of both financial and physical capital; however, the primary emphasis of Chapter 15 is on physical capital. Interest rates (rates of return on capital) serve to allocate physical capital among competing uses. Interest rates also represent the opportunity costs of capital. The return to capital, when compared with its opportunity cost, signals firms to either expand or contract their capital stock. The rent on land is demand-determined since the supply of land is fixed. The land rental rate responds to the demand for different uses and productivities of the factor. The marginal value products of land and capital determine the demand for these resources.

Chapter 15 is organized so that you first are introduced to the concepts of rental payments for capital services, interest rates, and asset prices. It continues through a discussion of the market for capital services, capital asset ownership, and the land market and concludes with a discussion of factor proportions and the rate of return on capital.

Chapter 15 begins by making a distinction between stocks and flows and between the rental payment for capital services and the asset price of capital ownership. You must master the present value concept to understand Chapter 15. Present value is the value of future payments received from a capital asset which may be either rented or owned. The present value of an asset is affected by the productivity of capital.

In the market for capital services, the demand for the services in a particular industry determines the equilibrium rental rate since in the short run, supply is fixed. When the use of other inputs is held constant, the demand for capital services depends on the marginal value product of capital $MVPK$. The $MVPK$, like the marginal value product for labor (presented in Chapter 14), is determined by capital's productivity and the firm's output price. Given the supply of capital services, the equilibrium rental rate is established at the intersection of the $MVPK$ and the supply curves. In order to attain an equilibrium capital stock, capital owners must receive a rental rate such that no gains or losses are incurred. The rate at which this occurs is the required rental rate of capital.

The demand for a capital asset is determined by the present discounted value of the net revenue streams generated by various levels of capital. The demand price of a capital asset is the net revenue from the asset per time period divided by the interest rate. In the short run, the supply of capital assets is perfectly inelastic, but over the long run, the supply is responsive to price changes. A capital asset market equilibrium occurs when the demand price and supply price of capital are equal.

The supply of land is perfectly inelastic, and so rental rates change in response to changes in demand. The demand for land's services is determined by the marginal value product of land. Since land's productivity varies with different uses, the demand for the resource and the rental rate paid for the use of land also vary. As different uses compete for land, urban landscapes and agricultural and natural areas change.

The final section of Chapter 15 is a discussion of the rate of return on capital in the United States. The after-tax return has been about 5 to 8 percent since 1941. During the decade of the 1970s, the rate of return decreased as a result of high unemployment and slow growth in the economy. The rate of investment during the 1970s did not decline drastically. The explanation for this phenomenon lies in the distinction between the average rate of return and the marginal rate of return on capital.

CHAPTER OUTLINE

1. Tangible wealth consists of physical capital (consumer capital, producer capital, and inventories) as well as land and provides a flow of services useful in production or consumption. The composition of tangible capital among nations varies and reflects the economic well-being of each country. Poor nations hold most of their tangible wealth in the form of land, while in rich nations,

wealth exists primarily in the form of structures, producer capital, and consumer durables. Three measures of the role of tangible wealth are the ratio of tangible wealth to national income, the income of tangible wealth as a share of national income, and tangible wealth per worker. Any measure of the current capital stock is difficult to obtain since capital may have a life of many years.

2. In capital markets, it is possible to determine either the rental rate (the cost of using capital services) or the asset price of capital. The asset price of capital is the cost incurred by purchasing the capital, while the rental rate is determined only for the use of capital's services. In order to calculate the asset price, it is necessary to determine an asset's present value as well as nominal and real interest rates.

   a. An asset earns a return over future time periods. The return is based on the prevailing rate of interest. The value of an earning asset today is less than it would be if the asset has had sufficient time to earn a return. The present value of future return (payment) on an asset is the amount of money that would have to be invested today in order to generate exactly the future return (payment) on some specified date in the future. The interest rate and the length of time over which payment takes place determine an asset's present value. At low interest rates and over short periods of time, the present value of an asset is high relative to that asset's present value with high interest rates and longer periods of time.

   b. An asset's price is equal to the sum of the present values for each of the payments in future time periods plus the present value of the scrap value of the asset. The future payments and scrap value must be discounted in order to determine today's present value of the asset. A perpetuity is an asset yielding payments over many future time periods. The perpetuity's price is determined by dividing the annual income from one time period by the interest rate. The size of the interest rate (a measure of the opportunity cost of capital) can affect an asset's price greatly.

   c. The nominal rate of interest is expressed in dollars, while the real rate of interest measures interest rates in terms of what can be bought rather than in dollars. The real rate of interest is approximately equal to the nominal rate minus the inflation rate and may be positive, negative, or zero. The real and nominal interest rates for calculating an asset's present value depend on the specification of the asset's future payments.

   d. The real rate of interest is usually positive because lenders want to receive positive interest for saving and making investment funds available and because productive capital permits borrowers to make a profit after paying for the use of savers' money.

3. The marginal value product of capital $MVPK$ is the contribution to output value resulting from the addition of 1 more unit of capital. Other things equal, the $MVPK$ falls as more capital is added to a given amount of labor and other factors because of diminishing marginal returns to capital. Given a schedule of rental rates, the $MVPK$ curve is the firm's demand curve for capital services, and so the firm hires capital up to the point at which $MVPK$ equals the rental rate paid. Since the firm's demand for capital services is a derived demand, changes in the demand for the firm's output (as well as changes in the market conditions for all other inputs) affect the firm's demand for capital. This causes the $MVPK$ curve to shift. The elasticity of the $MVPK$ curve is influenced by the elasticity of demand for the firm's output. As the level of other inputs (especially labor) increases relative to capital, capital becomes more productive, and so the $MVPK$ curve shifts. The industry demand for capital is obtained by adding the individual firms' demand curves, and so the industry demand curve takes essentially the same shape.

4. The supply of capital changes from the short run to the long run and from the industry to the economy level.

   a. The short-run supply of capital is fixed since an expansion of the capital stock takes time. Thus, the short-run supply curve of capital for the economy is inelastic (vertical). At the industry level, however, the short-run supply curve is vertical only if a specialized type of capital is used. Otherwise, the supply curve is upward-sloping.

   b. In the long run, both the stock of capital and the amount of capital services supplied change. Specialized capital inputs are less important for the industry in the long run because any necessary adjustments can be made.

      (1) The required rental rate on capital is the rental rate that allows the owner of capital to just cover the opportunity cost of owning the capital. At this rental rate, owners of capital receive neither a positive nor a negative gain because the costs to the owners of supplying the capital services are just covered.

      (2) The three factors determining the required rental rate are the price of the

capital good, the real interest rate, and depreciation. If we assume that the interest and depreciation rates are constant, the variable determinant of the required rental rate is the purchase price.

   (3) In the long run, the supply curve for capital services shows the required rental rate on capital at each level of capital services supplied. There are two possibilities. If only the price of capital goods affects the required rental and the economy produces as much capital as it wants at the going price, the required rental rate is constant. Thus, the long-run supply curve of capital is perfectly elastic. On the other hand, if the economy produces more capital only at higher prices, the long-run supply curve is upward-sloping. Both the price of capital and the required rental rate rise as more capital is supplied.

   (4) For a small industry with the ability to purchase its capital at a constant price, the long-run supply curve for capital services faced by the industry is perfectly elastic (horizontal). Thus, the required rental rate is constant.

5. A long-run equilibrium exists in the market for capital services when the quantity supplied equals the quantity demanded. At this equilibrium, the required rental rate and quantity of capital services used in the industry are established.
   a. For any change in the use of other inputs, the demand for capital services changes, and a new equilibrium rental rate and quantity are established. The adjustment process includes both a cost effect and a substitution effect since relative input prices change. The ability to substitute inputs determines the net effect on the demand for capital services when alternative input usage and prices change.
   b. The industry's long-run equilibrium adjustment involves a change in the long-run quantity and the long-run rental rate for capital services as either disinvestment or capital accumulation occurs. For the special case of a completely elastic long-run supply curve, only the quantity adjusts. In the long run, the rental rate of capital services must equal the rate of return on assets in other sectors of the economy; capital's opportunity costs must be covered.
   c. In the short run, most capital is sector-specific, and so it cannot be moved easily into either sectors. The rental rate is primarily demand-determined. In the long run, capital may be highly mobile, and so both demand and supply conditions determine the rental rate.

6. The asset price, as opposed to the rental rate for capital services, is the purchase price of capital. If an asset yields a constant stream of payments over a period of time, the demand price for a capital asset is the present discounted value of the future income stream (after the expenses of owning the asset are deducted from the stream). The present value changes if either future rental rates or the real interest rate changes. The long-run equilibrium price of an asset equals the cost of producing the asset. This equals the present discounted value of rental payments received by the owner. The adjustment process from a short-run to a long-run equilibrium includes expansions and contractions of the capital stock.

7. The demand curve for land is derived from the marginal product of land and the price of the output produced by using the land input. The demand curve for land slopes downward and to the right. Since the quantity of land is fixed, its supply curve is vertical. The equilibrium rental rate for land is established by the intersection of the demand and supply curves. Any change in the productivity of land or the market demand for land's output causes the demand curve for the factor to shift and a new rental rate to be established.

8. The asset price of land is determined by the demand for the land's output and productivity. This is obtained by discounting future rental payments to get the land's present value. Land competes among many uses, and diminishing marginal productivity of the factor causes the demand curve to slope downward. If the marginal productivity in one use exceeds that obtained from other uses, the asset price of land will be higher, and land will be switched from one type of production into another. When real estate development competes with agriculture for land use, the asset price of land increases.

9. Most U.S. industries have experienced an increase in their capital-labor ratios since the 1950s as more cost-effective methods have been developed and the growth rate of saving and investment has exceeded the growth rate of the labor force. Increasing the economywide capital-labor ratio increases labor productivity and the wage-rental ratio.

10. The rate of return on capital expresses the income accruing to capital as a function of the value of the capital stock. Since the 1930s, the average rates of return have fluctuated both upward and downward. Even when the average rates of return are

CAPITAL AND LAND

declining (or even negative), the marginal rate of return on new investment may be very high.

IMPORTANT TERMS AND THEIR MEANING

Match the following terms with the correct definition or phrase.

1. _____ A gift of nature; one of the factors of production in fixed supply over the long run

2. _____ The total income accruing to capital as a fraction of the value of the capital stock

3. _____ Wealth that can be touched; consists of capital and land

4. _____ Occurs over a period of time; describes the service of capital

5. _____ The payment made for the use of the services of capital or land

6. _____ The value of payment today as opposed to a payment at some point in the future

7. _____ The rate of interest expressed in dollars

8. _____ Represented by the interest rate; reflects the value of alternatives forgone by using resources to buy capital assets

9. _____ The rate of return on capital which just covers the asset's cost so that the owners of capital incur neither gains nor losses

10. _____ The price paid for the purchase of capital; the present discounted value of the flow of rental payments

11. _____ A measure of the interest rate in terms of the goods that can be bought rather than in terms of the money that changes hands

12. _____ The ability of capital to produce or add to the production of an output; the productivity of capital

13. _____ The accumulation of a commodity, asset, or flow of payments; in general, the accumulation of any flow at a particular point in time

14. _____ The price of labor relative to the price of capital

15. _____ The rate of return expected on new or additional investment expenditures

16. _____ The wearing out of capital over time

17. _____ An input into the production process which does not directly satisfy a consumer want; consists of such items as bulldozers, record-processing equipment, and delivery trucks

18. _____ Examples are currency and bank accounts which can be converted into tangible assets

19. _____ Describes the impact on the industry supply of commodities as a result of some or all input prices changing

20. _____ The value created for a producer as a result of hiring 1 more unit of capital

21. _____ Describes a change in the input combinations as a result of one input price changing relative to the price of other inputs

22. _____ Describes the combination of capital and labor in production

a. Present value
b. Stock
c. Asset price
d. Real interest rate
e. Physical capital
f. Opportunity cost of capital
g. Wage-rental ratio
h. Average rate of return of capital
i. Depreciation
j. Cost effect
k. Rental rate
l. Land
m. Flow
n. Marginal value product of capital
o. Nominal interest rate
p. Substitution effect
q. Tangible wealth
r. Required rental rate
s. Capital-labor ratio
t. Marginal rate of return to capital
u. Financial wealth
v. Services of capital

EXERCISES

1. Table 15-1 contains the present values of a $1 payment received at a future date for discount (interest) rates of 10 percent and 15 percent.

   a. Assume that you are the president of a firm and have two capital investment opportunities: alternatives A and B. Each investment alternative has a one-time cost of $5000, and the expected life of each piece of capital is 5 years. At the end of its productive life, the capital equipment has scrap value of $1000 for each piece. The expected flow of rental receipts from each investment is presented in Table 15-2.

TABLE 15-1
PRESENT VALUE OF $1

YEAR	DISCOUNT (INTEREST) RATE	
	10%	15%
0	$1.00	$1.00
1	.91	.87
2	.83	.76
3	.75	.66
4	.68	.57
6	.62	.50

TABLE 15-2

YEAR	ALTERNATIVE A	ALTERNATIVE B
1	$ 5000	$ 2000
2	4000	3000
3	3000	4000
4	2000	5000
5	1000	6000
Total income	$15,000	$20,000

The total expected flow of receipts from investing in alternative A is $15,000, while the flow from alternative B is $20,000. However, alternative B has a greater degree of risk associated with it. The interest (discount) rate for alternative A is 10 percent, while the more risky alternative B must be evaluated at an interest rate of 15 percent. Using the discount rates presented in Table 15-2, complete Table 15-3 and determine which investment alternative you should undertake.

Total present value of
   receipts   _____   _____
Minus: cost of investment
   (−$5000)   −_____ −_____
Plus: present value of
   scrap   +_____ +_____
Net present value of
   investment $_____ $_____

   b. Based on your computations, you should undertake investment alternative _____ since a value of $_____ is contributed to the overall value of the firm.

   c. The marginal rate of return on both investment projects is (positive/negative) _____.

2. Table 15-4 presents input, output, and revenue data for the rental of capital services.

   a. Complete the third column by determining the marginal product of capital, assuming all other inputs are held constant.

   b. If the product can be sold on the market at a price of $10 per each unit, compute total revenue and enter each value in the table. Also, compute and enter the marginal value product of capital.

   c. Plot the firm's marginal value product of capital curve on your graph paper. Label the vertical axis "dollars" and the horizontal axis "number of machine-days" rented. Be sure to plot the marginal values at the midpoints on the horizontal axis.

   d. Using the information computed in (a) and (b), complete Table 15-5.

Table 15-5 is the (demand/supply) _____ schedule for capital and (is/is not) _____ the MVP_K schedule computed in (b) above. If the market rental rate for capital is $80 per day, the firm will employ _____ machine-days.

   e. If the price of the firm's output increased or the machines (capital) became more productive, the MVP_K curve would shift (to the right/to the left) _____, and (more/less) _____ capital would be used at each rental rate.

3. Figure 15-1 shows four demand curves for a fixed amount of land in an urban area. The area has a central city and surrounding fringes. The demand for land varies according to its use, and thus the rents users are willing to pay differ. On the graph, the rental rates which individuals are willing to pay for a particular use of the land are presented on the vertical axis. The horizontal axis measures the quantity of land demanded

TABLE 15-3

	ALTERNATIVE A				ALTERNATIVE B		
YEAR	RECEIPTS	PRESENT VALUE OF $1 @ 10% (I-A)	PRESENT VALUE OF RENTAL RECEIPTS (II-A)	YEAR	RECEIPTS	PRESENT VALUE OF $1 @ 15% (I-B)	PRESENT VALUE RENTAL (II-B)
1	$5000	$_____	$_____	1	$2000	$_____	$_____
2	4000	_____	_____	2	3000	_____	_____
3	3000	_____	_____	3	4000	_____	_____
4	2000	_____	_____	4	5000	_____	_____
5	1000	_____	_____	5	6000	_____	_____

CAPITAL AND LAND

TABLE 15-4

NUMBER OF MACHINE-DAYS RENTED	OUTPUT	MARGINAL PRODUCT OF CAPITAL (MP_k)	TOTAL REVENUE (TR)	MVPK
0	0			
1	14			
2	26			
3	36			
4	44			
5	50			
6	54			
7	56			

TABLE 15-5

MACHINE RENTAL RATE PER DAY, $	QUANTITY OF MACHINE-DAYS DEMANDED (Q_d)
150	
140	
120	
100	
80	
60	
40	
20	

in square feet per person. The quantity measure is actually a measure of the density and intensity of land use. For instance, a high-rise apartment building may cover one-fourth of a city block and yet house 1000 people. A single-family residence may be placed on a building lot of 20,000 square feet and house a family of four. Clearly, the apartment uses land more intensely and has a higher land use density. The lower the square feet per person, the more intensely the land is used. Also measured on the horizontal axis is the distance from the central city. The origin represents the city's center; the farther a point is from the origin horizontally, the more distant it is from the city's center. Each of the four demand curves represents a different use of the land, and all users compete for the fixed quantity available. Demand curve AB is for users who have to be close to the city's center. We can call this the contact function. Major office buildings, banks, and stock brokerage houses as well as some retail establishments are examples. Demand curve CD is for users supplying the firms in the center. We can call this the support function of the city. Such users might include suppliers of office products, restaurants, or any firm needing to be in daily contact with the firms whose demand curve is reflected by AB. Demand curve EF reflects the households, or residential land use. The final demand curve GH reflects agricultural use and is farthest away from the city's center. Based on the above information and Figure 15-1, complete the following questions.

a. For any land rental rate between X and Y dollars per square foot, the land is used in the (contact/support) _____ function, while for rental rates between Y and Z dollars per square foot, land is used in the (support/residential) _____ function. For rental rates above X dollars, the (contact/support) _____ function prevails.

b. Land use is (more/less) _____ dense in the support function than in household use.

c. The city's boundary is encountered at a distance of _____ miles from the city's center as land in _____ use commands a higher rent than could be obtained from the residential function, and the number of square feet per person is (greater than/less than) _____ that for any of the other three functions.

d. If the demand for residential use of the land increased, we would expect demand curve _____ to shift upward; more houses would be provided primarily at the expense of the _____

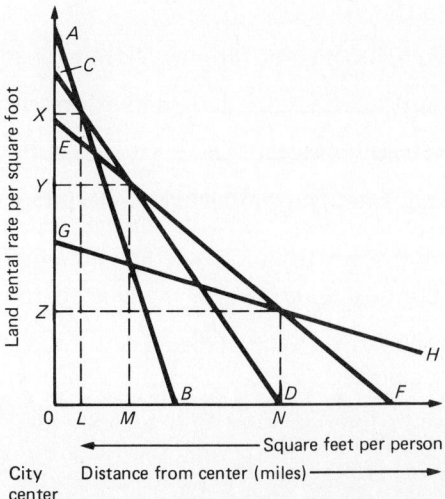

FIGURE 15-1

function, and so the city's boundary would (expand/contract) _____.

e. You should now develop a demand curve for land use in an urban area. On the diagram, darken the relevant segments of each demand curve depending on whether that particular function gets the use of the land.

f. The fact that the demand curve for land in this example is segmented reflects (constant/different) _____ marginal value products of land in various uses.

4. Figure 15-2 shows the long-run adjustment process of capital services in response to an increase in the average wage rate paid to labor. In Figure 15-2, the initial rental rate is R_o and the initial equilibrium quantity is K_o.

a. In response to an increase in the wage rate, there is a(n) (increase/decrease) _____ in the demand for capital services, and the (cost/substitution) _____ effect is dominant.

b. The short-run supply curve of capital services (is/is not) _____ perfectly inelastic, and as a result, any increase in the demand for capital services is initially reflected only by (an increase/a decrease) _____ in the rental rate.

c. The new short-run equilibrium rental rate is _____, and this is (above/below) _____ the long-run rental rate. As a result, (more/less) _____ capital services will be supplied, and the rental rate will (rise/fall) _____.

d. The new long-run equilibrium rental rate is established at _____, and the new equilibrium quantity is _____. The long-run supply curve of capital SS' (is/is not) _____ perfectly elastic since more capital services will be forthcoming onto the market only at a (higher/lower) _____ rental rate.

e. At the rental rate R_2 and quantity K_2, there (will/will not) _____ be a perfectly inelastic short-run supply of capital services curves parallel to SS and intersecting the quantity axis at K_2.

f. In this example, capital and labor (are/are not) _____ substitutes.

FILL-IN QUESTIONS

1. Automobiles, stoves, lawn mowers, and television sets are all examples of (consumer/producer) _____ capital and are considered to be (tangible/intangible) _____ wealth.

2. A characteristic of less-developed countries is that (more/less) _____ of their tangible wealth is held in the form of land than in the industrialized nations.

3. The services provided by capital goods over a period of time are an example of (stock/flow) _____, while the value of capital goods available at a particular time is a (stock/flow) _____.

4. By using the "rule of 72," it is possible to determine the length of _____ necessary to (double/spend) _____ the value of a money asset, given a particular interest rate.

5. In order to calculate the value today of a payment on some future date, it is necessary to _____ the future payment by using a particular _____ rate.

6. If an asset yields an income forever, it is known as a (perpetuity/bond) _____, and its present value is calculated by dividing the _____ by the _____ rate. The quotient also determines the asset's _____.

7. When the nominal interest rate is adjusted for inflation, an approximate measure of the _____ interest rate is obtained.

8. An increase in interest rates and an extended period of time serve to (increase/decrease) _____ the present value of an asset.

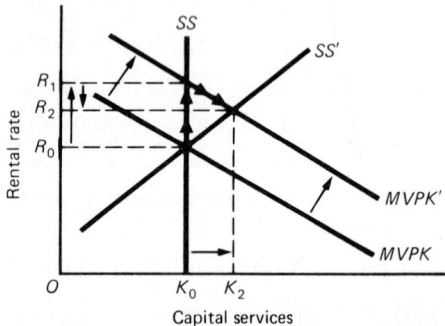

FIGURE 15-2

9. Human impatience and the productivity of capital are two forces which explain why interest rates are (positive/negative) _____.

10. The *MVPK* curve shows the firm's (demand for/supply of) _____ capital's services, and the curve is based on the marginal _____ of capital and the market _____ of the firm's output.

11. In the short run, the quantity of capital available for use (is/is not) _____ fixed, and in the long run, the quantity of capital (can/cannot) _____ be varied.

12. In the capital market, an equilibrium exists when the _____ for capital services equals the _____ of these services.

13. Capital that is sector-specific usually is present in the (short/long) _____ run and (can/cannot) _____ be used easily in other sectors.

14. The _____ price of capital, as opposed to the rental price, is the relevant price when a firm purchases capital.

15. The demand curve for a capital asset represents the (present/historical) _____ value of the net revenue streams from different levels of capital.

16. The supply of land in an economic system is essentially (fixed/variable) _____; hence, the supply curve for land is (vertical/horizontal) _____.

17. The higher the marginal value product of land, the (higher/lower) _____ the land's use.

18. The (marginal/average) _____ rate of return on capital reflects the expected return on new investment expenditures.

TRUE-FALSE QUESTIONS

1. ____ Since the Great Depression, the after-tax rates of return to capital have been between 5 percent and 8 percent.

2. ____ One of the fastest growing capital-labor ratios can be found in the agricultural industry.

3. ____ One factor which accounts for part of the increase in food prices is that because land rents are higher, the products of land are higher.

4. ____ Technological progress in the capital goods industry has the effect of reducing the long-run supply price of capital.

5. ____ The demand price of an asset is the sum of all future revenue expected from the use of the asset.

6. ____ The asset price of capital is that rental rate which must be paid by producers in order to ensure that they will continue to have use of capital services.

7. ____ The cost of capital defines that rental rate which generates neither gains nor losses for the owners of capital.

8. ____ In the short run, the rental rate for capital is primarily supply-determined since the supply of capital is fixed.

9. ____ When the price of an input rises, there is both a cost effect and a substitution effect on the demand for alternative inputs.

10. ____ If the long-run equilibrium rental rate for capital is above the short-run market rate currently being paid by producers, the owners of capital will not change the amount of capital supplied.

11. ____ The demand for capital service increases as more and more capital is employed by the firm.

12. ____ If the nominal interest rate is 18 percent and the inflation rate is 6.2 percent, the real interest rate is approximately 11.8 percent.

13. ____ It is never possible for the real interest rate to be negative since it is irrational for a lender to make a loan today and receive a payment in the future which has less purchasing power than the original loan.

14. ____ For an asset having a very long life, the rate of interest has only a small influence on the asset's price.

15. ____ When the future revenue stream of an asset is discounted, it is possible to determine the present value of the asset.

16. ____ The rental rate for capital defines the cost of using capital's services.

17. ____ To say that an economic system has experienced a positive net investment means that new additions to the capital stock have exceeded the amount of the existing capital stock lost through depreciation.

18. ____ Tangible wealth consists of savings accounts, stocks, bonds, and certificates of deposit.

MULTIPLE-CHOICE QUESTIONS

Circle the correct answer.

1. All of the following are measures of the importance of tangible wealth in the economy except
   a. the share of national income accounted for by the stock of tangible wealth
   b. the ratio of the current value of all savings accounts, corporate stocks and bonds, certificates of deposit, and government securities to national income
   c. the ratio of land and capital to the value of national income
   d. the amount of tangible wealth per worker

2. If you invested $5000 in a savings certificate paying 9.25 percent interest per year, you could expect your investment to double in
   a. 5.6 years   c. 7.8 years
   b. 12 years   d. 6.5 years

3. The fact that a dollar today is not the same as a dollar tomorrow is the basis for the concept of
   a. capital rental rates
   b. present value
   c. interest accumulation
   d. none of the above

4. If a perpetuity yields an annual payment of $3000 per year forever, what is the asset worth if the interest rate is 6 percent?
   a. $18,000
   b. $5000
   c. $20,000
   d. $50,000
   e. cannot be determined from the above information

5. One of the primary reasons interest rates are nearly always positive is that
   a. surplus capital will be invested only if interest rates are greater than zero
   b. the net present value of capital assets can never be negative
   c. individuals who make financial capital available for capital investment are impatient to consume
   d. the market for capital services is always strong
   e. none of the above

6. The marginal value product of capital services depends on
   a. the amount of capital employed
   b. the productivity of capital
   c. the demand for and price of the firm's output
   d. the quantity and quality of all other factors of production employed
   e. all of the above

7. All of the following are methods by which an industry can reduce its capital stock except
   a. shutting down the capital equipment and permitting it to remain idle
   b. not replacing equipment as it wears out
   c. selling the equipment to another industry for use as is
   d. transforming the capital and selling to another sector

8. The rental rate at which capital services are supplied to an industry depends on
   a. the opportunity cost of capital to the industry
   b. the elasticity of supply of capital
   c. the marginal value product of capital
   d. all of the above
   e. none of the above

9. One of the major factors determining the long-run adjustment of capital is the
   a. complete inelasticity of the long-run supply of capital
   b. mobility of capital into and out of the industry
   c. rigidity of the rental rate of capital
   d. none of the above

10. If $25,000 can be borrowed at 12 percent real interest to purchase a machine which is then rented to a firm for $3500, how much do you have to make per year just to cover your cost, assuming a depreciation rate of 8 percent per year?
    a. $3000   c. $2000
    b. $1250   d. $5000

11. Which of the following factors is not a determinant of the required rental rate for capital?
    a. the price of the capital good
    b. the substitutability of capital and labor
    c. the real interest rate
    d. the depreciation rate

12. If an asset yields a net income stream of $12,000 per year for many years and the current interest rate is 8 percent, what is the demand price of the asset?
    a. $150,000   c. $93,000
    b. $9600   d. $15,000

13. An improvement in the technology of production of capital goods will
    a. shift the average total cost curve of capital downward
    b. lower the long-run supply price of capital goods
    c. shift the marginal cost of production of capital goods
    d. increase the supply of capital goods
    e. all of the above

14. In the market for land's use, the rental rate is determined by
   a. the demand for land by the various users of the resource
   b. the supply of other factors of production
   c. the rental rate on capital
   d. none of the above

15. In 1976, the highest value of capital per worker was in the
   a. petroleum industry
   b. public utilities industry
   c. leather industry
   d. chemical industry

AT THIS POINT YOU SHOULD BE ABLE TO...

1. Define tangible wealth, list the two major asset classes which make up the tangible wealth of an economy, and explain how the composition of tangible wealth by asset class differs between developed and underdeveloped economies.

2. List the three types of physical capital and give two examples of each.

3. Explain the meaning of the rental rate for capital services and state how it differs from the asset price of capital.

4. Explain the meaning of the present value of an asset and state the role of the interest rate and time period in the determination of an asset's present value.

5. Calculate the present value of an asset using the interest rates presented in your text and explain how the present value of an asset differs from the accumulation of interest over time.

6. Explain why the interest rate (rental rate of capital) is said to show the opportunity cost of capital.

7. Define the real interest rate and state a computational method designed to approximate the real interest rate.

8. Explain the role of the marginal value product of capital in the determination of the demand for capital services and state two determinants of the marginal value product of capital.

9. Explain the meaning of the supply of capital services, distinguish between the long-run and short-run supply of capital, and state three ways in which adjustment of the supply of capital in the long run can occur.

10. Define the cost effect and the substitution effect and explain how these two effects influence the adjustment process in the market for capital services.

11. Explain the meaning of the required rental rate and show how the annual costs of acquiring and renting out a piece of capital equipment are determined.

12. List three determinants of the required rental rate.

13. Explain and show how the asset price of capital is determined.

14. Describe the demand for land services, show graphically how competing uses of land set the equilibrium rental rate, and define the meaning of the long-run equilibrium allocation of land.

15. State a reason why the long-run capital-labor ratio has increased and explain why the ratios show such differences between various sectors of the economy.

QUESTIONS FOR THOUGHT

1. Why is the present value concept used in determining the asset price of a capital good? Why not simply sum all of the future income generated by the asset, subtract the total costs associated with acquisition and maintenance, and let this difference be the price we would be willing to pay?

2. Although we assume that the real interest rate is always positive, under what circumstances might it be possible for the real interest rate to be negative? What does it mean if the rate is negative? Explain.

3. Why is the rental rate of capital considered to be the opportunity cost of capital? Explain.

4. The mobility of capital among industries is one of the most important factors in attaining a long-run equilibrium in the capital market. Explain this statement.

5. Distinguish between the demand for capital as an asset and the demand for capital's services.

6. Given a fixed supply of land, explain how competition among different users of land determines the rental rate of land and how it can determine the physical appearance of the landscape.

APPENDIX: THE SIMPLE ALGEBRA OF PRESENT VALUES AND DISCOUNTING

Contained in the appendix to Chapter 15 are the algebraic derivations and explanations of three basic formulas used in the determination of present values. The formulas are used to compute the present value of a one-time payment in the future, the present value of a stream of unequal future payments, and the present value of a perpetuity. When tables are available, present values can be determined by finding the appropriate discount factor and multiplying that factor by the value of the future payment. When present value tables are not available, however, these formulas provide an easy method of discounting in order to obtain the value today of a future payment.

CHAPTER OUTLINE

1. A sum of money invested today at a given interest rate per period of time returns the principal (the sum originally invested) plus interest earned at the end of the period. If the present investment is $K, and the interest rate is i percent per period, at the end of the period, the investor will receive $K(1 + i)$.
2. In order to calculate the present value today of a sum to be received at a future date, the sum is discounted since the face value of a future receipt of money is greater than what the sum is worth today. If a future payment is worth $K(1 + i)$, today it is worth $K(1 + i)$ divided by $(1 + i)$, or $K. The future payment has been discounted to establish its present value.
3. It is possible to calculate the present value of a payment to be made after several time periods have elapsed. The present value of $1 to be received k years from now is determined by the equation

$$PV_k = \$1/(1 + i)^k$$

This equation has the effect of repeating the present value computation for a payment to be received one time period from now.
4. To calculate the present value of a stream of payments over several time periods, it is necessary to sum the present values of each of the future payments. Assuming that three unequal payments (R_1, R_2, and R_3) are to be made, one in each of three time periods, the present value of the stream of future payments is given by the equation

$$PV = \frac{R_1}{(1+i)^1} + \frac{R_2}{(1+i)^2} + \frac{R_3}{(1+i)^3}$$

In general, if payments are to continue over k time periods, the equation becomes

$$PV = \frac{R_1}{(1+i)^1} + \frac{R_2}{(1+i)^2} + \cdots + \frac{R_k}{(i+i)^k}$$

The present value of a stream of unequal payments is thus nothing more than the sum of the present values of each individual component of the stream.
5. In order to calculate the present value of a stream of payments of $R per time period forever, the following equation is used:

Present value of a perpetuity of $R per year $= \dfrac{\$R}{i}$

The present value of payments received further into the future is worth almost nothing (or very little) today.

IMPORTANT TERMS AND THEIR MEANING

1. Principal: The initial amount of an investment earning a rate of return in the form of interest
2. Discounting: A reduction in the face value of a future receipt in order to find the present value of the future payment

EXERCISES

1. Suppose that for the next 6 years you will receive the following payments from an investment you made before enrolling in college.

YEAR	RECEIPTS, $
1	1000
2	850
3	2500
4	1500
5	500
6	3000

If the interest rate is 10 percent, what is the stream of future payments worth to you today? At the end of the 6 years, how much money will you have received?

2. You are given two alternatives. You may receive $2000 today, or after 8 years you may receive $4000. If the interest rate is 9 percent, which alternative would you choose? Why?

3. Suppose you are offered $5000 at the end of 3 years or $X today. If you received the $X today, you could put it in a savings account and earn 8 percent interest on the funds. What is the minimum amount X must be in order for you to wait for $5000 3 years from now?

4. Assume that you inherited a bond with a current market value of $7692.31. The bond has a rate of return of 6½ percent per year and pays an annual dollar sum once a year. What is the value of each annual payment?

16
Applied Economics in Action

Chapter 16 contains economic analysis applied to some contemporary issues and problems. The tools of analysis have been developed in previous chapters, and so they should not be difficult for you. Chapter 16 answers questions you may have asked about the relevance of the study of economics. As you study Chapter 16, you will see that in many cases economic sense makes common sense.

Chapter 16 begins with a discussion of the maximum-hours laws for women passed in the early part of this century for "humanitarian" purposes. The Landes hypothesis argues that by restricting the supply of labor, men promoted their best interest by increasing their access to higher wages and more hours of work. The maximum-hours laws are examined from the standpoint of supply and demand analysis, and Professors Fischer and Dornbusch show circumstances in which both male and female workers might benefit from the laws.

The allocation of scarce time between work and leisure is presented, and the authors show how individuals vary both the quantity and intensity of leisure consumption. The consumption of household appliances and the allocation of responsibilities of marriage partners represent very rational behavior on the part of individuals as they seek to maximize their well-being. Scarce time influences directly both the quantity and quality of children raised by modern parents.

The application of economic analysis to the problems of imperfect information in the marketplace shows that the existence of price differentials among competing products weakens the model of the competitive firm. Consumers and workers search in the marketplace to increase their information; however, the search is very seldom complete because of the costs involved. In fact, it is possible for asymmetric information to destroy a market.

Externalities exist as a result of failure in the marketplace, and because of this, resources are misallocated. Spillover effects in the form of social costs and benefits are examined by using marginal analysis. If society must bear part of the burden of private actions, it is possible to force private individuals to internalize any spillover cost by having the government undertake certain policies. Government can also pursue policies designed to correct any imbalance in the social and private benefits of consumption.

The final section of Chapter 16 examines crime and crime prevention by using the economist's tool kit. Criminals may make a rational choice in hopes of maximizing their welfare. Two of the factors considered by criminals before committing illegal acts are the probability of being apprehended and the severity of the sentence if convicted. Both economic sense and common sense suggest that crime deterrence might be improved by allocating more resources to the apprehension and conviction of criminals.

CHAPTER OUTLINE

1. The impact of maximum-hours laws for women passed during the early part of the twentieth century is analyzed on the basis of supply and demand theory. Using humanitarian reasons as a justification, these laws were designed to restrict the number of hours women could work at any wage rate and therefore restrict the supply of labor in the market. The Landes hypothesis argues that the laws were not humanitarian but simply gave male workers higher wages and more hours of work. Landes argues that men passed the laws to make themselves better off. The restriction of the number of hours worked at any wage rate caused the aggregate supply of labor curve to shift to the left, thus generating a higher equilibrium wage for a given market demand for labor. With fewer female hours of labor supplied, men worked more hours at a higher wage rate. The costs of maximum-hours laws were borne primarily by immigrant women. It is possible, however, that even though women worked fewer hours, they did so at a higher wage rate, and thus their actual incomes increased. As the male supply of labor and the market demand for labor became more inelastic, women were more likely to be better off.

    a. Like the maximum-hours laws, other protective legislation often may have goals other than those most apparent to the public. Many types of legislation designed to ensure safety, labor quality, and product quality may have the effect of restricting the supply of labor to an industry or output on a market.

2. The allocation of scarce time is analogous to, and in fact is a component of, the consumer's optimal consumption decisions. The consumer must allocate time among competing activities including market work, leisure, and household activities in the most cost-effective way. Price theory may be applied to the analysis of time allocation and to the economics of the family since financial obligations require the consumption of both time and resources.

    a. The opposite of work is leisure, and it is measured by the satisfaction consumers get from combining goods and time for pleasure. The wage rate reflects the opportunity cost of time and hence the price of leisure. The higher the wage rate, the more likely it is that leisure activities will be time-saving and purchased input intensive.

    b. If a household enjoys a high wage rate, it is rational behavior for the household to own time-saving appliances. The wage rate is important in the determination of the cost of time but not as an indicator of household income level. Households in a developed country will consume different amounts of time-saving appliances and have fewer domestic servants than identical households in a less-developed country.

    c. There are economies of scale in household operation which may serve to induce individuals into a marital relationship. The relationship is a trading arrangement, and so it may permit the specialization of labor if comparative advantages exist. Specialization and comparative advantage determine the length of time each partner or both partners spend in market work, leisure, and household activities. Also, the effect of children on the household's allocation of time influences the economy's labor supply.

    d. Children are a time-intensive source of utility. The number of children per household has been falling. With fewer children (given a parent's wage rate), the amount of investment in human capital in the children increases.

3. In a market economy, imperfect information exists. Reducing both the number and the degree of imperfections costs both time and money.

    a. Price differences exist in relatively competitive markets and for products with a high degree of similarity. The absence of perfect information promotes the existence of price dispersion.

    b. Price differences are present for frequently purchased commodities as well as those bought infrequently. The search problem faced by the consumer is how and where to look for low prices. The search process requires both time (the major cost component) and the cost of inputs which facilitate the search process. The primary benefit from searching is a reduction in product price. Although the marginal cost of searching can be viewed as remaining constant, the marginal benefit is subject to diminishing returns, and so it declines. The optimal search ends at the point where marginal cost equals marginal benefit. Since price differences exist for some commodities in relatively competitive markets, the differences may be due to differences in location or clientele so that buyers do not find it advantageous to search. The two main determinants of price dispersion are the frequency of purchase and the budget share claimed by that good.

    c. Imperfect information exists in the labor market, and so the search process is important in matching job vacancies with job applicants. Some unemployment is productive in the sense that the search activity occurs. Unemployment benefits lower the search cost for job seekers.

    d. Incomplete information, especially if it is one-sided, may effectively destroy a market. If information is asymmetric, a market cannot exist since either buyers or sellers (whoever has information that others do not have) are unwilling to perform their market function.

4. Externalities are present when prices exist at some level which allows either firms or households not to incur the full costs or receive the full benefits of their actions. When spillover effects are present, resource allocations are not optimal, and so society can be made better off.

    a. Spillover costs exist in the private choice of automobile ownership. Both spillover and private costs increase with vehicle size. Congestion is an example of a spillover cost. The optimal car size is determined by the equality of an increasing marginal cost and decreasing marginal benefit of ownership. The socially optimal car size internalizes the spillover costs of automobile ownership. The government can encourage buyers to consume automobiles of a socially optimal size by exercising its taxing and licensing function.

    b. Noise pollution may incur zero private costs of production; however, noise levels do spill over onto society and thus reflect a misallocation of resources. Society may adopt specific standards or manners in order to encourage people to internalize the social costs of their activities.

c. Even when resources are unowned, both social and private costs exist for the use of these resources. In order to adjust for the absence of private ownership and to attain a more socially desirable level of resource use, society engages in natural resource management.

5. Economists begin the study of criminal behavior by initially assuming that criminals are rational, welfare-maximizing individuals seeking the greatest return for the least possible cost. In order to deter crime, society should increase both the quantity of resources allocated for the apprehension and conviction of criminals and the severity of penalties. Such a social approach to crime prevention increases the costs of criminal behavior relative to its benefits.

IMPORTANT TERMS AND THEIR MEANING

Match the following terms with the correct definition or phrase.

1. _____ Information possessed by only one market sector (buyers or sellers) which may destroy a market

2. _____ The spread of prices in a market for goods; the goods may be either similar or different

3. _____ Services provided by economic agents designed to generate a money income

4. _____ Participants in the market process who must sell their product

5. _____ The argument that maximum-hours laws were not designed for humanitarian reasons but rather were designed to promote the well-being of male workers

6. _____ Not knowing everything about the environment in which the consumer or producer operates

7. _____ Describes the consumer's attempt to determine both how and where to purchase a commodity at the lowest price

8. _____ Workers searching for the right job and employers searching for the right worker for the job

a. Landes hypothesis

b. Market services

c. Imperfect information

d. Search problem

e. Price dispersion

f. Job matching

g. Asymmetric information

h. Distress sellers

EXERCISES

1. Figure 16-1 presents both private marginal benefits and marginal private and social costs for automobile size. It is assumed that external social costs increase with car size.

a. From the standpoint of the individual, optimal car size is _____, where marginal (private/social) _____ costs and marginal private benefits are _____ at a value of $_____.

b. At the optimal car size for the individual, marginal private costs equal _____, while marginal social costs equal _____ for that particular car size. Thus, the total marginal cost of the optimal car size ($MC_s + MC_p$) is the distance _____, which is (greater than/equal to/less than) _____ the marginal benefit.

c. To attain a socially optimal size of car, the size must be (increased/reduced) _____ to size _____. At this size of car, if there are no social costs, MC_p equals the distance _____, and this is (greater than/less than) _____ MB. As a result, the individual (would/would not) _____ remain with this size of car.

d. To achieve a reduction in car size to that which is socially optimal, the government may impose a tax in the amount of _____ per car, which (increases/decreases) _____ the marginal private cost of car ownership. Such a tax reflects an attempt by government to force private owners to

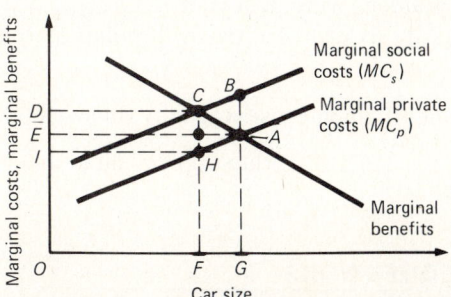

FIGURE 16-1

(internalize/externalize) _____ the marginal social cost of automobile size.

FILL-IN QUESTIONS

1. One of the marginal benefits in the search process takes the form of a (reduction/increase) _____ in the price which we expect to pay for a product.

2. Two important components of the job search process are information on job _____ and the _____ paid for certain jobs.

3. Externalities exist when households or firms (do/do not) _____ take into account the social costs and benefits of an action; thus, when externalities exist, the price mechanism (does/does not) _____ provide for an efficient allocation of resources.

4. An equilibrium is reached between criminals and their victims when the _____ and _____ of carrying out and preventing a crime are equal.

5. The term _____ is used to indicate the spread of prices both within and among industries.

6. As families have fewer children, the investment in human capital on each child generally (increases/decreases) _____ and the quality of the children rises.

7. The concept of (comparative/absolute) _____ advantage can be used to examine the allocation of _____ between market and nonmarket services provided by each partner in a marriage.

8. As an individual's wage rate increases, the _____ cost of time also increases, and as a result, leisure activities are (more/less) _____ time-saving.

9. The Landes hypothesis argues that maximum-hours laws for women (were/were not) _____ designed primarily to promote the well-being of the male worker.

10. Trade unions try to increase wages by (increasing/decreasing) _____ the supply of labor available in the market.

TRUE-FALSE QUESTIONS

1. ____ As the wage rate increases relative to the prices of household appliances, we expect households to purchase more of the appliances in an attempt to save time.

2. ____ Economies of scale do not play a significant role in the institution of marriage.

3. ____ Increasing the real wage tends to cause households to increase the demand for home- or self-generated leisure activities.

4. ____ A price dispersion ratio of 111 indicates that the spread in prices is small.

5. ____ If every consumer in the market knew what every seller charged for his product and then bought from the seller with the lowest price, no seller could charge more than the lowest price.

6. ____ The more frequently a good is purchased, the larger the dispersion in the good's price.

7. ____ In a secondhand market, distress sellers often are the cause of prices exceeding the fair-market price for a commodity.

8. ____ In a market economy, it may sometimes be the case that private utility maximization leads to a misallocation of resources.

9. ____ The socially optimal consumption of a commodity occurs when total marginal cost (marginal private cost plus marginal social cost) is less than the marginal private benefit in consumption.

10. ____ The evidence that capital punishment reduces the supply of murder is controversial and as yet not definitive.

MULTIPLE CHOICE QUESTIONS

Circle the correct answer.

1. Potential criminals look at all of the following aspects of their actions except the
   a. probability of arrest
   b. effect of the action on the victim
   c. probability of being convicted
   d. severity of the penalty

2. All of the following might appropriately be examined by the economics of the allocation of time except
   a. the length and intensity of leisure activities
   b. the allocation of household responsibilities among partners in a marriage
   c. the market search process
   d. optimal car size

3. One of the main reasons consumers do not take a more active role in market search is
   a. seller reluctance to give prices
   b. the time involved in the search

   c. the fact that prices generally do not exhibit large dispersion ratios
   d. in a modern economic system, information is usually relatively complete

4. A firm's location and clientele
   a. are not determinants of output price
   b. permit the firm to charge higher prices only if all other competitors increase prices
   c. may permit the firm to charge higher prices consistently
   d. none of the above

5. In the consumption of a commodity, if private costs equal social costs, then
   a. spillover costs are zero
   b. a social optimum has been attained
   c. there is a proper allocation of resources
   d. no taxes or subsidies should be placed on the consumption of the good
   e. all of the above

6. If resources are underallocated so that society's marginal benefit exceeds the marginal private benefit in consumption, an appropriate strategy for government would be to
   a. levy a tax to decrease private consumption
   b. subsidize private consumption of the commodity
   c. neither encourage nor discourage changes in consumption
   d. tax producers so that output falls

7. Which of the following price dispersion indices indicates the largest spread in price?
   a. 123   **c.** 183
   b. 157   **d.** 212

8. Recently, Congress prohibited the Federal Trade Commission from requiring that used auto dealers tell potential buyers of any defects in the cars being sold. This action by Congress promotes the existence of
   a. symmetric information
   b. complete market information
   c. asymmetric market information
   d. effective and efficient market operation

9. Washington, D.C.'s National Airport, as well as others around the country, prohibits commercial air traffic after a certain time at night because of jetliner noise over residential areas. This is an example of
   a. society setting standards to reduce the social costs of private actions
   b. both marginal social and marginal private costs equaling zero.
   c. private producers recognizing the marginal social costs of their operations and voluntarily restricting their activities
   d. society forcing the internalization of private costs.

AT THIS POINT YOU SHOULD BE ABLE TO . . .

1. Explain the Landes hypothesis.
2. Show graphically how reductions in the supply of labor because of maximum-hours law can raise the wage rate for all who remain unemployed.
3. Define the opportunity cost of leisure and explain in a few sentences the time allocation choices faced by individuals.
4. Explain how increased efficiency in time use can influence the decisions to marry, have families, purchase certain appliances, and have children.
5. Define imperfect information and price dispersion.
6. State the search problem and list two costs and the benefits of search in the marketplace.
7. Explain the meaning of job matching and state how imperfect information may influence employment.
8. Define asymmetric information and explain how it may cause a market to collapse.
9. State the meaning of externalities and describe how they may influence resource allocation in the market.
10. Graphically show and explain how society may force consumers to internalize an externality.
11. State how and why society should allocate its resources in order to reduce crime.

QUESTIONS FOR THOUGHT

1. It has been argued by Elizabeth Landes that maximum-hours laws for women only improved the well-being of male workers. Explain how and under what conditions all workers might be made better off by restricting the labor supply.

2. Suppose that two friends of yours are getting married but both experience high anxiety levels about how they will make it financially. Explain to them the economic rationale for marriage.

3. Through the process of searching, a consumer's welfare is increased. What is the effect of incomplete search in the market? Explain.

4. Fines for littering the highways often range from $10 to $100 for each offense. Is this an example of a tax designed to cause the internalization of external littering costs to society? Explain.

5. Suppose you had to present a brief talk on the economics of crime and crime prevention to your sociology class. Briefly prepare an outline of what you would plan to say.

17 The Government and Resource Allocation

The role of government in a market economy is presented in Chapter 17. Government intervention in a market system occurs because of market failure, a need to provide some public goods, and the presence of an unequal distribution of income generated by the price system. The goal of government intervention is the improvement of both market efficiency and equity; however, there are many strong differences of opinion about what role the government should actually play.

Government provides public goods and services because private markets find it difficult to produce the socially optimal amount. No one can be excluded from the consumption of a public good, and so it is possible for someone to enjoy the benefits gained from consumption of a public good without paying for it. This is the free rider problem, and it further limits the ability of private markets to provide the optimal quantity of public goods. The government does not have to produce public goods, but it has to specify the quantity to be produced and make the resources available.

Private markets often generate allocations of resources and incomes that are indifferent from those which society deems ideal. Government attempts to redistribute income by taxing the rich and transferring funds to the poor. A problem that is immediately encountered is how to determine an equitable income distribution. When government intervenes to redistribute income, it can make some citizens better off only if it makes others worse off.

Government policies and programs ideally should reflect the wishes of society; however, it is possible that through the very process of government, society's best interests are not fulfilled. The theory of public choice gives us a method of analyzing and predicting how the political system allocates resources. One aspect of this theory—the paradox of voting—states that it is not possible for society to rank its alternatives consistently by using the majority voting process.

A variety of taxes are imposed by different levels of government on citizens; however, the tax system is constrained by the principles of equity and efficiency. The equity aspect of taxation is concerned with the fairness of taxes, but the very meanings of "fairness" and "equity" are difficult to define. Thus, problems are encountered rapidly when government tries to develop an equitable tax system. People try to avoid taxes, and this results in society wasting some of its resources. In fact, taxes often create such a distortion in the marketplace that a socially optimal allocation of resources is not attained.

The late 1970s and early 1980s were years marked by public dissatisfaction with the current tax system. Many state governments passed laws limiting their power to spend and tax. A movement is currently under way to amend the Constitution so that federal spending can be controlled. The decade of the 1980s may be a period of both tax revolt and tax reform.

CHAPTER OUTLINE

1. Federal, state, and local governments together collect about one-third of total GNP in taxes. Government spends approximately 20 percent of GNP on goods and services, while 13 percent is disbursed as transfer payments from which the government receives no service or product.
   a. The major components of federal spending are national defense, Social Security and welfare, and interest on the national debt. The major expenditures by state governments include education, Social Security and welfare, and highways and transportation. At the local level, the major components of government spending are education, health and hospitals, and highways and transportation. Questions often arise about the government's function in a market economy.
   b. The primary source of government revenue is taxes. The federal government receives almost two-thirds of all tax revenue. Some federal tax receipts, however, are transferred back to state and local governments. The major source of federal tax revenue is the personal income tax, and this is followed in importance by payroll taxes. The major sources of revenue for state and local governments are the sales tax, property tax, and personal income tax.

2. Three areas in which government intervention into the marketplace may be beneficial are the reduction of market distortions, the provision of public goods, and the redistribution of income.
   a. A public good is one that is available for consumption by others after it has been consumed by one individual. A private good is available for consumption only by one individual. In general, no one can be excluded from the consumption of a public good.
      (1) The free rider problem makes it difficult for private markets to provide the correct amount of public goods. A free rider does not pay for the good consumed even though there is a cost of production involved in making the good available. A public good involves strong positive externalities, and so the private allocation of resources is not socially optimal because the goods are underproduced.
      (2) Society's demand curve for a public good is the vertical sum of individual member's demand curves and shows the marginal social benefit in consumption of additional units of the good. The demand curve shows the price society is willing to pay for additional units of the public good. Individual demand curves are added vertically because exclusion from consumption is not possible with public good, as it is with private goods. A social optimum for public goods occurs when some point on the demand curve equals the marginal cost of producing an extra unit of the good ($MSB = MC$).
      (3) A problem exists in establishing the correct level of public goods. If individuals are asked to reveal how much they would be willing to pay for the good, there is an incentive to be dishonest. Each individual may regard himself as a free rider. It is difficult to get individuals to reveal their preferences for public goods.
      (4) Although governments provide many goods and services, some are not public goods since the exclusion rule does not apply. State control and operation of liquor sales and stores is an example of a good and service which could be sold through the private sector.
      (5) Governments usually rely on the private sector for the actual production of public goods; however, governments specify the quantity and distribution of the goods. Although there is no reason why governments should not produce public goods, it is generally assumed that they would be less efficient than the private sector because there is no incentive for them to reduce costs.
   b. In a competitive market, the distribution of income depends on the ownership and utilization of society's resources. When income inequalities exist, government can intervene to promote a better distribution. The problem, however, is deciding what determines a good income distribution. Government intervention to alter the distribution of income and make someone better off can be achieved only by makng someone else worse off.
      (1) A trade-off exists between economic efficiency and output. The primary method of obtaining a more equitable income redistribution is through taxation; however, it is not possible to tax and maintain the marginal conditions necessary for an efficient allocation of resources.
      (2) That part of GNP spent on transfers represents an attempt by government to redistribute income to certain groups in society.
      (3) A merit good is a good which society thinks should be consumed by everyone regardless of income. These goods show a concern for society's general welfare and are partial public goods. There is no reason to expect that government should produce the merit good itself.
3. The objective of the theory of public choice is to understand and predict how voters in a political system choose to allocate resources, given the structure of the system and their own goals. Public decision making involves voters, politicians, and bureaucrats. A reasonable question arises as to whether the end result of the political process is actually what the voters wanted.
   a. If the voting process is based on majority rule, a problem can arise. The paradox of voting states that in some cases it is not possible for society to rank policy choices consistently by using majority voting. The paradox of voting also shows how the voters' preferences may become intransitive when three alternatives are presented. An implication of the paradox is that the outcome of majority voting may depend on the order in which society votes on the alternatives.
      (1) The median voter model shows that society can provide a consistent ranking of alternatives by using the majority rule. The ranking is the choice of the middle

voter. The median voter model provides consistent choices if voters' preferences are single-peaked. If preferences are double-peaked (not well defined), majority voting and the median voter model do not work.

    (2) Logrolling describes the situation in which voters without a majority agree on the outcome of each issue in a package of issues so that their position is improved by the entire package. When logrolling occurs, voters trade votes. Without logrolling, each separate issue could very well fail because none would receive a simple majority; however, the coalition of minority voters assures that all issues pass.

  b. Decision making in the legislative process involves compromise and vote trading. Although questions arise as to whether the legislator's goals and the political process result in decisions which reflect society's best interest, the assumption is that they do.

  c. Bureaucrats may influence the allocation of resources because they often administer the programs established by legislators; thus, they have some discretion over how funds are spent. Politicians also may be influenced by the advice of civil servants, which may not reflect the wishes of society.

4. The principles of taxation include types of taxes, equity, efficiency, and tax reform.

  a. Tax revenue is generated by taxes on income (payroll, personal income, and corporate profit taxes), assets (property and capital gains taxes), specific goods (alcohol, tobacco, and gasoline taxes), and specific transactions (retail sales tax and estate and gift taxes). A tax which is not used in the United States but is widely used in Europe is one levied and collected on the value created at each stage of production and distribution of a good. This value added tax (VAT) is like a general sales tax levied on all goods sold. The problems of equity and efficiency serve to constrain the tax system as it attempts to raise revenue for the government.

  b. Two considerations are horizontal equity and vertical equity. Horizontal equity states that equals should be treated equally under the law, while vertical equity says that unequals should be treated unequally. Included in the concept of vertical equity are the ability to pay and benefits received principles.

    (1) A problem often encountered is how to define equals and unequals. The principle of horizontal equity does not provide straightforward answers in many situations in which individuals are to be taxed equally.

    (2) The ability to pay principle states that taxes should be based on income or wealth, while the benefits received principle states that those receiving most of the benefits should pay more for them. The benefits principle suggests that government should not redistribute income. The ability to pay principle is the basis for a progressive tax structure since the after-tax inequality of economic well-being is reduced. Data indicate that progressive federal taxes reduce income inequality.

  c. The efficiency consideration involves the waste incurred by society as citizens try to avoid taxes. When the supply of labor (or any other factor) curve is elastic, taxes on labor income create a wedge between the marginal value of a worker to a firm and the income (marginal benefit) received by labor for working 1 more hour. A tax on labor income reduces the work effort and creates a distortion in the market. The incentive to work more is reduced by a tax on labor income. A waste of society's resources occurs because labor works less. This represents not only a loss to workers but a net waste because of government's tax collection. The waste to society is called the deadweight burden of the tax. If a factor's supply curve is completely inelastic, there is no waste to society because labor does not reduce the quantity of hours worked.

  d. It has been estimated that the waste per dollar of tax collected is 30 cents. This means that in order to spend $1, the government must collect $1.30.

  e. Because the value of imputed rents is not counted as income, investment in housing and in capital are treated differently by the tax laws. Return on investment in corporate capital is taxable income. Relative to the return on investment in private housing, the return on investment in corporate capital has been declining since 1965. A distortion is created in the market by taxing the two investment possibilities at different rates. Because financial capital can flow into either market, it is possible that investment in corporate capital and investment in private housing may eventually equalize.

  f. The incidence of taxation is borne by both the supply side and the demand side of the market. The more inelastic supply is relative to demand, the more the tax is borne by the supply side.

THE GOVERNMENT AND RESOURCE ALLOCATION

5. Current dissatisfaction and disillusionment with the U.S. tax system have caused some reform.
   a. A tax revolt began in California in the late 1970s and has spread to the rest of the country. Californians accepted propositions designed to reduce and roll back the rate of increase in property taxes and freeze real government spending. The propositions also reduced the level of services provided by state and local governments.
      (1) A federal constitutional amendment which would set limits on government spending was defeated by the Congress in 1982.
   b. The Laffer curve shows that after a particular tax rate, tax revenues fall as tax rates rise. In order to increase revenues, the Laffer curve suggests that tax rates should be reduced since some economists believe that the U.S. tax structure has surpassed the rate at which revenue in fact declines. In 1981, President Reagan introduced a 25 percent reduction in marginal tax rates to take effect over a 3-year period. The President argued that lower taxes would stimulate the economy, increase private investment, increase the work effort, and increase federal revenues. Other economists argue very strongly that the United States has not reached the point where further increases in the tax rates will yield less revenue.
   c. Two proposals for tax reform are to make the tax system inflation-proof and to impose a flat tax rate. The flat-tax-rate system would tax all incomes (after some exceptions) at the same rate. The taxes would be levied only on income and would eliminate some of the misallocations which currently exist. A major problem with the flat-rate system is that it is not a very progressive tax rate structure.

IMPORTANT TERMS AND THEIR MEANING

Match the following terms with the correct definition or phrase.

1. _____ Well-defined preferences with one alternative preferred over all others
2. _____ The rate at which taxes are paid on an extra dollar of income
3. _____ Says that equals should be treated equally by the tax laws
4. _____ Minorities get together and agree how they will vote on a particular package of issues so that they will benefit as a group
5. _____ Shows that tax revenues need not fall when tax rates are cut; used as a basis of President Reagan's 1981 tax cuts
6. _____ A tax levied on the value created at each stage of production of a product
7. _____ A proposal to charge a fixed tax rate on income regardless of the level of income
8. _____ The tax rate increases as the level of income increases; reduces the after-tax inequality of economic well-being
9. _____ Payments made by government for which no current service or product is returned by the recipient
10. _____ Someone who gets to consume a good that is costly to produce without paying for it
11. _____ The tax structure should be based on income or wealth; individuals who can pay their taxes should pay
12. _____ Goods which society thinks people should consume or receive, whatever their incomes
13. _____ The difference between the value of a worker to a firm and the amount received by the worker for working 1 hour more; arises because of a tax on wages
14. _____ A good which if consumed by one person cannot be consumed by another
15. _____ A tax imposed on the increased value of an asset when the asset is sold
16. _____ Argues that in some cases society is unable to rank policy choices consistently through a majority voting process

a. Progressivity
b. VAT
c. Benefit principle
d. Paradox of voting
e. Tax revolt
f. Wedge
g. Capital gains tax
h. Vertical equity
i. Merit goods
j. Single-peaked preferences
k. Corporate profit tax
l. Waste or deadweight burden
m. Horizontal equity
n. Flat-rate tax
o. Private good
p. Free rider

17. ____ A tax levied on the accounting profit of a corporation

18. ____ States that taxes should be paid by those receiving the benefits from government

19. ____ The net loss of resources because of misallocation of resources arising from taxes on wages or other factors of production

20. ____ Began in California during the late 1970s and resulted in the passage of Proposition 13 and Proposition 4

21. ____ Social Security taxes levied on labor income

22. ____ A tax levied on the sale of specific goods

23. ____ A good that if consumed by one individual is still available for consumption by others

24. ____ States that unequals should be treated unequally by the tax system

25. ____ A model of voting behavior which states that in some cases majority voting results in consistent choices, and so the choice will be that of the voter in the middle

q. Logrolling

r. Median voter

s. Marginal tax rate

t. Payroll tax

u. Public goods

v. Transfer payment

w. Laffer curve

x. Excise taxes

y. Ability to pay principle

EXERCISES

1. Table 17-1 presents the demand data for fire protection (a public good) for three different consumers.

a. On graph paper, plot the three demand curves. Label the appropriate curves D_1, D_2, and D_3.

TABLE 17-1

PRICE, $	QUANTITY 1	QUANTITY 2	QUANTITY 3
8	0	0	1
7	0	1	2
6	1	2	3
5	2	3	4
4	3	4	5
3	4	5	6
2	5	6	7
1	6	7	8

TABLE 17-2

PRICE, $	QUANTITY

b. On your graph, determine the demand for the public good. Draw the demand curve and label it DD.

c. Complete Table 17-2 by inserting the correct price and quantity data for the public good's demand schedule.

d. In order to determine the demand schedule for a public good, it is necessary to sum each individual demand curve (vertically/horizontally) _____ because it (is/is not) _____ possible to exclude anyone from the consumption of a public good.

e. The supply schedule for fire protection is presented in the table below. Plot this supply schedule on your graph.

Price	$9	$9	$9	$9	$9	$9	$9	$9	$9	$9	$9
Quantity	0	1	2	3	4	5	6	7	8	9	10

f. The optimal quantity of fire protection supplied is _____ units, and the optimal price is $_____.

2. Suppose a U.S. Senate subcommittee has to select from three alternative budgets one to recommend to the full Senate for approval. Budget 1 spends 50 percent on defense and 40 percent on social programs, and 10 percent is returned to the states. Budget 2 spends 10 percent on defense and 50 percent on social programs, and 40 percent is returned to the states. Budget 3 spends 40 percent on defense and 10 percent on social programs, and 50 percent is returned to the states. Each member of the subcommittee ranks the budgets in order of preference, and their rankings are presented in Table 17-3.

Using the majority rule criterion, answer the following questions.

TABLE 17-3

SENATOR	BUDGET 1	BUDGET 2	BUDGET 3
A	Third	First	Second
B	Second	Third	First
C	First	Second	Third

THE GOVERNMENT AND RESOURCE ALLOCATION

a. When the rankings of budgets 1 and 2 are compared, the majority ranks budget _____ higher than budget _____.

b. When the rankings of budgets 1 and 3 are compared, the majority ranks budget _____ higher than budget _____.

c. It logically follows from (a) and (b) that budget _____ is preferred to budget _____.

d. When the rankings of budgets 2 and 3 are compared, the majority ranks budget _____ higher than budget _____.

e. Table 17-3 reflects the (paradox of voting/median voter) _____, and it shows that a consistent ranking of the alternatives (is/is not) _____ possible.

f. If each senator could vote only for his most preferred budget, the voting would result in a _____.

3. Figure 17-1 represents a labor market in which the government has imposed a tax on labor income. The initial supply curve is SS.

a. At the initial equilibrium, the wage is $_____ and the quantity is _____ hours of work.

b. When the government imposes a tax; the supply curve _____ to SS' because at each market wage rate, worker take-home pay (rises/falls) _____, and so labor supplies (more/fewer) _____ hours at each wage.

c. After the tax, the new wage paid by employers is $_____ per unit of labor, but the take-home pay is $_____ per hour. The amount of labor supplied falls to _____ hours because the tax has (increased/reduced) _____ the work effort.

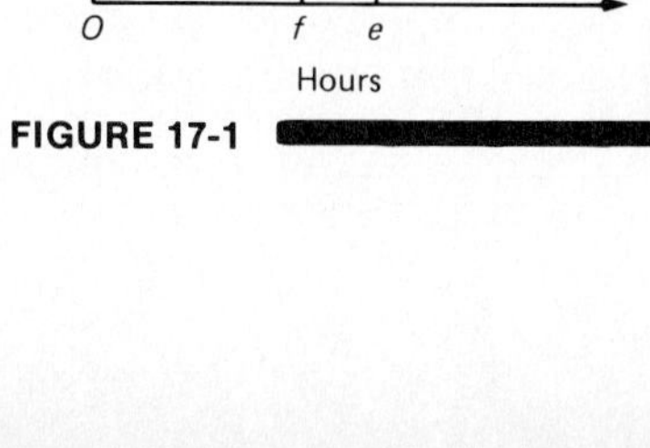

d. A wedge in the amount of (bc/gh) _____ has been driven between the value of the worker to the firm and the marginal benefit received by workers for another hour of labor. This wedge represents a _____ in the market, and it serves to (encourage/discourage) _____ workers to supply more labor.

e. The loss to society is the deadweight burden of the tax and is given by triangle _____. The revenue received by the government is shown by rectangle _____.

4. Tables 17-4 and 17-5 present two different tax structures.

TABLE 17-4
TAX STRUCTURE 1

TAXABLE INCOME, $	INCOME TAX PAID, $	AVERAGE TAX RATE (ATR-I), %	MARGINAL TAX RATE (MTR-I), %
1,000	147		
2,000	312		
3,000	505		
4,000	700		
5,000	905		
10,000	2,097		
15,000	3,528		
20,000	5,221		

TABLE 17-5
TAX STRUCTURE 2

TAXABLE INCOME, $	INCOME TAX PAID, $	AVERAGE TAX RATE (ATR-II), %	MARGINAL TAX RATE (MTR-II), %
1,000	200		
2,000	400		
3,000	600		
4,000	800		
5,000	1,000		
10,000	2,000		
15,000	3,000		
20,000	4,000		

a. Complete each table by computing and entering the marginal and average tax rates as income rises.

b. Of the two tax structures above, structure _____ is progressive because at higher levels of income, both the average and marginal tax rates _____.

c. When every income level is assessed the same

FIGURE 17-1

TABLE 17-6

PRODUCTION STAGE	SOLD TO	AT A PRICE OF, $	VALUE ADDED (VA), $	VALUE ADDED TAX (VAT), $
1. Mining	Gold processor	25	_____	_____
2. Alloys gold	Craftsman	75	_____	_____
3. Creates ring	Jewelry wholesaler	150	_____	_____
4. Distributes ring	Jeweler	200	_____	_____
5. Displays good/retailer	Customer	300	_____	_____

tax, it is called a _____ structure, and this is presented in structure _____. Both the marginal and average tax rates under this structure are _____ percent.

5. Assume that the government imposes a 5 percent value added tax. This tax is added on to the value created at each stage in the production of a good. Table 17-6 shows the stages involved in the production and distribution of a gold dinner ring.

a. Complete Table 17-6 by calculating value added and the value added tax.

b. The sum of the value added to the production of this good is $_____.

c. If the government had a single 5 percent sales tax levied on the retail price of the good, the tax would be $_____.

d. The sum of all of the value added taxes is $_____, and so both taxes yield (the same/a different) _____ amount of revenue.

FILL-IN QUESTIONS

1. Welfare and Social Security benefits are both examples of _____ payments since no good or service is provided by the recipient.

2. The major component of government revenue is _____; however, some revenue is earned from _____.

3. Government intervention into the market economy can help minimize or eliminate _____ arising from market failure, provide public _____, and _____ income.

4. Exclusion (is/is not) _____ possible in the consumption of private goods, but it (is/is not) _____ possible in the consumption of public goods.

5. In order to determine an aggregate demand curve for a public good, each individual demand curve is added (horizontally/vertically) _____ because of the impossibility of _____ anyone from consumption.

6. The paradox of voting argues that it (is/is not) _____ possible to determine consistent rankings by using the _____ rule voting criterion; however, the median voter model states that society's preferences will reflect those of the _____ voter.

7. If taxes are used to redistribute income, the trade-off between economic _____ and _____ becomes important.

8. Health, education, food, and shelter are examples of (public/merit) _____ goods because society thinks that citizens should receive them regardless of income.

9. If voter preferences are single-peaked, it (is/is not) _____ possible for _____ rule voting to bring about a sensible result and possible that that result will reflect the choice of the _____ voter.

10. Two ways in which bureaucrats may influence the allocation of resources are discretionary use of _____ and being influenced by the advice of _____.

11. Social Security taxes are an example of (a payroll/an excise/an income) _____ tax, while a tax on the increased value of an asset is (a corporate profit/a capital gain) _____ tax.

12. When an income tax is imposed, the marginal social costs and marginal social benefits of working are not equal, and so a _____ is created in the market.

THE GOVERNMENT AND RESOURCE ALLOCATION   161

13. The (ability to pay/benefits received) _____ principle argues that taxes should be based on income or wealth, while the (ability to pay/benefits received) _____ principle states that those receiving services from government should pay.

14. Taxes on wages (do/do not) _____ create a deadweight loss to society.

15. If the supply curve of a factor is perfectly (elastic/inelastic) _____, any imposition of a tax on wages is borne entirely by the worker since the quantity of hours worked (does/does not) _____ change.

16. The tax system (does/does not) _____ treat investment in capital and in private housing equally because of the _____ rent of home ownership.

17. In California, Proposition _____ advocated big cuts in state income taxes, and it (did/did not) _____ pass.

18. According to the Laffer curve, after a certain tax rate is reached, it is possible to increase tax revenues only by (increasing/decreasing) _____ the tax rate.

TRUE-FALSE QUESTIONS

1. _____ The paradox of voting is a serious problem because it means that it is not possible for society to make consistent choices under all circumstances by using majority voting.

2. _____ Quite often, government departments become the major proponents of the programs they administer.

3. _____ Since the early eighteenth century, the major source of revenue for the U.S. government has been the income tax.

4. _____ Social Security payments could more appropriately be called an insurance payment because they insure the worker against destitution in old age.

5. _____ A major difference between the U.S. and European tax structures is that the governments of Europe collect more revenue through the VAT than the United States does.

6. _____ To say that a tax system should reflect horizontal equity means that unequals should be treated unequally.

7. _____ The ability to pay principle supports the idea of the redistribution of income by government.

8. _____ The federal tax structure greatly enhances the inequality of income among citizens.

9. _____ When the government imposes a tax on wages, it drives a wedge between the productivity of labor and the disutility of labor, thus creating a distortion in the market.

10. _____ It has been suggested that the U.S. income tax system generates a minimal waste of resources.

11. _____ Relative to the return to owner-occupied housing, the return to investment in productive capital has fallen.

12. _____ For an elastic supply of labor curve, any tax on wages is borne by both workers and producers.

13. _____ Proposition 13 increased taxes and local government spending in California.

14. _____ Since Arthur Laffer introduced his curve showing that high tax rates can actually cause tax revenue to fall, most economists have strongly supported his arguments.

15. _____ The proposed tax rate of 19 percent for a flat-rate tax system would greatly simplify the individual tax return.

16. _____ At the state, local, and federal levels, government tax collections amount to about one-third of GNP.

17. _____ The federal property tax accounts for almost 1 percent of total government revenues.

18. _____ The federal government has a general sales tax on the sale of finished goods.

MULTIPLE-CHOICE QUESTIONS

Circle the correct answer.

1. The change in the amount of tax paid on an extra dollar of income is called the
    a. average tax rate   **c.** marginal tax rate
    b. flat-rate tax   **d.** value added tax

2. The largest single component of state government expenditure is
    a. education   **c.** health and hospitals
    b. police   **d.** highways

3. Local governments receive most of their revenue from
    a. corporate profits tax
    b. excise taxes
    c. customs duties
    d. capital gains tax
    e. none of the above

4. All of the following can be classified as a public good except
   a. the U.S. Navy
   b. clothes given to the Salvation Army
   c. police protection
   d. clean rivers and lakes

5. The free rider problem is encountered when
   a. all individuals who consume a public good pay for it
   b. individuals are willing to pay for what they consume
   c. all goods consumed and produced are private goods
   d. someone benefits from the consumption of a public good without paying his full share

6. The general presumption about government as a producer of goods is that
   a. it is less efficient than the private sector
   b. it is more efficient than the private sector
   c. it will be very innovative in new production technology
   d. it will be as efficient as the private sector

7. When the government intervenes in the marketplace in order to redistribute income,
   a. every citizen is made better off
   b. the well-being of all citizens remains unchanged
   c. some citizens are made better off at the expense of others
   d. all citizens are made worse off

8. All of the following can be considered a merit good except
   a. immunization from polio
   b. a high school education
   c. filet mignon once a week
   d. adequate housing

9. The function of a political lobby is to
   a. provide a place of rest and relaxation for senators
   b. influence politicians to vote a certain way
   c. promote the best interest of all voters
   d. ensure large voter turnout in major elections

10. A coalition by minorities agreeing on how they will vote on a package of issues so that all benefit is known as
    a. block voting
    b. the paradox of voting
    c. double-peaked preferences
    d. logrolling

11. Which of the following might be a motive for a legislator's behavior?
    a. desire for wealth
    b. desire to promote the voters' interest
    c. desire for power
    d. desire for popularity
    e. all of the above

12. Taxes on the income of the factors of production include all of the following except
    a. personal income tax
    b. estate tax
    c. corporate profit tax
    d. payroll tax

13. The incidence of taxation describes
    a. how often taxes are collected
    b. the amount of taxes collected
    c. who pays the tax
    d. which government agency receives the tax revenue

14. A leader of the tax revolt of the early 1970s was
    a. Howard Jarvis
    b. Arthur Laffer
    c. Tip O'Neill
    d. Jimmy Carter

15. The Laffer curve has been used in conjunction with
    a. the argument to increase taxes
    b. the argument for increased government spending
    c. supply side economics
    d. all of the above

16. The flat-rate tax proposal
    a. is proposed at 19 percent of income
    b. applies to both households and corporations
    c. is not levied on capital gains
    d. simplifies income tax reporting
    e. all of the above

AT THIS POINT YOU SHOULD BE ABLE TO . . .

1. Define both marginal and average tax rates and show how each is calculated, and define and give an example of the payroll tax.
2. State three major components of federal, state, and local government spending and three major sources of federal, state, and local revenue.
3. Define and distinguish between private and public goods, give examples of each, and explain the free rider problem.
4. Explain and show graphically how the aggregate demand curve for a public good is determined.
5. State an argument for and an argument against the government production of public goods.
6. Explain the trade-off between equity and efficiency as government attempts to redistribute income.

THE GOVERNMENT AND RESOURCE ALLOCATION

7. Define and give an example of a merit good.

8. State the general objective of the theory of public choice, explain the paradox of voting and the median voter model, and define single- and double-peaked preferences and explain their influence on majority voting decisions.

9. Explain the meaning of a value added tax and state how it differs from a retail sales tax; also, describe a progressive tax structure.

10. Explain the meaning of horizontal equity and vertical equity, state what role they play in tax policy, and give an example of the benefits received and the ability to pay principles of public finance.

11. Show graphically and explain how a tax on labor income generates a market distortion and a deadweight burden to society; identify the tax wedge.

12. Define imputed rent and compare the return to investment in private capital with the return from investment in owner-occupied housing.

13. List three propositions from the California tax revolt, give their major features and tell which have become law.

14. Draw the Laffer curve and explain the idea behind it; also, explain the proposed flat-rate tax system.

QUESTIONS FOR THOUGHT

1. The three levels of government in the United States receive hundreds of billions of dollars each year in tax revenue and often spend even more. What are the major sources of this revenue at each level of government? What are the major expenditure categories? Has government finance always been so large?

2. Why should government be concerned about the redistribution of income? What are the ethical considerations encountered when the tax system is used as a method of redistribution? Explain.

3. In a free-market economy, how can government intervention into the market ever be justified? What role do social and market valuations play in the decision of government to intervene? Explain.

4. What is the paradox of voting? What is meant by the median voter model? What effect would an even number of voters have on the paradox and the median voter model? Explain.

5. What is the difference between a public good and a private good? What role does the principle of exclusion from consumption play in your definition? Explain.

6. Explain how the free rider problem can influence the provision of public goods by the free market. How does the problem influence the allocation of resources in the market? Can the possibility of free riders be used to justify government intervention into the marketplace? Why or why not?

7. Exactly what is meant by tax progressivity? How would a flat-rate tax system differ? Can you give examples?

18

City Economics and the Problems of the Cities

Chapter 18 presents a discussion of some of the advantages and disadvantages of the urbanization of population. Cities are almost as old as history itself. When agriculture became so productive that one farmer could support himself and someone else, people began to leave the land and congregate in "cities." Once individuals no longer had to rely on their own labor for food and clothing, new skills and trades developed. Cities further promoted the development of skills and fostered trade among individuals. When people began to live in cities, though, the problems of urban living began. As in modern times, ancient cities faced such problems as overcrowding, crime, poverty, and housing. Cities in the United States face many of the same problems as ancient Rome. In Chapter 18, Professors Fischer and Dornbusch present the economic rationale for the development and structure of cities, the economic basis for many of the problems faced by today's metropolitan areas, and some proposed solutions to these problems.

Chapter 18 begins by asking, "Why cities?" In answering this question, two forces which promote the development of cities must be mentioned: the benefits from specialization and trade and the benefits from lower transportation costs. The location of economic activity in an urban area promotes economies of agglomeration, and these promote trade. Another important explanation for city development is the development of transportation methods which reduce the costs of moving goods, people, and information. These two forces encourage the concentration of people, which in turn promotes more scale economies, specialization, and trade. However, problems such as pollution, congestion, scarcity of space, and (eventually) rising transportation costs serve as a decentralizing force which causes the city to spread. When a city does spread outward, its land-rent and population density gradients flatten.

Lower transportation costs, higher incomes, and increased population have caused suburbanization in many metropolitan areas. When population moves away from a city's center, businesses and industry also move away. Some households leave the inner city to escape urban blight and a deteriorating downtown. Their leaving creates a vacuum that is filled by new immigrants into the city. These new immigrants are the rural poor who move to the city in search of better living conditions and job opportunities; however, because job vacancies are few, the immigrants often contribute to the increased deterioration of the downtown area.

In the central city, much of the housing available for the poor is not very desirable. Programs for the removal of slums and the development of public housing in which the government subsidizes construction have had only partial success because of the limited supply of housing units. Other approaches to the problem of urban housing include direct cash transfers to the poor for housing and rent control. Some economists argue that people should have unrestricted cash transfers in order to increase their income. Such a program of money transfer to the poor is called a negative income tax.

The primary method of urban transportation is the private automobile. The auto is also a source of major problems in the movement of people both within cities and between cities and suburbs. Automobiles pollute, generate tremendous amounts of congestion (especially during rush hours), and are inefficient relative to other types of transportation available within an urban area. It is difficult if not impossible to determine the price for using a road, and so the level of congestion created by the automobile is usually beyond the social optimum. For this reason, some have argued that public transportation should be subsidized and private use of the automobile discouraged.

The final section of Chapter 18 presents the problem of financing urban areas. Many of the nation's older cities have experienced or are currently experiencing serious financial problems. Cities must pay for education and other urban services with tax revenues from federal and state governments and the local property tax. A problem arises when the demand for services increases rapidly (especially with the influx of low-income households into the city's center) but the revenue does not grow at the same rate. As upper-income households and businesses leave the inner city, the tax base declines so that an important source of revenue falls. The financial crisis will force cities to reduce services, rely more on aid from the federal and state governments, or merge with other local governments.

CHAPTER OUTLINE

1. Two forces which combine to create cities are the benefits from specialization and transportation costs. Trade occurs because of differences in skills and ownership of resources and because of economies of scale in production. Economies of agglomeration (benefits accruing to all industries because of increased population in an area) also serve to concentrate economic activity. Some activities require a large population (market) for support, and so they usually are found only in cities. People migrate to cities because of increased productivity in agriculture and reduced transportation costs for both goods and individuals.
2. The size and location of cities are also determined by the benefits of concentration (specialization, scale economies, and increased choice) and transportation costs. Increased concentration creates problems associated with congestion. When a city grows, the average and marginal costs of production and transportation fall until some point is reached at which the marginal transportation costs to the edge of the city's effective market rise. Eventually, the marginal transportation costs exceed any benefits from scale economies, and so the delivery cost (price) of goods to distant markets increases. When the marginal costs of production and delivery reach a certain level, new central locations are formed, and the city begins to decentralize.
   a. City location is influenced by natural resources and natural barriers. Many older cities are located on or near navigible rivers, oceans, and railroads.
3. A high density of population defines a city. The population density is greatest at the city's center. A population density gradient is a curve which shows a negative relationship between densities and distance from the center of the city. A land-rent gradient (rents paid for the use of the land only) shows that the rent offered for the use of land decreases with distance from the city's center.
   a. Assuming that all land and households in an area are identical and that transportation costs depend on the distances from the city's center, the major reason why land rents decline with distance from the center is that transportation costs increase. The greater the distance, the higher the transportation costs, and so less is offered for the use of the land. In the city's center, consumers substitute other goods for space because rent is so high. This results in a high concentration (density) of population.
      (1) The rent gradient does not have to be smooth as it falls from the center of the city. Local centers of business activity and population within a city's area may well make the gradient undulate as it falls with distance.
      (2) The major determinant of the slope of the rent gradient (the rate at which it falls) is transportation costs.
      (3) The level of the rent gradient (and hence the city's land rents) is determined by the opportunity cost of land in agriculture. As the agricultural use of land decreases, its marginal product and opportunity costs increase, and so a higher rent has to be paid to bid more land away from agricultural use. As the city's boundaries expand, more land is forthcoming only at higher rents, and this generates an upward-sloping supply curve for land. The demand for land in cities slopes downward because of the diminishing marginal value product of land in urban use.
   b. Population densities vary among cities. Population density gradients for the United States are lower and flatter than in most countries. The gradients have become flatter over time because of continued reduction in transportation costs, an increase in the demand for land (space) resulting from higher incomes, and efficient decentralization of older cities.
4. The move to the suburbs occured as lower transportation costs, higher income, and a higher population flattened density gradients.
   a. As people move to the suburbs, so do businesses. The reasons which lead people to move out of the central city also cause businesses to move.
   b. The blight flight explanation of decentralization describes the movement of primarily white people to the suburbs in an attempt to escape deteriorating central cities. On leaving the central city, the middle- and upper-income families sold their households to less wealthy families who did not maintain the houses or neighborhoods. As the tax base deteriorated, so did city services. Flight to the suburbs to avoid blight actually made the deterioration worse. Rural poor blacks moved to the central cities and into inadequate housing. The substandard, low-rent housing of the central city has not

been maintained by the owners because of rising maintenance expenses. With its relatively low rents, this type of housing attracts the poor to the central city. Attempts at urban renewal in the 1960s were not very successful because slum housing was replaced by better, more expensive residential units. These newer units were priced above the affordable rent for many individuals. The decentralization of cities also can be attributed in part to racial prejudice as whites left the central city when the influx of minorities began.
5. City slums are one of the most visible signs of poverty. Attempts to improve the living standards of the inner-city poor have been made.
   a. The urban renewal program of the federal government had as its goal the removal of slums and the creation of an adequate supply of standard housing; however, the better housing attracted people with higher incomes.
   b. An alternative to slum clearance was the construction of low-cost public housing, with the federal government paying the cost of building the units. The aim of the public housing program was to shift the supply curve of housing and thus force down rents. The program has had limited success.
   c. Housing allowances provide a direct transfer of money from the government to individuals to use only for housing. A household's eligibility to receive this allowance is based on its income. The major benefit of giving money directly to individuals to spend on housing is that government remains out of the housing market. The major objection is that since housing supply is inelastic in the short run, housing allowances only drive up rents for everyone.
   d. The use of rent controls (establishing a ceiling rent) to ensure that people can afford housing creates a shortage of units because the short-run stock of housing is fixed. In the long run, rent controls serve as a negative incentive to either build more units or maintain the existing units adequately. The result is that existing housing deteriorates, the available stock declines, and the shortage is made even worse.
   e. Two reasons against giving people unrestricted cash transfers to obtain housing are that there is no assurance that the individual will use the money for housing and that externalities may exist in the housing market. These externalities arise because some urban residents are offended by the presence of slums, because the need for urban services is greater in poor neighborhoods, and because housing is a merit good. It has been argued that people should have a decent level of income and that they should be allowed to allocate it in any way they wish. The argument is that government should give money to the poor and not necessarily try to improve housing.
      (1) The negative income tax proposes that money should be given to low-income people. After income reaches a certain level, a positive income tax is collected.
6. The decline in urban transportation cost has encouraged people to move to the suburbs; however, transportation itself may be a problem in a city.
   a. People commute daily from suburb to city, city to suburb, and within suburbs. The primary means of commuting is the private automobile. Public transportation receives less commuter traffic.
   b. Some economists argue that automobile traffic should be discouraged because the auto pollutes, causes congestion, helps people leave the central city, and is energy-inefficient in comparison to mass transit. The use of automobiles in urban areas does generate externalities, especially pollution and congestion. A problem in dealing with congestion and fixed road capacity is that drivers cannot be forced to internalize this external cost of their actions. There appears to be no way to charge the correct price so that the marginal social cost and marginal private valuation of auto travel are equal, because there is no market for using roads. Through a change in social conventions, some of the costs arising from the absence of a market for automobile use of roads can be lowered. A complete cost-benefit analysis of urban transportation would probably reveal that the most efficient means of transportation is the bus.
7. Many cities have experienced major financial crises during the last decade, and the decade of the 1980s does not appear to be much brighter. There are four reasons why some older cities have or are likely to have a financial crisis. First, many urban services are labor-intensive, and labor costs are very high. Second, many central cities are substantially built up, and so any movement of population or business to the suburbs reduces the tax base and tax revenues. Third, some central cities have signed excessive wage and benefit packages in an attempt to ensure labor peace. Fourth, central-city residents are more likely than suburban residents to need the social services provided by the urban government. Since increasing taxes to raise revenue is both unpopular and discouraging to new construction, the central city could raise money by charging for

CITY ECONOMICS AND THE PROBLEMS OF THE CITIES

some services or by depending on the state and federal government for more funds. An alternative possibility is for the central city and wealthier suburbs to merge.

a. The Tiebout hypothesis states that central cities and suburbs should not merge because this would interfere with the free locational decisions of both people and business. Tiebout argued that each local government offers a particular package of services; the more local governments in an area, the greater the choice of packages. The merging of local governments reduces the selection of services. A problem with the Tiebout hypothesis is that newer cities are able to offer lower-cost services which the older cities cannot, and so the more affluent resident selects the newer city because he can afford to move.

b. Zoning regulations in the suburbs help keep out the poor who might use the area's services without paying for them. Zoning efficiently controls the consumption of goods. Economics does not justify limiting access for any reason other than the payment made for the local services provided.

IMPORTANT TERMS AND THEIR MEANING

Match the following terms with the correct definition or phrase.

1. _____ Setting a price for housing below the market equilibrium price; usually done by government

2. _____ The concentration of population in cities

3. _____ Shows how density of population changes with distance from the center of a city

4. _____ Argues that the movement of primarily white people to the suburbs happened because they were trying to escape deteriorating city centers

5. _____ Proposal to subsidize low-income people by giving them unrestricted money; but after a certain income level, they begin to pay taxes

6. _____ Regulations established by local authorities which state how the land in an area can be used

a. Slum clearance

b. Zoning regulations

c. Negative income tax

d. Urbanization

e. Economies of agglomeration

f. Land-rent gradient

7. _____ Since local government is a way of providing a package of services, central cities and suburbs should not merge because this would interfere with the locational decisions of people

8. _____ Benefits which accrue to all industries in an area because the population expands

9. _____ A curve showing how rents change with distance from the center of the city

10. _____ A characteristic of the urban renewal program of the 1960s in which old housing was destroyed and better housing was built

11. _____ The movement of people and businesses out of the central city and the establishment of local centers of economic activity

12. _____ A high density of automobile traffic reflected in overcrowded highways

13. _____ A direct payment of money to people for use only in securing better living accommodations

g. Congestion

h. Decentralization

i. Population density gradient

j. Tiebout hypothesis

k. Blight flight

l. Housing allowance

m. Rent controls

EXERCISES

1. Figure 18-1 presents one hypothesis explaining how a city grows.[1] Imagine that you have an aerial photograph of a metropolitan area from a high altitude. Looking directly down on the photo, you see a downtown area (represented by A) with its associated retail and office activities. Zone B supports the activities in zone A with supply, warehousing, storage, and a few retail activities. Zone C is a zone in transition and is associated with low-income households. This zone at one time consisted of middle- and upper-income residents; however, it now contains housing for low-income people. Zone D is made up of working-class households and some supporting retail establishments. Zones E and F are middle- and upper-income residences with supporting local retail businesses. The commuter lives in zone F. Below the set of rings, a rent gradient is shown; however, this gradient shows movement in two directions from the city. Based on the

[1] Earnest W. Burgess, "The Growth of the City," reprinted in Robert E. Pask, et al., *The City*, University of Chicago Press, Chicago, 1925.

168 CHAPTER 18

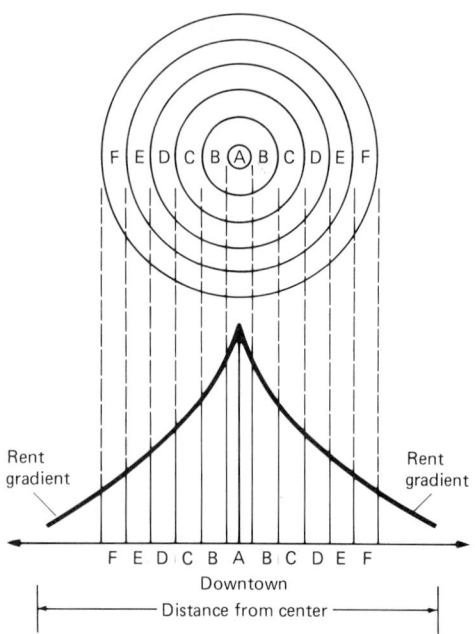

FIGURE 18-1

above information and Figure 18-1, answer the following questions.

a. The highest rent in this urban model is found in zone _____, and this zone also contains the (highest/lowest) _____ population density.

b. Blight flight from the area could best be represented by movement from zone(s) _____ to zone(s) _____.

c. As outmigration occurs, the rent paid (decreases/increases) _____, and it generally can be assumed that population becomes (more/less) _____ dense.

d. The agricultural function takes place after zone _____ since rents are (lower/higher) _____ than the rent charged for any of the urban functions; however, if the metropolitan area expands, the boundary of zone _____ expands and rental rates _____.

e. Listed below are several characteristics describing an urban area. Using Figure 18-1 and the zone designations, identify each activity by the zone in which you think the characteristic or activity occurs.

(1) fine restaurants, expensive clothing shops, major office functions, theater _____

(2) expensive single-family homes, well-kept lawns, private swimming pools _____

(3) middle- and high-income apartments, condominiums, some speciality shops and retail stores _____

(4) high crime rate, high concentration of minorities, poor or rapidly deteriorating housing _____

(5) storage buildings, railroad freight yards, supply houses _____

(6) ethnic neighborhoods, poor schools, high consumption of urban services _____

(7) houses primarily industrial workers; older but not deteriorated houses _____

(8) almost all residents commute to work; clearly a suburban area _____

2. Table 18-1 presents hypothetical income data and "guaranteed income." The guaranteed income is the amount the government permits you to keep after paying taxes or receiving money transfers.

a. Calculate the tax payment either to or from government and enter your computations in the appropriate column.

TABLE 18-1

GROSS INCOME, $	GUARANTEED INCOME, $	TAX PAYMENT TO (+) OR FROM (−) GOVERNMENT, $
0	2,000	
1,000	2,500	
2,000	3,000	
3,000	3,500	
4,000	4,000	
5,000	4,500	
6,000	5,000	
7,000	5,500	
8,000	6,000	
9,000	6,500	
10,000	7,000	

b. Table 18-1 provides an example of a _____ tax since below a certain income level, government (transfers/receives) _____ payments (to/from) _____ individuals.

c. At a guaranteed income of $_____, the tax payment from government is zero, but the payment to government (increases/decreases) _____.

d. If an individual had no income, he could be assured of receiving $_____ of (restricted/unrestricted) _____ income.

e. This proposed method of government assistance was first advanced by the well-known economist _____.

CITY ECONOMICS AND THE PROBLEMS OF THE CITIES 169

TABLE 18-2

PRICE PER TRIP, $	NUMBER OF CARS ENTERING PER HOUR, thousands	AVERAGE COST PER TRIP, $	MARGINAL COST PER TRIP, $
12	35	5.00	5.00
11	45	5.00	5.00
10	55	5.00	5.00
9	65	5.00	5.00
8	75	5.25	6.00
7	85	5.50	7.00
6	95	6.00	8.50
5	105	8.50	12.50

3. The data in Table 18-2 present price, quantity, and cost data for private automobiles using a highway near an urban area. The quantity data are in thousands.

 a. The average and marginal cost per journey is constant at $_____ per trip until _____ cars enter the road. When this number of cars enters the road, it is then filled to _____; however, the marginal private valuation is (greater than/less than) _____ the marginal social costs of travel. Thus, (more/fewer) _____ cars will enter the road.

 b. Drivers will continue to use their cars until _____ equals the _____ cost of the trip. At that point, _____ cars enter the road per hour. There (is/is not) _____ congestion according to the data.

 c. The optimal rate of cars entering the highway is _____ cars per hour since at this rate, the _____ cost of $_____ equals the marginal private valuation or _____ per trip.

 d. The above analysis indicates that auto traffic should be (increased/reduced) _____.

FILL-IN QUESTIONS

1. In the U.S., approximately (50/75) _____ percent of the population lives in towns or cities, and (10/18/100) _____ urban areas have populations in excess of 2 million or more.

2. The benefits of _____ and _____ costs are two important factors which combine to create cities.

3. If agriculture had not become so productive, it (would/would not) _____ have been possible for the United States to become such an urbanized nation.

4. A (land-rent/population density) _____ gradient measures the number of people per square mile, and the gradient (rises/falls) _____ as distance from the central city increases.

5. Sometimes a city's land-rent gradient is not smooth but undulates because there are _____ centers of both population concentration and retail activities, and this (would/would not) _____ influence land rents in the area surrounding the central city.

6. An increase in the population of an urban area causes the demand curve for land to (increase/decrease) _____ and the rents to (increase/decrease) _____ both at the center and the edge of the city, and so land will be shifted from (residential/agricultural) _____ use to urban use.

7. In 1950, _____ percent of the people living in cities lived in the central city, but by 1970 the number had fallen to _____ percent.

8. The movement of more affluent households out of the central city because of deteriorating conditions has been labeled _____, and this tends to attract (more/less) _____ poor families into the central city because housing rents are (higher/lower) _____.

9. _____ housing is usually built with federal money and operated by local governments to provide low-income housing; however, the program has had (no/limited) _____ success.

10. Rent controls can generate a serious long-run (surplus/shortage) _____ of housing because deteriorating housing (is/is not) _____ replaced.

11. One of the major reasons explaining the economics of cities is that transportation costs (rise/fall) _____, and this also permits the movement of the population to the (central city/suburbs) _____.

12. By far the most frequently used mode of urban transportation is the (bus/automobile/subway)

_____, and this leads to both air _____ and _____.

13. The two major sources of urban revenue are the _____ tax and _____, while the largest expenditure cities have to make is for (highways/education/sanitation) _____.

14. The _____ hypothesis argues that we should have (more/fewer) _____ local governments so that a better locational choice is possible.

15. Local governments often _____ land so that its use is restricted to certain activities.

TRUE-FALSE QUESTIONS

1. _____ A characteristic of most major cities in the past is that they were almost always located on a navigable waterway.

2. _____ The urbanization of America has resulted in a very rapid growth rate of some of our larger cities.

3. _____ Scale economies increase with city size and pull down the average and marginal costs of production.

4. _____ It is possible to regard trading centers and cities as forming a hierarchy of urban places ranging from small hamlets to world cities.

5. _____ Because people demand less space farther from the center of a city, the population density gradient increases as distance from the central city increases.

6. _____ In 1980, the population density in the United States was 57 people per square mile.

7. _____ One reason why population density gradients have been falling in recent years is that rail transportation permits people to lower their commuting costs.

8. _____ In suburban areas, property taxes are higher than in the central city because of the ability to pay principle.

9. _____ One reason why many poor families have moved to the cities from rural areas is that agriculture became more mechanized so that the demand for agricultural labor fell.

10. _____ Segregation is practically nonexistent in central-city housing because such areas contain so many ethnic groups.

11. _____ One reason why poverty in urban areas receives so much attention is that it is more visible than in rural areas.

12. _____ The urban renewal programs of the 1960s were very successful in providing a large supply of modern, low-income housing.

13. _____ If the government used a voucher system to provide a direct housing allowance to the poor, it would also have to subsidize new housing construction to increase the number of available housing units.

14. _____ Staggered working hours have helped reduce both the private and the social costs of traffic congestion.

15. _____ In many cities, the most economical form of public transportation is the bus.

16. _____ In New York City, most public welfare payments are the responsibility of the state of New York.

17. _____ According to the Tiebout hypothesis, urban efficiency in terms of administration and individual locational choice can best be achieved when local governments merge.

18. _____ The economics of zoning indicates that social welfare can be improved by limiting the access to certain areas on the basis of race or ethnic origin.

MULTIPLE-CHOICE QUESTIONS

Circle the correct answer.

1. When the costs of production fall because firms are located close to one another in an area with an expanding population, the firms are experiencing
    a. negative returns to scale
    b. constant returns to scale
    c. economies of agglomeration
    d. decreasing returns to scale

2. All the following forces tend to create cities except
    a. blight flight
    b. falling costs of transportation
    c. specialization
    d. choice and competition
    e. scale economies

3. Which of the following will not promote the decentralization of a city?
    a. the movement of business out of the central city
    b. high levels of congestion of both people and autos
    c. a well-developed network of highways around and in the city
    d. high transportation costs

4. A land-rent gradient shows
   a. the population per square mile in a particular area
   b. rent as a function of distance from the center of a city
   c. the population in an area as a function of distance from a city's center
   d. rental rates paid for the use of a fixed supply of land

5. Local centers of economic activity emerge in a metropolitan area because
   a. people move away from the central city
   b. transportation costs fall
   c. businesses move away from the city's center
   d. the central city becomes blighted
   e. all of the above

6. The demand curve for land in an urban area slopes downward when
   a. the value of an extra unit of land in either industrial production or private consumption decreases
   b. the quantity of land is fixed so that higher rents have to be paid in order to get more land to be forthcoming for use
   c. economies of agglomeration reduce the costs of operation of a firm so that it offers less for more land
   d. land rents at the edge of a city are higher than those at the city's center

7. In 1970, the percentage of the population of metropolitan areas living in the suburban ring was
   a. 57.3 percent   c. 56.9 percent
   b. 42.7 percent   d. 70.1 percent

8. In 1979, the official poverty level income for a family of four was slightly over
   a. $10,300   c. $8500
   b. $5800   d. $7400

9. Public housing programs
   a. have had only limited success
   b. have experienced very high construction costs
   c. have not increased the supply of housing units that much
   d. are usually funded by the federal government and operated by local governments
   e. all of the above

10. When the government establishes a limit on the amount of rent that can be charged for housing,
    a. every person who wants adequate housing can find it
    b. a serious long-run shortage of housing units develops
    c. there is an excess supply of housing in the short run
    d. the established rent will be above the market equilibrium rent
    e. none of the above

11. In 1975, the percentage of workers living outside a central city who drove to work alone in their private vehicles was
    a. 69.7 percent   c. 32.7 percent
    b. 75 percent   d. 56.2 percent

12. Which of the following would be included in a cost-benefit analysis of metropolitan commuting patterns?
    a. the nonmarket work time spent driving to and from work
    b. the comfort of commuting in a private auto
    c. the increased level of automobile emissions
    d. the price of a new car
    e. all of the above

13. The negative income tax
    a. could be used by everyone to reduce tax liabilities
    b. went into effect in 1978
    c. was first proposed by economist Paul Samuelson
    d. increases as income goes up
    e. none of the above

AT THIS POINT YOU SHOULD BE ABLE TO...

1. Define urbanization, state two forces which combine to create cities, and list two reasons for the existence of trade.
2. State the meaning of economies of agglomeration and give two examples of these economies.
3. List three forces which promote the centralization and three forces which promote the decentralization of economic activity; also, explain the role of natural resources in determining the location of older cities.
4. Define population density gradients and land-rent gradients and explain the general shape of each.
5. State the meaning and importance of local centers of economic activity in metropolitan areas, especially in terms of the shape of the land-rent gradient.
6. List three reasons why population density gradients have become less steep during the twentieth century.
7. Define blight flight and explain how such an exodus from the central city can actually cause more deterioration.
8. Describe three policies that have been followed in an attempt to improve the housing standards of the poor.
9. State three reasons which have been used to justify government intervention into the housing markets, and explain the idea of the negative income tax.

10. Explain two arguments which have been made against the current level of automobile use in urban areas.

11. List the major sources of revenue and the major categories of expenditures for urban governments.

12. Explain the Tiebout hypothesis.

QUESTIONS FOR THOUGHT

1. Why has trade between people been an important factor in the evolution of urban places? Do you think trade was important in the development and location of ancient cities? Why are economies of agglomeration important in urban areas? Do you think these economies were important in ancient cities? Explain.

2. As a city grows and matures, the decentralization of its central area begins. Explain the economic reasons why this might happen. Why have older cities not been able to cope with this decentralization as well as newer urban places?

3. Explain why a rent gradient may actually rise at the edge of the city. What conditions need to be present in the urban area before the gradient rises? Can the idea of efficient decentralization be used in your answer?

4. Explain the role of transportation cost in both the development of urban areas and the decentralization of these cities. How have automobiles and expressways been important?

5. Explain the concept of "blight flight." What kinds of households are usually involved? What kinds of businesses leave the central city? Can blight flight be used to explain the evolution of inner-city slums and ghettos? If so, how?

6. What is the urban housing problem? How did this problem come into being? Explain some steps that have been taken to improve inner-city urban housing.

7. What are the social costs of congestion? Is there an economic approach to explaining the overuse of private automobiles? If so, explain this approach. Why would it be difficult to determine the appropriate price to charge for road use so that the marginal benefits received equal the marginal costs incurred?

19
Uncertainty in Economic Life

In Chapter 19, you are introduced to the role of uncertainty in economics. Uncertainty occurs in our economic system for many different reasons, but for every action taken, there exists some uncertain future outcome. Some events occur randomly, while others, although unpredictable, are not random. Incomplete information about the process governing the occurrence of events or actions generates uncertainty and risk. Individuals' attitudes toward the risks they face generate certain predictable behavior patterns as they try to make decisions which maximize their well-being in a risky or uncertain environment. Chapter 19 presents the concepts of risk and uncertainty in economics and develops some principles of consumer (investor) behavior within uncertain markets.

Your first task should be to learn the three attitudes toward risk used frequently in economic analysis. Individuals can be risk-averse (attempt to avoid risky events), risk-neutral (indifferent toward risk), or risk-loving (seek out risky events). In economics, the general assumption is that people are risk-averse and attempt to reduce uncertainty. Economists also assume that people undertake risky ventures only if they are compensated for taking those risks.

One way in which individuals try to deal with the effects of uncertainty is to purchase insurance against loss resulting from a particular event. Insurance is based on the premise that risk can be spread or pooled over many people so that the uncertainty about the average outcome of the event is reduced. Through risk pooling, social risk is reduced practically to zero.

When an investor selects the assets to include in a portfolio, both the expected returns and the risks associated with these returns must be considered since uncertainty surrounds the assets' earnings. You should pay particular attention to the way investors react to risk. The risk-averse investor's portfolio contains assets of varying degrees of risk; however, the investor assumes more risk only if the expected returns increase. Through asset diversification, it is possible for the investor to reduce the overall degree of portfolio risk by including several different assets. The success of asset diversification in portfolio selection is influenced by the relationship between asset returns and the degree of risk of each asset. The returns to an asset are also influenced by changes in the overall level of activity in the asset market. A measure of the extent to which an asset's return moves with the returns of the market as a whole is known as beta. Beta is a useful measure when determining which assets to include in a portfolio.

An asset market equilibrium is determined by the interaction of buyers (demand) and sellers (supply). The willingness to either buy or sell assets is based on the expected rate of return. Beliefs about market rationality and efficiency influence the investor's portfolio choice and participation in the market.

The last major section of Chapter 19 presents two additional examples of the influences of uncertainty on the behavior of market participants. In the futures market, hedgers try to reduce their risk and uncertainty about the future, while speculators try to earn a profit by taking the risks which others do not want. The final example shows that in some occupations, the risk of personal injury or death is above average, and so a compensating differential is paid to labor.

CHAPTER OUTLINE

1. Consumers may be risk-averse (unwilling to take chances unless returns are very high), risk-neutral (not at all concerned with risk), or risk-loving (willing to take chances). In economics, risk occurs because of uncertainty; however, it is generally assumed that consumers exhibit risk-averse behavior. Risk-averse individuals try to reduce uncertainty and must be rewarded for bearing risks.

2. Individuals attempt to reduce the possibility of suffering a loss by purchasing insurance. In the event of a loss, the insuror pays the value (or insured amount) of the loss. If a loss does not occur, the individual loses a nonrefundable premium paid for the insurance coverage. Insurance companies spread risk among many individuals who face a particular type of risk during some time period. Spreading risk among many individuals is called risk pooling. This practice reduces the uncertainty about the average outcome. Those individuals who

purchase life insurance for a particular sum buy the insurance company's promise to pay a larger sum in the event of their death. If the company has a large number of policyholders, it can be relatively certain that all claims will not be due over a short period of time; the company spreads the risk over many people. The pooling of risks reduces the social risk to zero since society itself does not bear much risk. Risk pooling works when the risks faced by each individual are independent of each other, and so all individuals who buy a particular type of insurance are the source of funds for payment when a claim is made against an insurance company. A very large degree of uncertainty exists for some events. Should these events occur, losses are substantial, and so the risks are spread over many firms, with each firm offering to assume some but not all of the risk. Each firm offers partial insurance for part of the premium so that together the firms provide substantial insurance coverage. An example of risk spreading over many firms is the Lloyd's of London syndicate.

  a. The presence of insurance can influence human behavior, and it may make the insured more careless and more likely to take chances. This is known as the moral hazard phenomenon.
  b. Adverse selection describes the purchase of insurance against a specific loss by individuals who most likely will collect from the policy. Thus, the insurance companies must try to determine the degree of risk associated with each potential policyholder.
  c. The question of insurance companies' fairness in issuing their policies has been raised. Automobile insurance costs can be very high for drivers under a certain age. The companies argue that young drivers have more accidents and more claims; however, only a few young drivers are reckless. Should all drivers below a certain age pay high premiums? Another problem involves pensions paid to retired individuals. Since women live longer on average than men, should they both receive the same pension payment per month (assuming each paid into the fund for the same length of time)? If so, the average woman gets more per dollar contributed because she outlives the average man.

3. One common form of carrying wealth into the future is holding stocks and bonds. A Treasury bill is a short-term government bond which promises to pay a fixed rate of interest in the future, while a stock represents ownership in a company and earns a return in the form of both dividends and capital gains. These dividends and capital gains are not fixed but change with market conditions. The real rate of return on a stock or bond is its inflation-adjusted rate of return. The real rate of return is uncertain because it is difficult to predict the rate of inflation. For stocks, there also exists uncertainty about dividend payments and the value of the stock (capital gains) in the future. Thus, although stocks and bonds have an element of uncertainty about the real rate of return, the greater degree of risk is associated with stocks.

4. Because an investor can hold many potential assets, the portfolio selection problem focuses on how a risk-averse investor selects and divides wealth among the many alternatives. Portfolio selection is essentially a consumer maximization problem (see Chapter 5) in which attitude toward risk and expected returns to the assets are substituted for consumer tastes and the prices of goods.

  a. Investors' attitudes toward risk determine the level of return.
      (1) An investor who is risk-averse prefers high returns but dislikes risks, and so compensation (return) must be high if an asset is risky.
      (2) Investors' choices are determined by the combinations of returns on assets and the degree of risk associated with these returns.
      (3) An investor, unless he is totally unwilling to accept any risk, divides his wealth among assets with varying degrees of risk. The strength of the investor's risk aversion determines the allocation of wealth among the risky and less risky assets. It is generally expected that the larger the return to assets having a high risk relative to the return to those having much less risk, the larger the share of the investor's portfolio occupied by the more risky assets. If a risky asset's return is extremely variable, the risk-averse investor reduces that asset's share in his portfolio. The more risk-averse an investor, the greater the proportion of his portfolio held in less risky assets.
  b. When an investor faces several risky assets, he may reduce the risk (but not the rate of return) by diversifying his portfolio. When an investor diversifies, he spreads the investments across several assets and reduces risk because it is improbable that all asset performances are correlated perfectly. The more independent the assets' performance, the greater the reduction in risks. Diversification permits the investor to examine the risk associated with his entire portfolio, not just a single asset. The benefits of diversification are achieved by buying 9 to 10 stocks (assets) for a portfolio.

c. Assets' market performance suggests that their returns may be positively or negatively correlated. When the returns on assets move in the same direction, they are positively correlated. If the returns move in opposite directions, a negative correlation exists. When asset returns are positively correlated, the level of portfolio risk is not reduced because diversification doesn't work; all assets rise or fall at the same time. When asset returns are negatively correlated with each other, the overall level of portfolio risk can be reduced as the good performance of one asset compensates for the bad performance of another. Assets which are completely independent in their performance permit the investor to practically eliminate risk in the portfolio.

d. A measure of the extent to which an individual investment's (stock's) returns move relative to the asset (stock) market's returns is the beta coefficient. Beta may be large and positive (the asset fluctuates significantly more than the market but in the same direction), negative (the asset fluctuates in the opposite direction as the market), or equal to 1 (the asset moves in exactly the same way as the market). Assets with a high positive beta add risk to the portfolio, while assets with a negative beta reduce portfolio risk.

e. The principle of risk reduction through diversification can be applied not only to the portfolio problem but to other areas as well. As an example, most farmers do not rely only on one crop for their income—they diversify.

5. The equilibrium level of asset returns depends not only on the investor's attitude toward risk and return but on the interaction between his preferences for present and future consumption with the productivity of capital. Supply and demand forces in the asset market are influenced by the expected return on assets. In turn, these forces establish an equilibrium rate of return. For risky assets, beta is the best measure to use when estimating the equilibrium rate of return the market places on assets. The market prices of stocks, bonds, and other assets are established by supply and demand.

6. When markets are efficient as opposed to being speculative, they serve as processors of information so that the correct prices are paid for assets. This correct price reflects the risk and returns of those assets with respect to the income they produce. Some have argued that asset markets are not efficient but are irrational and speculative, implying that no economic forces determine the prices of assets. The speculative argument states that investors buy an asset on the basis of what they believe its selling price will be in the next time period, and so the emphasis is on the asset's potential capital gains. The efficiency argument states that asset prices accurately reflect all information relevant to the price of the asset. The primary focus of most research on asset pricing has been the stock market. Current research suggests that no method to beat the market exists.

a. If assets are accurately priced on the stock market, investors must decide whether to buy and hold stocks or sell stocks. An assumption of the buy and hold strategy is that the investor believes that the market reflects an accurate pricing mechanism. Since the desired portfolio is determined, it should be maintained. A problem arises if everyone follows the buy and hold strategy, since there will be no incentive to maintain the market's efficiency.

b. The issue of efficiency in asset markets is very important. If asset markets are efficient, society's investment decisions allocate capital resources properly. On the other hand, if asset markets are irrational, it may be argued that state planners can better decide how and what investments should be made.

7. Uncertainty is present in many of our economic activities. As a result, individuals try to find methods to reduce the associated risks. If risks cannot be reduced, individuals must be compensated.

a. A market exists when consumers (investors) contract today for the delivery of commodities at a specified date in the future at a specified price. Participants in the futures market may be hedgers (individuals using the market in an attempt to reduce risk) or speculators (individuals who expect to earn a profit by taking risks). When individuals hedge, they attempt to establish some certainty about the price at which they can buy or sell their commodity in the future. Often, speculators neither have nor want the commodity they trade; they try to guess the future behavior of the market by speculating on the future spot price (the price for immediate delivery) of a commodity. The future price of a commodity is an estimate of the spot price at which it will sell in the future. As a predictor of the future spot price of a commodity, current future prices have not performed very well.

b. In jobs where the risks of physical injury are high or in situations where the income associated with a job is uncertain, employees are paid a compensating differential in the form of higher wages. Studies indicate that the compensating differential for dangerous work is most strongly associated with unionized industries. Profits are often seen as the rewards to entrepreneurs for taking risks by entering new and unproven areas of the market.

IMPORTANT TERMS AND THEIR MEANING

Match the following terms with the correct definition or phrase.

1. _____ The existence of insurance makes people behave in ways that increase the likelihood that they will have the accident against which they are insuring

2. _____ The strategy of reducing risks by spreading investments across several assets

3. _____ A measure of the extent to which a stock's returns move with the returns of the stock market as a whole

4. _____ Describes an individual who is reluctant to take risks unless the returns are very high; one who devotes resources to reducing risks

5. _____ The spreading of risk across many people who face that risk, thus reducing the uncertainty about the average outcome

6. _____ In the market, the returns on two assets move in opposite directions and so the portfolio's risk is reduced

7. _____ The risk faced by society as a whole as opposed to individual risk

8. _____ Investors (consumers) who use the market to reduce the risk they face by making some contracts about future receipts or payments

9. _____ A problem faced by insurance companies because the people who want to buy insurance against a particular loss are those most likely to collect the actual payoff

10. _____ The price for the immediate delivery of a commodity

11. _____ Organized markets for the future delivery of many commodities and assets; in these markets, future prices and quantities for the commodities are determined

12. _____ Describes an individual who is indifferent to risk and is usually concerned with the average payoff of an activity

13. _____ Describes the investment behavior of an individual who assumes that the price of assets in a market are correct and thus does not want to change the existing asset portfolio

14. _____ Traders in the futures market who are not reducing any of their own risk by being in the market and who expect to earn profits by taking risks

15. _____ The difference in wages paid to some workers because their jobs involve a risk of injury or death

16. _____ In the market, the returns on two assets move in the same direction so that the portfolio's risk is not reduced at all through diversification

17. _____ A view of the stock market which states that it is a sensitive processor of information and responds quickly to each bit of new information which might influence the correct price that should be paid for stock

18. _____ An individual who is willing to pay to take risks even when the odds are against him

19. _____ Describes the movement of the returns on assets (stocks) when these returns move together either in the same direction or in opposite directions

a. Social risks
b. Beta
c. Risk-neutral
d. Adverse selection
e. Speculators
f. Spot price
g. Moral hazard
h. Buy and hold strategies
i. Compensating differentials
j. Diversification
k. Risk lover
l. Portfolio selection or choice
m. Efficient markets
n. Hedgers
o. Negatively correlated assets
p. Futures market
q. Risk pooling
r. Risk-averse
s. Correlated stock returns

20. ____ The manner in which an individual investor decides to divide wealth among the different ways of holding assets

t. Risk spreading

21. ____ A key concept in the insurance industry; describes how a company reduces risk by insuring many people who face the same risks; essentially the same as risk pooling

u. Positively correlated assets

EXERCISES

1. Suppose that you might make an offer to lease the coal mining rights on 5000 acres of land. You know what it will cost to lease the rights and begin mining operations. What you don't know is how much coal is present even though you have geologic reports on the area. If you begin operations, you might make money or lose money. You are going to risk your money. If you do lease the land and begin operation, there is a 50-50 chance that the coal will be of such poor quality and have such a high sulfur content that it will be worthless. In this case, you lose $750,000. There is a 20 percent chance that you will find only 2000 tons of poor but usable coal, in which case you lose $200,000. The chance of finding 4000 tons of medium-quality coal is 10 percent, and you gain $550,000. You also have a 10 percent chance of finding 5000 tons of good coal and making $1 million. Finally, if all goes as you hope, there is a 10 percent chance of mining 11,000 tons of an exceptional-quality product and making $2.5 million. Of course, if you don't lease the land and operate, you neither make nor lose anything. Table 19-1 presents the possibilities you face.

a. The first step in evaluating your two alternatives is to compute the expected monetary value of each. Complete Table 19-2 by computing what you

TABLE 19-1

ALTERNATIVE 1: PROCEED WITH VENTURE

OUTCOME OF MINING VENTURE	CHANCE OF OUTCOME, %	MONETARY VALUE OF OUTCOME, $
Poor quality, unusable	0.50	−750,000
Poor quality, usable (2000 tons)	0.20	−200,000
Medium quality (4000 tons)	0.10	+550,000
Good quality (5000 tons)	0.10	+1,000,000
Exceptional quality (11,000 tons)	0.10	+2,500,000
ALTERNATIVE 2: DO NOTHING		0

TABLE 19-2

ALTERNATIVE 1

OUTCOME	EXPECTED MONEY VALUE, $
Poor quality, unusable	____
Poor quality, usable (2000 tons)	____
Medium quality, usable (4000 tons)	____
Good quality, usable (5000 tons)	____
Exceptional quality (11,000 tons)	____
Sum of expected money value	____
ALTERNATIVE 2	0

would expect to gain or lose if a particular outcome occurred.

b. In order to compute the expected money value of each possible outcome, it is necessary to multiply the (chance/hazard) _____ of the event occurring by the (monetary/real) _____ value of the outcome.

c. In comparing alternatives, alternative 1 has an expected money value of _____, while alternative 2 has a value of _____.

d. Based on this analysis, you (should/should not) _____ undertake this venture.

2. The actions below describe the behavior of risk-averse (RA), risk-neutral (RN), and risk-loving (RL) individuals. Beside each action, indicate which type of person it best describes by placing RN, RA, or RL in the blank.

a. Offers a friend the opportunity to flip a coin and win $100 or lose $50 _____

b. Makes all long-distance phone calls person to person rather than station to station _____

c. Buys $100,000 worth of flight insurance for $5 on every flight taken _____

d. Pays $1000 for a gamble with a 1 percent chance to win $10 million, a 1 percent chance of losing $9,900,000 and a 98 percent chance of winning and losing nothing _____

e. Buys a $5 ticket in a raffle for the chance of winning a $15,000 car when 5000 tickets are sold _____

f. In Las Vegas, bets $1000 where the outcome is a 50 percent chance of winning $1010 or a 50 percent chance of winning $990 _____

FILL-IN QUESTIONS

1. Risk-averse individuals (will/will not) _____ use resources to reduce uncertainty and risk and will bear risk only if they are _____ for doing so.

2. In the insurance industry, risk pooling (does/does not) _____ work if the risks faced by individuals are dependent.

3. The return on stocks consists of _____ paid to the stockholders and _____ resulting from an increase in the value of the stock.

4. It is generally assumed in economics that individuals are (risk-averse/risk-neutral/risk lovers) _____ and that they will have a (large/small) _____ number of very risky stocks in their portfolio.

5. Even though an asset may be risky, its inclusion in a portfolio with many other assets can _____ the level of risk of the overall portfolio.

6. A stock can be called (cyclical/countercyclical) _____ if its returns move with the business cycle and (cyclical/countercyclical) _____ if its returns move against the cycle.

7. For a given expected rate of return, the desirable stocks have a (high/low) _____ beta since they are (more/less) _____ risky.

8. The most important determinant of the average rate of return on stocks is the consumer's _____ toward risk.

9. Some believe that the stock market is (rational/irrational) _____ in its activities and is really like a big casino, while others believe that it is (rational/irrational) _____ and determines the correct prices for assets efficiently.

10. A _____ bubble exists when the price of an asset is based largely on the expectations of what others will pay for the asset.

11. If a wheat farmer sells his crop for a specified price before it is harvested, he is (hedging/speculating) _____ by trying to reduce uncertainty about future wheat prices.

12. Some jobs (do/do not) _____ pay a higher wage because of the danger involved in the occupation.

TRUE-FALSE QUESTIONS

1. _____ Risk averters are willing to bear risks only if they are sufficiently compensated for doing so.

2. _____ One of the common assumptions in economics is that people are indifferent toward risk.

3. _____ Two components of the return on stocks are interest paid and capital gains.

4. _____ One of the basic distinctions between the theory of consumer behavior and the theory of portfolio selection is that the latter theory incorporates the consumer's attitudes toward risk as opposed to using the consumer's tastes and preferences for goods.

5. _____ When the returns to two stocks are positively correlated, they move in opposite directions.

6. _____ An example of lack of diversification is the U.S. Navy's emphasis on a fleet of super aircraft carriers as its primary source of oceangoing strength.

7. _____ It is possible that adding a risky asset to a portfolio can reduce the portfolio's overall level of risk.

8. _____ John Maynard Keynes argued very strongly that the stock market exhibited rational behavior and, over the long run, was very efficient in establishing an asset's price.

9. _____ If a trader in the futures market buys a contract today to deliver a commodity 6 months from now because he expects the commodity's price to be higher in 6 months, he is hedging.

10. _____ In his study of compensating differentials for dangerous jobs, Viscusi found that unions had very little influence on the wage differentials.

MULTIPLE-CHOICE QUESTIONS

Circle the correct answer.

1. When an individual with a terminal illness buys a $100,000 insurance policy, the insurance company faces the problem of
   a. risk spreading
   b. adverse selection
   c. social risk
   d. moral hazard

2. In selecting the portfolio, the risk-averse investor
   a. specializes in only one risky asset
   b. chooses only those assets which have a high degree of risk
   c. chooses some risky assets and some less risky assets
   d. does not select assets on the basis of risk but rather on the basis of expected future return

3. When an investor reduces risk by spreading investments over several assets, he is practicing

a. diversification
b. risk pooling
c. a buy and hold strategy
d. hedging

4. Which of the following statements is incorrect?
   a. if a stock has a beta coefficient equal to 1, it fluctuates independently of market fluctuations
   b. if a stock has a beta coefficient less than zero, its inclusion in a portfolio reduces the portfolio's risk
   c. a stock with a high beta coefficient fluctuates more than the market as a whole
   d. most stocks have betas close to 1

5. All of the following statements describe the behavior of investors as they adjust their portfolio except
   a. if investors think an asset's return is too low, they may no longer want to hold the asset
   b. investors may add a risky asset to their portfolios in order to improve the expected return on their overall investments
   c. if a stock has a high rate of return, investors can actually cause its rate of return to fall as they try to buy more of the asset
   d. when investors try to sell a stock, they never affect its rate of return

6. When an asset market is efficient,
   a. investors can improve their portfolios significantly by collecting and processing new information about assets
   b. asset prices are below equilibrium, and investors should follow a well-designed investment strategy
   c. investors should decide on their portfolio and then simply hold on to it
   d. none of the above

7. In the futures market, the price for the immediate sale and purchase of a commodity is its
   a. future price   c. historic price
   b. spot price   d. equilibrium price

8. If one accepts the hypothesis that markets are completely irrational, one may support which of the following statements?
   a. left alone, the asset market can correctly allocate capital to areas where it is needed most
   b. there is a predictable pattern of behavior of prices and quantities in the assets market
   c. even though the market may be inefficient, the interaction of buyers and sellers of assets will cause the market to approach an equilibrium
   d. government planners can best determine what investments should be undertaken

9. In 1974, total gambling outlays amounted to what percentage of GNP?

a. 1.5 percent   c. 11.2 percent
b. 0.9 percent   d. 9.4 percent

10. A risk-neutral individual
    a. will never gamble
    b. buys insurance to lower the risk of financial loss
    c. demands favorable odds on all bets
    d. takes bets even if the odds are not in his favor
    e. none of the above

AT THIS POINT YOU SHOULD BE ABLE TO . . .

1. Define risk-averse, risk-neutral, and risk-loving behavior and give an example of each.
2. Explain the concept of risk pooling in insurance, state how it eliminates social risk, and explain how moral hazard and adverse selection are problems for insurance companies.
3. Define the real rate of return on an asset, state the two components of the return on stocks, and explain how this return differs from that on a Treasury bill.
4. Describe how a risk-averse person may be induced to hold risky assets and list two sources of uncertainty about the returns on stocks.
5. Explain how the problem of portfolio selection is both similar to and different from the problem of consumer choice.
6. Define portfolio diversification and state how risk is reduced by diversifying.
7. Define positively correlated and negatively correlated asset returns and explain how the correlation of returns can influence the risk of a portfolio.
8. Explain the meaning of a beta coefficient and state how the coefficient can be used to estimate portfolio risk.
9. State the meaning of an asset market equilibrium and explain how such an equilibrium can be attained.
10. Explain the concept of an efficient asset market and an irrational asset market.
11. Explain the role of hedgers and speculators in the futures market and explain why compensating differentials exist in some occupations.

QUESTIONS FOR THOUGHT

1. Insurance companies are in business to make a profit, and so they have to minimize their risk of paying out huge claims to a large number of people. How do they do this? Why do many insurance policies prohibit claims resulting from war?

2. Why do stocks have a higher return than Treasury

bills? What are the sources of uncertainty for both types of investments? Explain.

3. In an uncertain asset market, how can a diversified portfolio have less risk than a specialized one? What is the underlying principle of asset diversification?

4. Why is the assumption that most individuals are risk-averse important in economics? Explain.

5. Explain the arguments about the efficiency versus the irrationality of the stock market. Why does it make a difference whether the market is efficient? Explain.

20

General Equilibrium and Welfare Economics

This is the last chapter in your study of microeconomics; it is also one of the more analytically rigorous chapters in the text. The major theme of Chapter 20 is that no one market stands alone in our capitalist system; all are interconnected. What happens in one market affects the activities in other markets so that prices and quantities in both the output and factor markets are linked together. The study of general equilibrium examines the linkage between the various markets and provides an overview of how the entire economy operates. Welfare economics examines the ways of allocating resources optimally within the entire economy. You should pay special attention to the order in which the material in Chapter 20 is presented. Make sure that you master one concept completely before moving on to another.

Chapter 20 begins with a discussion of how well the economic system meets consumers' wants, and so the first sections of the chapter are concerned with the "what" and "how" questions. By producing efficiently and allocating resources optimally, the economy operates on its production possibilities frontier (PPF). The frontier is derived from the production functions of industries producing different goods when at least one input is fixed. The PPF also shows the maximum amount of goods which can be produced by an economy; when one good is produced, other goods have to be given up. This trade-off among goods reflects the opportunity costs of specializing in one good and is formally called the marginal rate of transformation (MRT). Once the market behavior of consumers (demand) is considered, the "what" and "how" questions are answered.

The optimal allocation of resources occurs at the tangency point of the consumers' indifference curve and the PPF. At this point, the economy is producing efficiently and is producing exactly the combination of goods consumers want. Prices signal both producers and housholds to move to the point of tangency. For any set of prices (price ratio) other than the one required for equilibrium, the economy adjusts by changing the output combination, wages, employment, and price ratio so that the general equilibrium is attained at the tangency point.

General equilibrium analysis assumes that competitive firms face the same wages, experience diminishing returns to the variable input, and experience wage and price flexibility. The optimal allocation of resources established by a general competitive equilibrium is Pareto optimal since no one can be made better off without making someone else worse off. If, however, there are distortions in the market, a competitive equilibrium does not result in an optimal allocation of resources. Thus, overall welfare in the system is reduced.

The last section of Chapter 20 shows how the real rate of interest is established through savings and investment. The analysis is done within a general equilibrium framework in which producers and consumers face the choice of present versus future consumption and production. The productivity of investment and consumers' attitudes toward thrift determine the level of investment, the level of saving, and the real interest rate. In equilibrium, saving and investment will always be equal, thus establishing the equilibrium interest rate.

CHAPTER OUTLINE

1. In the simple case in which an economy produces only two goods and resources are allocated optimally, production occurs on the production possibilities frontier (PPF). The frontier shows the maximum amount of one good that can be produced, given the production level of the other good and a fixed level of resources. The PPF establishes a limit beyond which the economic system cannot move; however, if some resources are unemployed, production may occur at points below the frontier. Any output combination below the PPF is not optimal, because more of both outputs could be produced. The frontier's negative slope shows that a trade-off exists between the two commodities. In order to obtain more of one type of good, some of the other has to be given up. The PPF is bowed

outward because as an additional unit of one output is produced, more and more of the other output has to be given up; there are increasing opportunity costs to producing one good rather than another. Opportunity costs increase because as resources are shifted more and more into the production of one good, diminishing returns set in.
2. The PPF for an economic system is derived from the economy's production functions. For the two-good case, each good has a short-run production function with some inputs fixed, and so each function exhibits diminishing returns. The PPF is generated by shifting a unit of the variable input from the production of one good to the other so that the output of one good increases as the output of the other decreases. All points on the PPF can be generated in this manner.
    a. The shape of the two-good PPF reflects the trade-off between the two goods (negative slope) and diminishing marginal returns to the inputs (the curve is bowed out). The trade-off is also called the marginal rate of transformation MRT, which is the ratio of the marginal product of the variable input used in the production of each good. This ratio also defines the slope of the PPF. The diminishing marginal productivity of the variable input thus generates a diminishing MRT.
3. The use of indifference curves (from the appendix to Chapter 5) along with the PPF helps answer the question of what should be produced by an economic system so that an optimal allocation of resources is established. This optimal allocation of resources is established by the tangency of the PPF and an indifference curve. At this point, the system is producing just the quantity and type of goods society wants to consume in order to maximize (as best it can) its satisfaction. If consumption takes place at any combination of goods other than that at the point of tangency, resources are not optimally allocated, an incorrect combination of goods is being produced, and social welfare is not being maximized. Adam Smith's invisible hand concept is an analogy for the process by which a competitive price system in all markets attains optimality.
4. In a market economy, prices signal individual producers and consumers to make decisions about what and how much to produce and what and how much to consume. Wages (the price of labor) allocate labor between sectors of the economy and (assuming flexibility) move the economy toward full employment by signaling workers to move from sectors where the wage rate is low (demand for labor is low) to sectors where the rate is high (demand for labor is high). Ultimately, the labor market is in equilibrium when the marginal value products in all industries equal the wage rate. The economy attains full employment on the PPF when wages are flexible. The final equilibrium point on the PPF is determined by the market price of goods produced. Since firms hire labor up to the point at which the wage rate equals the marginal value product of the factor (price of the good times the marginal product of the factor), any change in the price of one good relative to the price of others changes the allocation of employment between the sectors, and so the system moves along the PPF. In equilibrium, the ratio of the prices of goods produced must equal the ratio of the marginal products in the industries. When one price changes relative to another, so does the ratio of marginal products, and so movement along the PPF occurs. The marginal rate of transformation for profit-maximizing firms equals the ratio of the inputs' marginal products, and this also equals the ratio of the goods' prices.
    a. Another way of showing the equilibrium condition of firms in a competitive market is to demonstrate that the marginal cost of production equals the ratio of the input price to the marginal product of the input. For a competitive firm in equilibrium, market price equals marginal cost. Thus, in a competitive market equilibrium, the marginal costs of production equal the market wage rate, and this equals the value of the marginal products in each industry. This equality establishes the fact that the marginal cost approach to a general producer equilibrium results in the same conclusion that the marginal rate of transformation equals the price ratio.
5. In order to determine the general equilibrium and establish the point on the PPF where the economy settles, consumer behavior must be added to the model.
    a. The economy attains a general equilibrium when the marginal rate of substitution (slope of the indifference curve) equals the marginal rate of transformation. Equilibrium occurs here because households establish the optimal choice of goods consumed when the marginal rate of substitution equals the ratio of the prices of the goods (appendix to Chapter 5). The ratio of goods' prices equals the marginal rate of transformation, and so the two curves are tangent at this particular combination of goods. The amount and type of goods households want to consume equals the amount and type of goods producers want to produce. At any price ratio other than the one which generates the tangency point, a general equilibrium is not established. Thus, society can be made better off if the market reallocates resources in pro-

duction, changes wages and prices, and changes the combination of goods consumed.
6. A general equilibrium supply curve is a modified supply curve because it takes into account all interactions within the economy. When using supply and demand analysis, only one market needs to be studied, because when it is in equilibrium, so are all other markets. A general equilibrium demand curve shows the marginal valuation consumers place on a particular good relative to another good at each point on the PPF. It is also modified to the extent that it is affected by economic activity. At the point of intersection of the supply and demand curves, the economy is in equilibrium because the price consumers are willing to pay exactly equals the price which producers require to supply the good. All markets are interrelated, and so activity in one influences the others; a change in the general equilibrium demand or supply curve in one market causes price and output changes in other markets.
7. The general equilibrium achieved in a competitive economy in which every market clears requires that all firms face the same wages, that wages and prices be flexible, that all industries experience diminishing returns to labor, and that economies of scale present no problems. The income distribution (welfare) in a market economy is determined by ownership of the factors of production, and so a market equilibrium implies a given distribution of income. Given this distribution for all members of the economy but one, the competitive allocation of resources makes this last individual as well off as possible. Since there are many possible competitive equilibria, it cannot be said that one allocation is better than the others. But it can be said that a competitive equilibrium is Pareto optimal since no one can be better off without making someone else worse off.
8. Distortions in the market drive a wedge between the marginal rate of substitution and the marginal rate of transformation. Thus, an optimal allocation of resources is not attained. A tax on commodities is an example of a distortion. Imposing a tax on a commodity does not change the PPF, and producers still produce at some point on the curve. A difference emerges, however, between the price paid by consumers and the price received by producers, and so the output of the good is reduced (output of other goods increases). Consumers are then forced onto a lower indifference curve. A tax on commodities generates an overall reduction in welfare.
9. The real rate of interest serves as an important price in determining the optimal allocation of resources in competitive markets.

a. The PPF may be used to describe the trade-off between current and future consumption since what is not consumed today is invested for consumption in the future. When investment takes place, society's capital stock increases. Movements along the PPF (when the alternatives are present as opposed to future consumption) show how much current consumption must be given up in order to achieve a higher level of investment; however, the rate at which this substitution takes place diminishes. The marginal rate of transformation between current and future consumption (the slope of the PPF) diminishes because of the diminishing marginal productivity of capital. A measure of the percentage rate of return on investment uses the marginal rate of transformation and is defined as $(MRT - 1) \times 100$ percent. This percentage (which may be either positive or negative) shows the increase in future consumption gained by giving up 1 unit of current consumption. The rate of return on investment becomes negative when the unit of current consumption given up does not generate even 1 unit of future consumption (recall diminishing returns to capital). The rate of return on investment provides a measure of the productivity of investment.

b. Consumers' preferences toward current and future consumption are shown with a typical indifference curve since a trade-off exists between the two. The trade-off is not constant because the curve exhibits diminishing marginal rates of substitution. The optimal level of current and future consumption (investment) is established at the tangency of an indifference curve and the PPF.

c. In equilibrium, saving and investment are equal. Saving by consumers is that part of income which is not spent on current consumption, while investment is that part of current production set aside to produce future consumption. Since the value generated in production (investment plus sales for current consumption) must equal income (saving plus current consumption), current consumption by households equals sales by producers. Thus, saving must equal investment. In the market, the level of saving and investment is determined by the interest rate. For households a positive relationship exists between saving and the interest rate, while for firms the relationship between investment and the interest rate is negative. Firms undertake investments up to the point at which the rate of return on their investment just equals the interest rate. The rate of return on investment is determined by its productivity, while the consumers' attitude toward thrift determines the availability of savings for investment use. The interest rate causes households and producers to adjust their investment and saving activities so that at the equilibrium real interest rate, the desired level of saving equals the desired level of investment.

IMPORTANT TERMS AND THEIR MEANING

Match the following terms with the correct definition or phrase.

1. _____ The situation in which no one in the economy can be made better off without at least one person being made worse off

2. _____ The study of optimal ways of allocating resources so that society's well-being is maximized

3. _____ Describes the condition where for any given output level of a particular good, the amount of another good produced is the maximum possible, given the economy's resources

4. _____ The rate at which a consumer can tradeoff one good for another; also defines the slope of an indifference curve

5. _____ The amount of one good which has to be given up in order to produce an extra unit of another good

6. _____ States that in a competitive market, as firms and households attempt to promote their own self-interest and well-being, the best interest of society is promoted

7. _____ Describes an economic system in which the decisions concerning "what," "how," and "for whom" questions are answered by a central planner

8. _____ The point of tangency between a PPF and an indifference curve which represents the amount of goods consumers should consume if they are to maximize satisfaction, the amount of goods produced for the consumers, and the amount of inputs used to produce these goods

9. _____ The slope of a PPF which shows the trade-off possible between goods; calculated as the ratio of the marginal products of the inputs

10. _____ Exist where market prices do not equal both the marginal social valuation of a good and the marginal social cost of producing a good; cause the MRS and MRT to differ

11. _____ Describes how income is divided among the households in the economy

12. _____ That part of income which is not currently consumed by households; represents a claim on future consumption

13. _____ A measure of the productivity of investment calculated by $(MRT - 1) \times 100$ percent, where MRT is the trade-off between present and future consumption

14. _____ Shows how the output of one good changes when the relative price ratio changes and firms move along the PPF; incorporates all the interactions taking place in the economy

15. _____ Arises because of diminishing marginal productivity and shows that the trade-off between goods on a PPF is not constant but decreases

16. _____ That part of current production which firms do not sell but add to the capital stock to provide for future consumption

17. _____ Describes the condition in which all markets are in balance in terms of price, output, and resource employment

a. Distortions
b. Opportunity costs
c. Saving
d. Pareto optimal
e. Marginal rate of transformation
f. General equilibrium
g. Diminishing marginal rate of transformation
h. Rate of return on investment
i. General equilibrium supply curve
j. Welfare economics
k. Invisible hand
l. Investment
m. Marginal rate of substitution
n. Command economy
o. General equilibrium demand curve
p. Distribution of income
q. Optimal allocation of resources

18. _____ Shows the marginal valuation consumers place on one good relative to another at each point on the PPF; all interactions in the economy are taken into account

r. Production efficiency

EXERCISES

1. Figure 20-1 presents a simple two-good economy operating in competitive markets. The PPF and "social" indifference curves are shown. The equilibrium relative price ratio is shown by PP'. Answer the questions on the basis of Figure 20-1.

a. This economy is in a general equilibrium at point _____ in Figure 20-1, with _____ units of good X being produced and consumed and _____ units of good Y being produced and consumed.

b. At the point of equilibrium, the MRT and MRS (are/are not) _____ equal, and the relative price ratio (does/does not) _____ signal firms and households to make changes.

c. Point K below the PPF indicates that the economy (is/is not) _____ operating at full employment and full production since (more/the same amount/less) _____ of either or both goods could be produced with the existing level of resources and technology. Point K (is/is not) _____ an optimal allocation of resources.

d. Point M represents a combination of _____ units of good X and _____ units of good Y, but the economy (can/cannot) _____ produce this level of output, given existing resources and technology.

e. If the price of good X increases relative to Y, the relative price ratio (increases/decreases) _____, and this is shown by line _____. The new price ratio (is/is not) _____ optimal since producers now want to produce _____ units of good X and _____ units of good Y but consumers want to maximize their well-being by consuming _____ units of X and _____ units of Y as shown by point N on I_3. There is an excess demand for good _____ and an excess supply of good _____. The price of good _____ falls, while the price of good _____ rises, and so the entire price ratio (increases/decreases) _____ until an equilibrium is approached.

f. At point L, there (is/is not) _____ an optimal allocation of resources since the MRS is (greater than/less than/equal to) _____ the MRT, and so resources will move out of the production of good _____ and into the production of good _____.

2. The table below presents a production possibilities schedule showing the trade-off between current and future consumption. It is assumed initially that some positive level of investment takes place even when most resources are used to satisfy current consumption.

	POSSIBILITY					
	A	B	C	D	E	F	G
Current consumption	6	5	4	3	2	1	0
Future consumption	1	6	10	13	15	16	16.5

a. Complete Table 20-1 by calculating the real return to investment as current consumption is forgone in order to have more future consumption.

TABLE 20-1

FROM POSSIBILITY	RATE OF RETURN ON INVESTMENT, %
A to B	_____
B to C	_____
C to D	_____
D to E	_____
E to F	_____
F to G	_____

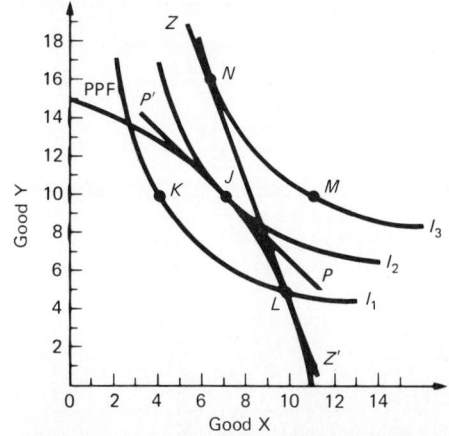

FIGURE 20-1

b. A zero rate of return is earned as society moves from alternative _____ to _____ because it must give up _____ unit of current consumption in order to get _____ unit of future consumption.

c. If the system moves from possibility F to possibility G, it encounters a (positive/negative) _____ rate of return because it costs (more/the same/less) _____ in current consumption than is gained in the future.

d. As the economy moves from possibility A to possibility G, the rate of return falls because of _____ returns to investment; the system obtains (too much/too little) _____ investment.

e. In order to determine the optimal level of investment (future consumption), it is necessary to have information about society's _____ toward spending and saving.

3. In the spaces below, list five major points of a general equilibrium.

a. _____

b. _____

c. _____

d. _____

e. _____

FILL-IN QUESTIONS

1. On the PPF, the diminishing marginal rate of transformation is due to _____ returns to the factors of production, and this causes the PPF to be _____ outward.

2. The points along a production possibilities frontier show the limits of what the economy (can/does) _____ produce, and any point beyond the frontier (is/is not) _____ attainable.

3. The PPF has a (positive/negative) _____ slope because as production of one good increases, production of other goods must _____.

4. In a general equilibrium setting, the optimal allocation of resources occurs where the _____ is tangent to an _____ reflecting society's preference because at this point, society (can/cannot) _____ be made any better off and all markets (are/are not) _____ cleared.

5. In a competitive market system, wages (distort/allocate/reduce) _____ labor between sectors and, if they are flexible, _____ full employment.

6. A profit-maximizing firm seeks the point on the PPF at which the *MRT* equals the ratio of output _____, and this is also the point at which the *MRT* equals the ratio of the (marginal/average/total) _____ products of the variable inputs used.

7. A tax imposed on a good creates a _____ in the market, and it causes resources to be _____.

8. The difference between the income received by households and the amount spent in consumption is _____ and these funds become available for firms to _____ in order to provide more goods and services in the future.

9. A firm undertakes investment up to the point at which the _____ on the investment just equals the _____ rate since at any point other than this equality, profits (are/are not) _____ maximized.

10. In equilibrium, _____ always equals _____, and this determines the equilibrium _____ rate.

11. Any change in the _____ of investment or the attitude toward _____ on the part of consumers causes a change in the _____ rate because both the saving and investment schedules (shift/remain the same) _____.

TRUE-FALSE QUESTIONS

1. ____ To say that a competitive equilibrium is Pareto optimal means that it is possible for at least one individual in the economy to improve his well-being while not making anyone else worse off.

2. _____ Behind the general equilibrium demand curve, the assumption that "everything else remains constant" has been removed.

3. _____ In order for a consumer to maximize satisfaction, it is necessary that the marginal rate of substitution of the goods exceed the ratio of the goods' prices.

4. _____ In a competitive market with firms attempting to maximize their profits, labor market equilibrium ensures that as the price of one good increases relative to the prices of other goods, labor moves from industries with the lower prices to the industry with the relatively higher price.

5. _____ Prices serve the important function of signaling households and firms in a competitive market to move toward the economy's equilibrium.

6. _____ Since consumers can be at any point on the PPF, they do not prefer one point to another.

7. _____ On the PPF, the opportunity cost of producing 1 more unit of a good is the amount of the other good that must be given up, and it is measured by the marginal rate of transformation.

8. _____ In a two-good economy, the PPF can be derived from the production functions of each good as long as these functions exhibit increasing returns to the factors of production.

9. _____ If the PPF for a two-good economy is a straight line, there is an increasing marginal rate of transformation between the two goods.

10. _____ There can be many different competitive equilibria, with each corresponding to a different initial distribution of resources.

11. _____ Because the real interest rate expresses the terms on which current consumption can be substituted for future consumption, the rate must be taken into account when future economic events or problems are analyzed.

12. _____ At very low levels of investment (future consumption), a 1-unit reduction in current consumption adds almost nothing to the goods available in the future.

13. _____ Consumers' indifference curves show that a diminishing marginal rate of substitution does not exist when one is faced with the choice between present and future consumption.

14. _____ When the interest rate is high, future consumption has a low opportunity cost in terms of current consumption.

MULTIPLE CHOICE QUESTIONS

Circle the correct answer.

1. If the current level of income for an economy in equilibrium is $900 billion and the current level of consumption is $750 billion (assuming no government taxes), the level of investment is
   a. $1650 billion
   b. $150 billion
   c. $750 billion
   d. $900 billion
   e. cannot be determined from the information given

2. Which of the following statements is incorrect with regard to a two-good economy (goods A and B) in a general equilibrium?
   a. $\dfrac{MPL_a}{MPL_b} = \dfrac{P_b}{P_a}$
   b. $MRS = \dfrac{P_b}{P_a}$
   c. $P_a MPL_a > P_b MPL_b$
   d. $MRS = MRT$

3. The production possibilities frontier for a two-good economy is derived from
   a. each industry's production function
   b. the individual's indifference curve
   c. the demand curve faced by the industry in each market
   d. the supply curve in each market

4. In the absence of market distortions, perfect competition
   a. sometimes leads to a point on the PPF
   b. never leads to a point on the PPF
   c. always leads to a point on the PPF
   d. always leads to a point below the PPF

5. If government levies a tax on a commodity,
   a. the relative price ratio faced by the consumer changes
   b. the PPF does not change its shape
   c. firms do not produce where the $MRS = MRT$
   d. consumers are forced to a lower indifference curve
   e. all of the above

6. If future output is increased by $3.05 billion when current consumption is reduced by $2.8 billion, the rate of return on investment is
   a. 25 percent   c. 108 percent
   b. 8.9 percent   d. 0.09 percent

Answer the next two questions on the basis of Figure 20-2, which shows a PPF and an indifference curve.

7. The socially optimal allocation of resources occurs at point
   a. C   c. A
   b. D   d. B

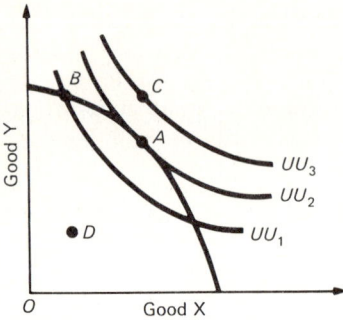

FIGURE 20-2

8. Given the three indifference curves, an unconstrained consumer's most preferred point is
   a. D   c. A
   b. C   d. B

9. For a perfectly competitive economy in a state of general equilibrium, all of the following are true except that
   a. each firm maximizes its profits, given the level of technology, resource availability, and prices
   b. each household supplies the factors of production it chooses given factor prices
   c. all markets for both inputs and outputs clear at the established prices
   d. consumers do not face an income constraint in selecting their optimal combination of goods

10. The theory of general equilibrium argues that
    a. when a shortage exists in one market, a shortage must exist in another market as well
    b. the price system connects all markets, simultaneously ensuring full employment and answering the "what" and "how" questions
    c. the role of prices becomes less important when all sectors of the economy are examined together
    d. the market system may not ensure the optimal allocation of resources

AT THIS POINT YOU SHOULD BE ABLE TO . . .

1. Define the meaning of general equilibrium analysis and state how it differs from the partial equilibrium analysis approach taken in earlier chapters of the text.
2. Draw a production possibilities frontier, describe its characteristics, and explain how it reflects the opportunity costs of specializing in one good or the other.
3. State the relationship between the production functions of two goods and the production possibilities frontier and explain how the shape of these functions influences the shape of the frontier.
4. Show graphically, using indifference curves and the production possibilities frontier, the optimal allocation of resources and explain why it is optimal.
5. State the firms' equilibrium conditions in the labor market, explain the role of prices in this market, and explain why when competitive firms maximize profits, the labor market clears and the MRT equals the relative price ratio.
6. Show how the firms' marginal cost of production can be related to the MRT.
7. Explain why in a state of general equilibrium all markets (outputs and factors) must clear and state how prices affect this general equilibrium.
8. Show graphically and explain the meaning of general equilibrium by using a supply and demand diagram; list four assumptions which were made in order to show that the market allocation of resources is optimal.
9. Define the meaning of Pareto optimality; also, explain how distortions in a competitive market cause the system to move from the optimal allocation of resources and reduce overall welfare.
10. Show graphically and explain a PPF having investment as one of the alternatives, explain what is meant by the rate of return on investment, and show how this rate can be calculated.
11. Explain and show graphically how the equilibrium interest rate is determined, and explain why, in equilibrium, savings always equal investments.

QUESTIONS FOR THOUGHT

1. In terms of a general equilibrium and welfare analysis, why is it that a monopoly is not as socially desirable as competitive markets? Explain why it is said that a monopolist imposes a tax on consumers.

2. What is meant by Adam Smith's invisible hand concept? How can the concept be used in the study of an economic system's general equilibrium?

3. Are competitive markets both necessary and sufficient to generate a general equilibrium? Explain why or why not.

4. What is a command economy? What is the function of an "idealized" planner in such an economy? Explain.

5. In 1981 and 1982, President Reagan and the Congress reduced the marginal income tax rates so that households received more spendable income. From the standpoint of a general equilibrium analysis, what effect do you think the tax reduction might have on the economy? Why?

6. In equilibrium, why must the amount households save equal the amount firms invest? What happens if they are not equal? Explain.

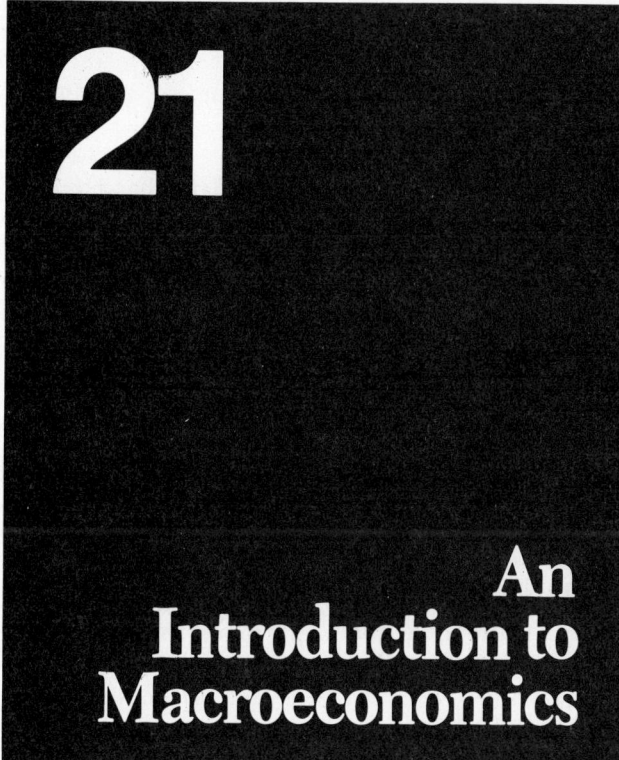

21 An Introduction to Macroeconomics

Chapter 21 is your introduction to the study of macroeconomics and presents an overview of some key concepts and questions studied by aggregate economic analysis. As opposed to microeconomics (the study of individual economic units), macroeconomics is the study of the whole. Economic problems such as unemployment, inflation, and growth as well as the ability of government to solve these problems are studied in macroeconomics.

Chapter 21 begins with a discussion of the interdependence of a macroeconomy. The activities and decisions of both households and firms determine the level of total output, income, employment, and spending. The circular flow model of economic activity shows how households and firms are interrelated, since decisions by firms to produce require the hiring of the factors of production from households. Once these factors are hired, a flow of income is generated, and so households can purchase the output of firms. If for some reason firms cannot sell all they produce, unemployment, lower incomes, and slower growth are expected. If households try to consume more output than firms produce, prices begin to increase, and inflation results. A central topic of macroeconomics is how growth can be promoted without encountering the problems of unemployment and inflation. When an economic system grows, its production possibilities frontier shifts outward. Growth is promoted by increasing either the quantity of the factors of production or the productivity of existing factors.

The consumer price index expresses current prices in terms of the prices in some base year. The index shows that in the United States there have been periods of primarily rising prices, while deflation has occurred during some other periods. In recent years, the United States and many of the world's industrialized countries have faced the problem of inflation. When inflation is a problem, a country's growth rate of real GNP may be very low (or even negative) at the same time that its nominal GNP is increasing. The level and growth of real aggregate output (and income) is a major issue in macroeconomics since it signals a period of prosperity or recession. Even though GNP serves as a measure of an economy's well-being, per capital real GNP provides a better indication of the standard of living within an economy.

When an economy grows, the problem of unemployment diminishes. When growth slows, human resources are used very inefficiently. Not only do the unemployed bear the cost of no jobs, society loses as well. When labor is not working, society is not producing at its maximum level, and so it forgoes potential output. Often, high levels of unemployment are not restricted to one country but spill over onto other nations as well.

The study of macroeconomic activity focuses on these problems of unemployment, growth, and inflation. The next few chapters are devoted to developing the linkages between households and firms and showing how they influence each other. Once these links have been developed, the problems of unemployment, inflation, and low growth are presented. The role and effect of government in the macroeconomy are sometimes less than expected and perhaps detrimental to aggregate activity.

For your study of macroeconomics to be successful, you should realize that no sector or market is totally independent of the activities in other markets. As you study the following chapters, keep these interdependencies in mind.

CHAPTER OUTLINE

1. An aggregate economic system is made up of millions of independent households, each deciding how much to work and buy, and firms, each deciding how much to produce and how many workers to hire. The total of these decisions by households and firms constitutes the economy's aggregate spending and production. Households own the factors of production (resources used in production) which are used (hired) by firms to produce an output. When firms hire the factors, households are paid primarily in the form of wages and profits, which are the major source of house-

hold income. This income is then used by households as they make their spending decisions about how much and which of the firms' outputs to buy. Household spending in turn provides the source of revenue for firms, and this spending is then used to hire more factors of production. The circular flow model (assuming no government participation, no foreign trade, and no sales by some firms to other firms) shows the flow of payments to households as they provide the factors of production to firms and the flow of payments from households as they purchase the firms' output. The circular flow shows the interdependence between the goods and factor markets and the generation of money flows from which the abilities to buy and supply goods are created.

a. When workers become unemployed, they may be willing to work but cannot find a job. Unemployment frequently occurs when firms cannot sell all of their output and thus have to reduce production and hire fewer workers. When unemployment increases, the level of income available for spending decreases, and so firms face an even greater reduction in sales. Unemployment again increases. The problem becomes one of pumping up the economy so that the fall in unemployment and production decreases. When unemployment is present, the economy is operating below its production possibilities frontier (PPF), and so society is wasting its labor resources.

b. If the economy is operating at full employment and is on its PPF, any increase in consumer demand leads to higher prices, resulting in inflation as producers try to reconcile the scarcity of goods with the increase in demand. Inflation may, however, occur even if the economy is not at full employment.

c. Economic growth occurs when there is an increase in the economy's production of goods and services. Two circumstances can cause growth. First, unemployed resources are put back to work, and second, the PPF shifts outward. An improvement in the quality (productivity) or quantity of the factors of production shifts the PPF outward. Macroeconomic analysis shows how growth can be increased and the standard of living improved.

d. When the independent decisions made by households and firms do not generate a full-employment, noninflationary level of output, macroeconomic problems occur. Unlike microeconomics, macroeconomics emphasizes the interactions between households and firms since the decisions of one affect the other.

2. The consumer price index (CPI) is an index of prices for a basket of goods and is the most common measure of price behavior. Inflation reflects increasing average prices, while deflation describes falling average prices. Statistics show that since 1929, the general price level has increased almost sixfold; however, during this time period, there were also periods when the average price level fell. The rate at which prices increase over time is the inflation rate. This rate is computed by the formula

Inflation rate per year

$$= \frac{\text{CPI in year 2} - \text{CPI in year 1}}{\text{CPI in year 1}} \times 100 \text{ percent}$$

The same formula is used to compute inflation rates for any two time periods.

a. Inflation is not unique to the United States. In fact, the inflation experienced by the United States between 1970 and 1979 has been low relative to that of many other countries.

3. The value of all final goods and services produced in the economy in a given year is nominal gross national product. Nominal GNP changes because either prices or quantity of output produced or both change. Real GNP measures the value of goods and services produced in a given year in terms of the prices of a given base year. If real GNP changes, it is because output, not price, changes. If real GNP declines (a negative growth rate), the economy experiences a recession, while prosperity (a boom) is reflected by a sustained period of expanding real output. The growth rate in real GNP is computed like the inflation rate; however, real GNP values for the particular years under investigation are substituted into the expression in place of the price index. By dividing real GNP by the population, a measure of the real output per person is obtained. This is called per capita real GNP and is an indicator of an economy's standard of living.

4. An individual is considered unemployed if he is 16 years old or older and is recorded as being unable to find a job. The economy's unemployment rate is that fraction of the labor force age 16 or older who want to work but cannot find a job. The unemployment rate serves as an indicator of the economy's well-being. If the unemployment rate is high, the economy is performing poorly. Unemployment strikes some groups harder than others. Young, nonwhite, and female workers all have higher unemployment rates than white men over age 20. Unemployment, like inflation, is an international problem.

5. Inflation, unemployment, and growth are related. During a recession, the economy experiences low growth, high unemployment, and slowing rates of inflation. During periods of prosperity, the economy experiences low unemployment, increased growth, and more rapid inflation. Even though the inflation rate slows during periods of recession, once the economy recovers, the problem of accelerating prices may be present. During inflationary periods, people worry because inflation creates an atmosphere of uncertainty about future prices and decreases the purchasing power of their wages. Economists are divided on whether people should worry about inflation. During periods of high or rapid growth, unemployment rates decrease; however, when real GNP falls, so does the level of employment. The high unemployment rates of 1982 were caused in part by low growth rates in real GNP.

6. During the 1970s, many countries experienced the problems of slow growth, high unemployment, and inflation. During the early 1980s, however, many governments began programs to reduce inflation and promote higher growth rates.

IMPORTANT TERMS AND THEIR MEANING

Match the following terms with the correct definition or phrase.

1. ____ A sustained period of economic prosperity and growth

2. ____ A fall in the average price level

3. ____ The dollar value of all goods and services produced in the economy during a given time period

4. ____ The study of the operation of the entire economy; concerned with aggregate economic behavior

5. ____ The value of goods and services produced in a given year expressed in terms of the prices in a given base year

6. ____ Increases in the average price level

7. ____ A measurement of the cost (price) over time of a representative basket of goods and services

8. ____ An increase in the economy's goods and services

9. ____ Goods and services useful in production, including labor, buildings, and machines

10. ____ Consists of government actions designed to affect the economy through the use of policy instruments.

11. ____ $\dfrac{\text{GNP in year 1} - \text{GNP in year 0}}{\text{GNP in year 0}} \times 100$ per year

12. ____ Shows the flow of the factors of production and spending from households to firms and the flow of incomes and goods from firms to households

13. ____ A period of low or negative growth, high unemployment, and declining rates of inflation

14. ____ The decisions of firms (households) about how much to produce (consume) are what determine the income (revenue) of households (firms); the essential difference between microeconomics and macroeconomics

15. ____ Defines the maximum quantities which a fully employed economic system can produce and shows the rate of trade-off the system faces in choosing its priorities

16. ____ The payments to households in exchange for their providing factors of production

17. ____ The year serving as a point of reference for prices in other years

18. ____ Describes individuals who are 16 years old or older and want to work but cannot find a job

19. ____ Dividing aggregate data by the population in order to get a per person statistic

a. Real GNP
b. Economic policy
c. Interactions
d. Inflation
e. Growth rate
f. Base year
g. PPF
h. Nominal GNP
i. Recession
j. Per capita
k. Income
l. Consumer price index
m. Unemployment
n. Ouput
o. Boom
p. Macroeconomics
q. Circular flow diagram
r. Factors of production
s. Growth

20. _____ The goods and services produced by firms when they use the factors of production

t. Deflation

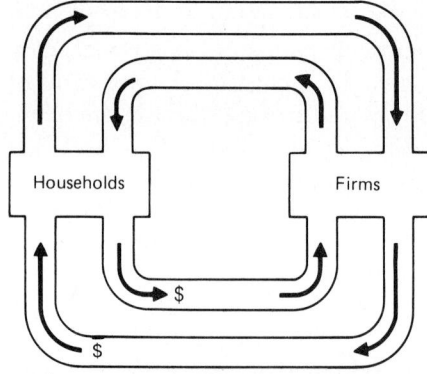

FIGURE 21-1

EXERCISES

1. Table 21-1 presents nominal GNP data over a 5-year period. Also presented are five price indices, one for each year. All data are hypothetical.

  a. Compute real GNP, the inflation rate per year, and the growth rate of both nominal and real GNP. Enter your calculations in the appropriate columns.

  b. For every year presented in Table 21-1, nominal GNP (increased/decreased) _____, and the growth rate was (positive/negative) _____.

  c. Real GNP (increases/decreases) _____ up to year 4. The growth rate in real GNP between years 3 and 4 is (positive/negative) _____, while the growth rate in nominal GNP remains _____.

  d. Real output (increased/decreased) _____ between years 3 and 4, and so the increase in nominal GNP must be the result of _____.

  e. The lowest rate of inflation occurred between years _____ and _____.

  f. The base year used in Table 21-1 is year _____, and for any year prior to the base year, nominal GNP is (greater than/less than) _____ real GNP since the price level is (greater/less) _____ than that in the base year.

  g. From Table 21-1, this hypothetical economy experienced a fall in real output in year _____.

2. The circular flow model in Figure 21-1 shows the interdependence between the goods market and the factor markets. There are four channels of activity between the sectors. Two of the channels are in terms of dollars or money flows, and two are in terms of products and factors (real flows). Complete Figure 21-1 by filling in each channel with the appropriate flow.

FILL-IN QUESTIONS

1. The _____ index measures the cost of a representative basket of goods bought over a period of time.

2. In order to calculate real GNP, it is necessary to divide nominal GNP by the _____, and this has the effect of holding prices _____ so that any change in real GNP occurs only because aggregate _____ changes.

3. The study of aggregate economic behavior and hence the operation of the economy as a whole is called _____.

4. The term (inflation/deflation) _____ defines increasing average prices.

5. If the price level increased and the level of output remained constant, (real/nominal) _____ GNP would increase, but (real/nominal) _____ GNP would remain unchanged.

6. During the decade of the 1970s, most of the western industrialized nations (did/did not) _____ experience stable prices and economic growth.

7. If the average price level should suddenly begin to fall and continue to fall over several time periods, we would be experiencing _____; everything

TABLE 21-1

YEAR	NOMINAL GNP	PRICE INDEX	REAL GNP	INFLATION RATE PER YEAR	GROWTH RATE OF NOMINAL GNP	GROWTH RATE OF REAL GNP
1	250	75	_____			
2	325	92	_____	_____	_____	_____
3	380	100	_____	_____	_____	_____
4	450	125	_____	_____	_____	_____
5	600	150	_____	_____	_____	_____

else constant, the real measure of output and income would (increase/decrease) _____.

8. In the circular flow model, the upper flows show how the economy (produces/pays for) _____ goods and services, while the lower flows show how the economy (produces/pays for) _____ these transactions.

9. Unemployment is a problem for both the _____ and _____ because scarce labor resources are wasted.

10. The PPF shifts outward because of changes in either the _____ or _____ of resources.

11. When spending by households falls, firms (are/are not) _____ able to sell all of their goods, and so unemployment can be expected to (increase/decrease) _____.

TRUE-FALSE QUESTIONS

1. _____ The inflation of the 1970s and early 1980s in the United States represents the only periods in our history when prices were not stable.

2. _____ To say that real income for 1983 is $1800 billion in 1972 dollars means that the total income in 1983 would purchase $1800 billion worth of goods in 1972.

3. _____ In the United States, from 1960 through 1981, the average real growth rate in GNP was 8.7 percent per year.

4. _____ The circular flow model shows the interactions of firms and households; the firms supply the factors of production and demand goods, while the households supply goods and demand factors.

5. _____ Unlike microeconomics, macroeconomics is not concerned with the price and output determination for a particular firm or industry.

6. _____ To say that the consumer price index today has almost tripled since 1967 means that what cost $1 in 1967 costs almost $3 today.

7. _____ Most macroeconomic models emphasize the interactions between the various sectors of the economy.

8. _____ An individual is considered in the unemployed statistics if he is over 16 years old, is not working, and does not want to work.

9. _____ It is reasonable to expect the rate of employment to decline if firms begin to have large inventories of unsold goods.

10. _____ When nominal GNP increases, we know that the price level has fallen or real output has gone up.

11. _____ Unemployment rates are calculated from estimates of the civilian labor force, which is made up only of those individuals who are either working or unemployed and looking for work.

12. _____ When compared with many countries throughout the world, the United States had a relatively low inflation rate in the 1970s.

MULTIPLE CHOICE QUESTIONS

Circle the correct answer.

1. All of the following are within the scope of macroeconomics except
   a. government tax policies
   b. national growth rates
   c. deflation
   d. the wage rate of an individual worker

2. Using index numbers in macroeconomics permits us to
   a. examine price fluctuations for specific industries
   b. summarize what has happened to average prices
   c. determine the price for particular items
   d. examine the effect of price changes for a good on the market demand for other goods

3. All of the following describe some aspect of the CPI except
   a. the index is based on a representative basket of goods bought by the typical consumer
   b. the index expresses current prices in terms of some base year
   c. the base period used in the CPI changes yearly
   d. the index equals 100 during the base period

4. If the price index was 263 in April 1981 and was 283 in April 1982, the inflation rate for the year was
   a. 7.6 percent
   b. 20 percent
   c. 0.076 percent
   d. 0.20 percent
   e. cannot be determined from the data supplied

5. When real output falls for two consecutive quarters,
   a. nominal output may be either rising or falling
   b. average prices may be either rising or falling
   c. the economy is experiencing a recession
   d. all of the above may occur

6. Which of the following statements is incorrect?
   a. macroeconomics is concerned with the interaction among the goods and factor markets
   b. macroeconomic policies designed specifically for one market may very well spill over into the other market
   c. the factor markets are linked to the goods market
   d. all of the above are incorrect

7. If consumer demand increases when the economy is producing on its production possibilities frontier, we would expect all of the following except
   a. the output of firms to increase
   b. the average level of prices to increase
   c. unemployment to decrease
   d. some consumer demand to be unsatisfied

8. Which of the following would not cause an outward shift of the PPF and thus would not stimulate economic growth?
   a. an abundant supply of a key resource is discovered
   b. the education and skill levels of the average worker increase
   c. 20 percent of the existing capital stock becomes obsolete
   d. improved technology makes all workers more productive

9. Which of the following statements is incorrect?
   a. increases in economic growth result in decreases in unemployment
   b. when unemployment decreases, income increases along with the consumption of goods and services
   c. during a recession, we would expect increasing unemployment and deflation
   d. when firms want to produce more goods, they hire more labor and increase incomes
   e. all of the above are incorrect

AT THIS POINT YOU SHOULD BE ABLE TO . . .

1. Define macroeconomics, state how it differs from microeconomics, and list three topics studied by macroeconomists.
2. Define the unemployment rate, inflation rate, and growth rate and show how each is calculated.
3. Define the consumer price index and state how it is used.
4. Define inflation and deflation and describe how price levels in one year can be compared with price levels in other years.
5. Distinguish between nominal and real GNP and explain how inflation can cause nominal GNP to increase while real GNP falls.
6. Describe the role of market (sector) interdependence in macroeconomics.
7. Draw and explain the circular flow diagram and explain how households and firms influence each other's activities.
8. Show the production possibilities frontier and state two circumstances in which economic growth occurs.
9. Explain the meaning of negative growth in real GNP.
10. Define real GNP per capita and state why it can be used as an indicator of an economy's standard of living.

QUESTIONS FOR THOUGHT

1. Suppose you are asked to present a talk to a local civic group on the subject of the interdependence of markets from a macroeconomic standpoint. Briefly list the major points of your speech.

2. Briefly explain some of the major differences between the micro and macro approaches to economic analysis. Can you think of ways in which the two approaches are similar?

3. In macroeconomic analysis, much of the aggregate data presented or used are in real terms as opposed to nominal measures. Why do you think using real data is preferred to using data expressed simply in money terms? Briefly explain.

4. The circular flow model presents the interactions between households and firms. Do you see any problems with the model? How would we show the effects of government programs on the circular flow model?

5. Professors Fischer and Dornbusch state that "the essential difference between microeconomics and macroeconomics consists of the interactions in the circular flow diagram." What do you think they mean? Explain your answer.

22
National Income Accounting

Chapter 22 focuses on the meaning and uses of a system of national income accounting. The circular flow model presented in Chapter 21 set the stage for the material presented here. National income accounting measures the dollar value of the flow of product (output) and income. The dollar value of all final goods and services produced during a particular time period is called gross national product (GNP). By definition, GNP must equal the total income (plus indirect business taxes and depreciation) of all the factors of production used to produce the final output. It is this total, or national, income which after certain adjustments gives a measure of households' personal disposable income. GNP must equal the sum of expenditures for private consumption C, business investment I, government spending G, and net foreign trade NX. What else could happen to output produced if it didn't fall into one of these expenditure categories? Chapter 22 shows how GNP is related to a variety of other income measures and shows how the expenditures on final goods and services are related to the value of the output produced.

Although GNP is the most frequently used measure of an economy's performance, there are inherent problems in using GNP as the sole criterion. Some goods and services are not produced in a market setting. These activities are excluded from GNP calculations, and so GNP understates the real level of economic activity. The effect of inflation on GNP is another problem. By using the GNP deflator, it is possible to dampen the influence of price changes. But using real GNP as a measure of economic welfare also has its shortcomings.

A more recent measure is net economic welfare (NEW). NEW attempts to remove the value of nuisance goods (disproducts) and include the value of leisure time since these factors affect our overall well-being. Although not estimated regularly, NEW serves as a remainder of the problems encountered when using GNP as a measure of social welfare.

Chapter 22 lays the foundation for your study of aggregate economic analysis presented in the next several chapters. Be sure that you know how the GNP and other income accounts presented in Chapter 22 are calculated and that you are very familiar with the components of each account. You should be able to estimate gross national product by using either the total expenditure or the factor income method.

CHAPTER OUTLINE

1. GNP is a measure of the market value of all final sales of goods and services produced within a given time period by domestically owned factors of production. Five features of GNP must be clarified. First, double counting must be avoided in the estimation of GNP since it makes no sense to count the same production twice. Double counting can be avoided by adding only the value contributed by firms at each stage of production. By deducting the value of all intermediate goods used in the production process, it is possible to obtain only the value added by a firm's labor and capital inputs. Second, GNP should include the value of all output produced in the economy. Because some output is not sold through the market system, it is difficult to determine its value. Illegal activities, the value of housework, and the activities of the "underground" economy are examples of economic activities not included in the GNP accounts. Home ownership provides the owner a value in the use of his residence even though no rent is paid. The statistician estimates this current rent value, labels it imputed rent, and puts this value in the GNP accounts. A third point is that GNP includes only estimates of currently produced goods and services. Existing assets (a previously constructed house or a previously owned car, for instance) are not included. Fourth, GNP measures the value of output produced by domestically owned resources. If some output is produced abroad but is produced by U.S.-owned resources, the GNP of the United States increases (income earned by foreign-owned resources producing in the United States is not counted in the U.S. GNP). Gross domestic product (GDP) measures the value of output produced domestically without regard to ownership of the factors of production. Fifth, GNP measures the market value of final goods. Any applicable taxes are included in the final value of these goods. The value of government services is determined by the wages paid to government employees.

a. Dividing nominal GNP by the nation's population gives per capita GNP (GNP per person). Per capita GNP varies greatly from country to country; however, interpreting such international comparisons is difficult because of the different types of goods produced across countries and the value of the different monetary units in which the outputs are measured. In the United States, 1981 per capita GNP was $12,733.

b. Data covering U.S. GNP are collected and published on a regular basis by the Commerce Department. Although not perfect, two statistical procedures are used to estimate GNP. Government economists can get a measure of GNP either by computing the overall value of production or by obtaining the value of incomes earned by the factors of production. The value of production equals the value of incomes earned (assuming no leakages from or injections into the circular flow).

c. GNP measures the value of final sales of goods and services and, with some modification, measures the income accruing to households as owners of the factors of production.

2. Two adjustments must be made to GNP in order to get a measure of national income. First, the amount of capital used up (depreciation) in the production of the final goods and services is deducted from GNP. This capital consumption allowance reflects a cost of production that is not part of current output. Deducting the capital consumption allowance provides an estimate of net national product (NNP). When indirect taxes are deducted from and any subsidies are added to NNP, a measure of national income (NI) is obtained. These indirect taxes are taxes levied on the value of goods prior to or at final sale, and so they are not included in the firm's income. The market price for goods receiving subsidies is lower than the income received by sellers. National income is the income flowing to the factors of production. In 1981, national income was $2344 billion.

a. Income from labor (including proprietors' income) is the major component of national income. The other major source of national income is income derived from property. Included in property income are rents, corporate profits, and net interest.

3. National income is not the level of income households have to spend. Personal disposable income is the income available for household spending. In order to obtain personal disposable income, deduct all corporate profits from national income and then add that part of the profits paid to stockholders as dividends. Next, any interest receipts by households which are not part of national income must be added. Finally, deduct personal taxes and add transfer payments to households. Personal disposable income is

National income − corporate profits + stockholder dividends + interest receipts − personal taxes + transfer payments = personal disposable income

In 1981, per capita disposable income was about $8800.

a. Household consumption expenditures on goods and services (excluding the purchase of houses) account for over 92 percent of personal disposable income. Of the other 8 percent, part is used to pay interest on debt (2.5 percent), and the remainder is saved. Personal saving is that part of disposable income which households use to add to their wealth. The share of disposable income allocated to saving is the personal saving rate. The United States currently has the lowest saving rate among the major industrialized economies.

4. GNP can be defined in terms of what each sector spends to exhaust the total value of output. GNP is sold to four sectors: households, businesses, government and the rest of the world. Household spending is called consumption (C) and accounts for the largest share of GNP. Business spending for goods (excluding intermediate goods) is called investment (I), which takes the form of either inventories or physical capital. Spending by all levels of government (G) includes the purchase of both goods and labor services. The last sector to purchase some of GNP is the foreign sector. Some goods are bought domestically but are imported, while other goods are produced domestically but are exported. The difference between exports and imports (net exports) is the last source of demand for GNP. Thus, $GNP = C + I + G + NX$.

a. The demand for GNP shows which part of aggregate output each sector wants. Investment, however, is an exception since some investment spending may not have been desired at all. If firms produce goods but cannot sell them, these goods are added to inventory.

Since producers already have a desired level of inventories which they want to maintain, any surplus of goods produced but not sold represents an unwanted increase in inventories and unwanted (unplanned) investment.

5. The following relationships summarize national income accounting:

   GNP = the sum of all final sales of goods and services produced in a given time period

   Aggregate spending = $C + I + G + NX$ = GNP

   GNP = gross domestic product + net factor income from abroad

   NNP = GNP − depreciation (capital consumption allowance)

   NI = NNP − indirect taxes + any subsidies on goods

   Shares to factors of production = compensation of employees + proprietors' income + profits + interest and rents = NI

6. GNP is one of the most frequently used measures of aggregate economic performance; however, there are limitations to the use of these data.
   a. Nominal GNP measures the market value of output in terms of current prices. Real GNP measures the value of current production in terms of prices in some base year. When nominal GNP increases, it is due to increases in final output, increases in the price level, or both. Increases in real GNP occur only because final output increases; the price level is held constant. When a comparison of an economy's output is made over time, real GNP should be used.
      (1) The GNP deflator and the CPI are the two measures most frequently used to measure inflation. The GNP deflator is the ratio of nominal to real GNP expressed as an index. The deflator provides a good estimate of the average behavior of prices. The inflation rate may be calculated as simply the growth rate of the GNP deflator, since the index applies to a broad range of goods and prices.
   b. Growth of per capita real GNP is often used as a measure of changes in an economy's standard of living. However, two caveats must be stated. First, it is possible that changing population growth distorts the growth of real GNP so that some adjustment to population growth rates is necessary in order to compare real GNP growth rates across time periods or countries. Second, it is possible that even though per capita real GNP grows over time, the distribution of income changes so that some people are actually worse off.
   c. The comprehensiveness of the GNP accounts is reduced because the production of output involves the production of some nuisance goods which ideally should be subtracted from GNP. It is difficult to determine the cost of these goods because they are not traded in the market. Some economic activities are not included in GNP because they do not occur in the marketplace.
      (1) An alternative measure of society's overall well-being is called net economic welfare (NEW). NEW includes estimates of the value of nonmarket activities and the value of leisure time enjoyed and deducts the costs of nuisance goods. The value of NEW is larger than that of GNP; however, it has grown at a slower rate.

IMPORTANT TERMS AND THEIR MEANING

Match the following terms with the correct definition or phrase.

1. _____ Expenditures by households on all goods and services except the purchase of houses

2. _____ The total amount earned by the economy's factors of production

3. _____ An index used to measure inflation; defined as the ratio of nominal GNP to real GNP

4. _____ The value of our goods sold to foreigners (exports) minus the value of goods we buy from foreigners (imports)

5. _____ The market value of final goods and services produced minus the capital-consumption allowance

6. _____ The income available for spending by households

7. _____ The value of GNP measured in terms of the price level during some base year; prices are held constant

8. _____ A measure of the economy's production of goods and services which deducts the

a. Net exports

b. Intermediate goods

c. Real GNP

d. Value added

e. Personal saving

f. Nuisance goods

g. Transfer payments

h. Depreciation

estimated value of nuisance goods and includes estimates of the value of nonmarket activities and leisure

9. ____ The value of GNP in an economy divided by the population; a measure of the value of output per person

10. ____ Goods used in the production of final goods and services; these goods are not finished consumer goods

11. ____ The increase in the value of goods resulting from progressing through the various stages of production

12. ____ That part of economic activity which escapes official statistics and may well be illegal

13. ____ That part of personal disposable income which is not consumed; households use it to add to their wealth

14. ____ Payments received by households from government and business for which no services are provided in return

15. ____ Measures the value of output produced by factors of production located in the economy which, when added to net factor income from abroad, equals GNP

16. ____ In measuring GNP, the problem faced if some production is counted twice

17. ____ The wearing out of capital equipment during the process of production; also called the capital consumption allowance

18. ____ A measure of the market value of all final goods and services produced in an economy during a particular time period

19. ____ The share of personal disposable income going to personal saving

i. National income (NI)

j. Saving rate

k. GNP deflator

l. Double counting

m. Consumption expenditure

n. Net economic welfare (NEW)

o. Gross national product (GNP)

p. Personal disposable income

q. Nominal GNP

r. Imputed income

s. Underground economy

20. ____ Some output of production such as noise, pollution, and congestion which tends to reduce overall welfare

21. ____ A measure of GNP in terms of current prices; not adjusted for inflation.

22. ____ Benefits derived from the ownership of certain physical assets (such as houses) which would generate an income in the marketplace so that inclusion in GNP is reasonable

t. Net national product (NNP)

u. Gross domestic product (GDP)

v. Per capita GNP

EXERCISES

1. Table 22-1 presents data (in billions of dollars) obtained from the May 1982 *Federal Reserve Bulletin* on national product and income for 1979.

TABLE 22-1

Corporate profits	$ 196
Exports	281
Federal government purchases	168
Personal consumption	1511
Indirect business taxes minus subsidies	197
Personal taxes	534
Imports	268
Change in business inventories	18
Transfer payments	294
State and local government purchases	306
Capital consumption allowance	254
Dividends	49
Interest adjustment	66
Fixed investment	398
Rental income	31

a. Using the relevant data in Table 22-1, calculate the value of GNP. All of the data will not be needed for this calculation.

b. Enter your answer in Table 22-2. Next, make the appropriate adjustment to GNP in order to derive NNP. In the blank followed by a question mark, write the account which goes in the blank. In the blank to the right, enter the correct dollar amount. Complete the table until you determine personal disposable income.

c. If households paid $45 billion as interest payments to businesses and their consumption expenditures [from (a)] were $_____ billion, they saved $_____ billion of their personal disposable income.

d. The saving rate for households in 1979 was _____ percent of disposable income.

NATIONAL INCOME ACCOUNTING

TABLE 22-2

Gross national product		$_____
Less _____ ?		(−)_____
Equals: Net national product		_____
Less _____ ?		(−)_____
Equals: National income		_____
Less _____ ?		(−)_____
Plus _____ ?		(+)_____
Plus _____ ?		(+)_____
Less _____ ?		(−)_____
Plus _____ ?		(+)_____
Equals: Personal disposable income		_____

TABLE 22-3

YEAR	NOMINAL GNP, $ billions	REAL GNP, $ billions	GNP DEFLATOR	RATE OF INFLATION, %
1972	1171	1171	_____	
1973	1307	1235	_____	_____
1974	1413	1214	_____	_____
1975	1516	1192	_____	_____
1976	1702	1273	_____	_____
1977	1900	1341	_____	_____
1978	2128	1399	_____	_____
1979	2414	1483	_____	_____
1980	2626	1481	_____	_____
1981	2926	1510	_____	_____

2. From your study of Chapter 22, you now know that some economic transactions are included in the derivation of GNP and that some are not. Listed below are several transactions, and you are to determine whether they are included in GNP. If the transaction is included, place a check (√), and if it is not, place an X in the blank.

a. You win $100 in a "friendly" poker game _____
b. You rent two pieces of property to tenants _____
c. You buy a new $100,000 house _____
d. The government purchases a new cruise missile _____
e. You sell your old house _____
f. Before you sold your house, you repainted and installed new gutters _____
g. A low-income family receives a welfare check _____
h. You purchase $1 million worth of General Motors stock _____
i. The Soviet Union purchases $10 million of U.S. wheat _____
j. You purchase an eighteenth-century antique chest _____
k. A dentist and an attorney agree to provide services to each other as a "professional courtesy" _____
l. The stock of unsold new homes increases _____

3. Table 22-3 presents both nominal and real GNP data (obtained from the *Federal Reserve Bulletin*) for the period 1972–1981. The data have been rounded to the nearest whole number. Your task is to complete Table 22-3 by first calculating the GNP deflator for each year and then computing the rate of inflation from one year to the next. Enter your computations in the appropriate blanks.

a. From 1974–1975, real GNP (increased/decreased) _____ even though nominal GNP _____.

b. During the period 1974–1975, the GNP deflator (increased/decreased) _____, and so a decline in a real GNP means that aggregate output (rose/fell) _____.

c. From the data in Table 22-3, it appears that the economy experienced slowdowns in the years _____, _____, and _____. During two of these years, the rate of inflation (increased/decreased) _____.

d. According to the GNP deflator, the economy (did/did not) _____ experience deflationary periods.

FILL-IN QUESTIONS

1. Noise, pollution, and congestion are examples of _____ goods created in the process of production, and they (are/are not) _____ easily included in a comprehensive measure of GNP.

2. As presented by Professors Nordhaus and Tobin, a measure of net economic welfare (NEW) would adjust GNP by deducting _____ goods, adding the value of _____ activities, and including the value of _____ time.

3. If a country's population grows more rapidly than its real GNP, per capita real GNP (increases/decreases) _____ because total production must be shared among (more/fewer) _____ people.

4. (GNP/GDP) _____ is a measure of the output produced by factors of production located in the domestic economy regardless of who owns the factors.

5. If _____ is deducted from GNP, the resulting statistic measures net national product. If we subtract _____ from NNP, a measure of the income received by the owners of the factors of production is obtained.

6. The two basic types of income are income from _____ and income from _____, with the largest percentage of national income being derived from _____.

7. The income available for consumption by households is called _____, and it is (greater than/equal to/less than) _____ national income.

8. The share of disposable income allocated to personal saving is known as the _____; in the United States, this share is among the (highest/lowest) _____ of the major industrialized countries.

9. In the United States, the major component of aggregate demand for current output is (household consumption/business investment/government spending/net foreign trade) _____, while the smallest component is that generated by the _____ sector.

10. It (is/is not) _____ possible for some investment demand to be unwanted.

11. When we want to compare the money value of output, the appropriate measure is (nominal/real) _____ GNP; however, if we want to compare the economy's physical production of goods, the appropriate measure is (nominal/real) _____ GNP.

TRUE-FALSE QUESTIONS

1. _____ The most widely used measure of inflation is the growth rate of the GNP deflator.

2. _____ When the value added approach is used to measure the value of goods resulting from production, the problem of double counting is removed.

3. _____ In estimating a nation's per capita GNP, total output is divided by the number of people in the labor force who actually contribute to the production of final goods and services.

4. _____ Because GNP data are published by the U.S. Commerce Department and are based on elaborate statistical techniques, these data can generally be considered highly accurate.

5. _____ Net national product measures the final market value of goods produced during a year after adjustment has been made for any capital used up in the production of the goods.

6. _____ Net interest income is the smallest component of national income.

7. _____ In 1981, 92.2 percent of disposable income was used as consumption expenditures, and so 7.8 percent must have been saved.

8. _____ If an economy imports $20.5 billion of goods and exports $18.7 billion, net exports are −$1.8 billion.

9. _____ Unwanted inventories arise as a component of aggregate investment because firms produce a certain amount of goods expecting to sell all of them and then cannot.

10. _____ As a measure of a nation's standard of living, nominal GNP is the best available statistic.

11. _____ When a country experiences a rapid growth in its population, GNP must grow at least as fast just to keep each person equally well off.

12. _____ One problem encountered in trying to assign a cost to nuisance goods is that these goods are not traded in a market, and so the value of their damage is very difficult to determine.

MULTIPLE CHOICE QUESTIONS

Circle the correct answer.

1. If the value of the steel, paint, insulation, and all other components used in making an electric stove is included in measuring GNP, the measure is
   a. accurate because each individual component is involved in a market transaction
   b. too high because of the problem of double counting
   c. too low because of the problem of double counting
   d. unaffected because the various parts were initially a part of some producer's inventory

2. If $C = \$400$ billion, $I = \$70$ billion, $G = \$50$ billion, and imports = $25 billion, GNP equals
   a. $545 billion   c. $495 billion
   b. $520 billion   d. cannot be determined

3. All of the following statements are correct except
   a. gross national product equals personal disposable income plus depreciation
   b. national income equals the income received by the owners of the factors of production during a period of time

NATIONAL INCOME ACCOUNTING

    c. net national product equals gross national product minus the capital consumption allowance
    d. national income equals personal disposable income minus transfer payments, dividends, and interest adjustments plus corporate profits and personal taxes

4. For a real GNP of $1750 billion and a GNP price deflator of 160, nominal GNP must be
    a. $1100 billion   **d.** $1750 billion
    b. $1570 billion   **e.** cannot be determined
    c. $2800 billion

5. The GNP account would reflect all of the following transactions except
    a. a 6 percent commission paid to a real estate agent for selling a previously owned house
    b. $100 won on the Super Bowl game
    c. newly constructed but unsold houses
    d. the wages paid to a plumber for replacing a leaky faucet

6. The major component of U.S. national income is
    a. rental income
    b. proprietors' income
    c. corporate profits
    d. interest income
    e. none of the above

Answer the next three questions on the basis of Table 22-4 for a hypothetical economy.

TABLE 22-4

	$ BILLIONS
Consumption	1925
Net exports	44
Interest adjustment	81
Personal taxes	500
Depreciation	300
Investment	650
Imports	30
Government spending	800
Indirect business taxes minus subsidies	150
Corporate profits	170
Dividends	50
Transfer payments	200

7. Based on the information in Table 22-4, GNP is
    a. $3389 billion   **c.** $3419 billion
    b. $2775 billion   **d.** $3134 billion

8. Personal disposable income is
    a. $2630 billion   **c.** $3389 billion
    b. $3119 billion   **d.** $2969 billion

9. If households pay $40 billion to businesses in interest, the personal saving rate is
    a. 21.3 percent   **c.** 19.6 percent
    b. 25.3 percent   **d.** 22.4 percent

10. If prices in the current year are less than prices in the base year,
    a. real GNP equals nominal GNP
    b. real GNP is less than nominal GNP
    c. real and nominal GNP are the same thing
    d. real GNP exceeds nominal GNP

11. Which of the following adjustments would not have to be made to GNP in order to get a measure of net economic welfare (NEW)?
    a. the value of leisure time would have to be added to GNP
    b. the costs of pollution would have to be deducted from GNP
    c. the value of all secondhand transactions would have to be added to GNP
    d. the value of nonmarket incomes would have to be added to GNP

AT THIS POINT YOU SHOULD BE ABLE TO . . .

1. Define the concept of GNP and state why such a measure is important in aggregate economic analysis.
2. List five points about GNP as a measure of aggregate output and state why each feature is important.
3. Compute GNP by using the aggregate expenditure approach.
4. Derive net national product, national income, and disposable personal income by making the proper adjustments to GNP.
5. Explain why depreciation must be removed from GNP in order to measure net national product.
6. List the three major components of national income.
7. Explain why the sum of the components of aggregate demand equals GNP.
8. Explain why there are problems using GNP as a measure of social well-being.
9. Define nominal GNP, real GNP, and the GNP deflator; explain how this deflator can be calculated; and use the deflator to calculate the rate of inflation.
10. Explain why a measure of net economic welfare (NEW) might be a better measure of social well-being than GNP.

QUESTIONS FOR THOUGHT

1. Why is it important not to include the value of intermediate goods in the computation of gross national product? What would be the result of including such goods? Explain one method of estimating GNP which solves the problem of intermediate goods.

2. In computing NNP, an allowance must be made for the capital used up in the production of current output.

Why is such an adjustment necessary? Do you think that this is an important adjustment? Explain why or why not.

3. When would it be appropriate to measure GNP in nominal terms? In real terms? Why is the distinction between real and nominal GNP important?

4. In terms of GNP and per capita GNP, how can these statistics be used to identify a recession? An expanding economy? Which measure (and why) would you use as an indicator of a nation's standard of living?

5. GNP is by no means a perfect measure of aggregate well-being. Discuss some of the problems and possible solutions for improving the comprehensiveness of GNP and enhancing its usefulness as a measure of economic welfare.

6. The expression $C + I + G + NX = $ GNP states that the value of aggregate demand equals the value of final aggregate output. Explain this equation in terms of the circular flow model presented in Chapter 21.

23 The Business Cycle, Output, and Aggregate Demand

The major purpose of Chapter 23 is to develop a simplified model for the determination of aggregate output (income) and demand. The model is based on the circular flow concept; however, the concept is extended to show how the flow attains an equilibrium and what happens if a disequilibrium occurs. The analysis developed in Chapter 23 is Keynesian, and a central conclusion is that once an economy attains an aggregate equilibrium at which there is neither excess demand nor excess output, there is no reason to expect this to be a full-employment equilibrium. The level of aggregate demand essentially determines the level of output, income, and employment; if this demand is less than what is required to achieve full employment, nothing automatically guarantees that the resulting unemployment will be eliminated.

Chapter 23 begins with a discussion of the consumption and investment components of aggregate demand, since in the initial model these are assumed to be the only sources of spending. Household consumption is a function of the level of personal disposable income, which in turn depends on the level of output. The consumption and saving functions are relatively stable over time, and data indicate that higher levels of income induce increases in consumption and saving. Investment spending is assumed constant regardless of the level of income. This, however, is a strong assumption which is relaxed in later chapters. Aggregate demand is the sum of consumption and investment spending. Only at the point at which this demand equals the value of the output produced is the economy in equilibrium. For any output other than this equilibrium level, adjustments take place which push the system toward equilibrium. These adjustments take place through the investment component of aggregate demand as firms alter their inventories, which in turn change output, employment, and income. Only at equilibrium does the value of the inventories firms intend to hold equal the actual level held. Any change in the aggregate demand function causes output (income) to change by some multiple of the change in aggregate demand as a new equilibrium is established. The multiplier shows how much output changes for any change in aggregate demand. Its value is determined by the marginal propensity to consume.

Chapter 23 concludes with a discussion of the paradox of thrift and Keynes's hypothesis of investment. The paradox is that when households try to increase saving, employment and output fall so that the actual level of saving may not change at all. Keynes argued that the major source of changes in output arises from changes in investment demand. Investment spending is influenced by, among other things, firms' expectations about the future. But the future is uncertain, and so investment demand is strongly influenced by the "animal spirits" of the investors.

The model is expanded in Chapter 24 to include government spending. In Chapter 24, you see how the Keynesians argued that if an economy was in an unemployment equilibrium, it could very well remain there unless the government participated actively in the economic system.

CHAPTER OUTLINE

1. Within the context of the circular flow model, any reduction in spending by households results in a reduced demand for firms' output, and so overall economic activity contracts, production decreases, and unemployment increases. Both income and demand continue to decline, and the output gap widens. This contraction in the circular flow activity, however, does not continue forever.
2. In an economy with no foreign trade and no government spending, aggregate demand consists of household consumption and investment demand.
   a. If it is assumed that households make no interest payments to firms, all of personal disposable income is divided between consumption and saving. Many factors affect the consumption decisions of a particular household at a particular time. The major influence on household consumption is the level of personal disposable income. Data indicate that a strong, positive relationship exists between

consumption spending and households' income.
- (1) The consumption function specifies the level of consumption for each level of personal disposable income. The consumption function presented in Chapter 23 is linear, with consumption being proportional to income, and so the graph of the function is a straight line passing through the origin formed by the intersection of the consumption and income axes. The slope of the consumption function is called the marginal propensity to consume MPC. The MPC shows how much of each extra dollar of income received by households is spent. The part of the extra dollar of income which is not spent is saved. This fraction of extra income saved is called the marginal propensity to save MPS. Once the consumption function and the MPC are determined, so are the saving function and the MPS, since $MPC + MPS = 1$.
- b. The level of investment demand consists of firms' desired (planned) additions to physical capital and inventories, and it depends to a large extent on the expected demand for output in the future. This expected product demand is influenced by the current level of income and demand. The model developed in Chapter 23 assumes that the level of investment demand is constant and independent of the level of income.

3. For an economy with no foreign trade and no government sending, aggregate demand is determined by the amount firms and households plan to spend on goods and services at each level of income.
- a. The aggregate demand schedule is derived by adding consumption at each level of income (the consumption function) to the given investment demand at each level of income. The sum shows aggregate demand. Because the level of investment is assumed to be independent of income, any change in aggregate demand occurs because of changes in consumption. The MPC shows how much consumption changes when income changes, and it also shows how much aggregate demand changes as a result of changes in income.
- b. A useful tool in graphically analyzing the determination of the level of output and income is the 45° line. This line has the special property of being the same distance from both the vertical and horizontal axes so that any point on the line corresponds to a point of equal spending and income. When the aggregate demand line crosses the 45° line, income and spending are equal.

4. Using the assumptions that GNP equals personal disposable income (this removes the effects of depreciation, taxes, retained earnings by corporations, interest, and transfer payments) and that all prices are given and constant, an equilibrium in the goods market is established.
- a. The goods market is in equilibrium when at a given level of prices, the level of output supplied equals the level of aggregate demand. For any level of output or spending other than that at equilibrium, there will be either an excess demand for or an excess supply of goods and services. Only at equilibrium does the demand for goods equal the output produced.
- b. If output is below its equilibrium level, aggregate demand exceeds current production. Firms begin to reduce their inventories or turn away customers in order to satisfy this excess demand. Because firms have some desired level of inventories which they wish to maintain, as they draw down their stocks of goods, they also increase production, and so output and employment increase. On the other hand, if current production exceeds aggregate demand, firms cannot sell all they produce and begin to accumulate unwanted inventories. Firms respond by cutting production, causing aggregate output and employment to fall.
  - (1) Even though an economy may achieve an aggregate equilibrium at which firms sell all the goods they produce and households buy all the goods they want, there is no guarantee that the economy will attain this equilibrium at full employment. Actual output may very well lie below potential output. Firms have no incentives to produce more, and households have no incentives to spend more.

5. Still assuming no government intervention and no foreign trade, at equilibrium, the amount saved by households equals the amount invested by firms. Income minus consumption equals investment, and income minus consumption equals savings; thus, saving equals investment. For any output above the equilibrium level, saving exceeds desired investment, and unwanted inventories build up. Firms reduce production and output. When output is below the equilibrium level, saving is less than firms expect, and so there is a decline in the level of desired inventories.

6. Any change (shift) in the consumption function or the level of investment demand (previously assumed to be constant) causes the aggregate demand

curve to shift. A decrease in investment demand causes aggregate demand to be lower at every level of income. The fall in aggregate demand is greater than the initial fall in investment spending because firms begin to reduce production in response to the decreasing demand and accumulating inventories. This in turn leads to reduced employment, income, and consumption and an even lower aggregate demand. This adjustment process continues until a new equilibrium is reached and no unwanted inventories are present. Thus, when investment demand initially decreases, aggregate demand falls by a multiple of this decrease.

7. The multiplier shows how much output changes when there is a shift in aggregate demand. A multiplier with a value greater than 1 means that any change in investment demand initiates even further changes in consumer spending. It is the response of households and their consumption behavior which ultimately decide the size of the multiplier, because the multiplier is related to the MPC. The multiplier is calculated as $[1/(1 - MPC)]$, and so the larger the MPC, the larger the multiplier.
    a. Since $MPC + MPS = 1$, the multiplier can also be expressed as $(1/MPS)$. The higher the MPS, the lower the multiplier.

8. The paradox of thrift occurs when a change in households' saving behavior has no effect at all on the level of aggregate saving yet may lead to a change in the aggregate income level. If households save more during periods of recession, aggregate demand falls and compounds the severity of the recession. For an economy at full employment, an increase in the saving rate may lead to increased actual saving.

9. In Keynesian analysis, the main source of changes in aggregate output and income are changes in the level of investment demand; the consumption function is considered relatively stable over time. Because investment demand is influenced strongly by expectations about the future, there is some uncertainty and risk associated with investment spending, and so it can fluctuate. Investment also changes in response to new discoveries and innovations.

IMPORTANT TERMS AND THEIR MEANING

Match the following terms with the correct definition or phrase.

1. ____ Keynes's belief that investment demand is bound to be affected strongly by the pessimism and optimism of investors

2. ____ Describes the process of a household spending more than its income by drawing down assets

3. ____ The amount saved out of each additional (extra) dollar of income

4. ____ Consists of more or less regular and coordinated movements in GNP relative to trends, unemployment, inflation, interest rates, and other economic variables

5. ____ The amount of aggregate output added to (deducted from) inventories as a result of aggregate demand falling short of (exceeding) producers' expectations

6. ____ The amount firms and households plan to spend on goods and services at each level of income

7. ____ The output level the economy would produce if there were full employment

8. ____ Specifies the level of consumption for each level of (personal disposable) income

9. ____ Measures the amount of output lost through the unemployment of resources; corresponds to an economy operating inside its production possibilities frontier

10. ____ Occurs when a change in the amount households want to save ends up having no effect at all on saving but changes the level of income

11. ____ An analytical tool which bisects the X,Y plane with the property that the value of the variable on the horizontal axis is equal to the value of the variable on the vertical axis

12. ____ Shows the effect on output when there is a shift in the aggregate demand schedule; calculated by the expression $(1/MPS)$.

a. Dissaving
b. Aggregate demand
c. Paradox of thrift
d. Potential output
e. 45° line
f. Animal spirits
g. Marginal propensity to consume (MPC)
h. Business cycle
i. Multiplier
j. Aggregate demand schedule
k. Output gap
l. Goods market equilibrium

TABLE 23-1

OUTPUT LEVEL (INCOME), billions of $	PERSONAL CONSUMPTION, billions of $	PERSONAL SAVING, billions of $ (PS)	MPC	MPS
100	80	_____		
200	160	_____	_____	_____
300	240	_____	_____	_____
400	320	_____	_____	_____
500	400	_____	_____	_____
600	480	_____	_____	_____
700	560	_____	_____	_____

13. _____ The amount consumed out of each extra dollar of income

14. _____ A schedule showing the planned level of total spending on goods and services at each level of income

15. _____ Established when (at the going level of prices) the level of output supplied is equal to aggregate demand, or planned aggregate spending

m. Consumption function

n. Marginal propensity to save (MPS)

o. Undesired or unplanned inventory adjustment

EXERCISES

1. Table 23-1 presents aggregate demand and output data for a hypothetical economy. In this economy, it is assumed that prices are constant, taxes are zero, transfers are zero, and the only component of aggregate demand is consumption.

a. Calculate the level of personal saving PS at each level of income and enter your answers in the appropriate column.

b. Calculate both MPC and MPS at each level of income and enter your answers in the appropriate columns.

c. The MPC (does/does not) _____ change as the level of income changes. Neither does the _____, and their sum equals _____ since each extra dollar must be _____ or _____.

d. If the consumption function presented in Table 23-1 was graphed, it would have a slope of _____.

e. On graph paper, plot both the consumption function and the saving function. Plot the income-consumption relationship and label the curve C = AD. Plot the income-saving relationship and label the curve S. Be sure to draw the 45° line.

2. Suppose the planned investment component of aggregate demand is $60 billion at each level of income. Table 23-2 presents the income and consumption data from Exercise 1, and so the same assumptions hold.

a. Record from Exercise 1a the level of personal saving at each level of income in the appropriate column. Also, enter the level of planned investment spending in its appropriate column.

b. Calculate the level of aggregate demand at each output level and enter it in the appropriate column.

c. As a result of the investment component being added to aggregate demand, an equilibrium is attained at an output level of $_____ billion.

d. For any output level below the equilibrium, aggregate spending is (more/less) _____ than producers expect, and so inventories (increase/

TABLE 23-2

OUTPUT LEVEL (INCOME), billions of $	PERSONAL CONSUMPTION, billions of $	PERSONAL SAVING, billions of $ (PS)	PLANNED INVESTMENT, billions of $ (PI)	AGGREGATE DEMAND, billions of $ (AD)	INVENTORY ADJUSTMENT (IA)	OUTPUT ADJUSTMENT (OA)
100	80	_____	_____	_____	_____	_____
200	160	_____	_____	_____	_____	_____
300	240	_____	_____	_____	_____	_____
400	320	_____	_____	_____	_____	_____
500	400	_____	_____	_____	_____	_____
600	480	_____	_____	_____	_____	_____
700	560	_____	_____	_____	_____	_____

decrease) _____; because of inventory adjustment, the actual level of investment is (greater than/equal to/less than) _____ planned investment. Thus, aggregate output (increases/decreases) _____.

   e. In Table 23-2, show the inventory and output adjustment at each income level. If inventories or output is increasing as a result of changing incomes, designate this increase by a plus sign. If they are falling, use a minus sign.

   f. When the economy is in equilibrium, inventories and output (do/do not) _____ change; however, for any output level greater than the equilibrium level, producers (do/do not) _____ have unwanted inventories, and so aggregate output (increases/decreases) _____.

   g. On the graphs you drew for Exercise 1e, plot a new aggregate demand curve which reflects the $60 billion investment expenditure. Label this new curve $C + I = AD'$. Also, plot the investment function on the same graph with your saving function. Do the graphic results confirm your tabular analysis? _____

   h. If the full-employment equilibrium occurs at an output level of $700 billion, with an equilibrium in the goods market of $300 billion, an _____ gap exists because the value of (actual/potential) _____ output exceeds the value of (actual/potential) _____ output.

   i. Suppose investment spending increases from $60 billion at each level of income to $80 billion. The change in aggregate demand is (greater than/less than/equal to) _____ the change in investment spending because of the _____, which has a value of _____. The new equilibrium level of income is $_____ billion, and the aggregate demand curve (shifts/rotates) _____ upward.

3. On Figure 23-1, the saving function S shows an economy initially in equilibrium at point E at an aggregate income level of $700 billion. At point E, saving and investment are equal to $50 billion.

   a. Suppose households suddenly have a change in attitude toward saving and want to save $25 billion more at each level of income. On Figure 23-1, plot the points which would reflect the $25 billion in increased saving for income levels 525, 700, and 900. Since the saving function is linear, draw a line connecting these new points. Label the new curve S'.

   b. As a result of this increased desire to save, the saving function has made a _____ shift upward, and this corresponds to the aggregate demand curve shifting (upward/downward) _____ since (more/less) _____ is being consumed at each income level.

   c. At the original equilibrium (point E), saving is now (greater than/equal to/less than) _____ investment, and so inventories begin to (increase/decrease) _____ even though producers (do/do not) _____ want this change in inventories to occur.

   d. Firms (increase/decrease) _____ production, and aggregate income (rises/falls) _____.

   e. The new equilibrium is reached at an income (output) level of $_____ billion, and the level of actual saving has (increased/remained constant/decreased) _____. This demonstrates the _____.

   f. When desired saving increased by $25 billion, the level of aggregate income changed by $_____ billion. This suggests that the value of the multiplier is _____ and that the MPS is _____.

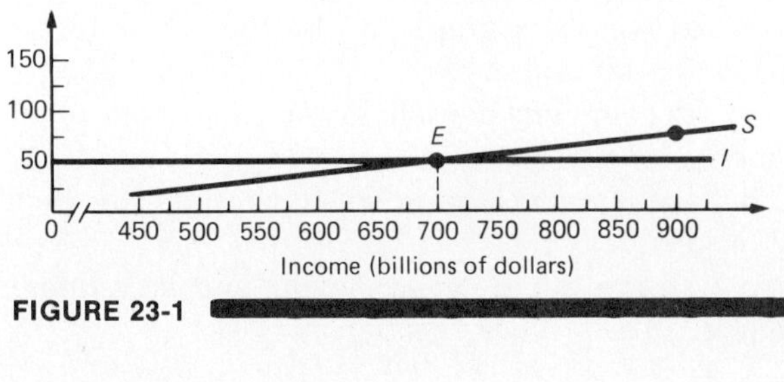

FILL-IN QUESTIONS

1. An output gap occurs when _____ does not equal _____.

2. The business cycle consists of the four phases: _____, _____, _____, and _____. These cycles (are/are not) _____ irregular in their frequency of occurrence.

3. In the simplified model of aggregate demand developed in Chapter 23, it is assumed that investment demand (is/is not) _____ a function of the

FIGURE 23-1

level of income, while household consumption (is/is not) _____.

4. The _____ expresses the relationship between consumption expenditures and disposable income.

5. The *MPC* shows how much _____ changes when there is a change in _____.

6. It (is/is not) _____ possible for households' consumption expenditures to exceed their level of income because they can (save/dissave) _____.

7. An increase in the rate of growth in technology probably will cause a(n) (increase/decrease) _____ in the rate of investment demand.

8. The _____ line is a visual aid used in studying aggregate economic analysis because at any point along the line, quantities on the vertical and horizontal axes are _____.

9. When aggregate demand equals output, the level of saving equals the level of _____ spending, and there (is/is not) _____ any change in desired inventories.

10. If the level of planned spending on output is greater than the level of output, output (increases/decreases) _____ as long as there (is/is not) _____ full employment.

11. When aggregate demand and output are equal, inventories are (increasing/constant/decreasing) _____, output is (increasing/constant/decreasing) _____, and _____ equals investment.

12. The multiplier shows how much _____ changes when there is a shift in _____; the larger the *MPS*, the (larger/smaller) _____ the multiplier.

TRUE-FALSE QUESTIONS

1. ____ Business cycles are predictable because they occur with very regular frequency.

2. ____ If potential real GNP output is $950 billion and actual output is $1 trillion, an output gap of $50 billion exists, and the economy is in a recession.

3. ____ In the simple circular flow model, a reduction in aggregate investment (everything else constant) causes a contraction of economic activity.

4. ____ Together, consumption expenditures and investment spending account for almost 80 percent of aggregate demand.

5. ____ If a household's income is $X per week, it is not possible for its consumption to exceed $X.

6. ____ For a consumption function of the form $C = 0.85Y$, the marginal propensity to consume is 85 cents out of each dollar of additional income.

7. ____ Although the rational producer's investment demand consists of planned additions to physical capital and inventories, it is possible for the firm to have investment spending that it doesn't want.

8. ____ The graph of the aggregate demand schedule is an upward-sloping straight line showing that aggregate demand increases with income; its slope is equal to *MPC*.

9. ____ If corporate retained earnings, depreciation, taxes, interest payments, and transfer payments are assumed away, disposable personal income will be greater than GNP.

10. ____ During a period when aggregate demand exceeds the level of aggregate output, it is reasonable to expect firms to reduce production and employment in order to increase the prices of their goods and their profit levels.

11. ____ Aggregate equilibrium will always occur when the level of savings held by households equals the level of investment by firms.

12. ____ A decrease in the level of desired investment at every level of income causes aggregate demand to fall, but by less than the decrease in investment.

13. ____ The multiplier can be easily calculated as $[1/(1 + MPC)]$.

14. ____ During periods of high unemployment, an increase in the overall level of saving will result in an increase in aggregate demand and output because the increased saving is made available for investment spending.

MULTIPLE CHOICE QUESTIONS

Circle the correct answer.

1. When we use a graph to plot the consumption function, the 45° line shows
   a. the amounts households save at each level of income
   b. the amounts households consume at each level of income
   c. all the points where saving and investment are equal

d. all points where spending by households equals income

2. In Keynesian analysis, the main source of movements in aggregate output is attributed to
   a. changes in the MPC
   b. changes in investment demand
   c. changes in consumption spending
   d. changes in the MPS

3. The permanent income hypothesis argues that
   a. consumption is proportional to income but not to current income
   b. consumption is proportional to the income received over an entire lifetime
   c. consumption is negatively related to the current level of saving
   d. consumption is proportional to the frequency of income receipts

4. Which of the following statements is incorrect?
   a. at higher levels of income, aggregate demand increases, and so households consume more out of each extra dollar of income
   b. aggregate demand is the amount both households and firms plan to spend on goods and services at each level of income
   c. an upward shift of the consumption function means that the aggregate demand curve shifts upward
   d. if the saving function shifts upward, the aggregate demand curve shifts downward

5. When the economy is at an equilibrium level of output,
   a. firms still face the problem of unwanted inventory increases
   b. the amount that households plan to (and do) save equals the level of investment which firms plan to (and do) undertake
   c. the spending by both households and firms exceeds the value of goods produced
   d. firms have unwanted inventories, and so they reduce their level of investment spending

6. All of the following statements are correct except
   a. an aggregate equilibrium does not guarantee a full-employment output
   b. during the Great Depression, the United States may have experienced an unemployment equilibrium
   c. at a full-employment equilibrium, actual output is less than potential output
   d. in equilibrium, the value of actual output equals the value of potential output

7. If households save 10 cents out of each extra dollar of income received, the multiplier is
   a. 4   **c.** 9
   b. 5   **d.** 10

TABLE 23-3

OUTPUT (INCOME), billions of $	CONSUMPTION, billions of $
225	220
300	270
375	320
450	370
525	420
600	470

Answer the next three questions on the basis of the data in Table 23-3.

8. If investment spending is $30 billion at each level of income, the equilibrium level of output (income) is
   a. $225 billion   **d.** $450 billion
   b. $300 billion   **e.** $225 billion
   c. $375 billion

9. The marginal propensity to consume is
   a. 1/3   **c.** 2/3
   b. 1/2   **d.** 3/4

10. Based on Table 23-3, the multiplier is
   a. 3   **c.** 7.5
   b. 5   **d.** 1.0

AT THIS POINT YOU SHOULD BE ABLE TO . . .

1. Define the meaning of a business cycle and describe economic activity during each of its phases.

2. Explain how actual output can exceed potential output.

3. State how the circular flow model is used in the analysis of aggregate income (output) determination, describe the relationship between consumer spending and income, and explain how the marginal propensity to consume is derived from the consumption function.

4. Once the consumption function is known, state why the saving function is also known; also, define the marginal propensity to save.

5. State the two major components of investment demand and explain how a firm's planned investment may not equal its actual investment.

6. Explain the meaning of aggregate demand, graph an aggregate demand schedule, and explain why the 45° line is useful in analyzing aggregate demand graphically.

7. State the conditions of an aggregate equilibrium in the goods market, show this equilibrium graphically, and explain how the economy adjusts when output is at a level other than the level required for an equilibrium.

8. Explain and show graphically how equilibrium in the goods market does not guarantee full employment.

9. Using the saving and investment approach, show how a goods market equilibrium is achieved; explain why this approach results in the same outcome as the outcome that is achieved when aggregate demand equals output.

10. Show graphically and explain what happens to aggregate demand and output when investment demand increases (decreases); explain the concept of the multiplier and, when given appropriate data, calculate this multiplier.

11. Explain and show graphically how an increased willingness to save can result in lower output and no change in the level of saving.

12. Explain why Keynesian economists emphasize changes in investment demand as the major source of changes in aggregate output.

13. List three of the assumptions on which the analysis in Chapter 23 is based.

QUESTIONS FOR THOUGHT

1. In Figure 23-2 of your text, there were periods during the 1960s when the actual level of output exceeded the potential output for the economy. At first sight, this doesn't seem possible. Explain how and under what conditions actual GNP can be greater than potential GNP.

2. The consumption function presented in Chapter 23 stated that the level of consumption was positively related to the level of current income. Milton Friedman and Modigliani and Ando disagree with this concept. Explain both Friedman's and Modigliani and Ando's approaches to the relationship between consumption and income.

3. Explain in a few sentences how the basic model of the determination of aggregate output is built around the circular flow model.

4. When aggregate output exceeds aggregate demand, the economy is not in an equilibrium position. Explain what causes the economy to move toward its equilibrium. What happens to saving and investment?

5. The level of investment demand was assumed constant. What do you think the implications might be if investment demand changed with the level of aggregate income? Do you think the assumption of a constant level of investment spending is reasonable? Explain.

6. What is meant by the multiplier? Explain how the multiplier is related to the marginal propensities to consume and save. Can you think of something that might change the size of the multiplier?

7. What is the paradox in the paradox of thrift? Explain how and why this paradox might exist.

8. Explain what you think Keynes meant when he stated that investment demand was strongly influenced by the "animal spirits" of investors. Also, does technology play any role in investment demand? Explain.

24

The Budget, Fiscal Policy, and Aggregate Demand

Chapter 24 introduces the government component into the macroeconomic model of income determination. Government spending *G*, consumer spending *C*, and investment spending *I* are the major components of aggregate demand. Once *G* is included, the model is almost complete. When government spending is introduced, aggregate demand changes in two ways. First, the government directly adds to aggregate demand by purchasing goods and services. Second, when the government levies taxes or makes transfer payments, disposable income changes, and so does consumption. The government's decisions about spending and taxing are known as fiscal policy. The type of fiscal policy pursued by the government affects aggregate spending, employment, and output. As you read Chapter 24, remember that the price level is still assumed constant and that the economic system does not engage in foreign trade.

Chapter 24 begins with a discussion of the two ways in which government spending enters the circular flow. Government purchases (assumed to be independent of the level of income) directly change aggregate demand for goods and services since they are an injection into the spending stream. This spending for goods and services causes the aggregate demand curve to shift, and as a result, output changes. The change in aggregate output and income is greater than the change in government spending because of the multiplier. The second way in which government spending enters the circular flow is through taxing and transfer payments. Taxes are a leakage from the circular flow which reduce household disposable income. As their income falls, households reduce their spending. The *MPC* out of national income declines when the government imposes taxes, causing a change in the consumption function. Transfer payments enter the circular flow as an injection and increase the level of disposable income and consumption. Net taxes are proportional to income and are defined as the difference between taxes and transfer payments which determines how much consumption changes.

Spending and taxes are the tools the government uses to implement its policies in an attempt to stabilize the economy at or near full employment. Increases in government spending and decreases in taxes represent an expansionary fiscal policy since they cause aggregate demand to increase. An equal increase in both taxes and government spending is also expansionary because of the balanced budget multiplier.

When the government taxes and spends, it does so within the framework of a budget. This budget is in balance only when government's outlays equal its receipts. Every year since the late 1960s, the government has maintained a budget deficit because it has spent more money than it has received. When the government pursues an expansionary fiscal policy, unemployment is reduced and economic growth is promoted; however, this causes the deficit to increase. In fact, the deficit can change because of automatic stabilizers which Congress has built into the system. The operation of these stabilizers dampens the effects of recessions and booms on national income.

As you study Chapter 24, pay particular attention to how aggregate demand and output change when the government spends on goods and services and how taxes affect the consumption function. Remember too that the multiplier operates when government participates in the economy actively. You should also be able to explain how the government's fiscal policy seeks to stabilize the economy, what effect this policy can have on the budget deficit, and what the real problem is with a large national debt.

CHAPTER OUTLINE

1. Government spending, taxes, and transfer payments directly influence the circular flow of income, output, and spending.
    a. Government spending directly changes aggregate demand. In the United States, most government spending on goods and services is done by state and local governments, while more than half the federal outlays consist of transfer payments, grants to state and local governments, and interest payments on the national debt.

b. Government taxes and transfer payments enter the circular flow and affect aggregate demand by changing the level and distribution of disposable income. Most federal transfer payments are Social Security benefits, while the largest component of tax receipts is the federal personal income tax. Social Security contributions are the second largest source of federal revenue. State and local governments derive most of their revenue from property and sales taxes.

2. When the government purchases goods and services, the expenditures are added directly into the aggregate demand equation. The model developed in Chapter 24 assumes that government spending is independent of the level of income. Taxes and transfer payments affect aggregate demand through the consumption function. Net taxes (taxes minus transfer payments) reduce personal disposable income and are assumed to be proportional to national income. When proportional taxes are included, the slope of the consumption function MPC changes, and so the level of consumption falls. The MPC out of national income is lower after taxes are included.

   a. In the absence of taxes, an increase in government spending shifts the aggregate demand curve upward, and so the equilibrium level of output and national income increases. Because of the multiplier, this increase in output and income is larger than the increase in government spending.

   b. With an unchanged investment demand and no government spending, an increase in the tax rate pivots the consumption function, and consumption spending falls at each level of national income. The aggregate demand curve pivots, and so output and income fall.

   c. For a given level of investment spending, a change in both the level of government spending and the tax rate changes the level of income and output.
      (1) When both tax receipts and government spending increase by an equal amount, the overall effect is not zero. Equal increases in government spending and tax receipts cause an increase in aggregate output. The reason for this increase in output is the fact that although disposable income is reduced by the full amount of the tax increase, the MPC causes a reduction in consumption equal to only a percentage of the reduction in income. At the same time, the total increase in government spending is added directly to aggregate demand. These changes cause aggregate demand to increase by an amount equal to the difference between higher government spending and lower consumption. The balanced budget multiplier states that the combined effects of equal increases in government spending and taxes on aggregate demand cause output to increase.

   d. Proportional taxes reduce the MPC out of national income, and so the multiplier is also reduced. For a given change in national income, higher proportional tax rates cause smaller changes in disposable income and consumption. This causes the MPC out of national income to fall.

3. The government's budget shows its spending and financing plans. If the government's revenue (primarily from taxes) is less than its expenditures on goods, services, and transfer payments, a budget deficit exists. The government incurs a budget surplus when its revenues exceed its outlays. The tax rate, the level of government spending, and the level of national income determine whether a budget surplus or deficit exists.

   a. For a given tax rate, altering the level of government spending causes the level of income and the budget deficit to change in the same direction. Because of changing tax revenues, the deficit does not change by an amount equal to the change in government spending. The government affects both the deficit and the level of income by changing its tax rates.

   b. Government and investment spending are injections into, while net taxes and saving are leakages from, the circular flow of output and income. In equilibrium, the value of leakages equals the value of injections; when the government has neither a budget deficit nor a surplus, saving equals investment. If a budget deficit exists, government spending exceeds revenues *and* saving exceeds investment by the same amount. This occurs because the government borrows funds from households which would otherwise go into investment spending. The amount firms borrow for investment and the amount government borrows to finance its deficits equals saving. With investment independent of the level of income, an increase in government spending increases the deficit.

4. An active fiscal policy involves changes in both government spending programs and tax rates. Fiscal policy is expansionary if its aim is an increase in GNP and contractionary if its goal is to reduce GNP. Two questions which are frequently asked about the active use of fiscal policy are whether it really can be successful in stabilizing output and whether the status of the government budget

deficit is a good measure of the type of fiscal policy being pursued. The deficit changes for reasons other than changes in government spending and tax rates.
   a. The full-employment budget calculates the level the budget surplus or deficit would be if the economy were at full employment, and so it is a better indicator of the type of fiscal policy being pursued by the government than the actual budget deficit or surplus. Since 1955, the actual budget deficit has been greater than the full-employment deficit because output has been below its potential level.
5. Two problems which may limit the success of an active fiscal policy in maintaining stability and full employment are the uncertainty surrounding economic events and the time lags involved in implementing policy effectively. Economists are unable to predict exactly when a boom or recession will begin or state precisely the impact of world events on the economy, and so it is very difficult to determine the type of policy to pursue until the recession or boom is under way. Even then it often is difficult to determine the size of desired changes in government spending or taxes. Once policy decisions are made, it may take months for these decisions to be felt in the economy. The effects of fiscal policy changes are not instantaneous.
   a. Automatic stabilizers reduce the response of GNP to shocks in the economy. The main stabilizers are the income tax and unemployment benefits. When the economy is expanding rapidly, the income tax dampens consumption and aggregate demand. During periods of recession, unemployment benefits and lower taxes keep aggregate demand from falling as much as it would without these benefits. The automatic stabilizers are designed to work without any direct decision being made about when they should be implemented. This is an important advantage over active fiscal policy.
6. At the end of 1981, the outstanding national debt was about $800 billion. There are two reasons why a large national debt may be a problem. First, when people lend the government money to finance this debt, they choose not to invest as much in physical capital, and so the stock of productive capital is lower than it would be if the government did not borrow savers' money. Second, a big debt requires big interest payments to the holders of the debt. If the government borrows to make its interest payments, both the debt and interest payments increase. The basis of the fear about a large public debt is that the government may print money to finance its spending programs and thus increase the money supply. This increase in the money supply may lead to serious inflationary problems.
7. Efforts are currently under way by some citizens and members of Congress to pass a constitutional amendment which would require the federal government to operate with a balanced budget except under very unusual conditions. Economists generally believe that there are economic conditions under which budget deficits are beneficial. Small deficits do not present a problem; however, most economists agree that large deficits cannot be maintained easily over a long period of time. Many proponents of a balanced budget amendment may actually want to reduce the size of government.

IMPORTANT TERMS AND THEIR MEANING

1. _____ An increase in government spending and an equal increase in taxes result in an increase in output.

   a. Government outlays

2. _____ The percentage of each dollar of income paid as taxes

   b. Net taxes

3. _____ Total spending by all levels of government, including transfer payments

   c. Burden of the debt

4. _____ Deliberately changing tax rates and government spending in an attempt to reach full employment and attain economic stability

   d. Budget deficit

5. _____ The federal government's total outstanding debts

   e. Contractionary fiscal policy

6. _____ Occurs when the government's outlays are greater than its revenue

   f. Leakages

7. _____ Part of the flow of income that is taken out of the circular flow and does not get put back into the aggregate demand for goods

   g. Full-employment budget

8. _____ Policy designed to increase GNP; may consist of increased government spending and lower taxes

   h. Tax rate

9. _____ Shows what the level of the budget surplus or deficit would be if the economy were at full employment

   i. Budget surplus

10. ____ An addition to aggregate demand which does not come from the circular flow because it does not depend on the level of income

11. ____ A description of the spending and financing plans of an individual, business, or government

12. ____ Arises because the debts of the U.S. government are ultimately debts of the taxpayers

13. ____ Occurs when the government's outlays are less than its revenue

14. ____ Total tax receipts minus transfer payments

15. ____ Policy designed to reduce GNP; may consist of reduced government spending and higher taxes

16. ____ Mechanisms (primarily the income tax and unemployment benefits) which reduce the response of GNP to shocks

j. Automatic stabilizers

k. Fiscal policy

l. National debt

m. Injections

n. Balanced budget multiplier

o. Expansionary fiscal policy

p. Budget

EXERCISES

1. Table 24-1 shows various levels of income and output for a hypothetical economy. Government spending and investment are $100 and $60, respectively, and are assumed constant at all levels of income. The letter Y designates national income. It is assumed that the government does not collect taxes and that consumers spend 75 cents out of each extra dollar received as income.

   a. Compute the level of consumption C and saving S at each level of income; enter your answers in the appropriate column. (1) As income increases, both consumption and saving (increase/decrease) _____.
   (2) The MPC is _____, and the MPS is _____.

   b. Calculate the level of aggregate demand AD at each level of income. Enter your answers in the appropriate column. (1) The equilibrium level of spending and output occurs between an aggregate income of $_____ and $_____.
   (2) In order to determine the equilibrium output specifically, recall that in equilibrium, leakages from spending must equal injections into the system. The only leakage is _____, while both _____ and _____ are injections. The value of total injections is $_____. (3) The equilibrium expression $S = I + G$ implies that $S = 160$ when aggregate demand and output are equal. From part **a**, the MPS is equal to _____, and so we could write $0.25Y = 160$ as a statement of the saving equilibrium. The value of output (income) which causes the leakages and injections to be equal is $_____. (4) In equilibrium, $C = \$_____$, $S = _____$, and $AD = \$_____$.

   c. Suppose government spending increases by $50 for each level of income. This causes the overall level of aggregate demand to increase. In the column labeled "new AD," enter the new value of aggregate demand for each level of income. (1) The equilibrium level of spending and output now occurs between an aggregate income of $_____ and $_____.
   (2) The value of total injections is now $_____, and this implies that the total leakages must be $_____ for the economy to be in equilibrium.
   (3) Again using the relationship $S = 0.25Y = 210$ as a statement of saving equilibrium, the value of output (income) which causes the leakages and injections to be equal is $_____. (4) This new equilibrium

TABLE 24-1

Y, $	C, $	S, $	I, $	G, $	AD, $	NEW AD, $
100	___	___	60	100	___	___
200	___	___	60	100	___	___
300	___	___	60	100	___	___
400	___	___	60	100	___	___
500	___	___	60	100	___	___
600	___	___	60	100	___	___
700	___	___	60	100	___	___
800	___	___	60	100	___	___
900	___	___	60	100	___	___
1000	___	___	60	100	___	___

THE BUDGET, FISCAL POLICY, AND AGGREGATE DEMAND

TABLE 24-2

Y, $	T, $	Y_d, $	C', $	S', $	I, $	G, $	AD', $
100					60	100	
200					60	100	
300					60	100	
400					60	100	
500					60	100	
600					60	100	
700					60	100	
800					60	100	
900					60	100	
1000					60	100	

income shows a change in national income of $_____ even though the increase in government spending was only $50. This happens because of the _____ effect. (5) Given the MPS of 0.25, the multiplier is _____, and so the changes in income equals the change in government spending ($50) times the multiplier.

2. Suppose the government levies a 20 percent income tax on each level of income. Some of the macroeconomic relationships presented in Exercise 1 change because consumption and saving are a function of disposable income (income minus taxes). The symbols AD', C', and S' designate the new aggregate demand, consumption, and saving levels after the effect of taxes. Table 24-2 reproduces the Y, I, and G entries from Table 24-1.

a. Compute the level of taxes T, disposable income Y_d, consumption C', and saving S'. Enter your calculations in the appropriate columns. (1) As the level of income increases, the dollar amount of income paid as taxes (increases/decreases) _____. (2) The MPC (MPC') out of national income after the tax is imposed is _____, and the MPS (MPS') is _____. (3) The MPC and MPS out of disposable income (Y_d) are _____ and _____, respectively.

b. Calculate the level of aggregate demand AD' at each level of income. Enter your answers in the appropriate column. (1) The equilibrium level of spending and income is $_____, and this is (higher/lower) _____ than the equilibrium income established in part **b**. (2) Aggregate demand falls at each level of income because (consumption/investment/government spending) _____ falls at each level of income.

c. Complete Table 24-3 by listing the leakages from and injections into the system at each level of

TABLE 24-3

Y, $	S' + T, $	I + G, $
100		
200		
300		
400		
500		
600		
700		
800		
900		
1000		

income. (1) Leakages are the sum of _____ and _____, while injections are the sum of _____ and _____. (2) Using the leakages and injections approach, an equilibrium income is established at $_____, which is the same as the income determined by the aggregate demand and output approach. (3) At any income level lower than equilibrium, leakages are (greater than/less than) _____ injections, and this tends to (increase/decrease) _____ output; however, for any income level greater than the equilibrium level, leakages are (greater than/less than) _____ injections.

3. On your graph paper, plot two separate graphs. First, plot AD ($C + I + G$), which you computed in Exercise 1b. Next, plot AD' ($C' + I + G$), which you calculated in Exercise 2b. When you draw the AD' curve, remember that the MPC' is less than the MPC. and so the curve has a different slope than AD. Be sure to draw the 45° line. Directly below this graph, construct another one to show how equilibrium is established, using the leakages and injections approach. In the second graph, plot $I + G$, S, and $S' + T$.

a. On both the graphs, before any taxes are levied, equilibrium output (income) is $_____.

b. When the government imposes the 20 percent

proportional tax rate, both the aggregate demand and saving curve (shift/rotate) _____ because the (intercept/slope) _____ of the consumption function changes.

c. After the tax levy, the new equilibrium is $_____.

4. Table 24-4 shows the different income levels presented in Exercise 2. When government spending G is $100 and there is a 20 percent proportional income tax, there is only one level of aggregate income at which the budget is in balance. Complete Table 24-4 by transferring the tax receipts T you calculated in Exercise 2a to the table. Assuming that government spending is constant at $100, calculate the size of the government surplus or deficit $(G - T)$. If a deficit exists, place a minus sign before your answer. If a surplus is present, indicate that with a plus sign.

TABLE 24-4

Y, $	T, $	G, $	G − T, $
100			
200			
300			
400			
500			
600			
700			
800			
900			
1000			

a. The government budget is in balance at an income level of $_____.

b. At any income level lower than equilibrium, there is a budget (surplus/deficit) _____ because government spending is (greater than/less than) _____ tax receipts.

c. If the economy were in equilibrium at $400 but full employment occurred at an income (output) level of $700, the full-employment budget would show a (surplus/deficit) _____ of $_____, but the actual budget (surplus/deficit) _____ would be $_____.

d. In an equilibrium of $400, the government appears to be pursuing a(n) (contractionary/expansionary) _____ fiscal policy even though its spending and tax rates (have/have not) _____ changed.

5. (*Optional*) In Exercises 1 and 2, you worked with two simple models of an economic system. In this exercise, see if you can formulate the basic algebraic statements of the economic relationships presented in Exercises 1 and 2. Table 24-5 is based on Exercise 1, and Table 24-6 is based on the relationships in Exercise 2.

a. Complete each equation.

TABLE 24-5

Aggregate demand	$AD = \_\_\_ + \_\_\_ + \_\_\_$
Consumption function	$C = \_\_\_$
Saving function	$S = \_\_\_$
Investment (assumed constant)	$I = \$60$
Government spending (assumed constant)	$G = \$100$

TABLE 24-6

New aggregate demand	$AD' = \_\_\_ + \_\_\_ + \_\_\_$
New consumption function	$C' = \_\_\_$
New saving function	$S' = \_\_\_$
Disposable income	$Y_d = \_\_\_ - \_\_\_$
Tax function	$T = \_\_\_$
Investment (assumed constant)	$I = \$60$
Government spending (assumed constant)	$G = \$100$

b. After the 20 percent income tax on each level of income, some of the macroeconomic relationships change. Supply the missing information to complete each equation.

FILL-IN QUESTIONS

1. Government intervention in the economy generates a leakage from the circular flow in the form of _____, but the government also generates injections when it makes _____ payments and _____ goods and services.

2. The two major sources of revenue for the federal government are the _____ tax and _____ contributions.

3. If transfer payments are larger than tax receipts, net taxes are (positive/zero/negative) _____, and personal disposable income (increases/remains constant/decreases) _____.

4. The equation $MPC' = MPC \times (1 - t)$ tells us that when taxes are included in the macroeconomic model, the amount consumed out of each extra dollar of income (increases/decreases) _____, and so the graph of the consumption function (shifts/

THE BUDGET, FISCAL POLICY, AND AGGREGATE DEMAND

rotates) _____ and (more/less) _____ is consumed at each level of income.

5. An increase in government spending causes the aggregate demand curve to (shift/rotate) _____ and increases output and income by an amount larger than the change in spending because of the _____.

6. An increase in government spending and tax receipts by the same amount (does/does not) _____ increase the level of output and income because consumers (do/do not) _____ reduce their consumption by an amount equal to the increased tax.

7. A high tax rate causes the *MPC* to (rise/fall) _____, and so the value of the multiplier (increases/decreases) _____.

8. The government _____ describes what goods and services the government will buy during the coming year, what transfers it will make, and how it will pay for them.

9. Initially, a fall in the tax rate will cause the budget deficit to (rise/fall) _____ and the level of output and income to (rise/fall) _____.

10. Savings and net taxes are (leakages from/injections into) _____ the circular flow, and they must equal _____ purchases and _____ when the economy is in equilibrium.

11. A _____ fiscal policy would include such actions as reduced government spending and higher taxes because its aim is to (increase/decrease) _____ GNP.

12. The _____ budget shows what the budget surplus or deficit would be if the economy were at full employment; it (is/is not) _____ a more appropriate guide to the direction of fiscal policy.

13. Two reasons why fiscal policy does not always work as it should are _____ about economic events and the time _____ involved before a policy can be implemented effectively.

14. The income tax and unemployment benefits are examples of _____ stabilizers because each (enhances/dampens) _____ the response of GNP to shocks.

15. The federal government's total outstanding debts are known as the _____ debt; on average, the debt has been (increasing/decreasing) _____ relative to the GNP.

16. A balanced budget amendment to the Constitution would require that the government's _____ equal its _____ except under exceptional circumstances.

TRUE-FALSE QUESTIONS

1. _____ It is a fundamental principle of economics that for periods other than the very short run, government deficits are inherently bad and should be avoided.

2. _____ The per capita national debt has been falling steadily since 1965.

3. _____ One important advantage which automatic stabilizers have over active fiscal policy is that they work without anyone deciding when they should go into effect.

4. _____ One problem encountered by policymakers when they attempt to pursue an active fiscal policy is that it is often impossible to know exactly how much output should be changed; therefore, it is difficult to know how much taxes and spending should be changed.

5. _____ For most of the period since 1955, the full-employment deficit has been smaller than the actual deficit because output has been below its potential level.

6. _____ The best indicator of the type of fiscal policy being pursued by the government is whether the actual budget has a deficit or a surplus.

7. _____ In equilibrium, total borrowing by the government and firms equals the level of saving in the economy.

8. _____ For a given level of government spending, an increase in the income tax rate causes both output and income to rise; however, the deficit gets smaller.

9. _____ Government pays for most of its spending and transfer programs by borrowing directly from the public.

10. _____ When an income tax is imposed, the size of the multiplier falls because the *MPC* falls.

11. _____ When both government spending (an injection) and taxes (a leakage) increase by the same dollar amount, they cancel each other out, and there is no impact on output and income.

12. _____ The balanced budget multiplier is usually higher than the simple investment expenditure multi-

plier because taxes are not included when there is a change in investment spending.

13. _____ Taxes are one tool of fiscal policy which can be used to help keep output near its potential level.

14. _____ An increase in government spending has a multiplier effect on output and income.

15. _____ Personal taxes collected by the government are computed by subtracting taxes from transfer payments.

16. _____ The tax on corporate income is the greatest single source of federal revenue.

17. _____ The federal government spends less on goods and services than state and local governments do.

18. _____ When the government spends money to buy goods, aggregate demand is increased at all levels of income.

MULTIPLE CHOICE QUESTIONS

Circle the correct answer.

1. In 1981, most of the federal government's purchases were for
  a. education   c. transfer payments
  b. defense   d. highways

2. The largest component of total transfer payments by the federal government is
  a. unemployment benefits
  b. food stamps
  c. veterans benefits
  d. Social Security benefits

3. If the *MPC* out of national income is 0.9, and the government imposes a 25 percent proportional income tax, the new *MPC* becomes
  a. 0.675   c. 1.15
  b. 0.5   d. 0.75

4. Which of the following statements is incorrect?
  a. an increase in the tax rate causes both the consumption function and the aggregate demand function to pivot downward
  b. an increase in taxes changes output because consumption expenditures rise at each level of disposable income
  c. an increase in government spending causes the aggregate demand curve to shift upward
  d. taxes reduce personal disposable income at each level of national income

5. If the economy is in equilibrium when government spending and taxes both increase by $500, and the *MPC* out of disposable income is 0.8,
  a. aggregate demand remains unchanged at its initial equilibrium level
  b. aggregate demand falls at its initial equilibrium level by $100
  c. aggregate demand increases at its initial equilibrium level by $100
  d. aggregate demand increases at its initial equilibrium level by $200
  e. none of the above

6. If the *MPC* is 0.8, and the proportional tax rate is 0.25, when government increases both spending and taxes by $500, the total change in aggregate income is
  a. an increase of $100
  b. an increase of $250
  c. a decrease of $100
  d. an increase of $500

7. Which of the following is a determinant of the government's surplus or deficit?
  a. the level of government spending
  b. the tax rate
  c. the number of people working
  d. the level of aggregate income
  e. all of the above

8. In an economy with a proportional tax rate less than 1, an increase in government spending
  a. increases tax receipts by an amount lower than the increase in government spending
  b. increases tax receipts by an amount greater than the increase in government spending
  c. decreases the size of the government's deficit
  d. increases tax receipts by an amount equal to the increase in government spending

9. All of the following are correct statements for an economy in equilibrium except
  a. $S - I = G - T$ c. $S + G = I + T$
  b. $S + T = G + I$ d. $S = (G - T) + I$

10. If the economy were in a recessionary period, which of the following would be an appropriate fiscal policy?
  a. reduce expenditures for defense and social programs
  b. increase taxes and reduce spending in order to balance the budget
  c. reduce taxes, increase spending, and increase the government's deficit
  d. support a congressional pay increase

11. If the government experiences a budget deficit, it can be concluded that
  a. government is pursuing an expansionary fiscal policy
  b. nothing can be said about the type of fiscal policy being pursued

c. government is pursuing a contractionary fiscal policy

d. the full-employment budget has experienced a larger deficit

12. Automatic stabilizers

a. require no congressional or administrative actions to operate

b. guarantee full employment

c. consist primarily of unemployment benefits

d. may serve to strengthen the business cycle

AT THIS POINT YOU SHOULD BE ABLE TO . . .

1. Explain how government outlays influence the circular flow of income and distinguish between government purchases of goods and services and transfer payments.

2. Describe how net taxes influence the circular flow of income.

3. Show graphically how both government spending and net taxes change the consumption and aggregate demand functions; also, show how output changes.

4. Explain the meaning and operation of the balanced budget multiplier.

5. Calculate the equilibrium level of output and income, given the appropriate data on consumption, investment, and government spending.

6. Compute a multiplier showing the effect of taxes and explain why this multiplier differs from the simple investment expenditure multiplier.

7. Define "budget deficit" and "budget surplus" and explain how the tax rate, the level of income, and the level of government spending determine whether the government's budget has a surplus or a deficit.

8. State the condition for an equilibrium level of income, using saving, investment spending, government spending, and taxes; explain why this is an equilibrium condition.

9. Explain under what conditions the government might pursue an expansionary fiscal policy or a contractionary fiscal policy; give an example of each type of policy.

10. Explain why the status of the full-employment budget is a more appropriate guide to the direction of fiscal policy than the actual budget surplus or deficit.

11. State the purpose of automatic stabilizers, explain their advantage over an active fiscal policy, and list the two major stabilizers.

12. Explain why we should or should not be concerned with the size of the national debt.

13. Give the goals of a balanced budget amendment to the Constitution.

QUESTIONS FOR THOUGHT

1. How is it possible for equal increases in government spending and taxes to increase aggregate output and income? Why don't the two simply cancel each other out? What happens if both government spending and taxes fall by the same amount? Explain.

2. How do proportional taxes affect the multiplier? Explain why a proportional tax rate will influence the size of the multiplier.

3. What exactly does it mean when someone says that the government is pursuing an active fiscal policy?

4. Is it possible with a given tax rate for an increase in government spending to reduce the budget deficit? Explain why or why not. What about an increase in the tax rate?

5. Is it important to make a distinction between the actual budget and the full-employment budget? Explain why or why not.

6. In equilibrium without government intervention into the economy, $S = I$; however, saving does not equal investment unless the budget is balanced. Explain why and state what pressures are in the economy if injections exceed the leakages from the circular flow. If the level of income rises, must the deficit rise?

7. How can recessions and booms affect the federal deficit?

8. When the government pursues an active fiscal policy to combat a business cycle, the results may not be what was expected. What problems are encountered by policymakers which could reduce the effectiveness of fiscal policy? Does the time factor play any role? Explain.

9. How can automatic stabilizers dampen the business cycle, and what advantage do these stabilizers have over an active fiscal policy?

10. Suppose you are scheduled to make a talk to a local civic club about the national debt. List and briefly explain two reasons why the debt may not be as serious a problem as many people assume. Next, list and briefly explain two reasons why the debt may be a problem.

APPENDIX: FOREIGN TRADE AND INCOME DETERMINATION

In this appendix, the assumption of a closed economy is removed, and foreign trade is added directly to the macroeconomic model. Imports are a leakage from and exports are an injection into the economic system, and so the foreign sector also affects the equilibrium level of income, employment, and output. Net exports represent the excess of the injections (exports) over the leakages (imports). It is this value which is added to the consumption, investment, and government spending components to arrive at an equilibrium condition that takes all components into account. When exports increase, equilibrium income increases (this occurs because of the marginal propensity to import MPQ), but the increase in income is less than it would be if the economy did not engage in foreign trade. The MPQ lowers the value of the expenditure multiplier since as income rises, so does the level of imports. Although it is argued frequently that increased imports lower domestic employment, restricting imports could cause retaliation by trading partners against our exports.

CHAPTER OUTLINE

1. The total demand for goods produced in the domestic economy is the sum of consumption spending by households, investment spending by firms, government spending on goods and services, and net exports. Net exports (trade surplus) are the total exports X we sell abroad minus what we import Q from the rest of the world. The new aggregate spending equation is $Y = C + I + G + (X - Q)$.
   a. Net exports account for a relatively small percentage of GNP; however, during the 1970s, both exports and imports increased substantially. Most exports from and imports into the United States are manufactured goods; however, almost one-third of the value of our imports is accounted for by oil purchases.
   b. Exports of U.S. goods are determined by foreign demand conditions, but imports are determined by our domestic income level.
   c. The marginal propensity to import MPQ is the change in imports per dollar change in national income. The MPQ is smaller than the MPC. Similar in function to the MPC, the MPQ defines the slope of the import function. The MPQ rises or falls when tax rates increase or decrease, because those rates affect disposable income.
2. At lower levels of income, exports exceed imports; but as income rises, so do imports, and net exports fall. At high levels of income, imports exceed exports. In an aggregate equilibrium, aggregate demand $[C + I + G + (X - Q)]$ equals aggregate income. When imports are included, an increase in income raises our demand for domestically produced goods by an amount less than it would if we did not import. This happens because the MPQ causes some of the increased income to leak out of the economy for increased imports.
3. When the foreign sector is considered, the value of the multiplier changes. The new multiplier becomes $[1/(1 - MPC' + MPQ)]$. The multiplier falls because part of any increase in domestic spending is spent on foreign goods.
4. Any change in exports changes the equilibrium level of income, output, and employment as well as the trade balance. An increase in exports causes a greater increase in income because of the multiplier effect. When exports increase, the trade balance changes by an amount smaller than the change in exports, because imports increase as income rises.
5. Through reducing or restricting the level of imports, the demand for domestically produced goods increases, and so output and employment rise. A policy designed to restrict the level of imports may cause our trading partners to retaliate against our exports and cause worldwide trade to decrease. The end result is that no country gains employment and worldwide trade disappears.

IMPORTANT TERMS AND THEIR MEANING

Match the following terms with the correct definition or phrase.

1. _____ The increase in imports per dollar increase in national income

2. _____ The value of goods produced domestically but sold abroad

3. _____ The value of goods produced abroad but sold domestically; determined primarily by the level of national income

4. _____ The difference between what is produced domestically but sold abroad and what is produced abroad but sold domestically; may be positive, negative, or zero

a. Imports

b. Trade balance

c. Marginal propensity to import

d. Exports

EXERCISES

1. The following model assumes an open economy trading with the rest of the world. Also, government spends but does not tax.

THE BUDGET, FISCAL POLICY, AND AGGREGATE DEMAND

Consumption function $\quad C = 0.7Y$
Investment (assumed constant) $\quad I = 50$
Government spending (assumed constant) $\quad G = 50$
Exports (assumed constant) $\quad X = 50$
Imports $\quad Q = .2Y$
Equilibrium condition $\quad C + I + G + (X - Q) = Y$

Note: Y denotes income.

a. Complete Table 24-7 by computing the values for consumption, net exports, and aggregate demand. Enter your computations in the appropriate columns. Be sure to look at your model when computing C and Q.

b. The aggregate economy is in equilibrium when aggregate demand equals $_____$.

c. When the economy is in equilibrium, there is a trade (surplus/deficit) _____ in the amount of $_____. This occurs because (imports/exports) _____ exceed (imports/exports) _____.

d. If income increased by a dollar, _____ cents would be spent on domestically produced goods and _____ cents would be spend on imports because the marginal propensity to import is _____.

e. Imports equal exports at an income level of $_____, but aggregate demand exceeds the level of income and output, and so the income expands and imports (increase/decrease) _____.

2. Using the same data presented in Exercise 1, let exports increase by $25 and complete Table 24-8.

a. When exports increase, the new equilibrium level of income is $_____.

b. In equilibrium, there is a trade (surplus/deficit) _____ of $_____.

c. The multiplier has a value of _____, and this would be (larger/smaller) _____ if the MPQ increased.

TABLE 24-7

Y	C	I	G	NET EXPORTS (X − Q), $	AGGREGATE DEMAND (AD), $
100	___	50	50	___	___
150	___	50	50	___	___
200	___	50	50	___	___
250	___	50	50	___	___
300	___	50	50	___	___
350	___	50	50	___	___
400	___	50	50	___	___
450	___	50	50	___	___
500	___	50	50	___	___

TABLE 24-8

Y, $	C + I + G, $	NET EXPORTS (X − Q), $	AGGREGATE DEMAND (AD), $
100	170	___	___
150	205	___	___
200	240	___	___
250	275	___	___
300	310	___	___
350	345	___	___
400	380	___	___
450	415	___	___
500	450	___	___

FILL-IN QUESTIONS

1. Exports are a component of aggregate demand because they represent the _____ demand for goods produced domestically, while imports represent the _____ demand for goods produced abroad.

2. With exports remaining constant, an increase in imports causes the balance of trade to (increase/decrease) _____.

3. The level of imports is dependent on the level of (investment/income) _____.

4. The MPQ (is/is not) _____ affected by the income tax rate, and so higher tax rates (do/do not) _____ change the level of import demand.

5. The presence of foreign goods in the United States (increases/decreases) _____ the MPC for domestic goods and causes the value of the multiplier to (rise/fall) _____.

TRUE-FALSE QUESTIONS

1. _____ A fall in the propensity to import causes the equilibrium level of income and output to increase.

2. ____ An increase in exports from the United States has the opposite effect on output and income of an increase in government spending.

3. ____ The correct formula for the foreign trade-adjusted multiplier is $1/[(MPC' - 1)] + MPQ$.

4. ____ As income levels increase, the level of imports into the domestic economy increases.

5. ____ The United States exports primarily raw materials and imports primarily manufactured goods.

MULTIPLE CHOICE QUESTIONS

Circle the correct answer.

1. In 1981, exports of goods and services from the United States accounted for what percentage of GNP?
- **a.** 0.8
- **b.** 11.7
- **c.** 12.5
- **d.** 9.9

2. If imports increase by $22 when a national income increases by $100, the marginal propensity to import is
- **a.** 0.22
- **b.** 2.2
- **c.** 4.5
- **d.** 4.0
- **e.** cannot be determined

3. All of the following statements are correct except
- **a.** the chance that net exports are positive is greater at lower levels of national income than at higher levels
- **b.** in equilibrium, $C + I + G + (X - Q)$ equals income
- **c.** at higher levels of income, net exports may be zero or even negative
- **d.** none of the above statements is correct

4. If the value of MPC' is 0.5 and for every $100 of increased national income, imports increase by $30, the value of the trade-amended multiplier is
- **a.** 5.0
- **b.** 1.25
- **c.** 4.5
- **d.** 2.5

5. For a nation experiencing a $50 million trade deficit, an MPC' of 0.8, and and MPQ of 0.3, a $10 million increase in exports changes the trade deficit by a
- **a.** $4 million decrease
- **b.** $10 million increase
- **c.** $8 million increase
- **d.** $6 million decrease

AT THIS POINT YOU SHOULD BE ABLE TO . . .

1. State why net exports are a component of aggregate demand and explain why if net exports are not considered, $C + I + G$ is an overstatement of spending on domestically produced goods.

2. Show graphically and explain the relationship between the level of income and the level of national income.

3. Describe how the trade-amended multiplier differs from the investment and government spending multiplier; also, use this amended multiplier to calculate the impact of a change in exports on national income.

4. Using the MPC and MPQ, explain why an increase in national income causes the demand for domestically produced goods to increase by a smaller amount than it would if we did not engage in foreign trade.

5. Describe the effect an increase in exports has on the trade balance.

6. State the major reason why restricting imports may not be good for domestic employment.

QUESTIONS FOR THOUGHT

1. Why should we consider the foreign component in our aggregate demand equation? If foreign trade were ignored, do you think it would significantly affect the equilibrium income level determined in Chapter 24? Explain.

2. In an open economy, the effect of an increase in government or investment spending on income is dampened. Explain why this happens.

3. Suppose you and a union member were in a heated discussion about limiting the imports of foreign autos and steel into the United States. The union member strongly supports trade restrictions as a way to save jobs. How would you counter that argument?

25

Money and Banking

Chapter 25 is an introduction to the role of money and banking in a modern economic system. Societies have used money for thousands of years, and in modern industrialized economies a highly developed banking system is a prerequisite for stability and growth. Chapter 25 examines the reasons why society wants and uses money and the role played by banks in the monetary system. It presents the background material you will need for Chapters 26 and 27, in which central banking and its role in the monetary system are examined and the effects of money on a society's economic well-being are presented.

In the first section of Chapter 25, money is defined and the four functions of money are stated. Anything that is used as money must serve as a medium of exchange, a store of value, a unit of account, and a standard of deferred payment. If an item does not perform these functions, it isn't money. Money's role as a medium of exchange is by far its most important function, since if it is not present, goods and services must be traded physically. This type of economy is called a barter economy and is not at all conducive to specialization and efficiency. Money does not have to be intrinsically valuable, but it must have value in exchange. In fact, money in most economic systems is token money; it has value because its supply is controlled carefully.

The fable of the goldsmiths provides an interesting and somewhat factual introduction to both the evolution and the role of banks in a monetary system. As safekeepers of gold deposits, goldsmiths made loans and accepted letters of transfer (an early form of checks) against the deposits they held. When loans were made by goldsmiths, the money stock increased.

Modern banks are profit-making financial intermediaries which serve as both borrowers and lenders of funds. Commercial banks, however, have a distinguishing characteristic from other financial institutions; some of their liabilities are widely accepted as a form of payment and as such are a major component of the money stock. These bank liabilities (which are part of the money supply) are called demand deposits (checkable deposits). Commercial banks earn most of their income from the interest received from loans made against their deposits. It is unlikely that all depositors will want their money at one time, and so banks hold only a fraction of their total deposit liabilities in reserve to meet the withdrawal demands of customers; the remainder is loaned out, and the money stock increases. This banking practice is known as fractional reserve banking. The required ratio of reserves to deposit liabilities is established by the Federal Reserve System (the Fed). The Fed serves as a bankers' bank and facilitates check clearing between banks in different locations. The Fed's most important function, though, is regulation of the money supply by controlling commercial banks' lending ability.

The final section of Chapter 25 examines the role of near-monies within a monetary system. These near-monies are not spendable like checks, currency, or traveler's checks; however, they can be converted into a spendable form with little difficulty. This conversion makes it possible for the stock of near-monies to affect the rate of inflation and economic activity.

In Chapter 25, you should pay very close attention to the definitions and terms presented and should become very familiar with the concepts of fractional reserve banking and how the banking system actually creates money through the loan process. You will see these concepts again later.

CHAPTER OUTLINE

1. Money serves as a common medium of exchange, a unit of account, a store of value, and a standard of deferred payment; however, its most important function is that of a medium of exchange.
   a. Money is the primary means through which goods and services are exchanged between people. In the absence of money, a barter economy would exist in which some goods are physically traded for other goods. A barter system requires that a double coincidence of wants exist before trade takes place, because each individual participant has to want some-

thing that the other has to offer. Otherwise, trade cannot take place. A barter economy is very inefficient. When money is introduced into a barter economy and is accepted by everyone in exchange for goods, exchange is simplified. Money permits an increase in specialization and productivity because resources which would have been used in trading are free to be used in other productive activities.

- **b.** When money serves as a unit of account, it is the common denominator in which prices are quoted and accounts are kept. As a store of value, money can be used to make purchases in the future; it retains most of its worth in terms of goods and services over time. The store of value function is necessary if money is to be accepted as a medium of exchange; however, money is not the only store of value. When payments to be made in the future are expressed in terms of money, money is performing its function as a standard of deferred payment.
- **c.** Anything that performs the functions of money, but especially those things which serve as a medium of exchange, are defined as money.
  - **(1)** When commodity money is used as a medium of exchange, it is bought and sold as an ordinary good since it has some value both in use and in exchange.
  - **(2)** Token monies are those means of payment whose face value as money is greater than their cost of production or value in alternative uses. Token money exists because its supply is controlled tightly in order to maintain its value. The private production of token money is illegal, and the forces of supply and demand keep the value of this money above its cost of production. If the government declares that something is money, it is fiat money or legal tender. Legal tender is money that must be accepted in exchange and is required by law to be accepted in payment of debts. If an economic system experiences very high inflation rates, sellers of goods may refuse to accept legal tender in payment because its value falls so rapidly.
  - **(3)** An IOU money is a medium of exchange that is the debt of a private firm or person. This type of money accounts for most of the money used in modern economies. An example of an IOU money is traveler's checks.

2. The fable of the goldsmiths states that in the fifteenth and sixteenth centuries, gold was the major form of money, and people often deposited their coins and bullion with goldsmiths for safekeeping. Such transactions were the beginning of banking.
   - **a.** With their gold on deposit, the owners of this wealth found that they could transfer ownership to others simply by issuing a letter instructing the goldsmith to pay the bearer. The goldsmith would either give the letter bearer physical gold or transfer the gold to the bearer's account. These letters of transfer were checks and soon became acceptable as payment for purchases. Goldsmiths also discovered that although they kept large quantities of gold in their vaults, depositors never came by to actually see their gold. All the goldsmith had to do was be able to give gold to those individuals who wanted to withdraw some or all of their deposits.
   - **b.** The goldsmiths soon felt confident that all depositors would not want their money at one time, and so they lent part of the gold held on deposit to individuals who on some specified date repaid the amount borrowed plus interest. The goldsmith's assets and liabilities both remained unchanged when a loan was made.
     - **(1)** If the borrower did not want to take the actual gold, the goldsmith simply entered a deposit on his books for the amount of the loan. The goldsmith's assets and liabilities were still equal even if the borrower wrote a check against his deposit.
   - **c.** Because the goldsmith did not believe that all depositors would claim their gold simultaneously, he was able to make loans; however, he did hold some gold as reserves to be immediately available to meet depositors' demands. The reserve ratio is the ratio of reserves to deposits. When the reserve ratio was less than 100 percent, the goldsmith faced the possibility of insolvency. The lower the ratio, the greater the possibility of having to declare bankruptcy. The goldsmith (in the role of banker) would estimate the level of reserves needed, based on the types of loans made and the unpredictability of demands for gold withdrawal.
   - **d.** The stock of money is the value of the generally accepted means of payment. The stock consists of money in circulation, money on deposit, and the value of loans (in the example of the goldsmiths, the money stock was gold in circulation plus gold held by goldsmiths plus gold-

smiths' loans). Thus, the money stock is increased when loans are made because money which had been deposited is put back into circulation. The amount of loans rises as the reserve ratio falls, and so the money stock increases as the reserve ratio falls. In the goldsmith example, the money stock exceeds the amount of gold in the economy.

    e. A financial panic develops when holders of bank deposits believe that they can no longer get their money from the bank. As everyone tries to withdraw deposits, a run on the bank occurs. When this happens, there usually is not enough money to pay all of the depositors because some of their money has been lent out, and so the bank fails. When banks fail, so do other businesses and a panic begins.

3. Modern banks are the economy's major financial intermediaries. A financial intermediary is an institution which stands between borrowers and lenders by borrowing and then lending these funds to borrowers. Bank liabilities are often used as a means of payment (checking accounts) and thus are part of the money stock.

    a. A state or federal charter permits commercial banks to accept checkable deposits and other types of deposits (such as time deposits) and to make loans. The balance sheet of a commercial bank consists of both assets and liabilities. Asset consist of cash (currency, coins, and reserves on deposit with the Fed), loans and securities (investments made by the bank are primarily in the form of various types of loans and interest-bearing claims on both the federal and foreign governments), and other assets (assets which do not fit into either cash or loans and securities). Liabilities consist primarily of deposits (checkable demand deposits and noncheckable saving and time deposits), borrowing (selling IOUs or notes directly to the public), and miscellaneous liabilities. The commercial bank's cash assets are the main source of its reserves which are left available to meet claims by the bank's depositors. A bank's demand deposit liabilities are subject to withdrawal without notice, while notice must usually be given before saving and time deposits are withdrawn.

    b. Banks are in business to make (and if possible maximize) profits. To do this, they borrow money primarily from depositors and then lend most of what they borrow to customers. Banks make a profit when the cost of borrowing is less than the income received from loans to customers. In this manner, banks serve as a financial intermediary by providing depositors with a means of holding assets which they find attractive and a source of interest income for those who have earned profits for the bank. Banks also earn income by charging fees for many of the services they provide; however, most income is derived from making loans.

    c. Fractional reserve banking is a practice whereby banks do not hold all of their deposit liabilities in the form of cash but keep only a fraction on reserve to meet their depositors' demands. The amount banks must hold as reserves (the reserve ratio) is determined primarily by the Federal Reserve System, which has established minimum reserve requirements for banks. The minimum reserve requirement a bank faces will depend on its size and the types of deposits held. The Fed has also established maximum limits on the amount of interest that can be paid to depositors.

4. Commercial banks (the largest group of financial intermediaries) have the unique characteristic that their deposit liabilities serve as a means of payment which substantially lowers the cost of trade. By issuing checks against their deposits, consumers do not have to transfer currency to a seller physically since the banking system provides a method of check collection. Banks belonging to the Federal Reserve System keep some of their reserves on deposit at the Fed and can make payments from those accounts. When a check deposited in one bank is drawn against another bank, the bank in which it is deposited has a claim against the bank on which it is drawn. The bank in which the check was deposited has an increase in assets (reserves) and liabilities (deposits), while the bank on which the check is drawn loses assets (reserves) and liabilities (deposits). Most transactions between intercity banks are cleared through the Fed; however, some banks in major cities still maintain a local clearing system.

5. Money is broadly defined as those means of payment which are used for unrestricted payments. More specifically, money is defined as currency (coins and bills), checkable deposits, and traveler's checks. This is known as M1.

    a. Because checkable deposits are part of the money stock (M1), when banks make loans to customers, the money stock increases. A borrower may receive the proceeds of a loan either in currency or in the form of a checkable deposit. If the borrower receives currency, the bank's reserves (an asset) fall, but this is offset by the increase in an earning asset (loans). The bank's liabilities do not change. The money supply increases because currency previously held by the bank (not part of the money stock) is now in circulation. If the borrower receives a checkable deposit, both the bank's assets (loans) and its liabilities (deposits) change by the amount of the loan. The money stock increases because checkable deposits are a component of M1. Economists pay close attention to the banks' ability to create money because this process can affect spending decisions by households and production decisions by firms.

6. Assets which do not fully possess all of the functions of money are called near-monies. Such assets are near-monies because they are not as liquid (spendable) as money. Examples of near-monies are savings accounts and money market mutual fund shares. If individuals regard near-monies as being very close to money, these assets influence economic activity. These near-monies are included in the broader monetary aggregates of M2 and M3.

IMPORTANT TERMS AND THEIR MEANING

Match the following terms with the correct definition or phrase.

1. _____ A function of money which permits it to be used to make purchases in the future

2. _____ Consists of coins (issued by the U.S. Treasury) and paper money (issued by the Federal Reserve)

3. _____ Any generally acceptable means of payment in exchange for goods and services and acceptable in payment of debts

4. _____ Anything declared by the government to be money; hence, it is money

5. _____ A narrow range of financial assets consisting of currency, checkable deposits, and traveler's checks

6. _____ Defines the most important function of money as being the means through which goods and services are exchanged between people in the economy

7. _____ A type of money which is used as a medium of exchange and bought and sold as an ordinary good

8. _____ Assets which do not fully possess all of the functions that money must fulfill; they are "almost" as good as money

9. _____ One of the functions of money which establishes the unit in which prices are quoted and accounts kept

10. _____ Those means of payment whose value or purchasing power as money exceeds the cost of production and the value in alternative use

11. _____ Money which the government has declared must be accepted in exchange and which is a lawful way of paying off debts

12. _____ A medium of exchange that is the debt of a private person or firm

13. _____ The amount of a bank's deposit liabilities held to meet depositors' withdrawal demands

14. _____ A set of arrangements in which debts among banks are settled by adding up all transactions within a given period and paying the net amounts needed to balance the accounts

15. _____ An institution that stands between lenders and borrowers; it borrows and then relends those funds to the borrowers

16. _____ An economy in which no commonly accepted medium of exchange is present; goods are physically traded for other goods

17. _____ The value of generally accepted means of payment

18. _____ Before exchange can take place, each buyer and seller must want something the other has to offer

a. Commodity money
b. M1
c. Unit of account
d. Stock of money
e. Reserves
f. Legal tender
g. Money
h. Financial intermediary
i. Store of value
j. IOU money
k. Clearing system
l. Token money
m. Currency
n. Double coincidence of wants
o. Medium of exchange
p. Near-monies
q. Fractional reserve banking
r. Barter economy

19. ____ A practice whereby banks hold only part of their deposit liabilities in reserve to meet the withdrawal demands of their customers

s. Fiat money

EXERCISES

1. In Exercise 1, you are to show what happens to the Zebina National Bank's balance sheet for each of the following transactions. Remember that the assets and liabilities must be equal after each transaction.

a. A group of local citizens get together and form the Zebina National Bank. They put up $250,000 of their own money (net worth), buy a building, purchase supplies (bank premises and equipment) for $75,000, and use all of the remaining cash for cash reserves. Enter these figures into the appropriate accounts for transaction 1.

TRANSACTION 1

ASSETS		LIABILITIES AND NET WORTH	
Reserves	$____	Net worth	$____
Bank premises and equipment	____		

b. The bank accepts $75,000 in checkable demand deposits, and this increases both its _____ and _____. Enter this information into the appropriate accounts for transaction 2.

TRANSACTION 2

ASSETS		LIABILITIES AND NET WORTH	
Reserves	$____	Demand deposits	$____
Bank premises and equipment	____	Net worth	____

c. The bank makes a $15,000 cash loan to a customer. This cash loan changes the composition of the bank's _____ but does not change its _____. Enter the effect of this loan transaction into the appropriate accounts for transaction 3.

TRANSACTION 3

ASSETS		LIABILITIES AND NET WORTH	
Reserves	$____	Demand deposits	$____
Loans	____	Net worth	____
Bank premises and equipment	____		

d. Another customer borrows $10,000 from the bank and takes the proceeds of the loan in the form of a checkable demand deposit. Enter the effect of this loan under transaction 4. The assets and liabilities (have/have not) _____ changed. After transactions 3 and 4, the money stock (has/has not) _____ changed.

TRANSACTION 4

ASSETS		LIABILITIES AND NET WORTH	
Reserves	$____	Demand deposits	$____
Loans	____	Net worth	____
Bank premises and equipment	____		

e. The recipient of the $15,000 cash loan repays $5000. Enter the effects of this repayment under transaction 5. Has the money stock changed? ____

TRANSACTION 5

ASSETS		LIABILITIES AND NET WORTH	
Reserves	$____	Demand deposits	$____
Loans	____	Net worth	____
Bank premises and equipment	____		

f. Tables 25-1a and 25-1b are the balance sheets for a Federal Reserve bank and for the Bald Eagle Bank (located 300 miles from the Zebina Bank). While on vacation, a depositor at the Zebina Bank makes a $5000

TABLE 25-1a

FEDERAL RESERVE BANK: Balance Sheet

ASSETS		LIABILITIES AND NET WORTH	
Cash	$1,000,000	Reserve deposit, Zebina National Bank	$240,000
Bank property	500,000	Reserve deposit, Bald Eagle National Bank	300,000
		Other reserves	560,000
		Net worth	400,000

TABLE 25-1b

BALD EAGLE NATIONAL BANK: Balance Sheet

ASSETS		LIABILITIES AND NET WORTH	
Reserves	$300,000	Demand deposits	$250,000
Loans	50,000	Net worth	200,000
Bank premises and equipment	100,000		

TABLE 25-2a
FEDERAL RESERVE BANK

ASSETS		LIABILITIES AND NET WORTH	
Cash	$_____	Reserve deposits, Zebina National Bank	$_____
Bank property	_____	Reserve deposits, Bald Eagle National Bank	_____
		Other reserves	_____
		Net worth	_____

TABLE 25-2b
BALD EAGLE NATIONAL BANK

ASSETS		LIABILITIES AND NET WORTH	
Reserves	$_____	Demand deposits	$_____
Loans	_____	Net worth	_____
Bank premises and equipment	_____		

sailboat purchase and pays with a check drawn against his account. The check is deposited in the seller's checking account in the Bald Eagle National Bank, which presents the check to the Fed for collection. Show the effects of this transaction on the balance sheets for the Fed (Table 25-2a) and the Bald Eagle National Bank (Table 25-2b) by entering the new accounts in the appropriate places. Show the effects of this transaction by entering the new amounts into the appropriate accounts for the Zebina National Bank under transaction 6.

TRANSACTION 6

ASSETS		LIABILITIES AND NET WORTH	
Reserves	$_____	Demand deposits	$_____
Loans	_____	Net worth	_____
Bank premises and equipment	_____		

2. Below you are presented with several situations in which the various functions of money are illustrated. Using the symbols MX (medium of exchange), SV (store of value), SP (standard of deferred payment), and UA (unit of account), identify the particular function of money in each instance.

   a. You put $2000 of summer earnings into a savings account to help pay for next year's schooling. _____

   b. You must pay $2500 on your student loan 2 years after you graduate. _____

   c. Your roommate told you that her grandparents once buried $10,000 in their backyard because they feared another Great Depression. _____

   d. You pay $28 for a new sweater. _____

   e. At the end of the month, you balance your checkbook. _____

   f. When you graduate, your parents have agreed to give you $3000 for a trip to Europe. _____

   g. Your friend tells you that the price of a theater ticket is now $10. _____

   h. You go to the store and buy a piece of bubble gum for a nickel. _____

FILL-IN QUESTIONS

1. In their role as _____, modern banks stand between lenders and borrowers by borrowing funds and then relending these funds to borrowers.

2. _____ banks have a state or federal charter which authorizes them to accept _____ and make _____.

3. A _____ deposit can be withdrawn from a bank at once, while _____ and _____ deposits may require notice of a specified period before withdrawal.

4. When a bank practices _____ banking, it keeps only a portion of its total deposits on hand to meet customers' withdrawals.

5. Assuming no excess reserves, if a bank's reserve ratio increases, it (increases/decreases) _____ the amount of loans made, while if the ratio falls, the amount of the bank's loans (increases/decreases) _____.

6. In some major cities, banks still use a _____ system of settling (especially checking accounts), while nationwide, the _____ System collects and settles checks between banks.

7. When the money stock is defined as M1, it consists of _____, _____, and _____.

8. Besides M1, other aggregate monetary measures are _____ and _____; however, these (are/are not) _____ as spendable as M1.

9. When an individual buys an item and pays for it

upon receipt, money is serving its _____ function.

10. If two individuals each want what the other has, it can be said that a _____ exists, and this has to be present for exchange to take place in a _____ economy.

11. A U.S. Federal Reserve note is an example of a (commodity/fiat/near-) _____ money, and it (is/is not) _____ legal tender.

12. It is quite possible that some of history's earliest bankers were the _____ since they both accepted _____ and made _____.

13. To say that the Federal Reserve banks are bankers' banks means that they accept _____ from and make _____ to banks.

14. A _____ panic may develop when depositors believe that they cannot get their money from a bank, and this may lead to a _____ on the bank as everyone tries to withdraw his money.

15. In the banking system of the goldsmiths, it (was/was not) _____ possible for the money stock to exceed the total amount of gold in the economy as long as the reserves held were less than the value of their _____.

TRUE-FALSE QUESTIONS

1. _____ If the value of money in use exceeds its value in exchange, it is called a commodity money.

2. _____ The reason that a token money maintains its value is because its production and supply are controlled strictly.

3. _____ When a loan is in the form of a bank deposit into an individual's checkable account, the money stock goes up.

4. _____ When a goldsmith's reserve ratio was 50 percent, every dollar lent out or kept on deposit was backed by gold.

5. _____ Currency in circulation consists of bills ($1, $10, etc.), coins, and checkable (demand) deposits.

6. _____ Any banking system which holds 100 percent reserves does not face the problem of insolvency.

7. _____ In the United States, the major financial intermediaries are commercial banks.

8. _____ Although commercial banks hold some of their assets in the form of U.S. government securities, there really is no well-developed market for these securities, and it may be difficult to turn them into cash quickly.

9. _____ When an individual makes a deposit in a commercial bank, he is lending the bank money.

10. _____ Banks usually establish their reserve ratios by carefully weighing the benefits in terms of higher earnings from a lower ratio versus the risks of insolvency.

11. _____ One of the distinguishing characteristics of commercial banks as financial intermediaries is that their liabilities serve as a means of payment.

12. _____ The major component of the U.S. money supply (M1) in 1981 was currency (paper money and coin).

13. _____ Whether an individual takes the proceeds of a loan in cash or as a checkable deposit, the issuing bank's demand deposit liabilities always increase.

14. _____ When a financial institution sells shares to the public and uses the proceeds to invest in short-term interest-bearing securities, it essentially is performing the functions of a commercial bank.

MULTIPLE CHOICE QUESTIONS

Circle the correct answer

1. All of the following are examples of near-monies except
   a. large time deposits
   b. traveler's checks
   c. U.S. savings bonds
   d. passbook savings accounts

2. The largest part of the U.S. money supply (M1) is
   a. $1 bills
   b. all currency and coins
   c. traveler's checks
   d. demand deposits at banks

3. Suppose a bank has a required reserve ratio of 15 percent, as established by the Fed. If an individual deposits $10,000 in a demand deposit account, how much of this deposit can be lent out by the bank?
   a. $1500   c. $8500
   b. $10,000   d. $11,500

4. In its role of a financial intermediary, which of the following functions could a bank be expected to perform?
   a. accept checkable deposits
   b. make new car loans

c. finance a color TV
d. accept saving and time deposits
e. all of the above

5. The most important function of money is that of a
   a. medium of exchange
   b. store of value
   c. unit of account
   d. standard of deferred payment

6. A distinguishing factor of banks among all financial intermediaries is that
   a. they purchase government securities
   b. a deposit is an asset for the depositor but a liability for the bank
   c. their checkable deposit liabilities are part of the money supply
   d. they try to make a profit
   e. none of the above

7. Which of the following could possibly cause a run on a bank?
   a. a major industry in a town very frequently overdrew its checking account
   b. numerous loans made by the bank were suddenly placed in default
   c. the amount of money people put in their saving accounts declined
   d. there was a sharp decrease in the consumer price index

8. The stock of money is
   a. not constant and changes with banking activities
   b. the value of the generally accepted means of payment
   c. changed when the banking system makes loans
   d. reduced when loans are repaid to banks
   e. all of the above

9. In the fable of the goldsmiths, all of the following were important to the emergence of banks except
   a. the creation of paper currency
   b. the need of people to have a place to keep their gold safely
   c. the fact that depositors found that they could transfer ownership of their gold by checks
   d. the fact that goldsmiths discovered that all people would not want their gold at the same time

10. A ten dollar bill is an example of
    a. fiat money
    b. legal tender
    c. token money
    d. a medium of exchange
    e. all of the above

11. When money is sewn into a mattress, it is performing its
    a. medium of exchange function
    b. store of value function
    c. unit of account function
    d. standard of deferred payment function
    e. none of the above

12. The major source of profit for commercial banks is
    a. interest received on loans
    b. fees charged for writing checks
    c. rental of safety-deposit boxes
    d. fees charged for overdrawing an account
    e. none of the above

AT THIS POINT YOU SHOULD BE ABLE TO . . .

1. State a general definition of money, list and explain the four functions of money, and give an example of each function.
2. Explain how, in the absence of money, a barter economy operates.
3. List three different kinds of money and give an example of each, explain how token monies can exist, and state when such money may be removed from circulation.
4. Define reserves and the reserve ratio and explain the relationship between reserves, solvency, and the profitability of banks.
5. Give both a general and a specific definition of the money supply.
6. Explain the meaning of a financial panic and describe how one might begin; also, state the major reason why a run on a bank might begin.
7. State the major function of financial intermediaries and explain what distinguishes banks from the other intermediaries.
8. List the major assets and liabilities of U.S. commercial banks, give a one- or two-sentence explanation of each, and list three services provided by banks in their role as financial intermediaries.
9. Explain the concept of fractional reserve banking and state how the reserve ratio is usually determined.
10. Explain how a check drawn against one bank but deposited in another bank in another town clears; also, describe the effect the check-clearing process has on each bank's balance sheet.
11. Explain how and why when a commercial bank makes a loan, the money supply changes.
12. List the major components of M1, M2, and M3.
13. Define and give two examples of near-monies and explain why a share in a money market mutual fund might be considered a near-money.

QUESTIONS FOR THOUGHT

1. Suppose that you are scheduled to speak before your high school's honor society and that your assigned

topic is "the money-creating role of banks in an industrialized society." You have a few days to prepare; list the major points that you plan to make. Can you anticipate any questions which students might ask you? List them and jot down short answers.

2. It has been said that money is the grease that makes the wheels of commerce turn. What does this statement mean? What problems would be encountered in a moneyless society?

3. Explain why we no longer see a silver dime, a silver dollar, or a twenty dollar gold piece (just to name a few coins) in circulation? What kind of money were these coins? The government now is about to mint a zinc penny. Do you think that the price of copper has influenced its decision? Explain.

4. What do you think backs the money supply in the United States? Do you think that gold plays a role? Explain why or why not.

5. Why do you think checkable (demand) deposits and traveler's checks are included in the definition of the money supply (M1)?

6. What is the meaning of fractional reserve banking? Explain how it works and how it influences the money stock.

26

Central Banking and the Monetary System

This is the second of three chapters in which the role of money and banking in an aggregate economy is examined. More specifically, Chapter 26 presents a discussion of the organization, structure, function, and operation of the Federal Reserve System. The Federal Reserve system is the central bank of the United States, and so it must promote the smooth operation of our commercial banking system and must determine monetary policy. The Federal Reserve Board of Governors affects macroeconomic stability through the implementation of monetary policies. Chapter 26 prepares you for the analysis of the impact of money on aggregate demand that is presented in Chapter 27.

Chapter 26 begins with an overview of the structure and major functions of the Federal Reserve System. The system is directed by a seven-member Board of Governors who, along with other members of the Fed Open Market Committee, make decisions about monetary policy in the United States. The country is divided into 12 districts, each containing a Federal Reserve bank. These banks are responsible for implementing the Fed's decisions and regulations. The Fed serves as a bankers' bank by accepting the deposits of and making loans to depository institutions. Thus, its balance sheet shows both assets and liabilities. But the Fed's liabilities are unique since they form the basis of the nation's money supply and can be issued in unlimited quantities.

Three instruments used by the Fed to control the money supply are the required reserve ratio, the discount rate, and open market operations. Of these three, however, open market operations are the most frequently used. When the Fed buys and sells government securities on the open market, it changes the economy's monetary base directly (high-powered money), and so the money supply changes. The change in the money supply, however, exceeds the change in the monetary base because of the money multiplier. This multiplier incorporates both the primary and secondary effects of a change in the stock of high-powered money.

Early in the 1930s, the Fed failed to perform effectively its role as the lender of last resort when some banks started to fail, and the financial panic which followed was compounded in its severity. During this period, the money supply fell by 25 percent, while the commercial banking system deliberately increased its excess reserves in an attempt to meet depositors' demands. As a result, the banking system practically collapsed. The Fed should have stepped in and made loans to banks in trouble so that a panic could have been avoided.

The Fed has been criticized by many economists and financial experts who argue that the central bank has failed to maintain a low and stable growth rate of the money supply. The critics argue that the Fed actually has promoted increases in the inflation rate. Two alternatives offered to current monetary policy are the use of monetary rules and the gold standard. The constant money growth rule would not permit the Fed to follow an active countercyclical monetary policy but would require it to set the rate of growth in the money stock at a level low enough to avoid inflation. The gold standard fixes the price of a nation's currency in terms of gold, and the money stock grows only as the stock of gold grows.

Be sure that you understand how the Fed changes the money supply by using its policy instruments. In particular, you should be able to follow the effects of an open market transaction by using the commercial banking system's T-accounts. As the theory of aggregate demand is developed in Chapter 27, the tools of monetary analysis and policy are used.

CHAPTER OUTLINE

1. To ensure the smooth operation of the nation's banking and financial system and to create an institution which would determine monetary policy, the U.S. Congress in 1913 created the Federal Reserve System (FRS).
   a. In 1980, over 5000 of the nearly 16,000 commercial banks were members of the FRS. Members of the FRS must clear checks at par and abide by the Fed's regulations. In return, members may borrow from the Fed and use its

check-clearing system. The FRS is directed by a seven-member Board of Governors, each appointed by the President and approved by the Senate for a 14-year term. The chairman of the Board of Governors (one of the governors) heads the board and is appointed by the President for a 4-year term. The system is made up of 12 districts, each having a Federal Reserve Bank which creates the Fed's check-clearing system, implements the Fed's policy and regulations, and undertakes research on local economic conditions. The Fed Open Market Committee (FOMC) is made up of the seven governors, the president of the Federal Reserve bank of New York, and four presidents from the other district Federal Reserve banks. The FOMC makes decisions about the nation's monetary policy which are carried out by the Fed's New York open market desk.
   b. In fulfilling its functions of maintaining the smooth operation of the monetary and financial system and conducting monetary policy, the Fed serves as a bankers' bank, supervises the banking system, and controls the money stock.
2. The balance sheet of the Federal Reserve System as of March 31, 1981, showed assets and liabilities of $158,078 million.
   a. The major liabilities of the Federal Reserve System are the deposits of the U.S. Treasury, foreign governments, and commercial banks as well as Federal Reserve notes (paper currency).
      (1) As paying agent for the U.S. Treasury, the Fed holds Treasury deposits. Any checks written by the Treasury are drawn on the Federal Reserve System.
      (2) Commercial bank deposits at the Fed must be held in U.S. dollars since they serve as the bank's reserves against its liabilities. These reserves may be drawn down by the banks (as long as there are reserves in excess of the required amount) when needed, and they facilitate the Fed's check-clearing system.
   b. The major asset of the Fed is government securities. By purchasing and selling these securities, the Fed directly affects the lending ability of commercial banks, which in turn changes the stock of money. Other assets include gold (no longer has any monetary role at all), loans and acceptances (loans to commercial banks which must be repaid with interest), and other miscellaneous assets.
3. Because the Federal Reserve System controls the money supply, it can influence overall economic activity significantly.
   a. When traveler's checks are excluded, the money supply (M1) is defined as currency plus demand deposits, and so it consists of liabilities of the Fed (currency in circulation) and liabilities of commercial banks (checkable deposits).
      (1) Member banks of the Federal Reserve System must hold some percentage of their reserves on deposit with the Fed. They may hold more than this minimum (excess reserves), but they cannot hold any less. This percentage is the required reserve ratio. By changing the required ratio of reserves to deposits, the Fed changes the money stock by making it either easier (as the ratio declines) or more difficult (as the ratio rises) for commercial banks to make loans. Should a bank's reserves on deposit at the Fed fall below its required reserves, it may have to reduce loans and thus reduce one component of M1.
      (2) The Fed either encourages or discourages money stock expansion by changing its discount rate. This is the rate at which depository institutions borrow from the Fed in order to meet reserve shortfalls. If the discount rate increases, member banks are more reluctant to borrow from the Fed, and so they try to increase their reserves in order to ensure that they do not fall below the required reserve. When the discount rate changes, changes in the money stock usually follow. The discount rate and the reserve requirement are now infrequently used instruments of monetary policy.
   b. When the Fed decides to buy or sell government securities in the financial market, the open market desk at the Federal Reserve Bank of New York implements the instructions of the FOMC. These open market operations change the money stock and are the primary instrument of monetary policy. When the Fed buys securities on the open market from commercial banks, the initial impact is an increase of the banks' deposits at the Fed. Because of the purchase by the Fed, the commercial banking system's reserve deposits increase, and so it has more excess reserves and adjusts its loans to reflect this change. When the Fed buys securities on the open market from the public, the initial impact is an increase in M1.
   c. The money multiplier determines the change

in the money stock per dollar of change in an open market operation. It takes into account both the primary and secondary effects of the Fed's securities trading. The secondary effects are determined by the banks' reserve deposit ratio and by the way in which the public divides its money between currency and checkable deposits.

d. Open market operations alter the stock of high-powered money (the monetary base). High-powered money consists of currency outstanding plus depository institutions' deposits (reserves) at the Fed (the two major liabilities of the Federal Reserve System). When the Fed buys or sells securities on the open market, it increases or decreases the monetary base by changing its liabilities, and so there is a multiple expansion or contraction of the money stock. Thus, the Fed can alter the money stock by changing the monetary base (through open market operations) or changing the size of the money multiplier (through changes in the reserve requirement and the discount rate).

e. The monetary stock depends on high-powered money. Currency is counted directly in M1, but bank reserves are used to generate larger amounts of checkable deposits by the banks; thus, a lower reserve ratio means that more deposits can be created. Currency plus these checkable deposits makes up M1. The ratio of M1 to high-powered money is the money multiplier. The Fed controls the money supply primarily through its open market operations (which change the amount of high-powered money) and through its ability to change the money multiplier.

4. Although the Fed has almost complete control over high-powered money, it has less control over the money multiplier. Public attitudes about the proportion of their money held as currency relative to deposits may cause significant changes in the stock of money.

a. During the Great Depression, the money multiplier fell significantly, and the money stock contracted by 25 percent. The money multiplier fell for two reasons. First, the public feared that banks were no longer safe places to keep their money, and so they held a large amount of currency. As the public withdrew currency, more banks failed. Second, banks tried to increase their reserves in order to cover the increased withdrawal of deposits. Had the Fed acted in its role of lender of the last resort, many banks would not have collapsed.

b. In its role as lender of last resort, the Fed should have made loans to the financial institutions which were faced with the possibility of failure. By making loans of high-powered money, the Fed would have restored the public's confidence in the banking system, probably prevented many bank failures, and relieved the panic atmosphere. Today the Fed stands ready to fill its role as lender of last resort at the first sign of financial panic.

c. The Federal Deposit Insurance Corporation (FDIC) guarantees depositors that if a bank goes bankrupt, they will be paid up to a certain maximum amount. The FDIC removes the risk of depositors losing their money because of a bank's failure, and so it is a major factor in preventing financial panics.

5. The Fed is independent of the U.S. Treasury, but this is not enough to guarantee that it will not use its power to create money in order to finance government deficits. Since the major way of financing a government deficit is for the Treasury to borrow from the public by selling securities, if the Fed buys these securities, it increases the stock of high-powered money. This in turn increases the money stock (M1). A similar increase in the money stock occurs if the Fed provides the financial system with reserves that allow it to buy this government debt. Thus, the Fed must exercise caution to ensure that it does not finance government deficits by creating money.

6. Critics of the Fed's monetary policy argue that it has not maintained a low and stable growth rate of the money stock. Professor Milton Friedman argues that money growth increased significantly over the past years and that this growth rate has been very unstable. The critics claim that this fluctuating and even increasing growth in the money stock is the source of inflation. A system of monetary rules and a gold standard have been offered as possible alternatives to the Fed.

a. Friedman argues that the Fed should not pursue an active monetary policy in an attempt to prevent recessions or booms but rather should follow a constant money growth rule. This rule would permit the money supply to grow at a constant rate that is low enough to prevent inflation. Since 1979, the growth rates for nominal M1 in the United States have declined slightly. These growth rates have not, however, been stable.

b. When an economic system is on a gold standard, gold serves as the monetary base, and its price is fixed in terms of the system's currency. In theory, the monetary base grows only as a result of purchases or new discoveries of gold, keeping the rate of inflation down. A major advantage of a gold standard appears to be a

CENTRAL BANKING AND THE MONETARY SYSTEM

low rate of inflation, while the disadvantage is that it wastes scarce resources. Also, changes in the gold supply are very uncertain. The gold standard will not reemerge as the basis for a monetary system in today's modern economies.

IMPORTANT TERMS AND THEIR MEANING

Match the following terms with the correct definition or phrase.

1. _____ Argues that the Fed should not pursue an active monetary policy but should promote a constant growth rate in the money supply which would be low enough to avoid inflation

2. _____ Describes the Fed's policy of making loans to financial institutions and firms at times when panic threatens the financial system

3. _____ Consists of seven members, each appointed by the President to serve a 14-year term, and directs the Federal Reserve System

4. _____ Indicates how much the money stock changes per dollar in an open market operation

5. _____ The ratio of reserves to deposits that the Fed requires banks to hold as a minimum

6. _____ The rate at which the Fed lends funds to banks that borrow to meet reserve shortfalls

7. _____ The total amount of money banks have on deposit at the Fed

8. _____ The practice of a nation defining its money in terms of a specific quantity of gold; the monetary base consists of gold

9. _____ The sum of currency outstanding plus bank deposits at the Fed; when multiplied by the money multiplier, it defines the money stock

10. _____ Makes decisions about U.S. monetary policy; consists of the Fed's seven governors, the president of the Federal Reserve Bank of New York, and four presidents of the remaining 11 Federal Reserve banks

11. _____ Insures bank deposits by guaranteeing depositors that they will be paid off up to a certain amount if the bank in which they have their money goes bankrupt

12. _____ That part of a bank's reserves which are greater than the required reserves

13. _____ The buying or selling of government securities in the financial market by the Fed's open market desk

a. Money multiplier

b. Discount rate

c. Excess reserves

d. Gold standard

e. High-powered money (monetary base)

f. Lender of last resort

g. Bank reserves

h. Monetary rules

i. Open market operations

j. Federal Deposit Insurance Corporation (FDIC)

k. Federal Reserve Board

l. Required reserve ratio

m. Federal Open Market Committee

EXERCISES

1. The following accounts (obtained from the May 1982 issue of the *Federal Reserve Bulletin*) show the condition of the Federal Reserve System at the end of April 1982. Examine the accounts and decide which are assets of the Federal Reserve, which are liabilities, and which show the system's net worth (capital accounts).

Acceptances	$ 768
Bank premises	514
Deposits of foreign government	966
Other liabilities	9439
U.S. government securities	134,257
Gold certificates	11,149
Foreign currencies	5591
Deposits from depository institutions	24,702
Loans to depository institutions	1799
Other deposits	450
Coins	411
Other assets	9103
Deposits of the U.S. Treasury	12,239
Federal Reserve notes	130,189
Net worth (capital accounts)	3064
U.S. government obligations purchased	9008
Cash in process of collection	8449

   a. Complete the balance sheet (Table 26-1) by entering the appropriate accounts and amounts in the "Assets" and "Liabilities and Net Worth" columns. All entries are in millions of dollars.

   b. The balance sheet of the Fed shows that its major asset is _____, which amount to $_____ million, while its greatest single liability is _____.

TABLE 26-1

FEDERAL RESERVE SYSTEM BALANCE SHEET
(millions of dollars, April 30, 1982)

ASSETS	LIABILITIES AND NET WORTH (CAPITAL ASSETS)

c. Assume that all commercial banks are loaned up (there are no excess reserves in the system) and that the reserves on deposit with the Fed are just enough to meet the Fed's reserve requirement. If the required reserve ratio is 20 percent, the commercial banking system has a total demand deposit liability of $_____ million.

2. Listed below are several actions or situations which may or may not eventually change the money supply. Some of the actions have a rather quick impact on M1. For others, the initial impact is very small, but there is a significant eventual effect. In the space beside each action, indicate both the initial and eventual effects of the action on M1. Indicate an increase in the money supply by a plus sign, a decrease by a minus sign, and an unchanged M1 by a zero.

	INITIAL IMPACT	EVENTUAL IMPACT
a. The public decides to hold more of its money in the form of currency.	____	____
b. The Fed purchases government securities on the open market from commercial banks.	____	____
c. The university lends you $3000 for this year's expenses.	____	____
d. The discount rate imposed by the Fed is lowered.	____	____
e. A major gold discovery is made in California (assume that gold is not monetized).	____	____
f. The Fed sells $10 million worth of government securities to the public.	____	____
g. An individual converts $50,000 worth of gold coins to currency and then deposits this currency in a commercial bank.	____	____
h. The required reserve ratio is raised by the Fed.	____	____

3. The simplified T-account in Table 26-2 is for the Federal Reserve System, and the one in Table 26-3 is for all commercial banks. The commercial banks are assumed to be loaned up, and no excess reserves exist.

TABLE 26-2

FEDERAL RESERVE SYSTEM
(millions of dollars)

ASSETS		LIABILITIES	
Loans to banks	$ 2	Federal Reserve notes	
Government securities	134	Currency held by public	$ 80
Other assets	19	Vault cash of banks	50
		Deposits of banks	25

TABLE 26-3

ALL COMMERCIAL BANKS
(millions of dollars)

ASSETS		LIABILITIES	
Reserves		Checkable deposits	$375
Deposits at Fed	$ 25	Loans from Fed	2
Vault cash	50		
Loans and securities	302		

a. Since the Fed includes the vault cash of banks as part of the banks' reserves and since it is assumed that the banking system is loaned up, the required reserve ratio is _____ percent.

b. From the Fed's T-account, the monetary base (high-powered money) is $_____ million, and the total money stock (M1) is $_____ million.

c. From part *b*, it is possible to determine the money multiplier as being _____.

d. Assume that the Fed wants to undertake an expansionary monetary policy and purchases $10 million of government securities from the commercial banking system. In Tables 26-4 and 26-5, indicate the initial impact on the Fed as it receives the securities and pays for them by putting the new values in the appropriate accounts. Also, show the new T-accounts for the commercial banking system.

TABLE 26-4
FEDERAL RESERVE SYSTEM
(millions of dollars)

ASSETS		LIABILITIES	
Loans to banks	$____	Federal Reserve notes	
Government securities	____	Currency held by public	$____
Other assets	____	Vault cash of banks	____
		Deposits of banks	____

TABLE 26-5
ALL COMMERCIAL BANKS
(millions of dollars)

ASSETS		LIABILITIES	
Reserves		Checkable deposits	$____
Deposits at Fed	$____	Loans from Fed	____
Vault cash	____		
Loans and securities			

As a result of this transaction, the monetary base has (increased/decreased) _____ by the amount of $_____ million.

e. The money stock (has/has not) _____ increased because of the Fed's open market operations; however, banks now have _____ reserves in the amount of $_____ millions since their checkable deposits have not changed.

f. Suppose the banking system creates new loans in the form of demand deposits for all of the $10 million it just received from the sale of the securities. Complete the commercial banks' balance sheet (Table 26-6) by showing the initial impact of these loans.

TABLE 26-6
ALL COMMERCIAL BANKS,
(millions of dollars)

ASSETS		LIABILITIES	
Reserves		Checkable deposits	$____
Deposits at Fed	$____	Loans from Fed	____
Vault cash	____		
Loans and securities	____		

The initial impact on the money stock of these loans is to increase the banking systems' _____ deposits by $_____ million.

g. When the $10 million is lent out, the commercial banking system (does/does not) _____ have excess reserves since given the required reserve ratio computed in part *a*, the system should have a total of $_____ million on deposit with the Fed to meet its new reserve requirement.

h. The money supply (will/will not) _____ continue to expand until the banking system has no _____ reserves.

i. When all secondary effects have taken place, the money stock (M1) will be approximately $_____ million, which represents an increase of $_____ million.

FILL-IN QUESTIONS

1. The Federal Reserve System is organized into _____ districts, and in each district there is a _____ bank.

2. The largest assets owned by the Fed are _____ and _____, while its greatest liability is _____.

3. Commercial banks' deposits at the Fed are part of the required _____ which the banks must maintain against their own liabilities and must be in the form of U.S. _____.

4. If a single bank has excess _____ on deposit with the Fed, it (can/cannot) _____ expand the money supply by an amount equal to its _____; however, if the banking system has an excess in its reserve account, it can (expand/contract) _____ the money stock by (a greater amount than/a lesser amount than/the same amount as) _____ this excess.

5. The _____ ratio is the ratio of reserves to deposits which the Fed requires banks to hold; if the banking system just meets this ratio, it (can/cannot) _____ make more loans.

6. Three tools with which the Fed can exercise

control over the money stock are _____, _____, and _____.

7. If the Fed sells government securities on the open market, we would expect the money supply to (increase/decrease) _____ because banks' reserves (increase/decrease) _____ as people pay for the securities, and this causes the banks to (expand/contract) _____ their lending operations.

8. The _____ base is also called _____ money and is the sum of _____ outstanding plus _____ at the Fed.

9. When the banking system as a whole experiences a change in the monetary base, there will be both _____ and _____ effects as the money _____ changes the money stock by more than the change in the base.

10. When the Fed lends money to financial institutions in trouble in order to prevent a panic, it is performing the role of _____ of last resort.

11. During the Great Depression, the money multiplier (increased/decreased) _____ because banks wanted to increase their holdings of reserves.

12. The _____ insures the bank accounts of depositors against a bank's failure.

13. In the United States, the Treasury (does/does not) _____ issue money, and so it can finance government deficits only by (lending to/borrowing from) _____ the public or the Fed.

14. A strong advocate of the constant money growth rule is Nobel Prize-winning economist _____, who argues that the Fed (should/should not) _____ try to pursue an active monetary policy.

15. The United States (is/is not) _____ currently under a _____ standard, and its monetary base (does/does not) _____ consist of gold.

TRUE-FALSE QUESTIONS

1. _____ The instrument of monetary policy most frequently used by the Fed is changing the required reserve ratio faced by member banks.

2. _____ That part of M1 which is made up of some of the liabilities of the Fed is the currency held by the public.

3. _____ If a commercial bank belongs to the Fed and just meets its reserve requirement of 16 percent with $100,000 on deposit with the Federal Reserve Bank, its total deposit liabilities are $1,600,000.

4. _____ When the Fed raises the discount rate, banks suddenly have excess reserves, and so they make more loans and expand the money supply.

5. _____ If the banking system is loaned up (has no excess reserves), the sale of government securities by the Fed in the open market will cause banks to call in loans, sell off assets, and contract the money supply.

6. _____ The immediate effect of the Fed's open market operations is to change the monetary base.

7. _____ The Board of Governors consists of 14 members, each appointed by the President of the United States and serving for a term of 7 years.

8. _____ During the Great Depression, banks tried to hold large excess reserves because many loans were risky and the chance of customers trying to withdraw their deposits was great.

9. _____ The Fed, like any other financial institution, faces the possibility of insolvency if the value of its liabilities approaches or exceeds the value of its assets.

10. _____ To say that the Federal Reserve acts as a payment agent for the U.S. Treasury means that when a check is written by the Treasury, it is drawn on an account at the Federal Reserve.

11. _____ Because gold is still considered part of the U.S. money stock, it is included as an asset on the Fed's balance sheet.

12. _____ The least important role of the Fed in the economy is its control over the money supply.

13. _____ During the Great Depression, the Fed failed to perform its function as lender of last resort.

14. _____ One primary function of the FDIC is to generate a sense of security for bank depositors so that the likelihood of financial panics is reduced.

15. _____ Since the U.S. Treasury does not issue money, the formal independence of the Fed from the U.S. government is sufficient to guarantee that government deficits will not be financed through the printing of money or expansion of the money supply.

16. _____ During the period 1880–1895, while the United States operated on a gold standard, growth in the money supply was not very stable.

CENTRAL BANKING AND THE MONETARY SYSTEM

17. _____ The Fed is often charged with promoting inflation because it has failed to maintain a low and stable growth rate of the money supply.

18. _____ To say that the Fed is a banker for the banking system means that it accepts deposits from and makes loans to commercial banks.

MULTIPLE CHOICE QUESTIONS

Circle the correct answer.

1. All of the following are functions of a central bank except
   a. serving as a lender of last resort
   b. accepting deposits from the public
   c. promoting full employment and low inflation by controlling the money supply
   d. preventing financial panics

2. Which of the following is not a part of the Federal Reserve System?
   a. Federal Open Market Committee
   b. Federal Reserve Bank
   c. Board of Governors
   d. Federal Deposit Insurance Corporation
   e. The open market desk at the New York Fed

3. In 1980, the assets of member banks in the Federal Reserve System were
   a. $1137 billion   c. $914 billion
   b. $393.2 billion   d. $542 billion

4. A feature of the Fed's liabilities is that
   a. they are backed by gold holdings which appear as an asset
   b. like commercial banks, the Fed can have liabilities only to the extent to which it has assets
   c. an unlimited quantity can be created because there is no possibility of bankruptcy
   d. most are created because the Fed holds U.S. Treasury deposits

5. When commercial banks hold deposits at the Fed, these deposits
   a. are held as reserves against the bank's deposit liabilities
   b. may be in U.S. dollars or some other type of asset
   c. help simplify the Fed's check-clearing and payment system
   d. are the major liability of the Fed
   e. a and c above
   f. b and d above

6. If a commercial bank needs to increase its reserves, it can do this by
   a. making loans so that its assets increase
   b. selling securities on the open market
   c. lowering the discount rate
   d. reducing the required reserve ratio

7. Suppose a commercial bank faces a 20 percent required reserve ratio and is just meeting that requirement when $5000 in cash is withdrawn. The bank must now
   a. decrease its reserves by $1000
   b. increase its demand deposits by $4000
   c. increase its reserves by $4000
   d. decrease its demand deposits by $1000

8. If the Fed reduced the discount rate by 2 percent, which of the following statements would most likely be correct?
   a. commercial banks increase their borrowing from the Fed, lower their required reserves, make fewer loans, and increase the money supply
   b. commercial banks reduce their borrowing from the Fed, lower their excess reserves, make fewer loans, and decrease the money supply
   c. commercial banks reduce their borrowing from the Fed, increase their excess reserves, make more loans, and reduce the money supply
   d. commercial banks increase their borrowing from the Fed, increase their excess reserves, make more loans, and increase the money supply

9. If the monetary base is $200 billion and M1 is $600 billion, the value of the money multiplier is
   a. 3.0   d. 2.0
   b. 3.33   e. cannot be determined
   c. 2.9

10. For a money multiplier of 2.4, if the Fed buys $8 million in securities on the open market, the money stock could potentially
    a. increase by $19.2 million
    b. increase by $8 million
    c. decrease by $19.2 million
    d. decrease by $16.5 million

11. Which of the following events might cause a disturbance in the money stock?
    a. commercial banks deliberately increase their excess reserves
    b. individuals suddenly want to hold more currency
    c. a large percentage of the commercial banking system's loans to customers goes bad
    d. the Fed increases the required reserve ratio
    e. all of the above

12. Which of the following has not been a criticism of the Fed's performance in recent years?
    a. the growth rate in the money stock has been very erratic
    b. the Fed has contributed directly to current inflation through its active monetary policy

c. the Fed has promoted an efficient payment system in the U.S. economy

d. the Fed has not pursued its task of maintaining economic stability

13. A constant money growth rule would

a. limit the Fed's pursuit of an active monetary policy when it tries to ease recessions or limit expansions

b. contribute directly to the nation's inflation rate

c. give the commercial banking system practically unlimited lending ability

d. make the Fed and the monetary system in general highly vulnerable to political pressure

14. Which of the following statements is incorrect?

a. when the United States was on a gold standard, even though the growth rate in the money stock fluctuated, inflation rates were low compared with those of today

b. because the world's supply of gold is known, the return to a gold standard promotes very stable prices

c. even when most of the world was on a gold standard, the standard was abandoned during periods of war

d. under a gold standard, the price of gold is fixed in terms of a nation's currency

AT THIS POINT YOU SHOULD BE ABLE TO . . .

1. Describe the structure and organization of the Federal Reserve System and list two primary functions of the Fed.

2. List and describe two major assets and two major liabilities on the Fed's balance sheet; also, explain in what way the liabilities of the Fed are unique and why it is impossible for the Fed to go bankrupt.

3. Explain the two major functions of commercial bank deposits held at the Fed.

4. Define the meaning of the required reserve ratio, the discount rate, and open market operations and explain the role of each as an instrument of the Fed's monetary policy.

5. Using T-accounts, show and explain how a change in the required reserve ratio and participation by the Fed in open market operations change the money stock.

6. Explain how and why there are both primary and secondary effects on the money stock as a result of the Fed's participation in open market operations; also, define the money multiplier and explain why a $1 change in an open market operation results in a greater change in the overall money stock.

7. Explain the role of high-powered money in the determination of the aggregate monetary stock and discuss the effect of changes in the reserve ratio, the discount rate, and the Fed's open market operations on the money base.

8. Given a level of M1 and the monetary base, calculate the banking multiplier.

9. Describe two channels through which monetary policy works.

10. Describe the major function of the FDIC and state why it contributes to the stability of the banking system.

11. Explain why the formal independence of the Fed from the Treasury does not guarantee that government deficits will not be financed by expansions of the money supply.

12. State two major criticisms of the Fed's performance, define the constant growth money rule, and explain how such a rule might lead to stability in the monetary system.

13. Define the meaning of a gold standard and state a reason for and a reason against a modern economy operating under such a standard.

QUESTIONS FOR THOUGHT

1. In its open market operations, the Fed can buy or sell government securities to both commercial banks and the general public. Suppose the banking system is all loaned up (has no excess reserves) and faces a required reserve ratio of 15 percent. If the Fed buys $1 milllion worth of securities from commercial banks, what is the impact on the banking system's excess reserves, its lending capabilities, and the money supply? If the bank sold the same bonds to private citizens (rather than commercial banks) who then deposited their payments into their checking accounts, would the effect be any different? What would happen to the banking system's reserves and lending capabilities and to the money supply? Explain.

2. The Fed is described as the lender of last resort to the financial system. Why is this function of the Fed so important in maintaining financial stability? Explain why the likelihood of financial panics increases if the Fed does not serve as lender of last resort.

3. In 1980, almost 64 percent of the commercial banks in the country did not belong to the Federal Reserve System. What are some of the advantages of membership in the system? With so many of the banks not members, do you think the Fed's ability to perform its functions is reduced? Explain why or why not.

4. The Fed makes monetary policy in the United States by using primarily three instruments. Explain each of these instruments and identify the one most frequently used. Also, explain why there are both primary and secondary effects on the money stock when the Fed uses these instruments of monetary policy.

5. Explain the concept of high-powered money and the banking multiplier to a friend who knows absolutely nothing about banking. What major points should you make?

6. The United States has incurred large budget deficits each year for many years. If the Fed were simply an extension of the Treasury, how do you think these deficits might be financed? What problems might this create for the economy? Even though the Fed is formally independent of the Treasury, might the central bank still create problems when it helps to finance the federal deficit by purchasing securities directly from the Treasury? Explain.

7. Discuss the major criticisms of the Fed's performance on monetary policy. Do you think it would be wise for the country to return to a gold standard? Why or why not?

APPENDIX: THE MONEY SUPPLY AND THE MONEY MULTIPLIER

In Chapter 26, you saw that an increase in the stock of high-powered money caused a multiple increase in the money supply because of the money multiplier. In this appendix, the logic of the multiplier is presented as Professors Fischer and Dornbusch illustrate three expansionary rounds of the money stock. These rounds originate because of an initial open market operation by the Fed and continue because of the interaction between the public and the banking system. The formula for the money multiplier incorporates the nonbanking public's currency to deposit ratio and the commercial banking system's required reserve ratio.

CHAPTER OUTLINE

1. When the Fed increases the stock of high-powered money (monetary base), the money stock increases by a multiple of the change in the monetary base. The money multiplier shows by how much the money stock changes when there is a $1 change in the monetary base. Changing the money stock involves the interaction of the Fed, commercial banks, and the public.

2. The Fed's open market operations are the most frequently used channel through which the monetary base is changed. When the Fed buys securities directly from the public, the monetary base and the money stock initially increases by an equal amount. The public holds some fraction of its money in currency and the remainder as checkable deposits. When the Fed buys securities, some of the money received in payment of the public is held as currency, but the remainder is deposited in commercial banks. The commercial banks must hold some fraction of their deposit liabilities on reserve with the Fed (required reserves), and so when the public makes new deposits, the banks have the ability to make new loans. As the banks expand their loans, the level of checkable deposits and the amount of currency held by the public increase, and so the money stock increases. With each lending round, however, the ability of banks to make new loans decreases because the amount of their extra reserves decreases, and so the rate of increase in the money stock slows down. After all loans have been made (the banks are loaned up), the banking system has no extra reserves. The money stock (currency plus deposits) has increased by an amount greater than the initial change in the monetary base.

3. The money multiplier is greater than 1 because the banking system expands its loans, using high-powered money as reserves. The rate of increase in the money stock falls with successive lending rounds because the public keeps some of their increased money as currency and because banks must keep part of any new deposits as reserves. Any change in the amount of currency held by the public or the required reserves held by the banks changes the money multiplier.

IMPORTANT TERMS

1. Currency-deposit ratio: The ratio of total currency held by the public to the public's total deposits in banks. The ratio shows the percentage held as currency for every dollar on deposit.

EXERCISE

1. Suppose the Fed requires commercial banks to keep $20 on reserve for every $100 of their deposit liabilities. The public holds $30 for every $100 on deposit as currency. Using this information, answer the following questions.

   a. If the Fed buys $500 million of securities from the public, the initial change in the money stock is (an increase/a decrease) _____ of $_____.

   b. The money multiplier is _____, and so the eventual effect of the Fed's open market operation is to (increase/decrease) _____ the money stock by $_____.

c. If the public decides to reduce its currency holdings from $30 to $20 for every $100 on deposit, the money multiplier (increases/decreases) _____ from _____ to _____.

TRUE-FALSE QUESTIONS

1. _____ The reason why the increase in the money stock becomes smaller with each successive lending round is that the level of banks' excess reserves falls and the public holds some money as currency.

2. _____ A currency to deposit ratio of 25 percent means that for every dollar households receive as income, 25 cents is put in checkable deposits.

3. _____ If the money multiplier is 3, a $5 million reduction in the monetary base lowers the money stock by $15 million.

4. _____ An increase in the required reserve ratio which banks must keep on deposit at the Fed causes the money multiplier to decrease.

5. _____ The only role played by the commercial banking system in expanding the money stock is that of simply accepting deposits from the nonbanking public.

6. _____ The monetary base consists of all currency in circulation plus the checkable deposits of the non-banking public.

7. _____ If a bank's actual reserves fall below its required reserves, the bank must call in loans.

8. _____ As soon as the Fed increases the monetary base by purchasing securities from the nonbanking public, the money stock goes up by an amount equal to the change in the base.

9. _____ If the public decides to hold more currency for each dollar on deposit with the banks, the money multiplier falls.

10. _____ It is easier for the Fed to control the public's currency-deposit ratio than the banking system's required reserve ratio.

QUESTIONS FOR THOUGHT

1. Why is the money multiplier greater than 1? Can you foresee a situation in which the multiplier might be less than 1? What would such a multiplier mean?

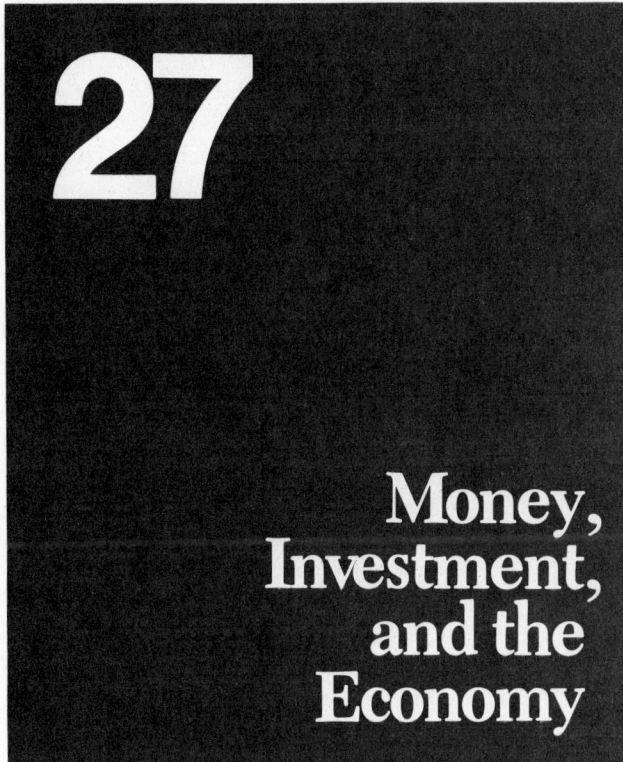

27

Money, Investment, and the Economy

Chapters 25 and 26 described the nature and function of money, the role of the banking system in a modern economy, and the structure, organization, and functions of the Federal Reserve System. Chapter 27 discusses the importance of the Fed and the stock of money. The demand for and the supply of money affect the market interest rate, which in turn influences businesses' investment spending decisions and families' residential housing spending decisions. When the level of investment spending changes, the level of aggregate demand, output, employment, and income changes. The interaction between the asset market and the goods market is presented, and the overall structure of a macroeconomic system is clarified. You should pay particular attention to the link between the control over the money supply and the aggregate demand for goods, since this is the method by which the Fed influences economic activity.

Chapter 27 begins with an examination of the determinants of money demand. It is quickly established that the demand for money is the demand for a spendable asset. Thus, it is actually a demand for real balances. Households demand real balances up to the point at which the marginal cost of holding an extra dollar just equals the marginal benefit gained from holding that dollar. The interest rate reflects the opportunity cost of holding money; when there is a change in this opportunity cost, the amount of real balances held moves in the opposite direction. The price level and nominal income level also affect the amount of money people hold, because a change in either prices or real income changes the purchasing power of the money balances held.

The money supply is controlled by the Fed primarily through its open market operations, but it may also be adjusted through the use of the discount rate and the required reserve ratio. When the Fed engages in open market operations, the stock of high-powered money changes, and so the money supply changes by some multiple of the change in the monetary base. With an established demand for money, an equilibrium is established in the money market at the point at which the quantity of real balances demanded equals the quantity supplied. At this equilibrium, the market interest rate and the optimal level of real money balances held are established. Any change in the money stock or the demand for real balances changes the interest rate, the quantity of balances held, or both.

Investment spending adds to the economy's stock of physical capital. Firms invest as long as the return from the extra dollar spent is greater than the extra cost (including interest) incurred. When the interest rate increases, fewer projects are profitable, and so investment spending falls. Because of the Fed's ability to control the money stock and influence the interest rate, its policies affect the level of investment spending. Since investment spending is a component of aggregate demand, any change in the interest rate which alters investment spending by firms also changes aggregate demand, output, employment, and income. There are, however, dampening effects of monetary actions on aggregate demand since if real income changes, so does the demand for real balances. This causes the demand for money to change, and so there are secondary effects on the interest rates which feed back onto investment.

If the government pursues an expansionary fiscal policy while the stock of real balances remains unchanged, the attempt to expand aggregate output through fiscal actions is dampened. This occurs because the fiscal expansion increases the rate of interest so that both real and financial private investment spending are crowded out of the market. The overall effect of fiscal policy in the absence of an appropriate monetary policy is weakened, and so what is needed is a complementary fiscal and monetary policy mix.

CHAPTER OUTLINE

1. The per capita demand for money in the United States changes over time. Three factors which affect money holdings are the interest rate, the price level, and the level of real income.
   a. The reason people hold or want to hold money is to spend it, and the rate at which they spend money influences the amount they want to

hold. People can hold their wealth in interest-earning assets such as bonds or equities. The interest rate reflects the opportunity cost of holding money since it is the amount of income given up by holding money instead of an interest-earning asset. An individual's optimal level of money holdings (everything else constant) is established at the point at which the marginal cost of holding an extra dollar (the interest forgone) just equals the marginal benefit of holding the extra dollar. At a given interest rate, the marginal cost of holding money is constant whatever the level of real balances; however, the marginal benefit declines for higher levels of money holdings. At higher rates of interest (marginal cost), people hold less money (real money balances).
   b. When people hold money, they do so primarily because it functions as a means of payment, and so the demand for money is a demand for real balances (its purchasing power). When everything else remains constant, as the price level changes, people change their nominal money holdings proportionately and in the same direction so that their real balances remain unchanged.
   c. If households' real income increases, their level of spending increases. When households increase spending, their demand for real balances also increases so that they can pay for the higher level of consumption conveniently. This increase in the demand for real balances occurs at every interest rate, and so it serves to shift the marginal benefit schedule for money holdings to the right.
   d. Although the per capita demand for nominal money balances increased between 1969 and 1981, the demand for real balances fell. Increases in prices and real income over this period should have caused this demand to increase; however, the almost 250 percent increase in the interest rate caused households to manage their assets better and thus reduce their money holdings. Other recently developed alternatives to money holdings help explain in part the reduction in per capita real balances. Interest rates, the price level, and real income levels, however, remain the most important explanatory factors for the quantity of money demanded.
2. The Fed, through its ability to control the money supply, affects interest rates. With changing interest rates, the level of aggregate demand, employment, income, and equilibrium output changes.
   a. When the Fed participates in open market operations, it changes the stock of high-powered money. As the stock of high-powered money changes, so does the stock of real money balances in the economy. With a given demand schedule for real balances (showing the negative relationship between quantity demanded and the interest rate), a change in supply causes a new equilibrium in the money market. The equilibrium interest rate is established at the point at which the quantity of real balances demanded equals the quantity supplied (existing money stock). The real money supply schedule is vertical because it is assumed to be completely interest-inelastic; the Fed determines the money stock.
   b. The Fed's purchase of securities in the open market increases the stock of high-powered money, increases the nominal money stock, and (assuming a constant price level) increases the real money stock. This causes the supply curve of real balances to shift to the right. With a given demand schedule for real balances, a surplus of real balances exists, and so the interest rate falls. The overall result of an increase in the real money stock by the Fed is a lower interest rate and more real balances held.
   c. For a given money stock and price level, an increase in real income increases the marginal benefit of holding money at every interest rate, and so the demand curve for real balances shifts to the right. Assuming a constant money stock, this shift generates an excess demand until a new equilibrium is reached. A decline in real income has the opposite effect, with interest rates falling.
3. Within the confines of the GNP accounts, investment spending consists of expenditures for additions to plant and equipment, additions to inventories of goods, and residential housing construction. The level of investment spending is negatively related to the interest rate, and so any actions by the Fed which change the rate of interest also change the level of investment.
   a. During periods of recession, investment falls relative to GNP, while during periods of prosperity, it rises. The major component of aggregate investment is expenditures for plant and equipment; however, the most volatile component is investment in housing. During the period 1979–1981, residential construction fell by over 25 percent as interest rates reached new highs.
   b. When investment spending occurs, any amount over the amount required to replace capital used in production adds to the economy's stock of physical capital. The capital stock is expanded because firms believe that the benefits

of an increased scale of operation or more efficient plant and equipment will exceed the cost of the investment. Through this capital acquisition, firms expect to increase their profits. If the interest rate (and interest payment) increases, some investment opportunities which would have been undertaken at lower interest rates will no longer be considered because they are no longer profitable. As a result, overall investment declines since only those alternatives which cover *all* costs are undertaken. This negative relationship between the interest rate and investment demand is shown by the investment demand schedule. At high interest rates, a firm is less willing to invest its own funds in physical capital.

4. If everything else is held constant, the Fed's monetary policy changes the stock of money. The change in the money supply causes a change in the interest rate and the level of income so that neither an excess demand nor an excess supply of money remains on the money market. When the interest rate changes, so does the level of investment spending. Since investment is a component of aggregate demand, aggregate demand changes, and firms change their output and employment levels. As the level of employment changes, the level of aggregate income changes. An expansionary monetary policy leads to lower interest rates, increased investment spending, and increased output, employment, and income. A restrictive monetary policy has the opposite effect.

   a. The overall effect of an expansionary monetary policy is dampened because as aggregate income rises, so does the demand for money balances. This leads to a slight decrease in the interest rate and some slowing of investment demand. Even with these second-round adjustments in money demand, an expansionary monetary policy still results in an increased aggregate output as long as excess capacity exists.

      (1) An application of the impact of the Fed's tight monetary policy on investment can be seen in the residential housing market during 1979–1980. The Fed tightened money in late 1979, and interest rates increased sharply. All components of investment spending declined, but the housing sector was especially hurt. The economy moved into a recession, and housing starts fell by more than 500,000 units between October 1979 and May 1980.

5. When there is excess capacity and the government pursues an expansionary fiscal policy, aggregate demand, output, and income increase. As income increases, the interactions between the goods and money markets (when the real money stock remains unchanged) ultimately cause investment spending to fall. The effects of an expansionary fiscal policy are thus dampened.

   a. An increase in government spending or a reduction in taxes causes aggregate demand, output, and income to expand; however, when real income increases, so does the demand for real money balances. With a constant money stock and a higher demand for real balances, interest rates rise and planned investment begins to fall. As a result of the expansionary fiscal policy, some private investment is crowded out of the market. This crowding out should theoretically end when the reduction in investment equals the change in fiscal variables; however, it is unlikely that crowding out will be complete in practice.

   b. The composition of aggregate demand is affected by the application of monetary and fiscal policy. When the Fed's monetary policy results in lower interest rates, the investment component increases. An expansionary fiscal policy such as lower personal taxes or higher government spending lowers investment. The application of both a tight monetary and a tight fiscal policy serves to slow economic activity and aggregate demand rapidly without affecting its composition significantly. The monetary-fiscal policy mix employed and the resulting composition of aggregate demand are important issues because they influence the economy's willingness to increase its stock of physical capital.

   c. It is possible for the government to pursue a special type of expansionary fiscal policy while monetary policy remains unchanged, thus causing investment spending to increase. This is done by providing an investment tax credit to firms. Such a credit permits firms to deduct some percentage of their investment costs from their tax liabilities, and so investment, aggregate demand, employment, and income expand.

6. During the 1960s, Keynesian economics was used actively in directing U.S. economic policy. This "new economics" stressed active expansionary monetary and (especially) fiscal policies to fight recessions and expand employment and incomes. Although this policy reduced unemployment by the end of the 1960s, there was a gradual buildup of inflationary pressures, both realized and anticipated. Keynesian economics works on the assumption that the price level remains unchanged even

when the government pursues active economic policies. If an economy is near full employment, an increase in aggregate demand and an expansionary monetary policy may simply lead to higher prices. A major criticism of Keynesian economics is that it does not show the inflationary effects of changes in monetary and fiscal policy. A more complete model of macroeconomic activity should incorporate both aggregate demand and aggregate supply. With such a model, aggregate output and the price level are determined.

IMPORTANT TERMS AND THEIR MEANING

Match the following terms with the correct definition or phrase.

1. _____ Permits firms to deduct a percentage of the costs of an investment from the taxes they owe the government, thereby reducing the cost of investing

2. _____ Using both monetary and fiscal policies to achieve desired economic goals

3. _____ The economic policy of the 1960s which stressed active monetary and fiscal policies to achieve high levels of employment and fight recessions

4. _____ The purchasing power of money held by households and businesses

5. _____ A reduction in the level of private investment caused by an expansionary fiscal policy and an increase in the interest rate

6. _____ A decrease in the money stock which reflects a restrictive monetary policy and causes interest rates to increase

7. _____ Holding wealth in the form of shares of ownership in companies, entitling the owner to a share in the profits

8. _____ Economic policy of the government characterized by lower taxes and higher government spending

9. _____ Describes the situation in which households want to hold a greater level of money balances than is supplied, resulting in an increase in the interest rate

10. _____ The amount of interest given up by holding money rather than some interest-earning asset

11. _____ Describes the situation in which the quantity of real balances demanded equals the quantity supplied

12. _____ The face value of money held; not adjusted for the price level

13. _____ Economic policy of the government characterized by high taxes and low government spending

14. _____ A schedule which shows the amount of investment firms wish to undertake at each rate of interest

15. _____ Describes the monetary policy in which the Fed increases the money stock and causes interest rates to fall

16. _____ The market in which shares of ownership in corporations are traded

a. Equities
b. "New economics"
c. Crowding out
d. Stock market
e. Nominal balances
f. Easy money
g. Excess demand for money
h. Real balances
i. Monetary-fiscal policy mix
j. Tight money
k. Investment demand schedule
l. Easy fiscal policy
m. Money market equilibrium
n. Tight fiscal policy
o. Investment tax credit
p. Opportunity cost of holding money

EXERCISES

Exercises 1 through 3 are designed to show how a change in the money stock affects aggregate income, and so you will have to use the answers from Exercise 1 to solve Exercises 2 and 3. The exercises assume that everything remains constant except the factors under analysis. Also, don't consider any dampening effects as you work through the first three exercises.

1. Table 27-1 presents information about the interest rate in an economic system, the demand for real money balances, the prevailing money supply, and an aggregate investment demand schedule.

   a. On graph paper, plot the demand curve for money balances. Label the vertical axis "interest rate," the horizontal axis "real money balances," and the demand curve LL.

MONEY, INVESTMENT, AND THE ECONOMY

TABLE 27-1

MONEY SUPPLY, billions of $	INTEREST RATE, %	REAL MONEY BALANCES, billions of $	INVESTMENT DEMAND, billions of $
220	20	10	5
220	18	40	10
220	16	70	15
220	14	100	20
220	12	130	25
220	10	160	30
220	8	190	35
220	6	220	40
220	4	250	45
220	2	280	50

b. The (positive/negative) _____ relationship between the money balances demanded and the interest rate reflects the fact that at lower rates of interest, the _____ cost of holding money (increases/decreases) _____, and so households hold higher balances.

c. On the same graph, plot the money supply curve and label it MS_0. This curve is a (vertical/horizontal) _____ line which shows that the money supply (is/is not) _____ dependent on the interest rate.

d. The money market equilibrium rate of interest and the level of real balances held are _____ percent and $_____ billion.

e. At any rate of interest above the equilibrium rate, there is an excess (demand for/supply of) _____ money balances, and so with everything else constant, there is pressure on the interest rate to (rise/fall) _____ until the quantity of real balances _____ equals the quantity _____.

f. Suppose the Fed sold securities on the open market and decreased the money supply to $160 billion. Draw this new curve on your graph and label it MS_1. When the money stock is reduced and everything else remains the same, the interest rate (rises/falls) _____ while the real balances held by households (increase/decrease) _____. For households, the opportunity cost of holding money (increases/decreases) _____, and so they hold less.

2. a. From the data in table 27-1 in Exercise 1, plot the investment demand schedule. Label the vertical axis "interest rate," the horizontal axis "investment" (billions of $), and the curve II.

b. When the money supply (from Exercise 1) is $220 billion, the interest rate is _____ percent, and so the level of planned investment spending is $_____ billion. At this interest rate, it (is/is not) _____ profitable to undertake more investment projects because the extra _____ of doing so will be (greater than/equal to/less than) _____ the extra returns from the investment.

c. If the money stock decreases (as in Exercise 1f), the interest rate (increases/decreases) _____, and so (more/less) _____ investment spending takes place. When the interest rate rises to 10 percent, the new quantity of investment spending is $_____ billion, and some projects are no longer undertaken.

3. Table 27-2 contains data on aggregate income, consumption, and saving. Prices are assumed to be constant, and the money market is presented by the data in Table 27-1.

a. With a money stock of $220 billion, the investment demand schedule and a demand for real balances are presented in Table 27-1. You determined the

TABLE 27-2

AGGREGATE INCOME, billions of $	CONSUMPTION, billions of $	INVESTMENT, billions of $	SAVING, billions of $	AGGREGATE DEMAND, billions of $
200	180	_____	20	_____
250	225	_____	25	_____
300	270	_____	30	_____
350	315	_____	35	_____
400	360	_____	40	_____
450	405	_____	45	_____
500	450	_____	50	_____
550	495	_____	55	_____
600	540	_____	60	_____
650	585	_____	65	_____

equilibrium interest rate in Exercise 1d and the level of investment spending at this interest rate in Exercise 2b. Enter this level of investment associated with a money stock of $220 billion in the column labeled "investment" in Table 27-2. Next, compute the aggregate demand associated with each level of income and enter your calculations in the appropriate column.

    b. On graph paper, plot the graph of both consumption C and consumption plus investment C + I. Label the vertical axis "aggregate demand (billions of $)" and the horizontal axis "income (billions of $)." Make sure that you measure both the income and the aggregate demand axes in the same units (i.e., 200, 250, 300, etc.). This will require you to estimate most of the aggregate demand points. Also, don't forget to draw the 45° line.

    c. Equilibrium income is $_____ billion. At this point, saving equals _____.

    d. Suppose the Fed decides to pursue a restrictive monetary policy and reduces the money stock by $60 billion to $160 billion. From your answers to Exercises 1f and 2b, the interest rate (increases/decreases) _____ to _____ percent, and as a result, investment spending (increases/decreases) _____ to $_____ billion.

    e. Complete Table 27-3, using the new level of investment brought about by the reduction in the money stock by entering the new investment data and computing the new aggregate demand.

    f. Because of the decrease in the money supply, equilibrium aggregate income has (increased/decreased) _____ to $_____ billion even though aggregate investment fell by only $_____ billion. The increase in the _____ rate is the mechanism which drove aggregate demand and income down.

    g. On your graph developed in Exercise 2b, sketch the new aggregate demand curve and label it (C + I)'.

4. Suppose the federal government undertakes an expansionary fiscal policy by reducing taxes and increasing government spending, but the money supply does not change. Listed below are several events that probably will occur as a result of the government's actions. Based on the linkages and assumptions discussed in Chapter 27 of your text, rank 1 (first) through 8 (last) the sequence in which you think the events will occur.

    a. _____ The equilibrium rate of interest rises.

    b. _____ Aggregate income employment and output decrease.

    c. _____ The government reduces taxes and increases its level of spending.

    d. _____ The demand for real balances increases.

    e. _____ Planned investment spending falls.

    f. _____ Real income, output, and employment increase.

    g. _____ Expansionary effects of fiscal policy are dampened.

    h. _____ Aggregate demand falls.

    i. This sequence of events shows that if the money supply does not change, expansionary fiscal policy _____ out private investment.

FILL-IN QUESTIONS

1. A(n) (easy/tight) _____ monetary policy means that the Fed decreases the money stock, and with everything else constant, interest rates can be expected to (rise/fall) _____.

2. As the economy approaches full employment, the composition of aggregate demand (is/is not)

TABLE 27-3

AGGREGATE INCOME, billions of $	CONSUMPTION, billions of $	INVESTMENT, billions of $	AGGREGATE DEMAND, billions of $
200	180		
250	225		
300	270		
350	315		
400	360		
450	405		
500	450		
550	495		
600	540		
650	585		

_____ important because it (can/cannot) _____ affect future production and employment.

3. If the government grants businesses investment tax credits while the money stock remains unchanged, we would expect investment spending to (increase/decrease) _____, aggregate demand to (increase/decrease) _____, employment and income to (increase/decrease) _____, and interest rates to (increase/decrease) _____.

4. The _____ of the 1960s stressed active monetary and fiscal policies to fight recessions and achieve full employment; however, one of the negative effects of this policy was (depression/inflation) _____.

5. People hold money because they want to _____ it on goods and services.

6. The interest rate serves as a measure of the (total/opportunity/average) _____ cost of holding money; if this cost becomes higher, (more/less) _____ money is held in real balances.

7. The _____ power of money is the amount of goods and services it will buy.

8. If the nominal income of households increases while everything else remains constant, the (marginal cost/marginal benefit) _____ of holding money (increases/decreases) _____ because the level of spending rises, and so people hold (more/less) _____ in real balances.

9. Suppose the demand curve for money shifts upward and to the right; now there is pressure on interest rates to (rise/fall) _____, and so the Fed must (increase/decrease) _____ the money stock if interest rates are to remain unchanged.

10. Three primary types of investment spending are firms' addition to _____, construction of new _____, and changes in business _____.

11. A firm (will/will not) _____ invest if the present discounted value of the investment project's returns exceeds the present discounted value of the project's _____.

12. When everything else remains constant, an increase in the money supply by the Fed (increases/decreases) _____ aggregate demand because interest rates (rise/fall) _____, and so investment (increases/decreases) _____.

13. If the economy is threatened by a very serious recession, an appropriate mix of fiscal and monetary policy would be to (ease/tighten) _____ monetary and (ease/tighten) _____ fiscal activities.

14. Aggregate demand consists of _____, plus _____, plus _____ plus _____; however, the two components through which monetary policy affects activity are _____ demand and _____ demand.

15. If the Fed wanted to pursue an expansionary monetary policy designed to lower the interest rate and encourge private investment, it might (buy/sell) _____ securities on the open market, (raise/lower) _____ the discount rate, and (raise/lower) _____ the reserve requirement for depository institutions.

TRUE-FALSE QUESTIONS

1. _____ When the money stock falls, there is less money available for people to hold, and so the interest rate falls.

2. _____ The critical link between the Fed's control of the money stock and changes in aggregate demand is the interest rate.

3. _____ The largest component of private investment in the United States is expenditure by firms on plant and equipment.

4. _____ If a firm plans to use its own money to undertake an expansion of its plant, it does not really have to be concerned about the interest rate in the money market.

5. _____ The connection between interest rates and the value of stocks as assets is the expected dividend to be paid out.

6. _____ When a monetary expansion leads to an increase in aggregate output and income, interest rates fall at first and then rise somewhat.

7. _____ The amount of money people hold is related to the rate at which they spend it.

8. ____ In the U.S. economy, there is only one interest rate, and it is determined by the monetary actions of the Federal Reserve System.

9. ____ If all prices fall by 50 percent and nominal incomes fall by one-half, the typical household will try to double the amount of real balances held.

10. ____ When real income increases, the typical household buys more, and so it holds less in real balances.

11. ____ In 1981, real balances per capita had fallen compared with the amount held in 1965. One possible explanation is that the interest rates had more than doubled.

12. ____ By changing the stock of high-powered money, the Fed controls the supply of nominal balances.

13. ____ If real income falls, the demand for money schedule shifts to the left, and a shortage of money exists.

14. ____ When there is an increase in the money stock, the interest rate falls; investment, aggregate demand, income, and output all increase, but the level of employment falls.

15. ____ The Fed followed a tight monetary policy in late 1979, and as a result, housing starts fell.

MULTIPLE CHOICE QUESTIONS

Circle the correct answer.

1. If you could earn 14 percent interest by investing your money but instead keep it in a special checking account which pays 4½ percent, your opportunity cost of holding money is
    a. 14 percent   **c.** 9½ percent
    b. 18½ percent   **d.** 4½ percent

2. Which of the following will not directly affect the level of real money balances held?
    a. the number of Federal Reserve districts in the nation
    b. the level of real income
    c. the price level
    d. the interest rate

3. If the level of spending by households increases, we would expect
    a. the demand for real balances to fall
    b. the supply of real balances to increase
    c. the demand for real balances to remain unchanged
    d. the demand for real balances to increase
    e. the supply of real balances to fall

4. The reduction in the demand for real balances between 1965 and 1981 can be explained in part because
    a. aggregate income increased
    b. interest rates increased
    c. the purchasing power of money increased
    d. aggregate output increased

5. When an investment demand schedule is drawn, all of the following are held constant except
    a. the state of technology
    b. the rate of interest
    c. the wages paid to labor
    d. expectations about future product demand

6. For an increase in the money stock with constant prices, the mechanism through which aggregate demand will increase is
    a. increase in money stock → decrease in real balances → increase in the interest rate → decrease in private investment spending → increase in aggregate income and output
    b. increase in the money stock → increase in real balances → decrease in the interest rate → decrease in private investment spending → increase in aggregate income and output
    c. increase in the money stock → decrease in real balances → decrease in the interest rate → increase in private investment spending → increase in aggregate income and output
    d. increase in the money stock → increase in real balances → decrease in the interest rate → increase in private investment spending → increase in aggregate income and output

7. In order for crowding out to be complete, it is necessary that
    a. the level of aggregate income remain essentially constant
    b. a reduction in the stock of real balances occur as a result of price increases
    c the interest rate increase
    d. the reduction investment demand equal the increase in government spending
    e. none of the above

8. The most interest-sensitive component of investment is
    a. expenditures for housing construction
    b. expenditures for inventory acquisition
    c. expenditures for plant expansion
    d. expenditures for new equipment

9. When the goods and money markets interact, an expansionary fiscal policy combined with an unchanged money stock will
    a. have no impact on the new equilibrium aggregate output

b. cause the demand for real balances to fall
   c. increase interest rates and reduce investment
   d. cause the supply of real money balances to decrease

10. When both fiscal policy and monetary policy are expansionary, we would expect
   a. a recession and a decline in aggregate output and income
   b. most of the increase in employment and output to be crowded out since private investment falls
   c. the overall effect to be very small since one offsets the other
   d. increasing output, employment, income, and prosperity

11. An investment tax credit is more likely to be used when the government wants
   a. an easy monetary and an easy fiscal policy
   b. a tight monetary and an easy fiscal policy
   c. a tight monetary and a tight fiscal policy
   d. an easy monetary and a tight fiscal policy

12. Which of the following is a criticism of the type of Keynesian analysis presented in Chapter 27?
   a. the analysis is based on the assumption that the price level is given
   b. it is doubtful that the effects of fiscal policies can be predicted well enough for them to be useful for stabilizing the economy
   c. the analysis does not allow for the inflationary effects of monetary and fiscal policy changes
   d. all of the above
   e. none of the above

AT THIS POINT YOU SHOULD BE ABLE TO . . .

1. Explain the relationship between the interest rate and the opportunity cost of holding money, state the main reason why people hold money, and list three factors which affect these money holdings.

2. Define the marginal cost and marginal benefit of holding money, show graphically how the optimal level of money holding is established, and explain why the demand for money is actually a demand for real balances.

3. Describe the effect of changes in real income on the demand for real balances.

4. Explain the effects of changes in the price level and changes in the interest rate on the demand for both nominal balances and real balances, show these changes graphically, and explain the meaning of a money market equilibrium.

5. Describe both the demand for real money balances and the supply of money curves, show graphically the effects of an increase in the money stock on both the level of real balances held and the market interest rate, and explain how the equilibrium interest rate is determined.

6. List the three primary components of private investment spending, draw and explain an investment demand schedule, and explain why a negative relationship exists between investment spending and the interest rate.

7. Explain the channels through which the Fed can influence aggregate demand; also, show graphically how a reduction in interest rates shifts the aggregate demand function.

8. Describe how the effect of a monetary expansion on aggregate demand can be dampened.

9. Explain the meaning of crowding out and show how it occurs; show graphically how this affects the aggregate demand curve.

10. State the meaning of both a tight and an easy monetary and fiscal policy and identify one way in which the government can pursue an easier fiscal policy while at the same time the Fed does not change the stock of money.

11. Explain why the composition of aggregate demand is an important issue when an economic system is near full employment.

12. Define the term "Keynesian economics" and state when it has been applied in the United States; also, explain the major criticism of Keynesian economics.

QUESTIONS FOR THOUGHT

1. Suppose the Fed increases the discount rate in order to implement its monetary policy. What will be the eventual effect on the monetary base? The money stock? Will the market rate of interest be influenced? Explain.

2. If the economy is in a serious recession, both the Fed and the government may pursue an easier fiscal and monetary policy. What are the objectives of such a policy mix? How might an easier fiscal and monetary policy be implemented? Will crowding out be a problem? Explain why or why not.

3. In Chapter 27, the money supply curve is shown as a vertical line. Why do you think this supply curve is drawn vertically? Explain why the demand for real money balances curve is drawn as a downward-sloping line. How are the equilibrium interest rate and level of real money holdings established?

4. Explain why there is a negative relationship between investment spending and the interest rate. Does the interest rate influence the type of investment expenditures made? Explain.

5. Suppose you are to be interviewed on the "Phil Donahue" television show. You expect to be asked to explain how and why an increase in the money supply by the Fed can increase the level of national employment and income. You will be allowed to have one 3 by 5 note card. Briefly, state the causal chain beginning with the Fed buying securities on the open market and ending with an increase in income. What qualifications do you need to make? Remember, you must be very concise.

6. Do you think crowding out poses a problem for an expansionary fiscal policy? Why should it cause policymakers concern? Explain.

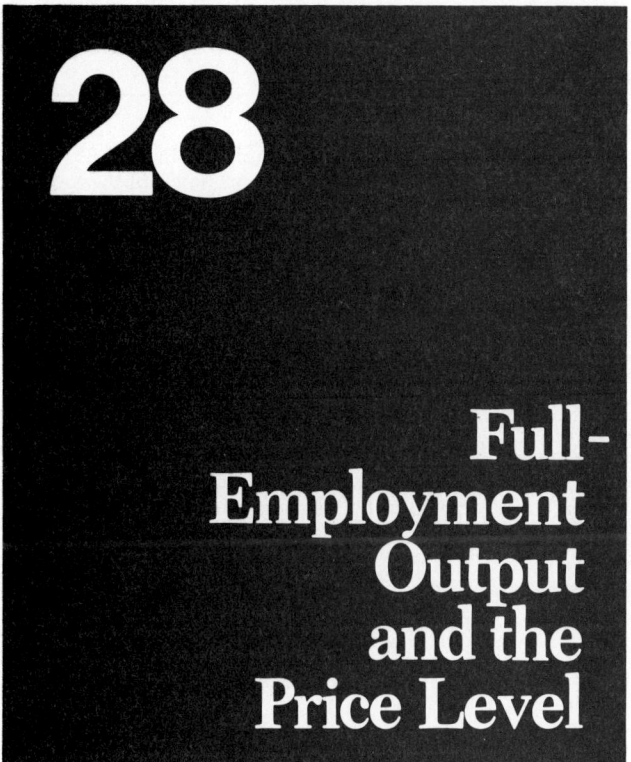

28 Full-Employment Output and the Price Level

Chapter 28 develops the classical model of macroeconomics. The classical model shows how aggregate supply is determined in an economic system. The Keynesian model developed in earlier chapters, on the other hand, emphasizes aggregate demand and doesn't treat the concept of aggregate supply adequately. Neither the Keynesian model alone nor the classical model alone provides a complete picture of both the aggregate price and the output level. The underlying assumptions and policy recommendations for achieving macroeconomic stability are very different for each model. You should pay particular attention to these assumptions as well as the effects of monetary and fiscal policy on the price and output level suggested by both models.

Chapter 28 begins with a discussion of the relationship between the price level and aggregate demand. Changes in the price level (given a constant nominal money stock) cause changes in the rate of interest, and so investment demand changes. Variation in investment produces changes in aggregate demand and output. The macroeconomic demand schedule shows the equilibrium level of output corresponding to each level of prices at which planned spending equals income.

The aggregate supply schedule shows the quantity of output firms want to supply at each price level. The first step in deriving an aggregate supply schedule is an analysis of the labor market. Workers exhibit a preference between work and leisure, and so a trade-off exists between income and leisure. Given the level of the capital stock and the productivity of labor, firms hire labor up to the point at which the real wage equals the marginal product of labor. The real wage also determines how much labor is supplied. Labor market equilibrium is established when the amount of labor firms demand equals the amount supplied. At equilibrium, full employment exists because everyone who wants to work is working, and so the level of potential output is established. Assuming no money illusion and flexible money wages, any change in the price level not caused by a shift in the macroeconomic demand or supply schedule does not change the real wage. With a constant real wage, the level of employment and output remains unchanged even when prices change. The aggregate supply curve is vertical at the potential output level.

The equilibrium price level in the classical model is established at the point where aggregate supply equals macroeconomic demand. At this price level, all markets clear, and there is equilibrium in the goods, labor, and money markets.

The classical model argues that increases in the nominal money stock shift the macroeconomic demand curve and change only the price level (not output) when the economy is in equilibrium. Increases in government spending shift the macroeconomic demand curve, which causes both the nominal interest rate and the price level to rise. The result of increased government spending is no change in output and a crowding out of private spending exactly equal to the increase in government spending.

The classical model argues that a reduction in the income tax can increase output and employment by increasing the work effort. Both saving and investment rise too, because incomes increase as output and employment increase. Supply side economics advocates a tax reduction and a decrease in government regulations in order to increase aggregate employment and output.

In Chapter 29, the classical model is combined with the Keynesian model developed earlier so that a complete analysis of how the economy actually operates is presented. Be sure you understand the effects of flexible wages and prices presented in Chapter 28 because the model presented in Chapter 29 incorporates both this assumption and the Keynesian notion of fixed prices and wages. Table 28-1 compares some of the more important aspects of the Keynesian and classical models. Table 28-1 also shows (in items 10 through 14) how each model views the role of fiscal and monetary policy. Study this table since it will be useful in both this chapter and Chapter 29.

CHAPTER OUTLINE

1. Changes in the real money stock change both the interest rate and the stock of real balances. Any

TABLE 28-1

ITEM	KEYNESIAN	CLASSICAL
1. Time frame	Short run	Long run
2. Aggregate output (income)	Determined by the level of aggregate demand	Determined by the production function, employment, and the firm's decision to produce
3. Demand for labor	Determined by the wage rate and the marginal value product of labor; firms hire workers up to the point where $MVPL$ = wage or, the same thing, where the marginal product of labor equals the real wage	Same as in the Keynesian system
4. Supply of labor	Only at full employment is the supply of labor a function of the real wage. When there is unemployment, labor is available at the prevailing wage in whatever quantity is demanded.	The real wage determines the supply of labor; at higher real wages, workers supply more labor, while at lower real wages, they supply less
5. Wages	Nominal wages are rigid (especially downward); Keynes assumed an autonomously determined money wage at less than full employment	Nominal wages are completely flexible both upward and downward; the real wage is determined by the demand for and supply of labor; once the real wage is determined, the labor market is in equilibrium because there is neither a surplus nor a shortage in the labor market
6. Prices	Prices are based primarily on wages and therefore adjust slowly	Price are flexible (moving either upward or downward)
7. Demand for money	The demand for money depends on both the level of income and the interest rate; there is a negative relationship between the overall demand for money and the interest rate; a positive relationship exists between the level of income and the demand for money	The demand for money depends on the level of income
8. Saving	Aggregate saving (consumption) is determined by the level of aggregate income; in equilibrium, planned saving equals planned investment	Saving is determined by the interest rate; in equilibrium, planned saving equals planned investment
9. Investment	Investment spending is negatively related to the interest rate because this affects the expected profitability of the additional investment	Same as in the Keynesian system
10. Effects of fiscal policy	Fiscal policy is an effective tool for stabilization and growth of aggregate demand and output	Fiscal policy is not an effective tool because of the crowding out effect
11. Effects of monetary policy	Monetary policy affects output; although not powerful, monetary policy works by affecting interest rates, investment, and aggregate demand	Monetary policy directly affects only the price level
12. Equilibrium	Achieved when aggregate demand equals the value of output produced; equilibrium may or may not occur at full employment	Achieved when aggregate demand equals aggregate supply; because of flexible wages and prices, equilibrium always occurs at full employment
13. The stock of money	Logically, the stock of money affects output, but it is not a very powerful influence	The stock of money is the most important determinant of nominal GNP
14. Stability of the system	Private spending may be (animal spirits) unstable, and so variation of fiscal policy is needed to maintain full employment	Private spending is stable, and so there is no need for discretionary fiscal policy

change in the stock of real balances changes the interest rate, and so investment spending also changes. When spending changes, so do the levels of aggregate demand and income. Changes in the real money stock occur when either the nominal money stock or the price level changes.

    a. Given a constant nominal stock of money, price level, and level of income, there is some interest rate at which the quantity demanded and the quantity supplied of real balances are equal. An increase in the price level (nominal balances remaining unchanged) causes the real stock of money balances to decrease. At the initial interest rate, there is an excess demand for real balances, and so the interest rate rises and investment spending falls.

    b. Any change in the price level affects both the goods and assets markets, and this causes a change in equilibrium income. The macroeconomic demand schedule shows the equilibrium level of output corresponding to each price level at which planned spending equals income Also, any point on this schedule represents an equilibrium income level at which there is equilibrium in the money (assets) market. For each price level, there is a different level of income and employment at which the goods and money markets clear.

2. The aggregate supply schedule shows the output levels firms want to supply at each price level. It is based on the interaction of households and firms.
   a. There is a negative relationship between the real wage and the quantity of labor a firm hires. The firm hires additional units of labor up to the point at which the increase in output produced by the last worker employed (the marginal product of labor) equals the real wage paid. If the marginal product of the last worker hired does not equal the real wage, the firm can increase its profits by adjusting the number of workers hired. The firm's demand curve for labor slopes downward because as the number of workers hired increases, each additional unit of labor produces less. The firm hires more labor only at lower real wages.
   b. Statistical evidence suggests that a positive relationship exists between the real wage and the quantity of labor supplied in the market. At higher real wages, workers trade off leisure for income, and so they work more.
      (1) Equilibrium in the labor market is established at that real wage rate at which the quantity of labor firms want to hire equals the quantity of labor workers want to supply. At this equilibrium real wage, there is neither a surplus nor a shortage of labor on the market; everyone who wants to work does work. Any disequilibrium causes real wages to adjust until the labor market is again in balance. Full employment occurs when the labor market is in equilibrium.
      (2) Neither workers nor firms suffer from money illusion because they realize that changes in real wages, not money wages, affect their well-being. Because there is no money illusion, any movement in the price level that is not caused by a change in labor supply or demand causes money wages to change so that real wages remain constant. A constant real wage means that the level of employment does not change. This shows that a price level change that is not induced by labor market activities does not change the equilibrium level of employment. The real wage determines labor market equilibrium.
   c. With a given stock of capital, firms produce some output level for a given level of employment. When the labor force is at full employment, firms produce the potential output level. When firms produce their potential output, this is independent of the price level. This independence of output and prices happens (remember that prices and wages are flexible and that there is no money illusion) because employment is independent of the price level. The aggregate supply schedule shows the amount of output supplied at each level of prices. Since potential output is independent of prices, aggregate supply equals potential output. This relationship is the classical aggregate supply schedule.

3. The intersection of the macroeconomic demand and aggregate supply schedules establishes the price level at which macroeconomic demand and aggregate supply are equal so that all markets clear. This is a price level which generates equilibrium in the goods, money, and labor markets. If prices are at some level other than the level required for equilibrium, adjustments in real balances, interest rates, aggregate demand, employment demand, wages, and output move the price level back toward equilibrium. This is the classical model of macroeconomic equilibrium.
   a. The potential level of output is influenced by labor supply conditions (workers willing to work at a particular wage) and the productivity of labor. The productivity of labor in turn is influenced by the availability of capital. A change in either one of these factors can shift the aggregate supply curve and change the price level. Macroeconomic demand is influenced by both the nominal money stock and fiscal policy. A change in the nominal money stock or in the government's fiscal policy shifts the macroeconomic demand schedule and changes the equilibrium price level.

4. A change in the government's fiscal policy or the Fed's monetary policy shifts the macroeconomic demand curve and changes the level of aggregate demand at each price level.
   a. Initially, for a given price level and full employment, a change in the nominal money supply changes the stock of real balances, and so the equilibrium interest rate changes. In response to changes in the interest rate, investment spending changes. This leads to changes in

aggregate demand, equilibrium income, and spending. The macroeconomic demand curve shifts, and so the price level changes. The adjustment process in the economy continues until real balances return to their original level, interest rates return to their original level, and aggregate spending again equals the level of potential output. In the long run, the classical model shows there is no effect on interest rates or output.
b. The Keynesian model argues that an increase in the nominal money stock increases aggregate demand and leads to an increase in output as long as unemployment exists. Prices don't increase. Decreases in the nominal money stock reduce aggregate demand and output. In the Keynesian system, output, employment, and income change. The classical model argues that no unemployment exists (there is full employment), and so price, not output, changes when the nominal money stock changes. The Keynesian model does not consider long-run adjustments of wages and prices; to the Keynesians, wages and prices are given or change only slowly.
c. The classical model argues that the effect of an increase in government spending is simply to crowd out an equal amount of private spending so that long-run output is unchanged. Private investment is crowded out because when the economy is operating at its potential output, an increase in government spending shifts the macroeconomic demand schedule, and excess demand results. This excess demand raises prices; the real money stock falls, interest rates rise, and private investment falls until total aggregate spending declines to its initial level. The result is that total spending and output remain at their initial levels, but the government's spending displaces an equal amount of private spending. In the Keynesian model, an increase in government spending increases interest rates and reduces investment spending, but output still expands because unemployment may exist.
d. The analysis presented from Chapter 23 up to this point has provided a macroeconomic model which permits the simultaneous determination of the price level and aggregate output.
5. Aggregate supply and demand together establish the price level and equilibrium output. Supply side economics argues that policies operating through the tax system can have beneficial effects on the economy.

a. Supply siders argue that a cut in the marginal tax rate (the fraction of an extra dollar in income paid as taxes) increases the supply of labor and the quantity demanded of labor. Workers are willing to supply more labor at the same before-tax wage because they receive higher take-home pay. The labor supply schedule increases (shifts), causing the equilibrium real wage paid by firms to fall so that they hire more workers, and aggregate output (supply) increases. Aggregate spending rises because households' disposable incomes increase when the government takes less in income taxes. The macroeconomic demand schedule increases (shifts), and a new equilibrium is achieved. The change in the price level is indeterminate, but potential output increases so that equilibrium income rises. There is no reason to expect a tax cut to crowd out private investment.
b. Supply side economics proposes tax cuts not only on individuals' income but on firms' income.
(1) In the short run, an investment tax credit affects aggregate demand but does not increase the capital stock significantly. The short-run effects increase the price level and interest rates because macroeconomic demand, not potential output, increases. Investment may increase only if consumption decreases (government spending remains unchanged). If saving increases in response to higher interest rates, then investment spending, the capital stock, and output increase over a period of time.
(2) At full employment, the supply siders argue that saving is the key factor in the ability of the investment tax credit to trigger rising output. It is not certain exactly how saving responds to the interest rate. Data do not indicate a strong response of saving to an increase in the interest rate.
c. Supply siders argue that taxes drive a wedge between prices, wages, and interest payments made by firms using the factors of production and the incomes received by the suppliers of these factors. As a result of the wedge, potential output is reduced. Thus, supply side economics argues that the wedge must be reduced if output is to be increased. Removal of the wedge means that saving, investment, and employment increase. Reducing taxes, though, most probably would reduce many of the services we expect government to provide.

FULL-EMPLOYMENT OUTPUT AND THE PRICE LEVEL

IMPORTANT TERMS AND THEIR MEANING

Match the following terms with the correct definition or phrase.

1. _____ The gap (caused by taxes) between what the users of the factors of production pay for these factors and what the suppliers receive as income

2. _____ Shows the equilibrium level of output corresponding to each level of prices at which planned spending equals income

3. _____ Nominal money stock divided by the price level

4. _____ Describes the operation of an economy when wages and prices are fully flexible; argues that all markets clear and that full employment is guaranteed

5. _____ The displacement of private investment spending which results from increases in government spending and increases in the interest rate

6. _____ The increase in total output produced by employing another worker

7. _____ The fraction of an extra dollar of income that has to be paid in taxes

8. _____ Present when a change in money wages leads people to change their behavior even though real wages have not changed

9. _____ Argues that tax cuts will generate anti-inflationary effects by expanding output; emphasizes the effects of government policy on incentives for people to work and invest

10. _____ Shows the quantity of output firms want to supply at each price level

11. _____ The amount of goods and services a given money wage will buy

a. Classical model of macroeconomics

b. Money illusion

c. Crowding out

d. Real wage

e. The wedge

f. Supply side economics

g. Real money stock

h. Wage and price flexibility

i. Aggregate supply schedule

j. Marginal tax rates

k. Macroeconomic demand schedule

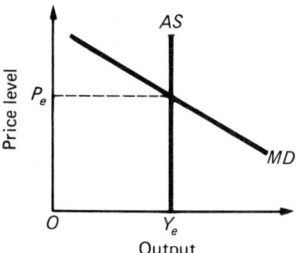

FIGURE 28-1

12. _____ The price paid for goods and the wages paid for labor are not fixed; they can either increase or decrease

l. Marginal product of labor

EXERCISES

1. Figure 28-1 shows the classical case's macroeconomic equilibrium. At the equilibrium price P_e and output Y_e, the goods, money, and labor markets clear. Below, you are presented certain events which may affect the position of the aggregate supply curve AS or macroeconomic demand curve MD. Even though the events may shift the curves, remember that the classical model argues that full employment always exists in the long run. Your task is to determine what effect each of the events has on aggregate output Y, aggregate supply AS, macroeconomic demand MD, and the price level P after all adjustments have occurred. To show an increase, use ↑; for a decrease, use ↓; and if there is no change, use 0. If the change cannot be determined, use a question mark.

	MD	AS	P	Y
a. The Fed reduces the nominal money stock.	___	___	___	___
b. The government increases defense spending by $1.5 billion.	___	___	___	___
c. The government reduces personal income taxes.	___	___	___	___
d. The price level falls.	___	___	___	___
e. The Fed increases the nominal money stock.	___	___	___	___
f. The productivity of labor decreases.	___	___	___	___
g. Government increases the tax rate, and both aggregate demand and the willingness of labor to work at the going wage rate fall.	___	___	___	___

2. Listed below are eight statements about the effects of monetary and fiscal policy changes on macroeconomic equilibrium. In the blank beside each statement,

identify it as belonging to either the Keynesian or the classical approach.

  a. When actual output is less than potential output, an increase in the nominal money supply increases aggregate demand and output but not prices. _____

  b. In the long run, an increase in government spending crowds out an equal amount of private investment, and so output doesn't increase. _____

  c. The level of aggregate output is supply-determined. _____

  d. An increase in government spending may crowd out some private investment, but income and output still expand. _____

  e. When the economy is at full employment with a given level of government spending, in order to increase investment spending, consumption must be reduced, and so an income tax increase is needed to prevent a price rise. _____

  f. At full employment with flexible prices and wages, an increase in the nominal money stock has no effect on output; only prices increase. _____

  g. The level of output is demand-determined, and so policies must be designed to change aggregate demand. _____

  h. Reducing income taxes encourages saving, investment, and work effort and increases the level of potential output. _____

3. Figure 28-2 shows the demand for and the supply of labor. The equilibrium real wage is W_o, and the full-employment level is N_o. The actual level of employment is N. Assume that the government taxes labor income.

  a. At the actual level of employment, the wage paid by employers is ($W_1/W_2/W_o$) _____, but the wage received by employees is ($W_1/W_2/W_o$) _____. The cost of hiring an additional worker is (greater than/equal to/less than) _____ the wage the additional worker receives.

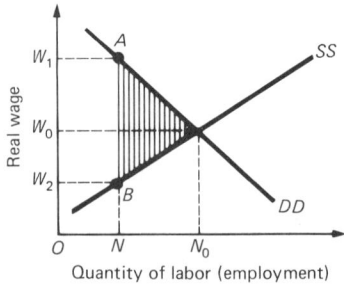

FIGURE 28-2

  b. Rectangle W_2W_1AB shows the government's tax _____ and is the amount of income labor loses.

  c. If the government reduces the income tax, the wage paid by the firm (increases/decreases) _____, the wage received by labor (increases/decreases) _____, and the level of employment (increases/decreases) _____.

  d. Supply siders argue that removal of the tax wedge (increases/decreases) _____ potential output.

FILL-IN QUESTIONS

1. The (classical/Keynesian) _____ model of macroeconomic activity assumes that wages and prices are fixed and that there (can/cannot) _____ be unemployment.

2. The real money stock is the _____ money stock divided by the _____ level.

3. The _____ demand schedule shows the equilibrium level of output corresponding to each level of prices at which _____ spending equals _____.

4. In making its decision to hire an additional worker, the firm compares the (marginal revenue/marginal product) _____ of labor with the (real/nominal) _____ wage and should hire labor up to the point at which the two (are/are not) _____ equal.

5. The classical model argues that for a given (nominal/real) _____ wage, there (is/is not) _____ always full employment in the long run.

6. If all prices (but not money wages) double and workers do not change the amount of hours worked, they (do/do not) _____ suffer from money illusion because the purchasing power of their money wages has (increased/decreased) _____.

7. In the absence of the money illusion and with flexible wages, an increase in the price level (does/does not) _____ cause the equilibrium real wage to change since there is an (equal/unequal) _____

increase in _____ wages so that the level of employment (does/does not) _____ change.

8. In the classical case with flexible wages and prices and no money illusion, the _____ schedule shows the level of output supplied, and it (is/is not) _____ independent of prices.

9. In the classical case, if prices are higher than the equilibrium price level, the real money stock is not in equilibrium because it is (higher/lower) _____ than it should be, interest rates are (higher/lower) _____, aggregate demand is (higher/lower) _____, and so eventually interest rates (increase/decrease) _____ and prices (rise/fall) _____.

10. According to the classical model, the equilibrium level of prices is established at the point where the _____ demand schedule and the _____ supply schedule intersect; at this point, (all/some) _____ markets clear.

11. An increase in the nominal money stock (shifts/rotates) _____ the macroeconomic demand schedule (upward/downward) _____, and aggregate supply (does/does not) _____ change.

12. The economists who argue that tax cuts can have an expansionary effect on potential output without causing inflationary pressures are known as _____.

13. The _____ tax rate is the fraction of an extra dollar of income that has to be paid in taxes, and it (increases/decreases) _____ as income levels rise if the tax structure is progressive.

14. Supply side economics argues that an investment tax credit (does/does not) _____ cause an immediate change in the capital stock; potential output (increases/remains constant/decreases) _____, and the price level (rises/falls) _____.

15. A major argument of supply side economics is that taxes drive a _____ between the prices paid by the users of the factors of production and the income received by the suppliers of these factors.

TRUE-FALSE QUESTIONS

1. ____ The real money stock will decline when the stock of nominal balances falls or the price level increases.

2. ____ The macroeconomic demand schedule shows that a decrease in prices causes a reduction in equilibrium income and spending.

3. ____ The level of aggregate employment does not play a very important role in the determination of aggregate supply because it is the price level, not employment, which determines supply.

4. ____ Economists cannot be certain that an increase in the real wage will cause workers to supply more labor.

5. ____ If firms and workers change their behavior when the real wage (not the money wage) changes, they suffer from money illusion.

6. ____ The equilibrium level of employment is not affected by changes in the aggregate price level; neither is the level of output.

7. ____ Keynesians argue that with given prices and a demand-determined output level, expansionary fiscal and monetary policies do not affect output and employment.

8. ____ According to the classical model, a reduction in the nominal money stock causes a fall in the price level after all adjustments have taken place.

9. ____ The classical model's analysis only describes the short run, while the Keynesian model evaluates long-run effects.

10. ____ An effective macroeconomic model requires the interaction of the goods, assets, and labor markets.

11. ____ According to supply siders, a reduction in marginal income tax rates causes both aggregate output and demand to increase.

12. ____ Supply siders argue that the appropriate policy needed for a very rapid increase in an economy's capital stock is an investment tax credit.

13. ____ Economists are certain that as interest rates increase, the level of saving increases.

MULTIPLE CHOICE QUESTIONS

Circle the correct answer.

1. All of the following statements are correct except
   a. supply side economists argue that removing the tax wedge will cause potential output to decrease

b. the tax wedge causes the wage paid for labor by firms and the wage received by labor to differ

c. the presence of taxes on income causes the labor market to be in a state of disequilibrium

d. if taxes are reduced, some households may be made worse off

2. According to supply side economics, the short-run effect of an investment tax credit is almost entirely a matter of
   a. increasing the capital stock
   b. reducing aggregate demand
   c. increasing aggregate demand
   d. lowering interest rates
   e. none of the above

3. If an individual's income increases from $23,500 to $28,500 and his tax liability increases from $4837 to $6587, the marginal tax rate is
   a. 22 percent
   b. 35 percent
   c. 40 percent
   d. 31 percent
   e. cannot be determined from the information given

4. Which of the following statements is incorrect?
   a. supply side economists argue that a reduction in taxes can expand aggregate output without the damaging effects of inflation
   b. to determine the price level in a complete macroeconomic model requires information on both aggregate supply and demand
   c. an income tax reduction can affect aggregate labor supply, aggregate demand, and potential output
   d. all of the above statements are incorrect

5. The classical model argues that an increase in government spending, with a constant nominal money stock,
   a. increases real output and employment
   b. causes an increase in the price level but not in aggregate output
   c. causes the interest rate to fall
   d. causes the interest rate to rise and private investment to be crowded out
   e. b and d above
   f. a and c above

6. Assuming that the aggregate supply curve is vertical and that there initially is an equilibrium price and output level, an increase in the nominal stock of money causes the movement of the aggregate demand curve. Which of the following statements about the effect of a change in the aggregate money stock is correct?
   a. there is too much money chasing too few goods, and so the price level rises
   b. there is an excess demand for goods, and so the price level falls
   c. the change in aggregate demand causes interest rates to rise and investment spending to fall
   d. the long-run effect of the change in the money stock is an increase in interest rates

7. A change in fiscal or monetary policy
   a. rotates the macroeconomic demand curve about the equilibrium price level
   b. has no effect on the macroeconomic demand curve
   c. shifts the macroeconomic demand curve either upward or downward
   d. none of the above

8. In the classical model, the equilibrium price level
   a. is determined by the intersection of the aggregate supply and macro demand curves
   b. clears the goods market
   c. clears the money market
   d. clears the labor market
   e. all of the above

9. When the labor market is in equilibrium, the classical case argues that
   a. some workers who want to work at the market real wage cannot find a job
   b. there is full employment
   c. job vacancies exist because firms cannot hire all the labor they need
   d. the tax wedge allows the labor market to achieve an efficient allocation of labor

Use the following table to answer Questions 10 and 11.

NUMBER OF UNITS OF LABOR	MP_L
1	12
2	10
3	8
4	6
5	4
6	2

10. Suppose a producer is manufacturing widgets and faces the above schedule of the marginal product of labor. If the producer pays $20 per unit of labor in wages and can sell his product on the market for $5, how many units of labor will the firm hire?
    a. 2   d. 5
    b. 3   e. 6
    c. 4

11. Using the price of widgets to represent the price level, what will be the real wage paid for the optimal number of workers?
    a. 8 widgets   c. 6 widgets
    b. 4 widgets   d. 2 widgets

FULL-EMPLOYMENT OUTPUT AND THE PRICE LEVEL

12. For a given nominal money stock, an increase in the price level
    a. causes the level of investment spending to increase
    b. increases the stock of real balances
    c. causes the equilibrium interest rate to increase
    d. has no effect on the stock of real balances or the equilibrium interest rate

13. All of the following were assumptions made by the classical economists except
    a. the economy is continuously at full employment
    b. government should manage aggregate demand
    c. through the price mechanism, the goods market is cleared
    d. wages are flexible both upward and downward

AT THIS POINT YOU SHOULD BE ABLE TO . . .

1. Explain how changes in the nominal stock of money or changes in the price level affect the interest rate and the level of investment.

2. Describe the macroeconomic demand curve and explain the linkage between prices and aggregate demand.

3. Explain why the demand for labor curve slopes downward, why the supply of labor curve slopes upward, and how a labor market equilibrium is established.

4. Define and give an example of money illusion, explain why the classical case emphasizes real wages instead of nominal wages, and state the effect of price changes on the real wage and aggregate output when money wages are completely flexible.

5. Describe the aggregate supply curve presented by the classical model and explain why it represents a full-employment level of output.

6. Explain price, output, and employment determination, using the macroeconomic demand and aggregate supply curves presented in the classical case.

7. List two reasons why the macroeconomic demand and aggregate supply curves may shift, and explain the effect such a shift would have on prices, output, and employment.

8. Compare the assumptions of the Keynesian model with those of the classical model and explain how the determination of a macroeconomic equilibrium differs for each model.

9. Explain why crowding out of private investment spending differs between the classical case and the Keynesian case.

10. Describe the role of reduced taxes in supply side economics and explain how a new equilibrium output, employment, and price level are established.

11. Explain the short-run and long-run effects of an investment tax credit on the capital stock and describe the role of saving in determining the success of an investment tax credit in increasing aggregate output.

12. Explain the Keynesian view and the classical (supply side) view on using fiscal policy to achieve a macroeconomic equilibrium.

13. Describe the tax wedge.

QUESTIONS FOR THOUGHT

1. The classical case argues that when the labor market is in equilibrium, there is always full employment. Explain how this can happen. How does this differ from the Keynesian argument about full employment?

2. Aggregate supply depends on three factors, while there are two primary determinants of aggregate demand in the classical model. Explain how each of these factors affects supply or demand. These factors also play a role in the determination of the equilibrium price level. Explain.

3. A monetary expansion has different short-run and long-run effects. What are these effects? Describe the adjustment process after a monetary expansion has taken place.

4. Briefly describe the major differences between the Keynesian and classical approaches to macroeconomic equilibrium. What does each approach say about the effectiveness of fiscal and monetary policy?

5. The labor tax wedge model presented in Chapter 28 argues that in order to increase employment, the government should reduce the taxes on labor since both employers and employees would benefit. Do you think a capital tax wedge exists in capital markets? Explain.

6. Is it necessary to have policies which effectively deal with both aggregate demand and aggregate supply in order to promote economic stability and growth? Explain why or why not.

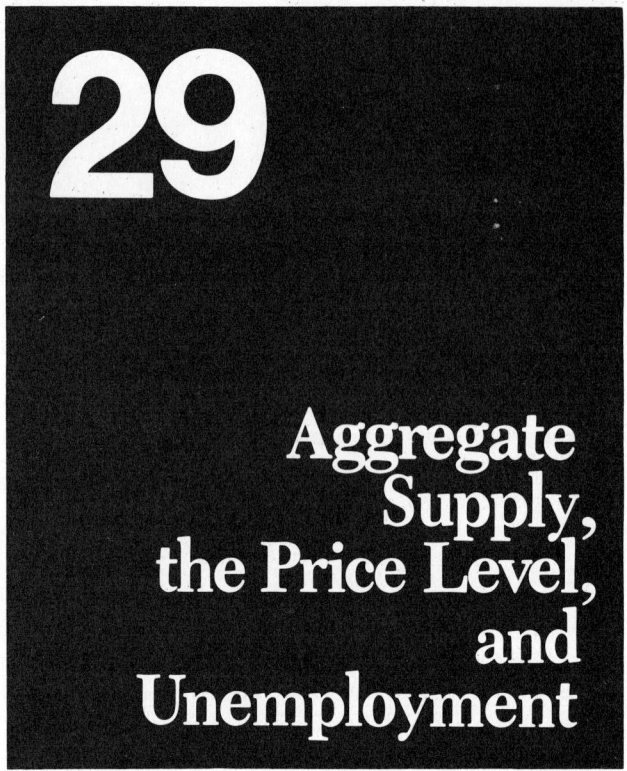

29

Aggregate Supply, the Price Level, and Unemployment

Chapter 29 shows how the economy adjusts when there are disturbances to aggregate demand or aggregate supply. The major point of Chapter 29 is that both the Keynesian and classical models are necessary to explain both the adjustment process and why persistent unemployment or inflation exists. The Keynesian model shows that with fixed wages and prices, unemployment can persist. The classical model, on the other hand, shows that when wages and prices are completely flexible, unemployment can't exist for very long. In most industrialized countries, it is not uncommon to have long periods of unemployment or inflation when some disturbance moves the economy from its equilibrium position.

The Keynesian model best describes the short-run effects of an aggregate disequilibrium, while the long-run effects are best described by the classical model. But neither model adequately explains the adjustment process from the short run to the long run. This adjustment process and the combination of ideas from both the Keynesian and classical models are what you learn about in Chapter 29.

As you read Chapter 29, pay particular attention as the links between the Keynesian and classical models are established. These linkages connect the behavior of output, employment, wages, and prices in both the long run and the short run. Once the links are established and understood, much of your foundation for studying current macroeconomic events is in place. An additional tool you must master is the upward-sloping aggregate supply schedule because it is critical to the adjustment process. The upward-sloping aggregate supply schedule links the output and labor markets because it is assumed that wages (labor costs) are the largest component of production costs. Thus, if events affect the labor market equilibrium and wages, the prices of goods in the output market are also affected.

The first sections of Chapter 29 describe employment and wage behavior. It is here that wages and the costs of production are linked to prices in the output market and the important role played by wages is presented. In the short run, the amount of labor used in production is determined primarily by firms. The adjustment process utilized here assumes that short-run wages and the level of employment do not change greatly. Firms and workers view jobs as a long-term commitment, and they both incur a cost when job turnovers are frequent; thus, wages change very slowly in response to changes in aggregate demand and unemployment. During periods of recession, layoffs and a shorter workweek are used more frequently than decreases in wages; thus, unemployment can exist in the short run. During periods of high aggregate demand (booms), the use of overtime and recalled workers (who were previously laid off) are the more common responses by business rather than an expansion of the firm's work force.

In the medium term, firms use a different adjustment process to an excess demand for labor (shortage) or unemployment (surplus). During this intermediate period between the short run and the long run, wages and the level of employment change. Firms and workers adjust both the number of hours worked and the number of people working. If producers expect the change in aggregate demand to be prolonged, they change their work force and wages. Thus, wages change over time as the level of output changes. As the firm's wage costs change, its costs of production change, and these are passed on as higher prices.

In the long run, the labor market clears at the equilibrium wage. This wage is determined by the demand for and the supply of labor. There is neither unemployment nor overemployment. All workers who want to work at the equilibrium wage have a job and work the normal workweek.

The short-run aggregate supply schedule is the connector between wages, prices, and output. The schedule shows the price (based on labor costs) firms charge at each level of output, and it shifts over time as long as actual output and potential output are different. This aggregate supply schedule also shows that changes in aggregate demand can lead to changes in output and prices as the labor market moves toward its full-employment level.

AGGREGATE SUPPLY, THE PRICE LEVEL, AND UNEMPLOYMENT

CHAPTER OUTLINE

1. The firm's demand for and the worker's supply of labor define the labor market. At any particular time in the labor market, there is full employment, unemployment, or a shortage of workers. The response of wages to changes in aggregate demand and unemployment occurs in the labor market.

   a. Because of the costs involved, firms are reluctant to hire and fire workers quickly. Also, there is a cost to labor when workers quit jobs frequently. The firm and the worker view employment as a long-term commitment, and so each wants some implicit or explicit agreement about the terms of the work.

   b. Given the state of technology and labor productivity (the amount of output per unit of labor input), the firm decides how much labor input it needs to produce the desired level of output. Total labor input is equal to the hours worked per worker times the number of workers hired. The firm changes total labor input by changing the number of hours each worker is on the job or changing the number of workers employed. A change in demand for its output causes the firm to change the demand for the labor input. There is both a short-run effect and a long-run effect on total labor input as the firm responds to changes in product demand. In the short run, the firm adjusts the length of the workweek (either overtime or fewer hours per week), and the size of the work force remains relatively constant. The short-run adjustment is transitory. If the firm believes that a permanent change has occurred in its product demand, the size of the work force is changed. In the long run, the firm returns to a normal workweek with an adjusted work force.

   c. Because the employees of most firms possess some firm-specific skills, employers may hoard labor in the short run by keeping more workers than are necessary to produce the current level of output. If the demand for a firm's production falls and remains low, the firm lays off some or all of its workers. A layoff is a temporary separation of an employee from the firm, and it causes the firm's payroll to decline during a period of weak product demand. When demand increases, the worker is recalled to the job.

   d. As the firm adjusts its level of production in the short run, workers adjust the amount and intensity of their work. Each firm's wage is changed only rarely so that the firm's competitiveness with other producers who are using the same kind of labor is maintained.

   e. Wages don't usually fall when there is unemployment in the short run, because firms are reluctant to reduce the wage for their current workers. If a firm reduces wages when unemployment is high, worker productivity and morale may be damaged. The likely response of a firm in the presence of unemployment is that wages will grow only slowly if at all. Those workers who do not have jobs do not provide much direct competition for those who are employed.

   f. The wage in the short run is largely fixed and unresponsive to changes in output, but in the long run it is completely flexible and clears the labor market.

2. The prevailing wage at any point in time can be expressed as

   Current wage = last period's wage
   + current cyclical adjustment + other

   The cyclical adjustment affects current wages because it is the component which incorporates the economy's deviation from full employment. The current wage equation shows that if the economy is at full employment, the wage currently paid is simply the wage paid during the last period. If there is unemployment and falling output, the cyclical adjustment (because of the reduced workweek or layoffs) makes today's wage somewhat lower than last period's. If output is above the full-employment level, this period's wage is higher than last period's. During the medium run, wages do adjust somewhat to changing conditions in the economy, and so the average wage changes. When output is continuously above the normal level, the average wage rises and the wage schedule shifts upward. If there is continuous unemployment, the wage schedule shifts downward and wages fall because output is below its potential level.

3. The seller of a product usually sets the product's price on the basis of market conditions and the costs of production. Labor costs are the major component of the firm's cost of production, and so any change in labor productivity, the wage rate, or the number of hours worked changes the firm's labor costs. When these costs change, the firm changes product price. If labor productivity and the length of the workweek are assumed constant, the wage rate determines the firm's product price. Although long-run aggregate supply at full employment is independent of the price level, the short-run supply curve shows how much firms charge for their

products at each output level. This price is determined by labor costs. The short-run aggregate supply schedule shows a weak positive relationship between price and output because wages respond slowly to changes in the labor market over the business cycle. Nevertheless, changes in employment have some effect on prices. When changes in labor market conditions occur continuously over time, the aggregate supply schedule shifts because wages, costs, and prices change continuously.

4. An increase in macroeconomic demand above the full-employment level causes the demand schedule to shift upward. The long-run effects are higher prices but a constant equilibrium output and employment. The short-run effects, however, permit increased prices (inflation) and an expansion of output. Given a short-run aggregate supply schedule, an increase in macroeconomic demand causes an increase in output and employment beyond the potential level. Wages increase as employment and production expand, and so the firm's costs increase. These costs are passed on in the form of rising prices. With the labor force still overemployed, pressure on wages increases so that the short-run aggregate supply curve shifts upward. Output falls, but prices increase. The short-run aggregate supply schedule continues to shift upward until output again reaches its potential level, the price level again equates long-run aggregate supply and macroeconomic demand, and the economy is again at full employment.

5. A shift in the long-run aggregate supply curve changes long-run equilibrium prices, output, and employment. An increase in aggregate supply causes prices to fall and output to increase; however, these results are not instantaneous. The short-run adjustments to an increase in the level of potential output involve gradually falling prices (deflation) and expanding output as the short-run aggregate supply curve shifts slowly downward. Spending also increases because as prices fall, real balances increase (assuming a constant money stock) and interest rates fall. The new long-run equilibrium is attained when the new long-run aggregate supply curve intersects the existing macroeconomic demand curve. At this intersection, prices are lower and output is higher. An increase in the level of potential output (long-run aggregate supply) is caused by a permanent lowering of firms' production costs per unit of output at each output level.

   a. An adverse supply shock is a disturbance which increases firms' costs of production. At any given wage, when the costs of production increase, firms pass these increases on to consumers in the form of higher prices. The short-run aggregate supply curve shifts upward, and output falls. Real balances fall, interest rates rise, and aggregate spending falls, resulting in a lower equilibrium level of output and employment. As the level of employment falls, wages fall and the short-run aggregate supply curve shifts downward toward the long-run equilibrium output and price levels. Unless the disturbance represents a permanent change in the economy, the long-run aggregate supply schedule doesn't shift, and so the long-run equilibrium price, employment, and output remain the same.

6. The underlying source of any business cycle is shifts in macroeconomic demand and aggregate supply. Changes in monetary and fiscal policy as well as private sector spending disturb macroeconomic demand, and the disturbances take time to work themselves out. During the adjustment period, prices, output, and employment change. In the long run, aggregate supply can change. Disturbances and shocks to the economic system occur at irregular intervals, and so business cycles are irregular.

   a. Data indicate that inflation is persistent even though unemployment may be high. Firms are reluctant to cut their employees' money wage during a recession. In fact, employers often give some wage increases to the workers they want to keep as a way of compensating for inflation. These increased wages increase the firms' costs, which are passed on in the form of higher prices. The Fed's policy of expanding the money stock during recessions also contributes to persistent inflation.

IMPORTANT TERMS AND THEIR MEANING

Match the following terms with the correct definition or phrase.

1. _____ Recurrent but irregular periods of expanding or contracting economic activity

   a. Adjustment paths

2. _____ A rise in the price of the inputs of production which in the short run increases firms' operating costs, lowers output, and raises prices

   b. Recalls

3. _____ A temporary separation of the worker from the firm

   c. Business cycle

4. _____ The amount of output produced per unit of labor input; output per labor hour

   d. Labor productivity

AGGREGATE SUPPLY, THE PRICE LEVEL, AND UNEMPLOYMENT

5. _____ The view held by both firms and workers that employment is not a transitory arrangement

6. _____ The level of output that would be produced if the economy were at full employment

7. _____ Opening jobs back up to workers who were previously laid off

8. _____ Shows the transitory changes in prices, output, and employment as the economy recovers from short-run shocks and approaches its long-run equilibrium

9. _____ A rather flat schedule which shows the price firms charge at each level of output

10. _____ The number of hours worked by an employee per week

11. _____ A short-run change (either internal or external) in the economy which disturbs aggregate supply and affects costs, prices, output, employment, and aggregate spending

e. Short-run aggregate supply curve

f. Materials price increase

g. Workweek

h. Layoffs

i. Potential output

j. Supply shocks

k. Long-term commitment

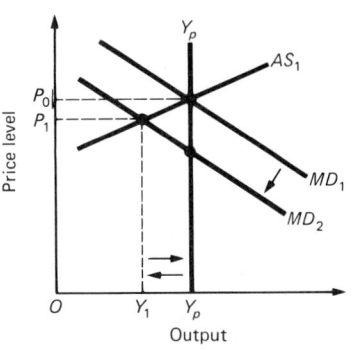

FIGURE 29-1

EXERCISES

1. Table 29-2 of your text shows the effects on output, prices, and inflation of shifts in the aggregate supply and macroeconomic demand curves. These effects are reproduced here in Table 29-1, except that some of the effects have been left out. Without looking back at the text, complete Table 29-1. Your possible answers are increase, none, higher, lower, more, or less.

2. This exercise is divided into two main parts. Each part shows the effects on long-run equilibrium of a shock to the economy. Your task is to trace the effects of the shock.

   a. Figure 29-1 shows the long-term effects of a decrease in the money stock. The long-run output level is Y_p, and the initial equilibrium price is P_0. The initial short-run aggregate supply curve is AS_1. (1) Draw the ending short-run aggregate supply curve and label it AS_3. (2) Draw one short-run aggregate supply curve (between AS_1 and AS_3) which shows the medium term of the adjustment process. Label this curve AS_2. Identify the medium-term price and output by labeling them P_2 and Y_2, respectively. (3) Label the ending price level P_3. (4) Once you have drawn the short-run aggregate supply curves, draw arrows to show the adjustment path of the economy as it attains a new long-run equilibrium. (5) Figure 29-1 shows that if the money stock decreases, the price level (rises/falls) _____ and aggregate output in the long run (increases/remains constant/decreases) _____. (6) When the money stock is reduced, real balances initially (rise/fall) _____, the interest rate (rises/falls) _____, investment (rises/falls) _____, and so aggregate spending (increases/decreases) _____. (7) The economy produces (above/at/below) _____ its

TABLE 29-1
EFFECTS OF SHIFTS IN THE AGGREGATE SUPPLY AND DEMAND CURVES

	EFFECTS ON OUTPUT		EFFECTS ON PRICE LEVEL		EFFECTS ON INFLATION	
TYPE OF SHIFT	SHORT RUN	LONG RUN	SHORT RUN	LONG RUN	SHORT RUN	LONG RUN
Demand curve shifts to the right	a. _____	None	Higher	b. _____	More	c. _____
Supply curve shifts to the right	Increase	d. _____	e. _____	Lower	f. _____	g. _____

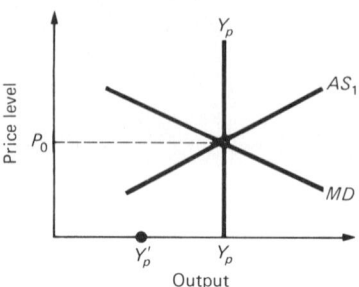

FIGURE 29-2

potential output level, employment and wages (rise/fall) _____, and the short-run aggregate supply curve shifts (upward/downward) _____ over time because producers' costs (rise/fall) _____. (8) As the short-run aggregate schedule shifts and prices fall, real balances begin to (rise/fall) _____ and interest rates (rise/fall) _____. The rate of deflation (accelerates/slows down) _____ as the adjustment process slows down and output again approaches its potential level.

  b. Figure 29-2 shows an economy initially in equilibrium with long-run aggregate supply and macroeconomic demand equal at Y_p and price level P_0. The short-run supply curve initially is AS_1. Suppose the government increases both income taxes and Social Security taxes. In completing the following questions, disregard any changes in macroeconomic demand. (1) Draw the new long-run aggregate supply curve at output level Y'_p and label the new price P_3. (2) Draw the short-run aggregate supply curve associated with this new long-run equilibrium and label it AS_3. (3) Draw one short-run aggregate supply between AS_1 and AS_3 and use arrows to indicate the adjustment of price and output as the economy approaches its new long-run equilibrium. (4) The increase in taxes (increases/decreases) _____ labor supply, and so potential output (rises/falls) _____. (5) The adjustment process (is/is not) _____ instantaneous because labor supply and output change (gradually/rapidly) _____, as shown by the (upward/downward) _____ shift of short-run aggregate supply.

FILL-IN QUESTIONS

  1. The behavior of (wages/interest rates) _____ makes prices respond slowly to changes in aggregate demand.

  2. Workers and firms view job arrangements as (long/short) _____-term commitments, and so when aggregate demand falls, firms are (willing/reluctant) _____ to fire excess labor.

  3. Firms can adjust the amount of labor input used by changing either the _____ of workers on the payroll or the number of _____ per worker.

  4. When there are unemployed workers in the labor market, wages (do/do not) _____ fall rapidly because the firm (is/is not) _____ willing to reduce the wages of its existing workers.

  5. If there is full employment in the economy, the wage in the current period equals the wage in the _____ since cyclical adjustments are (equal to/greater than) _____ zero.

  6. When firms experience increasing labor costs, it is reasonable to assume that these costs will lead to (higher/lower/unchanged) _____ output prices in the future.

  7. The short-run _____ schedule shows the price firms charge at each level of otuput, and it graphs as (a vertical/an upward-sloping) _____ line.

  8. An increase in the nominal money stock causes macroeconomic demand to (increase/decrease) _____ at every price level; in the short run, both output and prices (rise/fall/remain constant) _____. However, as the short-run aggregate supply schedule shifts (downward/upward) _____, prices (rise/fall) _____ and output (rises/falls) _____ as the economy adjusts to a new long-run equilibrium with a (higher/lower) _____ price level and no change in full-employment _____.

  9. An increase in the full-employment potential output with a given macroeconomic demand schedule causes long-run output to (increase/decrease) _____ and long-run inflation to (increase/remain unchanged/decrease) _____.

  10. An adverse supply shock which raises firms' costs of production causes the real money stock to (rise/fall)

AGGREGATE SUPPLY, THE PRICE LEVEL, AND UNEMPLOYMENT

_____, and so employment and output (rise/fall) _____.

11. The underlying sources of the business cycle are shifts in aggregate _____ or _____.

TRUE-FALSE QUESTIONS

1. _____ The policy of the Fed expanding the money supply during periods of unemployment actually helps keep prices up.

2. _____ The regularity and predictability of business cycles results from the regularity and predictability of disturbances which hit the economy.

3. _____ An example of an adverse supply shock is a fall in the real wage rate.

4. _____ When the macroeconomic demand schedule shifts to the right, the short-run effects are an increase in both output and prices.

5. _____ Since an increase in the nominal money stock increases employment and output in the short run, printing money is one way we could enjoy long-term economic stability and full employment.

6. _____ If the economy is in a sustained boom, the short-run aggregate supply schedule shifts upward because wages are rising.

7. _____ The cyclical component of the market's current wage is an adjustment for current market conditions when the economy is not at full employment.

8. _____ Wages are largely given in the short run, and this supports the Keynesian argument about rigid wages; however, in the long run, wages are completely flexible, and this supports the classical position.

9. _____ The rational businessperson will never raise employee wages during periods of high unemployment.

10. _____ One way in which employees adjust to changing levels of production by a firm is to vary the intensity of their work effort.

11. _____ When a worker is laid off, he is simply fired and has no chance of going back to work with the firm.

12. _____ The time required by a firm to change its work force is less with unskilled labor than with skilled craftsmen.

MULTIPLE CHOICE QUESTIONS

Circle the correct answer.

1. The aggregate supply schedule is essential to the adjustment processes in an economy because

   a. it links the demand for money with the labor markets
   b. it links the interest rate with the goods market
   c. it links the goods and labor markets
   d. it links macroeconomic demand with the price level

2. All of the following statements are correct except
   a. firms can easily hire and fire workers because there is very little cost involved in changing the labor force
   b. workers and firms often try to reach some implicit or explicit agreement about the terms of the work
   c. firms often think of their labor force as being reasonably attached to them
   d. workers usually expect to stay with an employer for some time when they take a job

3. If two workers produce 240 widgets in 6 hours, the productivity of labor is
   a. 40 widgets per hour
   b. 20 widgets per hour
   c. 120 widgets per worker
   d. 120 widgets per hour
   e. cannot be determined

4. All of the following could be considered a transitory adjustment except
   a. the firm cuts the workweek to 36 hours
   b. the firm hires more workers as demand for its product grows
   c. the firm uses 4 hours of overtime per worker per week
   d. the firm requires its workers to work half a day on Saturdays

5. In the short run, a firm responds to a reduction in the demand for its output by
   a. reducing output and cutting wages
   b. reducing output and raising wages
   c. leaving output unchanged and lowering wages
   d. lowering output, lowering the number of hours worked by labor, and leaving wages unchanged

6. In most markets, the prices are set by
   a. auctions   **d.** buyers
   b. sellers   **e.** b and d
   c. government

7. The model developed in Chapter 29 shows that the short-run effect of a decrease in the nominal money stock is to
   a. decrease short-run prices
   b. decrease short-run output
   c. decrease inflation
   d. all of the above

8. If the government pursued expansionary fiscal and monetary policies, we would expect
   a. high aggregate demand, low unemployment, and some inflationary pressures
   b. high aggregate demand, high unemployment, and inflationary pressures
   c. low aggregate demand, high unemployment, and low inflation
   d. low aggregate demand, low unemployment, and high inflation

AT THIS POINT YOU SHOULD BE ABLE TO . . .

1. Explain why both employers and workers prefer a stable work relationship.
2. Define the firm's total labor input and explain how this can be adjusted in both the short run and the long run if the firm wants to expand or contract the amount of labor used in production.
3. Distinguish between a layoff and a firing of labor and explain why the firm may prefer to lay off workers rather than fire them.
4. Explain why wages are not very flexible even though there may be unemployment in the short run but do change in the long run.
5. Identify the three components of the current period's wage and explain how each can affect the wage rate.
6. Define the short-run aggregate supply schedule, state how it is affected by the level of employment and the wage rate, and explain the two features which make it relevant to the long-run adjustment process.
7. Using diagrams, show and explain how the economy adjusts to a disturbance on the demand side; then show the adjustment process when there is a supply side disturbance.
8. Explain the meaning and effects of an adverse supply stock.
9. Explain why shifts in aggregate supply and demand are the underlying source of the business cycle; also, state why it is possible to have both unemployment and inflation at the same time.
10. Describe the role played by wages in both the short-run and the long-run adjustment process in an aggregate economy.

QUESTIONS FOR THOUGHT

1. Professors Fischer and Dornbusch make the statement that layoffs make sense for the workers. What exactly do they mean? During periods of high unemployment, what alternative do workers face that makes a layoff in their best interest? Explain.

2. During periods of high unemployment, why can't firms easily cut wages and reduce their costs of production? Is the labor market less susceptible to price (wage) cutting than the market for wheat? Explain.

3. The long-run effect of a change in the nominal money stock is a change in the price level and no change in potential output; however, in the short run, output does change along with prices. Explain how and why this happens. What roles do price and wage flexibility play in the adjustment process?

4. Depending on whether the macroeconomic demand schedule or the aggregate supply schedule shifts, the results are not the same. What are the different effects on output, prices, and the rate of inflation?

5. What is meant by an adverse shock? How does such a shock disturb aggregate equilibrium? Explain.

6. How does the model presented in Chapter 29 differ from the classical model developed in Chapter 28? Are there any similarities between the two models? Does the Keynesian model developed earlier play any role in the model developed here? Explain.

30

Unemployment

In the previous three chapters, you learned the relationship between the level of aggregate demand, aggregate supply, income, and employment. You saw how changes in aggregate demand or supply changed the level of output and employment. Chapter 30 examines the problem of unemployment from a descriptive standpoint rather than from the standpoint of the macroeconomic models presented earlier. Although these models provide the theoretical basis for analyzing unemployment, in Chapter 30 you will learn who is unemployed, the different types of unemployment, and how unemployment is defined and measured. You will also learn that unemployment imposes both an economic and a social cost.

As you read Chapter 30, pay particular attention to how unemployment is defined and how the government obtains unemployment data. Be sure that you understand why employment and unemployment can be viewed as flows of people into and out of both jobs and the labor force. Also, you will want to know why the effect of the duration of unemployment on the unemployed is an important consideration when policies are designed to reduce the level of jobless workers. Finally, as you study the distribution of unemployment, ask yourself why certain groups are unemployed more than others and whether the economy can realistically reduce unemployment so that no one group is hurt more than others.

Chapter 30 begins with a discussion of Okun's law. This law establishes a numerical relationship between the rate of real GNP growth and reductions in the level of unemployment. Okun's law, however, generally applies only to cyclical unemployment. There is some natural rate of unemployment in the economy which represents the full-employment level of unemployment. This natural rate changes as the composition of the labor force changes. Although the natural rate is only an estimate, it is difficult to reduce unemployment below the natural rate.

Individuals move in and out of jobs and in and out of the labor force. If an individual cannot find a job after searching a long time or believes that no job exists for him and drops out of the labor force, he is called a discouraged worker. Discouraged workers are not counted as unemployed because they are not currently seeking employment; hence, they are not included in the labor force. When unemployment is measured, it includes only those workers who did not work during the past week but actually looked for a job during the previous 4 weeks.

Unemployment changes over the business cycle. During periods of recession, unemployment increases as aggregate demand falls. Workers who lose their jobs are entitled to unemployment benefits. These benefits last for a given length of time and are given to the workers for the purpose of reducing the economic hardships caused by unemployment.

All groups are affected by unemployment; however, some are hit harder than others. The highest unemployment rates are for black teenagers, while white males 20 years old or older have the lowest rates. All teenagers have higher unemployment rates than other workers. One reason offered for high unemployment among teens is that without marketable skills, members of this group change jobs frequently, and so employers often do not make good jobs available to them. Another reason is the minimum wage. Employers would be willing to hire more unskilled workers at lower real wages, but they do not make as many job offers at higher wage rates. As long as the minimum wage is above the equilibrium real wage, unemployment is higher than it would be otherwise.

CHAPTER OUTLINE

1. An accurate picture of unemployment in an industrialized economy describes the following: who the unemployed are, how they become unemployed, how long they remain unemployed, and exactly how unemployment is defined and measured. The nature of unemployment determines the types of policies used to improve employment conditions.
    a. The rate of unemployment changes over the business cycle. Okun's law shows the relationship between economic activity and unem-

ployment. The law states that if GNP grows 3 percent annually, there is no change in the unemployment rate. When the growth rate of real GNP changes by 2 percentage points annually, the unemployment rate changes in the opposite direction by 1 percentage point. Okun's law shows how much the economy must grow just to keep the unemployment rate constant and how the unemployment rate is affected when the GNP growth rate differs from 3 percent per year.

  b. Even when an economy is said to be at full employment, some unemployment exists. This is the natural rate of unemployment. There is always some unemployment because when people change jobs or look for a first job, there often is some time difference between when one job is left and another is begun. The natural rate of unemployment is an estimate, and most economists think that it has risen since the 1960s.

2. An individual is considered unemployed if he did not work during the previous week but looked for work during the previous 4 weeks. An individual is not considered in the labor force if he stops looking for work, and so he is not counted as unemployed.

  a. The labor force consists of those individuals who are working or are currently unemployed but looking for work. People become unemployed because they permanently lose a job, are temporarily laid off, or quit a job. Also, if an individual enters the labor force but does not have a job, he is counted as being unemployed. Individuals are continuously entering and leaving the ranks of the unemployed.

  b. Individuals leave unemployment because they either find work or drop out of the labor force. An individual who drops out of the labor force because he believes that no job exists for him is called a discouraged worker. In any one period, about the same number of people drop out of the labor force as find jobs; however, individuals usually do not remain out of the labor force for very long periods.

  c. The unemployment rate increases during recessions and falls during periods of recovery and prosperity. If more people flow into unemployment than flow out, the unemployment rate increases. If more people find jobs or leave the labor force than flow into unemployment, the unemployment rate falls. Unemployment rates differ between different cities and regions of the country.

3. The duration of unemployment is the length of time a worker is unemployed. In the United States, most unemployment is accounted for by some people being unemployed for a long period rather than by a lot of people being unemployed for a short period.

  a. When an individual loses a job, he is entitled to collect unemployment insurance (benefits). These benefits are payable to workers who have been fired or laid off as long as they continue to look for a job. If a worker receives unemployment benefits, the financial hardships of not having a job are reduced; however, these benefits last only about 6 months. Thus, if unemployment is long-term, the unemployed will suffer because the benefits eventually run out. The amount and length of unemployment benefits vary from state to state and from individual to individual. When recessions are severe, the federal government usually lengthens the number of weeks an individual can receive benefits. One problem with increasing the amount of unemployment benefits so that workers have less of a financial burden is that the incentive to find a job is reduced as the benefits increase.

4. Unemployment in the United States is distributed unevenly by age, race, sex, and occupation. The group exhibiting the lowest unemployment rate in December 1981 was white males 20 years old or older. The group with the highest unemployment rate in the same period was black teenagers. In general, teenagers have the highest unemployment rate, followed by black males and females. Also, white-collar workers generally have a lower unemployment rate than blue-collar workers. One possible explanation for these unemployment patterns is that employers often consider teenagers as temporary members of the labor force, and so firms don't make them good job offers. The high unemployment rates among blacks are partially explained by the fact that they hold a larger percentage of blue-collar jobs than whites. Blue-collar jobs are more susceptible to the business cycle than white-collar jobs.

5. The natural rate of unemployment is often called the full-employment unemployment rate and is estimated to be between 5 and 6 percent. This natural unemployment is based on the observation that a time difference exists between the time when a person leaves one job and the time when he starts a new one. Also, there is a time difference between when a person enters the labor force to find a job and when he actually finds one. The natural rate of unemployment reflects the process of matching workers to jobs, and so it indicates an efficient operation of the labor market.

6. The unemployment associated with a recession is called cyclical unemployment. During a recession,

real GNP falls and cyclical unemployment rises. This unemployment can be considered a waste (assuming that people prefer to work and that there has been no major change in the economy) because the unemployed could be working and producing an output.
  a. Even though some unemployment serves a useful purpose by promoting a more efficient job search and a better matching of workers to jobs, some groups of the unemployed are hit especially hard.
  b. Most research shows that the minimum wage actually increases unemployment. This happens because some workers who could find jobs at lower wages (teenagers, for example) are not employable at the minimum wage. Thus, the minimum wage has the unintended effect of creating a surplus of workers.
  c. The natural rate of unemployment has been increasing over time primarily because of the changing composition of the labor force.
7. Unemployment rates differ significantly among nations. The reasons for the international differences are diverse and range from the stability of labor demand, the cost of firing workers, and the unemployment benefits paid to workers to the institutional structure of the country. Nevertheless, when a country experiences a fall in aggregate demand and the demand for labor, its unemployment rate rises.

IMPORTANT TERMS AND THEIR MEANING

Match the following terms with the correct definition or phrase.

1. ____ A payment by state government made to people who have lost their jobs; the size of the payment varies from state to state, and it lasts some specific period of time

   a. Recalls

2. ____ Established by the federal government as the least a worker can be paid for performing most jobs; applies to nonsupervisory employees and covers about 75 percent of the labor force

   b. Duration of unemployment

3. ____ Opening jobs back up to workers who were previously laid off

   c. Layoff

4. ____ Unemployed workers who drop out of the labor force because they believe that no jobs exist for them

   d. Natural rate of unemployment

5. ____ The length of time a person is unemployed

   e. Okun's law

6. ____ A worker did not work in the previous week but looked for work during the past 4 weeks

   f. Unemployment benefits

7. ____ States that annual GNP growth of 3 percent keeps the unemployment rate constant; the unemployment rate falls 1 percentage point for every 2 percentage points of extra GNP growth above 3 percent.

   g. Quits

8. ____ A temporary separation of the worker from the firm

   h. Minimum wage

9. ____ Voluntary separation from a job and becoming unemployed

   i. Discouraged workers

10. ____ The unemployment rate that corresponds to full employment in the economy

    j. Unemployed worker

EXERCISES

1. Listed in Table 30-1 are several situations in which an individual may or may not be working. You are to identify first whether the individual is in the labor force. If the individual is in the labor force, identify whether he is employed or unemployed. Finally, if the individual is unemployed, identify whether it is cyclical or transitory unemployment by placing an X where appropriate. Transitory unemployment represents the natural rate of employment.

2. Table 30-2 presents labor force, employment, and unemployment data for January, February, March, and April 1982. The data are in thousands of persons and are taken from the *Federal Reserve Bulletin*, vol. 68, May 1982.
   a. Complete Table 30-2 by supplying the missing statistics.
   b. During the first 4 months of 1982, the level of employment first (increased/decreased) _____ and then (increased/decreased) _____, while the level of unemployment (increased/decreased) _____ for each month.
   c. The labor force (increased/decreased) _____ each month, while the percentage of the population not in the labor force (rose/fell) _____. This indicates that there was a net flow (into/out of) _____ the labor force

TABLE 30-1

SITUATION	IN LABOR FORCE (YES OR NO)	UNEMPLOYED (YES OR NO)	CYCLICAL UNEMPLOYMENT	TRANSITORY UNEMPLOYMENT
a. An autoworker is laid off because the sales of new cars fall				
b. A housewife begins a job search in order to supplement the family income				
c. A construction worker fired when the company he worked for went bankrupt looks for a new job for 6 months and then gives up				
d. A college English professor with a Ph.D. is laid off and gets a job as a cook at Hamburger City				
e. The government cancels the CETA program, and so some program administrators are fired				
f. A steelworker loses his job because the demand for domestic steel falls				
g. In May, a high school junior finds a job which begins in June				
h. A househusband bakes and sells cakes to friends in his spare time				

and (could/could not) _____ explain some of the rising unemployment.

    d. If the full-employment rate of unemployment is 6 percent, the economy (was/was not) _____ at full employment because the natural rate of unemployment was (greater than/less than) _____ the actual rate by at least _____ percent.

3. Table 30-3 presents hypothetical demand, supply, and wage data for the labor market.

    a. In this hypothetical labor market, the equilibrium real wage is _____, and the market clears with _____ people working.

    b. If the market is completely free of any government intervention or regulation, everyone who wants to work at the equilibrium wage rate (does/does not) _____ have a job. Full employment (is/is not) _____ established at the equilibrium wage.

TABLE 30-3

REAL WAGE (per unit of labor)	LABOR DEMAND (number of workers)	LABOR SUPPLY (number of workers)
1	3600	2800
2	3500	2900
3	3400	3000
4	3300	3100
5	3200	3200
6	3100	3300
7	3000	3400
8	2900	3500
9	2800	3600

    c. If the government imposes a minimum real wage of 7 per unit of labor, the quantity of labor demanded (rises/falls) _____ to _____ units of labor, while the quantity supplied (rises/falls) _____ to _____ units of labor.

    d. The minimum wage (does/does not) _____ generate a disequilibrium in the labor market, and the level of unemployment increases

TABLE 30-2

	1982			
CATEGORY	JANUARY	FEBRUARY	MARCH	APRIL
Population 16 years old or older	173,494	173,657	173,842	174,019
Labor force (including military)	111,038	111,333	111,521	111,823
Civilian labor force	108,879	109,165	109,346	109,648
Employment	99,581		99,493	
Unemployment of civilian labor force	_____	9,575	_____	10,307
Unemployment rate (percentage of civilian labor force)	_____%	_____%	_____%	_____%
Not in labor force	62,456	62,324	62,321	62,196
Percentage not in labor force (including military)	_____%	_____%	_____%	_____%

from _____ to _____ workers.

e. The level of employment in this economy has (increased/decreased) _____, and some workers are made worse off; however the 3000 workers who would have worked for _____ per unit of labor now get 7, and so they are better off.

FILL-IN QUESTIONS

1. Okun's law describes how much growth in _____ is needed just to keep the unemployment rate from changing, and it implies that the unemployment rates (are/are not) _____ a result of cumulative high or low economic growth.

2. Even when the economy is working at full production and full employment, there (is/is not) _____ some unemployment, and so it (does/does not) _____ make sense to claim that the unemployment rate can be reduced to zero.

3. For a person to be classified as unemployed, that individual must not have worked during the previous _____ but must have looked for work during the past _____.

4. The labor force is made up of individuals who are either _____ or _____, and its composition (does/does not) _____ change frequently.

5. People who drop out of the labor market because they believe that no jobs exist for them are called _____ workers and (are/are not) _____ included in the unemployment statistics.

6. The length of time a person is unemployed is called the _____ of unemployment.

7. Unemployment benefits usually last about _____ months, (vary/are the same) _____ from state to state, and (are/are not) _____ taxable.

8. The group usually experiencing the highest unemployment rate in the United States is _____, while the lowest rates are for _____ males, 20 years old or older.

9. The unemployment usually associated with recessions is called _____ unemployment, and this type (is/is not) _____ generally considered a waste of resources.

10. Most evidence shows that the minimum wage (does/does not) _____ increase unemployment among workers who can find jobs at (higher/lower) _____ wages.

TRUE-FALSE QUESTIONS

1. _____ In recent years, the minimum wage has been slightly greater than the average paid in manufacturing.

2. _____ One reason why the natural rate of unemployment has been increasing since the 1960s is that the composition of the labor force has been changing.

3. _____ In 1973, Germany had one of the highest unemployment rates of the industrialized countries.

4. _____ One reason why the unemployment rate for teenagers is so high is that a large proportion of them frequently enter and reenter the labor force.

5. _____ Even though unemployment increases during recessions, there may be some positive benefits to society as the economy adjusts to any structural changes in production and employment.

6. _____ When estimating the natural rate of unemployment, it is necessary to use some benchmark period when the economy had full employment and stable prices.

7. _____ If a person who has held a job for a long time becomes unemployed, he is likely to be unemployed for only a short time.

8. _____ The only loss suffered by the unemployed is the economic loss resulting from the difference between what they were making while employed and their unemployment benefits.

9. _____ In 1975, over half of all unemployment was accounted for by people who had been unemployed at least half the year.

10. _____ Although unemployment varies from one region of the country to another, it is generally the same for cities having approximately the same population.

11. _____ More people leave the labor force than find jobs.

12. _____ If a person loses his job and can't find new employment within 3 weeks, he is considered to have dropped out of the labor force.

13. _____ Unemployment statistics in the United States are obtained primarily from a sample survey of households.

14. _____ If the unemployment rate in an economy equals its natural rate, full employment exists.

15. _____ Okun's law establishes a numerical relationship between the rate of growth of GNP in an economy and the rate of change in unemployment.

MULTIPLE CHOICE QUESTIONS

Circle the correct answer.

1. If the unemployment rate is 10 percent and the natural rate is 6 percent, real GNP in the economy must grow at what annual rate for the economy to be at full employment in 2 years?
   a. 5 percent   **d.** 9 percent
   b. 4 percent   **e.** none of the above
   c. 7 percent

2. All of the following statements are correct about the natural role of unemployment except
   a. the natural rate of unemployment includes those individuals who have dropped out of the labor force but not those who are cyclically unemployed
   b. the natural rate of unemployment has been rising over the past two decades
   c. there is a range of natural rates because no one knows for sure exactly what the rate is
   d. currently, the natural rate of unemployment is between 5 and 6 percent

3. Which of the following statements is correct?
   a. a person is considered unemployed if he did not work during the previous week or looked for a job during the previous 4 weeks
   b. a person currently not working is not considered unemployed if he is waiting to take a job within the next 30 days
   c. if a person did not work the previous week because of a severe snowstorm, he is considered temporarily unemployed
   d. when an unemployed person gives up the job search, he is no longer counted as being unemployed

4. When people enter unemployment from out of the labor force, there is a tendency for the unemployment rate to
   a. fall   **c.** remain constant
   b. rise   **d.** none of the above

5. The rate of unemployment is calculated as
   a. number of unemployed workers divided by number of employed workers
   b. number of workers in the labor force divided by number of unemployed
   c. number of unemployed divided by number of workers in the labor force
   d. number of employed workers divided by number of unemployed workers

6. Unemployment benefits
   a. are designed to ease the economic hardship for those who have lost their jobs
   b. usually last for a definite period
   c. are not the same in all states
   d. are not paid to those who have dropped out of the labor force
   e. all of the above

7. In December 1981, the unemployment rate among blue-collar workers was
   a. 6.4 percent   **c.** 7.0 percent
   b. 4.5 percent   **d.** 12.7 percent

8. Increased participation in the labor force by women has
   a. increased the natural rate of unemployment
   b. caused the percentage of the population in the labor force to fall
   c. decreased the natural rate of unemployment
   d. had no effect on the natural rate of unemployment

9. Which of the following is not covered by the minimum wage law?
   a. an interstate truck driver
   b. a licensed practical nurse in a hospital
   c. the foreman in a drapery-manufacturing plant
   d. a subway operator in New York City

AT THIS POINT YOU SHOULD BE ABLE TO . . .

1. Define unemployment and full employment and explain when a person is classified as unemployed.

2. State Okun's law and, when given the data, compute the growth rates of real GNP required to attain full employment.

3. Define the natural rate of unemployment, explain why it is sometimes called full-employment unemployment, list three points about the estimation of the natural rate, and state how it is affected by the composition of the labor force.

4. Describe three ways in which a person can leave employment and become unemployed, and explain why the labor market activities can be described as flows.

5. Identify the discouraged worker, state why he is not counted as unemployed, and explain how the unemployment rate changes as people enter and leave the labor force.

6. Define the duration of unemployment, explain why the duration is an important concept, describe the role of unemployment benefits in easing the economic hardships of unemployment, and explain what noneconomic costs may be involved in unemployment.

7. Describe the distribution of unemployment by age, sex, race, and occupation.

8. Present the argument and show graphically how the minimum wage can increase the level of unemployment.

9. Explain the effect of teenage unemployment on the natural rate of unemployment.

10. List four factors which influence the unemployment rate in different countries.

QUESTIONS FOR THOUGHT

1. Okun's law shows a numerical relationship of 2:1 between increased growth and reduced unemployment. What is the basis of this law? Why do you think it takes a 2 percent increase in real GNP just to get unemployment down by 1 percent? Explain.

2. Why will there always be some people unemployed? Realistically, how far do you think our economy should try to reduce unemployment? What do you think would happen if we tried to go below this rate? Explain.

3. In terms of unemployment benefits, why is the duration of unemployment important? Can unemployment benefits affect an individual's willingness to work? Explain.

4. Professors Fischer and Dornbusch talk about the "typical patterns of job holding in the United States" when describing the distribution of unemployment. What do you think they mean? What is the pattern, and how does it affect the distribution of unemployment?

5. Does the natural rate of unemployment reflect the efficient matching of people and jobs in the labor market? Explain.

6. Should we have a goal of reducing unemployment? Why is some unemployment considered a waste while some is not?

31 The Inflation Problem

Chapter 31 discusses one of the more aggravating problems faced by the U.S. economy over the last 30 years: persistent inflation. The average price level in the United States has increased continually since 1955. Unless consumers' nominal incomes rise by at least the same rate as the price level, real income falls. This means that households' claim on the economy's real output declines.

Price stability is one of the primary goals of the U.S. economic system, but it seems to elude policymakers. From previous chapters, you have learned the basic analytical tools of aggregate demand, aggregate supply, fiscal policy, and monetary policy. You saw how a short-run aggregate disequilibrium affects the level of prices. The application of fiscal and monetary policies designed to change aggregate demand or aggregate supply seems ineffective in reducing inflation. Chapter 31 offers some suggestions about why these policies have been ineffective. Inflation may be caused not only by excess aggregate demand, increased production costs, and structural factors which prevent wages and prices from falling; it can also be caused by expectations. If workers and firms build expectations of inflation into the decision-making process, prices become even more difficult to control. The lack of a credible government economic policy affects expectations and may even promote price increases. As you read Chapter 31, remember that inflation has many causes and that everyone is affected by it in some way.

The structure of Chapter 31 is straightforward. Professors Fischer and Dornbusch state in the introduction that they want to discover some of the causes of persistent inflation, its costs (or benefits), and how it can be controlled. They begin with an examination of price behavior since 1960. During the 1960s, many economists and policymakers felt that a trade-off existed between the rate of unemployment and the rate of inflation. This relationship became known as the Phillips curve. Expansionary monetary and fiscal policies were pursued in an attempt to maintain full employment, promote economic growth, and incur only slight increases in prices. The Phillips curve seemed to provide many combinations of inflation and unemployment from which policymakers could choose.

Unfortunately, during the 1960s, inflationary pressure began to build in the economy. As prices continued to rise into the 1970s, a series of supply shocks jolted the system, and inflation increased rapidly. During the 1970s and early 1980s, periods of stagflation were experienced, with high prices and a stagnant economy. Monetary and fiscal policy flip-flopped from promoting full employment to fighting inflation. The Phillips curve relationship was questioned when policymakers realized that it was easier to move up the curve (and reduce unemployment) than down it. Both people and institutions began to regard inflation as normal, and they adjusted their expectations and behavior in the market to reflect this condition. In late 1982, the rate of inflation was moderating, but unemployment was at its highest level since the Great Depression.

Real costs are incurred when prices rise. Depending on how much inflation is expected and the degree to which the economy has adapted to the inflationary process, the costs of a rising price level vary. The costs range from the time and expense involved in personal money management and changing the shelf price of goods when inflation is expected and the adjustment is complete to the redistribution of wealth that takes place when adjustment is incomplete. Unanticipated inflation and incomplete institutional adjustment allow rising prices to have an adverse effect on the financial system, the tax structure, and the taxation of capital.

There are three approaches to the problem of inflation. The first approach is to get rid of it. The second involves the introduction of changes that make it difficult for inflation to begin again. The last approach is simply to learn to live with rising prices. Each of these approaches has its weaknesses, leaving the fundamental problem unsolved.

As you read Chapter 31, pay particular attention to the effect of government policies in the 1960s, for it was during that period that today's inflation began. Be sure that you know the effects and costs of both expected and unexpected inflation and that you can explain how incomplete institutional adjustment also imposes a cost as prices rise.

THE INFLATION PROBLEM

CHAPTER OUTLINE

1. The current inflation in the United States began during the 1960s. Attempts to slow inflation during the past 20 years slowed the rate of growth in prices but increased the level of unemployment. In general, however, the United States has experienced both rising prices and higher unemployment since 1961.

   a. The Phillips curve shows a negative relationship between the inflation rate and the unemployment rate; it suggests that a trade-off exists between inflation and unemployment. During the 1960s, the Phillips curve was the basis for much of the government's economic policy. When unemployment was high, policymakers advocated an increase in aggregate demand which caused output to rise and unemployment to fall. With falling unemployment, pressures on wages and prices led to increases in the rate of inflation.

   b. The Nixon administration changed the emphasis of economic policy from reducing unemployment to reducing inflation. As a result of restrictive monetary and fiscal policies designed to lower aggregate demand and reduce prices, unemployment rose. Prices, however, didn't fall. The economy suffered from stagflation (inflation accompanied by a slowing of economic activity) from 1969 to 1971. Restrictive policies increased unemployment but had essentially no effect on prices because people, especially workers, changed their expectations of inflation. They expected inflation to continue, and so workers negotiated wage increases which were based on the expected rate of inflation and then were fixed by union contract. Thus, higher wages continued to be paid even as output and employment fell. Prices continued to rise, and the continued inflation reinforced workers' expectations about the future. Even though government policy may attempt to lower inflation, if individuals expect the price behavior of the past to continue in the future, they are less likely to accept lower wages now. Stagflation showed that the inflation-unemployment trade-off was not as straightforward as the Phillips curve would suggest.

   c. During the period 1973-1975, a series of supply shocks (increases in the world prices of oil, food, and raw materials) caused the inflation rate to increase sharply again. As prices rose, monetary and fiscal policies did not respond to compensate for the increased inflation, and so real balances fell. As interest rates increased, aggregate demand fell, and the economy again suffered stagflation.

   d. By 1976, inflation had slowed but unemployment had increased. Government policy again was directed toward reducing unemployment. By 1979, a rising price level caused the government to follow more restrictive policies; however, inflation didn't fall significantly. During 1982, unemployment rates were the highest they had been in decades, and the inflation rate finally began to fall. One explanation offered by many economists for unemployment and inflation is that government lacks credibility in its economic policy. Recent history shows that goverment policies often change, and so it is difficult to judge how serious the government is about reducing inflation, especially since it is committed to reducing high levels of unemployment.

   e. It has been estimated that it would take 20 years, many with unemployment at or above 10 percent, to bring the U.S. inflation rate down to 0 percent.

   f. The estimates of the length of time and the unemployment costs necessary to reduce inflation are not certain. If a credible antiinflationary policy were pursued continuously, wages and prices (because of expectations) would eventually begin to fall rapidly.

2. Most industrialized countries have experienced high rates of inflation since 1970. Differences in labor force composition, collective bargaining techniques, government policies, and general attitudes toward inflation and unemployment can affect a country's inflation experience.

3. Most people dislike rising prices because rising prices lower their purchasing power, but inflation also imposes other costs on people.

   a. People may have an illusion about inflation if they look only at how it affects spending. When prices are rising, workers' wages and nominal income usually rise also. Increases in nominal income serve as a compensating adjustment to inflation, and so people should compare changes in both their income and spending to see whether they are better or worse off.

   b. If people fully expect the actual rate of inflation and all institutions adapt fully to that rate, the costs and effects of inflation are reduced.

   c. In an economy in which inflation is fully expected and there is complete institutional and government adjustment, changes in nominal wages (income) and nominal interest rates occur in such a manner that real wages and interest rates are unaffected. The tax system changes so that real tax payments remain the same, and the capital market adjusts through the interest rate so that inflation has no effect on the decision to hold wealth in various types of assets. Capital gains are not taxed if they arise solely because of inflation.

  (1) Perfect adaptation of interest rates means that the inflation adjustment is incorporated into the nominal interest rate. This nominal rate is the interest rate expressed in terms of the money payments made on a loan, while the real interest rate is the return or cost of a loan expressed in terms of goods or services. When the interest rates adjust completely to inflation, the real interest rate equals the nominal rate minus the inflation adjustment component. Even when the economy adjusts completely to inflation, there are still some costs.
  (2) As inflation increases, the cost of holding currency increases, and so people hold less. The cost of holding currency is the interest rate. Because people hold less currency, they must go to the bank more often, which costs them time. In turn, the bank must hire more workers to handle the extra business, which increases the bank's labor cost. These costs are called the shoe-leather costs of inflation.
  (3) The menu costs of inflation describe the costs incurred by firms as a result of the necessity of frequent changes in the prices of the goods they sell. During inflationary periods, prices of goods have to be changed often, and so these menu costs can be substantial for some firms.
d. When there is a lag in the adaptation of institutions to expected inflation, substantial costs arise.
  (1) If interest rates and capital markets do not adjust fully as prices rise, individuals experience a decline in the real value of some of their assets, and so the shoe-leather costs go up as people spend time managing their money. As the adjustments to expected inflation continue, new institutions develop so that people can earn higher interest rates to compensate for rising prices.
  (2) The tax system adjusts very slowly to expected inflation. This also imposes a cost on people. As prices rise, nominal income usually goes up, pushing people into higher income tax brackets. Higher inflation and nominal income forces individuals to pay higher income taxes even though their real income has not changed. This is called bracket creep.
  (3) There are two ways to remove the effects of bracket creep. The tax rate schedules can be readjusted periodically, or the tax rates can be indexed to inflation so that taxes are paid on the value of real income.
  (4) Bracket creep allows the government to increase its share of national income without congressional approval.
  (5) Taxes cause a distortion in the capital market if capital is taxed at its inflated value when the market has not adjusted completely to inflation. This distortion may cause the after-tax real rate of interest to be negative.
e. When inflation is unanticipated, one of the resulting costs is a redistribution of income and wealth among different sectors of the economy.
  (1) An unexpected increase in the price level causes a gain for those who borrow money and a loss for lenders, because the real value of payments declines. When prices fall, borrowers lose and lenders gain. The gains and losses incurred by borrowers and lenders basically cancel out as prices rise; however, income is redistributed. Inflation also causes a redistribution of wealth from the private sector to the public sector, because a rising price level reduces the real value of the government's debt held by private citizens. Holders of high-powered money also lose when the inflation rate increases, because the real value of currency and bank reserves falls.
  (2) Because they have relatively fewer debts and live off past savings or pensions, the elderly are made poor in real terms when prices rise. The young have more debts than any other age group and gain from unexpected inflation.
  (3) Little evidence exists to support the proposition that inflation redistributes income from the poor to the rich.
  (4) Evidence indicates that higher inflation increases uncertainty about future inflation rates so that planning for the future becomes more difficult. This may also be one of the costs of inflation.
f. In most countries, expectations of inflation are incorrect or the adjustment process is incomplete, and so their economies bear all of the costs of inflation.

4. Three methods of dealing with inflation are to try to get rid of it, change the economy so that it cannot begin easily, or learn to live with it.
   a. Restrictive monetary and fiscal policies designed to get rid of inflation by reducing aggregate demand may increase the level of unemployment significantly. Two approaches which may be used to assist monetary and fiscal actions in both reducing inflation and preventing it from starting again are incomes policies and tax-based incomes policies.
      (1) An income policy is a direct attempt to influence wages and other income. The justification for using an incomes policy is that wages are slow to respond to changes in aggregate demand, which reduces the possibility of a rapid slowdown of inflation. Wage and price controls are laws passed by the government which attempt to regulate the wages and prices that firms are allowed to pay and charge. Except during wars, incomes policies have not been successful. Incomes policies have been used as a substitute for (not a complement to) macroeconomic policies that would remove the source of inflationary pressures. Wage and price controls are almost impossible to administer effectively.
      (2) Tax-based incomes policies (TIPs) are designed to reward or penalize firms and workers through the tax system according to the increase in prices or wages they receive. Taxes would be used to penalize firms and workers if they increased prices or wages above a certain percentage. If their increases stayed below the established percentage, tax rates would not rise. TIPs have not yet been used in the United States.
   b. In the long run, inflation can be controlled better if the money supply is permitted to grow only as rapidly as the rate of economic growth.
      (1) Controlling the money supply means controlling the Fed, and so Congress may have to set a limit to the growth of the money supply or establish a monetary rule within which the Fed will operate. As long as the Fed controls the relevant money supply and lets it grow at some low rate, the possibility of serious future inflation is reduced.
      (2) A few economists argue that the way to prevent inflation is to return to the gold standard. If gold backed the money supply and people could get gold for their dollars, the Fed would be limited in the amount of money it could create because the supply of gold is limited. Thus, with a restricted money supply, inflation would be reduced.
   c. If we must live with inflation, the economy's institutions must adapt. Some adjustments are already under way. The federal personal tax rates, for instance, will be indexed by 1985 so that tax payments are automatically adjusted for the effects of inflation. Other adjustments include the indexation of some labor contracts, private pensions, and Social Security.
      (1) Indexation is not a solution to inflation; it only makes it a bit easier for some people. Indexation is difficult to implement because of the time lags involved in the adjustment process. If people simply accept inflation and the adjustments that the economy makes as a fact of life, prices will continue to rise, and this could lead to very high future inflation.

IMPORTANT TERMS AND THEIR MEANING

Match the following terms with the correct definition or phrase.

1. ____ Occurs when rising prices put people into higher tax brackets even though their real income has not changed

2. ____ Laws which attempt to limit and regulate the wages and prices that firms are allowed to pay and charge

3. ____ Having gold serve as the basis of the money supply; obligates the Fed to buy and sell at a price fixed in dollars

4. ____ The costs incurred as people try to reduce their holdings of dollars during periods of inflation; a deadweight cost

5. ____ A period of increasing prices combined with a recession or stagnation of economic activity

6. ____ A system in which firms are rewarded or penalized through the tax system in accordance with increasing prices or wages

a. Gold standard
b. Indexation
c. Credibility
d. Phillips curve
e. Unexpected inflation
f. Institutional adaptation to inflation

7. ____ The automatic adjustment of payments for the effects of inflation

8. ____ The complete adjustment of all institutions, both public and private, to the effects of inflation; the costs of rising prices are reduced greatly

9. ____ The cost of changing prices frequently during inflationary periods; a deadweight cost

10. ____ A negative relationship between the inflation rate and the unemployment rate; the higher the rate of inflation, the lower the level of unemployment

11. ____ Argues that the Fed should promote a constant growth rate of the money supply which would be low enough to avoid inflation

12. ____ The believability of government policy; policies would be more effective if the public didn't believe that government goals would be changed frequently

13. ____ People believe that inflation will be at one rate, but it turns out to be at another

14. ____ The real interest rate; the nominal interest rate minus the rate of inflation

15. ____ Government policies which are designed to lower unemployment but which also increase the inflation rate

g. Stagflation

h. Monetary rules

i. Shoe-leather costs

j. Accommodation

k. Bracket creep

l. Menu costs

m. Inflation-adjusted interest rate

n. Wage and price controls

o. Tax-based incomes policy

FIGURE 31-1

goal of the economy, (more and more/less and less) _____ unemployment must be accepted. (2) When prices are stable, the unemployment rate is _____ percent. An attempt to reduce unemployment below this level causes prices to (increase/decrease) _____. This level of unemployment might be called the (cyclical/natural) _____ rate of unemployment. (3) If the economy accepts an unemployment rate of 7.5 percent, the rate of inflation is (positive/negative) _____, which means that prices are (rising/falling) _____.

  b. Suppose the Phillips curve shifts to curve II. Compared with curve I, there is a (higher/lower) _____ rate of inflation associated with each level of unemployment. (1) A restrictive monetary and fiscal policy designed to keep the rate of inflation at 2 percent per year causes unemployment to (increase/decrease) _____ from _____ percent to _____ percent, while if unemployment is held constant at 4½ percent, the rate of inflation (increases/decreases) _____ to _____ percent. (2) On the new Phillips curve, stable prices occur at an unemployment rate of _____ percent.

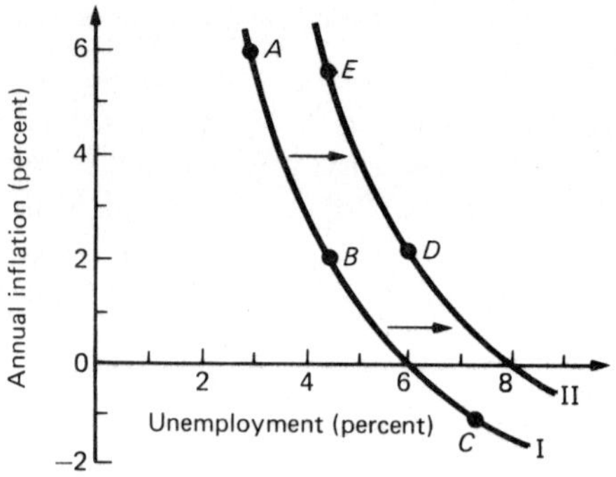

EXERCISES

1. Figure 31-1 shows a hypothetical Phillips curve for an economy. This Phillips curve shows the short-run trade-off between inflation and unemployment.
  a. According to Phillips curve I, the economy will have _____ percent inflation if it accepts an unemployment rate of 3 percent. This is shown by point _____ on the curve. (1) The trade-off between inflation and unemployment (is/is not) _____ constant. If less inflation is the

2. Suppose you are an investment analyst and one of your clients has $10,000 to invest in bonds for 1 year. It is your responsibility to make an analysis of the alternatives. There are two alternatives available. Alternative A is a high-quality corporate bond which pays 13 percent per year. The income from this bond is taxable at the rate of 30 percent. The other alternative is a municipal bond which pays 9.25 percent per year. The income from the municipal bond is tax-exempt. The two possible inflation rates are 12 percent and 4 percent.
  a. To help make your evaluation, complete Table 31-1.

THE INFLATION PROBLEM

TABLE 31-1

INVESTMENT ALTERNATIVE	NOMINAL INTEREST RATE	EXPECTED INFLATION RATE		PRETAX REAL INTEREST RATE WHEN INFLATION IS		TAX RATE	AFTER-TAX NOMINAL INTEREST RATE WHEN INFLATION IS		AFTER-TAX REAL INTEREST RATE WHEN INFLATION IS	
				12%	4%		12%	4%	12%	4%
A	13%	12%	4%	___	___	30%	___	___	___	___
B	9.25%	12%	4%	___	___	0%	___	___	___	___

b. Table 31-2 is designed to show the expected dollar return or loss from each $10,000 investment alternative. Complete Table 31-2 by estimating the after-tax dollar return for the alternatives and entering your calculations in the appropriate cells. There is an extra column for stable prices. Estimate the after-tax real income earned on the investment when there is no inflation.

TABLE 31-2

ALTERNATIVE	INFLATION RATE		
	12%	4%	0%
A			
B			

c. The recommendation to your client should be to purchase bond alternative (A/B) _____ because losses are minimized or gains are maximized.

d. The effects of inflation (increase/decrease) _____ the real return on each alternative, and once the tax is considered, the return can be negative. A negative return means that the purchasing power of the initial dollar investment at the end of the period is (greater/less) _____ than it was when the investment was made.

FILL-IN QUESTIONS

1. During the early 1960s, the rate of inflation in the United States was (high/low) _____, and economists thought that a trade-off existed between inflation and _____.

2. The Phillips curve shows a (positive/negative) _____ relationship between unemployment and inflation; as prices rise, unemployment _____.

3. During periods of _____, the economy suffers from continued inflation and recession at the same time.

4. If people expect inflation to continue, prices (are/are not) _____ likely to fall rapidly even though aggregate demand declines.

5. The U.S. inflationary experience of the 1970s (has/has not) _____ been confined to this country.

6. People think that inflation is bad because their _____ power falls as prices rise; however, their nominal _____ usually increases too. To look only at the effect of rising prices on spending means that people suffer from an inflationary _____.

7. When expectations are correct and there is complete adjustment by the economy to inflation, (real/nominal) _____ incomes and (nominal/relative) _____ prices are constant, and tax payments are based on (real/nominal) _____ incomes.

8. During periods of inflation, the _____ interest rate is lower than the nominal rate.

9. Shoe-leather costs arise because inflation makes it more expensive to hold _____, while the costs incurred when frequently changing the shelf price of goods when there is inflation are called _____.

10. Inflation causes bracket creep since rising prices usually are accompanied by (rising/falling) _____ incomes, and so people have to pay (more/less) _____ taxes on this income even though their (real/nominal) _____ income may actually fall.

11. When there is inflation, an individual owing money (gains/loses) _____ because the (nominal/real) _____ value of the payment

(rises/falls) _____, but a person who is owed money (gains/loses) _____.

12. _____ and _____ controls represent a type of _____ policy in which the government directly controls what firms are allowed to pay and charge.

13. Some economists argue that the United States should not develop a policy of indexation of payments because such a policy is (easy/difficult) _____ to implement, which means that the inflation problem probably (will/will not) _____ be solved.

TRUE-FALSE QUESTIONS

1. _____ Social Security payments currently are indexed to the inflation rate, and so increases in the cost of living do not reduce the elderly's purchasing power by as much as it otherwise would be reduced.

2. _____ Most economists believe that we should simply index all payments and forget about trying to reduce inflation.

3. _____ If a monetary rule were imposed by Congress which required the Fed to keep a tight control on the money supply so that it grew very slowly, it is possible that people might begin using other assets as money.

4. _____ If the money supply were allowed to grow rapidly, inflation would decline because people would have a larger stock of real balances.

5. _____ An example of a tax-based incomes policy is wage and price controls.

6. _____ Most economists agree that wage and price controls are more successful during peacetime than during wartime.

7. _____ In most industrialized economies, it is extremely difficult to predict the rate of inflation from one year to the next.

8. _____ There is substantial evidence available which supports the argument that inflation redistributes wealth from the poor to the rich.

9. _____ During periods of inflation, businesses find it more difficult to plan for the future.

10. _____ The holders of high-powered money have little to worry about when prices rise because the real value of their holdings is not affected.

11. _____ The effects of unexpected inflation are essentially the same as the effects when inflation is totally predictable.

12. _____ Because of bracket creep, the government is able to increase its share of national income without formal legislative approval.

13. _____ One way to adjust for bracket creep is indexation of tax brackets so that the effects of inflation are removed and taxes are paid on the value of real income.

14. _____ When financial institutions do not adjust completely to inflation, people willingly hold more currency.

15. _____ In some firms, menu costs may be small.

16. _____ If inflation causes the interest rate to rise, the cost of holding currency increases.

17. _____ Although expectations of inflation are important in terms of explaining price behavior during the current time period, these expectations have little if any effect on future prices.

18. _____ Most people who fall victim to the inflation illusion do so because they fail to see how inflation increases their nominal income.

19. _____ In Germany, the government participates in the collective bargaining process and announces its intentions with respect to economic policy for the coming year so that policy can affect wage agreements.

20. _____ During the first half of 1982, both the Reagan administration and the Fed followed extremely restrictive policies designed to lower inflation.

21. _____ Over the last 20 years, the only time inflation followed a business cycle was in 1975.

22. _____ The inflation and unemployment experience of the early 1970s showed economists that the economy could move easily either up or down the Phillips curve.

23. _____ The origins of today's inflation can be traced back to the Great Depression of the 1930s.

24. _____ A major problem in getting rid of inflation is that conventional restrictive aggregate demand policies cause prolonged unemployment.

MULTIPLE CHOICE QUESTIONS

Circle the correct answer.

1. The Phillips curve shows
   a. an exact quantitative relationship between the rate of inflation and the rate of unemployment
   b. a negative relationship between the inflation rate and the unemployment rate
   c. that if inflation increases, unemployment increases also

    d. that price stability is achieved only at low levels of unemployment
    e. none of the above

2. All of the following statements are correct except
    a. during periods of sustained inflation, people come to expect continued price increases
    b. moving down the Phillips curve is not as easy as moving up it
    c. what workers and firms expect about future fiscal and monetary policy can affect current and future wages
    d. once unemployment starts to increase, prices and the rate of inflation fall quickly

3. The primary reason why prices increased rapidly during 1973–1975 is that
    a. oil prices increased by over 300 percent
    b. the world price of food increased sharply
    c. raw materials prices rose sharply
    d. the supply shock of increasing costs of production caused firms to pass these costs on as higher prices
    e. all of the above

4. To say that a government policy is credible means that
    a. it is believable
    b. it is not believable
    c. it is irrelevant
    d. the policies change frequently

5. If people anticipate inflation correctly and there is complete institutional adjustment, which of the following do we expect to happen?
    a. all prices and incomes rise at the same rate
    b. tax payments are based on real, not nominal, terms
    c. the decision about holding different types of wealth is unaffected
    d. any capital gains arising solely from inflation are not taxed
    e. all of the above

6. If the annual inflation rate is 12 percent and you lend someone $100 today but want to receive $105 in real terms at the end of 1 year, what nominal interest rate must you charge?
    a. 12 percent   **c.** 13.3 percent
    b. 17.6 percent   **d.** 5 percent

7. With an annual interest rate of 13 percent, how much does it cost you to carry around $50 in cash?
    a. $6.50   **d.** $10.00
    b. $5.00   **e.** nothing
    c. $1.50

8. The menu costs of inflation are high in all of the following cases except
    a. parking meters
    b. J. C. Penney catalogs
    c. grocery store prices
    d. vending machines

9. Suppose you were employed in 1975, earned a salary of $5000, and paid 10 percent in income taxes. In 1983, you are still employed, earn $10,000, and pay 20 percent of your income in taxes. Assume that prices have doubled since 1975. How much extra tax do you pay because of bracket creep?
    a. $1000
    b. $1700
    c. $250
    d. $500
    e. cannot be determined from the information given

10. If the tax system does not make adjustments, the effect of inflation on the taxation of capital is to
    a. increase the real returns to capital
    b. lower or perhaps even make negative the real return to capital
    c. attract more funds for investment in capital
    d. leave the amount of national income invested in capital assets virtually unchanged

11. Which of the following statements is incorrect?
    a. it is better to borrow money during periods of unanticipated inflation than during periods of unanticipated deflation
    b. when there is inflation, the real value of the government debt falls
    c. during periods of unexpected inflation, young families are hurt more than the elderly
    d. when there is unexpected inflation, an atmosphere of uncertainty is created

12. Wage and price controls
    a. have never been applied in the United States except during wartime
    b. are very difficult to administer and usually fail to control peacetime inflation
    c. are always used along with appropriate macroeconomic policies to lower inflation
    d. are usually welcomed by the business community as a method of lowering production costs

13. Those who support a return to the gold standard argue that
    a. with gold backing the money supply, inflation would fall
    b. the Fed would be limited in the amount of paper currency it could create
    c. during periods when the United States was on the gold standard, there was less inflation
    d. the Fed would be obligated to buy and sell gold at a fixed price in dollars
    e. all of the above

AT THIS POINT YOU SHOULD BE ABLE TO . . .

1. State in a few sentences the U.S. inflation experience since the 1960s, draw and define the Phillips curve, explain why economists in the 1960s thought that the curve provided them with a broad selection of inflation and unemployment combinations from which to pick, and explain why their attitudes changed during the late 1970s and early 1980s.

2. Describe how expectations of inflation and supply shocks affect both current and future inflationary processes.

3. Explain why it is important to have a credible government policy if inflation is to be reduced.

4. Identify two industrialized countries which have had a greater problem with inflation than the United States since 1972.

5. State why most people suffer from an inflation illusion.

6. Identify and describe the effects and costs of inflation when expectations and institutions are completely adjusted to rising prices.

7. Identify and describe the effects and costs of inflation when there is incomplete adjustment of both expectations and institutions.

8. Given the data, show how bracket creep causes people to pay more taxes even though their real incomes may have fallen; also, explain how it is possible to have a negative after-tax real interest rate.

9. Describe the shoe-leather costs, menu costs, and redistribution effects of inflation.

10. List and describe three ways of dealing with inflation and state the limitations of each.

11. Define the term "incomes policy" and distinguish between wage and price controls and a tax-based incomes policy.

QUESTIONS FOR THOUGHT

1. We could simply give up the fight and learn to live with inflation. Is this an acceptable approach to take? Explain why or why not. What might be the consequences?

2. In what sense does the Phillips curve represent a trade-off between inflation and unemployment? If you were a policymaker, would it present you with a dilemma? Explain.

3. Explain why expectations of inflation can affect the rate of inflation both in the current period and in the future.

4. In the November 1982 congressional elections, Republicans argued that we should "stay the course" with President Reagan's anti-inflationary program. Democrats, on the other hand, condemned the President's program and argued that we should try to put people back to work. Do you think such campaigning might affect expectations of inflation? Does it affect the credibility of government policy? Explain.

5. How does inflation increase the cost of holding money? Does this really inflict a cost on an individual? Explain.

6. When inflation is unexpected or adjustments are incomplete, there is a redistribution effect. Explain this effect and identify those who might gain or lose by rising prices.

7. What is the idea behind an incomes policy? Why do many economists argue that incomes policies have never succeeded? Are wage and price controls an incomes policy? Explain. What is a TIP?

8. Explain three approaches to dealing with inflation. What are the advantages and disadvantages of each?

9. Describe how bracket creep and the taxation of capital during periods of inflation can present serious problems in both the short run and the long run.

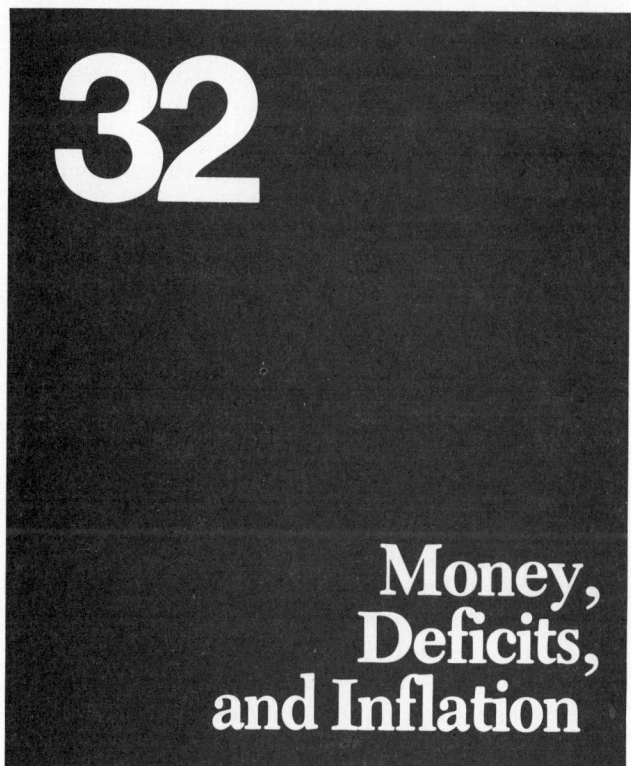

32

Money, Deficits, and Inflation

In Chapter 32, Professors Fischer and Dornbusch examine three issues. First, they look for a link between nominal money growth and inflation. Next, they examine the relationship between government budget deficits and inflation. Finally, they again explore the link between changes in the price level and changes in the interest rate. The first two issues represent popular explanations for inflation. As such, they receive much publicity when politicians, economists, and business leaders debate the causes of rising prices. The issues are presented in Chapter 32 first by asking what economic theory says about the relationship and then by examining the evidence.

Chapter 32 begins with a discussion of the relationship between prices and the nominal quantity of money. The quantity theory of money states that increases in the price level are primarily the result of prior increases in the nominal stock of money. Data over the short run for moderate changes in the nominal money stock (M1) do not strongly support this argument because of the change in real money demand. When the nominal money stock grows rapidly, though, prices do increase. If monetary growth is very rapid and large, the inflation rate may rise to exceptionally high levels. In such a situation, the monetary and market systems break down. Money becomes worthless, and real money demand tumbles as people attempt to get rid of their money balances. Hyperinflation redistributes wealth to debtors, and the value of all nominal assets falls at an increasing rate.

Evidence shows that for the United States there is little if any direct link between the government's budget deficit and the inflation rate. One reason is that the government's debt is financed primarily by borrowing from the private sector. If the Fed financed the debt by purchasing bonds directly from the Treasury, the stock of high-powered money and the nominal supply would increase. Such procedures establish an indirect link between the deficit, the money supply, and prices.

The final issue presented in Chapter 32 is an examination of the relationship between inflation and the nominal rate of interest. Because lenders require that the money they lend maintain its purchasing power over the period of the loan, the nominal interest rate includes an inflation premium. This premium compensates for the anticipated reduction in purchasing power as prices rise. Thus, as the rate of inflation increases, so does the inflation premium. This pulls the nominal rate up. The Fisher effect describes the relationship between inflation and the nominal rate of interest. Evidence suggests that the Fisher effect exists in the United States and in most other countries.

CHAPTER OUTLINE

1. Real money demand is determined primarily by the level of real income and the opportunity cost (real rate of interest) of holding money. A positive relationship exists between the level of real income and real money demand, while real money demand and the opportunity cost of holding money are negatively related.

   a. Monetary equilibrium is established when the demand for real balances equals the real money stock (nominal money supply divided by the price level). The price level can be defined as the ratio of the nominal money stock to real money demand. This definition links prices directly to the nominal money supply. The quantity theory of money states that changes in the price level are caused largely by changes in the nominal quantity of money. Evidence suggests, however, that no close relationship exists between the nominal money stock and prices unless changes in real money demand are considered.

   (1) Changes in real money demand occur over time for three primary reasons. First, changes in real income change the demand for real balances in the same direction, and with other things equal, prices change. An increase in the nominal money stock puts pressure on prices to rise, while an increase in real income puts pressure on prices to fall. The net effect on prices

of these two forces depends on which one is the stronger of the two. The second reason is that real interest rates change so that the opportunity cost of holding money balances changes. Changes in the interest rate and the demand for real balances move in opposite directions. When the demand for real balances falls, the price level rises. The third reason is that financial innovations have introduced near-monies and methods with which households can make transactions while holding lower real balances. These innovations put pressure on prices to rise. Changes in real money demand help explain why prices, the nominal money stock, and real income can increase at the same time.

   b. In a monetary equilibrium, the inflation rate is determined by the difference between the growth rate of the nominal money stock and the growth rate of real money demand. At extremely high rates of monetary growth, inflation appears to be caused by increases in the money stock, and so some support is given to the quantity theory. For short periods of time and for relatively low growth in the money stock, the quantity theory is much weaker.

   c. Although both the money stock and inflation have increased in the United States since the 1960s, there appears to be no clear-cut short-run relationship between money growth and inflation. In the long run, however, such a relationship may exist.

2. Some countries have experienced periods of hyperinflation in the past during which the inflation rate exceeded 1000 percent per year. Hyperinflation disorganizes markets, destabilizes prices, and redistributes income and wealth drastically. The most famous hyperinflation of this century occurred in Germany during the 1920s.

   a. In the early 1920s, Germany faced a large war debt, low tax revenue, and large government expenditures. Thus, the government simply began to print money to finance its budget deficit. Prices rose quickly. In fact, prices increased faster than the increase in the money stock during 1923. In late 1923, prices doubled every other day, and people began to hold goods rather than money.

   b. During the German hyperinflation, people tried to hold as little money as possible because of the rapid decline in its purchasing power. Individuals tried to hold real assets in order to protect their wealth, and money became practically worthless. The real balances held by Germans fell drastically so that in late 1923 less than 12 percent of purchasing power was held as money. There was a flight from money as everyone tried to hold lower real balances because of inflation. This decline in real money demand promoted price increases since citizens exchanged more and more money for a limited amount of goods.

   c. During periods of hyperinflation, the value of all nominal assets falls at an increasing rate, as do any contracts that are not indexed to the price level. The gainers during periods of hyperinflation are debtors because their debts fall substantially. The German government's liabilities became worthless as wealth was redistributed from creditors to debtors. Society was so destabilized that this actually promoted the rise of the Nazi regime. Germany sought a political system that would bring order out of chaos and establish some stability.

3. Fiscal policies designed to increase aggregate demand may increase the budget deficit. Evidence suggests that no close relationship exists in the United States or in other industrialized countries between the actual budget deficit and the rate of inflation.

   a. Budget deficits are financed by the government borrowing from the public or creating money. The U.S. budget deficits have been financed by borrowing since the Civil War. Any government bonds bought by the Fed increase the stock of high-powered money so that the nominal money supply increases. Given the money growth-inflation relationship, prices rise, and so there may be an indirect connection between the size of the budget deficit and the rate of inflation.

      (1) Financing the deficit by creating money imposes an inflation tax on society since there is a cost to people in maintaining their real balances. As prices rise, the purchasing power of these real balances falls. People increase their nominal money holdings in order to purchase the same goods as they did before the inflation. Thus, more of their income is held. The part of nominal income that is held to maintain the desired real balances is the inflation tax.

      (2) In the United States, there is no strong or automatic relationship between the size and growth of the budget deficit and the growth in the nominal money supply.

Evidence from other industrialized countries also suggests the absence of a direct link between budgetary deficits and growth in the money stock.

4. The Fisher effect describes the relationship between the inflation rate and the interest rate. As the price level increases, so do interest rates. Interest is the price paid for borrowing money. Rising prices decrease the real value of money, and this causes lenders to require a larger payment from borrowers. The nominal interest rate rises as lenders increase the inflation premium (the rate of inflation expected over the life of the loan) for loans. The real interest rate is the nominal interest rate minus the inflation premium; for a positive real interest rate, the nominal rate must be no lower than the rate of inflation.

   a. Both cross section and time series data tend to support the existence of the Fisher effect. In many industrialized countries, the relationship between higher inflation rates and higher nominal interest rates is strong but not exact. This suggests that the nominal interest rate is influenced not only by the inflation rate but by other determinants as well.

IMPORTANT TERMS AND THEIR MEANING

Match the following terms with the correct definition or phrase.

1. _____ Measures the deficit as it would be if the economy were at the level of potential output
2. _____ The economizing on real balances that occurs on a massive scale when inflation makes it costly to hold money
3. _____ States that a positive relationship exists between inflation and the nominal interest rate; they increase together
4. _____ The method of financing the government when its expenditures exceed its revenues
5. _____ The cost to money holders of maintaining the purchasing power of their real balances in the face of inflation
6. _____ The interest rate expressed in terms of its purchasing power
7. _____ Periods in which inflation rates exceed 1000 percent per year
8. _____ States that movements in the price level are determined largely by movements in the nominal quantity of money
9. _____ The interest rate expressed in terms of dollars; not adjusted for inflation

a. Fisher effect
b. Real interest rate
c. Inflation tax
d. Hyperinflation
e. Full-employment deficit
f. Quantity theory of money
g. Flight from money
h. Nominal interest rate
i. Deficit financing

EXERCISES

1. Table 32-1 shows the effects of inflation on a $1000 loan you made to your best friend. Included in Table 32-1 are five different expected inflation rates. It is assumed that the loan earns you a nominal interest rate of 12 percent per year.

   a. Complete columns A and B by computing the loss attributable to the rising price level and by determining the inflation premium which must be charged just to keep the purchasing power constant.

   b. Complete columns C and D by first computing the real interest rate and then estimating the gain or loss you incur for each of the expected inflation rates.

   c. If the inflation rate is less than _____ percent, you make some money on the loan because the purchasing power you receive once the loan is repaid is (greater than/less than) _____ what you lost because of inflation.

   d. For any rate of inflation higher than _____ percent, you lose purchasing power when the loan is

TABLE 32-1

AMOUNT OF LOAN, $	EXPECTED INFLATION, %	(A) LOSS BECAUSE OF INFLATION, $	NOMINAL INTEREST RATE, %	(B) INFLATION PREMIUM, %	(C) REAL INTEREST RATE, %	(D) GAIN (+) OR LOSS (−), $
1000	8	_____	12	_____	_____	_____
1000	10	_____	12	_____	_____	_____
1000	12	_____	12	_____	_____	_____
1000	14	_____	12	_____	_____	_____
1000	16	_____	12	_____	_____	_____

repaid. In fact, the real rate of interest is (positive/negative) _____.

  e. The inflation premium is equal to the rate of _____, since once this compensation is added, you neither gain nor lose.

  f. If you had to make $50 in real interest, the nominal rate of interest would have to (rise/fall) _____ as the inflation rate increased.

  g. Complete Table 32-2 on the basis of your requirement of a $50 real return. Note the behavior of the required nominal interest rate when the expected rate of inflation increases.

TABLE 32-2

AMOUNT OF LOAN, $	EXPECTED RATE OF INFLATION, %	REQUIRED NOMINAL RATE, %	REAL INTEREST RATE, %
1000	8		
1000	10		
1000	12		
1000	14		
1000	16		

2. Table 32-2 presents data for the economy of Betania. Included in Table 32-3 are data for the country's nominal money supply and an index of prices for 6 years. As you perform the required computations, round off the numbers.

  a. Your first task is to complete column A and enter your estimates of the country's real balances for each year. Next, complete column B by computing a nominal money index. This index is computed by expressing 1978–1982 in terms of the nominal money supply in the base year. (In your computation for columns A and B, be sure to multiply your quotient by 100.) Compute an index of real balances and enter your estimates in column C. This index may be estimated by the nominal money index divided by the price level.

  b. As the price level rises, individuals hold (more/less) _____ money, as indicated by the (increase/decrease) _____ in the index of real balances.

  c. The economy of Betania experienced an (increase/decrease) _____ in the real money demand, and this effect is described as the _____ from money.

  d. We (would/would not) _____ expect people to change their payment habits in Betania as a result of the falling index of real balances.

  e. Calculate the inflation rate and enter your answers in column D. In column E, calculate and enter the growth rate of the nominal money stock (round the answers to the nearest whole number).

  f. In Betania, the nominal money stock increased at a (faster/slower) _____ rate than inflation. Because people try to hold (greater/lower) _____ real money balances, they (increase/decrease) _____ their demand for goods, and this leads to an (increase/decrease) _____ in the price level.

FILL-IN QUESTIONS

1. The demand for real balances (increases/decreases) _____ as the level of real income rises because people buy (more/less) _____ goods.

2. Changes in real money demand over time occur primarily because of changes in (nominal/real) _____ income, changes in the (unemployment/interest/jobless) _____ rate, or _____ innovations.

3. When money growth is very high, inflation over

TABLE 32-3

YEAR ENDING	NOMINAL MONEY SUPPLY, (millions $)	PRICE LEVEL INDEX (1977 = 100)	(A) REAL MONEY BALANCES	(B) NOMINAL MONEY INDEX (1977 = 100)	(C) INDEX OF REAL BALANCES (1977 = 100)	(D) INFLATION RATE, %	(E) GROWTH RATE OF NOMINAL MONEY STOCK, %
Dec. 31, 1977	$337	100					
Dec. 31, 1978	363	117					
Dec. 31, 1979	389	147					
Dec. 31, 1980	415	195					
Dec. 31, 1981	441	258					
Dec. 31, 1982	478	365					

MONEY, DEFICITS, AND INFLATION

long periods (is/is not) _____ determined by money growth, while in the short run, there (is/is not) _____ a clear-cut relationship between money growth and inflation.

4. One of the best known cases of hyperinflation occurred in _____ during the 1920s, and as a result, citizens tried to hold (more/less) _____ money.

5. When people try to reduce their real balances, the real value of the money stock (rises/falls) _____ .

6. Hyperinflation (increases/decreases/leaves unchanged) _____ the value of nominal assets unless the value of an asset is _____ to the price level.

7. There (are/are not) _____ strong, simple links between budget deficits and money growth because budgetary decisions are made by _____ and money growth is controlled by the _____ ; however, there may be (direct/indirect) _____ links.

8. The _____ effect describes the relationship between the inflation rate and the _____ rate.

9. It (is/is not) _____ possible for the real interest rate to be negative.

10. The (insurance/inflation/unemployment) _____ premium is part of the _____ rate that compensates lenders for any fall in the value of their loans over time.

TRUE-FALSE QUESTIONS

1. _____ In the United States, the average real yield on Treasury bills has been approximately zero during the last 50 years.

2. _____ For the real interest rate to be positive, the nominal interest rate must be lower than the inflation rate.

3. _____ The Fed can link budget deficits and money growth indirectly by open market purchases during periods of increased government spending.

4. _____ When the Fed finances the budget deficit by creating money, it is essentially creating another form of taxation because citizens must hold money just to maintain the purchasing power of their real balances as prices rise.

5. _____ In the United States, the Treasury always finances its deficit by creating money.

6. _____ Between 1965 and 1981, a strong relationship was present between the actual government deficit and the inflation rate.

7. _____ During periods of recession, we expect both the inflation rate and the budget deficit to be high.

8. _____ During periods of hyperinflation, debtors benefit.

9. _____ When inflation is severe, the flight from money actually promotes continued increases in the price level.

10. _____ One characteristic of the hyperinflation in Germany during the 1920s was that the money stock rose faster than prices.

11. _____ Chile experienced a period of hyperinflation during the early 1970s.

12. _____ Although current inflation in the United States may have been caused by money growth over the last 2 or 3 years, there is no evidence of such well-specified lags.

13. _____ Increases in the nominal money stock over time tend to reduce the price level, while increases in real income tend to raise the price level.

14. _____ Monetarists argue that changes in the money stock do not affect the price level.

MULTIPLE CHOICE QUESTIONS

Circle the correct answer.

1. In a monetary equilibrium
   a. the nominal money supply equals the ratio of real money demand to the price level
   b. the nominal money stock exceeds the real money demand
   c. real money demand equals the ratio of the nominal money supply to the price level
   d. the nominal money stock is lower than the real money demand
   e. none of the above

2. Which of the following statements best describes the quantity theory of money?
   a. movements in the price level are determined largely by movements in the nominal quantity of money
   b. an increase in the nominal stock of money reduces the price level
   c. movements in the price level are determined largely by movements in the real stock of money
   d. a decrease in the nominal stock of money increases the price level

3. The demand for real balances
   a. falls as the level of real income rises
   b. is unaffected by the level of real income
   c. falls as the interest rate falls
   d. rises as the level of real income rises

4. All of the following will influence real money demand except
   a. credit cards
   b. checkable savings accounts
   c. lowering the silver content of coins
   d. money market mutual funds

5. If the inflation rate is 9 percent per year and the nominal money stock grows at 4 percent per year, with other things constant, the growth rate of real money demand is
   a. −5 percent   c. 13 percent
   b. 5 percent   d. −4 percent

6. One reason for the hyperinflation in Germany during the early 1920s was that
   a. the Germans financed their war debt by selling government bonds, and this drove prices up
   b. France refused to pay Germany for the losses it suffered during World War I
   c. Germany's tax revenue exceeded its expenditures, and so prices rose
   d. Germany financed much of its war debt simply by printing money

7. In the final stages of the German hyperinflation,
   a. money became practically worthless
   b. there was a flight from money
   c. citizens' payment habits changed dramatically
   d. the demand for real balances fell dramatically
   e. all of the above

8. The government's full-employment budget deficit
   a. has no effect on the level of inflation
   b. moves in the same direction as the actual deficit
   c. can affect the rate of inflation
   d. none of the above

9. If the government finances its deficit by borrowing from the private sector,
   a. there will be a direct effect on inflation
   b. inflation increases rapidly
   c. there will be little direct effect on inflation
   d. inflation increases by a larger percentage than the budget deficit

10. If you had $1000 on January 1, 1983, and the price level increases by 15 percent during 1983, in order to maintain the real value of your money balances, an inflation tax is imposed in the amount of
    a. $1500   c. $1000
    b. $150   d. $100

11. Evidence on the Fisher effect suggests that
    a. there is a relationship between the nominal interest rate and inflation, but it is a weak one
    b. there is no relationship between the nominal interest rate and inflation
    c. there is a strong but negative relationship between the nominal interest rate and inflation
    d. there is a strong relationship between the nominal interest rate and inflation

AT THIS POINT YOU SHOULD BE ABLE TO . . .

1. State both the basic equation of inflation economics and the quantity theory of money.
2. List and explain three reasons why the real money demand changes and state the relationship between this real money demand and the inflation rate.
3. Explain why there appears to be no short-run relationship between growth in the nominal money stock and inflation in the United States.
4. Describe some of the causes and effects of the hyperinflation in Germany during the early 1920s and explain why rapidly rising prices promote a flight from money.
5. Explain some overall effects of hyperinflation.
6. Explain how a budget deficit which is financed through money creation can increase the inflation rate, state the relationship between the deficit and inflation in the United States, and explain why financing the deficit by borrowing from the private sector does not establish a strong, direct link to inflation.
7. State the meaning of an inflation tax and give an example.
8. Explain which Fed actions can link budget deficits to the rate of growth of the nominal money supply and inflation in the United States.
9. Describe the Fisher effect and explain why such an effect exists.
10. Show and explain how and why an inflation premium is included in the nominal interest rate.

QUESTIONS FOR THOUGHT

1. How does real income growth affect changes in the price level when the nominal money stock is increasing? Is there any evidence to support the argument that real income growth plays a role? Explain.

2. Your text states that during the short run, there is no evidence that a relationship exists between slow money

growth and inflation. Is this true for the long run or with rapid increases in the nominal money stock? Explain.

3. How does hyperinflation redistribute wealth? Explain who is hurt and who benefits. Does hyperinflation threaten the social order? Explain.

4. Describe the effects on inflation of the Fed financing a large percentage of the government's deficit through the purchase of bonds.

5. Why is there a very close relationship between the nominal interest rate and the rate of inflation? Explain.

33 Growth and Investment

Chapter 33 introduces the principles of economic growth. When an economy grows, more goods are produced, more people have jobs, real incomes rise more rapidly, and the overall standard of living improves. A growing economy uses more inputs of production and rapidly incorporates improvements in technology into the production process. Technological change in turn promotes more growth. One question some economists ask is whether there are limits to the growth of an economic system. In the 1960s, the U.S. economy and that of most of the industrialized world grew at a rapid rate. But the late 1970s were at best a period of sluggish growth. Professors Fischer and Dornbusch examine the reasons why the world economy experienced such an abrupt reduction in the rate of growth during the 1970s.

The conventional measure of economic growth is the rate of change in real gross national product (or gross domestic product) per capita. Per capita real GNP is used as an estimate of economic welfare, but it does not provide a completely accurate measure because some components of society's welfare can't be included in the statistic. A problem also arises when comparisons of per capita GNP are made over time, because the combination of goods that makes up the GNP measure changes. One measure that has been used to compare standards of living over time is individual life expectancy.

The basis of economic growth in any nation is the stock and quality of the factors of production, the state of technical knowledge, and economies of scale. These variables affect an economy's productive capacity and also influence the efficiency with which the production process takes place. Improvements in capital, land, labor, and technology all promote growth. A problem, though, is the availability of usable factors of production. Some resources are renewable, and so there is no fear of running out of them in the foreseeable future. Other resources are depletable and may present a limit to growth. For many of these depletable resources, technological progress and the use of substitutes may avoid a growth crisis (or at least shift the limits way back).

Society has at any point in time a stock of available technical knowledge. It is this knowledge which is so important to economic growth. Invention, innovation, and technological advances improve the productivity of resources so that more output is produced. The growth process itself promotes more technological development and greater research expenditures.

Much of the growth in the United States during the 1960s can be accounted for by improvements in knowledge and large investments in the capital stock. In the 1970s, though, new technological discoveries slowed, the rate of growth of capital diminished, and labor productivity declined. Thus, the rate of economic growth fell. Data indicate, however, that the rate of U.S. growth during the 1970s, when placed in historical perspective, is not that different from the norm. What is unusual is the exceptional growth experienced between 1960 and 1973. The high growth rate during those years led many to expect this type of economic performance in the future.

As you study Chapter 33, make sure that you know what factors contribute to economic growth. You should be able to explain the role of population increases in investment spending and the effect of research and development spending on a growing economy. You should also be familiar with the effect of government policies on factor productivity and how the government can promote growth by reevaluating some of its policies and regulations.

CHAPTER OUTLINE

1. Both national and international comparisons of income changes over long time intervals are based on either GNP or GDP measures. These comparisons are difficult to interpret because the measures of GNP and GDP are imperfect.
    a. GNP measures the market value of all final goods and services produced by an economy during a specific time period, and so it is a nominal measurement. All nonmonetary and monetary transactions covering illegal and used

goods are excluded from GNP. A measure of economic welfare (MEW) adjusts GNP for the increased value of leisure enjoyed by citizens and for the estimated costs imposed on society by the production of goods when these costs are not internalized by the producer. Another statistic which can be used to measure society's well-being is changes in consumption; however, consumption is affected by government tax and transfer policies which alter disposable income.

   b. The major conceptual problem faced when measuring GNP over long periods of time is accounting for new goods produced in the economy. The changing combination of goods made available over time weakens the comparability of long-term GNP and consumption data.
   c. GNP can serve as a measure of happiness only if material goods directly make people happy and better off.
   d. Although GNP and GDP are used to compare average incomes, these measures indicate nothing about the distribution of income within an economic sytem. The average income level is not the same concept as the distribution of income. Since the nineteenth century, the distribution of income in the industrialized countries has become more equal.
      (1) Another statistic besides GNP which can be used to compare living standards over time is individual life expectancy.
   e. Data for growth patterns in per capita incomes for the industrialized countries are no more than a few hundred years old. The industrial revolution and the mechanization of production were the beginnings of modern growth. The rapid growth in output and income over the past few decades is attributable primarily to rapid changes in technology.

2. The production function shows the maximum level of output that can be produced by using any specified combination of inputs and given technology. The inputs (also called the factors of production) are land, labor, capital, and raw materials. When either the availability of inputs or the body of technological knowledge expands, growth is possible.
   a. Capital consists of buildings, equipment, and inventories. In 1980, the capital stock of the United States was over $6.8 trillion. The largest components of the capital stock are plant, equipment, and housing.
   b. Production increases when the rate of labor input increases. One reason for the increase in per capita output over the last 100 years is that the quality of labor has improved through investment in human capital.
      (1) Human capital describes the skills and knowledge embodied in individuals. The stock of human capital increases because of both formal education and on-the-job training. As the stock of human capital rises, the quality and productivity of labor go up. This means that labor produces more output per worker with fewer hours of work.
   c. In less-developed countries and before the industrial revolution, agriculture dominated economic life, and the overall standard of living was low. The amount of land available for production is more important in an agricultural society than in a society which is industrialized.
      (1) Some nineteenth-century economists believed that the limit to economic growth was determined by the availability and productivity of land. Reverend Thomas Malthus argued that population increases at a geometric rate but that agricultural output increases only arithmetically because of diminishing returns to both labor and land. Therefore, per capita food output falls. Eventually there is starvation and a decline in the population. This is the Malthusian trap. Malthus's predictions have not come true because of the tremendous gains made in agricultural productivity.
   d. For a given level of all other inputs, output increases with the increasing use of raw materials. In production, raw materials are often substituted for each other without reducing the level of output. Some raw materials are depletable, which can affect economic growth.
      (1) Raw materials are either renewable or depletable. It is possible that depletable resources will be exhausted in the future, which raises fears about limits to growth. The prices of depletable resources, which should rise as a result of their increasing scarcity, have not risen much over time because of new discoveries, improved technology, and the development of substitutes. From the standpoint of growth, the use of depletable resources at current levels has not restricted growth. Technology and the development of substitutes may make it possible to avoid future limits to growth.
   e. The contribution to output from increases in

the use of a factor of production by 1 more unit is called the variable factor's marginal product. The value of each factor's marginal product equals the price paid for that factor, and so the price of an input is a measure of that input's contribution to the value of output.
  - (1) If all factors of production in an economic system are increased in the same proportion, aggregate output changes. Output will increase by an amount greater than, equal to, or less than the proportionate increase in all inputs, depending on whether the economy experiences economies of scale, constant returns to scale, or diseconomies of scale. In general, there is no way of knowing whether a particular economy experiences economies or diseconomies of scale.
3. Invention (the discovery of new knowledge) and innovation (the development of new methods for applying existing knowledge) promote the expansion of knowledge and economic growth.
  a. The invention of ways to generate power from animals and then machines was one of the most important developments in the process of economic growth. As machines replaced animals, the industrial age began. Inventions that improved agricultural productivity released humans from the land, and this allowed industrial economies to develop.
    - (1) Before inventions and innovations can affect economic growth, there must be investment in both physical and human capital to incorporate the newly discovered knowledge. Once this is done, production and output change.
    - (2) As workers perform the same job over a period of time, they become specialized, and so job experience promotes both increased productivity and improved technical knowledge. The Hordonal effect describes such improvements in labor productivity resulting from job experience.
    - (3) Once invention and innovation begin to increase productivity and growth, other inventions and technological advances promote even more growth.
  b. Profits, curiosity, and the desire to find easier and better ways of doing things promote technological change.
  c. The rate and amount of technological change depend in part on the amount of resources allocated by a society for research and development. Society always takes a risk in committing scarce resources to research and development, but the financial and real economic rewards can be large. In the United States, the patent system grants a 17-year monopoly to inventors as an incentive to expand knowledge. The inventor is assured that the financial rewards are his for a specific period of time. It may or may not be in society's best interest to award a temporary monopoly to inventors since once knowledge is expanded, society may be better off if everyone has access to it. In many countries, most research and development is conducted by the government.
    - (1) As a percentage of GNP, the United States spends as much on research and development as any other country except the Soviet Union. In absolute terms, the United States spends more on research and development than any other country.
    - (2) Evidence indicates that the rate of return on research and development spending is high. Substantial risks are also involved in research and development projects, and so the actual rate of return is uncertain.
4. Growth in the United States and other countries is accounted for by increases in the factors of production, economies of scale, and technological change. Of these, technological improvement is of major importance.
  a. Since the mid-1970s, a substantial slowing down of U.S. economic growth has occurred. Falling labor productivity is one of the main reasons for declining growth rates. Labor productivity fell because of a sharply declining growth rate in the capital stock (investment spending fell) and a rapid increase in the labor supply. Also causing the nation's growth rate to fall were declining contributions to knowledge (technological advances) and government regulations which increased producers' costs of operation.
    - (1) The effect of rising petroleum prices during the 1970s on reducing productivity and growth is still not certain. Although the direct effect of higher oil prices was to reduce oil use, the price increases may have affected productivity in other ways.
  b. The late 1970s was not a period of poor growth; by historical standards (since 1870), the per capita GDP grew at approximately the average historical rate. What makes the country's recent growth experience look bad is that it is often compared to the 1960–1973 period. The 1960s was a decade of extraordinary growth.
    - (1) The growth patterns of the United States

during the 1960s and the last half of the 1970s were shared by all major industrialized countries.
5. The United States, along with the rest of the industrialized world, is searching for policies to get its economy growing again and raise its living standards without increasing population.
   a. Evidence indicates that an extra 4 percent of GNP diverted into investment spending could increase the growth rate by 0.5 percent and move the country toward a better growth performance. A problem, however, is that it will take a substantial effort to allocate an additional 4 percent of GNP to investment. Thus, investment should not be viewed as the only means of growth.
   b. Government policies can promote a return to a higher rate of economic growth. First, government could remove or reduce current policies and regulations which hinder economic growth. Second, government could actively encourage research and development spending and spending on capital goods by amending current tax laws. Government support of basic research for which financial rewards may be limited could be especially beneficial.
   c. Because economic policy in the 1980s encouraged investment and research and development and reduced regulation and because it is unlikely that the U.S. economy will again be hit as hard by external shocks as it was during the first half of the 1970s, the expected rate of growth lies somewhere between what was experienced during exceptional 1960s and the low growth of the 1970s.

IMPORTANT TERMS AND THEIR MEANING

Match the following terms with the correct definition or phrase.

1. ____ Improvements in technical knowledge because of on-the-job experience; workers get better at doing the job the more often they do it

2. ____ The creation of new knowledge and the development of changes in knowledge and technology

3. ____ Designed to provide incentives for invention by granting inventors a monopoly for a period of 17 years

4. ____ Overall improvement or advances in the state of the technical arts; permits more output to be produced from the same amount of factor inputs

5. ____ Present if output more than doubles when all inputs double

6. ____ Raw materials which cannot be renewed; use of these raw materials reduces the amount that can potentially be used in the future

7. ____ Society's stock of knowledge about ways of producing goods

8. ____ The knowledge used to produce or enhance either physical or human capital so that production is affected

9. ____ Describes the situation in which increasing agricultural output causes an increase in the population but pressure on the land resource eventually causes agricultural output to fall; as a result, people starve

10. ____ Present when a doubling of all inputs does not double output

11. ____ An average measure of output; output per unit of input

12. ____ A reduction in the rate of economic growth resulting in part from a fall in the output of labor

a. Diseconomies of scale
b. Productivity
c. Malthusian trap
d. Research and development
e. Patent system
f. Technical knowledge
g. Production slowdown
h. Economies of scale
i. Learning by doing
j. Technical progress
k. Embodied technical knowledge
l. Depletable resources

EXERCISES

1. Assume that a hypothetical economy has an initial capital stock of $1000 and an initial potential output level of $300. Also assume that the marginal and average products of the inputs are constant so that diminishing returns don't exist. In this economy, potential output depends only on the capital stock. Over several periods, the level of net investment is positive but falling.
   a. Calculate the level of the capital stock for each time period and enter the results in the (K) column.

TABLE 33-1

TIME PERIOD	LEVEL OF NET INVESTMENT, $	CAPITAL STOCK (K), $	POTENTIAL OUTPUT (Y_p), $	GROWTH RATE OF POTENTIAL OUTPUT (GR), %
1	60	1000	300	
2	50			
3	40			
4	30			
5	20			
6	10			

    b. Assuming that the marginal product of capital is 0.3, compute the new level of potential output for each time period and enter the results in the (Y_p) column.

    c. Calculate the growth rate of potential output and enter your computations in the (GR) column.

    d. As the level of net investment falls, the level of potential output (increases/decreases) _____ but at (an increasing/a decreasing) _____ rate.

    e. This economy experiences a (rising/falling) _____ growth rate, and so we would expect the standard of living to (rise more slowly/remain constant/fall) _____.

    f. An increase in the productivity of capital resulting from technological progress would (increase/decrease/leave unchanged) _____ the marginal productivity of capital, and so the growth rate of potential output would (rise/fall) _____.

FILL-IN QUESTIONS

1. Productive capital consists of _____, _____, and _____ of produced goods.

2. The recent slowdown in the growth of the U.S. economy occurred primarily because of the (increase/decrease) _____ in the labor productivity rate, (an increasing/a decreasing) _____ growth rate in the capital stock, a (rise/fall) _____ in the contribution of new knowledge, and too (much/little) _____ government regulation.

3. The _____ function gives the maximum amount of output that can be produced using a given state of (technology/income/consumption) _____.

4. Most economists (are/are not) _____ concerned with the predictions of Malthus because of the significant increases in _____ productivity.

5. Two aspects of the development of technical knowledge are _____ and _____, and each (does/does not) _____ promote economic growth.

6. The _____ system is designed to provide incentives for invention by giving the inventor a monopoly for a period of 17 years.

7. One statistic which may be used to compare standards of living across time periods is _____ expectancy.

8. The growth in incomes over the past 125 years (is/is not) _____ historically exceptional and had its beginnings when (animals/machines) _____ came to be used in production.

TRUE-FALSE QUESTIONS

1. _____ The most important contributing factor to U.S. growth during the period 1929–1969 was increased knowledge.

2. _____ The major difficulty of the U.S. economy during the 1970s was deficient aggregate demand.

3. _____ There is no evidence that the oil price increases of the 1970s affected U.S. economic growth.

4. _____ Economic growth during the years 1960–1973 in the United States was not typical from a historical standpoint of the nation's overall growth patterns.

5. _____ Most industrialized countries experienced a fall in their aggregate growth rates during the 1970s.

6. _____ The only way an economic system can reverse a period of sluggish growth and make significant gains in its GNP is to encourage investment.

7. _____ One way in which government can promote economic growth is to encourage private spending on research and development by giving firms better tax treatment.

8. _____ Most economists are certain that given proper support from the government, the economy can return to or exceed the growth rate of the 1960s.

9. _____ The emphasis in the industrialized nations is to promote policies which increase the rate of economic growth so that the rate of labor force expansion will increase.

10. _____ The anticipated rate of return to research and development spending in the United States is in the neighborhood of 30 percent.

MULTIPLE CHOICE QUESTIONS

Circle the correct answer.

1. All of the following countries spent more than 2 percent of their GNP on R&D in 1977 except
    a. Japan   **c.** Soviet Union
    b. United States   **d.** Germany

2. Improvements in technical knowledge
    a. result only from formal education
    b. have little effect on the economy's output
    c. can result from on-the-job training
    d. were not an influence on the growth rate of the 1960s

3. Invention and innovation are most frequently motivated by
    a. human curiosity
    b. the desire to make money and get ahead
    c. the desire to do a better and more efficient job
    d. all of the above
    e. none of the above

4. All of the following statements are correct except
    a. major inventions have to be embodied in capital before they have effects on production
    b. technological progress in agriculture has been essential to economic growth because it freed man from the land.
    c. the generation of power from machines marked the beginning of the industrial age
    d. at any point in time, society has a stock of knowledge about ways of producing things
    e. all of the above statements are incorrect

5. If all inputs in an economy are doubled, and as a result, the economy's output doubles,
    a. there are economies of scale present
    b. there are constant returns to scale present
    c. there are diseconomies of scale present
    d. there are increasing returns to scale present

6. One weakness of using GNP as a measure of economic well-being is that
    a. GNP doesn't take into account the social costs of production
    b. GNP is not a measure of happiness
    c. GNP ignores the increased amount of leisure time
    d. GNP fails to pick up changes in the type of goods produced
    e. all of the above

7. Since the nineteenth century, the distribution of income in the industrialized countries
    a. has become more unequal
    b. has remained essentially constant
    c. has become more equal
    d. is easily measured by GNP

8. All of the following are factors of production except
    a. a bulldozer
    b. 500 shares of stock in the IBM Corporation
    c. a carpenter
    d. $100,000 worth of nuts and bolts held in a warehouse

9. Investment in human capital
    a. increases the skill and knowledge embodied in the minds and hands of the population
    b. improves the quality of labor
    c. makes physical capital more productive
    d. may take the form of on-the-job training or formal schooling
    e. all of the above

10. Coal and petroleum are examples of
    a. depletable resources
    b. capital resources
    c. renewable resources
    d. independent resources

AT THIS POINT YOU SHOULD BE ABLE TO . . .

1. State three problems encountered when GNP and GDP are used as a measure of economic well-being and explain the adjustments which can be made to the measure so that it reflects social welfare more accurately.

2. Define the production function; also, list and give examples of the four factors of production.

3. Explain the Malthusian trap and describe the conditions which Malthus thought would eventually lead the population to starvation.

4. Distinguish between renewable and depletable raw materials and explain what the evidence suggests about running out of resources as a limit to growth.

5. Define the concept of technical knowledge, describe the embodiment of technical knowledge in capital, and explain the roles of invention, innovation, and research and development in promoting growth.

6. Explain why the growth rate of the 1960s and early 1970s in the United States is not considered typical when compared with growth rates over a long period of time.

7. List the three sources of economic growth in the United States between 1929 and 1960; also, state and explain three reasons for the productivity slowdown of the 1970s.

8. Explain capital's role in promoting economic growth and state why our economy should not emphasize only capital investment.

9. Describe two policy issues which the government might pursue to encourage technical progress and economic growth.

10. Describe the outlook for U.S. economic growth through the end of this century.

QUESTIONS FOR THOUGHT

1. Why haven't the predictions of Malthus come to pass? Can your foresee when the Malthusian trap might exist? Do you think Malthus's predictions are applicable to some less-developed countries? Explain.

2. What effect did the energy crisis of the 1970s have on the growth of the industrialized world? Did it tell us anything about our depletable resources? Explain.

3. Why is spending on research and development like an investment in capital? Do you think invention and innovation still play as important a role in economic growth as in the past? Explain.

4. What can government do to get the economy growing again? Is government activity one reason why we have had such slow growth in recent years? Explain. Give some examples of government programs that might promote growth.

5. What are some of the difficulties encountered when economists attempt to compare incomes or standards of living over a period of time? What shortcomings does GNP have as a measure of living standards? Explain.

34

International Trade and the Balance of Payments

Practically all nations engage in trade with each other. Improvements in communications and the transportation of goods have made nations more interdependent within the world economy. Chapter 34 is the first of three chapters in which Professors Fischer and Dornbusch examine the principles of international trade. As you will see in Chapter 35, trade between countries permits countries to specialize. This specialization increases productivity, employment, and income.

When you begin reading Chapter 34, you will see that two distinguishing features of international trade are that the traders live in different countries and that they use different currencies. The emphasis in Chapter 34 is placed on foreign exchange markets, where the different currencies are priced, and on a nation's balance of payments.

World traders use different monies to pay for the goods and services they buy and sell. The foreign exchange market serves the function of establishing the price of one currency in terms of another. If this exchange rate is free of government intervention, it is determined by the demand for and the supply of different currencies. When the rate at which one nation's currency can be exchanged for another changes, the nation experiences a change in the prices of both its exports and its imports. Such price changes on the international market affect domestic economic activity, and so it is not uncommon for a government to intervene in the foreign exchange market by adjusting its currency's exchange rate.

A country's balance of payments account shows the transactions between that country and the rest of the world. As nations trade with each other, money and wealth flow between them. At any given time, a nation may have either a surplus or a deficit in the current account portion of its balance of payments. When a nation has a surplus in its current account, its capital account increases along with its claims on the rest of the world. A balance of payments deficit means that the country has imported more than it has exported, and so some method of financing the excess of imports must be found. A country cannot persistently have a balance of payments deficit without some action being taken by its government. In the long run, a country must be in balance both internally and externally.

CHAPTER OUTLINE

1. A nation's exports are the goods and services produced by domestic residents and sold to residents of foreign countries, while a nation's imports are the value of purchases of foreign-produced goods by domestic residents. World trade consists of imports and exports, because one country's exports are another's imports. This is a distinguishing feature of international trade.
   a. In real terms, world trade has increased since 1950, implying that nations are becoming more interdependent. During the period between the Great Depression and World War II, international trade was almost destroyed.
   b. Data on trade patterns show that most world trade takes place among the industrialized nations. Industrialized countries also receive a large percentage of the oil-producing countries' and less-developed countries' exports. The major trading patterns of the Soviet Union and its eastern bloc nations are limited to their own sphere. The less-developed countries (LDCs) primarily export raw materials to the industrialized nations.
   c. Over half (58 percent) of world trade consists of manufactured products, while the remainder consists of primary commodities. The types of primary and manufactured commodities traded have changed significantly since 1935.
   d. One-third of U.S. exports are primary commodities, while the remaining two-thirds are manufactured items. Most of the primary exports are agricultural, and most of the manufactured exports are engineering products. The

largest category of primary commodities imported by the United States is fuel. Most of Japan's imports are primary commodities, and most of that country's exports are manufactured engineering products. The non-oil-producing LDCs export primary commodities and import manufactured products. The largest import category for the LDCs is engineering products.

   e. Four facts are emphasized in international trade. First, in the United States GNP has not increased as fast as world trade. Second, world trade centers on the industrialized countries. Third, 60 percent of world trade is in manufactured products. Fourth, the LDCs are primary commodity exporters and importers of manufactured goods. These facts are used to explain three current trade policy issues.

      (1) The LDCs want higher prices for their raw materials because they believe that the industrialized countries pay them too little for their exports and charge too much for manufactured goods.

      (2) Some newly industrialized countries (NICs) export manufactured goods to the industrialized countries. The older industrialized countries often complain that cheap foreign labor threatens domestic employment.

      (3) Intra-industry trade disputes often arise in world trade when an industry in one country becomes more efficient relative to those in other countries and begins to dominate world trade in that industry.

2. When people of different countries engage in international trade, different monies are used. The use of different currencies is a second distinguishing feature of international trade. In the foreign exchange market, one currency is exchanged for another. The price of one currency is expressed in terms of how much of another currency it buys. This price is called the exchange rate. The exchange rate is established in the foreign exchange market by the forces of supply and demand. When the price of one currency rises relative to another, it takes more of the cheaper currency to buy 1 unit of the more expensive currency. The exchange rate adjusts when currency prices change because of changes in either the demand for or the supply of the currencies. As the price of one currency rises in terms of another, it appreciates in value, while the other currency depreciates.

   a. It is not unusual for a nation's central bank to enter the foreign exchange market to buy or sell foreign currencies in order to support its currency's exchange rate. Such intervention means that the central bank raises or lowers the exchange rate by changing either the demand for or the supply of its national currency so that it either appreciates or depreciates in value. A central bank may intervene in the foreign exchange market to change rates because movements in the exchange rate affect both the volume of a country's international trade and the rate of domestic inflation.

3. A country's balance of payments accounts show all the transactions between the residents of that country and the rest of the world.

   a. An individual's balance of payments accounts are like those for a country, except on a much smaller scale. The individual's balance of payments account shows a current account containing income (money flowing in) and expenditures (money flowing out). If spending exceeds income, there is a current account deficit which must be financed. When income exceeds spending, there is a current account surplus. The individual's capital account shows all transactions in terms of financial assets. From this capital account, all current account deficits are financed by selling assets and borrowing.

      (1) When an individual's or country's income exceeds its spending, its current account has a surplus because there are increased money holdings in the asset account. A current account deficit occurs when spending exceeds income.

   b. A nation's current account portion of the balance of payments measures the difference between its exports (income flowing in) and its imports (payments flowing out). When exports exceed imports, there is a current account surplus, but if imports exceed exports, the current account is in a deficit position. For the world as a whole, exports equal imports, and so one nation's current account deficit is another nation's surplus.

      (1) If a nation experiences a current account deficit, it must finance this deficit by selling assets or borrowing. When assets are sold, the country reduces its net claims on the rest of the world. A surplus in the current account is used to reduce net liabilities or increase assets and claims on the rest of the world. A country's current account surplus equals its increase in net foreign assets.

   c. The government plays a role in a nation's balance of payments because when the current account is in deficit, both the central bank and the private sector must reduce their ownership

of foreign assets or increase borrowing. If a nation has a current account surplus, the central bank's holdings of foreign assets increase. Thus, a balance of payments surplus or deficit equals the increase or decrease of the central bank's holdings of foreign assets.
   d. When a country continually has a current account deficit in its balance of payments, a point is reached at which the deficit can no longer be financed. The country must make adjustments by producing more goods, reducing imports, reducing domestic consumption, reducing investment, or lowering government spending so that more goods are left for export. If a country cannot remove its current account deficit, it will face a balance of payments crisis.
   e. By maintaining its currency's existing exchange rate with other currencies, a country can affect its balance of payments problem. When exchange rates change to reflect foreign exchange market conditions, the balance of payments surplus or deficit changes. A central bank, however, will often intervene to keep its currency's exchange rate relatively stable.
4. The international exchange rate system is affected by the policies of governments and central banks.
   a. During the decade of the 1950s, most countries fixed their currencies' exchange rates against the dollar, and the central banks stood ready to intervene in order to keep the exchange rate fixed.
   b. When a central bank believes that the exchange rate for its currency is not at an equilibrium level, it adjusts the rate. This is the adjustable peg exchange rate system. If the exchange rate is persistently too high and there is a continuing current account deficit, the central bank devalues its currency and lowers the exchange rate. The central bank lowers the price at which it buys and sells the nation's currency, and so the currency depreciates. If there is a continuing current account surplus, the central bank can revalue its currency and move the exchange rate upward. A revaluation means that the central bank is willing to pay more for its currency, and so the price rises.
   c. When there are completely free floating exchange rates (clean floating), central banks do not intervene in the foreign exchange markets. Thus, a country's exchange rate is determined solely by the international demand for and supply of its currency. Under a system of clean floating exchange rates, there are no persistent balance of payments problems. Currently, the exchange rates of most countries are allowed to float and adjust to conditions in the foreign exchange market; however, central banks do intervene in order to prevent any large or rapid changes in their currencies' exchange rates. This is called a managed (dirty) float system. A central bank wants to prevent major changes in its currency's exchange rate because domestic exports, imports, production, employment, and inflation are affected.
   d. There is no strong evidence to support the adjustable peg system over a clean float system or vice versa. Some international financial experts argue that a clean floating system promotes an efficient foreign exchange market, while others claim that central bank intervention could have prevented some of the large changes in rates that were experienced during the 1970s.
   e. An international gold standard requires governments in each country to fix the value of their currencies in terms of gold and stand ready to buy or sell gold at that price. A gold standard automatically determines and stabilizes exchange rates. Proponents of the gold standard argue that by fixing the price of currency in terms of gold, nations can reduce the possibility of a sustained period of inflation.
5. There are links between the conditions of a nation's economy and its balance of payments accounts.
   a. The internal balance of a country is the full-employment sustaining level of aggregate demand. When a country's current account balances (imports equal exports), it is in external balance. Although short-run deviations are possible, a country must be in both internal and external balance in the long run.
   b. Internal and external balance are affected by changes in domestic spending, changes in world demand for or world supply of domestically produced goods, discovery of new export products, and the development of new export markets. Most disturbances affecting a nation's internal balance also have external effects.
   c. Forces exist to promote a return to both internal and external equilibrium automatically after a disturbance; however, because of both the length of time involved in the adjustment process and the effects on unemployment and inflation, government policies to reduce the imbalances may be necessary. Monetary and fiscal policy, tariffs, and currency revaluation are parts of a policy mix which is undertaken by governments to affect both the level and composition of spending in an attempt to remove any imbalances.

IMPORTANT TERMS AND THEIR MEANING

Match the following terms with the correct definition or phrase.

1. _____ The current account of a country is in balance; the value of its exports equals the value of its imports
2. _____ The price at which currencies are exchanged
3. _____ A country's excess of exports over imports during a given time period from all transactions with the rest of the world
4. _____ The combination of policies affecting two or more different targets
5. _____ Exchange rates change from day to day or minute to minute in response to the demand for or supply of currencies
6. _____ Newly industrialized countries such as Mexico, Brazil, and Taiwan
7. _____ A fall in the value of one currency in terms of another currency
8. _____ Describes a country's current account when exports exceed imports during a given time period
9. _____ A systematic record of all transactions between the residents of one country and the rest of the world
10. _____ The level of demand for a country's goods which sustains full employment
11. _____ Less-developed countries such as China or India
12. _____ Goods bought by domestic residents from foreigners
13. _____ A system in which the government in each country fixes the value of its currency in terms of gold and is willing to buy and sell gold at that price
14. _____ Describes a central bank's intervention into the foreign exchange market to affect its currency's floating exchange rate
15. _____ An official action by government to depreciate its currency on the foreign exchange market
16. _____ Describes a country's current account when imports exceed exports during a given time period
17. _____ Exchange rates are kept constant by the central banks of different countries buying and selling foreign currencies at fixed prices
18. _____ Goods sold by domestic residents to foreigners
19. _____ A rise in the value of one currency in terms of another currency
20. _____ Shows all the transactions in financial assets made by a country during a given time period
21. _____ Either selling assets or borrowing to remove a current account deficit
22. _____ Describes floating exchange rates when central banks do not enter the foreign exchange markets at all
23. _____ Describes the exchange rate system in which central banks were committed to keeping the exchange rate fixed at any one time but changed the rate when necessary to move toward an equilibrium
24. _____ Describes a central bank entering the foreign exchange market and buying any surplus or selling its currency in order to affect the exchange rate
25. _____ Actions taken by a country in order to remove persistent current account deficits and avoid a balance of payments crisis

a. Current account surplus
b. Flexible exchange rate
c. Internal balance
d. Imports
e. Adjustment
f. Dirty floating
g. LDCs
h. Devaluation
i. Policy mix
j. Exports
k. Capital account
l. Current account deficit
m. Exchange rate
n. Appreciation
o. Adjustable peg
p. Gold standard
q. External balance
r. NICs
s. Balance of payments
t. Financing
u. Depreciation
v. Current account
w. Intervention
x. Clean floating
y. Fixed exchange rate

INTERNATIONAL TRADE AND THE BALANCE OF PAYMENTS

EXERCISES

1. Table 34-1 shows data for the small but highly developed country of Alphania. The country engages in international trade, and so it will have a balance of payments.

TABLE 34-1

ACCOUNT	MILLIONS OF ALPHANIAN DOLLARS
Automobile exports	1.0
Imports of agricultural commodities	1.0
Spending by Alphanian tourists in Europe	8.5
Imports of foreign automobiles	30.4
Exports of Alphanian adding machines	15.2
Exports of military hardware	7.1
Imports of foreign oil	10.5
Sale of gold by the central bank to foreigners	1.0
Sale of Alphanian government bonds	4.0
Sale of Alphanian corporate stock to foreigners	2.1
Exports of Alphanian wheat	20.0

a. In Table 34-2, construct the Alphanian balance of payments. Be sure to include both the current account balance and the capital account balance.

TABLE 34-2
ALPHANIA'S BALANCE OF PAYMENTS, 1983

Current account

   Exports:

   Total exports

   Imports:

   Total imports:

Current account balance

Capital account

   Sale of assets:

Capital account balance

Total

b. Alphania experienced a current account (surplus/deficit) _____ in 1983 because _____ exceeded _____ by $_____.

c. It (is/is not) _____ necessary for the Alphanian government to finance the current account.

d. The government (increases/decreases) _____ its assets by selling them from its (current/capital) _____ account.

e. The net sale of assets (is/is not) _____ just enough to (adjust/finance) _____ Alphania's current account deficit.

FILL-IN QUESTIONS

1. As economies became more (independent/interdependent) _____ after World War II, world trade among nations (increased/decreased) _____.

2. Most international trade is organized around the (industrialized/developing/less-developed) _____ countries.

3. The LDCs export mostly _____ materials and import mostly _____ goods.

4. Two distinguishing features of world trade are that consumers involved in international trade live in (the same/different) _____ countries and that (the same/different) _____ monies are often used.

5. If the value of a dollar falls in terms of the British pound, the pound has (appreciated/been devalued/depreciated) _____ in value, while the dollar has (appreciated/been devalued/depreciated) _____; we can expect the foreign exchange rate in terms of trading pounds for dollars to (rise/fall) _____.

6. When a country has a surplus in its current account, its (imports/exports) _____ have exceeded its (imports/exports) _____, and so expect the country's claims on the rest of the world to (increase/decrease) _____ or its liabilities to the rest of the world to (rise/fall) _____.

7. When a nation's central bank lowers the price of its currency in the foreign exchange market, the currency is said to have been (revalued/devalued) _____, and so the values of other currencies (rise/fall) _____.

8. The foreign exchange markets are _____ floating when central banks do not intervene and the forces of supply and demand determine _____ rates.

9. The return to an international gold standard by all countries would have the effect of _____ the value of a currency in terms of gold so that foreign exchange rates (do/do not) _____ fluctuate.

10. An economy (can/cannot) _____ depart from both an internal and an external balance for short periods of time, but it (can/cannot) _____ over long periods.

TRUE-FALSE QUESTIONS

1. _____ When an economy is in both an internal and an external disequilibrium, there are forces of adjustment which automatically take the economy back to equilibrium in a short period of time.

2. _____ Devaluation, tariffs, and tax changes are policies which affect both the level and the composition of a nation's imports and exports.

3. _____ A balance of payments surplus in a country can be generated either by a current account or by a capital account surplus.

4. _____ When a country's income from foreign trade exceeds its expenditures, there is an increase in money holdings in the current account but a deficit in the capital account.

5. _____ Any surplus in an individual's current account is financed by a deficit in the capital account.

6. _____ One reason why central banks intervene in the foreign exchange market is that if a country's currency depreciates, inflation at home increases.

7. _____ Exchange rates typically are expressed as the price of a domestic currency in terms of 1 unit of a foreign currency.

8. _____ When one country increases its efficiency in production, all other countries producing the same good benefit because they can lower their production and purchase the good at a lower price from the more efficient country.

9. _____ Most industrialized countries are pleased to see the NICs develop their own manufacturing sectors because this promotes international competition.

10. _____ The largest percentage of primary commodities imported into the United States is accounted for by fuels.

11. _____ Since 1955, international trade in manufactured goods has increased.

12. _____ It is very unusual for a central bank to intervene in the foreign exchange markets to support its own currency.

13. _____ Most statistical evidence indicates that flexible exchange rates have helped smooth the adjustment of current account deficits.

MULTIPLE CHOICE QUESTIONS

1. All of the following statements are correct except
   a. one country's exports are another country's imports
   b. when domestic residents sell goods to foreigners, they are exporting goods
   c. when domestic residents buy goods from foreigners, they are importing goods
   d. when a Canadian tourist visits Disney World in Florida, the admission fee is a U.S. export
   e. all of the above statements are incorrect

2. The less-developed countries are
   a. primarily exporters of raw materials and importers of manufactured goods
   b. primarily exporters of manufactured goods and importers of raw materials
   c. feel that they are exploiting the industrialized countries because of the sharp increase in raw materials prices
   d. none of the above

3. When a country faces a persistent current account deficit,
   a. it should increase its imports and reduce its exports so that more money flows into the economy
   b. it should revalue its currency upward on the international markets to encourage more exports
   c. it should tax imports, subsidize exports, and devalue its currency
   d. it should continue to finance the deficit by borrowing more from foreign governments

4. During the late 1950s and early 1960s,
   a. exchange rates were allowed to float freely and were determined by the supply of and demand for currencies
   b. most exchange rates were kept fixed
   c. exchange rates were allowed to clean float
   d. central banks played no role in the foreign exchange markets

5. The foreign exchange system in which central banks are not formally committed to fixing exchange

rates but often do intervene to affect the rates is known as
   a. adjustable peg   c. free floating
   b. clean floating   d. managed floating

6. All of the following statements are correct except
   a. a gold standard has no effect on exchange rates in the foreign exchange markets
   b. proponents of the gold standard argue that it will reduce inflation
   c. currently, no countries are on a gold standard
   d. the gold standard would have almost the same effect as a common world currency

7. In the short run, it is possible for an economy to experience
   a. a recession in the domestic economy and a current account deficit
   b. a level of high employment and output domestically and a current account deficit
   c. high unemployment domestically and a current account surplus
   d. high employment and output domestically and a current account surplus
   e. all of the above

8. A country is in external balance when
   a. aggregate demand equals aggregate supply
   b. there is no unemployment in the economy
   c. exports equal imports
   d. more money flows into the economy than flows out

AT THIS POINT YOU SHOULD BE ABLE TO . . .

1. Give a general description of world trade patterns, with emphasis on trade between industrialized countries and less-developed countries.
2. Explain the role of the foreign exchange market, describe how exchange rates are established between two different currencies, and explain why a currency appreciates or depreciates.
3. State how governments can affect the foreign exchange rate through intervention in the market.
4. Define the balance of payments, compare both an individual's and a country's balance of payments accounts, construct the balance of payments accounts when given the appropriate data, and explain the effects of both a surplus and a deficit on a country's capital and current accounts.
5. Explain why a country cannot incur a deficit continually in its current account.
6. Distinguish between fixed, clean floating, and dirty floating exchange rate systems; also, describe the adjustable peg system of exchange rates.
7. Calculate the exchange rate between two currencies when given the appropriate data.
8. Describe the effects of an international gold standard on the foreign exchange markets and state two reasons why proponents favor a return to the gold standard.
9. Explain what it means when an economy is in both internal and external balance; also, state the meaning and give an example of an internal and an external disequilibrium.
10. Explain why a mix of policies is often more effective in restoring an internal and external equilibrium than a single policy.

QUESTIONS FOR THOUGHT

1. What does it mean when one currency appreciates or depreciates against other currencies? How can this happen? Does it have any effect on international trade? Does it affect domestic economic activity? Explain.

2. It is not unusual for central banks to enter the foreign exchange market. Why do the banks intervene? Does the intervention affect the operation of the market? Explain.

3. Why do countries keep balance of payments accounts? Is it ever possible for all countries engaging in international trade to have current account deficits at the same time? Explain.

4. When a country builds up a current account surplus, it increases its ownership of the rest of the world. Describe how this can happen.

5. When a country has a balance of payments problem, it must make adjustments. Explain why. What are some of the adjustments the country can make?

6. Professors Fischer and Dornbusch state in the text that "without central banks there are no balance of payments problems." Explain how this can be true. Is it always true? Why?

7. How does the adjustable peg system of foreign exchange rates differ from a system of floating rates? What type of system is most of the world on today?

8. Why is a policy mix often more desirable than a single policy when the economy faces both an internal and an external disequilibrium? What kind of basic adjustments can policy promote?

35

The Gains from Trade and Problems of Trade

Chapter 35 is organized around two major themes: specialization and government activity in the international market. Countries specialize in the production of certain goods because of the law of comparative advantage. Comparative advantage means that one country produces a particular good at a lower relative cost than another country. Thus, specialization permits a more efficient use of the world's resources. But when each country specializes in production, an excess of goods is produced. This excess of goods is the basis for trade between nations. As nations trade, they obtain goods which are produced as efficiently as possible. Each nation has more goods available for consumption than it would if all goods were produced at home. Thus, trading may generate gains for the entire world because world output increases and resource waste is reduced.

The second major theme of Chapter 35 is government reaction to problems in international trade. Although countries are made better off trading, some groups within a country may be hurt. These groups want to reduce trade to better their positions. In the past, governments relied primarily on tariffs to restrict trade. Although tariffs increase government revenue and protect some industries, they also impose a social cost because there is a loss of consumers' surplus and because producers waste resources. This social cost is a deadweight loss to society.

As you study Chapter 35, one of the first concepts you must master is comparative advantage, since it is used throughout the chapter. The world economy is more integrated now than at any time in history, and so our daily lives are affected not only by the U.S. economy but by the economies of other countries as well. There is little indication that the members of the world economy will return to the protectionist ideology of the early twentieth century and before. In fact, economies may become even more integrated.

CHAPTER OUTLINE

1. When countries use different production techniques, they specialize in producing those goods which they can produce at relatively lower costs. This is the law of comparative advantage.
   a. For any two countries producing the same goods (even if one country has an overall productivity advantage over the other), as long as there are *relative* productivity differences, there is a basis for trade.
   b. When two countries that use different currencies and have relative productivity differences trade in free international markets, an equilibrium exchange rate is established between the two different monies. The foreign exchange market attains an equilibrium when the demand for and the supply of each currency are equal.
   c. When one country produces a good at a lower relative cost than another country, it specializes in that good, and both countries gain from trading. Even if one country produces all goods more efficiently than the other, the less efficient country may still specialize and receive gains from trade.
   d. The law of comparative advantage tells how countries will specialize when the relative productivities of the inputs and costs of producing the same goods differ. Consideration of only a country's absolute advantage in producing all goods creates an inefficient allocation of resources which results in higher production costs for some goods.
   e. The returns to production, specialization, and trade between two countries (each with a comparative advantage in producing one good) are influenced by the relative sizes of the countries.
   f. When a country specializes in production and trade with the rest of the world, that country gains while making its trading partners no worse off. This happens because the country specializing in production exports those goods which it produces more efficiently and imports those goods which it produces less efficiently. Thus, trade permits the country specializing in

production to have more of the imported good than it could produce directly.
  g. The law of comparative advantage and trade holds for the two-good case or the many-goods case. Specialization and the patterns of international trade are determined primarily by labor productivity differences among countries.
2. The principle of comparative advantage (as developed by Ricardo) emphasizes differences in relative labor productivity; however, differences in the relative costs of production are the most important contributors to trade between countries. These differences in relative costs are determined by differences in both technology and factor endowments.
  a. When one country has relatively more of one factor than another country, it exports those goods which require a production technique that uses the relatively abundant factor intensely and imports goods which require the use of the relatively scarce factor. Countries with a high capital-labor ratio export capital-intensive goods and import labor-intensive goods.
  b. Data indicate that countries with high capital-labor ratios do in fact export goods that are more capital-intensive and import goods that are more labor-intensive. This evidence supports the principle of comparative advantage.
3. When goods are differentiated (especially finished goods), intra-industry trade occurs between countries so that the role of comparative advantage is diminished. Even though the same good is produced by the same industry in different countries, the effects of product differentiation dominate the relative production cost advantage experienced by the different countries. There are three reasons for this. First, consumer preferences create a demand for a broad range of goods. Second, economies of scale in an industry may make it possible for the industry to produce both for domestic and for foreign consumption. Third, these economies of scale lower the long-run average cost of production enough to offset the cost of transporting the goods to foreign markets; otherwise, the country produces only for its domestic market. For primary commodities, the patterns of trade are determined by comparative advantage and relative factor availability.
4. Even though countries trade in the international economy, some people may not be better off. Two examples are the effect of Argentina's emergence as an exporter of beef and Japan's increasing prominence as an automobile exporter.
  a. The development of refrigerated transportation allowed Argentina to become a major producer and exporter of beef. The cattle industry in Argentina gained, but other land-using producers and domestic consumers were made worse off because land prices (rents) and beef prices increased. In the United States, beef prices fell, and so American consumers gained but U.S. beef producers lost.
  b. Japanese workers and American consumers gain from the importation of cars produced in Japan, but domestic autoworkers and stockholders of the automobile industry lose. It has been suggested that the U.S. government should restrict foreign car imports to make more jobs in the auto industry for American workers. When domestic industries are threatened by foreign competition, they often advocate a commercial policy by government that affects trade directly. Such a policy may include taxes, subsidies, and direct restrictions on imports and exports.
5. The tariff is a common type of trade restriction that requires the importer to pay a specified percentage of the world price of the imported good to the government. The tariff raises the price to consumers above the world price of the good.
  a. If the world price of a good is below its domestic equilibrium price, there is a shortage of the good in the domestic market which is satisfied by imports (as long as the goods are perfect substitutes).
  b. A tariff on imports raises the prices of a commodity above the world price in the home market. Thus, domestic producers supply more at this tariff-inclusive price, and the quantity demanded by consumers falls. The tariff allows domestic firms to be less efficient and produce at a higher marginal cost, and it acts as a subsidy to the home firms. The level of imports declines because of the increase in domestic production and the decrease in quantity demanded.
  c. The imposition of tariffs on imported goods results in both a transfer of income and a deadweight loss of welfare to society. First, because the tariff-inclusive price of the good is above the world price, there is a transfer of income from consumers to producers in the form of higher profits. Second, there is a transfer of income to the government in the form of tariff revenue. Neither of these transfers represents a net cost to society. Third, because production is less efficient, domestic production costs are above world production costs. Thus, resources are not used efficiently. This resource waste represents a cost to society. Fourth, there is a loss of consumers' surplus

because the social value of an extra unit of the good is greater than its costs. The loss of consumers' surplus and the resource waste represent a net cost to society (a deadweight loss).

6. To promote the nation's best interest, a tariff should bring about a socially desirable objective with the least waste relative to other available instruments. If there are other ways to achieve the objective at a lower cost to society, the tariff is a second-best solution.

   a. One argument for a tariff is that it should be used to protect the traditional way of life of certain producers or lower the consumption of imported luxury goods; however, a tariff raises the price to all consumers. A subsidy to the threatened producers and a consumption tax on the luxury good are better alternatives because they cost less.

   b. The infant industry argument for a tariff is that government should protect new industries from the threat of foreign competition. The argument is based on the notion that time is needed for new industries to become efficient in production. A tariff, however, has two weaknesses. First, it costs all consumers of that good while the firm is learning how to produce. Second, the industry may not become competitive if it is protected by a tariff. A government subsidy to the industry for a specified length of time during the learning period involves a lower cost to society. Thus, a tariff to protect infant industries is a second-best solution.

   c. Although tariffs have been a major source of government revenue in the past, today they are not. As a source of revenue, tariffs are second best.

   d. The argument that tariffs are needed to protect defense-related industries or industries which generate positive externalities is inadequate because the same goals can be accomplished with a production subsidy.

   e. The argument that domestic industries should be protected from cheap foreign labor is also no grounds for a tariff. Some countries have a comparative advantage in the production of certain products because labor is less expensive; to place a tariff on the goods produced in those countries means that the United States loses the benefits of trade. Some industries in the United States have lost their comparative advantage, and so the goods produced by these industries should be produced abroad.

   f. If foreign governments temporarily subsidize industries in order to assist them or give them an advantage in production, a tariff or some restriction of trade may be justified to alleviate the disruption to domestic industry. If a foreign producer sells output abroad at a price below the cost of production (dumps) and disrupts domestic production, a tariff to restrict such behavior may be justified.

   g. If a country exercises monopoly power and is able to influence the world price of commodities, the nation gains from a tariff because the world price is reduced. In the world market, however, resources are misallocated. This type of tariff is the optimal tariff.

   h. Although most tariffs are second-best solutions to world trade problems, they are still imposed by many nations.

      (1) One reason why tariffs are still imposed is that some groups which benefit from the restriction of trade are politically more powerful and better organized than those who are hurt by the tariff.

      (2) It is easier and much less obvious to taxpayers for the government simply to impose a tariff and restrict imports than to subsidize industries even though the subsidy involves a lower social cost.

   i. Although there may be occasions when a tariff, in principle, is in the social interest, in practice, tariffs impose a greater social cost than is necessary to achieve the desired goals. Thus, most economists oppose tariffs and are skeptical of their success.

7. In the United States and most of the industrialized world, tariffs are now lower than they have been in over a century. World trade is relatively free.

   a. The General Agreement on Tariffs and Trade (GATT) represents an attempt by the governments of most of the industrialized countries to promote free trade and follow the rules of "good behavior" in the world market.

8. Three nontariff instruments may be used as part of a country's commercial policy.

   a. Quotas restrict the quantity of imports which may come into a country. Quotas cause prices in the home country to rise (like a tariff) above the world price. Unlike tariffs, however, quotas exclude any effect of foreign competition on home prices, and they are more attractive to policymakers. When a quota is imposed on imports, domestic producers are removed from the threat of foreign competition.

   b. A government may impose nontariff barriers to limit imports into a home country. These barriers are administrative regulations which discriminate against imports, and they are used frequently by many countries.

   c. A third policy instrument used by governments

THE GAINS FROM TRADE AND PROBLEMS OF TRADE

is export taxes and subsidies. By subsidizing production of a good for export, by exempting the export from certain taxes, or by providing inexpensive credit, a country raises its exports at the expense of domestic consumers.

IMPORTANT TERMS AND THEIR MEANING

Match the following terms with the correct definition or phrase.

1. _____ A quantitative restriction on the amount or value of a particular good that can be imported into a home country

2. _____ The payment of money from the government to producers to encourage production or consumption of a good

3. _____ Describes a country having a greater productivity in the production of all goods; there is no relative advantage in the production of one good over another

4. _____ A tariff which lowers the price paid by the home country; foreign exporters pay part of the tariff because the home country exercises some monopoly power

5. _____ Two-way trade within an industry; a country both imports and exports the same good

6. _____ Government policies that influence trade through taxes, subsidies, and direct restrictions on imports and exports

7. _____ An international agreement to follow the rules of good behavior by not interfering with trade and by promoting reductions in tariffs

8. _____ Requires the importer of a good to pay a specific fraction of the good's world price to the government, thereby raising the price of the good to domestic consumers

9. _____ Occurs when foreign producers sell abroad at a price below what it costs to produce the good

10. _____ When two countries trade and one specializes in production, the country that specializes is made better off, with the other country being made no worse off

11. _____ The relative amounts of the factors of production a country has

12. _____ Countries specialize in the production of those goods which they can make at a relatively lower cost

13. _____ Administrative regulations that discriminate against foreign goods in favor of home goods

14. _____ States that firms acquire technical know-how and lower costs of production only by being in business; because there is learning by doing, government should protect new industries until they can compete on equal terms with more experienced foreign producers

15. _____ The social cost of a tariff arising from a loss of consumers' surplus and the excess cost of production incurred by firms because of inefficient operation

a. Tariff
b. GATT
c. Comparative advantage
d. Dumping
e. Deadweight loss
f. Infant industry argument
g. Gains from trade
h. Quota
i. Factor endowments
j. Absolute advantage
k. Commercial policy
l. Nontariff barriers
m. Optimal tariff
n. Subsidy
o. Intra-industry trade

EXERCISES

1. Suppose the small island nations of Alphania and Betania are located in the south Pacific. The islands are separated by 500 miles of ocean, and both produce pineapples and breadfruit. Labor is essentially the same in both countries and is the primary input in production. Over the relevant range of production for both countries, costs are constant because an increase in output doesn't cause the marginal and average costs to rise. Tables 35-1 and 35-2 show the production possibilities schedules for each country. (Remember, you studied the production possibilities frontier in Chapter 1.) Each country has six alternative output combinations.

   a. The production possibilities schedules show

TABLE 35-1
PRODUCTION POSSIBILITIES SCHEDULE FOR ALPHANIA

GOOD	ALTERNATIVE					
	A	B	C	D	E	F
Pineapples (bushels)	0	15	30	45	60	75
Breadfruit (bushels)	25	20	15	10	5	0

TABLE 35-2
PRODUCTION POSSIBILITIES SCHEDULE FOR BETANIA

GOOD	ALTERNATIVE					
	A	B	C	D	E	F
Pineapples (bushels)	0	20	40	60	80	100
Breadfruit (bushels)	50	40	30	20	10	0

that (Alphania/Betania) _____ has an absolute advantage in the production of (pineapples/breadfruit/both) _____.

b. In Alphania, 1 bushel of breadfruit costs _____ bushels of pineapples, and so 1 bushel of pineapples costs _____ bushel of breadfruit. In Betania, the cost of a bushel of breadfruit is _____ bushels of pineapples, and so 1 bushel of pineapples costs _____ bushel of breadfruit.

c. _____ has a comparative advantage in the production of breadfruit, while _____ has a comparative advantage in the production of pineapples.

d. If the countries decide to trade with each other, Alphania should specialize in _____, and Betania should specialize in _____.
Suppose that the countries do trade and decide to exchange 1 bushel of breadfruit for 2.5 bushels of pineapples. Each country finds this exchange rate acceptable because Alphania gets a bushel of breadfruit for 1/2 bushel less of pineapples than it would cost to reallocate its resources. Also, Betania gets 1/2 bushel more of pineapples for each bushel of breadfruit it gives up.

e. Assume that both countries were initially at alternative C on their production possibilities schedules, after specialization, and that Betania produces _____ bushels of breadfruit and Alphania produces _____ bushels of pineapples. If Betania now trades 17 bushels of breadfruit to Alphania for pineapples at the exchange rate of 1 bushel of breadfruit for 2.5 bushels of pineapples, Betania now has _____ bushels of pineapples and _____ bushels of breadfruit. Alphania now has _____ bushels of breadfruit and _____ bushels of pineapples.

f. In this case, there (are/are not) _____ positive gains from trade for both countries.

FILL-IN QUESTIONS

1. The basis for trade between nations is differences in the relative (size/productivity/origin) _____ of inputs, and these differences (do/do not) _____ affect the cost of the output.

2. A country always exports goods in which it has (an absolute/a total/a comparative) _____ advantage and (does/may or may not/does not) _____ produce only that good.

3. If two countries trade, there are (positive/negative) _____ gains from trade when one country is made better off and the other is not made any _____ off.

4. If country A has a high capital-labor ratio and country B has a high labor-capital ratio, we would expect A to export (capital/labor) _____-intensive goods while it imports goods which are (capital/labor) _____-intensive; country B has the (same/opposite) _____ trading patterns.

5. Consumers' preferences for _____, _____ of scale, and reduced _____ costs are forces which help explain intra-industry trade between nations.

6. A _____ requires the importer of a good to pay an import duty on the good so that the price charged in the home market (increases/decreases) _____, quantity demanded (increases/remains constant/decreases) _____, imports (rise/remain constant/fall) _____, and production of the output by domestic firms (rises/remains constant/falls) _____.

7. Some part of the increased consumer payments generated by a tariff is transferred to _____

THE GAINS FROM TRADE AND PROBLEMS OF TRADE   311

and to _____ in the form of higher profits, and these transfers (are/are not) _____ a net cost to society of the tariff.

8. Infant industries (are/are not) _____ as efficient as established industries, and so one argument for a tariff is that it helps the young industries become more (monopolistic/competitive) _____; however, society's costs are lower if the government gives a _____ to the new producers.

9. _____ describes the practice of foreign producers selling their output abroad at a price below what it costs to produce a unit of the good, and it usually takes place during periods of (prosperity/recession) _____ as one means to save _____.

10. The optimal tariff is in the best interest of (a nation/the world) _____, and it represents an international _____ of resources because the home country is able to exercise _____ power.

11. The trade experience of the 1930s (does/does not) _____ serve to encourage nations to support free international trade.

12. A subsidy for exported goods causes the domestic price of the goods to (rise/fall) _____, and so quantity demanded in the home country (rises/falls) _____.

TRUE-FALSE QUESTIONS

1. _____ When Argentina began to export beef in increasing quantities, U.S. exports fell; this shows that some countries may be made absolutely worse off through international trade.

2. _____ As long as the world price of a commodity is below the home country's equilibrium price, there will be some imports into the domestic market.

3. _____ When a tariff is imposed on an import, there is a transfer of revenue from the government to producers.

4. _____ A problem with using a tariff on imports to protect the livelihood of a particular group is that it penalizes consumers because they must pay a higher price for the good.

5. _____ During the 1700s, most governments relied on tariffs as their major source of revenue because tariffs were easy to collect.

6. _____ If two countries specialize in the production of goods they make at a relatively lower cost, each is pursuing its own absolute advantage in the world economy.

7. _____ For any two countries both trading with each other and using different currencies, an equilibrium exchange rate is attained only when all the goods are cheaper in one of the countries.

8. _____ The law of comparative advantage is based on differences in the relative costs of production between countries and has no basis in the productivities of the factors of production.

9. _____ Even though the law of comparative advantage and specialization laid the foundation for trade patterns, the actual patterns established depend mainly on the relative sizes of the countries.

10. _____ The law of comparative advantage holds without question for the simple two-good, two-country case; however, it breaks down when there are many goods and many countries.

11. _____ Both available technology and factor endowment affect a country's cost of production.

12. _____ The more independent world markets become and the greater the obstacles to international trade, the more countries tend to engage in intra-industry trade.

13. _____ When the government imposes trade restrictions, it is difficult to determine who benefits and who loses because these benefits and costs are so diffused throughout the economy.

14. _____ Most economists are opposed to tariffs because tariffs interfere with free trade.

15. _____ The United States has never had high tariffs, although import quotas have been imposed on foreign goods from time to time.

16. _____ When quotas are imposed on imported goods, domestic producers are removed from the threat of foreign competition.

MULTIPLE CHOICE QUESTIONS

1. All of the following might be a commercial policy of the United States except
   a. lending is restricted to Vietnam, and so it cannot buy American goods
   b. the Department of Agriculture supports milk prices so that farmers earn higher profits on dairy products

c. the number of cars imported from Japan is limited by the government
d. the price of imported steel is subject to a 30 percent tariff

2. If the government grants a subsidy on a domestically produced good,
   a. producers increase their level of production
   b. producers are able to operate at some output level other than the most efficient
   c. the subsidy is just like a negative tax to the producer
   d. producers increase their level of output
   e. all of the above

3. The deadweight loss of a tariff
   a. is not a social cost because it is transferred to both producers and government in the form of higher revenues
   b. is not a social cost because society as a whole doesn't pay for the loss
   c. is a social cost because it takes away some consumers' surplus and promotes inefficient production
   d. is a temporary social cost because the government eventually returns the revenue to the citizens in the form of social goods

4. For a tariff to be considered a "good tariff," it must
   a. attain a socially desirable objective with less waste to society than any other available instrument
   b. provide protection to infant industries, promote defense, and generate revenue better than other alternatives
   c. remove any externalities from international trade and promote competition in foreign markets
   d. none of the above

5. All of the following statements are false except
   a. the imposition of a tariff protects the home market from the unfair competition of goods made with cheap foreign labor
   b. one reason why labor is less expensive in some foreign countries is that it is less productive
   c. if foreign labor is cheap, it stands to reason that the goods produced by this labor are of inferior quality
   d. cheap foreign labor implies cheap foreign capital

6. Governments use tariffs more frequently than production subsidies because
   a. it is more difficult to determine who benefits with a tariff than with a subsidy
   b. it appears that only foreign producers are hurt by a tariff
   c. subsidies appear to be a government giveaway of taxpayers' money

d. all of the above
e. none of the above

7. All of the following are nontariff barriers to trade except
   a. the government establishes safety standards on imported products
   b. a duty of $2 is levied on every bottle of French wine imported into the country
   c. the government buys all of its products from domestic firms
   d. the Japanese inspect every American automobile shipped to Japan and reject an entire shipment if one is found to be below standard

Answer the next three questions on the basis of the following table, which shows the number of units of labor required to produce one small computer or one hand-cut glass bowl.

	U.S. LABOR REQUIREMENTS	BRITISH LABOR REQUIREMENTS
Computer	50	250
Glass bowl	20	40

8. The U.S. has an absolute advantage in the production of
   a. the small computer
   b. the glass bowl
   c. both the computer and the bowl
   d. neither good

9. Great Britain has a comparative advantage in the production of
   a. the glass bowl
   b. the small computer
   c. both the computer and the bowl
   d. neither good

10. U.S. labor is relatively more productive in the production of
    a. the glass bowl
    b. the small computer
    c. both the computer and the bowl
    d. neither good

AT THIS POINT YOU SHOULD BE ABLE TO . . .

1. State the law of comparative advantage from the standpoint of both relative costs and relative productivity; also, explain how comparative advantage promotes trade between nations and explain how countries gain from trade.
2. Explain the effect of factor endowments on a country's trade patterns and state how these endowments affect comparative advantage.
3. List three reasons why countries engage in intra-industry trade.

4. Describe how a country can both gain and lose from international trade; also, explain why trade sometimes may be a mixed blessing.

5. Explain and show graphically the effects of a tariff on a free trade equilibrium, describe the benefits and costs to society of imposing a tariff, and distinguish between the transfers and the deadweight losses which result from a tariff.

6. State four arguments for a tariff; state whether each is a best or a second-best argument and explain why.

7. Describe the optimal tariff and explain why governments often prefer a tariff to other alternatives.

8. Explain why trade is less restricted now than it has been in the past.

9. Explain three commercial policies which governments may pursue instead of a tariff.

QUESTIONS FOR THOUGHT

1. When countries using different currencies begin to trade with each other, an equilibrium exchange rate has to be established. Why is this important? What are the effects on trade if the exchange rates are in disequilibrium? Explain.

2. Explain why nations often specialize in the production of one good or a few goods. How is it possible for a nation to be better off by producing only a few goods and selling abroad what is not consumed domestically?

3. The United States exports relatively capital-intensive goods and imports relatively labor-intensive goods. Explain the economic rationale for this trade pattern. Why do LDCs export goods which are relatively more labor-intensive?

4. Western Europe consists of industrialized countries. Japan is also an industrialized country. But the patterns of trade exhibited by the European Economic Community and Japan are very different. How can this be explained? Do market integration and location play a role? Explain.

5. Explain both the distribution and transfer effects of a tariff. Do these effects represent a cost to society? What costs to society are involved in a tariff? Explain why governments often prefer a tariff to other instruments of commercial policy.

36
The Economics of Exchange Rates and International Finance

Chapter 34 was your introduction to the activities in international financial markets. In that chapter, you learned that traders use different monies, and so to facilitate trade, a foreign exchange market is established to determine the price of one currency in terms of another. These exchange rates are determined by the forces of supply and demand for different currencies as long as the government stays out of the market. The demand for and the supply of currencies are determined by importing and exporting goods, and so the status of a country's balance of payments accounts provides a good indication of how its currency will perform on the foreign exchange market. But government doesn't stay out, and the foreign exchange markets aren't completely free to respond to the signals sent by buyers and sellers. Chapter 36 extends the analysis of international financial markets and removes some of the "mysteries" surrounding foreign exchange.

The first sections of Chapter 36 further examine exchange rate systems which are used currently or have been used in the past. Under a system of free floating rates, governments do not maintain any specific value for their currencies, and the rate at which one currency is exchanged for another is determined by the market. Any excess demand for or supply of a currency causes an automatic adjustment, and so an equilibrium is attained between that currency and others. The gold standard was used during the nineteenth century and the early part of the twentieth century. Under the gold standard, the value of a country's currency is fixed in terms of gold. This par value of the currency fixes its value in international exchange. Governments stand willing to buy or sell gold at the currency's official par value, which establishes the exchange rates between currencies. Also under the gold standard, a nation's domestic money supply is linked to its supply of gold. Thus, any change in the stock of gold has a direct effect on the home country's money stock. Any disequilibrium in a country's exchange rates and external accounts is moved automatically toward equilibrium; however, this adjustment process is not instantaneous. The third exchange rate system presented in Chapter 36 is the adjustable peg system used by most of the world during the 1950s and 1960s. Under this system, a government lets its currency float but does intervene in the foreign exchange market from time to time to affect the currency's exchange rate. During the 1960s, most of the world was on a dollar standard. Under this standard, the values of foreign currencies were fixed in terms of the dollar, and dollars served as international reserves. The dollar standard was much like the gold standard; however, a major difference was that a nation's money supply was not linked to the amount of dollars it had.

You should be thoroughly familiar with the exchange rate systems presented in the first half of Chapter 36 before you proceed, because Professors Fischer and Dornbusch next describe the effects of international capital flows and speculation on exchange rates. Capital flows between countries primarily because of interest rate differentials and the relative values of different currencies. Speculators who believe that a currency is about to be devalued may create such an excess supply of that currency on the exchange market that the central bank has no choice but to devalue.

Make sure that you learn the new terms presented in Chapter 36, because you can't really understand international financial markets unless you understand the language used. Also, you should know the characteristics, strengths, and weaknesses of each of the three exchange rate systems presented. Be able to describe each and know how it affects the domestic economy.

CHAPTER OUTLINE

1. Assuming that both domestic and foreign prices are constant, a nation's imports affect its demand for foreign currencies, while the level of its exports determines the supply of foreign currencies available. When exchange rates are completely flexible and government does not intervene, the foreign exchange market achieves an equilibrium. This equilibrium exchange rate equates the quantity demanded and the quantity supplied of currencies.
    a. Any change in the demand for imports or the

supply of exports in a country causes a disequilibrium in the foreign exchange market, and so the relative prices of goods on the international market change. The country's balance of payments is initially in disequilibrium. But with completely flexible exchange rates, the international value of currencies and import and export patterns change. The balance of payments adjusts automatically until a new equilibrium exchange rate is attained.
2. The gold standard has three distinguishing features. First, its par value is fixed by government. Second, domestic currency is completely convertible into gold. Third, gold is linked directly to a nation's money supply since money is backed by gold (100 percent cover). Any change in the gold stock changes the money stock.
   a. If countries that trade with each other were on the gold standard and the exchange rates between currencies were calculated from the relative price of gold (gold parity), an imbalance in the balance of payments accounts would eventually adjust itself, so that countries would end up in a position of external equilibrium. This happens because the international flow of gold affects each nation's money supply, which in turn affects spending on domestically produced goods, imports, and exports. The adjustment process on a gold standard is automatic.
   b. The nineteenth century (when most of the world was on a gold standard) was a period of above-average unemployment and below-average inflation.
3. Since World War II, exchange rates have been determined by either the adjustable peg or the managed float system.
   a. Under the adjustable peg system of the 1960s, most exchange rates were fixed against the U.S. dollar. This dollar standard was much like the gold standard because the values of foreign currencies were fixed in terms of dollars, currencies supposedly were convertible into dollars, and central banks supposedly used dollars for their international reserves to meet their citizens' demands for foreign currency. The major difference between the dollar and gold standards was that no automatic adjustment existed under the dollar standard.
   b. If a country on the dollar standard lost international reserves because of a balance of payments deficit, the losses were sterilized if the central bank of that country simply engaged in an open market operation and bought bonds from the public. If the open market operation increased the money supply enough to offset the decrease which would have occurred because of the loss of reserves, the loss was sterilized. If a country had a surplus in its balance of payments, it sold bonds and reduced the money supply. Sterilization prevented the automatic adjustment process of the gold standard. Eventually, a country had to adjust its currency's exchange rate because there was a limit to sterilization.
   c. If a country devalues its currency in order to ease its balance of payments problems, it must be a real devaluation. A real devaluation requires that the country's goods become relatively cheaper than those of its trading partners so that imports fall and exports rise as devaluation occurs. The country must also reduce its spending (especially on imports) by contractionary monetary and fiscal policies. If prices within the country increase by as much as the nation's currency is devalued, there is no change in the relative prices of goods on the international market. It is difficult to achieve a real devaluation.
4. When individuals in one country sell assets to or buy assets from another, there is an international flow of capital through the countries' capital accounts of their balance of payments. Capital flows affect both the supply of and the demand for foreign currencies, and so exchange rates change as the countries experience a capital account deficit or surplus. A surplus (inflow) or deficit (outflow) in a country's capital account intensifies the balance of payments account surplus or deficit which results from its current account. A capital outflow or inflow for a country depends primarily on the relative rate of return (interest rates paid) to asset ownership in that country; however, the expectation of an official currency devaluation or revaluation greatly affects the capital flow for a country. In fact, if hot money flows out of a country because of an anticipated devaluation, it may actually force the government to devalue.
   a. Governments may try to limit the outflow of capital and thus dampen the negative effects on foreign exchange markets; however, individuals can usually find ways around government restrictions on the flow of money out of a country.
5. Domestic and international inflation, capital flows, and trade disturbances affect exchange rates.
   a. If a nation's inflation rate is high relative to that of other countries, ultimately it must depreciate its currency in the international markets. This depreciation maintains purchasing power parity (PPP) if it exactly offsets the country's inflation rate so that the prices of that country's

goods relative to the prices of goods produced in other countries remain unchanged. PPP leaves the level of imports and exports between countries unchanged.

b. If a country becomes more self-sufficient in meeting domestic demand or more dependent on the rest of the world, its foreign exchange rates change. In fact, any trade disturbance affects a country's exchange rate.

c. The types of fiscal and monetary policies pursued by a country affect its exchange rate. Restrictive policies lower import demand, lower balance of payments deficits, encourage exports, and tend to appreciate a country's exchange rate. Expansionary policies increase imports, lower exports, and tend to depreciate a country's currency.

d. When a nation pursues a tight monetary policy, domestic interest rates rise, and so there is an inflow of capital from other countries. A policy of easy money relative to the rest of the world lowers interest rates and encourages capital to flow out of the country. These capital flows affect the international demand for and supply of currencies, and so exchange rates rise or fall to reflect the new foreign exchange market. As the exchange rates move, trade flows change.

e. A central bank's intervention in the foreign exchange market in an attempt to affect its currency's exchange rate with other currencies is called dirty floating. It is difficult to determine whether central bank intervention is designed to change the exchange rate significantly or simply to smooth out short-term fluctuations.

6. It is still debated in international financial circles whether the world should be on a fixed or a flexible exchange rate system.

a. One argument is that if flexible rates promote speculation and create wide speculative swings in exchange rates, the rates should be fixed. On the other hand, if the fluctuations in the rates are the result of real forces in international trade, the flexible rates promote efficient trade. A recent argument is that under a fixed-rate system, central banks pursue more stable policies in both the domestic and the international economies. A third argument examines whether a fixed or a flexible exchange rate system promotes a greater degree of freedom of trade. The evidence is mixed on the first two issues but suggests flexible rates for the third.

b. It is unlikely that an economy will return to the gold standard because it is unlikely that society wants to control the domestic money stock through the balance of payments. Also, the production and storage of gold wastes resources. The money stock may be controlled more strictly by means other than the gold standard.

IMPORTANT TERMS AND THEIR MEANING

Match the following terms with the correct definition or phrase.

1. _____ Countries fix the value of their currencies in terms of dollars, and so the exchange rates are fixed in terms of dollars

2. _____ A country's foreign currencies and other assets which are used to meet its citizens' demand for foreign currencies

3. _____ The movement of capital either into or out of a country; determined by the size of its capital account surplus or deficit

4. _____ The face value (nominal value) of an asset; for gold, it is the metal's price in terms of currency

5. _____ Given the face value of a currency, there is an equal amount of gold to cover the value of the currency

6. _____ The ability to exchange currency for gold; on demand, a government buys or sells its home currency for gold at the par value

7. _____ A central bank neutralizes the effect of reserve gains or losses on the domestic money supply by undertaking open market sales or purchases that exactly balance the reserve changes

8. _____ Large flows of capital out of a country as a result of people expecting the home currency to be devalued; such large flows of hot money can cause a devaluation

9. _____ The money supply of a country is determined by the amount of gold it possesses

a. 100 percent cover
b. Sterilization
c. Freely flexible exchange rates
d. Speculative attack
e. Par value
f. Dollar standard
g. Purchasing power parity
h. Convertibility
i. Capital inflows and outflows

THE ECONOMICS OF EXCHANGE RATES AND INTERNATIONAL FINANCE

10. ____ The exchange rate that maintains the relative prices of goods in two countries at a constant level

11. ____ A flexible exchange rate system in which rates adjust automatically to the demand for and supply of currencies; there is no government intervention

j. Gold backing

k. International reserves

EXERCISES

1. Table 36-1 shows the exchange rates for five different currencies for the years 1979 and 1982. The data are expressed in terms of the number of the foreign currency units necessary to buy a U.S. dollar. Study the data in Table 36-1. This exercise is designed to show the appreciation or depreciation of currencies.

    a. Complete column A by converting the exchange rates from currency units per dollar to dollars per currency unit. This allows you to see what 1 foreign currency unit costs in U.S. dollars.

    b. Complete column B by determining whether the U.S. dollar appreciated or depreciated in value against each foreign currency. If the dollar appreciated, enter a plus sign corresponding to the appropriate currency. If the dollar depreciated against a currency, enter a minus sign.

    c. Complete column C by determining whether each foreign currency unit appreciated or depreciated against the U.S. dollar. Enter a plus sign for appreciation and a minus sign for depreciation.

    d. Over the 2 years shown, the dollar appreciated against all currencies except the _____ and _____.

    e. When the dollar appreciates against a particular currency, that currency _____ against the dollar.

FILL-IN QUESTIONS

1. If the world is on a gold standard with 100 percent cover, convertibility, and a par value of gold, a surplus in a country's balance of payments accounts (does/does not) _____ lead to an automatic adjustment since the domestic money supply (increases/decreases) _____, interest rates (rise/fall) _____, and spending (increases/decreases) _____.

2. When countries fixed the price of their currencies in terms of the U.S. dollar, they were under the _____ standard, and this (was/was not) _____ exactly the same as the gold standard.

3. When a country has a real devaluation of its currency, imports become (more/less) _____ expensive, while exports (rise/fall) _____ in price, and so we expect any balance of payments deficit to (increase/decrease) _____.

4. A country with high interest rates will generally have an (inflow/outflow) _____ of capital; however, if there is exchange rate speculation in a country, the capital flows tend to become (stabilized/destabilized) _____.

5. In order to maintain _____ between two currencies, the exchange rate must keep the relative prices of goods in the countries (constant/low) _____.

6. Restrictive monetary and fiscal policies tend to (increase/decrease) _____ the demand for imports, (increase/decrease) _____ exports, and (increase/decrease) _____ a balance of payments deficit.

TABLE 36-1

FOREIGN CURRENCY UNIT	CURRENCY UNITS PER DOLLAR		(A) DOLLARS PER CURRENCY UNIT		(B) CHANGE IN VALUE OF DOLLAR IN TERMS OF CURRENCY UNIT	(C) CHANGE IN VALUE OF CURRENCY UNIT IN TERMS OF DOLLAR
	1979	1981	1979	1981		
Australian dollar	1.12	1.46				
South African rand	1.19	1.14				
Indian rupee	8.12	8.68				
Norwegian krone	5.07	5.74				
New Zealand dollar	1.02	.87				

Source: Federal Reserve Bulletin, May 1982, p. A68.

7. Under a clean floating foreign exchange system, the exchange rate between currencies is determined solely by the forces of _____ and _____, and the government (does/does not) _____ intervene to support its currency's value in the international markets.

TRUE-FALSE QUESTIONS

1. _____ During the period when most of the world was on a gold standard, there were periods of high inflation (besides wartime) and high unemployment.

2. _____ The adjustable peg and gold standard exchange rate systems are pure forms of exchange rates because only the market establishes the value of one currency in terms of another.

3. _____ The only reason why countries were on the dollar standard during the 1960s was the automatic adjustment mechanism between a country's money stock and its balance of payments.

4. _____ When a central bank sterilizes the effects of a reserve gain on the money supply, it sells assets on the open market just enough to offset the reserve gain.

5. _____ A devaluation of a country's currency by 10 percent and an increase in domestic prices by the same percentage doesn't make the country's exports more competitive in foreign markets.

6. _____ The flow of capital between countries serves only to disrupt free trade, misallocate resources, and present policymakers with a serious problem.

7. _____ For any two countries using different currencies, the purchasing power parity exchange rate between the currencies changes if prices rise in one country and fall in the other.

8. _____ When Great Britain began to produce oil from the North Sea, the purchasing power parity exchange rate between the British pound and the U.S. dollar increased.

9. _____ If the French central bank followed a restrictive monetary policy while the Bank of England followed a policy of easy money, we would expect capital to flow from France to England.

10. _____ Central banks usually are able to distinguish between short-run fluctuations and fundamental changes in their countries' exchange rates.

11. _____ If society wants to affect inflation and unemployment through monetary policy, it cannot follow the gold standard rules.

12. _____ There is strong evidence that a flexible exchange rate system causes more inflation and unemployment than a system of fixed rates.

13. _____ Most economists do not consider the gold standard a realistic alternative for foreign exchange markets.

MULTIPLE CHOICE QUESTIONS

Circle the correct answer.

1. A depreciation of the dollar in the foreign exchange markets means that
   a. imported goods cost U.S. citizens less
   b. the dollar buys more in the foreign goods markets
   c. U.S. exports become less expensive for foreigners
   d. U.S. exports become more expensive for foreigners
   e. none of the above

2. When exchange rates are completely flexible and the government does not intervene in the foreign exchange system, an increase in domestic income
   a. leads to an increase in the demand for the dollar so that it appreciates against foreign currencies
   b. increases imports, promotes a balance of payments deficit, and leads to depreciation of the dollar
   c. leads to a reduction in spending on both domestically produced and imported goods, and so the balance of payments improves
   d. causes no change in the international value of the dollar because exports increase while imports decrease

3. All of the following are features of a complete gold standard except
   a. the only medium of exchange is gold
   b. the money stock is backed 100 percent by gold
   c. the government will buy or sell its home currency on demand for gold at a fixed rate
   d. the value of a country's currency is fixed in terms of gold
   e. all of the above are features of the gold standard

4. When the dollar standard was used during the 1960s,
   a. countries fixed the value of their currencies in terms of dollars
   b. There was an automatic adjustment between the amount of dollar reserves held by a country and that country's money stock
   c. currencies were supposedly convertible into dollars because countries used dollars as their international reserves

d. dollars were backed by gold
   e. **a** and **c** above
   f. **b** and **d** above

5. Under the dollar standard, if a country's international reserves increase by 18 percent and the central bank wants to sterilize the effect of the balance of payments surplus, it should
   a. buy enough bonds on the open market so that the money supply increases by 18 percent
   b. sell enough bonds on the open market so that the money supply decreases by 18 percent
   c. sell gold at par so that the amount of currency in circulation is reduced
   d. buy gold at par so that the amount of currency in circulation is increased
   e. none of the above

6. Suppose the exchange rate between the Japanese yen (¥) and the U.S. dollar is ¥200 per dollar and you buy a ¥200,000 bond paying 10 percent per year. If the yen is devalued during the year to ¥250 per dollar, how much would you earn on your investment at the end of 1 year?
   a. lose $120
   b. gain $100
   c. gain $120
   d. lose $100
   e. cannot be determined from the above information

7. An expansionary fiscal and monetary policy in a country has all of the following effects except to
   a. increase any existing balance of payments deficits
   b. increase the demand for imports
   c. increase the value of the country's currency on the foreign exchange market
   d. reduce any existing balance of payments surplus

8. If the United States and France are on a gold standard with the par value of gold in the United States at $25 per ounce and the par value in France at 180 francs per ounce, the gold parity is
   a. 13.8 francs per dollar
   b. 7.2 dollars per franc
   c. 0.5 dollar per franc
   d. 7.2 francs per dollar

AT THIS POINT YOU SHOULD BE ABLE TO . . .

1. Describe and show graphically how a system of free floating exchange rates adjusts the foreign exchange markets so that an equilibrium is established.
2. List three features of a gold standard and explain how under a gold standard adjustments occur so that no country has a balance of payments surplus or deficit.
3. Describe the similarities and differences between the dollar standard and the gold standard; also, explain how a country's central bank sterilizes the effect of changes in its international reserves on its money supply.
4. Distinguish between a currency devaluation and a depreciation and describe how a real devaluation corrects an imbalance in a country's external accounts.
5. Present a reason why capital flows between countries, describe the effects of an anticipated devaluation of a country's currency on its capital inflow and outflow, and explain how currency speculation may actually promote a devaluation.
6. Calculate the purchasing power parity between two currencies.
7. Explain how a country's domestic monetary and fiscal policies affect its exchange rate and level of international trade.
8. List two arguments for a fixed-rate system and two arguments for a flexible-rate system.

QUESTIONS FOR THOUGHT

1. Both the gold and dollar standards have been used by countries in the past. How are the two standards similar? How are they different? Do you think that international trade should use either of these standards again? Explain why or why not.

2. Professors Fischer and Dornbusch state that for a devaluation to work, it must be a real devaluation. What do they mean? Explain why a devaluation accompanied by a domestic price increase by the same percentage does not lead to an improvement in a country's balance of payments. What problems arise when a country tries to undertake a real devaluation?

3. Countries experience capital inflows and capital outflows. Do these flows serve any economic purpose? If so, what? When might the flows of capital be primarily speculative?

4. Explain how a country's domestic macroeconomic policies affect its level of international trade and its currency's exchange rates. Do interest rates play a role? If so, explain.

5. What does it mean to say that a currency is overvalued or undervalued? Under free floating exchange rates, is it possible for a currency to be undervalued or overvalued? Explain.

6. What is the link between a country's international reserves and its domestic money supply? Why might a country want to sterilize any increase or decrease in its reserves? Describe how sterilization works.

37
Problems of Developing Countries in the World Economy

Much of the world's population lives in the less-developed countries. The quality of life for the masses of people in these countries is much worse than that for people in developed countries. This difference in quality of life is present primarily because of the substantial income inequality which exists between countries. The differences between the rich and poor nations prompted the call for a New International Economic Order (NIEO) by the United Nations General Assembly in 1974. The movement for an NIEO is led almost entirely by the less-developed countries. In Chapter 37, Professors Fischer and Dornbusch discuss the problems of the LDCs, examine the role of international trade in establishing growth strategies, and discuss the effects of foreign aid as a vehicle for growth.

Chapter 37 begins with a description of the world distribution of income and the NIEO. Although substantially below the level in developed countries, the quality of life in the LDCs has improved since 1960. But the gap between the per capita income of the LDCs and that of the developed nations has continued to widen even though the growth rate of per capita income for the LDCs has been greater than that for the industrialized countries. Thus, it is questionable whether any relative improvements in the LDCs' position are attainable.

In the world market, almost half of the LDCs' exports are primary commodities. This reliance on primary commodity exports presents a problem because primary commodity prices are volatile and fluctuate greatly when there are disturbances in the market. This volatility is caused to a large extent by the inelastic demand for primary goods and agricultural products. Any change in supply causes a significant change in both price and export revenue for the LDCs. Since the 1960s, some of the less-developed countries have begun to industrialize and export manufactured goods in world markets. But this change in exports is also causing problems because the developed nations are reluctant to provide access to their markets. In fact, protectionist sentiments are growing in many industrialized countries.

Most LDCs have serious deficits that must be financed. These deficits arise because the LDCs import more than they export, and so this imbalance must be financed through borrowing, foreign aid, and direct investment from other countries. The most commonly used method of financing is borrowing in world financial markets., This borrowing, however, has led many countries to the brink of bankruptcy. Should the LDCs begin to default on their debts, the industrialized countries would be seriously affected because they are the major creditors of the LDCs.

CHAPTER OUTLINE

1. Much of the world's population lives in extreme poverty. This is one reason why the United Nations General Assembly voted in 1974 to approve a resolution calling for a new international economic order (NIEO). The NIEO involves a transfer of wealth from rich nations to poor nations.
    a. Over the past 20 years, the quality of life and the relative position of low-income countries have improved. Life expectancies, literacy rates, years of schooling, and diet have improved in the poor nations; however, the gap between per capita incomes in the rich and poor nations has been expanding.
    b. The LDCs view the northern hemisphere as rich and the southern hemisphere as poor. This north-south distinction is based on differences in income, not political or economic ideology.
    c. The third world nations of the south argue that there are four basic causes of their poverty. First, rich nations control most of the markets for the LDCs' primary commodity exports and keep the commodity prices too low, while at the same time, the prices of goods imported by the LDCs rise. Second, they are discouraged from industrializing and exporting manufactured goods because the rich nations are protectionists. Third, borrowing for investment and development is expensive, and the length of the loan period is too short. Fourth, they

claim that the rich nations should as a matter of justice provide aid for their future development.
2. The LDCs face a problem in world trade because the prices for their primary exports are volatile and because their exports of manufactured goods are being restricted in the markets of some developed nations.
   a. The prices of primary commodities experience very large swings. In addition to wide fluctuations in price, the prices of some raw materials have not increased as much as the prices of manufactured goods. For these primary commodities, their purchasing power falls.
      (1) The major cause of volatile prices for primary commodities is the low elasticity of demand and supply. When there is a disturbance in the market, these inelasticities cause a large effect on price. The low elasticities of demand are caused by the nature of the commodities. Primary commodities are either agricultural products or industrial inputs. When prices change in the short run, quantity demanded is not very responsive because of consumer habits or existing production patterns. Supply is inelastic primarily because of the time period required to increase or decrease output.
      (2) Another contributing factor to the problems faced by the LDCs in world trade is that these countries often overspecialize in a few commodities. Changes in the export prices of its goods cause changes in a country's income. With prices often unstable, so is the country's income from foreign trade. The world price of the LDCs' exports affects their domestic economies significantly more than developed nations are affected by their export prices. To solve this problem, many LDCs are attempting to diversify their production and export base.
      (3) New production techniques are causing an excess supply of some primary (especially agricultural) commodities, and this forces their real prices down. For some primary commodities (especially depletable resources), the long-run tendency is actually rising real prices. The future trend of primary exports, however, cannot be established definitively.
   b. In a few primary commodities, attempts have been made to stabilize export prices, which benefits both the individual producer and the nation. A stabilization program works when producers organize and jointly withhold any surplus of, or satisfy any excess demand for, a commodity. This organization (a buffer stock) sells when commodity prices are high and buys when prices are low. Through these actions, commodity prices stabilize, as do the incomes of the exporting countries. Two problems with stabilization programs are that it is not certain whether the stabilized price is sustainable in the long run, and that the organization of all actual and potential producers is very difficult. Should stabilization evolve into a system of price supports, inefficient production may be encouraged.
3. Because declining export prices and export markets affect a nation's domestic economy, many LDCs have started or are starting industrialization programs.
   a. From the Great Depression to the mid-1950s, many Latin American countries were building an industrial base through a process of replacing imports with domestically produced goods. It was believed that industrialization and substitution would benefit the developing countries because of an expected long-run relative decline in raw materials prices. Substitution of domestically produced goods for imports created jobs and higher income in new industries. Industrialization had a stabilizing effect because it promoted diversification. Some countries are now pursing a growth strategy which emphasizes increased exports rather than displaced imports.
   b. The newly industrializing countries (NICs) consist of a number of less-developed countries which have over the last 20 years developed a significant export sector. These countries have grown faster in real terms than the industrialized countries and have experienced a significant increase in their share of world trade. As their share of world trade increases, the NICs may cause a problem for the industrialized countries. One view is that the NICs will cause the extinction of many labor-intensive industries in the developed countries; however, another view is that all LDCs control only an insignificant share of world trade so that no threat exists. The LDCs, though, are increasing their share of the international market.
   c. Many of the developed nations are now following a more protectionist ideology in their dealings with the LDCs. Trade between the developed and the underdeveloped countries

is becoming less free because of the imposition of quotas, nontariff barriers, and voluntary export restrictions on certain goods. This demise of free, open trade between the north and south goes against the law of comparative advantage, and so world resources are not allocated in the most efficient manner. Because the costs of protectionism usually exceed its benefits, some countries are providing financial assistance to firms and labor hurt by lower-priced imports and are phasing out production in inefficient plants.

4. Because the LDCs spend more than their income, they frequently borrow money in the world financial markets. Since the early 1970s, the debts of third world nations have been increasing primarily because the prices of imported goods (especially oil) have increased while the countries' consumption of these goods has not declined. At the same time, the prices of many commodities fell, causing the countries' income to decline. Aggregate saving has not been adequate to finance both domestic investment and the growing current account deficit, and so this deficit must be financed primarily by borrowing from other countries.

   a. The LDCs finance most of their current account deficit by long-term borrowing from foreign governments, private institutions, and official institutions such as the World Bank. Other sources of debt financing are direct investment from firms in developed countries and by the OPEC countries as well as transfers and aid.

   b. The LDCs eventually will find it difficult to finance their deficits unless they set aside enough of any current trade surplus to pay the interest on their outstanding loans. Otherwise, more must be borrowed just to finance the interest, and so the debt will grow larger. Such a situation may cause a country to default on its loans. The ratio of the LDCs' debt to GNP and debt to exports has increased significantly since 1971. Some countries have been kept out of default only because the lenders have rescheduled their debts.

5. The LDCs of the south believe that the developed countries of the north should provide them aid in addition to loans. Most sound investment projects in the LDCs are financed through the international capital markets at market interest rates, and so there is little evidence that too little funding is going to the developing nations. Many LDCs want loans at special interest rates or some other form of aid. A fundamental issue in regard to the question of aid is whether the developed countries have the right or duty to provide aid to the poor countries.

   a. By actively encouraging trade with the LDCs, the developed countries provide markets for the exports of the south, which is one type of aid. Also, the governments of the northern countries may encourage the governments of the LDCs to follow sensible trade policies and allow their markets to adjust to supply and demand conditions. In some developing countries, aid may never get to the people for whom it was intended.

   b. An open world migration policy would make the world distribution of income more equitable as the poor moved to the rich countries; however, there is no indication that open door immigration policies are about to be implemented by any country.

IMPORTANT TERMS AND THEIR MEANING

Match the following terms with the correct definition or phrase.

1. ____ A measure of the nutrition level and food intake necessary for proper growth, development, and health

2. ____ An important source of development finance and of expertise on development policy; draws attention to world poverty, malnutrition, and disease and provides funds to combat these problems

3. ____ Corporations chartered in one country but doing business in other countries as well

4. ____ Stresses production and income growth through expanded exports rather than displacement of imports

5. ____ The movement or flow of people from one country to another, with the goal of establishing a new residence

6. ____ Some LDCs which are industrializing and have a high level of exports and high growth rates; Mexico, Brazil, and Taiwan are examples

a. Migration

b. Technology transfer

c. Price volatility

d. Buffer stock

e. World Bank

f. New protectionism

7. _____ A policy of replacing imports by domestic production under the protection of tariffs and quotas

8. _____ An organization established to stabilize a commodity market by selling when prices are high and buying when prices are low

9. _____ An association of nations established as part of the Bretton Woods System with the purpose of providing short-term loans to countries with balance of payments deficits in an attempt to maintain exchange rate stability

10. _____ Describes extreme changes in prices

11. _____ The prices of primary commodities which are used as inputs in the production process

12. _____ Consists of the LDCs (third world nations) and argues that the developed nations should give direct assistance or even transfer wealth to the LDCs

13. _____ The belief that the LDCs are making inroads in markets that are overcrowded with goods; thus, there are attempts by some nations to restrict the LDCs' access to their markets

14. _____ The flow of technology and technical knowledge to third world nations

15. _____ Making payments to labor and industries harmed by import competition and phasing out production in inefficient plants

g. New International Economic Order (NIEO)

h. Export-led growth

i. Raw materials prices

j. Adjustment assistance

k. Newly industrial- ing countries (NICs)

l. Calorie requirement

m. International Monetary Fund (IMF)

n. Import substitution

o. Multinational corporations

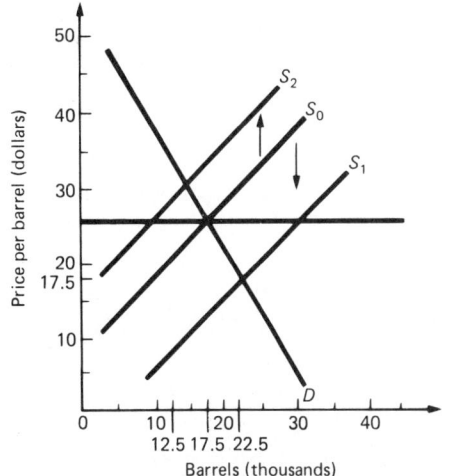

FIGURE 37-1

EXERCISES

1. Figure 37-1 describes the market for coconut oil produced and exported by the island of Alphania. Assume that the initial supply curve is S_0 and that the demand curve is D. Answer the following questions on the basis of Figure 37-1.

   a. The market is initially in equilibrium at a price of $_____ per barrel and a quantity of _____ barrels. There (is/is not) _____ excess demand or excess supply.

   b. If output increases because of a bumper crop, the supply curve (shifts/rotates) _____ to curve _____. At this new equilibrium, price (rises/falls) _____ to $_____ per barrel, and the new quantity is _____ barrels. Total revenue generated for Alphania from the sale of coconut oil (increases/decreases) _____ from $_____ to $_____.

   c. If output suddenly fell and the supply curve shifted to S_2, the price would (rise/fall) _____ to $_____ per barrel, and the equilibrium quantity would (rise/fall) _____ to _____ barrels. Total revenue would (increase/decrease) _____ to $_____.

   d. For Alphania, both the price of and the total revenue from coconut oil (are/are not) _____ stable.

   e. Suppose the producers decide to organize into a commodity buffer stock. The objective of such an organization is to stabilize both prices and revenue. When there is a bumper crop, as shown by S_1, the buffer stock (buys/sells) _____ an amount of coconut oil equal to _____ barrels at a price of $_____ per barrel. When the supply falls, the buffer stock (buys/sells) _____ an amount of oil equal to _____ barrels at a price of $_____ per barrel.

   f. Because of this buying and selling, total export revenues earned from coconut oil (are/are not) _____ stable.

2. Table 37-1 presents per capita GNP data for the countries of Alphania and Betania. Both countries have an annual growth rate of per capita GNP of 6 percent.

   a. Complete the Table 37-1 by calculating the new per capita GNP for each country; enter your answers in Table 37-1. (*Hint*: Multiply the per capita GNP in a given year by 1.06 to obtain the new GNP for the following year.)

TABLE 37-1

YEAR	ALPHANIA PER CAPITA GNP, $	BETANIA PER CAPITA GNP, $	DIFFERENCE, $
1	5000	600	4400
2			
3			
4			
5			
6			
7			
8			
9			
10			
11			
12			

   b. Compute the difference between the per capital GNP for each country for each year; enter your answers in the column marked "difference."

   c. Over the years given, the differences between the per capita GNP of the two countries (increased/decreased) _____ even though they have the same growth rate. All other things constant, there (is/is not) _____ the likelihood that the two countries will be equal in the future.

FILL-IN QUESTIONS

1. During the two decades since 1960, life expectancy in the low-income countries has (increased/decreased) _____, and this is an indication that the quality of life in these countries has _____.

2. Most LDCs are found in the (northern/southern) _____ hemisphere and are often designated as the _____ world nations.

3. Four specific complaints often made by the LDCs about the existing world economic order are:

   a. _____
   b. _____
   c. _____
   d. _____

4. The demand for food and primary commodities, which (are/are not) _____ important exports for the poor countries, is (elastic/inelastic) _____, and so any change in supply causes a (large/small) _____ change in the export's price.

5. When a country's exports are concentrated in one or two goods and these goods face an inelastic worldwide demand, any change in the commodities' world price (does/does not) _____ have large effects on the country's foreign trade revenue.

6. The world prices for exhaustible resources have been (rising/falling) _____ over the past 20 years, but the prices for primary commodities have been _____.

7. A major reason why exporters organize into a buffer stock is to stabilize both the world _____ of the commodities they produce and the export _____ received by the countries.

8. Import substitution requires that a country replace (domestically/foreign) _____ produced goods with goods produced _____, and this development strategy is used because it is believed by many LDCs that increasing employment and incomes are best provided by (primary/manufactured) _____ goods industries.

9. In most categories of manufactured goods, the LDCs account for a relatively (large/small) _____ share of the market; however, the one exception is _____.

10. An increase in import prices and a decrease in export prices causes the LDCs' current account deficit to (increase/decrease) _____, and this deficit must be (consumed/sold/financed) _____.

11. Three primary methods of financing the non-oil-producing LDCs' current account deficits are _____, _____, and _____.

12. The quickest way to equalize the world distribution of income is to permit free _____; however, most developed nations (are/are not) _____ reluctant to do this.

TRUE-FALSE QUESTIONS

1. _____ To say that a country has experienced an export-led growth pattern means that exports rather than the displacement of imports are the source of income growth.

2. _____ Even though the world price of an LDC's exports falls, the country should not be concerned because the effect on the entire economy is usually small.

3. _____ Two major advantages of forming a buffer stock are that organizing all actual and potential producers is relatively easy and that a certain price is maintained in the long run.

4. _____ One reason why long-run prices or primary commodities have been falling is that technology increases supply at a more rapid rate than demand increases.

5. _____ In many LDCs, the major macroeconomic variable is the world price of their exports.

6. _____ The demand for primary commodities is usually more elastic than the supply.

7. _____ In 1978, more than 50 percent of the LDCs' total exports were manufactured goods.

8. _____ The OECD is primarily a vehicle for giving financial aid directly to third world nations.

9. _____ The LDCs of the south believe that the only way for them to achieve satisfactory growth is to have completely free and unrestricted trade between themselves and the developed nations.

10. _____ In addition to being based on differences in wealth, the north-south differential also is based on differences in political and economic organization.

11. _____ One indication that the quality of life has improved in the LDCs over the last 20 years is the increase in life expectancy of the citizens.

12. _____ More than one-half of the world's population lives under conditions of extreme poverty.

13. _____ When the LDCs increase their market share of finished products, consumers in the developed countries usually benefit.

14. _____ One reason why the LDCs have traditionally been borrowers in the world financial markets is that their level of saving has exceeded their level of investment plus the budget deficit.

15. _____ The most important and largest method of financing the non-oil-producing LDCs' current account deficits is direct investment in these countries by the developed nations.

MULTIPLE CHOICE QUESTIONS

Circle the correct answer.

1. Which of the following statements does not describe a characteristic of the primary commodity export markets faced by the LDCs?
   a. these markets are controlled primarily by the developed countries
   b. the prices of nonexhaustible primary commodities have increased relative to the prices of other exports
   c. prices in the primary commodities markets are volatile
   d. price fluctuations in the primary commodities markets prevent serious long-term development planning by the LDCs

2. In 1979, the average per capita income in the low-income countries was
   a. $460   **c.** $946
   b. $540   **d.** $230

3. The militant and influential organization which has the responsibility of paying particular attention to trade and development in poor countries is
   a. UNCTAD   **c.** IMF
   b. OECD   **d.** World Bank

4. The main sources of disturbances on the demand side of the primary commodities markets are
   a. bad weather and harvest failures
   b. uncertainty and improvement in production technology
   c. the business cycle and inventory speculation
   d. increases in the prices of production inputs and government regulations

5. In many LDCs, the primary macroeconomic variable in the economy is the
   a. level of domestic investment
   b. price of its commodity exports on the world market
   c. domestic price of imported goods
   d. level of aggregate saving

6. Which of the following statements is incorrect?

   a. primary commodity producers and farmers act as if they were in a perfectly competitive market

   b. in the market for primary commodities, producers believe that their actions will not affect output price

   c. each producer of a primary commodity has only a negligible share of the market

   d. primary commodity producers try to increase their revenue by adjusting both product price and output levels

7. All of the following are characteristics of the NICs except

   a. an increasing share of world trade

   b. a very low per capita income

   c. relatively high real growth rates of GDP

   d. an increasing share of the export market for manufactured goods

8. Because of the increasing importance of the NICs in the international flow of goods,

   a. the developed nations are taking a more protectionist approach to world trade

   b. trade barriers are falling, thus promoting a more efficient flow of goods

   c. most developed nations have reduced or removed import quotas and nontariff barriers to trade

   d. none of the above

9. When a country reschedules its debt in order to avoid default, it

   a. selectively pays some creditors and dismisses the rest

   b. sterilizes the debt by selling bonds on the open market

   c. renegotiates the repayment period

   d. agrees to settle the debt for some amount less than what is owed to creditors

10. In most cases, private institutions

   a. are willing to make loans to underdeveloped countries only at usurious interest rates

   b. are usually willing to make loans to underdeveloped nations at market interest rates

   c. are very selective when lending money to underdeveloped nations

   d. do not make loans to LDCs

11. All of the following are arguments against foreign aid except

   a. aid programs do more for the elites of the developing countries than for the masses of poor citizens

   b. aid reinforces governments' policies and prevents adjustments which would make the economy more self-sufficient

   c. aid is always used correctly by the recipient country, and citizens of both the donor and the recipient countries are made better off

AT THIS POINT YOU SHOULD BE ABLE TO . . .

1. List three distinguishing features of the low-, middle-, and high-income countries and explain why the call for an NIEO is often put in terms of differences between countries in the north and the south.

2. State four complaints that the LDCs have against the existing world economic order.

3. Describe the effect of price volatility of primary commodities on the trade behavior of the LDCs and state two reasons why such prices are unstable.

4. Explain how a buffer stock may stabilize export prices and import revenue for producers; also, describe two problems encountered with such an organization.

5. Explain import substitution as a development strategy and compare this with export-led growth.

6. Distinguish between the NICs and LDCs, state why some economists argue that continued growth by the NICs may cause serious problems for the industrialized countries, and explain how a new protectionist attitude among the developed nations may be linked to the growth of the NICs.

7. State why external borrowing is important to the LDCs, describe the current financial situation of many third world countries, and identify three sources of financing the non-oil-producing LDCs' current account imbalances.

8. Explain the potential impact of debt defaults by all LDCs on the lending nations.

9. Describe the economic arguments often given for foreign aid and explain how migration may equalize the world distribution of income.

QUESTIONS FOR THOUGHT

1. Why do some third world nations want to diversify their production and exports? Does diversification stabilize overall export revenue for a country? Explain.

2. The buffer stock theoretically stabilizes export prices and revenues; however, there are problems with this type of organization. Explain these problems and describe how they may affect the buffer stock.

3. When countries pursue an import substitution development policy, the law of comparative advantage may be violated. How can this happen? Is there any justification for import substitution? How does this development strategy differ from export-led growth?

4. What problems potentially exist because of the growth and development of the NICs?

5. Poland, Mexico, Argentina, and Brazil have been

close to defaulting on billions of dollars in loans made by the industrialized nations; however, many of their loans have been rescheduled. What does this mean? What would be the effects of a default by these nations? In December 1982, Brazil asked its creditors for $4 billion more. Why might the creditors be willing to extend this new loan to a country in trouble?

6. Why is the north-south distinction often used when referring to the problems of LDCs and developed nations? Why has the south called for a NIEO?

7. Explain how the developed countries can help the underdeveloped nations. What types of direct and indirect aid can be given? Explain.

38
Income Distribution and Poverty in the United States

In Chapter 37, you learned that an inequitable distribution of income exists among the nations of the world; some countries have a large claim on the world's wealth, while others have to share a smaller portion. Income inequalities also exist within countries. In Chapter 38, you study the distribution of income in the United States. Although the United States is one of the richest nations, income inequality still exists here. Many of our citizens live in absolute poverty, while others live in affluence. The distribution of income in a society answers the "for whom" question, since income is the basis for both consumption and an individual's claim on the output of the economy. The role of the economist in studying the distribution of income is limited primarily to describing and explaining income inequality in a society. The economist does not tell us which income distribution is good or bad; don't expect to find one correct or best answer to the "for whom" question.

Most of Chapter 38 is not theoretical. The first section describes the functional distribution of income. Since most of national income accrues to the owners of labor and capital resources, Professors Fischer and Dornbusch emphasize the determination of labor's share of income in a competitive economy. Once you know the theory of how labor's income share is determined, you will understand the basic theory of how the income shares of the other factors of production are determined.

The personal distribution of income describes how aggregate income is broken down among individual economic units. A useful tool which you should master is the Lorenz curve. This curve shows the degree of income inequality in a society by plotting the cumulative percentage of income received against the cumulative percentage of households. The curvature of the Lorenz curve shows the degree of income inequality. As the income distribution becomes more unequal, the Lorenz curve bows out farther.

In the United States, there is both absolute poverty (households are unable to afford the necessities of life) and relative poverty (households are able to afford the necessities but not the amenities of life). You should be aware that income inequality and poverty are not the same thing and that government programs designed to solve one problem may be inappropriate for solving the other.

The highest incidence of poverty in this country occurs among black families, the elderly, and households headed by women. For some, poverty is only transitory because of a temporary disruption of income flows. For others, poverty is permanent, and there is a strong likelihood that it will continue over subsequent generations. The war on poverty, begun during the Johnson administration, had a goal of eliminating poverty in the United States. Using programs of income, education, and welfare assistance and programs to reduce discrimination, the war on poverty did reduce the number of families below the poverty line. The problem, though, is that it appears from recent evidence that this success was based primarily on income transfers, not on an improvement of poor people's earning ability. Such "success" may well reduce the allocative efficiency of the economy and create distortions in the marketplace.

CHAPTER OUTLINE

1. The functional distribution of income describes its distribution among the factors of production. The functional distribution depends on the quantity, quality, productivity, and mix of factors used in production. By examining only labor and capital resources (and assuming that both are homogeneous), we establish the determinants of the functional distribution.
   a. Labor's share of total income is the ratio of total labor income to total income; it is affected by the supply of labor, changes in the capital stock, and changes in production technology.
      (1) A negative relationship exists between the real wage and the quantity of labor demanded because of the law of diminishing returns. At any point in time, both the capital stock and the labor supply are given (quantity of labor supplied is inde-

pendent of the real wage), and so the equilibrium real wage is established at the point where quantity of labor demanded equals quantity supplied. The equilibrium real wage and the quantity of labor supplied at this wage determined total labor income.

(2) A shift in the supply of labor schedule, with a given capital stock, affects the real wage. An outward shift of the labor supply schedule results in a lower real wage, a higher quantity of labor demanded, and a higher level of output. If the demand for labor is inelastic and wages fall sharply when the supply of labor increases, labor's share of total income falls while capital's share rises. The demand for labor may be inelastic with a fixed capital stock because of the rapid decline in the marginal productivity of labor as more is hired. On the other hand, if capital and labor are highly substitutable in production, the demand for labor is more elastic so that wages exhibit only a small decline when the labor supply increases. In this case, labor's income rises relative to that of capital. The key determinant of labor's share of total income when the labor supply varies is the substitutability between capital and labor.

(3) The same analysis applies to changes in the capital stock with a given labor supply. The degree of substitutability of inputs again determines the effect on relative factor prices and the relative factor shares of total income. The effects of changes in either the capital market or the labor market are symmetric with respect to each other.

(4) When technology changes, the effect on the distribution of income is less clear because the change may or may not promote the use of one input at the expense of another.

  b. Data for the United States reveal that the capital-labor ratio has been increasing since 1889; however, the data do not permit an exact isolation of the effects of an increasing capital-labor ratio on the factor shares of total income. Nevertheless, the evidence suggests that labor's share of total income has increased since 1929.

2. The personal distribution of income describes how income is distributed among different members (income classes) of the economy.
  a. The Lorenz curve shows the cumulative distribution of income among households. On the graph, the vertical axis measures percentages of shares of total income, while the horizontal axis measures percentages showing the cumulative fraction of families. If income is distributed equally, the Lorenz curve is a diagonal line bisecting the origin of the two axes. In the United States, income is not equally distributed, and so the curve is nonlinear.
  b. The distribution of income provides an indication of the relative well-being of households in an economic system. There are, however, qualifications. First, since many income data are census data, they do not include transfers in kind or income in kind. Second, although the same data include transfer payments, the statistics do not include information on taxes. Progressive income taxes affect the distribution of income since one of the objectives of progressivity is the achievement of a more equitable distribution of income. Third, the income statistics report income by family; however, both family size and the number of employed family members increase as income levels increase. With more family members employed, family income rises.

3. The distribution of income provides information about the level of poverty in an economy.
  a. The definition of absolute poverty is based on the cost of maintaining a family at the margin between inadequate and adequate levels of food consumption. The poverty level income in 1979 was $7412 for a nonfarm family of four; however, this income level is adjusted as food prices change. During the same year, the median family income was $19,715. A household is relatively impoverished if it can afford all the necessities of life but cannot afford many of the amenities. In the United States, relative poverty is established at an income level equal to one-half the median family income.
  b. In the United States, the highest incidences of absolute poverty are for black families, the elderly, and families headed by women. Past social and sexual discrimination in the areas of education and quality of and access to jobs has promoted the existing pattern of inequality of both opportunity and income.
  c. Although it is important to know the composition of the poverty pool if appropriate assistance programs are to be developed, few data exist which identify the inflows to and outflows from the pool. For some, poverty is transitory, while for others (especially the elderly), poverty is permanent.

d. During the Johnson administration of the 1960s, the government began its war on poverty with the goal of essentially eliminating poverty. Programs to improve education, provide economic and welfare assistance break down discrimination, and enhance educational opportunities were all weapons used in the war. Almost 20 years later, however, the evidence shows that the causes of poverty were not removed. Rather, the level of poverty in this country was reduced primarily because of transfer payments; earnings did not show much relative improvement.

4. In the United States, a typical individual has about a 50-50 chance of socioeconomic mobility. An individual's economic success is affected by family, achievement, and luck. Family background influences socioeconomic status through hereditary factors, environmental effects, and economic effects. Achievement is often measured by years of schooling, since education serves as a screening device for the likelihood of future success. Finally, there is some element of luck in achieving economic success.

5. There is no general agreement about how income should be distributed in the United States or how much inequality society should accept. Through the political process, the distribution of income is affected through three channels: the tax system, the welfare system, and legal and social programs which promote equal opportunity. The progressive income tax does change the distribution of income somewhat; however, it is not efficient and involves costs. Providing welfare assistance may reduce the work incentive. An important problem is the reconciliation between the need for society to provide some income assurance and the need to promote the work incentive.

   a. The negative income tax would make cash payments to low-income households and replace other specific aid programs. The negative income tax would not provide a disincentive to work. Everyone's income would be taxed at a progressive rate. After a certain income level is attained, net receipts from the government disappear. At higher levels of income, there is a positive net tax liability.

   b. The flat-rate tax system proposes to tax every household at a fixed percentage of income; there would be no deductions. The flat-rate tax would alleviate much of the waste and confusion of the current progressive tax structure, and it has received widespread attention among politicians.

IMPORTANT TERMS AND THEIR MEANING

Match the following terms with the correct definition or phrase.

1. _____ Having the ability to purchase the necessities of life but not many of the amenities

2. _____ A proposal to have government make a cash payment to households so that all households have some guaranteed income

3. _____ Describes the distribution of income among different factors of production, especially capital and labor

4. _____ Argues that income redistribution cannot be carried out costlessly; most important is the conflict between provision of welfare benefits and preservation of incentives to work

5. _____ Proposes to tax all incomes at a fixed, specified rate; there would be not deductions

6. _____ The income of unincorporated businesses; consists of a return to both capital and labor

7. _____ A visual tool used to show the distribution of income in an economic system; can be used to show the degree of income inequality

8. _____ Being unable to afford the basic necessities of life; defined as an income equal to 3 times the dollar cost of a specified consumption basket

9. _____ The breakdown of aggregate income among individual economic units

10. _____ Any improvement in the equality of income in a society is made only by incurring a wasteful and inefficient allocation of resources

11. _____ The movement into higher social and economic levels; improving both income and social status

a. Okun's leaky bucket
b. Lorenz curve
c. Socioeconomic mobility
d. Negative income tax
e. Personal income distribution
f. Absolute poverty
g. Flat-rate tax
h. Equality and efficiency trade-off
i. Relative poverty
j. Functional distribution of income
k. Proprietors' income

INCOME DISTRIBUTION AND POVERTY IN THE UNITED STATES

EXERCISES

1. Figure 38-1 shows two different demand curves for labor, D_1 and D_2. It is assumed that the level of capital stock is given and that the labor supply L_s is constant at a particular point in time. Each of the demand curves reflects different elasticities of demand.

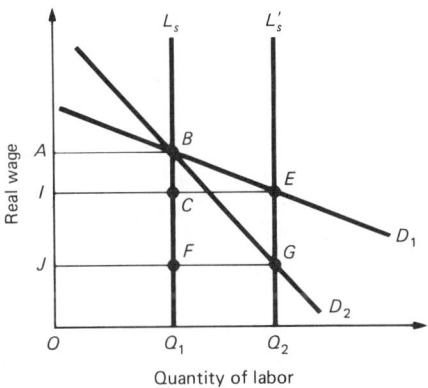

FIGURE 38-1

Answer the following questions on the basis of Figure 38-1.

a. With an initial labor supply of L_s, the equilibrium real wage in the market is _____, and labor's share of total income equals rectangle _____.

b. Demand curve D_1 is relatively (more/less) _____ elastic than demand curve D_2, and this suggests that capital and labor are better substitutes for the market demand described by curve _____ than for the demand described in curve _____.

c. Suppose an increase in the supply of labor shfits L_s to L'_s. Now the real wage associated with D_1 and L'_s is _____, and the equilibrium quantity is _____. Labor's share of total income now equals rectangle _____, and this is (greater than/less than) _____ labor's initial share. Labor (has/has not) _____ been substituted for capital, and this has caused capital's relative share of income to (increase/decrease) _____.

d. On demand curve D_2, in order to establish an equilibrium in the labor market, there is a large (increase/decrease) _____ in the real wage. The real wage has changed relatively (more/less) _____ than the change in quantity demanded, and so labor's share of total income has (increased/decreased) _____ by an amount equal to rectangle _____ minus rectangle _____. The marginal productivity of labor falls (more/less) _____ rapidly in the market associated with demand curve D_2 than in the market associated with D_1.

2. Table 38-1 of your text shows the effects of an economywide increase in the capital-labor ratio. That table is partially reproduced here as Table 38-1. Your task is to complete Table 38-1, assuming that the capital labor ratios *fall*; each unit of labor has less capital with which to work. Your possible choices are increase, decrease, and remain constant. Don't look back at the text.

3. Table 38-2 shows the income distributions in each of two hypothetical economies.

a. Complete Table 38-3 by calculating the cumulative income distribution for each country. Enter your answers in the appropriate columns.

TABLE 38-2

PERCENTAGE OF FAMILIES	PERCENTAGE OF INCOME
INCOME DISTRIBUTION FOR COUNTRY A	
Lowest 20%	1%
Second 20%	4%
Third 20%	5%
Fourth 20%	20%
Top 20%	70%
INCOME DISTRIBUTION FOR COUNTRY B	
Lowest 20%	20%
Second 20%	20%
Third 20%	20%
Fourth 20%	20%
Top 20%	20%

TABLE 38-1

	REAL WAGE	REAL RENTAL OF CAPITAL	LABOR INCOME	INCOME OF CAPITAL	LABOR'S SHARE OF INCOME
Substitutability:					
High	_____	_____	_____	_____	_____
Low	_____	_____	_____	_____	_____

TABLE 38-3

PERCENTAGE OF FAMILIES	PERCENTAGE OF INCOME	
	COUNTRY A	COUNTRY B
First 20%		
First 40%		
First 60%		
First 80%		
100%		

b. On your graph paper, plot the Lorenz curve for each country. Label the vertical axis "percentage of total income" and the horizontal axis "percentage of families."

c. Country A has the (less/more) _____ equitable distribution of income, because 80 percent of the families control _____ percent of income.

d. Absolute income equality is present in country _____, and this is shown by the (linear/nonlinear) _____ Lorenz curve bisecting the origin of the vertical and horizontal axes.

FILL-IN QUESTIONS

1. When economists discuss a nation's distribution of income, they are addressing the ("what"/"how"/"for whom") _____ question.

2. The largest component of the functional distribution of income is (wages/rents) _____, since the _____ factor of production is the most abundant.

3. When capital and labor are highly substitutable, the marginal product of labor (does/does not) _____ fall as fast as when they are poor substitutes, and so an increase in the supply of labor causes both absolute and relative income to (rise/fall) _____.

4. In the United States, over the long term, capital has been growing (faster/slower) _____ than labor, and so the capital-labor ratio has been (increasing/decreasing) _____ and labor's share of total income has (increased/decreased) _____.

5. The personal distribution of income is graphically presented by a _____ curve which shows the (absolute/relative/cumulative) _____ distribution. For the United States, the curve indicates that income (is/is not) _____ distributed equally.

6. Two qualifications to the personal distribution of income are that it doesn't include _____ and _____ that are not deducted.

7. The _____ family income level of an economy has half the families above and half below that level.

8. The incidence of poverty falls most heavily on (white/black) _____ households and households headed by _____.

9. Three determinants which affect economic success are _____, _____, and _____.

10. There (is/is not) _____ a general agreement among politicians and economists about the nation's distribution of income primarily because of the trade-off between _____ and _____.

11. A _____ tax structure increases a household's tax liability as its income increases; however, a _____ system imposes on every household the same percentage of income as a tax liability.

12. One major problem with public assistance programs is that the _____ to work is reduced, and this (is/is not) _____ a waste of society's resources.

TRUE-FALSE QUESTIONS

1. _____ According to recent studies, the war on poverty begun during the Johnson administration greatly improved the earning potential of many of the poor, raised income levels, and can be called a success.

2. _____ For some households, poverty is only transitory because incomes will increase in the future, but for others, poverty is permanent.

3. _____ Past discrimination in education, employment, and access to jobs is one reason why there is poverty in the United States today

4. _____ To say that a household is relatively poor means that it cannot afford the basic necessities of life.

5. _____ One argument which has been made against the negative income tax is that it does not solve the problem of a reduced work incentive among recipients of the cash payment.

6. _____ The Lorenz curve for the United States shows that income inequality is present.

7. _____ Since 1929, labor's share of GNP has been falling because the amount of capital spending has been increasing.

8. _____ To say that changes in capital and labor have symmetric effects means that when labor's share of income increases, so does capital's share, and vice versa.

9. _____ When capital and labor are good substitutes, the market demand curve for labor is relatively more elastic than it would be if they were poor substitutes.

10. _____ One way to make the functional distribution of income more equal is to impose a progressive income tax on everyone.

11. _____ A child with poor parents has very little chance in general of upward socioeconomic mobility.

12. _____ In the United States, there is neither a commonly accepted standard for income equality nor a standard to determine how much inequality society should accept.

13. _____ Under a flat-rate tax system, the marginal tax rate increases at a constant rate as incomes rise.

MULTIPLE CHOICE QUESTIONS

Circle the correct answer.

1. In 1979, the absolute and relative poverty levels for a family of four as defined by the government were
   a. $10,872 and $14,360, respectively
   b. $7412 and $9858, respectively
   c. $4981 and $8715, respectively
   d. $5540 and $7412, respectively
   e. none of the above

2. All of the following are factors which have contributed to long-standing poverty in the Unites States except
   a. the limited access of minorities to better paying jobs
   b. the denial of university admission on the basis of race or ethnic origin
   c. having parents who were poor
   d. the Civil Rights Act of 1964

3. All of the following statements are incorrect except
   a. the sources of poverty make no difference since a general antipoverty program raises all poor people's income
   b. for the elderly, poverty is usually regarded as only transitory
   c. there is no good source of data on inflows into and outflows from the poverty pool
   d. during a recession, the degree of relative poverty decreases

4. The war on poverty was begun during the administration of President
   a. Gerald Ford
   b. Lyndon Johnson
   c. Jimmy Carter
   d. Richard Nixon
   e. none of the above

5. If an economy is in equilibrium, with 1000 workers supplying 8 hours of work per day for 250 days at a wage rate of $6 per hour, labor's share of income is
   a. 28 percent
   b. 61 percent
   c. 37 percent
   d. 50 percent
   e. cannot be determined from the data supplied

6. When the real wage rate is low, firms find it advantageous to use
   a. relatively labor-intensive production processes
   b. relatively capital-intensive production processes
   c. an equal amount of both capital and labor
   d. more capital than labor

7. If the marginal product of labor falls rapidly and the capital stock is fixed, a decrease in the supply of labor causes
   a. a fall in the real wage of labor, more workers hired at every wage, and an increase in labor's share of total income
   b. no change in the real wage but more labor hired at the expense of capital
   c. an increase in the real wage, less labor used, and an increase in labor's relative share of income
   d. an increase in the real wage, more labor used, and a decrease in labor's relative share of income

8. If capital and labor are good substitutes, an increase in the stock of capital causes
   a. only slight changes in relative factor prices
   b. the rental rate of capital to fall, as does the real wage
   c. an excess demand for capital and a surplus of labor
   d. a shortage of both capital and labor

9. In 1981, labor's share of national income was
   a. 70.9 percent   c. 22.0 percent
   b. 18.7 percent   d. 75.6 percent

10. Which of the following is included in the functional distribution of income?

- **a.** wage income of labor
- **b.** interest income of capital
- **c.** rental income of land
- **d.** profits
- **e.** all of the above

11. If the Lorenz curve for the United States were linear,
- **a.** the distribution of income would be inefficient
- **b.** there would be an absolute inequality of income
- **c.** there would be an absolute equality of income
- **d.** nothing could be said about the distribution of income

AT THIS POINT YOU SHOULD BE ABLE TO . . .

1. Distinguish between the functional and personal distribution of income and describe how each is useful in answering the "for whom" question.

2. Using labor and capital as examples, explain how a factor's share of total income is determined; also, using diagrams, show and describe the effects of an increase in the labor supply when the stock of capital is fixed.

3. State the U.S. experience with factor income shares since 1929.

4. Describe how a Lorenz curve is constructed and explain how this curve shows the extent of income inequality.

5. List some shortcomings of the data describing personal income distribution and explain how this may cause a problem when the data are interpreted.

6. Distinguish between absolute and relative poverty and explain how each is measured.

7. Select and list data presented in your text which show who the poor are, explain the difference between transitory and permanent poverty, and state why it is necessary to identify the sources of poverty before appropriate antipoverty programs are developed.

8. State the overall objectives of the war on poverty and evaluate its overall results.

9. Explain the extent of socioeconomic mobility in the United States; also, identify and explain three factors which affect mobility between income classes.

10. Describe the trade-off between economic efficiency and income equality and explain how this trade-off affects the degree of income inequality present in our economic system.

11. Describe how a negative income tax would reduce the level of poverty in the United States and explain how such a tax system works.

QUESTIONS FOR THOUGHT

1. The Lorenz curve shows the personal distribution of income for an economy. What qualifications should be made to the personal distribution of income? If these qualifications are not made, how might the interpretation of the data be affected? How do taxes affect this distribution? Explain.

2. Why are there two definitions of poverty? Does it make sense to say that a household is not poor but is relatively poor? Explain.

3. In the United States, do we have an equal distribution of income? What do the data indicate about the personal distribution of income in this country?

4. During the 1960s and 1970s, the U.S. government spent billions of dollars for the war on poverty. Explain the goals of this war and describe the end results (success or failure) of the antipoverty programs. What weaknesses do you detect in the overall approach used by the government?

5. Do you think that we have a "culture of poverty" in the United States? What are the implications if such a culture does exist? Explain.

6. What did Arthur Okun mean when he stated that "we can transport money from the rich to the poor only in a leaky bucket"? Does this imply any inefficiencies in the redistribution of income? If so, elaborate on these inefficiencies. Is there a trade-off involved?

7. How might a negative income tax reduce both the level of poverty and the unequal distribution of income? Does a negative income tax have any effect on poor people's incentive to work? Explain.

8. How does the ease of factor substitution affect a factor's share of total income? During most of this century, how have the factor shares of national income changed?

39

Alternative Economic Approaches and Systems

Up to this point, your study of economics has focused primarily on the operation of a mixed capitalist system. The decisions of individual households, individual firms, and the government all interact to affect the way society answers the fundamental questions of "what," "how," and "for whom." In our mixed capitalist economy, most factors of production are owned by private individuals. These individuals are free within limits to enter the marketplace, where they purchase goods and dispose of their resources in any way they desire. Prices ration goods and resources, resulting in maximum overall well-being for society. But mixed capitalism with its system of markets is only one of many economic systems which currently exist throughout the world.

In Chapter 39, Professors Fischer and Dornbusch describe some of the alternative systems used by different countries. At one extreme is pure socialism, in which the state owns or controls all the factors of production and allocates resources according to a set of plans it develops. State planning answers the fundamental questions. At the other extreme, pure, or laissez-faire, capitalism answers the fundamental questions entirely through markets and prices; the decisions of households and firms are of primary importance. Neither of these two extremes exists. What we see throughout the world are systems with varying degrees of capitalism or socialism.

Chapter 39 begins by presenting some of the ideas of Marxian economic analysis. Marx argued that by its very nature, capitalism was self-destroying. He argued that labor was the only source of surplus value and that surplus value was the only source of profit. Thus, as capitalists tried to expand their profits and reduce their costs of production by using more labor-saving machines, they were simply destroying the foundation of their profits. Competition among capitalists, rising unemployment, falling wages, and the increasing misery of the workers would eventually lead to a revolution in which the capitalists would be destroyed. Marx envisioned a transitory socialist society with a strong central government. But over time, the government simply would wither away as society approached pure communism; everyone would produce and enjoy the benefits of collective production.

The two largest socialist nations are the Soviet Union and China. These nations are not in the Marxian sense purely communist because the state dominates most aspects of everyday life and because class distinctions are still present in both countries. In each country, a central planning authority allocates resources and sets the goals for most sectors of the economy. Even in China and the Soviet Union, though, central planning is not complete.

China and the Soviet Union both set rapid industrialization and a strong military as goals. The growth rates of both countries have been impressive; however, there have been some costs in terms of individual freedom and quality of life. Whether such growth can be sustained over a period of time is uncertain. In recent years, the growth rates of the Soviet and Chinese economies have slowed, as have the growth rates of the western industrialized nations.

CHAPTER OUTLINE

1. Karl Marx viewed history as a series of class struggles. Economic history was seen as a series of struggles between the bourgeoisie (capitalists) and the proletariat (workers). Marx argued that the conflict between the bourgeoisie and proletariat would eventually lead to revolution by the workers because the workers would be impoverished and face ever-increasing misery. According to Marx, labor is paid only a subsistence wage by capitalists. But labor creates more value for the firm than it receives in wages. This surplus value created by labor is the only source of the capitalists' profits. As capitalists try to maintain or improve their profits, they innovate and develop better production methods. These innovations use more capital and less labor. Capitalists use labor-saving production methods to lower their labor costs, and this lowers their overall costs of production. As the demand for labor falls, so does the wage rate. Unemployment increases, and a reserve army of the unemployed

emerges. As more laborers become unemployed, capitalists' profits fall because surplus value is the only source of profits. With fewer workers, the surplus value accruing to the capitalists falls. As profits fall, the whole process begins again, with the capitalist economies experiencing business cycles that increase in severity. Eventually, the workers revolt and expropriate the capitalists.

    a. Marxian economics includes themes other than predictions of communist revolution.

        (1) The labor theory of value states that the value of goods is derived from the labor embodied in them; labor is the only source of value. Thus, any profits received by the capitalists are the result of their exploitation of labor, since workers are paid a wage that is lower than the value they contribute in production. Implementation of this labor theory of value in planning caused problems for the Russian economy since planners did not want to include capital usage as a cost of production. As a result, many goods were underpriced.

        (2) Marx argued that firm size would increase and that production would become more complicated over time. In a capitalist system, industries and the economy would be dominated by a few very large firms. As production becomes more sophisticated, workers are alienated, and so labor feels no loyalty to producers.

        (3) Under a socialist system, the state owns the means of production and distribution and controls all economic activity. Under a communist system (pure Marxism), the state initially controls economic activity, but the government soon withers away. The state has no role in a pure communist system because everyone cooperates freely and society's best interests are served. Most of the communist nations as we know them have socialist systems.

    b. During the depression of the 1930s, many thought that Marx's predictions were correct, yet the modern mixed economies of the western industrialized nations stand as evidence that Marx's belief in the collapse of capitalism was wrong.

2. A pure command economy makes only limited use of markets since the state owns all productive capital. A central planner answers the "what," "how," and "for whom" questions. When the planning authority solves the "what" question, a position on the production possibilities frontier is located. This position is chosen on the basis of what the planner believes is the nation's best interest. The planner chooses how output is distributed so that the "for whom" question is answered. In order to meet the nation's production goals as established on the PPF, the central planner allocates resources and production capacity to each industry. This answers the "how" question. Once a central planning authority gets economic activity under way, the fundamental questions do not have to be answered anew. The planner may make corrections if necessary to the existing patterns of production and distribution. In practice, no pure command economies exist because of the difficulties involved in planning the operation of an entire economy; a large degree of decentralization is often necessary in both the planning and the production processes.

3. Although it is essential for the government of a socialist state to own the productive capital, it is not essential that markets be absent. If the central planner determines a set of prices which provides the desired allocation of resources, consumers may spend their incomes as they wish, firms may produce for a profit, and workers may select their jobs. Prices are used in the planning process because they are adjusted easily and create positive incentives for production. One problem is the selection of the proper allocation of resources by the planner. The primary distinction between capitalist and socialist economies with prices used to allocate resources lies in the ownership of productive capital.

4. The first country to organize its economy according to the Marxist-Leninist doctrine was the Soviet Union.

    a. During the last decades of czarist rule, Russia was rapidly industrializing. After the Bolshevik revolution in 1917 and the nationalization of productive capital, aggregate output fell significantly. The New Economic Policy allowed some private ownership of light industry and permitted its operation for profit. As a result, output increased. During the late 1920s and the 1930s, the Soviet government allocated vast amounts of resources and output for the development of heavy industry, coal, steel, and electric power generation. As a result, consumers suffered. The 5-year plans of the Soviet economy set broad goals to be achieved over a period of 5 years, while the annual plans provide managers of firms with an output target for each year. These are the two basic types of plans used in the Soviet economy.

    b. The first 5-year plan (1928) reduced consumer spending and allocated more resources for the production of military goods and capital investment. At this time, agriculture was also collectivized. The collectivization of Soviet agriculture has been unsuccessful, and the government often imports many agricultural products. The allocation of resources into capital investment and military goods has been successful. The Soviet Union is an industrialized nation with a GNP growth rate exceeding that of the United States for most of the years since World War II. During the late 1950s, Soviet workers were allowed to seek better jobs. Although wages are officially set by the government, firms do have some flexibility in the jobs and wage rates they offer. The Soviet economy allocates output by prices and by planning. Consumers, though, are given a relatively low priority in overall economic plans.

    c. Since the late 1960s, the growth rate of the Soviet economy has declined. This fall in the growth rate of GNP was caused by a slower growth of the labor force, a reduction in the number of people moving from agriculture to the industrial sector, and low agricultural productivity. Some Soviet authorities are beginning to question the effectiveness and relevance of planning as applied to a modern economy.

5. In just over 20 years under communist rule and central planning, China made substantial economic progress. Everyone worked for the benefit of the revolutionary state.
    a. Since 1949, China has experienced rapid growth in its industrial sector; however, most of the nation's population still works in agriculture. Unlike the Soviets, the Chinese did not restrict themselves to one development strategy but employed several strategies. The Great Leap Forward under Mao Tse-Tung emphasized a labor-intensive development strategy, but it did not succeed. During the early 1960s, a more orthodox style of communism was used, and GNP increased. During the Cultural Revolution, many basic institutions within the country were questioned, and in the ensuing confusion, both production and GNP fell. The 1970s marked a period of opening up. Trade and contact with the rest of the world increased. Since the Cultural Revolution, China has sought foreign technological expertise and resources.
    b. By the year 2000, China hopes to have modernized its national defense, economy, educational system, and political organization; however, it is uncertain whether the country can meet these goals.
    c. Although Chinese growth has been rapid, it has not been as rapid as that of Japan, Korea, and Taiwan. China's population, however, is much larger than the populations of these other countries. When the growth rates of China and India (similar populations) are compared, China's growth has exceeded India's.

6. Most communist bloc nations have used markets and prices to allocate resources more than either China or the Soviet Union. Of the eastern European nations, Yugoslavia relies more on prices, markets, and individual initiatives than the other countries. In Yugoslavia, workers manage the firms, share the profits, determine output levels, establish many prices, and determine the level of investment spending. Also, private ownership of some small firms is still allowed, and almost all of the agricultural sector is privately owned. Although Yugoslavia has a mixed economy, its markets are not completely free since the state controls some prices while others are fixed by producers. Yugoslavia's economy has grown rapidly, but it has also faced inflationary pressures. Hungary has also allowed prices to influence the allocation of resources. All communist bloc nations, though, use central planning to some degree.

7. In the noncommunist industrialized nations, the roles of the state and central planning vary. France and the Scandinavian countries have national ownership of major industrial sectors, and these governments use their control over taxes, banking, and investment to direct their economies toward meeting specified goals. In both West Germany and Japan, the government intervenes substantially in the economy. The growth of GNP in both countries, though, has been large. In Japan, economic growth is explained in part by effective managerial planning, government support of exports, and a loyal labor force. At the beginning of the 1980s, all industrialized countries experienced a slowdown of economic growth.

8. Although the governments of many developing countries call themselves socialist, socialism has not been that effective in promoting rapid growth. The LDCs which are experiencing substantial growth are those which emphasize markets and prices.

9. The convergence hypothesis states that over time, economies will become increasingly similar, with the market economies accepting more government intervention and the socialist economies relying more on markets. There is little evidence to support this hypothesis since many of the western economies are now moving away from government intervention and the communist bloc countries are not increasing their reliance on markets.

IMPORTANT TERMS AND THEIR MEANING

Match the following terms with the correct definition or phrase.

1. _____ An economic philosophy in which the state owns the means of production and directs all economic activity

2. _____ The workers

3. _____ An economy in which the government makes all decisions about production and consumption

4. _____ The state determines the goals of an economic system and decides how resources are allocated to meet these goals

5. _____ The value of goods is derived solely from the amount of labor embodied in them

6. _____ Introduced by the Bolshevik government in hopes of increasing Soviet GNP; permitted private ownership and operation of some light industry and agriculture for private profit

7. _____ The difference between the subsistence wage paid to a worker and the total value created by that worker; according to Marx, the only source of profits

8. _____ An economic system in which the state owns the stock of productive capital but markets and prices are the primary means of resource allocation

9. _____ Over time, economies become increasingly similar, with market economies accepting more government intervention and socialist economies relying more on markets

10. _____ The middle classes and the capitalists

11. _____ An economic system in which the factors of production are privately owned, markets and prices are the essential determinants of resource allocation, and the owners of the factors of production may use those factors as they wish

12. _____ According to Marx, as capitalists use more sophisticated methods of production, workers lose interest in their jobs and feel more like machines

13. _____ An economic system in which the allocation of society's resources is determined in part by the government and in part by the private sector

14. _____ An economic system in which all productive capital as well as land is owned by the state, central planning directs the economy, and individual freedoms are limited

15. _____ Arises because capitalists try to expand profits by using labor-saving machines so that the demand for labor falls and more and more workers cannot find jobs

a. Command economy
b. New Economic Policy
c. Alienation
d. Mixed economy
e. Market socialism
f. Reserve army of the unemployed
g. Socialism
h. Convergence hypothesis
i. Central planning
j. Communism
k. Labor theory of value
l. Capitalism
m. Proletariat
n. Surplus value
o. Bourgeoisie

EXERCISES

1. Listed in Table 39-1 are 11 characteristics of different economic systems. Your task is to identify which system is described by a particular characteristic by placing an X in the appropriate blank. Some characteristics may apply to more than one system.

2. Five false statements are presented below, each relating to some aspect of Marxian economics. In the space below each false statement, write the statement as it should be.

   a. As capitalists expand their use of machines, they demand more labor to operate these new machines; both the demand for labor and the real wage increase, making workers better off.

   _____

   _____

   b. As a society continues to industrialize, the bourgeoisie increase their profits, and this provides the

ALTERNATIVE ECONOMIC APPROACHES AND SYSTEMS

TABLE 39-1

CHARACTERISTICS	SYSTEM			
	PURE CAPITALISM	MIXED ECONOMY	MARKET SOCIALISM	PURE COMMUNISM
a. The state owns all productive capital, but markets and prices influence resource allocation	_____	_____	_____	_____
b. Prices adjust to ensure the efficient allocation of resources	_____	_____	_____	_____
c. Individuals are allowed to make profits	_____	_____	_____	_____
d. The state determines all production and distribution of goods, and so it determines the allocation of resources	_____	_____	_____	_____
e. There is a combination of both government and private decision making	_____	_____	_____	_____
f. If they exist, individual freedoms are severely limited	_____	_____	_____	_____
g. Producers are completely free to determine the type and amount of output produced	_____	_____	_____	_____
h. A central planning authority establishes a set of output prices and then allows the market to allocate resources within these price limits	_____	_____	_____	_____
i. Government regulates certain economic activities, but market forces are very important	_____	_____	_____	_____
j. The agricultural sector is owned and completely controlled by the state	_____	_____	_____	_____
k. Individuals are completely free to promote their own self-interest	_____	_____	_____	_____

foundation for increased production, employment, and income.

_____
_____
_____

c. After the proletarian revolution, a strong, permanent central government is needed, since class distinctions and antagonisms will be enhanced.

_____
_____
_____

d. Capitalists earn profits because they pay labor a wage equal to the value of the goods produced, and so workers are encouraged to increase their productivity and thus increase the revenue for the capitalist.

_____
_____
_____

e. In a capitalist economy, firms are by necessity small and have only a small portion of the overall market; otherwise, there would not be competition.

_____
_____
_____

FILL-IN QUESTIONS

1. Marx viewed history as a series of _____ struggles, and he saw economic history as a contest between the _____ and the _____.

2. In a command economy, the production plans are developed by a _____, and thus a point on the _____ frontier is chosen.

3. In a pure socialist economy, the _____ owns the productive capital, and there (is/is not) _____ use of markets.

4. The (New Economic Program/Great Leap Forward) _____ was introduced in the Soviet Union during the period when _____ headed the government, and this approach to development (did/did not) _____ allow private ownership of some means of production.

5. Two plans used in the Soviet economy are the _____ plan, which sets broad goals for growth over a period of years, and the _____ plans, which give short-term output targets for managers.

6. In Russia, the (dispersion/collectivization/aggregation) _____ of agriculture (was/was not) _____ successful, and Soviet farm production (is/is not) _____ as great as that in the United States.

7. China has set as a goal by the year 2000 the modernization of its _____, _____,

_____ organization, and _____ system.

8. In Yugoslavia, firms are managed by the (government/workers/planning board) _____; firms determine their own _____ levels, _____, and _____ levels. Most of the agricultural sector (is/is not) _____ privately owned.

9. For the underdeveloped nations, the appeal of socialism is that it promises a (more/less) _____ equitable distribution of wealth and income during the development process.

10. For most of the period between the end of World War II and the mid-1970s, the Soviet economy grew (slower/faster) _____ than the U.S. economy, and today Soviet GNP is about _____ percent of U.S. GNP.

TRUE-FALSE QUESTIONS

1. _____ In the Soviet Union, wages are set by the demand for and the supply of different types of labor.

2. _____ The United States economy is an example of a mixed capitalist system.

3. _____ Most socialist countries are prohibited from using markets and prices because of Marxian economic doctrines.

4. _____ The Soviet Union and China are examples of complete command economies.

5. _____ When a central planner determines what, how, and for whom output is produced, a position is being selected on the economy's production possibilities frontier.

6. _____ During the Great Depression, many economists and political scientists thought that capitalism was about to collapse.

7. _____ According to Marx, the dominant force in both socialism and communism is the state.

8. _____ The Lordstown, Ohio, General Motors plant during the 1970s provides a current example of worker alienation when confronted with sophisticated and automated production techniques.

9. _____ In Marxian economic analysis, labor, along with the productivity of capital, has little effect on the value of a commodity.

10. _____ Technological innovation played an insignificant role in Marx's analysis of the demise of capitalism.

11. _____ One reason why the growth of the Soviet economy is slowing is that productivity of the agricultural sector is high relative to that of the industrial sector.

12. _____ The effect of the Cultural Revolution on China's economy was a decrease in GNP.

13. _____ China's economy has grown faster than some mixed economies and slower than others.

14. _____ Because of their rapid growth, the communist bloc economies are catching up with the western economies.

15. _____ Historical data on economic growth do not indicate that centrally planned economies necessarily grow faster over the long term than market economies.

16. _____ Most of the developing countries favor an economy centered on markets because they believe that they can attain a higher growth rate.

MULTIPLE CHOICE QUESTIONS

Circle the correct answer.

1. Since the Bolshevik revolution, Soviet economic planning has been directed primarily toward
   a. a rapid buildup of the military and industrial base
   b. a rapid increase in the quantity, quality, and selection of consumer goods
   c. the incorporation of some aspects of a market system into the economy
   d. a rapid development of the agricultural sector
   e. none of the above

2. All of the following are reasons why Soviet economic growth has slowed in recent years except
   a. fewer Soviet citizens currently are leaving agriculture for industrial employment
   b. agricultural productivity has not increased as expected, and there has been a growing dependence on imported agricultural products
   c. the government has not changed its growth and development plans since 1925
   d. the labor force is growing at a much slower rate than in the past

3. The Greap Leap Forward implemented by the Chinese communists is best described by which of the following characteristics?
   a. labor was the basis for anticipated acceleration of economic growth
   b. the backyard steel furnace was a symbol of individual productivity and initiative
   c. emphasis was placed on labor-intensive, small-scale industries

ALTERNATIVE ECONOMIC APPROACHES AND SYSTEMS

    d. agriculture was to be totally collectivized
    e. all of the above

4. In Yugoslavia's economic system, there is
    a. total planning by government
    b. a large degree of worker involvement in the managerial decisions of firms
    c. complete collectivization of agriculture
    d. minimal trade with western countries
    e. none of the above

5. In the Soviet Union, workers
    a. are more productive than U.S. workers
    b. are told where to work
    c. may not change jobs
    d. earn a wage established by the supply of and demand for labor
    e. none of the above

6. All of the following have mixed economies except
    a. France   c. Albania
    b. West Germany   d. Great Britain

7. The convergence hypothesis argues that
    a. over time, capitalist and socialist economies will become more alike
    b. over time, most socialist economies will approach the true Marxian ideal of communism
    c. over time, the capitalist and socialist economies will become increasingly different
    d. over time, the capitalist nations will outproduce the socialist nations
    e. none of the above

8. All of the following statements are true except
    a. the *Communist Manifesto* was written by both Marx and Engels
    b. both Marx's and Adam Smith's views about the role of the capitalist in an industrial economy are identical
    c. the proletarian revolution would institute a heavy graduated income tax
    d. as capitalists increase their use of labor-saving machines, the reserve army of the unemployed increases

9. The labor theory of value suggests that
    a. profits are generated by using land, labor, and entrepreneurial ability but not capital
    b. the only source of a good's value is the amount of labor it takes to produce it
    c. capital and labor are the only sources of value
    d. the value of a good depends on both the demand for and supply of the commodity

10. Once a planner establishes a set of official prices under market socialism,
    a. consumers are allowed to spend their income as they wish
    b. firms are allowed to maximize profits
    c. workers are allowed to work where they wish
    d. all of the above
    e. none of the above

AT THIS POINT YOU SHOULD BE ABLE TO . . .

1. Describe Marx's interpretation of economic history as a series of class struggles, explain the ultimate outcome of these struggles, and explain a major flaw in Marx's analysis.

2. Describe the labor theory of value and explain why Marx claimed that surplus value was the only source of profits.

3. Distinguish between socialism, communism, and market socialism.

4. Explain how resources are allocated in a command economy and explain how once the resources are allocated, the "what," "how," and "for whom" questions are answered.

5. Describe the role of prices in market socialism and explain how it differs from the role of prices in a capitalist economy.

6. Describe the history and nature of Soviet economic planning and evaluate its success.

7. Describe the history and nature of Chinese economic planning, evaluate its success, and compare and contrast the Soviet and Chinese approaches to economic development.

8. Identify one communist bloc country which uses prices and individual initiative in its economy, describe its economic performance since World War II, and contrast this economy with that of the Soviet Union.

9. List three countries which have mixed economies and explain how these economies differ from purely capitalistic or purely socialistic economies.

10. Offer an explanation why many LDCs are pursuing a socialistic road to economic development and describe what the evidence suggests about such an approach.

QUESTIONS FOR THOUGHT

1. An important element of Marxian analysis is that wages fall and unemployment increases. On what basis did Marx reach these predictions? Why are they important within the framework of Marxian economics?

2. Pure communism, according to Marx, eventually leads to a society with everyone working for the common welfare and with minimal if any need for government. How does this compare with Adam

Smith's "invisible hand"? Are there any similarities? If so, what are they?

3. What two factors make economic planning not totally impossible? Once a plan is established for an economy, how can it be corrected?

4. What are the characteristics of market socialism? Are there any advantages of market socialism as opposed to pure socialism? If so, what are they?

5. What are the major objectives of economic planning in the Soviet Union? What sectors of the economy have received the greatest emphasis in Soviet economic development? Do prices and profits play any role in the Soviet economy? If so, explain.

6. Compare and contrast the historical record of economic planning and growth in the Soviet Union and in China. Do they approach economic planning differently? Explain.

7. What have the major gains and shortcomings of economic planning been in both the Soviet Union and China?

8. How has Yugoslavia's economic organization and performance differed from that of the other communist bloc economies and the Soviet Union?

9. Many of the western industrialized nations have mixed economies. Explain what this means. Overall, what has been their record of performance when compared with the communist bloc economies?

Answers

FIGURE A1-1

4. a. gross national product: the final value of all goods and services produced in a given time
   b. aggregate price level: a measure of the average price level of goods and services
   c. unemployment rate: percentage of labor force that cannot find a job

CHAPTER 1

Important Terms

1. i	8. r	15. t
2. q	9. f	16. h
3. e	10. n	17. m
4. o	11. g	18. j
5. a	12. c	19. d
6. s	13. k	20. b
7. l	14. p	

Exercises

1. a. can, positive
   b. 1
   c. more, steaks, movies, diminishing returns
   d. is not
   e. cost of movies: 1, 2, 3, 4, 5
   f. increases, is not
2. a. See Figure A1-1.
   b. on, below
   c. inefficiently, 9, 4
   d. straight, does not
3. a. P
   b. N
   c. N
   d. P
   e. P
   f. N

Fill-in Questions

1. unemployment rate
2. micro
3. what, how, for whom
4. oil price, more
5. government, individuals, self-interest
6. for whom
7. is, more
8. law of diminishing returns
9. was, self-interest
10. mixed, is
11. value

True-False Questions

1. T	5. F	8. F
2. F	6. F	9. T
3. T	7. T	10. F
4. T		

Multiple Choice Questions

1. e	5. d	9. c
2. b	6. c	10. b
3. a	7. a	11. a
4. b	8. c	12. d

CHAPTER 2

Important Terms

1. e
2. k
3. l
4. p
5. x
6. a
7. d
8. u
9. q
10. b
11. g
12. i
13. w
14. f
15. r
16. h
17. c
18. v
19. o
20. n
21. m
22. s
23. j
24. t

Exercises

1. time series data: b, e, g
   cross section data: a, c, d, f
2. **a.** See Table A2-1.

TABLE A2-1

UNEMPLOYMENT RATES AS A PERCENT OF THE LABOR FORCE

	1982		
	FEBRUARY	MARCH	APRIL
All workers	8.8	9.0	9.4
Adult men	7.6	7.9	8.2
Adult women	7.6	7.9	8.3
Teenagers	22.3	21.9	23.0

b. See Figure A2-1.

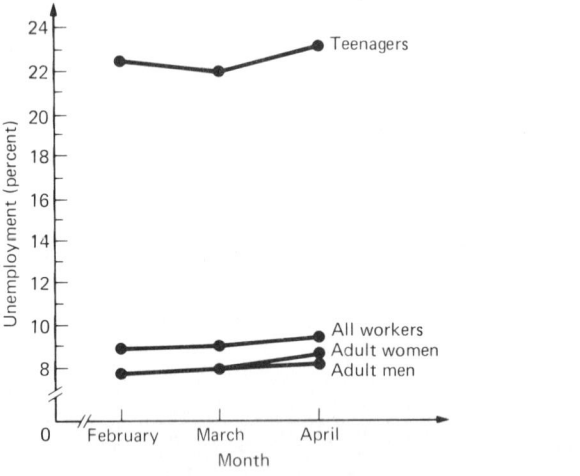

FIGURE A2-1

3. **a.** weighted component index (1980): 41.2, 129.2, 10.1, 36.4, 8.8, 6.6, 6.5; weighted component index (1981): 43.1, 135.7, 10.9, 37.4, 9.4, 7.2, 7.3; sum of the weights = 1.0
   b. weight
   c. 238.8, 251
   d. increased, 12.2, 5.1

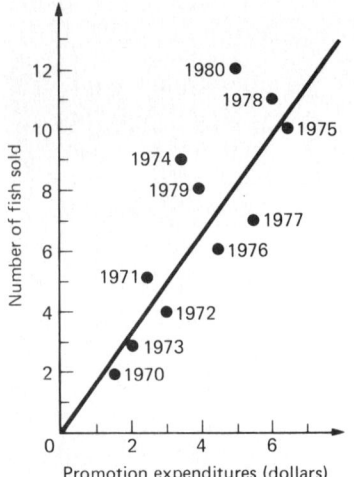

FIGURE A2-2

4. **a.** See Figure A2-2.
   b. time series, positive, increase
   c. hypothesis
   d. See Figure A2-2.
   e. is, positive, 1.5 (1.6), slope
5. **a, b.** See Figure A2-3.

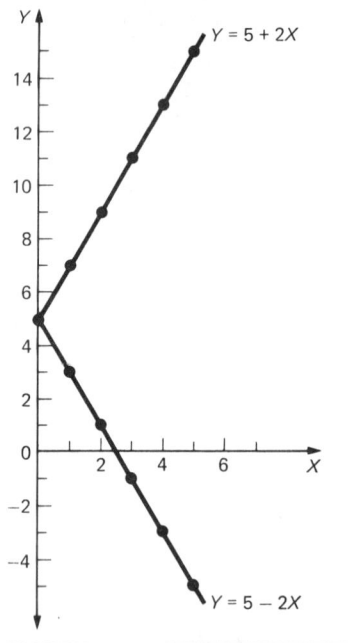

FIGURE A2-3

   c. positive, 5, +2, negative, 5, −2
6. **a, b.** See Figure A2-4.
7. **a.** observe the phenomena
   b. advance a theory that seeks to explain the phenomena
   c. test the theory by using real-world data

ANSWERS

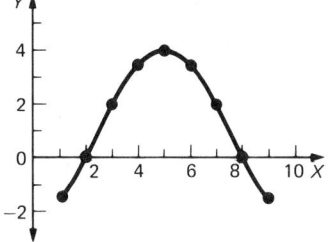

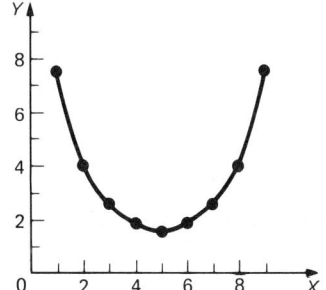

FIGURE A2-4

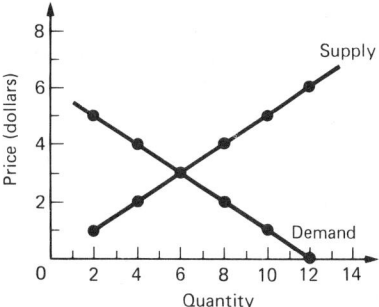

FIGURE A3-1

Exercises
1. a. See Figure A3-1.
   b. decreases, increases
   c. yes, $3, 6 units
   d. 4 units, 8 units, surplus, 4 units
   e. $3
2. a. See Figure A3-2.
   b. $4.50, 20
   c. See Figure A3-2.
   d. $5, 25, demand
   e. complements, shift to the right

Fill-in Questions
1. comparison
2. "other things equal"
3. model, is
4. tables, charts
5. *Statistical Abstract of the United States*
6. less
7. cross section, time series
8. median, mean
9. weighted
10. percentage, is not
11. statistical, scatter
12. econometrics
13. intercept, slope
14. excluded, will not
15. fact

True-False Questions
1. F
2. T
3. T
4. T
5. F
6. F
7. F
8. T
9. F
10. F
11. T
12. T
13. T
14. T
15. T

Multiple Choice Questions
1. b
2. d
3. a
4. c
5. c
6. d
7. b
8. a
9. c
10. e
11. c
12. a
13. d
14. b
15. c

CHAPTER 3

Important Terms
1. l
2. p
3. a
4. n
5. d
6. b
7. s
8. m
9. e
10. f
11. q
12. i
13. o
14. k
15. r
16. g
17. c
18. j
19. h

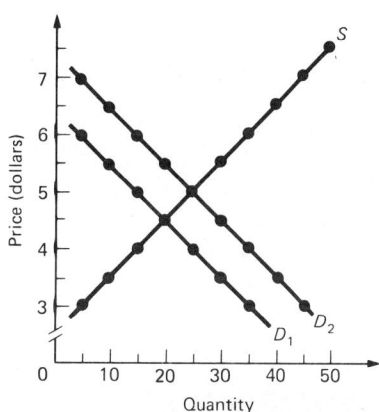

FIGURE A3-2

3. a. See Figure A3-3.
   b. $400, 9000
   c. would
   d. 11,000, 6000; See Figure A3-3.
   e. excess demand, 5000
   f. price ceiling, would not

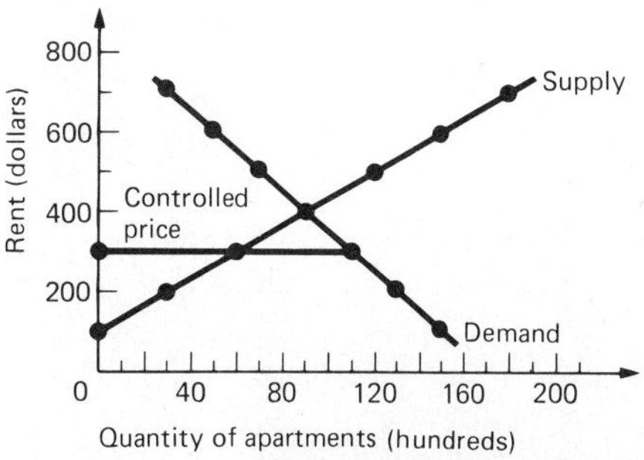

FIGURE A3-3

4. See Table A3-1.

TABLE A3-1

	DEMAND	SUPPLY	PRICE	QUANTITY
a.	✓	0	✓	✓
b.	✓	0	✓	✓
c.	0	✓	X	✓
d.	✓	0	✓	✓
e.	✓	0	✓	✓
f.	0	X	✓	X
g.	X	0	X	X

5. a. $6, 4
    b. excess supply (surplus), 2, excess demand (shortage), 2
    c. $6, $6

Fill-in Questions

1. negative, negative
2. normal
3. price floor
4. quantity demanded, quantity supplied
5. fall, above
6. an increase, fall, increase
7. left, less
8. is not
9. remain the same
10. 50, 10
11. would not
12. equilibrium
13. price, quantity, intersection
14. complementary, substitutes

True-False Questions

1. F
2. T
3. F
4. F
5. T
6. T
7. T
8. T
9. F
10. F
11. F
12. F
13. F
14. T
15. T
16. F
17. T

Multiple Choice Questions

1. b
2. c
3. a
4. d
5. c
6. c
7. d
8. b
9. c
10. a
11. d
12. e
13. a
14. b
15. b

CHAPTER 4

Important Terms

1. t
2. m
3. u
4. i
5. j
6. v
7. b
8. q
9. g
10. n
11. o
12. p
13. w
14. c
15. f
16. e
17. h
18. a
19. k
20. d
21. l
22. r
23. s

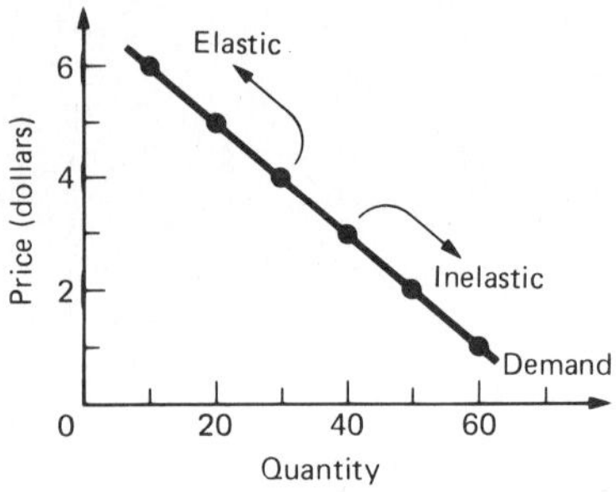

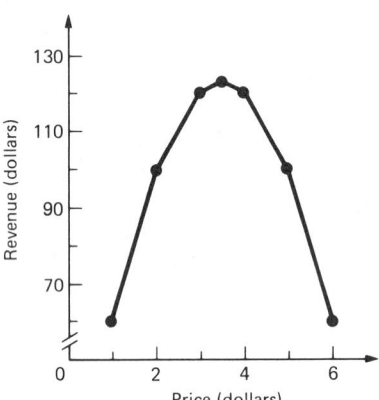

FIGURE A4-1

Exercises

1. a. See Figure A4-1.
    b. $60, $100, $120, $122.50, $120, $100, $60
    c. −6, −2.5, −1.3, −1, −.75, −.4
    d. See Figure A4-1.
    e. $3.50
2. See Figure A4-2.
    a. $3.50, −1.0
    b. increase, price-inelastic, decrease, price-elastic

FIGURE A4-2

3. a. is not, .56, is, 3.7
    b. 2, 3, 4, 5, 6, 7
    c. .46, 2.2
    d. See Figure A4-3.
4. a. DD_1, DD_2
    b. DD_2, DD_1
    c. highly elastic
5. 2.67

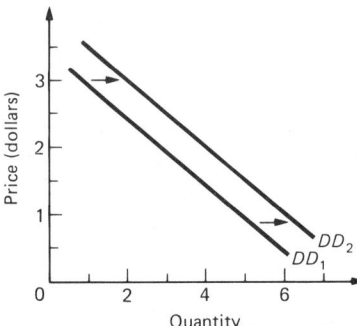

FIGURE A4-3

ANSWERS

Fill-in Questions
1. unitary-elastic, remain the same
2. short run
3. decreases
4. income
5. expenditure share
6. price
7. inferior
8. substitutes
9. elastic, fall
10. positive and greater than 1, increase, greater
11. less than, inelastic
12. loss, less than, gain
13. elastic, inelastic
14. loss, greater than, gain
15. complements

True-False Questions
1. F
2. F
3. T
4. T
5. T
6. T
7. F
8. T
9. F
10. T
11. T
12. F
13. T
14. F
15. T
16. F
17. T
18. F

Multiple Choice Questions
1. b
2. a
3. d
4. a
5. b
6. c
7. d
8. b
9. c
10. b
11. d
12. d
13. a
14. b
15. b
16. a
17. d

CHAPTER 5

Important Terms
1. q
2. k
3. e
4. l
5. g
6. d
7. m
8. c
9. t
10. a
11. r
12. h
13. j
14. i
15. o
16. s
17. n
18. b
19. p
20. f

Exercises
1. See Figure A5-1.
   a. *AOB*
   b. 5/8, slope
   c. rotate, inward, fewer
   d. See Figure A5-1, 1, −1
   e. See Figure A5-1.
2. a. See Figure A5-2.
   b. Triangle *KOM*, 1/2
   c. See Figure A5-2.

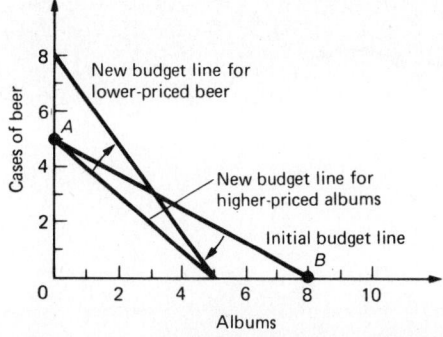

FIGURE A5-1

d. less preferred than; A and B; K, C, D, M, and K; M; is; are not; C; 6; 2; zero, D, is not
e. shift, 7, 14
f. is, 1/2

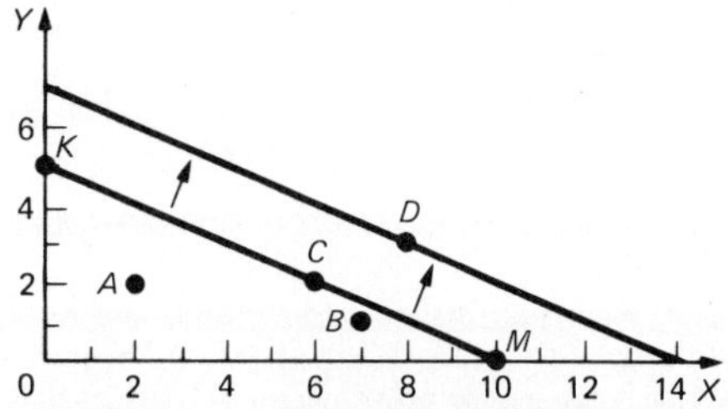

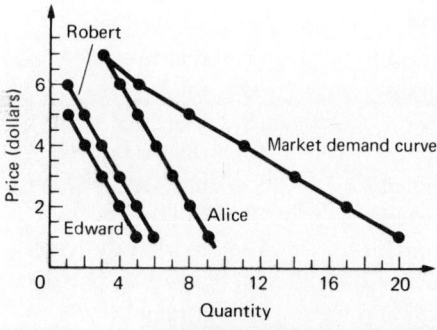

FIGURE A5-2

3. market demand: 3, 5, 8, 11, 14, 17, 20; See Figure A5-3.

FIGURE A5-3

4. marginal utility: 7, 6, 5, 4, 3, 2, 1, 0, −1; See Figure A5-4.
   a. does
   b. maximized, equal to
5. a, b, c. See Table A5-1.

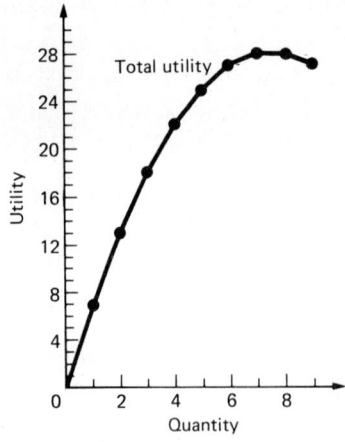

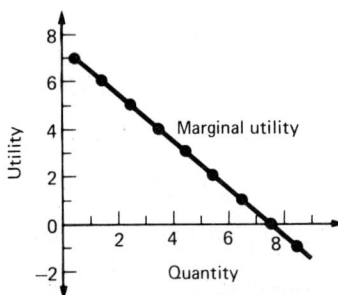

FIGURE A5-4

TABLE A5-1

ELASTICITY OF DEMAND FOR	WITH RESPECT TO THE PRICE OF		
	A	B	C
A	−1.71	−1.05	.76
B	−.76	−0.43	1.24
C	.55	.91	−1.0

Fill-in Questions

1. downward and to the left, remain constant
2. negative
3. complementarity
4. in-kind transfers, less, cash transfer
5. spillover, increase, shifts upward and to the right
6. steeper, flatter
7. relative price ratio
8. more, less, utility
9. marginal utility
10. relative price, increase, decrease
11. utility
12. market demand
13. positive, negative
14. attainable, unattainable
15. more, less, more

True-False Questions

1. F
2. T
3. T
4. T
5. F
6. T
7. F
8. F
9. T
10. T
11. T
12. F
13. F
14. T
15. T
16. F
17. T

Multiple Choice Questions

1. c
2. a
3. e
4. b
5. e
6. d
7. b
8. c
9. b
10. a

CHAPTER 5: APPENDIX

Important Terms

1. b
2. c
3. a

Exercises

1. a. See Figure A5-5.
   b. higher
   c. is, is not
   d. negative, diminishes, less
   e. is not

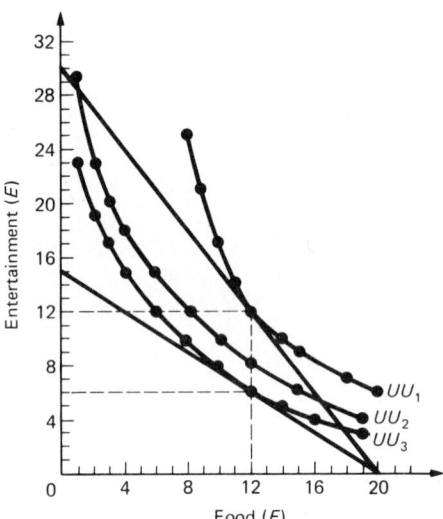

FIGURE A5-5

2. See Figure A5-5.
   a. 30, 20
   b. 30/20
   c. 12, 12, are
   d. $120, $180
   e. UU_1
   f. would not, would not
3. rotate; See Figure A5-6.
   a. 15, flatter, 15/20
   b. UU_3, 6, 12, decreased

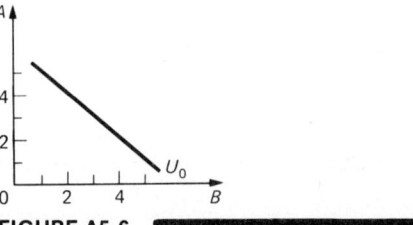

FIGURE A5-6

ANSWERS

4. See Figure A5-6.
   a. linear, does not
   b. perfect

Fill-in Questions
1. marginal, relative price
2. rotates, lower
3. utility, convex, decreases
4. income, prices
5. income, substitution
6. higher, more
7. tangent, unattainable, utility
8. decreases, diminishing marginal rate of substitution

True-False Questions
1. T
2. F
3. F
4. F
5. T
6. T

Multiple Choice Questions
1. c
2. a
3. b
4. a
5. d
6. b

CHAPTER 6

Important Terms
1. m
2. a
3. j
4. u
5. p
6. d
7. o
8. s
9. c
10. f
11. b
12. q
13. t
14. h
15. r
16. l
17. e
18. k
19. g
20. i
21. n

Exercises

1. a. See Table A6-1.

TABLE A6-1

WIDGET COMPANY
INCOME STATEMENT FOR THE YEAR ENDING
DECEMBER 31, 1983

Revenues:	
(200,000 units @ $4.00 each)	$800,000
Expenses:	
Wage expense (10,000 hours @ $8.00 per hour)	$ 80,000
Cost (expense) of materials in production	300,000
Rental expense on warehouse	100,000
Advertising and selling expense	60,000
Office supplies expense	10,000
Office operating expense	20,000
Total expenses	570,000
Net income (accounting profit)	$230,000

b. See Table A6-2.

TABLE A6-2

WIDGET COMPANY
BALANCE SHEET AS OF DECEMBER 31, 1983

ASSETS		LIABILITIES	
Cash in bank	$ 60,000	Accounts payable	$ 30,000
Accounts receivable	50,000	Loan from bank payable	240,000
Inventories	130,000		
Capital equipment (original value $800,000)	600,000	Real estate mortgage payable	50,000
		Wages payable	20,000
Real estate owned (original value $80,000)	70,000	Salaries payable	30,000
		Other current liabilities	80,000
Other current assets	10,000		
Total assets	$920,000	Total liabilities	$450,000
Total assets		$920,000	
Minus total liabilities		450,000	
Equals: Net worth		$470,000	

c. accounting, accounting, $230,000
d. $920,000, $450,000, $470,000, does not
e. $688,500, $111,500, $230,000; See Table A6-3.

TABLE A6-3

WIDGET COMPANY
ADJUSTED INCOME STATEMENT FOR YEAR
ENDING DECEMBER 31, 1983

Revenues:		
(200,000 units @ $4.00 each)		$800,000
Expenses:		
Accounting cost from unadjusted statement	$570,000	
Opportunity cost of owner's time	75,000	
Opportunity cost of financial capital ($300,000 @ 14.5%)	43,500	
Total accounting plus opportunity costs		688,500
Economic profit		$111,500

2. a. TR: $0, $11, $20, $27, $32, $35, $36, $35; MR: $11, $9, $7, $5, $3, $1, −$1
   b. positive, zero
   c. fall
   d. sixth unit

3. a. MC: $4, $3, $2, $5, $9, $14, $20
   b. decreases, increases, third and fourth
   c. increases
   d. $22

4. See Figure A6-1.
   a. third and fourth units, $8, $9
   b. second and third units

5. a. TR: $0, $18, $34, $48, $60, $70, $78, $84, $88; MR: $18, $16, $14, $12, $10, $8, $6, $4; MC: $10, $8, $6, $4, $6, $8, $10, $12; Π: −$20, −$12, −$4, $4, $12, $16, $16, $12, $4

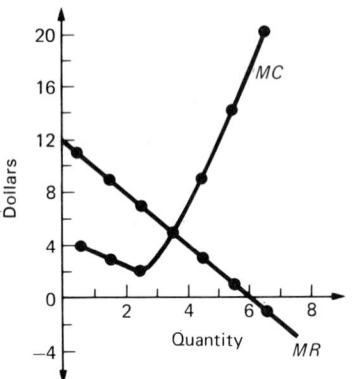

FIGURE A6-1

b. fifth and sixth units, $8, $8
c. total cost, total revenue, decrease, faster
d. $6, $10, $8, $8, zero

Fill-in Questions

1. maximize
2. marginal revenue, shift, increase
3. total cost, greatest
4. depreciate
5. net cash flow, negative
6. owner, dividends, capital gains
7. decrease, marginal revenue equals marginal cost, profits
8. limited liability
9. balance sheet, income statement
10. horizontal
11. opportunity costs
12. less than
13. high, fall, rise
14. inputs, costs
15. costs

True-False Questions

1. F
2. F
3. T
4. F
5. T
6. T
7. T
8. T
9. F
10. F
11. F
12. T
13. T
14. T
15. F
16. F
17. T
18. F
19. T
20. F

Multiple Choice Questions

1. d
2. b
3. c
4. b
5. c
6. a
7. d
8. b
9. d
10. c
11. b
12. a
13. d

CHAPTER 7

Important Terms

1. i
2. k
3. n
4. h
5. b
6. r
7. m
8. a
9. p
10. e
11. c
12. u
13. x
14. g
15. w
16. z
17. d
18. j
19. q
20. f
21. v
22. y
23. l
24. t
25. o
26. s

Exercises

1. MP_L: 3, 6, 5, 4, 3, 2, 1, 0, −1
   a. increases, 8
   b. second, third, decreases
   c. zero, decreases, negative
   d. capital, labor
   e. See Figure A7-1.

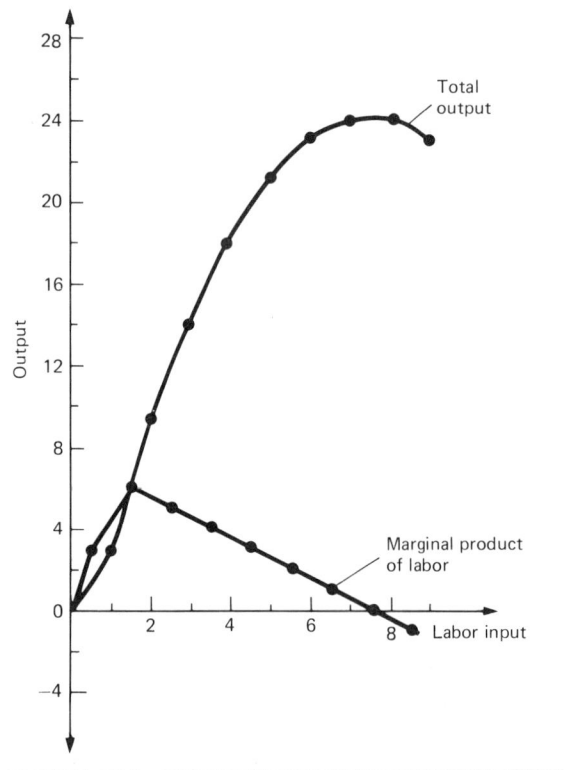

FIGURE A7-1

2. TCC: $800, $1600, $2400, $3200; TLC: $1750, $1250, $750, $250; TC: $2550, $2850, $3150, $3450
   a. 1, $2550
   b. capital, labor, 4, $2090
   c. 4, has not
3. a. STC: $10, $34, $49, $62, $73, $82, $92, $104, $118, $134, $152, $172
   $SATC$: $34, $24.50, $20.70, $18.30, $16.40,

ANSWERS

$15.30, $14.90, $14.80, $14.90, $15.20, $15.60
$SAFC$: $10, $5, $3.30, $2.50, $2, $1.60, $1.40, $1.30, $1.10, $1.00, $0.90
$SAVC$: $24, $19.50, $17.30, $15.80, $14.40, $13.70, $13.40, $13.50, $13.80, $14.20, $14.70
SMC: $24, $15, $13, $11, $9, $10, $12, $14, $16, $18, $20

b. increases, nonconstant
c. falls, decrease, minimum, increase
d. average fixed costs, diminishes
e. falls, increasing, rise, diminishing, $SATC$

4. See Figure A7-2.

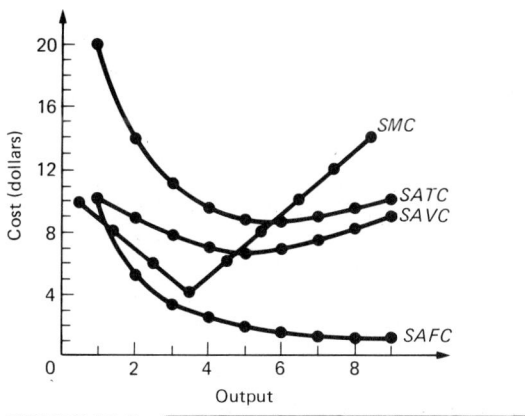

FIGURE A7-2

5. a. OS_1, OS_1
   b. would, loss
   c. average fixed
   d. would, fixed, variable
   e. profit
   f. total cost
6. a. economies of, decreased
   b. $SATC_3, OQ_3$
   c. $SATC_1, SATC_1, SATC_2$
   d. diseconomies
   e. See Figure A7-3.

Fill-in Questions

1. fixed, variable, variable
2. input
3. diminishing returns
4. economies, diseconomies
5. output, average fixed, average total
6. marginal
7. minimum
8. does not
9. production, input
10. marginal revenue, marginal cost, short-run average variable, should not
11. below, greater than, equal to
12. increasing, diminishing
13. sunk
14. plant
15. marginal costs, marginal revenue, price, long-run average

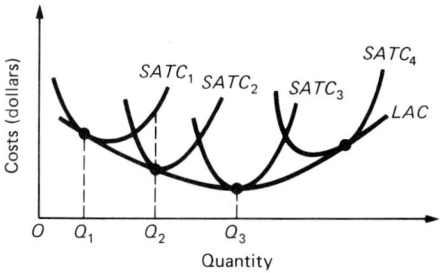

FIGURE A7-3

True-False Questions

1. T
2. T
3. F
4. T
5. F
6. F
7. F
8. F
9. T
10. F
11. T
12. T
13. T
14. T
15. F
16. F
17. T
18. F
19. T

Multiple Choice Questions

1. b
2. d
3. b
4. b
5. c
6. d
7. b
8. e
9. c
10. b
11. a
12. a
13. c
14. b
15. a
16. d

CHAPTER 8

Important Terms

1. d
2. o
3. m
4. a
5. r
6. q
7. b
8. e
9. s
10. c
11. j
12. i
13. g
14. p
15. h
16. k
17. n
18. f
19. l

Exercises

1. TR_1: $50, $100, $150, $200, $250, $300, $350, $400, $450, $500, $550, $600, $650
   Π_1: −$100, −$170, −$195, −$210, −$215, −$210, −$210, −$220, −$240, −$270, −$310, −$360, −$480, −$670
   TR_2: $90, $180, $270, $360, $450, $540, $630, $720, $810, $900, $990, $1080, $1170
   Π_2: −$100, −$130, −$115, −$90, −$55, −$10, $30, $60, $80, $90, $90, $80, $0, −$150
   TR_3: $240, $480, $720, $960, $1200, $1440, $1680, $1920, $2160, $2400, $2640, $2880, $3120
   Π_3: −$100, $20, $185, $360, $545, $740, $930, $1110, $1280, $1440, $1590, $1730, $1800, $1800

   a. shuts down, zero, $50, fifth and sixth, greater than, $67

    b. 10, $90, ninth and tenth
    c. twelfth and thirteenth, 13, $1800, would not, marginal, marginal
2. **a.** OS_1, average variable, marginal
    b. OS_3CQ_3, $OEDQ_3$, ES_3CD
    c. will, all, some, loss
    d. A
3. **a.** quantity supplied: 11, 10, 9, 8, 7, 6, 0, 0
    b. See Figure A8-1.
    c. $60
    d. average variable, marginal, falling, $100, $10.50, average total

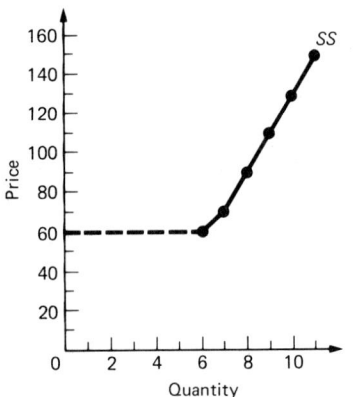

FIGURE A8-1

4. **a.** many
    b. none
    c. limited
    d. none
    e. few
    f. some
    g. more
    h. no entry
5. **a.** See Figure A8-2.
    b. $2.50, 225
    c. $562.50
    d. $4, $1, fall, $300
    e. See Figure A8-2.

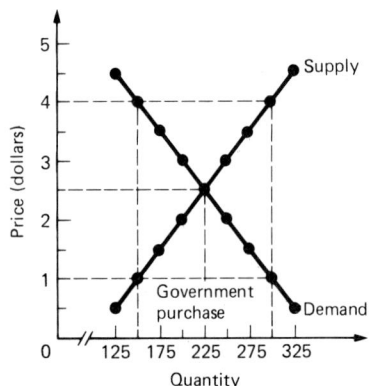

FIGURE A8-2

    f. 150, 150, $4, $1200, $900
    g. See Figure A8-2.
6. **a.** $8, 12
    b. Australia, 4, 4
    c. decrease, decrease, more
    d. decreases, $6, imports into, decrease, 1

Fill-in Questions

1. perfectly competitive, small
2. enter, removes, long-run average cost
3. SMC, MR, price, $SAVC$
4. sum, supply
5. is, has
6. increased, more
7. horizontal (perfectly elastic), quantity, price
8. do
9. tariffs, quotas, transportation costs, differentials
10. high, rise, fall, demanded, supplied
11. stabilize, inelastic
12. buyer, seller
13. parity, purchasing, price
14. MC, $SAVC$
15. increase, increase

True-False Questions

1. T	7. F	12. F
2. F	8. F	13. F
3. F	9. T	14. F
4. F	10. F	15. T
5. T	11. T	16. T
6. T		

Multiple Choice Questions

1. c	6. b	11. b
2. a	7. c	12. a
3. b	8. e	13. c
4. a	9. b	14. c
5. d	10. d	15. b

CHAPTER 9

Important Terms

1. i	7. l	13. c
2. f	8. b	14. n
3. o	9. j	15. q
4. k	10. d	16. r
5. a	11. g	17. e
6. h	12. p	18. m

Exercises

1. **a.** P_2, Q_2, quantity, quantity
    b. one, the same as
    c. less than
    d. MR, MC
    e. Q_1, P_1
    f. fall, increase

ANSWERS

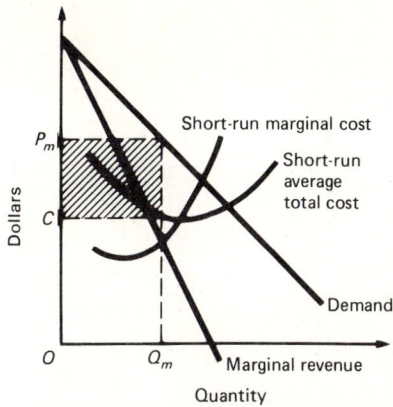

FIGURE A9-1

2. See Figure A9-1.
3. a. TR: $0, $140, $260, $360, $440, $500, $540, $560, $560, $540, $500, $440, $360, $260, $140
   MR: $140, $120, $100, $80, $60, $40, $20, $0, −$20, −$40, −$60, −$80, −$100, −$120
   b. See Figure A9-2.
   c. −4, −0.25
   d. $80, $70, 7, 8, zero

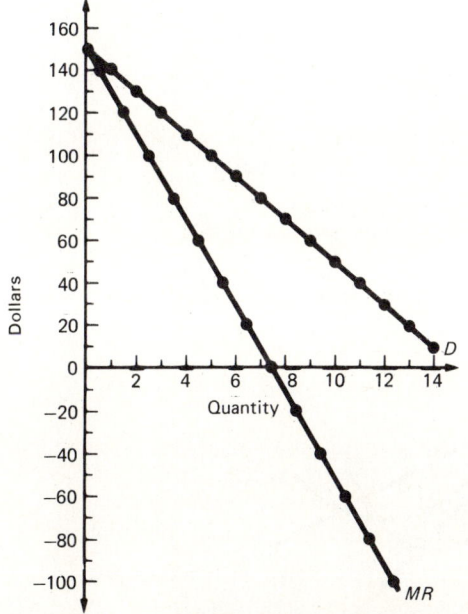

FIGURE A9-2

4. a. MR: $140, $120, $100, $80, $60, $40, $20, $0, −$20
   ATC: $140, $100, $80, $68, $66, $70, $79, $90, $107
   MC: $90, $60, $40, $30, $60, $90, $130, $170, $240
   Π: −$50, $0, $60, $120, $170, $170, $120, $10, −$160, −$420
   b. 5, $100, $170

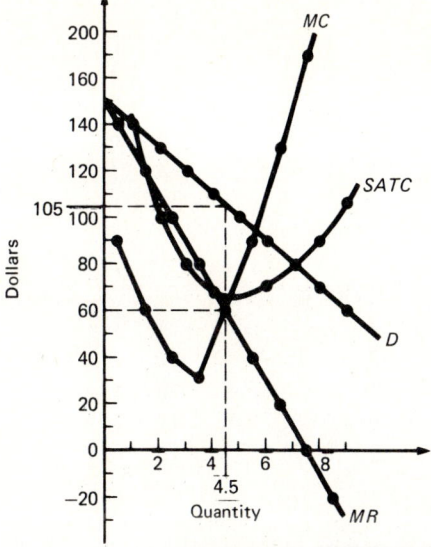

FIGURE A9-3

   c. fourth and fifth, $60
   d. See Figure A9-3
   e. 4.5, $105
   f. more, higher
   g. elastic, greater
5. a. 35, $115, $4025, $3150, $875
   b. $75, 65, are, zero
   c. 90, $45, $4050, $5850, loss, $1800, subsidy, $20
6. a. marginal, marginal, OZ
   b. OW, OX, OZ
   c. less, higher, less
   d. OA, OB, is
   e. OC
7. a. economies of scale
   b. control over scarce or essential resources
   c. government permission or authorization

Fill-in Questions

1. is, interactions
2. more, fewer
3. is not, do not
4. lower, greater than
5. zero, equal to, midpoint
6. MC, MR, greater than, average total, are not
7. setter, does
8. monopoly power
9. greater than, less
10. marginal valuation, price, marginal, price, marginal, competition
11. increase, decrease fall, fall
12. divide, price elasticity, lower
13. decreasing, cannot
14. patent
15. natural
16. does not, disappears
17. do

True-False Questions
1. F
2. F
3. T
4. T
5. T
6. T
7. F
8. F
9. F
10. T
11. F
12. F
13. T
14. F
15. F
16. T

Multiple Choice Questions
1. c
2. a
3. b
4. b
5. d
6. c
7. a
8. e
9. c
10. c
11. b
12. a
13. b
14. d
15. c

CHAPTER 9: APPENDIX

Important Terms
1. c
2. a
3. d
4. b

Exercises
1. a. See Figure A9-4.
   b. See Figure A9-4.
   c. Consumers' surplus = 4.5, producers' surplus = 4.5

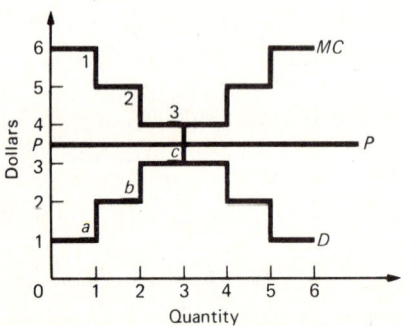

FIGURE A9-4

2. a. $AP_cB, CP_cB,$ is
   b. consumers' surplus, smaller
   c. consumers', producers', deadweight
   d. consumers' surplus, transferred, monopoly

True-False Questions
1. T
2. F
3. F
4. T
5. F
6. T
7. T
8. F
9. F
10. T

CHAPTER 10

Important Terms
1. q
2. g
3. i
4. n
5. r
6. u
7. a
8. e
9. d
10. s
11. p
12. b
13. f
14. t
15. v
16. j
17. c
18. o
19. h
20. l
21. m
22. k

Exercises
1. a. C
   b. O
   c. MC
   d. M
   e. MC
   f. O
   g. C
   h. M
   i. MC
2. a. DFD: —, —, 0, 6, 12, 18, 24, 30, 36, 42
      $TRDF$: —, —, 0, 42, 72, 90, 96, 90, 72, 42
      $MRDF$: —, 0, 7, 5, 3, 1, −1, −3, −5
   b. $6, 23
   c. 11, 12, 23
   d. decreases, 6, 12, 18, increases, $7
3. a. See Figure A10-1.
   b. marginal revenue, marginal
   c. See Figure A10-1.
   d. does not, is not, average total
   e. is
   f. entry of new firms, entry of new products

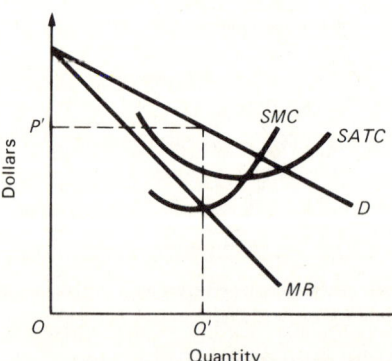

FIGURE A10-1

4. a. 60, $15
   b. $900, $540, $360
   c. $8.50
   d. 60, $15
   e. does not, sticky
   f. $180
   g. $13, decreases, increases

5. a. when collaboration is legally permitted and the firm can control entry
    b. ease of communication between firms
    c. ease of detection of cheating on established price
    d. difficult to maintain price when there are many firms
    e. different products are being sold
    f. changing costs and demand conditions
6. a. P_2, Q_2, marginal, marginal, $C_2 P_2 FL$
    b. $P_1, Q_1, C_1 P_1 EH, P_2$
    c. the same, $Q_2, RP_2 FG$, less than
    d. lose some or all
    e. Q_m

Fill-in Questions

1. barriers to entry, oligopoly profits
2. less than
3. cartel, profits
4. price leader
5. easy, large, similar
6. low, discouraged from entering
7. dominant
8. more difficult
9. competitive, competitive
10. kinked demand curve
11. different, variety
12. higher
13. monopolist
14. does not
15. the same, a lower, a higher

True-False Questions

1. F
2. F
3. T
4. T
5. F
6. F
7. F
8. T
9. F
10. T
11. T
12. T
13. F
14. F
15. T

Multiple Choice Questions

1. b
2. d
3. b
4. b
5. e
6. a
7. e
8. a
9. c
10. b
11. b
12. c
13. d
14. e

CHAPTER 11

Important Terms

1. f
2. k
3. h
4. b
5. l
6. a
7. n
8. c
9. m
10. d
11. i
12. e
13. g
14. j

Exercises

1. a. Section 7 of the Clayton Act. This section of the Clayton Act prohibits mergers of existing firms if the merger results in excessive concentration in an industry and a reduction in the level of competition.
    b. The FTC argued that the product extension merger permitted Procter and Gamble to enter into a market (liquid bleach) very close to those markets in which the company was already a leader (soaps and laundry detergents) so that essentially the markets were the same in terms of production and distribution.
    c. The goods are complements. Since Procter and Gamble had its advertising and distribution channels well established, the costs of adding liquid bleach to advertisements and distribution would be low. Also, P&G could identify both bleach and detergents together in its efforts, and this would impose a significant barrier which competitors or potential entrants would find difficult to surmount.
    d. The Supreme Court used economies (actual and potential) as a major factor in its decision to reverse the Court of Appeals. The economies might arise in the areas of production (the products of both companies were not that dissimilar), marketing, and advertising. Distribution (a major area) economies would probably be encountered. A new potential entrant into the liquid bleach market would find it very difficult and probably prohibitively expensive to establish a marketing, advertising, and distribution network to compete with P&G.
    e. P&G could reduce the price of Clorox bleach below the average cost of producing the product. Such a practice would serve to drive competitors out of the market and prohibit new firms from entering. Even though P&G would lose money on its bleach product, a part of the profits from other detergent products could be transferred to the bleach division.
    f. The industries are classified as oligopolies. Clorox controlled approximately 48 percent of the liquid bleach market, and P&G controlled approximately 55 percent of the laundry detergent market. The top four firms in each industry controlled almost 80 percent of each market.
2. a. Year 1 = (50 billion KWH potential) × (70% utilization rate) = 35 billion KWH
       Year 2 = (50 billion KWH potential) × (63% utilization rate) = 31.5 billion KWH
    b. Year 1: $1 billion var. costs + [(12.5%) × $4 billion asset value] = $1.5 billion
       Year 2: $1.2 billion var. cost + [(14%) × $4.1 billion asset value] = $1.774 billion
    c. Year 1: $1.5 billion/35 billion KWH = 4.3 cents per KWH

Year 2: $1774 billion/31.5 billion KWH = 5.6 cents per KWH

Fill-in Questions
1. loss
2. are not, is not
3. competition, welfare
4. 2, Clayton, costs
5. both civil and criminal, treble, may
6. predatory, denying
7. Justice, private citizens
8. cost
9. monopolies, distribution, cannot
10. two-part, marginal, does not
11. 9.5

True-False Questions
1. T
2. T
3. F
4. F
5. T
6. F
7. F
8. T
9. T
10. F
11. F
12. T
13. T
14. F
15. F

Multiple Choice Questions
1. a
2. c
3. a
4. d
5. c
6. b
7. d
8. a
9. c
10. b

CHAPTER 12

Important Terms
1. e
2. g
3. k
4. a
5. m
6. b
7. l
8. c
9. j
10. h
11. f
12. d
13. i

Exercises
1. a. CPSC
   b. OSHA
   c. EPA
   d. NHTSA
   e. FDA
   f. OSHA
   g. NTHSA
   h. CAB
   i. FDA
   j. CPSC
2. a. MC: $9.00, $9.10, $9.30, $9.60, $10.00, $10.50, $11.10, $11.80, $12.60
   b. $8.50, 11, $8.50
   c. negative, less than, overallocated
   d. $3.30, do not
   e. reduced, 9, increase, $10.50, price
3. a. MC: $1000, $500, $700, $900, $1100
      MB: $1300, $1000, $700, $400, $100
   b. 1.3, 2.0, 1.0, 0.44, 0.09
   c. should
   d. 4, 80%
   e. is, marginal costs, marginal benefit
   f. 1, 1, is not, costs, benefits
   g. should, greater than
4. a. See Figure A12-1.
   b. See Figure A12-1.
   c. underallocated, benefits
   d. larger
   e. ACB
   f. college education

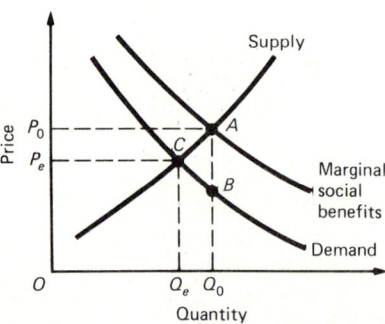

FIGURE A12-1

5. a. production of pollution would be efficiently allocated
   b. would not have to specify regulations for each firm
   c. difficult to measure amount of pollution for each firm
   d. difficult to determine correct price

Fill-in Questions
1. failure
2. price, optimal, valuation, costs
3. positive, negative
4. misallocation, is not
5. public
6. air pollution, water pollution, hazardous materials
7. benefits, costs, optimal, is not
8. expanded, information
9. FDA
10. higher, lower, decrease
11. Delaney
12. would not, costs
13. capture
14. airline, fallen, increased

True-False Questions
1. F
2. T
3. T
4. F
5. F
6. T
7. T
8. F
9. F
10. T
11. F
12. T
13. F
14. F
15. T

ANSWERS

Multiple Choice Questions
1. b
2. a
3. d
4. c
5. b
6. a
7. d
8. a
9. d
10. b
11. b
12. b

CHAPTER 13

Important Terms
1. h
2. o
3. i
4. j
5. d
6. m
7. c
8. l
9. k
10. g
11. a
12. b
13. e
14. f
15. n

Exercises
1. a. MP_L: 17, 15, 13, 11, 9, 7, 5, 3, 1
   b. TR: $0, $85, $160, $225, $280, $325, $360, $385, $400, $405
      $MVPL$: $85, $75, $65, $55, $45, $35, $25, $15, $5
   c. See Figure A13-1.
   d. quantity of labor demanded: 0, 1, 2, 3, 4, 5, 6, 7, 8, 9

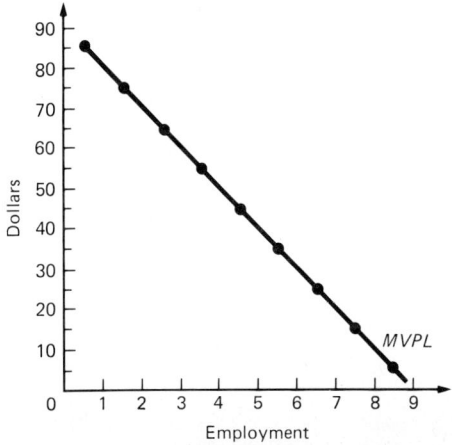

FIGURE A13-1

2. $MVPL$: $85, $75, $65, $55, $45, $35, $25, $15, $5
   contributions to profits: $60, $50, $40, $30, $20, $10, $0, −$10, −$20
   a. seventh, 8, 9, 7
   b. less than, fewer, 5
   c. competitive
3. a. W_e, Q_e, clears, can, can
   b. minimum, more, surplus, OQ_2-OQ_1
   c. wage, supply of
   d. floor
   e. would not, higher, will not
4. real wage: 6.80, 6, 5.20, 4.40, 3.60, 2.80, 2, 1.20, 0.80
   a. See Figure A13-2.

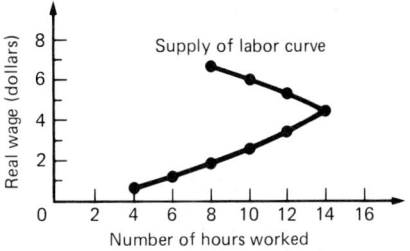

FIGURE A13-2

   b. substitution, income
   c. backward-bending
5. a. unit cost: $6, $5.40, $7.80, $8.10
      wage-rental: 0.67, 0.67, 1.17, 1.17
      capital-labor: 1.0, 0.33, 1.0, 0.33
   b. more, capital-labor
   c. 2
   d. 1, capital, capital-labor

Fill-in Questions
1. demand, marginal product, price
2. less, steeper
3. derived
4. substitution, income
5. upward-sloping, labor-force
6. cost (price), value (revenue)
7. is not
8. increase, increase, more
9. shift, movement along
10. demand, supply
11. human
12. economic rent

True-False Questions
1. F
2. T
3. F
4. T
5. T
6. F
7. T
8. F
9. T
10. F
11. F
12. T
13. F

Multiple Choice Questions
1. d
2. b
3. a
4. d
5. c
6. b
7. e
8. d
9. b
10. c

CHAPTER 13: APPENDIX

Exercises
1. a. See Figure A13-3, 30
   b. See Figure A13-3.
   c. above, greater
   d. 500, 18, 16, zero
   e. 1.125, 0.75
   f. See Figure A13-3; capital, labor, capital-labor
   g. rotate, 20, decreased, Q_2, decreased
   h. 10, 20, labor, capital, 1:2, flatter, 1:2
   i. more

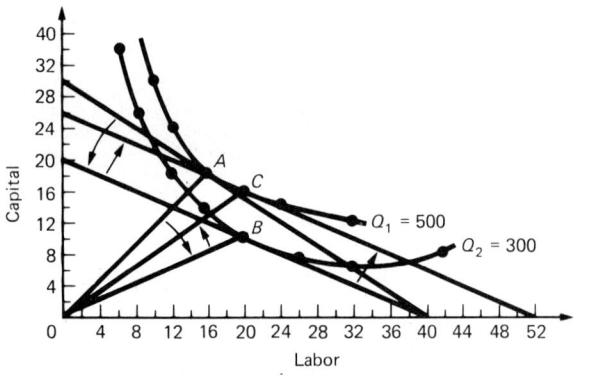

FIGURE A13-3

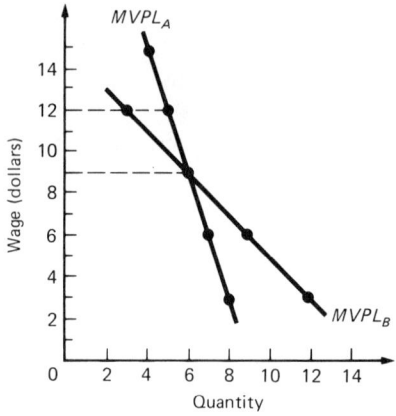

FIGURE A14-1

j. 16, 20, 0.8, steeper
k. 360, $1560

Fill-in Questions
1. technique
2. isoquant map
3. decreases, is not
4. isoquant, operating budget line
5. rotate, rental-wage, substitutes, does

True-False Questions
1. F
2. T
3. T
4. F
5. T

Multiple Choice Questions
1. b
2. e
3. b
4. c
5. a

CHAPTER 14

Important Terms
1. d
2. i
3. o
4. h
5. b
6. p
7. n
8. j
9. k
10. g
11. m
12. e
13. c
14. f
15. l
16. a

Exercises
1. a. projected income with college: $720,000, $1,116,000, $576,000, $1,800,000, $666,000
   projected income without college: $600,000, $600,000, $600,000, $600,000, $600,000
   total direct cost of education: $30,000, $30,000, $30,000, $30,000, $30,000
   net contribution: $90,000, $486,000, −$54,000, $1,170,000, $36,000
   b. D, $60,000
   c. negative, consumption
2. a. See Figure A14-1.
   b. less, less
   c. 6; See Figure A14-1.
   d. 5, 3, A, employment; See Figure A14-1.

Fill-in Questions
1. marginal
2. inelastic, horizontal
3. consumption, understated
4. real
5. General
6. may not
7. share of jobs, pay
8. group, reduce
9. differently
10. craft, industrial
11. Wagner Act
12. a monopolist, higher
13. right-to-work, more difficult
14. compensates
15. do not

True-False Questions
1. T
2. F
3. T
4. F
5. F
6. F
7. T
8. T
9. T
10. F
11. F
12. T
13. T
14. F
15. T
16. F
17. F

Multiple Choice Questions
1. a
2. d
3. c
4. d
5. b
6. e
7. b
8. d
9. c
10. b
11. a
12. a

CHAPTER 15

Important Terms
1. l
2. h
3. q
4. m
5. k
6. a
7. o
8. f
9. r
10. c
11. d
12. v
13. b
14. g
15. t
16. i
17. e
18. u
19. j
20. n
21. p
22. s

ANSWERS

Exercises

1. a. I-A: 0.91, 0.83, 0.75, 0.68, 0.62
      II-A: $4550, $3320, $2250, $1360, $620
      I-B: 0.87, 0.76, 0.66, 0.57, 0.50
      II-B: $1740, $2280, $2640, $2850, $3000
      net present value (A): $7720
      net present value (B): $8010
   b. B, $8010
   c. positive
2. a. MP_k: 14, 12, 10, 8, 6, 4, 2
   b. TR: $0, $140, $260, $360, $440, $500, $540, $560
      $MVPK$: $140, $120, $100, $80, $60, $40, $20
   c. See Figure A15-1.
   d. Q_d: 0, 1, 2, 3, 4, 5, 6, 7, demand, is not, 4
   e. to the right, more

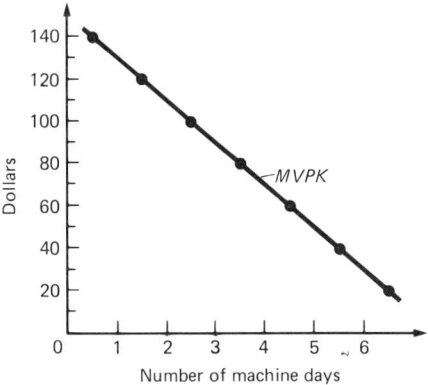

FIGURE A15-1

3. a. support, residential, contact
   b. more
   c. ON, agricultural, greater than
   d. EF, agricultural, expand
   e. See Figure A15-2.
   f. different

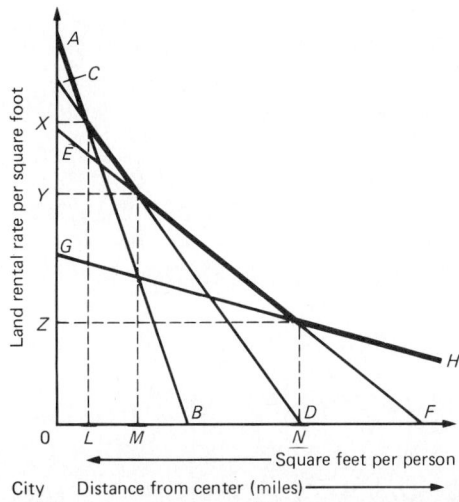

FIGURE A15-2

4. a. increase, substitution
   b. is, increase
   c. R_1, above, more, fall
   d. R_2, K_2, is not, higher
   e. will
   f. are

Fill-in Questions

1. consumer, tangible
2. more
3. flow, stock
4. time, double
5. discount, interest
6. perpetuity, annual payment, interest, price
7. real
8. decrease
9. positive
10. demand for, product, price
11. is, can
12. demand, supply
13. short, cannot
14. asset
15. present
16. fixed, vertical
17. higher
18. marginal

True-False Questions

1. T
2. T
3. F
4. T
5. F
6. F
7. T
8. F
9. T
10. F
11. F
12. T
13. F
14. F
15. T
16. T
17. T
18. F

Multiple Choice Questions

1. b
2. c
3. b
4. d
5. c
6. e
7. a
8. d
9. b
10. d
11. b
12. a
13. e
14. a
15. b

CHAPTER 15: APPENDIX

Exercises

1. $PV = \dfrac{\$1000}{(1+.1)} + \dfrac{\$850}{(1+.1)^2} + \dfrac{\$2500}{(1+.1)^3} + \dfrac{\$1500}{(1+.1)^4} + \dfrac{\$500}{(1+.1)^5} + \dfrac{\$3000}{(1+.1)^6}$

   $PV = \$909.09 + \$702.48 + \$1878.29 + \$1024.52 + \$310.46 + \$1693.42$

   $PV = \$6518.26$

   If you receive the six payments, total receipts equal $9350.

2. $PV = \dfrac{\$4000}{(1.09)^8} = \$2007.47$.

   Today, the $4000 payment in 8 years is worth $7.47 more than the $2000 payment.

3. $X = \dfrac{\$5000}{(1+.08)^3} = \$3969.16$ as the minimum amount acceptable to you

4. $7692.31 = \dfrac{X}{.065}$

$X = \$500$ payment each year forever

CHAPTER 16

Important Terms
1. g
2. e
3. b
4. h
5. a
6. c
7. d
8. f

Exercises
1.
   a. *OG*, private, equal, *OE*
   b. *OE* (*GA*), *AB*, *GB*, greater than
   c. reduced, *OF*, *HF* (*OI*), less than, would not
   d. *ID*, increases, internalize

Fill-in Questions
1. reduction
2. availability, wages
3. do not, does not
4. marginal cost, marginal benefits
5. price dispersion
6. increases
7. comparative, time
8. opportunity, more
9. were
10. decreasing

True-False Questions
1. T
2. F
3. F
4. T
5. T
6. F
7. F
8. T
9. F
10. T

Multiple Choice Questions
1. b
2. d
3. b
4. c
5. e
6. b
7. d
8. c
9. a

CHAPTER 17

Important Terms
1. j
2. s
3. m
4. q
5. w
6. b
7. n
8. a
9. v
10. p
11. y
12. i
13. f
14. o
15. g
16. d
17. k
18. c
19. l
20. e
21. t
22. x
23. u
24. h
25. r

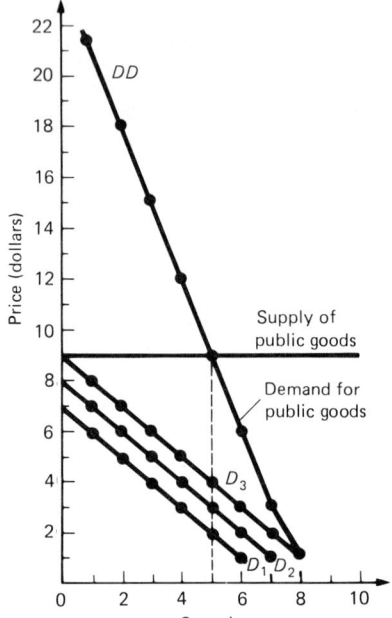

FIGURE A17-1

Exercises
1.
   a, b. See Figure A17-1.

   c.

Price	$21	$18	$15	$12	$9	$6	$3	$1
Quantity	1	2	3	4	5	6	7	8

   d. vertically, is not
   e. See Figure A17-1.
   f. 5, $9

2.
   a. 1, 2
   b. 3, 1
   c. 3, 2
   d. 2, 3
   e. paradox of voting, is not
   f. three-way tie

3.
   a. *Oh*, *Oe*
   b. shifts, falls, fewer
   c. *Oi*, *Og*, *Of*, reduced
   d. *bc*, distortion, discourage
   e. *bac*, *gibc*

4.
   a. ATR-I: 14.7, 15.6, 16.8, 17.5, 18.1, 21, 23.5, 26.1
   MTR-I: 16.5, 19.3, 19.5, 20.5, 23.8, 28.6, 33.9
   ATR-II: 20, 20, 20, 20, 20, 20, 20, 20
   MTR-II: 20, 20, 20, 20, 20, 20, 20
   b. 1, increase
   c. flat-rate, II, 20 percent

5.
   a. *VA*: $25, $50, $75, $50, $100
   VAT: $1.25, $2.50, $3.75, $2.50, $5
   b. $300
   c. $15
   d. $15, the same

ANSWERS

Fill-in Questions
1. transfer
2. taxes, fees and charges for services
3. distortions, goods, redistributed
4. is, is not
5. vertically, excluding
6. is not, majority, middle
7. efficiency, equity
8. merit
9. is, majority, median
10. funds, civil servants
11. a payroll, a capital gain
12. distortion
13. ability to pay, benefits received
14. do
15. inelastic, does not
16. does not, imputed
17. 9, did not
18. decreasing

True-False Questions
1. T
2. T
3. F
4. F
5. T
6. F
7. T
8. F
9. T
10. F
11. T
12. T
13. F
14. F
15. T
16. T
17. F
18. F

Multiple Choice Questions
1. c
2. a
3. e
4. b
5. d
6. a
7. c
8. c
9. b
10. d
11. e
12. b
13. c
14. a
15. c
16. e

CHAPTER 18

Important Terms
1. m
2. d
3. i
4. k
5. c
6. b
7. j
8. e
9. f
10. a
11. h
12. g
13. l

Exercises
1. a. A, highest
   b. C and D, E and F
   c. decreases, less
   d. F, lower, F, increase
   e. (1) A
      (2) F
      (3) E
      (4) C
      (5) B
      (6) C
      (7) D
      (8) F
2. a. *Tax Payment*: −$2000, −$1500, −$1000, −$500, 0, +$500, +$1000, +$1500, +$2000, +$2500, +$3000
   b. negative income, transfers, to
   c. $4000, increases
   d. $2000, unrestricted
   e. Milton Friedman
3. a. $5, 65,000, capacity, greater than, more
   b. price, average, 95,000, is
   c. 85,000, marginal, $7, price
   d. reduced

Fill-in Questions
1. 75%, 18
2. specialization, transportation
3. would not
4. population density, falls
5. local, would
6. increase, increase, agriculture
7. 57, 43 percent
8. blight flight, more, lower
9. public, limited
10. shortage, is not
11. fall, suburbs
12. automobile, pollution, congestion
13. property, federal and state governments, education
14. Tiebout, more
15. zone

True-False Questions
1. T
2. F
3. T
4. T
5. F
6. T
7. F
8. F
9. T
10. F
11. T
12. F
13. F
14. T
15. T
16. F
17. F
18. F

Multiple Choice Questions
1. c
2. a
3. d
4. b
5. e
6. a
7. c
8. d
9. e
10. b
11. a
12. e
13. e

CHAPTER 19

Important Terms
1. g
2. j
3. b
4. r
5. q
6. o
7. a
8. n
9. d
10. f
11. p
12. c
13. h
14. e
15. i
16. u
17. m
18. k
19. s
20. l
21. t

Exercises
1. a. See Table A19-1.

TABLE A19-1

ALTERNATIVE 1

OUTCOME	EXPECTED MONEY VALUE, $
Poor quality, unusable	−375,000
Poor quality, usable (2000 tons)	−40,000
Medium quality, usable (4000 tons)	+55,000
Good quality, usable (5000 tons)	+100,000
Exceptional quality (11,000 tons)	+250,000
Sum of expected money value	−10,000

ALTERNATIVE 2   0

   b. chance, monetary
   c. −$10,000, $0
   d. should not
2. a. RL
   b. RA
   c. RA
   d. RN
   e. RL
   f. RN

Fill-in Questions

1. will, rewarded
2. does not
3. dividends, capital gains
4. risk-averse, small
5. reduce
6. cyclical, countercyclical
7. low, less
8. attitude
9. irrational, rational
10. speculative
11. hedging
12. do

True-False Questions

1. T
2. F
3. F
4. T
5. F
6. T
7. T
8. F
9. F
10. F

Multiple Choice Questions

1. b
2. c
3. a
4. a
5. d
6. c
7. b
8. d
9. a
10. e

CHAPTER 20

Important Terms

1. d
2. j
3. r
4. m
5. b
6. k
7. n
8. q
9. e
10. a
11. p
12. c
13. h
14. i
15. g
16. l
17. f
18. o

Exercises

1. a. J, 7, 10
   b. are, does not
   c. is not, more, is not
   d. 11, 10, cannot
   e. increases, ZZ', is not, 10, 5, 6, 16, Y, X, X, Y, decreases
   f. is not, less than, X, Y
2. a. rate of return: 400%, 300%, 200%, 100%, 0, −50%
   b. E, F, 1, 1
   c. negative, more
   d. diminishing, too much
   e. preferences
3. a. Wage and price flexibility ensures labor market equilibrium at full employment; the economy is on the PPF
   b. Given prices, profit maximization by firms ensures that MRT = relative price ratio on PPF
   c. Given prices, consumers' MRS = relative price ratio
   d. Equilibrium occurs on the PPF where MRT = MRS = relative price ratio
   e. Competitive economy achieves a socially optimal allocation of resources

Fill-in Questions

1. diminishing, bowed
2. can, is not
3. negative, decrease
4. PPF, indifference curve, cannot, are
5. allocate, ensure
6. prices, marginal
7. distortion, misallocated
8. saving, invest
9. rate of return, interest, are not
10. saving, investment, interest
11. profitability, savings, interest, shift

True-False Questions

1. F
2. T
3. F
4. T
5. T
6. F
7. T
8. F
9. F
10. T
11. T
12. F
13. F
14. T

Multiple Choice Questions

1. b
2. c
3. a
4. c
5. e
6. b
7. c
8. b
9. d
10. b

CHAPTER 21

Important Terms

1. o
2. t
3. h
4. p
5. a
6. d

ANSWERS

7.	l	12.	q	17.	f
8.	s	13.	i	18.	m
9.	r	14.	c	19.	j
10.	b	15.	g	20.	n
11.	e	16.	k		

Exercises

1. **a.** Real GNP: 333, 353, 380, 360, 400
   Inflation rate per year: 22.3%, 8.7%, 25%, 20%
   Growth rate of nominal GNP: 30%, 17%, 18%, 33%
   Growth rate of real GNP: 6%, 7.6%, −5.3%, 11.1%
   b. increased, positive
   c. increases, negative, positive
   d. decreased, inflation
   e. 2, 3
   f. 3, greater than, less
   g. 4

2.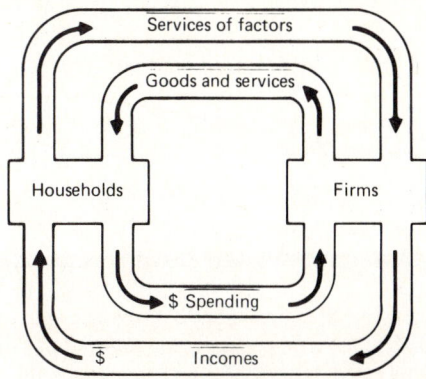

FIGURE A21-1

Fill-in Questions

1. consumer price
2. price index, constant, output
3. macroeconomics
4. inflation
5. nominal, real
6. did not
7. deflation, increase
8. produces, pays for
9. unemployed, society
10. quantity, productivity
11. are not, increase

True-False Questions

1.	F	5.	T	9.	T
2.	T	6.	T	10.	F
3.	F	7.	T	11.	T
4.	F	8.	F	12.	T

Multiple Choice Questions

1.	d	4.	a	7.	a
2.	b	5.	d	8.	c
3.	c	6.	d	9.	e

CHAPTER 22

Important Terms

1.	m	9.	v	16.	l
2.	i	10.	b	17.	h
3.	k	11.	d	18.	o
4.	a	12.	s	19.	j
5.	t	13.	e	20.	f
6.	p	14.	g	21.	q
7.	c	15.	u	22.	r
8.	n				

Exercises

1. **a.** $2414 billion
   b. See Table A22-1.

TABLE A22-1

Gross national product	$ 2414
Less capital consumption allowance	(−) 254
Equals: Net national product	2160
Less indirect business taxes minus subsidies	(−) 197
Equals: National income	1963
Less corporate profits	(−) 196
Plus dividends	(+) 49
Plus interest adjustment	(+) 66
Less personal taxes	(−) 534
Plus transfers	(+) 294
Equals: Personal disposable income	1642

  c. $1511 billion, $86 billion
  d. 5.2%

2. **a.** X
   b. ✓
   c. ✓
   d. ✓
   e. X
   f. X
   g. ✓
   h. X
   i. ✓
   j. X
   k. X
   l. ✓

3. GNP deflator: 100, 105.8, 116.4, 127.2, 133.7, 141.7, 152.1, 162.8, 177.3, 193.8
   rate of inflation: 5.8%, 10.0%, 9.3%, 5.1%, 6.0%, 7.3%, 7.0%, 8.9%, 9.3%
   a. decreased, increased
   b. increased, fell
   c. 1974, 1976, 1980, increased
   d. did not

Fill-in Questions

1. nuisance, are not
2. nuisance, nonmarket, leisure
3. decreases, more
4. GDP
5. depreciation, indirect business taxes minus subsidies

6. labor, property, labor
7. personal disposable income, less than
8. personal saving rate, lowest
9. household consumption, foreign
10. is
11. nominal, real

True-False Questions

1. F
2. T
3. F
4. F
5. T
6. F
7. F
8. T
9. T
10. F
11. T
12. T

Multiple Choice Questions

1. b
2. d
3. a
4. c
5. b
6. e
7. c
8. a
9. b
10. d
11. c

CHAPTER 23

Important Terms

1. f
2. a
3. n
4. h
5. o
6. b
7. d
8. m
9. k
10. c
11. e
12. i
13. g
14. j
15. l

Exercises

1. a. PS: $20, $40, $60, $80, $100, $120, $140
   b. MPC = 0.8 for all levels, MPC = 0.2 for all levels
   c. does not, MPS, 1, consumed, saved
   d. .8
   e. See Figure A23-1.
2. a. PS: $20, $40, $60, $80, $100, $120, $140
      PI: $60 billion at all levels
   b. AD: $140, $220, $300, $380, $460, $540, $620
   c. $300 billion
   d. more, decrease, less than, increases
   e. IA: −, −, 0, +, +, +, +
      OA: +, +, 0, −, −, −, −
   f. do not, do, decreases
   g. See Figure A23-2; yes
   h. output, potential, actual
   i. greater than, multiplier, 5, $400 billion, shifts
3. a. See Figure A23-3.
   b. parallel, downward, less
   c. greater than, increase, do not
   d. decrease, falls
   e. $525 billion, remained constant, paradox of thrift
   f. $175 billion, 7, 0.14

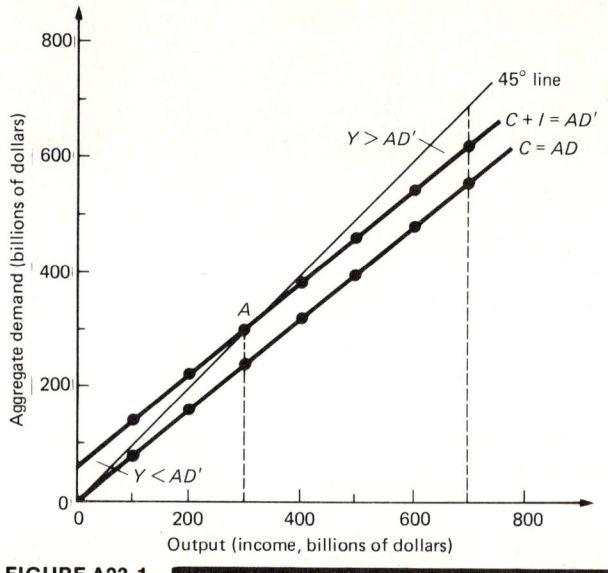
FIGURE A23-1

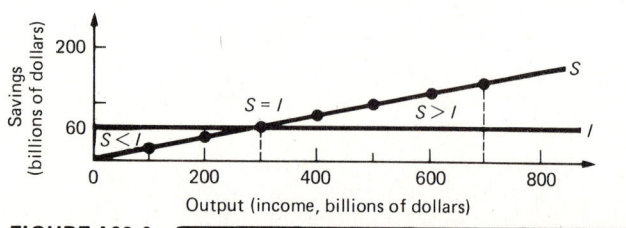
FIGURE A23-2

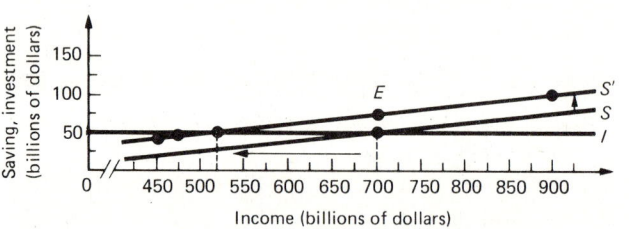
FIGURE A23-3

Fill-in Questions

1. potential output, actual output
2. recession, trough, recovery, peak, are
3. is not, is
4. consumption function
5. consumption, income
6. is, dissave
7. increase
8. 45°, equal
9. investment, is not
10. increases, is not
11. constant, constant, saving
12. output, aggregate demand, smaller

True-False Questions

1. F
2. F
3. T
4. T
5. F
6. T
7. T
8. T
9. F
10. F
11. T
12. F
13. F
14. F

ANSWERS

Multiple Choice Questions
1. d
2. b
3. a
4. a
5. b
6. c
7. d
8. b
9. c
10. a

CHAPTER 24

Important Terms
1. n
2. h
3. a
4. k
5. l
6. d
7. f
8. o
9. g
10. m
11. p
12. c
13. i
14. b
15. e
16. j

Exercises
1. **a.** C: $75, $150, $225, $300, $375, $450, $525, $600, $675, $750
   S: $25, $50, $75, $100, $125, $150, $175, $200, $225, $250
   (1) increase
   (2) 0.75, 0.25
   b. AD: $235, $310, $385, $460, $535, $610, $685, $760, $835, $910
   (1) $600, $700
   (2) saving, investment, government spending, $160
   (3) 0.25, $640
   (4) $480, $160, $640
   c. New AD: $285, $360, $435, $510, $585, $660, $735, $810, $885, $960
   (1) $800, $900
   (2) $210, $210
   (3) $840
   (4) $200, multiplier
   (5) 4
2. **a.** T: $20, $40, $60, $80, $100, $120, $140, $160, $180, $200
   Y_d: $80, $160, $240, $320, $400, $480, $560, $640, $720, $800
   C': $60, $120, $180, $240, $300, $360, $420, $480, $540, $600
   S': $20, $40, $60, $80, $100, $120, $140, $160, $180, $200
   (1) increases
   (2) 0.6, 0.2
   (3) 0.75, 0.25
   b. AD: $220, $280, $340, $400, $460, $520, $580, $640, $700, $760
   (1) $400, lower
   (2) consumption
   c. $S' + T$: $40, $80, $120, $160, $200, $240, $280, $320, $360, $400
   $I + G$: $160, $160, $160, $160, $160, $160, $160, $160, $160, $160
   (1) saving, taxes, investment, government spending
   (2) $400
   (3) less than, increase, greater than
3. See Figure A24-1.
   a. $640
   b. rotate, slope
   c. $400

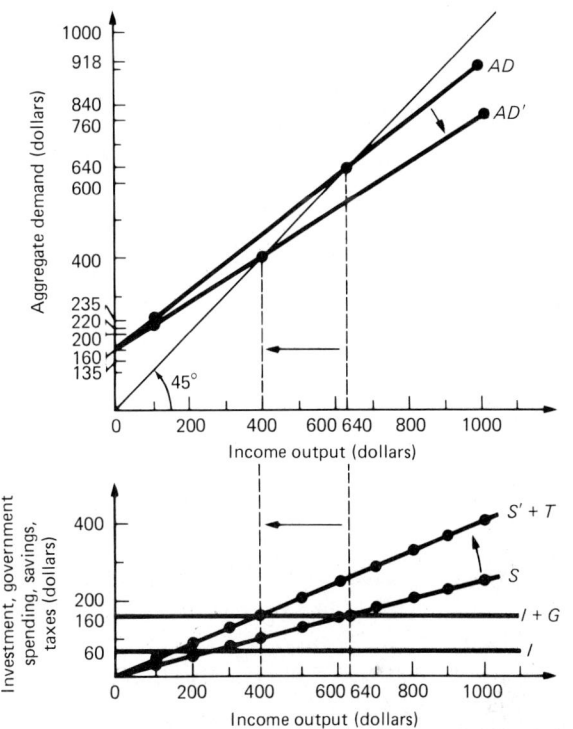

FIGURE A24-1

4. T: $20, $40, $60, $80, $100, $120, $140, $160, $180, $200
   $G - T$: −$80, −$60, −$40, −$20, 0, $20, $40, $60, $80, $100
   a. $500
   b. deficit, greater than
   c. surplus, $40, deficit, −$20
   d. expansionary, have not
5. **a.** $AD = C + I + G$, $C = 0.75Y$, $S = 0.25Y$
   b. $AD' = C' + I + G$, $C' = 0.75Y_d$, $S' = 0.25Y_d$, $Y_d = Y - T$, $T = 0.2Y$

Fill-in Questions
1. taxes, transfer, purchases
2. income, Social Security
3. negative, increases
4. decreases, rotates, less
5. shift, multiplier
6. does, does not
7. fall, decreases
8. budget
9. rise, rise

10. leakages from, government, investment
11. contractionary, decrease
12. full-employment, is
13. uncertainty, lags
14. automatic, dampens
15. national, decreasing
16. receipts, outlays

True-False Questions
1. F
2. F
3. T
4. T
5. T
6. F
7. T
8. F
9. F
10. T
11. F
12. F
13. T
14. T
15. F
16. F
17. T
18. T

Multiple Choice Questions
1. b
2. d
3. a
4. b
5. c
6. d
7. e
8. a
9. c
10. c
11. b
12. a

CHAPTER 24: APPENDIX

Important Terms
1. c
2. d
3. a
4. b

Exercises
1. a. C: $70, $105, $140, $175, $210, $245, $280, $315, $350
   $X - Q$: $30, $20, $10, 0, -$10, -$20, -$30, -$40, -$50
   AD: $200, $225, $250, $275, $300, $325, $350, $375, $400
   b. $300
   c. deficit, $10, imports, exports
   d. 50 cents, 20 cents, 0.2
   e. $250, increase
2. $X - Q$: $55, $45, $35, $25, $15, $5, -$5, -$15, -$25
   AD: $225, $250, $275, $300, $325, $350, $375, $400, $425
   a. $350
   b. surplus, 5
   c. 2, smaller

Fill-in Questions
1. foreign, domestic
2. decrease
3. income
4. is, do
5. decreases, fall

True-False Questions
1. T
2. F
3. F
4. T
5. F

Multiple Choice Questions
1. c
2. a
3. d
4. b
5. a

CHAPTER 25

Important Terms
1. i
2. m
3. g
4. s
5. b
6. o
7. a
8. p
9. c
10. l
11. f
12. j
13. e
14. k
15. h
16. r
17. d
18. n
19. q

Exercises
1. a.

TRANSACTION 1

ASSETS		LIABILITIES AND NET WORTH	
Reserves	$175,000	Net worth	$250,000
Bank premises and equipment	75,000		

b. assets (reserves), liabilities

TRANSACTION 2

ASSETS		LIABILITIES AND NET WORTH	
Reserves	$250,000	Demand deposits	$ 75,000
Bank premises and equipment	75,000	Net worth	250,000

c. assets, liabilities

TRANSACTION 3

ASSETS		LIABILITIES AND NET WORTH	
Reserves	$235,000	Demand deposits	$ 75,000
Loan	15,000	Net worth	250,000
Bank premises and equipment	75,000		

d. have, has

TRANSACTION 4

ASSETS		LIABILITIES AND NET WORTH	
Reserves	$235,000	Demand deposits	$ 85,000
Loans	25,000	Net worth	250,000
Bank premises and equipment	75,000		

e. yes

ANSWERS

TRANSACTION 5

ASSETS		LIABILITIES AND NET WORTH	
Reserves	$240,000	Demand deposits	$ 85,000
Loans	20,000	Net worth	250,000
Bank premises and equipment	75,000		

    f. See Tables A25-2*a* and A25-2*b*.

TRANSACTION 6

ASSETS		LIABILITIES AND NET WORTH	
Reserves	$235,000	Demand deposits	$ 80,000
Loans	20,000	Net worth	250,000
Bank premises and equipment	75,000		

TABLE A25-2*a*
FEDERAL RESERVE BANK

ASSETS		LIABILITIES AND NET WORTH	
Cash	$1,000,000	Reserve deposits, Zebina National Bank	$235,000
Bank property	500,000	Reserve deposits, Bald Eagle National Bank	305,000
		Other reserves	560,000
		Net worth	400,000

TABLE A25-2*b*
BALD EAGLE NATIONAL BANK

ASSETS		LIABILITIES AND NET WORTH	
Reserves	$305,000	Demand deposits	$255,000
Loans	50,000	Net worth	200,000
Bank premises and equipment	100,000		

2. a. SV
   b. SP
   c. SV
   d. MX
   e. UA
   f. SP
   g. UA
   h. MX

Fill-in Questions

1. financial intermediaries
2. commercial, deposits, loans
3. demand (checkable), saving, time
4. fractional reserve
5. decreases, increases
6. local clearing, Federal Reserve
7. currency, checkable deposits, traveler's checks
8. M2, M3, are not
9. medium of exchange
10. double coincidence of wants, barter
11. fiat, is
12. goldsmiths, deposits, loans
13. deposits, loans
14. financial, run
15. was, deposits

True-False Questions

1. F   6. T   11. T
2. T   7. T   12. F
3. T   8. F   13. F
4. F   9. T   14. F
5. F   10. F

Multiple Choice Questions

1. b   5. a   9. a
2. d   6. c   10. e
3. c   7. b   11. b
4. e   8. e   12. a

CHAPTER 26

Important Terms

1. h   6. b   10. m
2. f   7. g   11. j
3. k   8. d   12. c
4. a   9. e   13. i
5. l

Exercises

1. a. See Table A26-1.
   b. U.S. government securities, $134,257 million, Federal Reserve notes
   c. $123,510 million
2. a. 0, −
   b. 0, +
   c. 0, 0
   d. 0, +
   e. 0, 0
   f. −, −
   g. 0, +
   h. 0, −
3. a. 20
   b. $155 million, $455 million
   c. 2.94
   d. See Tables A26-4 and A26-5, increases, $10 million

TABLE A26-1

FEDERAL RESERVE SYSTEM BALANCE SHEET
(millions of dollars, April 30, 1982)

ASSETS		LIABILITIES AND NET WORTH (CAPITAL ASSETS)	
U.S. government securities	$134,257	Federal Reserve notes	$130,189
Gold	11,149	Deposits from depository institutions	24,702
U.S. government obligations purchased	9,008	Deposits from the U.S. Treasury	12,239
Cash in process of collection	8,449	Deposits from foreign governments	966
Foreign currencies	5,591	Other deposits	450
Loans to depository institutions	1,799	Other liabilities	9,439
Acceptances	768		
Bank premises	514	Total liabilities	$177,985
Coins	411	Net worth (capital assets)	3,064
Other assets	9,103		
		Total liabilities and net worth	$181,049
Total assets	$181,049		

TABLE A26-4

FEDERAL RESERVE SYSTEM, (millions of dollars)

ASSETS		LIABILITIES	
Loans to banks	$ 2	Federal Reserve notes	
Government securities	144	Currency held by public	$ 80
Other assets	19	Vault cash of banks	50
		Deposits of banks	35

TABLE A26-5

ALL COMMERCIAL BANKS, (millions of dollars)

ASSETS		LIABILITIES	
Reserves		Checkable deposits	$375
Deposits at Fed	$ 35	Loans from Fed	2
Vault cash	50		
Loans and securities	292		

TABLE A26-6

ALL COMMERCIAL BANKS, (millions of dollars)

ASSETS		LIABILITIES	
Reserves		Checkable deposits	$385
Deposits at Fed	$ 35	Loans from Fed	2
Vault cash	50		
Loans and securities	302		

    e. has not, excess, $10 million
    f. See Table A26-6, checkable deposits, $10 million
    g. does, $77 million
    h. will, excess
    i. $485 million, $30 million

Fill-in Questions

1. 12, Federal Reserve
2. gold, government securities, Federal Reserve notes
3. reserves, dollars
4. reserves, can, excess reserves, expand, a greater amount than
5. required reserve, cannot
6. changes in the discount rate, changes in the required reserve ratios, open market operations
7. decrease, decrease, contract
8. monetary, high-powered, currency, bank deposits
9. primary, secondary, multiplier
10. lender
11. decreased
12. FDIC
13. does not, borrowing from
14. Milton Friedman, should not
15. is not, gold, does not

True-False Questions

1. F	7. F	13. T
2. T	8. T	14. T
3. F	9. F	15. F
4. F	10. T	16. T
5. T	11. F	17. T
6. T	12. F	18. T

Multiple Choice Questions

1. b	6. b	11. e
2. d	7. c	12. c
3. a	8. d	13. a
4. c	9. a	14. b
5. e	10. a	

ANSWERS

CHAPTER 26: APPENDIX

Exercises

1. **a.** an increase, $500 million
   b. 2.6, increase, $1300 million
   c. increase, 2.6, 3

True-False Questions

1. T	5. F	8. T
2. F	6. F	9. T
3. T	7. T	10. F
4. T		

CHAPTER 27

Important Terms

1. o	7. a	12. e
2. i	8. l	13. n
3. b	9. g	14. k
4. h	10. p	15. f
5. c	11. m	16. d
6. j		

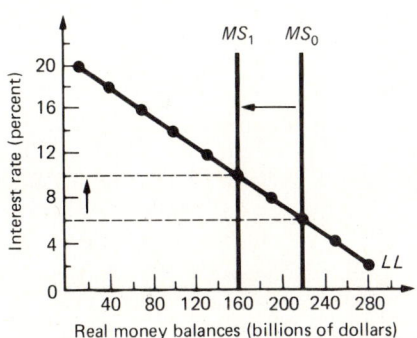

FIGURE A27-1

Exercises

1. **a.** See Figure A27-1.
   b. negative, opportunity, decreases
   c. vertical, is not
   d. 6%, $220 billion
   e. supply of, fall, demanded, supplied
   f. rises, decrease, increases
2. **a.** See Figure A27-2.
   b. 6%, $40 billion, is not, costs, greater than
   c. increases, less, $30 billion
3. **a.** investment: $40 billion at all levels of income
      aggregate demand: $220, $265, $310, $355, $400, $445, $490, $535, $580, $625
   b. See Figure A27-3.
   c. $400 billion, investment
   d. increases, 10%, decreases, $30 billion
   e. investment: $30 billion at all levels of income
      aggregate demand: $210, $255, $300, $345, $390, $435, $480, $525, $570, $615

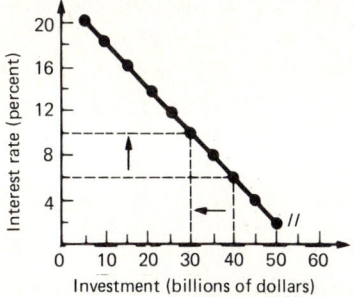

FIGURE A27-2

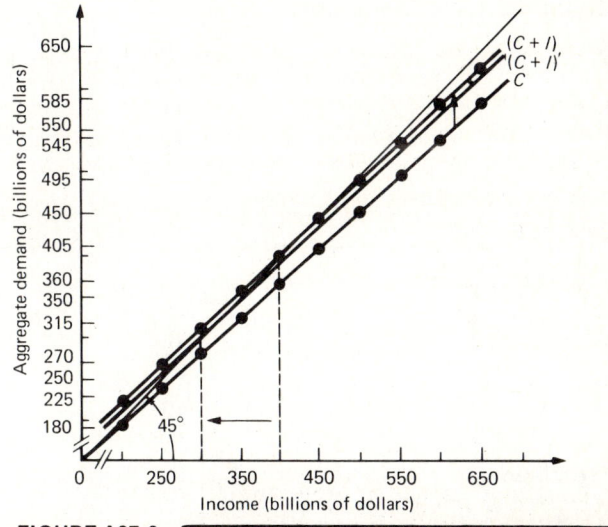

FIGURE A27-3

   f. decreased, $300 billion, $10 billion, interest
   g. See Figure A27-4.
4. **a.** 4
   b. 7
   c. 1
   d. 3
   e. 5
   f. 2
   g. 8
   h. 6
   i. crowds

Fill-in Questions

1. A tight, rise
2. is, can
3. increase, increase, increase, increase
4. "new economics," inflation
5. spend
6. opportunity, less
7. purchasing
8. marginal benefit, increases, more
9. rise, increase
10. plant and equipment, housing, inventories
11. will, costs
12. increases, fall, increases
13. ease, ease

14. consumption, investment, government spending, net exports, investment, consumption
15. buy, lower, lower

True-False Questions

1. F	6. T	11. T
2. T	7. T	12. T
3. T	8. F	13. F
4. F	9. F	14. F
5. T	10. F	15. T

Multiple Choice Questions

1. c	5. b	9. c
2. a	6. d	10. d
3. d	7. d	11. b
4. b	8. a	12. d

CHAPTER 28

Important Terms

1. e	5. c	9. f
2. k	6. l	10. i
3. g	7. j	11. d
4. a	8. b	12. h

Exercises

1.
   a. ↓, 0, ↓, 0
   b. ↑, 0, ↑, 0
   c. ↑, ↑, ?, ↑
   d. 0, 0, 0, 0
   e. ↑, 0, ↑, 0
   f. 0, ↓, ↑, ↓
   g. ↓, ↓, ?, ↓
2.
   a. Keynesian
   b. classical
   c. classical
   d. Keynesian
   e. Keynesian
   f. classical
   g. Keynesian
   h. classical
3.
   a. W_1, W_2, greater than
   b. revenue
   c. decreases, increases, increases
   d. increases

Fill-in Questions

1. Keynesian, can
2. nominal, price
3. macroeconomic, planned, income
4. marginal product, real, are
5. real, is
6. do, decreased
7. does not, equal, money, does not
8. aggregate supply, is
9. lower, higher, lower, decrease, fall
10. macroeconomic, aggregate, all
11. shifts, upward, does not
12. supply siders
13. marginal, increases
14. does not, remains constant, rises
15. wedge

True-False Questions

1. T	6. T	10. T
2. F	7. F	11. T
3. F	8. T	12. F
4. T	9. F	13. F
5. F		

Multiple Choice Questions

1. a	6. a	10. d
2. c	7. c	11. b
3. b	8. e	12. c
4. d	9. b	13. b
5. e		

CHAPTER 29

Important Terms

1. c	5. k	9. e
2. f	6. i	10. g
3. h	7. b	11. j
4. d	8. a	

Exercises

1.
   a. increase
   b. higher
   c. none
   d. increase
   e. lower
   f. less
   g. none
2.
   a. For (1) through (4), see Figure A29-1.
   (5) falls, remains constant
   (6) fall, rises, falls, decreases

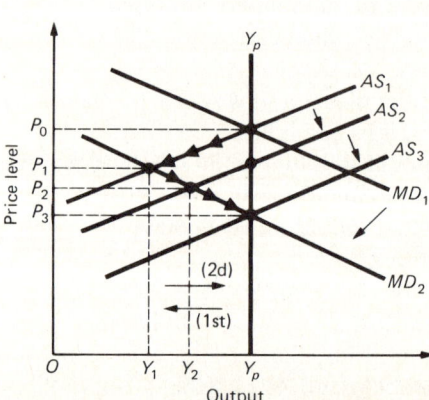

FIGURE A29-1

ANSWERS

(7) below, fall, downward, fall
(8) rise, fall, slows down

b. For (1) through (3), see Figure A29-2.
(4) decreases, falls
(5) is not, gradually, upward

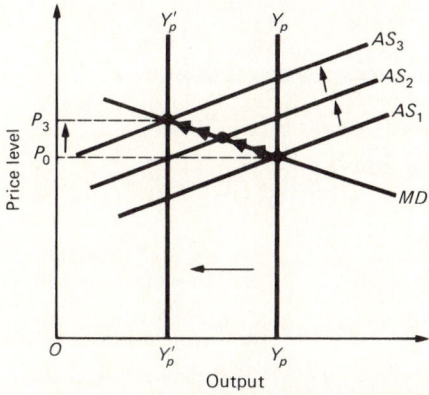

FIGURE A29-2

Fill-in Questions

1. wages
2. long, reluctant
3. number, hours
4. do not, is not
5. last period, equal to
6. higher
7. aggregate supply, an upward sloping
8. increase, rise, upward, rise, falls, higher, output
9. increase, remain unchanged
10. fall, fall
11. demand, supply

True-False Questions

1. T
2. F
3. F
4. T
5. F
6. T
7. T
8. T
9. F
10. T
11. F
12. T

Multiple Choice Questions

1. c
2. a
3. b
4. b
5. d
6. e
7. d
8. a

CHAPTER 30

Important Terms

1. f
2. h
3. a
4. i
5. b
6. j
7. e
8. c
9. g
10. d

Exercises

1. See Table A30-1.
2. **a.** Jan.: unemployment = 9298; unemployment rate = 8.5; percentage not in labor force = 56.2
   Feb.: employment = 99,590; unemployment rate = 8.8; percentage not in labor force = 55.9
   Mar.: unemployment = 9853; unemployment rate = 9.0; percentage not in labor force = 55.9
   Apr.: unemployment = 99,341; unemployment rate = 9.4; percentage not in labor force = 55.6
   b. increased, decreased, increased
   c. increased, fell, into, could
   d. was not, less than, 2.5%
3. **a.** 5, 3200
   b. does, is
   c. falls, 3000, rises, 3400

TABLE A30-1

SITUATION	IN LABOR FORCE (YES OR NO)	UNEMPLOYED (YES OR NO)	CYCLICAL UNEMPLOYMENT	TRANSITORY UNEMPLOYMENT
a. An autoworker is laid off because the sales of new cars falls	Yes	Yes	X	
b. A housewife begins a job search in order to supplement the family income	Yes	Yes		X
c. A construction worker fired when the company he worked for went bankrupt looks for a new job for 6 months and then gives up	No			
d. A college English professor with a Ph.D. is laid off and gets a job as a cook at Hamburger City	Yes	No		
e. The government cancels the CETA program, and so some program administrators are fired	Yes	Yes		X
f. A steelworker loses his job because the demand for domestic steel falls	Yes	Yes	X	
g. In May, a high school junior finds a job which begins in June	Yes	Yes		X
h. A househusband bakes and sells cakes to friends in his spare time	No			

d. does, zero, 400
e. decreased, 5

Fill-in Questions
1. GNP, are
2. is, does not
3. week, 4 weeks
4. employed, unemployed, does
5. discouraged, are not
6. duration
7. 6, vary, are not
8. black teenagers, white
9. cyclical, is
10. does, lower

True-False Questions
1. F
2. T
3. F
4. T
5. T
6. T
7. F
8. F
9. T
10. F
11. F
12. F
13. T
14. T
15. T

Multiple Choice Questions
1. c
2. a
3. d
4. b
5. c
6. e
7. d
8. a
9. c

CHAPTER 31

Important Terms
1. k
2. n
3. a
4. i
5. g
6. o
7. b
8. f
9. l
10. d
11. h
12. c
13. e
14. m
15. j

Exercises
1. a. 6, A
   (1) is not, more and more
   (2) 6, increase, natural
   (3) negative, falling
   b. higher
   (1) increase, 4.5, 6, increases, 5.5
   (2) 8
2. a. See Table A31-1.

TABLE A31-1

INVESTMENT ALTERNATIVE	NOMINAL INTEREST RATE	EXPECTED INFLATION RATE	PRETAX REAL INTEREST RATE WHEN INFLATION IS		TAX RATE	AFTER-TAX NOMINAL INTEREST RATE WHEN INFLATION IS		AFTER-TAX REAL INTEREST RATE WHEN INFLATION IS	
			12%	4%		12%	4%	12%	4%
A	13%	12% 4%	1%	9%	30%	9.1%	9.1%	−2.9%	5.1%
B	9.25%	12% 4%	−2.75%	5.25%	0%	9.25%	9.25%	−2.75%	5.25%

b. See Table A31-2.

TABLE A31-2

	INFLATION RATE		
ALTERNATIVE	12%	4%	0%
A	−$290	$510	$910
B	−$275	$525	$925

c. B
d. decreased, less

Fill-in Questions
1. low, unemployment
2. negative, falls
3. stagflation
4. are not
5. has not
6. purchasing, income, illusion
7. real, relative, real
8. real
9. currency, menu costs
10. rising, more, real
11. gains, real, falls, loses
12. wage, price, incomes
13. difficult, will not

True-False Questions
1. T
2. F
3. T
4. F
5. F
6. F
7. T
8. F
9. T
10. F
11. F
12. T
13. T
14. F
15. T
16. T
17. F
18. T
19. T
20. T
21. F
22. F
23. F
24. T

Multiple Choice Questions
1. b
2. d
3. e
4. a
5. e
6. b
7. a
8. c
9. d
10. b
11. c
12. b
13. e

ANSWERS

CHAPTER 32

Important Terms
1. e
2. g
3. a
4. i
5. c
6. b
7. d
8. f
9. h

Exercises
1. a. A: $80, $100, $120, $140, $160
      B: 8%, 10%, 12%, 14%, 16%
   b. C: 4%, 2%, 0, −2%, −4%
      D: $40, $20, 0, −$20, −$40
   c. 12%, greater than
   d. 12%, negative
   e. inflation
   f. rise
   g. required nominal rate: 13%, 15%, 17%, 19%, 21%
      real interest rate: 5%, 5%, 5%, 5%, 5%
2. a. A: 337, 310, 264, 213, 171, 131
      B: 100, 108, 115, 123, 131, 142
      C: 1.00, 0.92, 0.78, 0.63, 0.51, 0.39
   b. less, decrease
   c. decrease, flight
   d. would
   e. D: 17%, 26%, 33%, 32%, 41%
      E: 8%, 7%, 7%, 6%, 8%
   f. slower, lower, increase, increase

Fill-in Questions
1. increases, more
2. real, interest, financial
3. is, is not
4. Germany, less
5. falls
6. decreases, indexed
7. are not, Congress, Fed, indirect
8. Fisher, interest
9. is
10. inflation, interest

True-False Questions
1. T
2. F
3. T
4. T
5. F
6. F
7. F
8. T
9. T
10. F
11. T
12. T
13. F
14. F

Multiple Choice Questions
1. c
2. a
3. d
4. c
5. a
6. d
7. e
8. c
9. c
10. b
11. d

CHAPTER 33

Important Terms
1. i
2. d
3. e
4. j
5. h
6. l
7. f
8. k
9. c
10. a
11. b
12. g

Exercises
1. a. K: $1050, $1090, $1120, $1140, $1150
   b. Y_p: $300, $315, $327, $336, $342, $345
   c. GR: 5%, 3.8%, 2.8%, 1.8%, 0.9%
   d. increases, decreasing
   e. falling, rise more slowly
   f. increase, rise

Fill-in Questions
1. machines, buildings, inventories
2. decrease, a decreasing, fall, much
3. production, technology
4. are not, agricultural
5. invention, innovation, does
6. patent
7. life
8. is, machines

True-False Questions
1. T
2. F
3. F
4. T
5. T
6. F
7. T
8. F
9. F
10. T

Multiple Choice Questions
1. a
2. c
3. d
4. e
5. b
6. e
7. c
8. b
9. e
10. a

CHAPTER 34

Important Terms
1. q
2. m
3. v
4. i
5. b
6. r
7. u
8. a
9. s
10. c
11. g
12. d
13. p
14. f
15. h
16. l
17. y
18. j
19. n
20. k
21. t
22. x
23. o
24. w
25. e

Exercises
1. a. See Table A34-2

TABLE A34-2

ALPHANIA'S BALANCE OF PAYMENTS, 1983

Current account	
Exports:	
Automobile exports	$ 1.0
Adding machine exports	15.2
Military hardware	7.1
Wheat	20.0
Total Exports	$43.3
Imports:	
Agricultural commodities	$ 1.0
Spending by tourists in Europe	8.5
Automobile imports	30.4
Foreign oil	10.5
Total Imports	$50.4
Current Account Balance	−$ 7.1
Capital Account	
Sales of assets:	
Sales of Alphanian government bonds	$ 4.0
Sale of Alphanian corporate stock to foreigners	2.1
Sale of gold to foreigners by government	1.0
Capital Account Balance	$7.1
Total	0

  b. deficit, imports, exports, 7.1 million
  c. is
  d. decreases, capital
  e. is, finance

Fill-in Questions

1. interdependent, increased
2. industrialized
3. raw, manufactured
4. different, different
5. appreciated, depreciated, fall
6. exports, imports, increase, fall
7. devalued, rise
8. clean, foreign exchange
9. fixing, do not
10. can, cannot

True-False Questions

1.	F	6.	T	10.	T
2.	T	7.	T	11.	T
3.	T	8.	F	12.	F
4.	F	9.	F	13.	F
5.	F				

Multiple Choice Questions

1.	e	4.	b	7.	e
2.	a	5.	d	8.	c
3.	c	6.	a		

CHAPTER 35

Important Terms

1.	h	4.	m	7.	b
2.	n	5.	o	8.	a
3.	j	6.	k	9.	d
10.	g	12.	c	14.	f
11.	i	13.	l	15.	e

Exercises

1. **a.** Betania, both
   b. 3, 1/3, 2, 1/2
   c. Betania, Alphania
   d. pineapple, breadfruit
   e. 50, 75, 42.5, 33, 17, 32.5
   f. are

Fill-in Questions

1. productivity, do
2. a comparative, may or may not
3. positive, worse
4. capital, labor, opposite
5. diversity, economies, transportation
6. tariff, increases, decreases, fall, rises
7. government, firms, are not
8. are not, competitive, subsidy
9. Dumping, recession, jobs
10. a nation, misallocation, monopoly
11. does
12. rise, falls

True-False Questions

1.	F	7.	F	12.	F
2.	T	8.	F	13.	F
3.	F	9.	T	14.	T
4.	T	10.	F	15.	F
5.	T	11.	T	16.	T
6.	F				

Multiple Choice Questions

1.	b	5.	b	8.	c
2.	e	6.	d	9.	a
3.	c	7.	b	10.	b
4.	a				

CHAPTER 36

Important Terms

1.	f	5.	a	9.	j
2.	k	6.	h	10.	g
3.	i	7.	b	11.	c
4.	e	8.	d		

Exercises

1. **a.** A, 1979: 0.893, 0.840, 0.123, 0.197, 0.980
       1981: 0.685, 0.878, 0.115, 0.174, 1.149
   b. B: +, −, +, +, −
   c. C: −, +, −, −, +
   d. South African rand, New Zealand dollar
   e. depreciates

ANSWERS

Fill-in Questions
1. does, increases, fall, increases
2. dollar, was not
3. more, fall, decrease
4. inflow, destabilized
5. purchasing power parity, constant
6. decrease, increase, decrease
7. supply, demand, does not

True-False Questions
1. F
2. F
3. F
4. T
5. T
6. F
7. T
8. F
9. F
10. F
11. T
12. F
13. T

Multiple Choice Questions
1. c
2. b
3. a
4. e
5. b
6. a
7. c
8. d

CHAPTER 37

Important Terms
1. l
2. e
3. o
4. h
5. a
6. k
7. n
8. d
9. m
10. c
11. i
12. g
13. f
14. b
15. j

Exercises
1. a. $25, 17,500, is not
   b. shifts, S_1, falls, $17.50, 22,500, decreases, $437,500, $393,750
   c. rise, $30, fall, 1500, increase, $450,000
   d. are not
   e. buys, 12,500, $25, sells, 7500, $25
   f. are
2. a. Alphania's per capita GNP: $5300, $5618, $5955, $6312, ..., $8447, $8954, $9491
      Betania's per capita GNP: $636, $674, $715, $757, ..., $1013, $1074, $1139
   b. Difference: $4664, $4944, $5240, $5355, ..., $7434, $7880, $8352
   c. increased, is not

Fill-in Questions
1. increased, improved
2. southern, third
3. a. The prices for their exports (primary commodities) have been falling because the markets for the exports are controlled by rich nations.
   b. Markets for the industrial commodities they want to produce are closed by protectionism in the developed countries.
   c. The terms on which financial aid is provided are too stiff.
   d. Other countries should as a matter of justice provide aid to them for future development.
4. are, inelastic, large
5. does
6. rising, falling
7. price, revenue
8. foreign, domestically, manufactured
9. small, clothing
10. increase, financed
11. borrowing, direct investment, aid receipts
12. migration, are

True-False Questions
1. T
2. F
3. F
4. T
5. T
6. F
7. T
8. F
9. F
10. F
11. T
12. T
13. T
14. F
15. F

Multiple Choice Questions
1. b
2. d
3. a
4. c
5. b
6. d
7. b
8. a
9. c
10. b
11. c

CHAPTER 38

Important Terms
1. i
2. d
3. j
4. a
5. g
6. k
7. b
8. f
9. e
10. h
11. c

Exercises
1. a. OA, $OABQ_1$
   b. more, D_1, D_2
   c. OI, OQ_2, $OIEQ_2$, greater than, has, decrease
   d. decrease, more, decreased, $OBAQ_1$, $OJGQ_2$,
2. See Table A38-1

TABLE A38-1

	REAL WAGE	REAL RENTAL OF CAPITAL	LABOR INCOME	INCOME OF CAPITAL	LABOR'S SHARE OF INCOME
Substitutability:					
High	decrease	increase	decrease	decrease	increase
Low	decrease	increase	decrease	increase	decrease

3. **a.** Country A: 1%, 5%, 10%, 30%, 100%
   Country B: 20%, 40%, 60%, 80%, 100%
   b. See Figure A38-1.
   c. less, 30
   d. B, linear

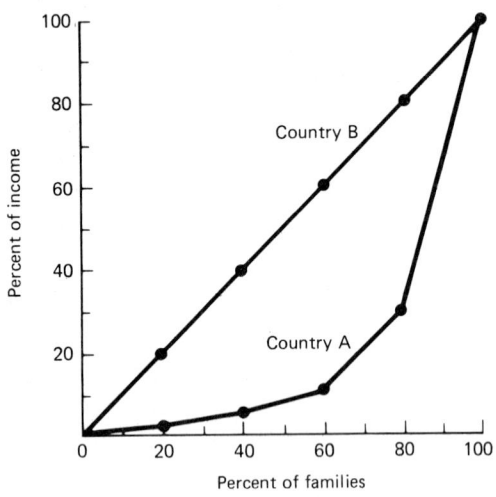

FIGURE A38-1

Fill-in Questions

1. "for whom"
2. wages, labor
3. does not, rise
4. faster, increasing, increased
5. Lorenz, cumulative, is not
6. income and transfers in kind, personal income taxes
7. median
8. black, women
9. family background, achievement, luck
10. is not, equality, efficiency
11. progressive, flat-rate tax
12. incentive, is

True-False Questions

1. F
2. T
3. T
4. F
5. F
6. T
7. F
8. F
9. T
10. F
11. T
12. T
13. F

Multiple Choice Questions

1. b
2. d
3. c
4. b
5. e
6. a
7. c
8. a
9. d
10. e
11. c

CHAPTER 39

Important Terms

1. g
2. m
3. a
4. i
5. k
6. b
7. n
8. e
9. h
10. o
11. l
12. c
13. d
14. j
15. f

Exercises

1. See Table A39-1.

TABLE A39-1

	SYSTEM			
	PURE CAPITALISM	MIXED ECONOMY	MARKET SOCIALISM	PURE COMMUNISM
a.			X	
b.	X			
c.	X	X	X	
d.				X
e.		X	X	
f.				X
g.	X			
h.			X	
i.		X		
j.				X
k.	X			

2. **a.** As capitalists expand their use of machines, the demand for labor falls since the machines are designed to be labor-saving; thus, wages and the level of employment fall, and workers are made worse off.
   b. As society continues to industrialize, the capitalists destroy the very foundation of their production and profit since they try to produce with less and less labor; unemployment increases.

ANSWERS

c. After the proletarian revolution, class distinctions and antagonisms disappear; everyone produces and receives the benefits of production, and so the government withers away.
d. Capitalists earn profits because they exploit labor by paying workers only a subsistence-level wage and taking away part of the value (surplus value) created by workers.
e. Capitalism encourages firms to become bigger and monopolistic, with the largest firms dominating their industries and the economy.

Fill-in Questions

1. class, bourgeoisie, proletariat
2. central planner, production possibilities
3. state, is not
4. New Economic Program, Lenin, did
5. 5-year, annual
6. collectivization, was not, is not
7. defense, economy, political, educational
8. workers, output, prices, investment, is
9. more
10. faster, 60

True-False Questions

1. F
2. T
3. F
4. F
5. T
6. T
7. F
8. T
9. F
10. F
11. F
12. T
13. T
14. F
15. T
16. F

Multiple Choice Questions

1. a
2. c
3. e
4. b
5. e
6. c
7. a
8. b
9. b
10. d